JUNNZARQ9

BOLLINGEN SERIES XCIX

NIETZSCHE'S
ZARATHUSTRA

NOTES OF THE SEMINAR

GIVEN IN 1934-1939 BY

C. G. JUNG

EDITED BY JAMES L. JARRETT

IN TWO VOLUMES

2

BOLLINGEN SERIES XCIX

PRINCETON UNIVERSITY PRESS

THIS EDITION OF THE NOTES OF JUNG'S
SEMINARS IS BEING PUBLISHED IN THE
UNITED STATES OF AMERICA BY PRINCETON
UNIVERSITY PRESS, AND IN ENGLAND BY
ROUTLEDGE & KEGAN PAUL, LTD. IN THE
AMERICAN EDITION, THE VOLUMES OF SEM-
INAR NOTES CONSTITUTE NUMBER XCIX IN
BOLLINGEN SERIES, SPONSORED BY BOL-
LINGEN FOUNDATION

The text here published is that of the
multigraphed version which Mary
Foote, its editor, issued privately in ten
volumes from approximately 1934 to
1940 (specific dates of issue are lacking).
Volumes 1 to 3, for the meetings from
May 1934 to March 1935, were originally issued in double-spaced typing,
and when depleted were reissued, with
minor corrections, in single-spaced for-
mat. The latter version and the remaining (single-spaced) volumes are the
source of the present text.

LIBRARY OF CONGRESS CATALOGUE CARD NUMBER: 87-32897
ISBN 0-691-09953-7

PRINTED IN THE UNITED STATES OF AMERICA
BY PRINCETON UNIVERSITY PRESS, PRINCETON, NEW JERSEY

TABLE OF CONTENTS
Volume 2

WINTER TERM

January / March 1936

LECTURE I

22 January 1936

Prof. Jung:

We have a question by Mr. Allemann: "In the last seminar you said that according to Analytical Psychology, Jesus was wrong when the tempter put him on the top of the temple not to jump down and so come into contact with the earth. Does this opinion take into account the fact that Jesus quite deliberately and consciously had rejected 'this world' and that he said that 'his kingdom was not of this world'? Would he not have left *his own way* if he had accepted the suggestion of the tempter? And would this not have been wrong also from the point of view of Analytical Psychology?"

Well, it all depends upon what aspect of Jesus we were speaking of. That is the trouble. You see, Jesus is such a symbolical figure that one cannot help mixing it up with one's own psychology. If we take him as a historical figure, sure enough he could not have acted differently; he had to be himself and naturally he rejected the world and the flesh. It would have been utterly wrong to cast himself down from the top of the temple; and it would have been a terrible nonsense because it is quite certain that anybody tempted by the devil to do such a thing would be smashed up: the devil makes promises only in order to destroy one. But if we speak of Jesus as a symbolical figure, a god or a symbol that has actual importance, then of course the situation is quite different, because then the devil belongs to the game and the world cannot be excluded. We have learned that it does not do to exclude the world, and moreover it is impossible; even those people who preach the exclusion of the world, the suppression of the flesh and so on, are unable to do it. It is a lie, an illusion. That kind of solution doesn't work; we no longer believe in it. So the idea or the figure of a savior must now be something or somebody who is acquainted with the life of the earth, and accepts the life of the earth. A young man who hasn't yet lived and experienced the world, who hasn't even married or had a profession, cannot possibly be a model of how to live. If all men

767

should imitate Christ, walking about and talking wisely and doing nothing at all, sometimes getting an ass somewhere in order to have a ride, it just wouldn't do; such people would nowadays land in the lunatic asylum. It is impossible for such a figure now to be a model or a solution or an answer. We shall soon come to a passage where Nietzsche says that Jesus died too early, when he was still a young man not having had experience of life. So to us he is a symbol. And inasmuch as Jesus is supposed to be the key, the real *clavis hermetica*, by which the gates of the great problems and secrets are unlocked, then the world and the devil cannot be excluded—nothing can be excluded. Then we must ask the *symbol* Jesus: "Now, would it not be better if you cast yourself down, if you would once try the earth and find out what the devil means by playing such a funny role? Is there not something quite reasonable in what he proposes? Should you not be closer to the earth perhaps and less in the air?" Of course, that is no longer the historical Jesus; to talk to Jesus like that means that you are surely no longer a Christian, but a philosopher arguing with Christ; as soon as Christ becomes a real symbol you are a philosopher, for Christianity has then come to an end. In Christianity, Christ is an entity, with substance; he is a historical figure first of all, and then he is a dogmatic figure. He is one third of God and nothing can be said about him.

Mrs. Sigg: I don't know whether we are so sure that what the Evangelists narrate is absolutely true; they might have omitted something in the real life of Christ.

Prof. Jung: Well, how can we judge it? We don't know whether the report is reliable because we cannot check it up. The only source is the Evangelical account and we have no means of comparison, so we cannot say whether it is really historically satisfactory or not.

Mrs. Sigg: We are not so sure whether he did not try the earth in some way; there is room for a little hope.

Prof. Jung: We know of nothing and his teaching doesn't point that way. The only thing we know is his baptism by John—nothing else, except that scene in the temple when he was a boy.

Mr. Allemann: Is it not curious that the founders of the two greatest religions both rejected the world? Buddha did the same thing.

Prof. Jung: Quite. It is an astonishing fact, but Buddha doesn't reject it to the same extent. He recognizes it more in that he acknowledges the necessity of a long development. The Christian attitude is far more resentful; the world is denied as sinful. The Buddhistic attitude is less so; of course, Buddha's *ultimate* attitude is just negative, but he agrees more with the world in accepting it as an illusion.

Miss Wolff: Buddha's life began when Christ's ended; he was about thirty years of age and had been in the world. He had married and had a child even, and his teaching was that a man ought to live first; only in the second half of life was he allowed to "retire."

Mrs. Crowley: Could you not say from the psychological point of view that the idea of the hermit, of isolating yourself or negating the world, was projected in order to find the world within—in other words, to individuate? Would that not be the real inner purpose in having rejected the world?

Prof. Jung: That would be very obvious in Buddhism, but not in Christianity.

Mrs. Crowley: But I mean from the angle of Christ, not as later Christianity taught; in his own attitude he was rejecting the world as it was at that time. He was rejecting the literal reality.

Prof. Jung: If you speak of the historical Jesus, that is true.

Mrs. Crowley: Yes, for we were speaking of the historical Buddha.

Prof. Jung: Ah yes, but Buddha's life was far more historical; it was not a drama. Buddha really lived a human life. He did not come to an end at thirty-three, but lived to be an old man. That of course makes a tremendous difference.

Prof. Fierz: In the first part of the Gospel, Jesus waits for the Messiah, not knowing whether he himself is the Messiah. If the disciples ask him, he forbids them to ask the question, and then he sends them out to say the Messiah will come. But he does not come, and it seems as if he then changed his mind and decided not to wait for a king from this world but from another world. There is a certain change in his teaching. When nothing comes he goes back to himself, and the final gospel is perhaps the result of the disappointment, a disillusion; he breaks down and then he dies. I think there is much to be said for that, except in St. John.

Prof. Jung: There are several places in the Gospel where one can see that disappointment but the Synoptic Gospels contain a good deal of historical truth about Jesus while the Gospel of St. John is entirely philosophical. There he is a symbol. Of course we get then an entirely different picture of the Christus, there he is really the God, not human.

Now we will go on to the next chapter, "Child and Marriage." In this last chapter there was the story of the snake that bit Zarathustra, and you remember that this *rencontre* between Zarathustra and the snake had the meaning that Zarathustra, being the Logos more or less, a mind only, had linked up with the serpent; or that the serpent, representing the lower nervous centers, the instinctive world, had linked up with him. The snake would represent the body, and with that a certain element of instinctiveness comes into the situation. Of course Zarathustra is always identical with Nietzsche; he is never clearly differentiated, and so practically every figure in *Thus Spake Zarathustra* is always in a way Nietzsche himself. There is no psychological discrimination; it is not an analytical piece of work. Zarathustra is an unconscious creation of which Nietzsche is as much the victim as he is the author. So when the snake bites Zarathustra, Nietzsche himself is bitten. For Zarathustra, it is not dangerous because he is also the snake, but Nietzsche is human and he is presumably poisoned. And we can be sure that whatever the serpent brings up from the depths of its own dark world would be things of *this* world. No wonder, then, that the next chapter has to do with a problem which must have been very near to Nietzsche, though it is not at all near to Zarathustra. Why should Zarathustra talk of child and marriage? He doesn't marry and he has nothing to do with children. This is Nietzsche's problem and it is a very negative one; there is trouble in Nietzsche's case. That the snake comes up and bites Zarathustra means that Nietzsche himself is reminded of the question of his possible marriage, a possible family, etc. Now this chapter begins:

> I have a question for thee alone, my brother: . . .

This is as if the serpent were speaking to Nietzsche.

> like a sounding-lead, cast I this question into thy soul, that I may know its depth.
> Thou art young, and desirest child and marriage. But I ask thee: Art thou a man *entitled* to desire a child?

He was infected as you know, which was of course a tremendous problem to him. And his relation to women was exceedingly poor. He did not know how to approach them. He was terribly clumsy and foolish when it came to women.

> Art thou the victorious one, the self-conqueror, the ruler of thy passions, the master of thy virtues? Thus do I ask thee.
> Or doth the animal speak in thy wish, and necessity? Or isolation? Or discord in thee?

This is an examination. The serpent is trying him, trying to make him conscious of possible motives for or against.

770

I would have thy victory and freedom long for a child. Living monuments shalt thou build to thy victory and emancipation.

Beyond thyself shalt thou build. But first of all must thou be built thyself, rectangular in body and soul.

Not only onward shalt thou propagate thyself, but upward! For that purpose may the garden of marriage help thee!

Here we see Nietzsche's peculiar bachelor psychology, and an attempt to make this very difficult and thorny problem of marriage more acceptable to himself—by contaminating it with philosophy, for instance. That makes it much nicer, you see. He can deal with philosophy, and if marriage could be linked up with it—if marriage could have a philosophical purpose and be a technique or a way of creating a higher body—then he might be able to deal with that also.

A higher body shalt thou create, a first movement, a spontaneously rolling wheel—a creating one shalt thou create.

Then marriage would look promising; otherwise it cannot be touched.

Marriage: so call I the will of the twain to create the one that is more than those who created it.

With such a definition it might be considered.

The reverence for one another, as those exercising such a will, call I marriage.

Let this be the significance and the truth of thy marriage. But that which the many-too-many call marriage, those superfluous ones—ah, what shall I call it?

Ah, the poverty of soul in the twain! Ah, the filth of soul in the twain! Ah, the pitiable self-complacency in the twain!

Marriage they call it all; and they say their marriages are made in heaven.

You see, in order to make something of marriage, they must assume that they are made in heaven, just as he must call it a philosophical business; something must be said in favor of marriage so that it can be tackled. Now, his particular idea is that marriage should provide a higher body, the birth of a first movement. What does he allude to here—that spontaneously rolling wheel?

Mrs. Crowley: I should have thought he meant the self.

Prof. Jung: Yes, what he means by "marriage" would be that two come together and create a superman, perhaps in the form of a child.

But of course in reality that won't do; it would be a very ordinary child to begin with, and the superman business would come very much later, if at all. Even Nietzsche could not imagine that if he had married Lou Salomé they would have created together anything more than an ordinary baby, and perhaps a little more pathological than another.

Mrs. Sigg: The actual fact is that in the moment when Nietzsche wrote this chapter his sister was trying to spoil the image of Lou Salomé. He says: "My sister treats Lou as a poisonous worm." He had made an offer of marriage to Lou but it was a very feeble offer, and after a while he had a suspicion that her health was not satisfactory.

Prof. Jung: I knew her and confirm that she was perfectly healthy and vigorous.

Mrs. Sigg: But she had no children afterwards, and Nietzsche said, "I think Miss Lou cannot live many years."[1]

Prof. Jung: He would not have lived, *he* would have given up. Well, obviously Nietzsche connects with marriage a philosophical idea of individuation which of course would not do; with such an idea in his head it could not possibly go. It would be a tremendous mistake because that would not meet with the approval of the ordinary biological man. And he has a doubt whether his idea is quite sound; he then projects the other possibility in all those "many-too-many" who also marry—marry like beasts. Of course he would not do that, yet the suspicion that marriage might be something that ordinary people do too creeps in somewhere; he reviles their marriages and tries to defend himself against such a failure of the ideal. But if he had married it would have been pretty much the same and he would soon have discovered it. He would also have discovered that he had reviled marriage. It is *not* like that.

> Well, I do not like it, that heaven of the superfluous! No, I do not like them, those animals tangled in the heavenly toils!
>
> Far from me also be the God who limpeth thither to bless what he hath not matched!
>
> Laugh not at such marriages!

Better not!

---

[1] In his letters Nietzsche repeatedly reported his sister's intense dislike for Lou Salomé, and even her deadly enmity toward her. See for instance the letter to Franz Overbeck, September 1882. Nietzsche's concern for Lou's fragility, as in the letter here quoted (to Peter Gast, 17 July 1882) was wholly unfounded: she proved to be a healthy, vigorous woman who outlived Nietzsche by some thirty-seven years. N/Letters/Fuss.

> What child hath not had reason to weep over its parents?
>
> Worthy did this man seem, and ripe for the meaning of the earth: but when I saw his wife, the earth seemed to me a home for madcaps.
>
> Yea, I would that the earth shook with convulsions when a saint and a goose mate with one another.

That is exactly what they do, and that is right. You see, it is the profound wisdom of nature that whenever there was a saint, there was also a goose ready for him and surely they mated. That is the necessary law of compensation; the high must be brought down and the low must be brought up. So that wonderful saint or whatever he was had an anima that was a goose.

> This one went forth in quest of truth as a hero, and at last got for himself a small decked-up lie: his marriage he calleth it.

In the Dionysian dithyrambs at the end of *Zarathustra*, there is a very interesting one about Dudu and Suleika who seemed to be nothing more than small, decked-up lies.[2]

> That one was reserved in intercourse and chose choicely. But one time he spoilt his company for all time: his marriage he calleth it.
>
> Another sought a handmaid with the virtues of an angel. But all at once he became the handmaid of a woman, and now would he need also to become an angel.
>
> Careful have I found all buyers, and all of them have astute eyes. But even the astutest of them buyeth his wife in a sack.

That must be so. That is very wise, because if a woman could see what a man was and if a man could see what a woman was they never would marry, or only under the utmost restrictions. You see, we would hardly touch other human beings if we knew ourselves better, or if we knew them better. One may well be frightened out of one's wits.

> Many short follies—that is called love by you. And your marriage putteth an end to many short follies, with one long stupidity.

Or, as in Nietzsche's case, with a complete absence of any kind of relationship.

[2] "Among Daughters of the Desert," Part IV, ch. 76.

Your love to woman, and woman's love to man—ah, would that it were sympathy for suffering and veiled deities!

That sounds very profound. Many people have speculated about what these suffering and veiled deities might be. What do you think? Who are they?

Mrs. Jung: The selves of the people.

Prof. Jung: Yes, the gods in them, the selves in them, are these suffering and veiled deities. You see, Nietzsche brings these problems together with that very practical problem in life, marriage. Whenever a philosophy is involved, or any other exceedingly impractical mixture takes place, the problem itself becomes practically impossible; you cannot deal with such a big problem by going to the *Standesamt*³ where you sign your names in the book that you are married, with the purpose of redeeming, for instance, suffering and veiled deities. You are Mr. and Mrs. So-and-So, and if you tell people that you are suffering and veiled deities, you will be sent to the lunatic asylum; if you mix up those two things, practical ordinary human life becomes unmanageable. Because so many people mix it up with a philosophical problem, a simple matter like marriage becomes clumsy. They assume that they naturally will marry that man or woman with whom they can climb to heaven, but with that idea they never will marry, or they will make a hellish blunder. And the idea that marriage exists in order to improve one another is worse: it then becomes a sort of classroom in which one is educated forever. Or any other ideal. That is not to be done; marriage is something quite different. It is a very practical and sober proposition which has to be looked at soberly and carefully. And then you must not be afraid of animals, a point which Nietzsche carefully excludes. For marriage in the first place, in spite of what idealistic people say about it, is what animals do too, and it needs much work and much suffering until people discover that there is something else behind it. The more people have high tones about marriage, the less they will be married; they will be careful not to disturb the harmony of their talk.

But generally two animals light on one another.

That is not so bad.

But even your best love is only an enraptured simile and a painful ardour. It is a torch to light you to loftier paths.

Beyond yourselves shall ye love some day! Then *learn* first of all

---

³ *Standesamt*: registry.

to love. And on that account ye had to drink the bitter cup of your love.

Bitterness is in the cup even of the best love; thus doth it cause longing for the Superman; thus doth it cause thirst in thee, the creating one!

Thirst in the creating one, arrow and longing for the Superman: tell me, my brother, is this thy will to marriage?

Holy call I such a will, and such a marriage.—

Thus spake Zarathustra.

The unfortunate thing is that such a marriage doesn't take place; because such big things have been said before, one cannot marry at all. It is the saddest thing to compare Nietzsche's fate with such marvelous teaching: the difference is too great. Now, this chapter about child and marriage has been a very hopeful chapter, a great attempt towards life and the continuation of life. But we come now to a chapter called "Voluntary Death." How do you account for this sudden turn? After a chapter on child and marriage, why should we land in a chapter about voluntary death?

Mrs. Stutz: Sometimes it is easier to die than to live one's life.

Prof. Jung: Under what conditions would you consider death easier than life?

Mrs. Stutz: When you cannot undertake the duties of life.

Miss Hannah: He would rather die than lose his high illusions; if he tried to live, he would have to smash them up.

Prof. Jung: Well, suppose you really meet somebody who makes a grand speech on the most idealistic aspect of marriage and children, and then suddenly begins to talk of suicide—what would you think?

Mrs. Crowley: That he was not convinced.

Prof. Jung: Yes, that he was evidently not quite convinced by his own talk, that there must be a flaw in the crystal. Therefore he confesses as much. He has the most wonderful ideas about marriage and its meaning, its goal, etc., yet he is so certain that this thing cannot come off that he prefers to die. You see, the one thing is exaggerated and the other is exaggerated. He makes of marriage such a rare and wonderful thing that it cannot easily happen, and he decides that if such a wonderful marriage is not possible he must choose death. That is the *enantiodromia* by which he reaches this chapter.

Mrs. Crowley: Is it not possible in the previous chapter on "Child and Marriage" that it was really Zarathustra who was preaching, and that he would be referring not to a psychical marriage but to the symbolic marriage of alchemy, just using that as a symbol?

Prof. Jung: Exactly. He identifies with Zarathustra's point of view and such a thing is unmanageable.

Mrs. Sigg: In actual reality, of the nine brothers and sisters in Nietzsche's family, five remained unmarried. That means something.

Prof. Jung: Rather!

Mrs. Jung: I think one should also consider a very simple meaning— that he admonishes people to be more conscious and responsible about marriage and that is actually what they are preaching in Germany now: an improvement of Rasse.[4] People must make a more careful choice, and are not allowed to marry without a certificate. In many other places also I think it is interesting to see that things have come about as Nietzsche said, but naturally in a more objective way, not in the spiritual way that he preaches.

Prof. Jung: Yes, there is still the difference that in Germany it is a hygienic question and with Nietzsche it is more spiritual.

Mrs. Stutz: I think we see this in Goethe himself who married a very simple woman.

Prof. Jung: That was too much contrary; the result was not very encouraging.

Miss Wolff: More like the saint and the goose!

Prof. Jung: Yes. Well, I think we will hurry on with these chapters, which are not particularly interesting.

Many die too late, and some die too early. Yet strange soundeth the precept: "Die at the right time!"

Die at the right time: so teacheth Zarathustra.

To be sure, he who never liveth at the right time, how could he ever die at the right time? Would that he might never be born!— Thus do I advise the superfluous ones.

But even the superfluous ones make much ado about their death, and even the hollowest nut wanteth to be cracked.

Every one regardeth dying as a great matter: but as yet death is not a festival. Not yet have people learned to inaugurate the finest festivals.

The consummating death I show unto you, which becometh a stimulus and promise to the living.

His death, dieth the consummating one triumphantly, surrounded by hoping and promising ones.

4 *Rasse*: race.

Thus should one learn to die; and there should be no festival at which such a dying one doth not consecrate the oaths of the living!

Thus to die is best; the next best, however, is to die in battle, and sacrifice a great soul.

But to the fighter equally hateful as to the victor, is your grinning death which stealeth night like a thief—and yet cometh as master.

My death, praise I unto you, the voluntary death, which cometh unto me because *I* want it.

What is your impression of this teaching? What is the remarkable thing?

Miss Wolff: It seems like a wish fulfilment. It is as if he had an intuition that his own death would not be like that, that his death would not come at the moment he would choose.

Prof. Jung: Well, it is like a superstition, or almost a conviction, that he was the one who would die when he wanted, but he was just the one who did not die when he wanted. He was dead before his body.

Mrs. Sigg: For a very long time when he was quite young, Nietzsche believed that he would die of the same disease and at the same age that his father died. He was very ill when he was thirty-six I think, and he was perfectly convinced that he would die, and he was also convinced that he would get this disease of the brain.[5]

Prof. Jung: You see, he is now making the same complication of death as he was making before with life: he links up or contaminates death, a natural occurrence, with a philosophy. The natural flow of events which life is and ought to be includes death; death is also a natural occurrence which comes flowing along. But he makes it a task, almost a decision. He says that he is going to die when he wants just as he is going to marry when he thinks best, not taking it as an event which comes along as the will of God, which is not his own will. One can fit in with the flow of events only when one can accept them, not when one makes them. There again is the identification with the archetype; the archetype prescribes what should be and Nietzsche backs it up. His inflation makes it his own conviction, so his idea is that one marries under such and such conditions and makes such and such a thing of it; and one chooses the right kind of death in the right moment, such a death as one wants and with the meaning one wants. You see, that is all

---

[5] In a letter to Carl von Gersdorff, 18 January 1876, Nietzsche recalled his father's dying at thirty-six from inflammation of the brain and said that such an affliction may take *him* off even earlier. He was then thirty-one.

violating the flow of events which he just cannot accept, so that even dying becomes clumsy and complicated. Such people cannot die naturally any longer. It is just as if one had to swallow in a certain kind of solemn way; then of course one cannot swallow at all. The simplest functions become absolutely impossible if one is on stilts: one cannot even die. "And when shall I want it?" But there is no choice. He can ask himself when he wants it as little as when he is going to marry.

Prof. Fierz: He speaks already of his heir but he never has one.

Prof. Jung: Yes, he says,

> And when shall I want it?—He that hath a goal and an heir, wanteth death at the right time for the goal and the heir.
>
> And out of reverence for the goal and the heir, he will hang up no more withered wreaths in the sanctuary of life.
>
> Verily, not the rope-makers will I resemble: they lengthen out their cord, and thereby go ever backward.

This is just tragic when one thinks how he died.

> Many a one, also, waxeth too old for his truths and triumphs; a toothless mouth hath no longer the right to every truth.
>
> And whoever wanteth to have fame, must take leave of honor betimes, and practise the difficult art of—going at the right time.
>
> One must discontinue being feasted upon when one tasteth best: that is known by those who want to be long loved.
>
> Sour apples are there, no doubt, whose lot is to wait until the last day of autumn: and at the same time they become ripe, yellow, and shrivelled.
>
> In some ageth the heart first, and in others the spirit. And some are hoary in youth, but the late young keep long young.
>
> To many men life is a failure; a poison-worm gnaweth at their heart. Then let them see to it that their dying is all the more a success.
>
> Many never become sweet; they rot even at the summer. It is cowardice that holdeth them fast to their branches.
>
> Far too many live, and far too long hang they on their branches. Would that a storm came and shook all this rottenness and worm-eatenness from the tree!
>
> Would that there came preachers of *speedy* death! Those would be the appropriate storms and agitators of the trees of life! But I hear only slow death preached, and patience with all that is "earthly."

Ah! ye preach patience with what is earthly? This earthly is it that hath too much patience with you, ye blasphemers!

Verily, too early died that Hebrew whom the preachers of slow death honour: and to many hath it proven a calamity that he died too early.

That is the passage I mentioned,

As yet had he known only tears, and the melancholy of the Hebrews, together with the hatred of the good and just—the Hebrew Jesus: then was he seized with the longing for death.

Had he but remained in the wilderness, and far from the good and just! Then, perhaps, would he have learned to live, and love the earth—and laughter also!

Believe it, my brethren! He died too early; he himself would have disavowed his doctrine had he attained to my age! Noble enough was he to disavow!

There is quite a famous book by George Moore, *The Brook Kerith*, in which Christ lived on.[6] It is an exceedingly poor book—you almost die before you reach something that has real substance—but there is one good substantial idea in it. He says that Christ was taken down from the cross and put into the grave by Joseph of Arimathea, and then the grave was opened by some of the disciples and Christ was discovered to be still alive; so they brought him back to Joseph where he recovered and became a shepherd again, as he had been before—he herded the sheep of Joseph. Then later on a very fanatical and excited man appeared who called himself Paul, a disciple of Jesus who was crucified. They told him they knew all about Jesus—he was saved, he is here, you can see him—and then they produced Jesus with the scars on his hands and feet from the crucifixion. But Paul did not believe it, because his Jesus had said he was the son of God, while this Jesus had understood that that was an error.

So the fact that Nietzsche feels that Christ died too early is a general idea only; we really have the need to ask the question: "What would Jesus have taught if he had been a married man, with eight children for instance? How would he have dealt with certain situations in life which only occur when you are in life, when you share it?" Of course he was in his own life but it was a very partial one—he was not really in

---

[6] Jung exaggerates the fame of this novel (1916) by George Moore (1852-1933), and probably was not acquainted with a better and more famous little novel on the same theme, D. H. Lawrence's *The Man Who Died* (London, 1932).

life as we know it. He would perhaps be a good teacher inasmuch as one is meant to live his particular life, the life of a philosophical tramp who really has the idealistic purpose of teaching a new saving truth, who recognizes no other responsibility. You see, he had no profession and no human connections which were valid to him. He separated himself from his family, was the lord of his disciples, who had to follow him while he had to follow no one, being under no obligations. This is an exceedingly simple situation, tragically simple, which is so rare that one cannot assume that the teaching coming from such a life can be possible or applicable to an entirely different type of life. Therefore, we may well ask how it would have been if Christ had had a responsible position. Would he have cast it away? How would he have behaved if he had had to earn money instead of catching a fish with a *stater* in its mouth, or if he only had to unhook an ass somewhere when he needed to ride? That is too simple. Also we could not live on the alms of other people; that would be against our grain. So in every way we are quite different from a man with such an attitude. We don't believe that the life of the earth will soon be finished, that the kingdom of heaven is to come, and that the legions of angels will fall upon the earth so that its power will be finished. And we have an entirely different idea of life in many other respects. And out of this comes the idea of Nietzsche: How would it have been if Christ had had to be responsible for so many children, or if he had been a responsible employee in the administration of Rome or Palestine, or if he had been born to be a priest who was responsible for the traditional creed—and so on? Nietzsche expresses this kind of feeling and so he expresses the need of finding a better key to unlock the problems which we find unanswerable.

Now, the real essence of this chapter is in the paragraph:

> Free for death, and free in death; a holy Nay-sayer, when there is no longer time for Yea: thus understandeth he about death and life.

He means of course a complete freedom even in reference to death. But death surely is an event which is not voluntarily chosen, any more than any great event in life which just comes along and has to be accepted. So what Zarathustra says here sounds like a tremendous exaggeration, unless we consider that it is just Zarathustra who is saying it. An archetype looks at life from the standpoint of Zarathustra—that life surely is an arrangement, that there are right moments in which something is chosen to happen, that even events are for a certain end. "Verily, a goal has Zarathustra." *He* can speak like that, can have a goal because it is the meaning of life in itself, but for a human being it is of course an exaggeration, making for an impossible complication. Then there is one other point in this chapter which needs some explanation:

> Verily, a goal had Zarathustra; he threw his ball. Now be ye friends the heirs of my goal; to you throw I the golden ball.
> Best of all, do I see you, my friends, throw the golden ball! And so tarry I still a little while on the earth—pardon me for it!
> Thus spake Zarathustra.

What does he mean by the golden ball?

Mrs. Sigg: You spoke in a former Seminar of a ceremony—I think it was a resurrection ceremony—at which the ball was used in church.

Mrs. Crowley: Le jeu de pelote.

Mrs. Sigg: But you gave one example of a certain ceremony in a church.

Prof. Jung: Oh yes, the burial of the Hallelujah at Easter. A lump of earth was buried, probably symbolizing the dead sun that is buried and given life again. As Christ dies on Good Friday, he is the sun of the past year, and then his resurrection takes place on Easter Day, marking the coming back of the sun. But you can read about the *jeu de pelota* in an early Seminar report; there I gave a full account of it.[7] It was a symbolic game with a peculiar meaning and it was played in the church. It was a system of relatedness among the figures of the Chapter, the bishop and the deacons and so on. In the way in which they threw the ball to each other they made a certain pattern; it was generally played standing in a circle and it had to do with the making of a mandala where the center moves from one to the other. The center, that ball which moves from the one to the other, is also a god, the god as a function of relationship; it swiftly moves around within the circle and it is the one thing upon which everybody is concentrated. You see, that golden ball is like the wheel which rolls out of itself, another analogy or parallel in *Zarathustra*, or like the dancing star. It is a symbol of the self. This pelote game also has a peculiar connection with depreciatory rumors about the ritual murder which was supposed to take place in Gnostic circles, as well as among the Christians and the Jews; it was said in antiquity that they played the game of pelote with a child that they threw to one another until it was dead. The child represented the god.

---

[7] See *Dream Sem.*, pp. 15-16, 21-22, 32-33, for a fuller account of *jeu de paume* or *pelota basque*, a ritual ball game popular in monasteries until the 13th century, and sometimes indulged thereafter, but with increasing disapproval from the higher clergy.

It was a sacrifice of the god and a human sacrifice in order to renew the life of the god. It was like putting to death the god of the past year, as Christ was put to death instead of Barabbas whom the people wanted to have released as the god of the coming year. Christ was condemned as the criminal representing the god of the past year, according to the old Babylonian custom. And the interesting thing is that Barabbas means "son of the father," just as Christ was the son of the Father; so it is one and the same—the god in its going down and in its coming up.

Now, this is all expressed by the *jeu de pelote*, and the ball is a symbol of the sun; it is the golden ball, an entirely round thing which expresses the state of perfection, of the highest value, of gold. In the next chapter it already appears in that light. There it is the golden top of a walking stick which Zarathustra receives from his disciples, a sun or a globe with a snake coiled round it. And the sun, the golden germ, the *Hiranyagarbha* as it is called in the Upanishads, is another symbol of the self; it is also called the golden child, the precious, perfect substance that is made by man or born out of man; and it is of course the alchemistic gold and the all-roundness of the Platonic being and the *sphairos*, the most blissful god of Empedocles.[8] That substance is played upon or handled in a mystic circle, the meaning being that such a circle of people, where there is that mystical relationship, are all held together by the sun germ, that one perfect golden ball—that germ which is moving among them, partially or chiefly moved by the people themselves, but according to a preexistent pattern. This is an exceedingly difficult picture, and of course we could not explain such an image out of *Zarathustra* if we did not have other materials by which to elucidate the peculiar symbolism.

It is the idea that the self is not identical with one particular individual. No individual can boast of having *the* self: there is only the self that can boast of having many individuals. You see, the self is an extraneous unit in one's existence. It is a center of personality, a center of gravity that does not coincide with the ego; it is as if it were something outside. Also, it is not *this* individual, but a connection with individuals. So one could say the self was the one thing, yet it is the many. It has a paradoxical existence which one cannot define and limit by any particular definition. It is a metaphysical concept. But we must create such a concept in order to express the peculiar psychological fact that one can

---

[8] Empedocles, a contemporary of Socrates who taught that the four elements—earth, air, fire, and water—were pulled apart and united by the force of strife and love. See also 4 May 1938, n. 6, below.

feel as the subject and one can also feel as the object: namely, I can feel I am doing this and that, and I can feel I am made to do it, am the instrument of it. Such-and-such an impetus in me makes my decision. I am feeling a principle which does not coincide with the ego. So, people often say that they can in a measure do what they like, but that the main thing is done by the will of God. God is doing it through them; that is, of course, the religious form of confessing the quality of the self. Therefore, my definition of the self is a non-personal center, the center of the psychical non-ego—of all that in the psyche which is not ego—and presumably it is to be found everywhere in all people. You can call it the center of the collective unconscious. It is as if our unconscious psychology or psyche were centered, just as our conscious psyche is centered in the ego consciousness. The very word *consciousness* is a term expressing association of the contents of a center to the ego, and the same would be the case with the unconscious, yet there it is obviously not *my* ego, because the unconscious *is* unconscious: it is not related to me. I am very much related to the unconscious because the unconscious can influence me all the time, yet I cannot influence the unconscious. It is just as if I were the *object* of a consciousness, as if somebody knew of me though I didn't know of him. That center, that other order of consciousness which to me is unconscious, would be the self, and that doesn't confine itself to myself, to my ego: it can include I don't know how many other people. And this peculiar psychological fact of being the same self with other people is expressed by the image of the pelote, the ball that is played in a certain pattern within a certain circle, symbolizing the relations going hither and thither.

Now, Zarathustra says here that his goal is connected with that ball. His goal is obviously to set that ball in motion, to create that wheel which moves out of itself. And he has thrown the ball among his brethren or disciples, which means that he is bringing up or instigating the self and setting it in motion. You see, there is a clear connection between this idea and the idea of the wheel in motion in Buddhistic literature; the teaching of the law is compared to a moving wheel, yet originally it was probably the same idea. As Zarathustra has thrown a ball, so Buddha brings a wheel among men and sets it in motion, a process which will eventually lead up to the Buddhistic idea of the most perfect condition—the condition of complete detachment, of nirvana.[9] It is also characteristic of Buddhism that it is considered to be a

[9] The Buddha's proclaiming the Dharma was often spoken of as setting in motion the wheel of the law.

spiritual merit to depict such a wheel, to make a drawing of it. It has spiritual value in that it helps towards one's own perfection. Of course a mandala is such a wheel, though that is again a somewhat different aspect. There we very clearly see that the mandalas mean the gods. As a mandala is the seat of the god, the center of the mandala is the deity. But a deity is simply a projected vision of the self. So this chapter leads us really to a very profound idea: namely, that to Zarathustra, being the archetype, life is a preestablished arrangement, a yea and a nay— it can be chosen—the beginning and the end and the way. And the chief meaning of that whole thing is like throwing the ball among a certain group of people who obviously are assembled, chosen by fate or by that unconscious consciousness to be together so that they produce this play of the golden ball. This is, I am afraid, quite obscure, but when it comes to matters of the unconscious, things *get* obscure because we are only partially conscious of them. But I am perfectly certain that such symbols refer to extraordinarily important things. You see, such things have been expressed in the Greek *to en to pan*, which means that the all is the one, or the one is the all,[10] represented by the *ouroboros*, the snake that makes the perfect circle by biting its own tail. That is the same idea, binding together the many into the one, and that one into the many.

Mr. Allemann: I think in India there is the same idea in *neti, neti.*

Prof. Jung: Yes, neither this nor that. It is, all around, the same idea. For instance, in Christian symbolic language Christ says, "I am the vine and ye are the grapes." You see, the supreme idea that Zarathustra is teaching is that the Superman is identical with a ball, and the ball is the globe, the all-perfect roundness expressing the primordial man, the man that *was* before he had been dismembered, cut up or separated— before he became two. And it is the idea of the alchemistic hermaphrodite that unites the sexes.[11] So the Superman is an exceedingly old, mystical idea which appears again and again in the course of the centuries. Of course Nietzsche was not aware of that, he knew almost

[10] The number *one* was perhaps first raised to *The One* by Heraclitus and continued important at least until Plotinus' famous "flight of the alone to the Alone" (*Enneads*, 6.9.70).

[11] An allusion to Aristophanes' speech in Plato's *Symposium* about how the sexes were created by the division of the original hermaphroditic, spherical creatures, whose power threatened the gods. The story is a favorite of Jung. See CW 11, par. 47n; 9 i, par. 138n; et al. In the Middle Ages, Sun/Moon and even the philosopher's stone were often represented as hermaphroditic. See CW 13, figs. B1-B4. Nietzsche of course knew well the Greek philosophers' writings, but probably not those of the alchemists.

nothing of the particular literature in antiquity which contains these symbols; it was not yet discovered, many things have been dug up since; he did not know of the medieval parallels, and he never would think that this ball had anything to do with the all-round primordial man of Plato, or with the *sphairos* of Empedocles. Yet these ideas keep on coming back again and again, and in that respect one could ask, "what is Nietzsche after all?" He is simply a repetition of one of the old alchemists. Nietzsche continues the alchemistic philosophy of the Middle Ages.

LECTURE II

29 January 1936

Prof. Jung:
We come now to a new chapter, a very famous one. The title, "The Bestowing Virtue," has become a sort of slogan. But before we dive into it I should like to know how Nietzsche comes from this particular theme of voluntary death to the idea of the bestowing virtue. What is the transition?

Miss Hannah: Is it not through the part at the end about tossing the golden ball?

Prof. Jung: It might be; usually in the end of a chapter one finds the idea which leads over to the next chapter. But what would be the connection exactly?

Mrs. Sigg: He might think that he really has to bestow something better on the world.

Prof. Jung: Than the idea of the voluntary death? Then you think of it as a sort of compensation?

Mrs. Sigg: I think that when he wrote that chapter in 1883, he had really given some good ideas to the world, so he gave up that idea of killing himself which he had had sometimes.

Prof. Jung: Sure enough, the idea of voluntary death is a pretty negative one. It would mean saying to oneself, "Well, if my life is unsuitable, if I have no chance, if I am no contribution to the life of the world, then it is better to make an end of it." Such an idea is of course exceedingly negative; many degenerate individuals have played with that chapter on voluntary death. It has a negative quality and a negative influence, and therefore we find in the end of it the positive idea of the golden ball as a sort of compensation. The golden ball is indeed an exceedingly positive symbol; even if we don't know exactly what it means, we have a certain idea as to what it refers. And it must be positive in itself or he would not use the attribute "golden" because gold, as he explains in the beginning of the next chapter, means value.

Mrs. Sigg: If the idea of death comes up from the unconscious, is it

786

not generally true that something has to die, not the whole individual, but something that is wrong inside?

Prof. Jung: Quite so, but what has to die in this particular moment of Nietzsche's development is a difficult question.

Prof. Reichstein: In connection with what Mrs. Sigg said, I would say that the chapter before was connected with the heavenly marriage and that idea is always connected with death; something has to die before. And the appearance of the golden ball would also be such a moment; this archetypal idea is always connected with something which has to die before.

Prof. Jung: Why?

Prof. Reichstein: Because it is a very great change in attitude. Perhaps you could say that the change would be that the earthly man has to die.

Prof. Jung: Yes, the "earthly man" being of course the biblical way of putting it; in psychological terms it would be the collective man because the golden ball refers to the self.

Miss Wolff: Last time we spoke of the meaning of the self, and in the end of the chapter on death there is quite a new idea: namely, that Zarathustra is intending to give over his purpose or his teaching to his disciples, so he would not be the only one who carries the idea. And the idea comes in here that one man alone cannot reach the self. In one of the last verses he says, "Now be ye friends the heirs of my goal; to you throw I the golden ball." I think this is a sort of analogy to the idea of the child, because the child, as Nietzsche puts it, is also something beyond, beyond the parents. So the idea is to carry on something.

Prof. Jung: So you would connect that passage of the golden ball with the symbolism we encountered before in "Child and Marriage"?

Miss Wolff: It is the same idea, that one person alone cannot achieve the self. It is phrased very differently, but it comes much nearer the meaning than the chapter on death, though he alludes here to that idea that the self is not one individual alone.

Prof. Jung: Well, when you go back through the chapters you find a sort of preparation, like a preparatory initiation, for this idea. For instance, begin with chapter 15—though it would be possible to begin before—"The Thousand and One Goals"; that is the idea of many goals with no certainty as to which is the right one. Then the sixteenth chapter is on neighbor love which means that something else must come in, a partner, a relationship. The seventeenth chapter is "The Way of the Creating One": something ought to be created. How can you create? Well, "Old and Young Women," chapter 18. Then if you have to do with women, there is chapter 19, "The Bite of the Adder": you will be bitten by the snake which is the reversed impregnation—poisoning. And what is the result? "Child and Marriage," chapter 20. That is voluntary death: namely, you go under in that relationship and you reappear as a child, because it is all the interior drama of the unconscious development. And so it comes to the chapter we have just dealt with, to the idea of the golden ball; that is the symbol for the thing he has created.

Mrs. Frost: In the third verse before the end Nietzsche says, "Thus will I die myself, that ye friends may love the earth more for my sake." If he dies that we may love the earth more, is it not the reaction against Christ who dies that we may go more into the spirit? And the loving of the earth is surely that love of the golden ball which he hands on.

Prof. Jung: Quite. This is a reaction against the Christian spirit, since Christ really did not die for the earth but for the spirit. The golden ball has that meaning; it symbolizes Nietzsche's most important idea, the relation to the earth. But that is not the whole thing. It is only the anti-Christian and the pro-earth aspect of the symbolism, and this same symbolism has also spiritual meaning. But Nietzsche does something new to it and we shall presently come to that.

Mrs. Sigg: I think Christ was not exactly anti-earth, because if people would really follow his teaching it would be possible for them to live in a deeper way too.

Prof. Jung: Well, what Christ himself meant is pretty obscure, with tremendous contradictions, and it is very difficult to make out. So in speaking of Christianity, we must speak of what has become of that teaching, the late Christian spirit as expressed in the churches or sects, and not be influenced by those very remote traces of the teaching which Christ might have given to the world. If you study carefully the teaching of Christ, you see that it is not a perfectly clear system, but full of allusions and profundities and depths which we don't quite understand: *Wer Ohren hat zu hören, der höre,* "who has ears to hear, let him hear." It was a mystery teaching. He says funny things sometimes: think of his cursing the fig tree, and the parable of the unjust steward, for instance. That cannot be understood without a knowledge of the mystery teaching of those days. Parsons carefully avoid those things, and they know very well why.

Mrs. Sigg: I think in many cases parsons know the truth and make falsifications. For instance, we have (Matthew 5:22) the expression "in danger of hellfire," although the word *Gehenna* that Christ uses there has certainly not that meaning. It is wrong for the parsons to say it is eternal hellfire.

Prof. Jung: Well, it makes little difference whether they explain it here as hellfire or not, because there are plenty of other passages in the Gospels where hell is established as a reality.

Mrs. Stutz: I think Zarathustra deals too much by will. He thinks he can arrange things in his own way; if he gave that up, so that the golden ball could fall in *its* way, then its virtue could give him something that he could not enjoy before.

Prof. Jung: You mean that this idea of the bestowing virtue is in opposition to his very wilful attitude? Sure enough, that is a new and a very important idea. Now we must really get on to the next chapter.

> When Zarathustra had taken leave of the town to which his heart was attached, the name of which is "The Pied Cow," there followed him many people who called themselves his disciples, and kept him company.

Here we learn that Zarathustra's heart was attached to the town called "The Pied Cow," an impression which we did not receive when we read the chapter about that town before. And it is not known that many disciples followed him and kept him company when he left that town, so it must be an entirely fantastical experience. Obviously Nietzsche is now attacked by love for people, for the world, for humanity—which is not usual. In many passages before he very openly declared his disinterestedness in humanity. Therefore, we can assume that in the course of the development of these images, he has become more and more isolated and feels his loneliness, so the end is the idea of voluntary death, which is often the case with people who have maneuvered themselves into complete solitude. Then when that moment is past, the other side comes up, the side of life, of humanity. Where have we a similar development—a condition of utter despair and a suicidal mood leading up to a similar transition? There is a famous case in literature.

Prof. Fierz: In Faust.

Prof. Jung: Yes, he also maneuvered himself into complete loneliness, and then comes the moment of suicide, and then suddenly a new mood surges up, the Easter mood, resurrection. One might call it the resurrection of the Christian spirit of life. The evidence that it is really a Christian mood in Faust is that he identifies with another famous personage of religious importance, Luther. And he translates the Evangel of John, which is rather astonishing because Faust had been very critical of Christianity before. But when he gets to the point of suicide, suddenly the Christian aspect comes back to him so strongly that he even identifies with Luther, the last thing one would have expected of such a man. Now this "bestowing virtue" is of course the blood that is poured out for mankind; in that all-embracing love one gives oneself to everybody: one is a present. It sounds almost like the Oxford Movement. You see, this is by no means an isolated case; one observes in practical life that when people come to a head with their existence, if they don't squeeze off their head they reappear in an old garment which they think is absolutely new. How is that?

Mrs. Sigg: It is the natural law that it must go in that way; it is what we call an *enantiodromia*.

Prof. Jung: It is an *enantiodromia* surely, and how do you explain it? How does such a thing happen? Suppose you have gotten yourself into a state of solitude and despair and are going to commit suicide, and then in the last moment you think better of it and come back to life, reappearing in a thoroughly Christian attitude.

Mr. Allemann: It would be an attitude of utter collectivity after utter isolation.

Prof. Jung: Exactly, that is one aspect of it. First you are absolutely isolated in your extreme individualism, cut off from the herd and on the way to death; you feel as if you were already dead. And then when you come back to life you will naturally begin where you gave it up; instead of going back to your individualism you go back to the earth—that is quite certain. Also from your former disbelief or criticism you come back to positive belief, and there is nothing to believe except what was there before, the general belief that exists everywhere. You might even have what people call an experience of Christ, or of God, *ein Gotteserlebnis*; you might have a vision, and you would then be thoroughly convinced that you had been saved by Christ in that moment. Unfortunately, we are not informed about Paul's mood when he was travelling to Damascus; perhaps he had been nervous and in a sort of despair and that led him to the vision of Christ. Of course it had a different meaning then, but in our days when Christ is an established truth, when it is *de rigueur* to believe in Christ, it is most probable that when you go so far on the one side, you will then go far in believing again what you believed before. This is a law, almost a mechanism, so it is quite understandable that Faust, having left all that his time believed in and hoped for, would return to it after he had given up the apparently inevitable idea of death.

That individualistic kind of development leads into isolation and death because one's life is no longer connected with the life of mankind. Life in one, single, isolated individual cannot be maintained because the roots are cut off; our roots are in mankind and if we give up that connection we are just like a plant with no roots. Therefore, if one wants to establish one's life one must return to the herd and to the given conditions. And our given condition, as it was with Goethe or Faust and as it was with Nietzsche, is the Christian humanity—that is the thing to which one inevitably returns. So this chapter and the idea of the bestowing virtue in itself, has not only a Christian aspect, but a Christian *value*, there is no doubt about it. You see, when Zarathustra, or Nietzsche, returns to life, he surely will be forced to participate in the life of mankind as it is in that moment, and then he will see the positive values of it. That is the reason why we come here to a rather unexpected Christian idea—unexpected with Nietzsche. Formerly he only mocked about that town and now we learn that he loves it, that his heart is attached to it. We were impressed with his utter loneliness before and did not know that he had so many disciples. That is an entirely new aspect from which we can conclude that he had felt quite positive there and had had a large audience. Now coming back to this situation leads him to a crossroad: "Thus came they to a cross-road." What about this?

Prof. Fierz: He is like Heracles, come now to a new dilemma.

Prof. Jung: Yes, and what would that be?

Prof. Reichstein: Whether to go with all his disciples, or to go alone.

Prof. Jung: Yes, either he goes with his disciples, which means going with the town of the Pied Cow, with the hitherto valid beliefs, or he goes alone; he has the choice of being absolutely collective or again alone. Now, people after such an experience very often decide not to be alone, but to remain with the herd which they then see in its positive aspect, and they think it is an advantage to have lost the loneliness. But then they have lost their last values, to speak in the words of Nietzsche. For the question is not to be either in the herd or isolated from the herd; it is to be in the herd and alone.

> Then Zarathustra told them that he now wanted to go alone; for he was fond of going alone. His disciples, however, presented him at his departure with a staff, on the golden handle of which a serpent twined round the sun. Zarathustra rejoiced on account of the staff, and supported himself thereon; . . .

He is obviously making up his mind to follow his road alone again because that is really his first love; his strongest tendency is to go alone, despite the very positive aspect of collectivity which he describes here. Now his disciples give him a sun symbol, the golden ball which he has thrown to them before. You see, in giving to his disciples something as precious as the golden ball, he has given them a positive value. What is that present, really?

Mrs. Crowley: It is the reconciling symbol.

Prof. Jung: Well, he has given them an important symbol; whether it is reconciling or not we still have to see. But a symbol is always an idea, so he has given them a really positive value. And this symbol means what?

Mr. Allemann: The self.

Prof. Jung: Yes, and the self appears to be a most valuable idea. The golden ball is the sun, also a divine symbol; it is what the sun used to be when it was the central god in old cults, the source of warmth and of life. Therefore, it must be an idea which has equal virtue, equal value, which for us, whether we believe it or not, is actually the sun, the source of warmth and life. So it *is* really a reconciling symbol, the symbol that solves conflicts, that overcomes the oppositions characterizing our lives—a symbol that creates peace and totality. The self is really expected to be able to do that. Of course in the west we have no philosophy of the self, but in the Upanishads you will find all these attributes; and you will see that the idea of the self is the most essential idea in their philosophy of Atman, for instance. A particularly beautiful example of that philosophy is the dialogue between Yajñavalkya and the king. I cannot quote it literally but you remember, the king asks him a series of questions about the light. For instance, when the people go out to do their work they return in the light of the sun, and then the king asks: But when the light of the sun is extinct, by what light shall they live?, and Yajñavalkya says by the light of the moon. Finally every light, every fire, comes to an end, and there would be utter darkness, but there is still left the light of the self, which is the supreme light.[1] That is the exact parallel of the idea of the golden ball. So in giving such teaching to his disciples, Zarathustra really gives them a golden present. And whatever you give returns to you; what you give, you have gained, but what you have acquired is lost. He gives a present to his disciples, and then it returns to him. This is not said by Nietzsche in so many words. I am not even convinced that he was conscious of it; it simply happens that his disciples are able to give him that present, and they would not have been able if they had not the means. Through the gold he has given to them, they can return in kind, and with an ad-

[1] Yajñavalkya, a great sage of the Upanishads, who told of the several kinds of light: sun, moon, fire—and finally Atman, the self.

dition which comes really from them, the serpent twined round the golden ball.

Mrs. Sigg: Nietzsche never was particularly intelligent when it came to his relation to people—not very practical—and the serpent being a symbol of cunning and wisdom might mean a leading principle to him in his relations to human beings.

Prof. Jung: Well, the serpent and the sun are general symbolism, and we must first know something of that before we can make an application to Nietzsche's case; otherwise, that interpretation looks far too personal and arbitrary.

Mrs. Baynes: Would it not be the Yin and the Yang?

Prof. Jung: Yes, in Chinese language it would be the Yin and the Yang, but there is a much nearer idea.

Mrs. Sigg: The Egyptian symbolism of the sun.

Prof. Jung: That is the closest analogy, the disc of the sun encoiled by the uraeus.[2]

Prof. Fierz: The Chinese universe with the dragon round it?

Prof. Jung: In China it is really the pearl and the dragon, and the strange thing is that the pearl there is the moon, the Yin, and the dragon is Yang. The symbolism is just reversed, and it is difficult to translate because in China the values are in a subtle way turned round; it is as if the real teacher there had been a woman. Everybody would say Yang was the sun, but the Chinaman says, not at all, it is a dragon. Everywhere else the dragon is a malevolent and dangerous beast, but in China it is a friendly thing; the Chinaman is a friend of the dragon. The only friend of the serpent we know is the woman; no man ever was the friend of the serpent unless he was a sorcerer and taught by a woman.

Mrs. Baynes: But it is true that the Chinese dragon can fly and the serpent cannot.

Prof. Jung: Yes, the dragon is a flying serpent. We have dragons but they are all bad while the Chinese dragon is a sign of happiness, of wealth and of health, of everything good. The sun is the important and positive thing to us, while there it is the dragon, and a moon that is very small, a pearl almost in the mouth of the dragon. As a rule the pearl is a little bit ahead so it looks as if in all eternity the dragon were not quite capable of catching that pearl, he is always after it but never quite

---

[2] "The disk of the sun . . . a vast dragon with its tail in its mouth mounted on seven powers and drawn by four others figures as horses" (from "The Books of the Savior" in Mead*, p. 510.

happy in its possession. If you follow up that thought and apply it to Chinese symbolism in general, you will see that it works. China has a peculiar twist; the earth plays another part there—it is unsurpassed. In Egypt the positive celestial body of the sun is the important thing; therefore in the time of Amenhotep IV the symbol was no longer the disc and the serpent, but was the disc of the sun rejoicing in its two horizons—the worship of the positive principle *par excellence*. Whereas the addition of the serpent is the earth lying in the sunshine, warming its cold body in the rays of the sun; that is the idea of the uraeus. Then we have another very direct parallel to the positive symbol of the sun and the encircling serpent.

Mrs. Baynes: The Kundalini Yoga.

Prof. Jung: Yes, the sun being the creative point, the bindu, and the Shakti is coiled round the phallic figure as in the *muladhara* mandala. Then there is the Orphic symbol of the egg round which the serpent is coiled, which is perhaps the nearest parallel to this *Zarathustra* symbolism. Now, what do the disciples convey in giving such a present to Zarathustra—what does it mean?

Miss Wolff: Perhaps a side of the problem which Zarathustra himself has not seen. It might be that snake which he has thrown out of his mouth to other people to handle, so they give it back to him, because without that the circle is not complete.

Prof. Jung: Yes, and besides the chapter about the bite of the adder, there is a chapter later where the snake crept into the shepherd's mouth.

Miss Wolff: I meant that chapter particularly—I anticipated.

Prof. Jung: Well, the serpent is rejected by Zarathustra. He loathes it because it is the earth, the darkness, the Yin, the female principle. Zarathustra is entirely masculine, the masculine archetype of the wise old man *par excellence*; and he is the *pneuma*, the wind-god, and therefore has to reject the serpent. That is the reason why he throws only the golden ball to his disciples; *they* add the serpent. And how does it come about that they are able to do that? You see, it is the *pelote* again.

Prof. Reichstein: They have the connection with the earth because they are also with collectivity.

Prof. Jung: Exactly. You see, when Zarathustra is in the circle of his disciples, he already represents that symbolism; one could say that the sun and the serpent symbolized his relation to his disciples. He is in the center, the *pneuma* surrounded by the circle of mankind, and mankind is the earth; so his disciples are his earth. He is rooted in his disciples. And in throwing the golden ball to them, he gives them himself, his own principle, and they receive it as the earth receives the seed. They form a circle round him like the earth snake that bites its own tail. It is the female that forms a ring round the male in the Tantric Yoga also; the Shakti in everlasting embrace with the god Shiva is an eternal symbol, and it is one of the most complete symbols of the self. The self conceived of as the superpersonal Atman (or the *Paramatman* or Prajapati or the *Purusha*) is alone, one could say; therefore, he emanates a world which is his mirror, the mirror being of course of a different substance from that which is mirrored. The mirror is the shakti that creates the real illusion, the veil of Maya, round the god; the god sees all his millions of faces mirrored in the magic mirror of Maya.[3]

That is the situation here, and there really could be no self if it were not in relation; the self and individualism exclude each other. The self *is* relatedness. Only when the self mirrors itself in so many mirrors does it really exist—then it has roots. You can never come to your self by building a meditation hut on top of Mount Everest; you will only be visited by your own ghosts and that is not individuation: you are all alone with yourself and *the* self doesn't exist. The self only exists inasmuch as you appear. Not that you *are*, but that you *do* is the self. The self appears in your deeds, and deeds always mean relationship; a deed is something that you produce which is practically outside of you, between yourself and your surroundings, between subject and object—there the self is visible. So the symbol is the sun encoiled by the serpent. That is what the disciples give back to him. It is the answer of the disciples, and it is a symbol of the union of Zarathustra and his disciples. That is the staff upon which he supports himself.

Then spake he thus to his disciples:
Tell me pray: how came gold to the highest value? Because it is uncommon, and unprofiting, and beaming, and soft in lustre; it always bestoweth itself.

This is a sort of interpretation of the symbolic idea of gold. The real gold is symbolic, therefore it is so highly praised. It has definite values but the main value is that which man gives to it; the use to which it is ordinarily put would never explain the fascination gold has in itself for man. In the hieratic language of the whole world, gold is used to designate something that is valuable. It is used in the same way in art—certain things are painted gold. And in alchemistic philosophy it is

---

[3] Atman knows itself by its creations, or as Jung taught, by one's projections.

known as *aurum nostrum non vulgi*.[4] So when gold appears in dreams it means value.

> Only as image of the highest virtue came gold to the highest value. Goldlike, beameth the glance of the bestower. Gold-lustre maketh peace between moon and sun.
> Uncommon is the highest virtue, and unprofiting, beaming is it, and soft of lustre: a bestowing virtue is the highest virtue.

Here we have the reconciling symbol, and a very interesting relation to the alchemistic symbolism: namely, the uncommon gold, the philosophical gold, is the child of the sun and moon, the male and the female. The gold or the philosopher's stone is even called the sun and moon child, or the hermaphroditic sun and moon child, the hermaphrodite symbolizing of course the union of male and female. One finds this idea practically everywhere.[5] The idea of the self under the aspect of a thing born out of man or out of the world is called in the Upanishads the *Hiranyagarbha*, which means the golden child or the golden germ; that is the philosophical gold which comes from the union of opposites. So if the lonely Zarathustra can be united to a circle of human beings then the golden child, the god, is born, *Hiranyagarbha*; then the golden ball appears with the serpent. The idea of the god being the reconciler and peacemaker is often symbolized also by the hermaphrodite; therefore, so many gods are represented as such. A very near analogy is the old Orphic *Phanēs*, whose very name denotes the rising sun. *Phanēs* means the appearing one, the one that is born at the beginning; it is the god of the beginning, hermaphroditic, with two bodies, and there are four symbolic animals. This is faintly analogous to the *quaternium* in Christian iconography, where the four pillars of the Gospels are represented as four animals and the figure of Christ is in the center; it is also called the *tetramorphos*, but that properly is the sort of monstrous animal with four heads that one sees in old illuminated manuscripts, the head of a lion, an ox, an eagle and an angel—the four Evangelists. And it has one leg of the lion, one of the ox, one of the eagle, and a human leg, and then the savior with a flag or emblem of the church is riding upon that animal. You see, the Orphic *Phanēs* is similar.[6]

Now, Frau Dr. Burgers has just told me that in China the horoscope

---

[4] "Our gold is not the vulgar [common] gold."

[5] See CW 12, *passim*, for further discussion of alchemical symbols for the hermaphroditic union of male and female.

[6] Phanes, the shining one, is an Eros, but bisexual. See CW 5, plate XII, for a reproduction of an Orphic relief showing this boy-god being born from the world egg.

is based on twenty-eight *moon* houses, not sun houses. And Professor Reichstein has pointed out to me that the currency of China is not based upon gold but on silver. They are trying some such stunt in America now and we shall see how that will influence the general welfare.

Mrs. Crowley: Is it not true that in the east voluntary death is quite a positive symbol?

Prof. Jung: Yes, and voluntary death was well received in Rome also; it was quite counted on. Now, we have a question by Mrs. Baynes: "When you say that the self cannot be reached in isolation, does that mean that the 'Forest philosophers' of India were deluded when they thought they had found the self?"

Oh well, when I said that you couldn't find the self without relationship, I didn't mean to exclude the other side. The forest philosophers don't go out into the forests in the beginning to try to find the self. They first live a full human life in the world and then comes the wood life. They are rooted in the world. They never shunned the individual social life, but gathered all the experience from their worldly existence, and then carried it into the wood. And that was the case in Buddha's own existence; he was a prince, a man of the world, and he had a wife, he had concubines, he had a child—then he went over to the saintly life. I could say just as well that you could never attain the self without isolation; it is both being alone and in relationship. But naturally we have to emphasize relationship with Zarathustra who was always on the lonely side; that Nietzsche was so isolated was the reason why things went so wrong, so he fell into the possession of *djins*. Of course one can rationalize that as coming from the syphilitic infection which caused the paralytic disease. But under that was a case of schizophrenia; he could have gone wrong in another way from being too much alone, not being capable of establishing roots—any plant dies that has no roots. It is not the roots alone, however, that make the plant; the flower must come too. It is the two things, being alone and connected.

> Verily, I divine you well, my disciples: ye strive like me for the bestowing virtue. What should ye have in common with cats and wolves?
>
> It is your thirst to become sacrifices and gifts yourselves: and therefore have ye the thirst to accumulate all riches in your soul.

This is somewhat involved. In throwing the golden ball to his disciples he obviously assumes that they are worthy disciples, that they are capable of taking his gift and putting it to the right use. He trusts that they are striving like him for the bestowing virtue, the virtue of the gold that is shining, beaming, radiating, giving its beauty and its fascination to everybody. "What should ye have in common with cats and wolves?" You see, those are rapacious animals of prey that devour and destroy. It is not the disciples' thirst to become cats and wolves, but to become sacrifices and gifts. Here comes in the Christian ideal that there is no rapacious instinct to steal, but rather to give and give to the utmost, to give oneself as a sacrifice. As Christ has given himself to mankind so Zarathustra and his disciples strive to become sacrifices to mankind. "And therefore have ye the thirst to accumulate all riches in your soul." That *therefore* doesn't belong there, it is not a logical conclusion, but is rather an immediate association; something should be said in between. For in order to be valuable gifts they must be gold first, and in order to be gold they must eat the gold in the world; they must acquire, appropriate, accumulate riches, and store them in their soul in order to become a rich gift. Many people think it is a gift when they give themselves. By no means! It is a burden. When a poor man gives me his last cent I am terribly burdened. Yes, if a rich man gives me out of his abundance, then I really have received a gift, but a beggar cannot give himself. What is he? Has he value? No, he is an empty sack. That all the empty sacks want to give themselves in order to be filled I can understand, but this is no gift; it is as if a tiger should say, I give myself entirely to you, and then eats you. So in order to be able to give something, one has to be something, one has to possess, one must consist of gold and not of hunger. Unfortunately most of the people who talk of giving themselves are just hungry wolves that want to eat your sheep. You see, that must be said between those two sentences.

> Insatiably striveth your soul for treasures and jewels, because your virtue is insatiable in desiring to bestow.

If there is a virtue that is desirous of bestowing, there must be also the means by which one can bestow; one cannot give emptiness. Riches must be accumulated first. One must be keen over treasures, jewels. One should be rapacious in accumulating in order to be able to give. Otherwise one is never quite certain whether one doesn't give hunger.

> Ye constrain all things to flow towards you and into you, so that they shall flow back again out of your fountain as the gifts of your love.

You see, this is the formula for what has happened: namely, Zarathustra threw the golden ball. He could give it because he had it, and then the ball came back to him.

Verily, an appropriator of all values must such bestowing love become; but healthy and holy, call I this selfishness.—

Another selfishness is there, an all-too-poor and hungry kind, which would always steal—the selfishness of the sick, the sickly selfishness.

Here is an important moral difference: when we speak of selfishness it sounds like a vice because we usually know only what Nietzsche calls sickly selfishness. We know selfishness as individualism, as a hungry or thirsty kind of craving to impose upon others, to steal from others, to take away their values; one can call it morbid—selfishness in the sense of egotism. But there is another selfishness which is holy, only nobody has any idea of it; this idea has died out for us since the early Middle Ages. We have the idea that when somebody withdraws into himself, when he does not allow other people to eat him, that he is morbid or terribly egotistical. This simply comes from the fact that late Christianity believes in the early teaching of Christ: "Love thy neighbor, "and then what Christ really taught, "as thyself," is never mentioned. But if you don't love yourself, how can you love anybody else? You come to him as a begging bowl, and he has to give. While if you love yourself, you are rich, you are warm, you have abundance; then you can say that you love because you are really a gift, you are agreeable. For you must feel well when you go to your friends; you must be able to give something in order to be a loving friend. Otherwise you are a burden. If you are black and hungry and thirsty you are just a damned nuisance, just an empty sack. That is what these Christians are; they are empty and they make demands upon one. They say, "We love you and you *ought to*"—those devils put one under an obligation. But I always point out that Christ said: "Love thy neighbor *as thyself*," so love yourself first.

And this is so difficult that for a long time you won't ask anybody to love you, because you know what an awful hell it is. You hate yourself, are despicable to yourself, cannot stand two hours in a room alone. Like the clergyman I told you about. He was occupied from seven in the morning till eleven at night with people, so he was quite empty and therefore suffered from all sorts of disturbances. You see, you must give something to yourself. How can you give to people when you don't understand yourself? Learn to understand yourself first. I had the greatest trouble in the world to teach that man that he should sometimes be alone with himself. He thought that if he read a book or played the piano with his wife he would be alone, and that if he were actually alone one hour every day he would get crazy and melancholic. If you cannot stand yourself for any length of time, you may be sure

799

that your room is full of animals—you develop an evil smell. And yet you demand that your neighbor should love you. It is just as if a dinner was served to you which was so bad you couldn't eat it, and then you say to your friend or mother or father, "Eat it, I love you, it is very bad." But no, you tell them it is very good, you cheat people.

You see, whoever is not able to love himself is unworthy of loving other people and people kick him out of the house. And they are quite right. It is very difficult to love oneself, as it is very difficult to really love other people. But inasmuch as you can love yourself you can love other people; the proof is *whether* you can love yourself, *whether* you can stand yourself. That is exceedingly difficult; there is no meal worse than one's own flesh. Try to eat it in a ritual way, try to celebrate communion with yourself, eat your own flesh and drink your own blood— see how the thing tastes. You will marvel. Then you see what you are to your friends and relations; just as bad as you seem to yourself are you to them. Of course they are all blindfolded, late Christians, so they may not see the poison they eat in loving you; but if you know this, you can understand how important it is to be alone sometimes. It is the only way in which you can establish decent relations to other people. Otherwise, it is always a question, not of give and take, but of stealing.

> With the eye of the thief it looketh upon all that is lustrous; with the craving of hunger it measureth him who hath abundance; and ever doth it prowl round the tables of bestowers.

That is the society of the empty sacks.

> Sickness speaketh in such craving, and invisible degeneration; of a sickly body, speaketh the larcenous craving of this selfishness.

What about this "sickly body"? Would it not be much nicer to say "of a sickly soul"? You know, to the late Christian you can convey the idea that one ought to be interested in oneself in the way, say, of a schoolmaster, or a doctor. They understand that one needs some education of the soul, some loving care of one's own spiritual welfare, provided that the body is excluded. The thing people are most afraid of is not so much the soul, which to them is practically non-existent, but the body. That is what they don't want to see, the animal or the evil spirit that is waiting to say something to them when they are alone. That is exceedingly disagreeable. So even if they agree that one could be a bit more careful with oneself, it is only with the guarantee that the body is excluded and has nothing to do with it. The body is the darkness, and very dangerous things could be called up. It is better to play the piano in order not to hear what the body says. So Zarathustra is quite right: it is not only a sickly soul, but is really a sickly body.

> Tell me, my brother, what do we think bad, and worst of all? Is it not degeneration?—And we always suspect degeneration when the bestowing soul is lacking.

You know, degeneration was much talked about in Nietzsche's time. There was a famous French book about degeneration (written by a Jew with a German name that I can't remember at the moment), which was a great thing in the eighties, and the word *degeneration* became a slogan.[7] Now, the meaning of *degeneration* is that the development deviates from the original pattern. A degenerate tiger would be a tiger that developed into a vegetarian, or a degenerate monkey would be one that specialized in sausages—such peculiarities. Singing birds sometimes show signs of degeneration; robins or even blackbirds in the neighborhood of railway lines begin to lose their own melody and imitate the whistle of the engine, or perhaps they learn human melodies; in the war, birds that lived near the trenches were observed whose song began to imitate the whistling of the bullets. *Genus* means the kind to which one belongs, and if you deviate from the pattern which constitutes that *genus* you suffer from degeneration.

Nietzsche uses this word, of course, in a very much wider sense. He means a deviation from the pattern which is in man, and that is the self; that is the individual condition or pattern or form which can be fulfilled according to its meaning. Or you can deviate from it. If you fulfil the pattern that is peculiar to yourself, you have loved yourself, you have accumulated and have abundance; you bestow virtue then because you have luster. You radiate; from your abundance something overflows. But if you hate and despise yourself—if you have not accepted your pattern—then there are hungry animals (prowling cats and other beasts and vermin) in your constitution which get at your neighbors like flies in order to satisfy the appetites which you have failed to satisfy. Therefore, Nietzsche says to those people who have not fulfilled their individual pattern that the bestowing soul is lacking. There is no radiation, no real warmth; there is hunger and secret stealing.

[7] Jung must have had in mind Max Simon Nordau's *Entartung*, which was so popular that it was almost immediately translated into *Degeneration* (London, 1920). In this book, Nordau (whose name was originally Max Simon Sudfeld) characterized Nietzsche as an imaginative sadist.

Upward goeth our course from genera on to supergenera. But a horror to us is the degenerating sense, which saith: "All for myself."

You see, that degenerate sense which says "all for myself" is unfulfilled destiny. That is somebody who did not live himself, did not give himself what he needed, did not toil for the fulfilment of the pattern which had been given him when he was born. Because that thing is one's *genus*, it ought to be fulfilled, and inasmuch as it is not, there is that hunger which says "all for myself." This is not love of oneself, but simply a hunger which demands for oneself, and one does not provide for the demand; one steals it, takes it from others, expects it as a sort of present from others, thinks it is their duty to give it. Our late Christian teaching has been like that. Love thy neighbor as Christ loves you, and if you are burdened by sins and all sorts of mental or moral troubles, eat his body and you will be cured: eat Christ in the form of the communion and you will be purified, fed, and fulfilled. People are educated in that way. If you have trouble, cast it on Christ as if he were the animal that carries your burdens, a scapegoat for your sins; and if you feel hungry, eat him. He will feed you. You see, you are thus taught an eternal babyhood where food is always ready; it comes from the mother church that has of course an everlasting supply of the sacred foodstuff in the substantial host and the wine. If you follow such a teaching exclusively, you get used to having most important things ready-made for you; you only have to go to church and there you get it. If something should be too difficult for you to carry, if you have done something of which you cannot stand the thought, you simply put it on the back of Christ and he will carry it away. He will remove it.

The Catholic practice of confession and repentance and absolution is just that: you repent and then you tell about it and are given absolution. You are washed of your sin, and then you can do it again—you are a clean slate so you can write on it once more. That is the reason the Reformation did away with confession, in one way fortunately, in another unfortunately, because people cannot get rid of their sins. And that is the reason *entre autres* for the success of the Oxford Movement, where you can hand over your sin to other people and they run away with it. But that is bad. The Protestant must be alone with his sin. He may confess it but he knows that doesn't give him absolution; even if he confesses ten thousand times, he can only familiarize himself with the fact that he should never lose sight of what he has done. That is good for him. He should arrive at a level where he can say, "Yes, I have done that thing, and I must curse myself for it." But I cannot be nice to a man who has given offence to me if I am not nice with myself. I must agree with my brother for my worst brother is myself. So I have to be patient, and I have to be very Christian *inside*. If I fulfil my pattern, then I can even accept my sinfulness and can say, "It is too bad, but it is so—I have to agree with it." And then I am fulfilled, then the gold begins to glow. You see, people who can agree with themselves are like gold. They taste very good. All the flies are after them.

LECTURE III

5 February 1936

Prof. Jung:

We were speaking last time of the idea of degeneration. Now he continues:

> Upward soareth our sense: thus is it a simile of our body, a simile of an elevation. Such similes of elevations are the names of the virtues.
>
> Thus goeth the body through history, a becomer and fighter. And the spirit—what is it to the body? Its fights' and victories' herald, its companion and echo.
>
> Similes, are all names of good and evil; they do not speak out, they only hint. A fool who seeketh knowledge from them!
>
> Give heed, my brethren, to every hour when your spirit would speak in similes: there is the origin of your virtue.
>
> Elevated is then your body, and raised up; with its delight, enraptureth it the spirit; so that it becometh creator, and valuer, and lover, and everything's benefactor.
>
> When your heart overfloweth broad and full like the river, a blessing and a danger to the lowlanders: there is the origin of your virtue.
>
> When ye are exalted above praise and blame, and your will would command all things, as a loving one's will: there is the origin of your virtue.
>
> When ye despise pleasant things, and the effeminate couch, and cannot couch far enough from the effeminate: there is the origin of your virtue.
>
> When ye are willers of one will, and when that change of every need is needful to you: there is the origin of your virtue.
>
> Verily, a new good and evil is it! Verily, a new deep murmuring and the voice of a new fountain!

Power is it, this new virtue; a ruling thought is it, and around it
a subtle soul: a golden sun, with the serpent of knowledge around
it.

The last part of this chapter is decidedly difficult but we get a hint in
that sentence, "Verily, a new good and evil is it! Verily, a new deep
murmuring, and the voice of a new fountain." To what would this refer?

Prof. Reichstein: To an impersonal center, not person. He says it is
different from the one who says "all for myself."

Prof. Jung: You mean that "all for myself" would be the egotistical
tendency and this would be an altruistic version?

Prof. Reichstein: He speaks of a new fountain.

Prof. Jung: But that might simply point to something like a new
fountain which hitherto has not played, to a new origin.

Mr. Allemann: It is new energy, new libido welling up from the unconscious.

Prof. Jung: That would be the exact formulation. We could also say
the new form of energy was welling up from a different region than
before. And under what conditions can such a thing happen?

Mrs. Crowley: When there is a reconciliation of the two opposite
sides.

Prof. Jung: Yes, a new energy could not spring up if there had not
been a conflict before, so there must have been an opposition somewhere, and then suddenly the pairs of opposites were reconciled, and
the energy which was invested in that tension is now released. And
what was that opposition?

Prof. Reichstein: The golden ball with the snake round it, meaning
the self and collectivity?

Prof. Jung: That would symbolize it. But throughout this chapter we
have allusions to a particular dilemma.

Mrs. Frost: Is it the opposition between the *Seele* which wants *ich will*,
and the one that says: "Do thus!"?

Prof. Jung: Yes, but it is said here in so many words.

Miss Hannah: The body and the spirit.

Prof. Jung: Exactly. He says, "And the spirit—what is it to the body?"
So we have the point of view of the spirit, and the physical or corporal
point of view. Now, spirit and body have long been in opposition, as
you know, but apparently Nietzsche has here found a reconciliation of
the two. Where is that indicated in the text of this chapter?

Mrs. Crowley: Is it not in this idea of the simile?

Prof. Jung: Yes. You see "similes are all names of good and evil; they do not speak out, they only hint. A fool who seeketh knowledge from them." So these similes really give nothing, give no knowledge in themselves, but there is another answer here in the words of Zarathustra.

Miss Hannah: Is it not, "Give heed, my brethren, to every hour when your spirit would speak in similes?"

Prof. Jung: Exactly. That is, the simile in itself is not a source of knowledge or understanding. The words mean nothing, they are mere words. The important thing is the hour in which the spirit speaks in similes. In other words, when the spirit speaks in similes then a new source of energy has opened up, and then, as the fruit or result of a certain psychological condition, the similes have meaning. It is not the similes themselves, then, that have meaning but that they do occur; that one speaks in parables is important, because that is a symptom of something that has happened. Now, under what particular conditions would you speak in similes?

Mrs. Crowley: In a creative condition. It seems to me that the simile is the thing that grows out of revelation, and the fact is the thing that is absolutely abstract, more a concept. So that creative process which goes on in similes is a kind of revealing form; it doesn't state, but allows one to perceive.

Prof. Jung: Yes, one speaks in similes or analogies, for instance, when unable to express a thing in clear, abstract language. This is one condition, but it is not exactly the condition which Nietzsche envisages.

Mr. Allemann: Would it be a state of *ekstasis*, exaltation?

Prof. Jung: Yes, in an ecstatic condition—as Mrs. Crowley has said, in the state of revelation—namely, when something is revealed to him which was not known or understood before. Then, unable to express that thing totally by the words that are given to him, he will add a long series of analogies. One very excellent example is the Sermon on the Mount, all those similes for the kingdom of heaven. You see, the idea of the kingdom of heaven was a great revelation, a reconciling symbol, the union of opposites. And when Christ tries to convey that revelation to his fellow beings, he uses that series of famous analogies of the kingdom of heaven, in order to characterize the essence of that peculiar idea which cannot be expressed by one word. For what is the kingdom of heaven? Of what does the kingdom of heaven consist? It is difficult to say; and still today, if you ask different people about this notion, they are not at one, not even the theologians. One will say it is to be found amongst human beings, and another, more true to the tradition, will say that it is within yourself, in your heart for instance. But if a man has no ears of the heart or of the mind, he does not get it, and then you must use a number of other analogies in order to convey the idea. So Nietzsche takes similes, inasmuch as they are mere names of good and evil, for words only, but words that are symptomatic of a certain ecstatic condition: namely, a condition in which the ordinary human being is suddenly seized by unconscious contents and made to speak out. He will produce similes as mere symptoms of an unconscious content, and then they have their value. So he continues logically, "Elevated is then your body, and raised up; with its delight enraptureth it the spirit; so that it becometh creator, and valuer, and lover, and everything's benefactor." This means that out of the unconscious, which is located in the body, flows the revelation and causes similes; one becomes creative, creates similes, and thereby conveys that state of grace, that stream of enlightenment or whatever it is, to one's fellow beings. One becomes everybody's benefactor because one is then the source of a new life, of a new energy. Now, it is interesting that Nietzsche says "elevated is then your body"; everybody else would say it was the spirit. Why is that?

Prof. Reichstein: Because he identifies with Zarathustra.

Prof. Jung: But then he would say "elevated is then the spirit," for Zarathustra is the spirit *par excellence*; he is not human.

Mrs. Crowley: Is it because the body *is* elevated when it has received this revelation or this word?

Prof. Jung: Why then in other cases do people always say "the spirit"?

Mrs. Crowley: Is it not just making that distinction? When it is unconscious it is the spirit, but when it is made conscious, that unconscious is then incorporated in the body.

Prof. Jung: That is all quite true, but usually people don't speak of the elevation of the body.

Mr. Allemann: In an ecstasy it looks as if the body were elevated; the saints were apparently lifted up.

Prof. Jung: Yes, that is a peculiar phenomenon which is reported by St. Francis for instance; in certain moments when they were praying before the altar they were lifted up and held suspended in mid-air in a sort of external manifestation of the *ekstasis*. But in the Christian understanding, they were lifted up in the spirit. That the physical body seems to have been elevated, in a way confirms what Nietzsche says, but none of the saints said that. They said that the spirit had been elevated.

Mrs. Jung: Is it not that the body *needs* elevation?

Prof. Jung: Yes, this is a peculiarity in Nietzsche's case which has to do with his type. He is chiefly an intuitive type with a complete neglect of the body; therefore his body always suffered from physical ailments. Half of the psychogenetic diseases occur where it is a matter of too much intuition, because intuition has this peculiar quality of taking people out of their ordinary reality. Intuitives are always ahead of themselves, never quite in the here-and-now, because they are nosing out possibilities which are to come off in the future. The body is the here-and-now *par excellence*, a prison in which we are here and now; but intuition is that faculty which removes one from the here-and-now in space and time. So as a compensation, the body is always reacting against morbidly intuitive people, who suffer from all sorts of ailments, particularly from disturbances in the abdomen or the stomach, ulcers in the stomach or the perineum for instance; it is as if the sympathetic nervous system, particularly the vegetative nervous system and the digestive tract, were producing spasms. Many such cases can be demonstrated which have the intention of calling the individual's attention to the reality of the body. It is almost dangerous to have so much intuition; such people forget entirely that they are in the here-and-now, and not in another country in the wonderful future.

That is exactly Nietzsche's case, so he is always at variance with his body; we dealt with that in connection with the rope-dancer and on several other occasions. Therefore when he tries to describe a real *ekstasis*, he naturally lays particular weight upon the body, because he realizes here that it is not the spirit in his case that gives the revelation. To an intuitive-intellectual the source of revelation is the body: the unconscious is then burdened with the body because the mind and the intuition don't take care of it. As Nietzsche is quite identified with Zarathustra, who is a pneumatic being, a breath, naturally he is always in the air above his body, and there he has nothing to eat but breath or air. So anything substantial that comes to him must come from the body, because the unconscious is identical with the body. Of course that is not so with a sensation type whose mind and consciousness are very much in the here-and-now; in such a case you would hear that the revelation comes from above, from the spirit. Now, inasmuch as the whole age is too much hypnotized or fascinated by the body, you naturally will be taught that the spirit always comes from above, out of the air. It is a light that comes from heaven, or it is a wind, and revelation takes place out of the breath.

Miss Wolff: I think the translation is not very good here; *auferstanden* means literally resurrected, and that may be a subtle reference to Christ, because Christ was raised up on the cross and then he was resurrected. So perhaps one could say it might be not only a problem of Nietzsche's time, but a problem of the whole Christian attitude, which is an intuitive attitude.

Prof. Jung: Well, that is just what I said, that it was a Christian teaching practically; that the revelation comes from the spirit and not from the body is a teaching that dates from antiquity, so it is coincidental with the spirit of Christian teaching. Therefore, Nietzsche is apt to express all his personal psychology by something which is general, collective, and traditional. Now the interesting thing is that when a revelation takes place in the kingdom of the spirit then the spirit is resurrected or healed, because it is then functioning; and when it happens from the side of the body, then that is resurrected and brought back to life. And then of course for Nietzsche as the intuitive, or for the good Christian which he represents, the functioning of the body is a true revelation. That the body is the here and the now if properly understood, is to the intuitive a true revelation; and inasmuch as the spirit of Christian teaching is thinking and intuition and identical with the air, it is a true revelation that there is a here and a now, and that it contains spirit, contains life, that it is something that really functions. To the intuitive the here and the now is nothing but the desolation of a prison, and that is of course exactly the old Christian teaching—that our body is the prison of the soul, that the here and the now is a valley of misery and humiliation, and that we are here in a prison where we only suffer, where we are not free, and only come into our existence in a future life.

Mrs. Frost: Doesn't Nietzsche in all these verses suggest a new synthesis? So far, there has only been the spirit, and here he means the body should join with the spirit in that new synthesis.

Prof. Jung: Absolutely, that is the great revelation, the union of the pairs of opposites, spirit and body. He brings about this union by a depreciation of the spirit in the nominalistic way. The Christian would say the spirit is the Logos, the word, and that it is full of life and revelation. But Nietzsche discovers and tells us that the spirit is Logos, but also that it means *nothing but* the word, and in so far the spirit is air. Of course, one could maintain that this is a very one-sided definition of the concept of the spirit, and that is exactly what *I* would say; the traditional meaning of *spiritos*, Logos, is surely a very one-sided idea. The original meaning of the word *Geist* in German points to something other than the Latin word *spiritus*, which is definitely a breath of air, as the Greek word *pneuma* is just the wind, and has taken on the spiritual meaning only under the influence of Christianity; in the Greek contemporary texts the word *pneuma* does not mean spirit, but means wind or air. So the Latin and Greek conception, or the word *spirit*, which we use, means definitely air, while *Geist* does not. The word *Geist*, as I have explained several times, has to do with something dynamic; it is a welling up, a new manifestation, like the foam that comes out of a champagne bottle. It is the volatile substance contained in the wine for instance, *Weingeist*; and *spiritus vini* is alcohol, the spirit coming back from the air. *Geist* had not the meaning of air originally, being a word that expresses a dynamic procedure, an outburst of something. In the New Testament, the descent of the Holy Ghost in the form of tongues of fire or a powerful wind, is the *dynamus* of the spirit; where it appears in a wind or in a storm you have the dynamic quality, but it has lost that quality, as the German word *Geist* has lost that meaning to a great extent. It perhaps still exists in the concept of *Geistreich*, which means that one is full of pep, that one produces, that one is brilliant; then one says *Er hat Geist* or is *Geistreich*, but that is faint. So you see, the original dynamic conception of *Geist* has really disappeared.

Mrs. Jung: I think the word *Gischt* has this dynamic quality.

Prof. Jung: Yes, the foam produced by a waterfall or the waves of the sea is called *Gischt*, and that is the same word.

Mrs. Baumann: Does the English word *geyser* not come from it?

Prof. Jung: A geyser is the welling up of hot water; that word is probably of the same origin, but I am not quite certain. It is Nordic, it comes from a Scandinavian root.[1]

Mrs. Sigg: I think just that heroic deed of Nietzsche, that he did write the first part of *Zarathustra*, was a *Rehabilitierung* of this *Geist*.

Prof. Jung: Yes, the whole of *Zarathustra*, its tremendous outburst, its élan and enthusiasm, is *Geist*, but in its most original form. He was overrun by it, the victim of this dynamic outburst. Like the disciples at Pentecost: when they came out into the streets, people thought they were drunk, but they were overcome by the *dynamis* of the spirit.[2] Our idea of the spirit has become quite lamed; in late Christianity it is lame and abstract. Now you see, he feels in this phenomenon that the body and what one called "spirit" have come together in a revelation that really to him comes from the body. So it is a sort of redemption of the body, something which has been lacking in Christianity, where the body, the here-and-now, has always been depreciated. One could say that in the moment when Nietzsche writes these words with his intui-

---

[1] *Geysir* (Icelandic): gusher, from old Norse *geysa*, "to rush forth."

[2] Ephesians 5:18.

tion and his whole world of thoughts, he feels that he is rushing into the here-and-now, and that is a revelation. Then the two things have come together and he feels that as portentous. For instance, he says, "Verily, a new good and evil is it! Verily, a new deep murmuring, and the voice of a new fountain!" *Ein neues tiefes Rauschen* is translated by "deep murmuring" but that is not very descriptive of the actual sound produced by an underground river rushing through rocks so that you hear a thunder-like noise in the depths. That sentence points to something which is still below the present moment; it is the future, and Nietzsche feels that he has heard something of the future. So what he feels as a new spring coming up from the ground is a sort of symptom, an anticipation of something very big that is to come.

Mrs. Frost: Rumbling would be the proper word, that is something which comes from below.

Prof. Jung: Would you speak of the rumbling of a river?

Mrs. Baumann: Roaring?

Prof. Jung: When there are stones in it, deep down in a big gorge, you hear a thunderous roar, like the roaring waters of Niagara.

Well now, the part we have been dealing with started from the idea of degeneration, and you remember I explained that as a sort of deviation from the *genus*, the particular kind to which the individual belongs. Now, when one has deviated from the law of the *genus*, it is as if one had left the center of the stream of life where the current is the swiftest, gradually drifted against the shore, struck ground, and come to a standstill. Now outside of life, one can look and see how the river passes, but one no longer moves or lives, because the actual process of living is an ever-renewed change, a change from day to day, hour to hour. For a time you can look at it from afar, but more and more life escapes you, and you feel it more and more as a loss; and the end will be that you feel that life is really leaving you, that you are dying. Degeneration leads therefore in a certain measure to death. But as soon as the lack of life is felt, the unconscious, being the balance or compensation, seeks to reestablish the former condition, so an unconscious seeking begins for the main current. Then the moment one comes into the current, one is also in the middle of the stream, in the middle position where right and left join, because in that act of kinetic energy is the act which unites the pairs of opposites; in the current the opposites come together. One is then moving, and this is a moment such as Nietzsche describes here. He feels that the spring has come, that the river is flowing; he is lifted from his feet and carried downstream. He feels therefore renewed; his spirit has been divorced from the body and now he has found it again. He is moving with the river of life.

That is an intensive, dynamic phenomenon, and in Nietzsche's case of course an individual occurrence, but as I said, it is also a collective phenomenon. In its origin, only one individual has clearly perceived it, but at the same time that that individual perceives that he is lifted up, he also hears the underground rumble and roar of a much more powerful stream which is greater than his individual spring. It is that stream from which his individual spring has come. This is a collective phenomenon which is still in the unconscious, not visible on the surface, but we shall see in the subsequent chapters that he feels it very much as the thing that will be in the future; in the future many will strike the current again and then it will be perhaps a very powerful river which will irresistibly move on and wash away whatever is in its path. I point this out particularly because it refers to what is happening in our days: we are witnessing under many different aspects the beginning of a new time and a new spirit, which older people have great difficulty in understanding. We are split up, uncertain about the meaning of our modern times, we observe many most peculiar phenomena around us and we don't know how to value them. For instance, that fact of going off the gold standard is one of the most remarkable of all times. That nations can break their word, we knew before, but that they should do it so easily is remarkable, when it is quite self-evident that both England and America pride themselves on being very moral and Christian. It is just as if I were owing a man a hundred francs and said, "Here, I pay you fifty, that is what I owe you." Then the man says, "No, you owe me a hundred." But I say it doesn't matter, take it or leave it; I have the power to cheat people and I make use of that power. And without blushing! Nobody feels anything particularly wrong about it—it is all for the betterment of one's own nation. What did the church say about it? Nothing. Nobody blushed about it.

Mrs. Frost: But you said that God should be bad too!

Miss Hughes: Have you not the parable of the unjust steward?

Prof. Jung: Exactly, exactly, and that I call the new spirit. But I say that if the churches believe in their own values, they should have said a word about it. But they did not, nobody dared to open their mouth, and this is an astonishing thing, though those same nations have a great deal to say about the morality of the proceeding when the Germans do such a thing, and we all opened our mouths when the Russians killed a million bourgeois. But the difference is slight, a bit more or less. Now this is decidedly something quite new. And I want to mention the interesting fact that Germany has at least the great merit of having formulated this new spirit. They say it is old Wotan, say they have become pagans. And when they broke into Belgium they said yes, we have violated the Treaty; yes, it *is* mean. That is what Bethmann-Hollweg always said; "We *have* broken our word," he confessed.[3] And then we said how cynical he was, and that the Germans were only pagans anyway. But they simply admit what the others think and do. So learn from that. Do it but never say it; then you are wise. Stay with the Archbishop of Canterbury and then it is an economic measure; cut the throat of somebody and then call it an economic measure. Believe in your church and then it is all right. You see, the Germans are moved by that new and strange spirit which is not good, and they are on top of all fools because they say so. But to us it is interesting that I must say that I am very grateful to the Germans for their paganistic movement, at the head of which is my friend Professor Hauer who taught us the Tantric Yoga, and who has now become a savior of the fools. And some of them are really so nice and honest; that they call it Wotan means of course that they are in a sort of dream state where they cannot help telling the truth. For it is Wotan[4] that is the interesting thing. A Swiss, Martin Ninck, has recently written a very interesting book called *Wodan und Germanischer Schicksalsglaube*[5] in which he collected all the material about Wotan as evidence that he is the personification of the moving spirit behind Hitler. Wotan is the noise in the wood, the rushing waters, the one who causes natural catastrophes, and wars among human beings. He is the great sorcerer. Quite rightly, the Romans identified him with Mercury—of course not as the god of merchants, but of sorcerers, of the people who go in the dark, who are surreptitious in a way, who are moved by dark purposes; and he is also the psychopompos, the leader of souls, the one that carries the souls into the ghostland, the god of revelation. Therefore one can say he is very similar to the Thracian Dionysos, the god of orgiastic enthusiasm. Now old Wotan is in the center of Europe; you can see all the psychological symptoms which he personifies, including his romantic character of

[3] Theodore von Bethmann Holweg (1856-1921) became Reichs Chancellor in 1900 and, in spite of many diplomatic blunders, lasted in office until 1917. Most famous for his dismissal of the treaty guaranteeing Belgium's neutrality as a "scrap of paper," he told the Reichstag in 1914 that Germany had been unjust to Belgium.

[4] J. W. Hauer gave the lectures on Kundalini Yoga in the Autumn of 1932, to which Jung added a psychological commentary. See 6 June 1934, n. 11, above. By now Hauer had identified with the Nazis.

[5] I.e., *Wotan and the German Belief in Destiny.* His work was published in 1935.

the sorcerer, the god of mysteries—all that is living again. As far as the German mentality reaches in Europe—and it reaches, as you know, from the Urals to Spain—we see religion upset; in the most Catholic of all countries, Spain, the church is completely overthrown. And that is old Wotan, you could not name it better, the wind came and blew the thing into bits. Fascism in Italy is old Wotan again; it is all Germanic blood down there, with no trace of the Romans; they are Langobards, and they all have that Germanic spirit. Of course Switzerland is still a little exception, you know! Oh, we have joined in but we were not so foolish as to say so.

Prof. Fierz: I should like to point out that one of the first acts of King Edward VIII was to receive Litvinov, who was one of the murderers of his cousin. If the poor Tzar could turn in his grave he would do so, but there was no fear of it because he was burned and buried in a well. He could not turn, so King Edward need have no fear.[6]

Prof. Jung: Yes, that is an economic measure like those the Italians follow out in Abyssinia. Well now, after this revelation

Here paused Zarathustra awhile, [I can understand!] and looked lovingly on his disciples. Then he continued to speak thus—and his voice had changed: [It would have changed!]

Remain true to the earth, my brethren, with the power of your virtue! Let your bestowing love and your knowledge be devoted to the meaning of the earth! Thus do I pray and conjure you.

Let it not fly away from the earthly and beat against eternal walls with its wings! Ah, there hath always been so much flown-away virtue!

Lead, like me, the flown-away virtue back to the earth—yea, back to body and life: that it may give to the earth its meaning, a human meaning!

A hundred times hitherto hath spirit as well as virtue flown away and blundered. Alas! in our body dwelleth still all this delusion and blundering: body and will hath it there become.

A hundred times hitherto hath spirit as well as virtue attempted

---

[6] Although his father, King George V, would never have done so, Edward VIII, shortly after taking the throne, received the Soviet ambassador, Maxim Litvinov (1875-1951), and had a long conversation with him, during which Litvinov explained why he considered it to have been necessary to kill Czar Nicholas II, his wife Alexandra (granddaughter of Queen Victoria), and their children. (It is, however, by no means clear that he himself had anything to do with this execution.) Litvinov told a reporter afterwards that Edward "impressed one as a mediocre Englishman who glances at one newspaper a day" (from *Time*, 10 Feb. 1936).

and erred. Yea, an attempt hath man been. Alas, much ignorance and error hath become embodied in us!

Not only the rationality of millenniums—also their madness, breaketh out in us. Dangerous is it to be an heir.

Still fight we step by step with the giant Chance, and over all mankind hath hitherto ruled nonsense, the lack-of-sense.

Let your spirit and your virtue be devoted to the sense of the earth, my brethren: let the value of everything be determined anew by you! Therefore shall ye be fighters! Therefore shall ye be creators!

This part of the chapter shows very clearly the meaning of the revelation: namely, the earth, the body, should become of spiritual value—of that value which formerly has been the exclusive prerogative of the spirit. Now, if the earth and the body assume the dignity of spiritual importance, then their peculiar essence has to be considered in the same way as the demands and the postulates of the spirit were formerly considered, and then naturally much that has been in the air with the spirit will return to the earth; many things which were kept in suspense, which were on the wings of the spirit, will now precipitate themselves in matter. You see, that people can keep themselves in suspense is the reason why they prefer to live in the spirit: they can live a provisional life with reference to the earth or the body; that may come about in the future but for the time being they are quite happy postponing it. It is like building one's house on a huge bird that never settles; if one never becomes, one can be anywhere. One is not in the here-and-now when living in the spirit, so one can postpone one's problems. But the moment that the here-and-now begins to suffer, when the individual body suffers, or political and economic circumstances become bad, then one is forced to land, and no sooner does the spirit touch the earth then one is caught. It is like that idea of the Gnosis, the *nous*, that beholds his own face in the ocean; he sees the beauty of the earth and that lovely woman's face and he is caught, entangled in the great problem of the world. Had he remained the *nous* or *pneuma*, he would have kept on the wing, would have been like the image of God that was floating over the waters and never touching them; but he did touch them and that was the beginning of human life, the beginning of the world with all its suffering and its beauty, its heavens and hells.[7] Of course what the Gnosis represented in this cosmo-

---

[7] In the *Corpus Hermeticum, Nous* or reason, bearing the name of Poimandres, "seeing reflected in the water this form resembling himself, which was appearing in nature, he

gonic myth as heaven and hell is what really happens again and again in human life. It is an archetypal picture.

And what happens here is really the same: The spirit beheld its image in matter, touched upon matter, and was caught; and it was a passionate embrace, apparently a moment of ecstasy, and the consequence will be that it is once more entangled in the earth. That expresses itself also in the circumstances of our time; if you compare our actual prevailing conditions with those that prevailed before the war, you see the difference. You can no longer travel from one country to another without a passport, and you have not the money you had before; you have to take into account that there is a difference in currency, new laws, and God knows what—so you are simply fettered. Our possibilities have been cut down tremendously; our free movement in quite ordinary ways has been enormously curtailed. All that is merely an expression or a symptom of what has happened: that one is in a way in the prison of the earth. Man has come down to the earth once more. Everybody talks of reducing and becoming simple, living a more natural and simpler life, and that means getting closer to the earth. Formerly one could afford to fly about, but now we have to remain right on the earth and one is very painfully reminded of the reality of the here-and-now. This is simply an external manifestation of the fact that the *nous* has once more come down from the heavens, has embraced the earth, and been caught in the earth. Naturally, that embrace seems at first to be all beauty and marvel, but if you think of the consequences, it is no longer so nice. And we will see in the end of *Zarathustra*—if we ever get there—what happens when he comes to the question of paying the account.

It seems ideal and beautiful: the body is being deified, we live again in the here-and-now, the earth and its vicinity, and we are friends of the next things. But wait until the next things come a little bit nearer and see whether you can remain friends with them. It is very doubtful. Hitherto, nothing but chance ruled the world, but since man has returned to his natural home on the earth his mind rules the world, and see how that works! More than ever, we are victims of mere chance; our politics since the war have been nothing but one big blunder. Man has proved absolutely inadequate to deal with the situation. Everybody was surprised by the development of things. Nobody clearly foresaw what would happen. They forgot all about the past and what very able

loved it and desired to dwell there!" Jean Doresse, *The Secret Books of the Egyptian Gnostics*, tr. Phillip Mariet (New York, 1960), p. 215.

people in the past knew would happen. So they created a situation where really nothing but chance can lead us out. Now Nietzsche thinks that man's mind, having come home to the earth, will deal with this giant chance and the nonsense that has ruled mankind hitherto, but the nonsense is greater than ever, the lack of sense. For this union of the spirit and the body, or the spirit and the earth, forms something which to man will lack sense forever because he is utterly inadequate. He never will understand what it is. If he did, he would know what life is and that is a mystery. And we don't know what the purpose of life is, don't even know whether it *has* purpose: we are quite safe in believing that this life is mere meaningless chaos because that is what we see. There may be sense here and there, and we can only hope that there is sense in general, but we don't know at all.

The only thing which seems absolutely sure is that the main feature is chance, though certain things are apparently law-abiding. We talk more of laws than abide by them, and when the law does not work—it never works exactly—we say, "Oh, that is mere chance." We belittle chance and don't admit that chance is the master. And when we want to make a natural law, we build laboratories and make very complicated experiments in order to exclude the chance that disturbs us. So when we observe life in the open, for a short stretch of the way it works *more or less*. You see, it is better that we see things as they appear to be. That is our only reality and it is better than to get angry over the non-observance of laws, for they don't work very clearly; the main thing is chaos and chance—that is a pretty fair picture of the world. We talk so much of law and reason because we wish to have something of it; it is so difficult to be reasonable, so difficult to observe the law. Therefore we talk of it. We usually talk of things as they ought to be and hate people who talk of things as they are; "you *ought to*," "you *should*," gives us peace of mind. If somebody tells us how we ought to do or say a thing, then reason is still ruling the world. Of course it doesn't work; things take their own way and we are singularly impotent to change them. Nietzsche says, "Let the value of everything be determined anew by you." But who is determining things? Are people reconciled even on the subject of the gold standard for instance? So Nietzsche says, "Therefore shall ye be fighters." You see, that leads directly into war and destruction. "And therefore shall ye be creators." Yes, when you are capable of creating something.

Mr. Allemann: Does not *Schaffende* mean the doer, the active one, rather than the creator?

Prof. Jung: Well, *der Schaffende* is in Nietzsche's language the creator, and nothing can be created without destruction. There is an old Latin sentence that expresses it very nicely: *Creatio unius est corruptio alterius,* "The creation of the one is the corruption of the other."

Mrs. Crowley: Is it not also expressed in the myth of the Phoenix?

Prof. Jung: Yes, the Phoenix burns itself up—that is destruction—and then it comes back recreated.

> Intelligently doth the body purify itself; attempting with intelligence it exalteth itself; to the discerners all impulses sanctify themselves; to the exalted the soul becometh joyful.

Well, let it be known generally to the discerners that all impulses sanctify themselves and you have the condition of Europe as it is today. "To the exalted the soul becometh joyful." You see when pairs of opposites come together, when you have struck the main current again, there is a spring of enthusiasm and life within you, which compensates to a great extent for the external difficulties you create for yourself. Generally, we have to look at fate in that way—that to a much greater extent than we assume, we are creating our fate. Even things which seem to come causally from another source than ourselves are of such an habitual kind that we must assume that they have to do with the deepest roots of our own being. So we can safely say, whatever one's experience in life, "That is *my* experience of life, simply my image; it is mirroring what I am." You see, when something evil happens to us, we can still assume that it comes from our own source, because it symbolizes exactly what we are. Therefore to certain people, always the same things happen; they are part of their scenery. They are like a theater with its different stage-sets, and one of them is just a series of things that habitually happen to them. If you look at things in this way, then you also have a chance to find perhaps a way by which you can avoid such an habitual fate. If it were only happening from without, with no connection with your character, then you would have absolutely no chance of changing anything; you could only run away and even that would not help you, because running round the next corner you would plunge into a situation which was habitually your own again, only worse. But if you accept this fact that fate is really created by your own self, then you are in the current; and then even if the external situation is bad, at least you have the spring flowing within. Then you can say, "To the exalted the soul becometh joyful," for if you are in the river of life you are joyful, and are lifted up by the river.

Now, the question is of course: Is it good to be in the current of life, or is it bad? I mean morally. And that is difficult to say. As a rule, it is good for others when I am not in the river of life because then I do nothing. I simply look on, and that might be better for others. But if I am outside, if I only look on, it is not so good for myself. Perhaps sometimes it is also good for certain reasons to be safe on the bank and not to touch the current; and usually those people who are onlookers, who have left the main current, are less offensive because they are inactive. You see, this is so in Buddhism. They try to leave the current of life because it is all illusion, and so they become inoffensive, and the evil they work is merely evil by deprivation—that they don't build hospitals, don't observe public hygiene, etc. They are chiefly concerned with their spiritual welfare. So whatever evil they work is simply the evil of deprivation, the absence of good; and that may be better than doing good like the active Europeans, for an active person is more likely to do damage, even if it is meant to be good. The worst people always have good intentions. They are just awful because the devil is behind their talk, all the time whispering, "Now do the good thing." And because they believe in it, they force other people to do the same and that is of course tyrannical, with a lot of power instinct in it. So one could hold that for other people the good thing would be for me to withdraw from life. But for myself it is not good. In order to prosper it is perhaps better to be in life, though the others will suffer because as soon as I step I crush the beetle upon the road; if I eat a certain loaf of bread nobody else can eat that loaf; if I take a seat nobody else can sit there. I am a nuisance right and left, and if I had great compassion I would withdraw from the current of life.

Now of course, one could ask, "But should one never withdraw?" Of course when the river begins to ebb low, it naturally ceases to flow, and then you cannot tell whether you are in the main current or in a by-water, in a swamp or a lagoon—or whether you are in the sea. Then you can and you naturally will withdraw, for if you depend on the movement of the river, what would be the use of trying to navigate a boat in a river that doesn't flow any longer? Then you might as well be on the shore. You see, when you begin to be static, when the world looks as it always has looked for all eternity, as soon as you see that in your own heart, then you can be on the mountain: you don't need the current. But this is only good teaching to older people. For the young people it is wrong; then the main current is everywhere and in everything, and then they should be everywhere and in everything. So if a Buddhist should withdraw into solitude as a very young man and live a passive life, unless he is called by God to be a particular saint, he surely would be making a mistake. But if he slowly goes out of life as

Buddha himself did, I should say that was natural and reasonable and good. Buddha really was good for other people, because he was no longer active. Inasmuch as you are active you are not so good for other people, and you will get your hands dirty; you cannot remain good. If you think you can be good and active, it is a great illusion: it is simply impossible.

Mrs. Frost: How about St. Francis of Assisi who was both good and active?

Prof. Jung: Well, he had had a pretty stiff dose of life before, I have heard. And his activity later is very doubtful. It was the activity of privation, a monk making friends with wolves and other animals is not living in the current of mankind. That doesn't pay, but is a kind of spiritual activity which I would call negative in the European sense of the word.

Mr. Allemann: What about preaching to the leaders of old Europe to be a bit less active?

Prof. Jung: That is pretty dangerous. We are already restricted in our activity by circumstances and we always shall be; and if one teaches anything to Europeans, they most probably will make the wrong use of it.

Mr. Allemann: I mean to people in the second part of life.

Prof. Jung: There it is something else. It is absolute necessity. You are forced by the psychological constitution of people when they are young to teach them a bit of life. And you must teach older people of the living inactivity, which is not mere lameness, but is the absence of movement. The inactivity which is characteristic in the second part of life is only inactivity in reference to people and circumstances. You see, when somebody sits on a mountain and reflects upon what is happening about him, he is very active—only other people don't see that.

LECTURE IV

12 February 1936

Prof. Jung:

Here is a question by Miss Hannah: "Last seminar you said, in connection with the verse on the giant Chance, that most things depend on Chance and that we can do very little about it. In connection with the next but one verse, you said that we create our fate ourselves to a far greater extent than we realize and that once we know this we can begin to alter it. Is this a paradox?" Yes, it is a paradox. "Or does one change into the other according to our state of consciousness? Or is it rather that what we call chance is really the doing of the self and that as we become more conscious we see that its pattern is our own, however little we may like it from an ego point of view?"

I am glad that Miss Hannah has brought up this point. You see, in saying "we," one speaks of a very complex fact, for there is always the conscious "we" and the total "we"; one should add that to explain the paradox. When one observes how people live, one sees how their totality lives, which is entirely different from the way the conscious lives. In many cases one cannot even make out whether people are conscious of what they do and live and say; one has to enquire and carefully investigate certain facts in order to find out. It is amazing how little people know of what they do; one would assume that they were quite conscious of it but as a matter of fact they are not. It is as if it were happening to somebody else. So one never can tell whether one's partner has done a thing consciously or not: one always has to enquire. Of course in ordinary speech one doesn't take these subtle differences into account. And that is again a paradox because they are shockingly evident; yet from another standpoint they are exceedingly subtle because one doesn't see the differences. So in saying "we" one means at one time the totality of what happens, while in another context one means more particularly the conscious ego. Now, it is a fact that the conscious ego can do very little. It is as if one were surrounded by all sorts of inevitable conditions so that one hardly knows how to move;

821

but if one speaks of that small circle in which the ego *can* move, it seems as if one could do quite a lot. Inasmuch, then, as one's fate is contained in the small circle of the ego, one can change it—one has free will within that little circle of one's personal reach. But outside of that— and our totality is mostly outside of it—not much can be done.

Then it is quite certain that if one increases the reach of one's consciousness, one will naturally have a much greater area in which to apply freedom of will, so to that extent one can also influence one's condition. But compared with the whole, it is very little. Therefore, even if one reaches a considerable extension of consciousness, one has to accept the lack of freedom, accept the fact that things are going against the grain, against the ego. And one reaches that frontier, I might say, in the moment when one discovers the inferior function, or the contrasting type. For instance, when an introvert discovers the possibility of his extraversion, his consciousness is extended to such an extent that he oversteps the limit of his freedom; for when he touches upon his inferior function his freedom is gone. The instinctive reaction is, therefore, to withdraw as soon as possible, to avoid the people who touch upon his inferiority, to avoid everything that could remind him of it, for nobody wants to be reminded of his defeat. One naturally reviles people and circumstances that remind one of one's inferiority, and that is in a way a sound instinct because one feels unable to cope with it. But if the process of the development of consciousness continues, one understands more and more that it doesn't help to avoid oneself; one is forced through oneself to accept even one's contrast and the lack of freedom. Anybody with a decent extension of consciousness will be forced to admit that in a certain way one is also not free, that one has to accept many things in oneself as facts which cannot be altered—at least not at the moment.

Then, if your extension of consciousness has forced you to accept your own contrast, you have thereby naturally overstepped the limit of a natural ego. That is exactly what Zarathustra is trying to teach here and still more in the subsequent chapters: namely, that we have not yet discovered man in his totality, despite the fact that we can see it externally. We see what other people live but *they* are unable to see that; and inasmuch as *we* only live it without seeing it, we don't know what we live. So within its own reach the ego can do a great deal, but beyond that very little, for then it steps over into the unconscious life where it can do nothing. Only when that area of unconsciousness can be covered by consciousness, when a part of formerly unconscious life is drawn into the sphere of consciousness, is it at all subject to your choice. If that is not the case, well, then it will be chosen for you: something will decide for you, and then you are of course not free. Now, though all that part of your life which is lived in an unconscious way is unfree, it is nevertheless your own because you are in it; you may not have chosen it yet there you are in a hole. And if you are a bit more conscious you see that you have maneuvered yourself into the boiling water; you have carefully picked your way until you found the hot water in which you are sitting. If you are not conscious of your own way, you say that somebody has surely played a trick on you and put a pot of boiling water just where you wanted to sit down. But with a bit more consciousness you see that *you* have done it, and with still more consciousness you will see that you could not *avoid* doing it: you had to do it for a certain purpose.

So you slowly come to the conclusion that many things which you formerly said were wrong and which some devil had arranged for you, were really just what you had sought and prepared and put there for your own use, for a purpose, and that your former idea that some enemy had worked the trick was a superstition. The more you have such experiences, the more you will be inclined to understand that this is the truth in all those cases which you don't understand. Things still happen to you; you have a certain fate which is not welcome, which disturbs you—or situations arise where you assume that somebody has worked against you. But now you are more able to say, "In so many cases I have seen that *I* was my so-called enemy, that *I* was the wise fellow who prepared such a fix for myself, that probably in this case I have worked the same trick—I really don't understand it yet." There really still seems to be something against you, but you are so impressed by your former experiences that you apply a new hypothesis. And so you slowly arrive at the idea that probably nothing in a human life is just against it; the whole thing has probably been a carefully worked out plan and there is no such thing as the giant chance. The giant is the self; the self has prepared it for a certain end. Then you may still say "we" have done so and so, but it is no longer exact; it is not an accurate use of speech, since it is the self.

Mrs. Crowley: In connection with that, you spoke of accepting life as if it were not only accepting the chaos but living it, as if there were nothing but chaos. That was so perplexing to me, because there is also the same idea in it that if you don't see that thread of the self in it, it would lead to frustration and ruthlessness.

823

Prof. Jung: Well, if you see nothing *but* chaos, it amounts to an unconscious condition, because that amount of life which you control by the ego surely is not chaos, but is already a little cosmos. Yet outside of that is something that seems to be chaos or chance, and anything else that is said about it is simply an assumption; you are allowed to say it is *not* chaos only when you have experienced the cosmos in it, the secret order. It is really true that unless you have experienced the order of things, they are a disorder; it is a wrong assumption to call it an order. Of course we are full of such assumptions, are taught to make them, to have optimistic conceptions and so on, and this is wrong. The world is an order only when somebody experiences that order, not before; it is a chaos if nobody experiences it as a cosmos. That has much to do with the Chinese idea of Tao. I always think of the story of the rainmaker of Kiau Tschou. If that fellow had not gone into Tao it would not have rained, yet there is no causality; the two things simply belong together, the order is only established when order is established. He had to experience the order in that chaos, in that disharmony of heaven and earth; and if he had not experienced the harmony, it would not have been.[1] Well, this is high Eastern philosophy; I am unable to explain to you this great paradox. Now we will continue:

> Physician, heal thyself: then wilt thou also heal thy patient. Let it be his best cure to see with his eyes him who maketh himself whole.

Nietzsche is realizing certain truths here which are highly important from a psychological point of view. "Physician, heal thyself" is particularly good teaching for our late Christianity. You see, he assumes that the real cure is made where it is most needed and most immediate. That is like the rainmaker of Kiau Tschou again. He does not curse the earth or pray to heaven to behave and produce rain. He says to himself that he was right when he left his village and when he got here he was wrong. This place is out of order so he is the one that is wrong; that wrong is nearest to him, and if he wants to do anything for the chaotic condition, it must be done in him—he is the immediate object of himself. So he asks for that little house and there he locks himself in and

---

[1] The story was told Jung by his friend Richard Wilhelm, who once lived in a region of China suffering from drought. The rain-maker, having been summoned, sequestered himself in a quiet house for three days and on the fourth there was a great snow. Asked to explain his powers, he denied being one who could make snow. Rather, since the country was in disorder, "I had to wait three days until I was back in Tao and then naturally the rain came." See CW 5, par. 604n.

works on himself; he remains shut in until he reconciles heaven and earth in himself, until he is in the right order, and then he has cured the situation: Tao is established. That is exactly the same idea. So the best cure for anybody is when the one who thinks about curing has cured himself; inasmuch as he cures himself it is a cure. If he is in Tao, he has established Tao, and whoever beholds him beholds Tao and enters Tao. This is a very Eastern idea. The Western idea—particularly late Christianity—is of course to cure your neighbor, to help him, with no consideration of the question, "*Who* is the helper?" Perhaps he is not a help, or perhaps he gives something which he takes back with the other hand. There are plenty of people nowadays who join the life of the community, assume responsibility, and all that stuff, but I say, "Who is assuming responsibility?" If my business is in a bad condition and a fellow comes along and says he will assume the responsibility and run the whole thing, I naturally ask him who he is—and then I find he has been bankrupt. Naturally I don't want one who is himself a beggar and has given evidence of his own incompetence. Those people who are very helpful need help. If they are physicians they should treat their own neurosis, otherwise they are just vampires and want to help other people for their own needs.

A thousand paths are there which have never yet been trodden; a thousand salubrities and hidden islands of life. Unexhausted and undiscovered is still man and man's world.

This is also an important item. But is that not a peculiar sequence? He was just speaking of the physician who should first heal himself and then suddenly "a thousand paths are there which have never yet been trodden." What is the connection?

Mr. Allemann: Perhaps he says, "Physician, heal thyself" because he sees that he himself has not trodden this path of which he speaks.

Prof. Jung: Exactly. And then the voice says, "*I* am ill, I should heal myself." But how can he heal himself if he does not know himself? So naturally he comes to the statement that any amount of things are still unknown: man is not yet discovered, but is still the great enigma. It should be: *I* am the great enigma, I have not found out anything about myself. That would lead him into a careful study of himself, for otherwise he would not be able to heal himself. You see, he does not apply that truth to himself, but teaches other people what he really should teach himself; he tries to be helpful, but in the wrong way. Of course it is good teaching for other people too; perhaps somebody else will draw conclusions from it.

Awake and hearken, ye lonesome ones.

It is Zarathustra who is lonesome, but being helpful and a good Christian, he talks to other people.

From the future come winds with stealthy pinions, and to fine ears good tidings are proclaimed.

Ye lonesome ones of today, ye seceding ones, ye shall one day be a people: out of you who have chosen yourselves, shall a chosen people arise:—and out of it the Superman.

This is really a sort of prophecy. It is as if he were hearing something of the future—the winds of the future with stealthy pinions and a new gospel with good tidings. That is the *euangelion*,[2] he scents faintly a new revelation, a new important truth which of course is connected with the undiscovered man. And what would that be?

Mrs. Sigg: The compensatory function of the unconscious.

Prof. Jung: Yes, the unconscious is not discovered—all the things that are unconscious to man. So the prophecy would be that good tidings are to be expected from that side because of the compensatory function of the unconscious. That would explain the idea of the thousand salubrities: namely, the helpful qualities of the unconscious which would produce a new health. And he announces these tidings particularly to the lonesome ones; for those who feel particularly separate and suffer from their separateness the good tidings in the air would be that they are lonesome and seceding today because they have more intuition or a certain premonition of what is to be expected in the future. And now comes the funny idea that they one day will be a people. What could one reasonably mean by that?

Mrs. Baynes: Could he mean the unification of the psyche into a whole man?

Prof. Jung: Well, psychologically that is surely true, for that has to do with the structure of the Superman. You see, the Superman really is "a people," not one man; that can be understood very literally. For if these lonely or seceding ones integrate their unconscious, they are of course different from other people insofar as their consciousness is more extended, and then it is as if they were uniting the statistics of a whole people in one psychology. Then they would recognize that they were not only this but also that, not only old but also young, not only good but also bad—there would be nothing, practically, which they were not. That is a condition which is usually only prevailing in a whole

[2] *Euangelion*: good tidings, evangels, gospels.

nation or in the population of a town at least, where one is the parson, another the doctor, another a workman, and so on; each has his specific role and is nothing else. The roles are well distributed on the surface. But when people integrate their unconscious, they see they are all those too. So it is as if one man were becoming a whole town; he would then find his former ego consciousness included in the consciousness of a whole population. Now, that is also a simile for the self; the self is often explained as being like a city containing thousands of people because the self only becomes visible in the experience of a greater consciousness. If one extends one's consciousness so that one sees that one is many things besides one's ego, one approaches a certain realization of the self. But it is also true in another way: namely, if an attempt at an extension of consciousness appears somewhere and is not realized, then it causes a sort of mental infection which draws people together in a sect, say, or it causes a mental epidemic such as one sees actually happening in Germany. That is the Superman on the level of non-realization; the whole people is like one man, and one man is shown as an emblem or symbol of the whole nation. That is the substitute for the integration of the consciousness of one individual. You see, Germany *should* be one individual but with an integrated consciousness; instead of that there is just no integration of the unconscious, but the whole people is integrated into one sacred figure—which nobody fully believes *could* be sacred. That is the unfortunate thing.

Mrs. Baumann: The actual phrase used here seems to really refer to Germany; it says a chosen people shall arise, and they call themselves a chosen people.

Prof. Jung: The German text is *soll ein auserwähltes Volk erwachsen*; you are quite right.

Mrs. Baynes: But surely you cannot accuse Nietzsche of that sort of chauvinism.

Prof. Jung: Oh heavens no—nobody was more critical than he; he is talking out of his unconscious. When you read his aphorisms, you understand that he never would have said such damned nonsense, but when the unconscious speaks it is a different matter—then it is in his blood. An integrated consciousness *is* of course the chosen one: "many are called but few are chosen." The integrated consciousness knows its meaning and therefore it is chosen, conscious of the choice that has been made before its birth. You see, the self is timeless, and that assembly of facts which characterizes the self has been chosen before time. Therefore, one cannot help having the feeling of being chosen, and that this whole thing is chosen, premeditated. There is no getting away from it: one is embedded in a course of events that is meaningful. Now, if that is not realized consciously, it simply spreads out unconsciously, and instead of the chosen self, realized by consciousness as the choice that has taken place before time, the whole people is chosen; and then you have that funny fact of a people imagining that it has a mission or something like that—that they are God's own people, chosen by God himself. That idea can be forgiven on a primitive level, but on a higher level it is absolutely out of the question; it is a psychological feeling that belongs in the individuation process, which has spread unconsciously by mental contagion because it has not been realized by the one individual.

Nietzsche's idea is perfectly clear to him. Those good tidings would be the idea of the Superman: namely, the idea that all those lonely people like himself will form a community, and out of them will come the future birth, the Superman. Nietzsche had the idea that civilization was declining and that something like a monastery might be created for people like himself. Keyserling has also preached that notion in *La Révolution Mondiale*—without mentioning his predecessor—that he himself might found such a monastery, a most amazing idea.[3] It is really very usual, however, when people are touching upon something vital, that they organize a society, assuming that they are the kernel perhaps of a great organization which will cover the whole world, and so the world will be renewed. That is the same mistake: it is a rationalization of a psychological fact which according to the principle of "Physician, heal thyself" should be dealt with in an entirely different way. For lacking wholeness of the individual a big organization is substituted. One thinks one is much bigger for belonging to a *Verein*, with ten thousand members, for instance. Of course the bigger an organization, the lower its morality and the more its psychology approaches mob psychology, but they don't see that; and that they would be working quite against the purpose of such an organization. So the idea Nietzsche plays with on the surface is of course the ordinary idea that all the lonely people of the world who smell a rat should be organized into one body.

Many such schemes were tried after the war. A woman named Dorothy Hunt[4] travelled all over Europe to collect the great names of Europe—not even the people—to organize them into a big hydrocepha-

---

[3] See p. 18n above.

[4] Dorothy Alice Bonavia Hunt (who also used the pseudonym Doric Collyer) was a minor English novelist. She brought out two books in 1937 (London), *Reflection* and *Unfettered*.

lus, and when she came to Bernard Shaw, he wrote in pencil at the bottom of her letter, "Don't try, Dorothy! Nothing doing." This is this kind of psychology. And then all these fine and lonely people—who cannot understand each other, but hate each other like poison, otherwise they never would be lonely—are all pressed together into one matchbox. By great good chance they might create a superman. But he would probably be a superman who would jump out of that box as soon as possible. Everyone would like to be a superman or imagines that he is one, but those people never go together. It is evidence of the amazing unconsciousness of good Christians to think that all good people should go together. They don't. They are competitors who hate each other. It is then not a case of being good, but of being better, and that is the worst.

Verily, a place of healing shall the earth become.

Oh God! Wouldn't that be awful?—the whole world a hospital filled with nurses and doctors—everybody healing everybody else.

And already is a new odour diffused around it, a salvation-bringing odour—and a new hope!

There is something decidedly late Christian about this, yet behind it there is a great truth. It would be really marvelous if the earth should become a place of healing, but it would be where people heal themselves, where everybody is concerned with their own health cure. That would be almost a paradise.

Mrs. Sigg: I don't think the translation is exactly healing, *Genesung.*

Prof. Fierz: Oh yes, it is even worse.

Prof. Jung: It doesn't make much difference, *Wahrlich, eine Stätte der Genesung soll noch die Erde werden*[5]—that might be a sanatorium you know!

Mrs. Baynes: Healing can also have the passive meaning in English. I understand Mrs. Sigg to mean that it is here used in the passive sense.

Prof. Jung: It is ambiguous, and on account of that it is as if the historical condition had misunderstood and had chosen just the wrong conclusion; one cannot even say *quite* wrong, but wrong from a psychological point of view.

Well now, I quite understand that my comments on the end of this second chapter have caused some discussion, so I want to make one

---

[5] Kaufmann* translates the sentence: "Verily, the earth shall yet become a site of recovery."

point clear, or rather two points: namely, that this whole chapter has a double bottom. Below the surface there is the teaching by Zarathustra. Now, Zarathustra is the archetype of the wise old man, the *nous* or the *pneuma*, as it always has been. And his message is right. But it is transmitted through a human brain. The man Nietzsche receives the message and lends it his own language, and then of course it becomes something else. Nietzsche is the man in time and space, the man who belongs to and is limited by certain conditions—time conditions, social conditions—and naturally these restricting conditions will modify the message. We can read the original message in his words. It is *contained* in the words, but Nietzsche's own time conditions and mental conditions come in too, so that the message comes out already in a modified way. It becomes still more so when it reaches the ears of the audience, because the audience modifies it again. One must always ask, to what time this truth has been taught—and then expect a peculiar modification.

For instance, compare the original meaning of Christ's teaching with what has become of it in the subsequent centuries. When Christianity was taught to a highly educated audience, it was made into a philosophy. If you have a certain idea how men like St. Augustine or Tertullian preached, or how a learned man like Origen understood Christianity, you realize that that makes all the difference in the world. One instance which I have often quoted is that St. Augustine compares the Virgin Mary to the earth: she is the earth fecundated by the spring rains, and from the earth, Christ, our truth, is born: he is the wheat.[6] That is the type of language which subsequent centuries would not have understood. It would have led back into a chthonic cult, but those men were talking to educated people who could take these things on the wing; an idea was not leaden, it lived. The antique Roman Christians didn't need dogma; their subtle minds could deal with analogies and symbolism. They understood things. Yet the same gospels taught to the barbarians became something quite different; the barbarian mind demands things cut and dried. Originally there was no question about the communion for instance, a sort of memorial rite. The idea of real flesh and blood only became dogma in about the ninth century when Paschasius Radbertus invented transubstantiation: that was a concession to the barbarous mind. He was the abbot of a monastery in

---

[6] See St. Augustine, p. 51n above. His mentor, St. Ambrose: "In the womb of the Virgin, grace increased like a heap of wheat and the lily" (*De Institutio Virginis*, cap. 14, cited in CW 6, par. 394.

Corbie, Picardie, one of the Frankish invaders. (The whole north of France was at that time Germanic.) A monk in the same monastery however, Radramndus, still held that it was a memorial meal. And Scotus Erigena, the abbot of Malmsbury, who died in 889, fought for this idea.[7]

So Zarathustra speaks to Nietzsche, but Nietzsche speaks out of his time. He is an advanced man of his time, yet he receives the message already with a certain modification. To reach the ears of an audience, he must speak the language of his surroundings, of his condition; and what people do to it afterwards, well, that remains to be seen. But already the fact that he is teaching somebody, even in the imagination, makes a great deal of difference. When I formulate a thought to myself alone, for instance, I can formulate it in a way that nobody would understand, in a mental shorthand, in a symbolic sort of way; and if I put that on paper and get it printed it will be incomprehensible. If I make up my mind to explain it, I must translate it into the language of my surroundings. I must imagine what people know and don't know, I have to come down to the ordinary conditions of communication, and that of course changes the original idea.

The underlying idea here is, of course, "Heal thyself!"—and then you are in Tao. Then Tao *is* and people are with you in Tao. But how do you get there? You have to explain yourself, have to become conscious of your unconscious, have to integrate your unconscious: you have still to discover yourself. So wake up, for there is a wonderful message in that, the *euangelion*, good tidings; and a lonely man like yourself will perhaps find companions. But these companions are all in yourself, and the more you find outside the less you are sure of your own truth. Find them first in yourself, integrate the people in yourself. There are figures, existences, in your unconscious that will come to you, that will integrate in you, so that you may perhaps come into a condition in which you don't know yourself. You will say, I am this, I am that, I am practically everywhere, I am exactly like a whole people—and when that doubt arises you are whole. But don't make the mistake of thinking you are whole when you are part of an organization, a *Verein der Gleichgesinnten*[8] or something of the sort.

This is the message but in the actual text he says, "Ye lonesome ones of today, ye seceding ones, ye shall one day be a people: out of you who have chosen yourselves, shall a chosen people arise:—and out of it the

---

[7] John Scotus Erigena, born in Ireland, flourished in the mid-9th century.

[8] *Verein der Gleichgesinnten*: Society of the Like-Minded.

Superman." Now, when Nietzsche is talking to Zarathustra, he perhaps understands the message, but the moment he begins to teach it to others it is already modified. In contradistinction to everything Nietzsche said before as an aphorist, it sounds exactly like the idea of a chosen people, or perhaps a *Kultur* monastery. You see, these lonely ones would not stand each other for two days: it is quite out of the question; far from being a salvation, it would be quite hellish. So the original message slowly, without any wrong intention, changes its meaning, becomes distorted, and finally you have the Catholic church.

And where is Christ's original teaching? Some say they go back to the true word of Christ himself, but then they falsify the Gospel very quietly. I discovered a really remarkable instance about two years ago which I have already mentioned. In the new revised text of the Greek and Latin New Testament, which is supposed to be without flaw, I found in the Lord's Prayer that God should not give us our ordinary daily bread, but the bread that is *supersubstantialis, das überwesentliche Brot*, the bread that is not of ordinary substance. I thought that surely this is amazing, knowing that the church had always asserted that it was the ordinary bread. But I happened to possess the first Greek edition of the New Testament by Erasmus of Rotterdam, the so-called *Textus rescriptus*, and there it was. And the other day Professor Karl Barth at his lecture in the university mentioned the fact that Erasmus held that *supersubstantialis* really was intended, that this was absolutely undeniable, and that it made much better sense than the word *bread*. He mentioned also that Calvin was against that; he even said that it was heresy and blasphemy to hold that it was not the ordinary bread.[9] Now why should it be so terrible? Moreover, it is a fact that the text of Matthew contains that word *epiousios*. (It is interesting that this Greek word *epiousios* only exists elsewhere in two doubtful places; but that doesn't matter; in this place it is an invention of the writer.) And St. Hieronymus, who made the *Vulgata*, the Latin translation of the New Testament,[10] took the trouble to find out the word for *epiousios* in the Aramaic text, where it means "the future thing." You see, *epi* means upon

[9] On supersubstantial (not just daily) bread, see 17 Oct. 1934, n. 1, above; on Barth, see 5 Dec. 1934, n. 9, above. Desiderius Erasmus (1466-1536) was the Dutch humanist whose book *The Praise of Folly* was the most popular work of the age. John Calvin (1509-1564), French Reformation leader, settled in Geneva.

[10] A Latin translation of the New Testament had been made in the time of the Apostles, but by the fourth century many variants had crept in, so there was a need for a new, commonly accepted translation, which was supplied by St. Hieronymus or St. Jerome (c. 340-420).

or after, and *ousios* means the being or the actual existence, so *epiousios* could mean the existence after. Just as the word *metaphysical* as used in Aristotle means that after the physical beings come the metaphysical beings, *meta* of course meaning "after."[11] St. Hieronymus assumed that that which follows after *ousios*, the natural existence, is the supersubstantial existence, and therefore he translated it as *supersubstantialis.* So the demand in the prayer would mean: give us that bread of the future kingdom *now*, today and every day—give us our daily supersubstantial bread, the spiritual food.

Now, the church is dead set against that. I read as a special commentary in a recognized work that it was quite evident from the surrounding text in Matthew that it must be the ordinary bread. I coud not remember that there was anything to prove that and found that the text of St. Matthew says very emphatically that only the heathens worry about food—what they shall eat and drink and what they shall wear—and that Christians should not do that. So I asked myself, why that resistance? Why the devil should the church be unable to admit that a good Christian should pray to God to give him his daily spiritual food, which is far more important than the ordinary food—though I admit that the ordinary food is very important?

Mrs. Sigg: The church wants to provide the spiritual bread herself.

Prof. Jung: Exactly, that is it.

Miss Wolff: Christ says in another passage, "I am the bread of life." So *he* is that supersubstantial bread, but one is only allowed to get it by way of the church.

Miss Hughes: That "man cannot live by bread alone" is another saying of Christ's, is it not? And that would confirm this, I should think.[12]

Prof. Jung: Absolutely. But the church, which is a human organization, claims, against the truth of the Gospel, that they alone can administer the food. They interfere between man and God, tell you obvious nonsense, and even cheat in order to blindfold you. You see, that is the difference between the needs and the morality of a great organization, and the other way, the integration of a human individual who is simply

[11] The usual story is that the editor of his treatises put Aristotle's long work on "First Philosophy" right after the work called "Physics"—hence, metaphysics doubly. Both Jung and Nietzsche professed disdain for metaphysics, Jung often calling it disguised psychology and Nietzsche "the science . . . which deals with the fundamental errors of mankind—but as if they were fundamental truths" (*Human All Too Human*, tr. Marion Faber with Stephen Schumann [Lincoln, Neb., 1984], p. 150).

[12] "I am the bread of life" (John 6:35). "Man cannot live by bread alone" (Matthew 4:4).

confronted with God, with no church and no organization in between. Of course, one can say there is the invisible church, the community of the saints, but that is only a saintly and invisible communion. Obviously as soon as they have a secretary and pay their annual tribute to the *Verein* it is no longer an invisible communion, but is an organized body which has to be registered. Then it is a world organization, and that is the tragedy of the church. Now, it is also obvious that when such an important thing as the integration of consciousness is not realized, not understood, yet is instigated by the message of the spirit, that thing simply spreads below the threshold of consciousness and causes a great mental disturbance which of course has certain social consequences. And then people will try to organize something because they cannot understand it otherwise. They think *good* and *sacred* and *true* are words which apply only to something in a church, so it must be an organization; and the church, the only truth, is the visibility of sacredness, so it must be visible. The symbolic bread and wine must be flesh and blood and the communion of the saints must be a visible organization, and whatever else there is is no good. Therefore, it is unavoidable that such a new movement in the unconscious is always in danger of being swallowed by the collective spirit in man, swallowed again by the collective unconscious. And that is what we see now everywhere—including the Oxford Movement. Now we go on to the next part of this chapter,

> When Zarathustra had spoken these words, he paused, like one who had not said his last word; and long did he balance the staff doubtfully in his hand. At last he spake thus—and his voice had changed:
> I now go alone, my disciples! Ye also now go away, and alone! So will I have it.

What has happened here?

Mrs. Crowley: It sounds as if he had realized something of this, as if he realized that it was an inner reality, that he had to integrate within.

Prof. Jung: Exactly. Now, this is really in contradiction with the teaching before, so here we see the two layers. You see, the message goes on and Zarathustra seems to correct himself, as if he realized that something wrong had been said on the surface, as if the message had gotten wrong. So he says, No, not an organization, neither a monastery nor a church nor a state, no visible body; going alone is what I mean.

Mrs. Jung: He said before, "Ye lonesome ones of today, ye seceding ones, ye shall one day be a people." So that would be a condition for becoming this chosen people, which is only in the future.

Prof. Jung: Yes, those who are lonely today will also become a chosen people: they form a community.

Mrs. Jung: So if he is seceding, it might be in order to prepare for this future community.

Prof. Jung: Exactly, but there is a peculiar emphasis on it which I think can only be explained by interpretation of a possible misunderstanding before, so he insists that not only is he going alone but that they also must go alone. "So will I have it." He would not speak like that if there had not been a certain tendency to substitute by an organization what they should do themselves. Of course, that is quite understandable, it is only too human; nobody chooses the integration of consciousness when he can get along much more cheaply: one is much too weak to stand alone. One makes organizations in order to have the grand feeling of being great by simply paying a certain tax or something like that.

> Verily, I advise you: depart from me, and guard yourselves against Zarathustra! And better still: be ashamed of him! Perhaps he hath deceived you.

You see, he makes it very strong in order that any idea of organization should be excluded. They must not trust him; they should even have a supreme doubt as to the veracity of the message. That can only be explained by the ambiguity of the message before, but now the real message breaks through and emphasizes its demand.

> The man of knowledge must be able not only to love his enemies, but also to hate his friends.

This is indeed very strong, but it expresses what kind of condition?

Mrs. Crowley: A paradoxical condition—that he could realize the two things. And I thought it might here have something to do with Nietzsche's own personal complex about friends, because he did not really understand friends in the right spirit.

Prof. Jung: Well, of course his difficulty in establishing relations is always everywhere.

Miss Taylor: Does he not advise them to be detached from him?

Prof. Jung: Yes, that is the idea. You see, it is the consciousness of the other thing that I am too, my own contrast. One person in me knows I love my friends, and the other person knows that he doesn't love my friends. The love is not absolute, but is only relative; it *is* only inasmuch as there is hatred. Now, that is a paradoxical consciousness which proves that consciousness has extended beyond the ego limitations and is now itself ambiguous. Therefore, the person which underlies that consciousness is ambiguous; no longer one, he is two, he is many, he is everywhere.

Mrs. Baumann: But could it not also be taken here that Zarathustra is warning him of his identification and pushing him away?

Prof. Jung: Well, the trouble is, Nietzsche is identical with Zarathustra, and doesn't make a difference. Zarathustra isn't talking to Nietzsche, but is talking to the imaginary disciples. You might take Nietzsche to be a disciple, but he is not. He is Zarathustra himself.

Prof. Reichstein: Is it not the idea of getting *Erkenntnis*, understanding, recognition, in contrast to the *Gläubigen*, the believers, which comes afterwards? Therefore, you must first detach yourself quite distinctly by hatred to get knowledge, a breaking up of the tradition.

Prof. Jung: Well, it is of course psychologically quite easy to understand why Zarathustra gives that particular teaching. If you are convinced that you do nothing but love, then you hold only one side and somebody else is doing the hating: then you are not an integrated consciousness. You must know that you are both, that you are the yea and the nay; if you are only conscious of the yea, then somebody else is doing the contrary, and it is merely projected. For the integration of consciousness it is necessary that one realizes positive and negative feeling. The extension of consciousness means of course an increase of knowledge, of understanding; otherwise it would be the original unconscious condition. For instance, if one sees a picture but has no relation to it, one could say one was not conscious of it. It would be only a perception.

> One requiteth a teacher badly if one remain merely a scholar.
> And why will ye not pluck at my wreath?

That of course means that they should accept his teaching to the extent of making it true: namely, that they take him at his word, that they realize themselves literally, and see what kind of feeling they have or what their real attitude is.

> Ye venerate me; but what if your veneration should some day collapse? Take heed lest a statue crush you!

You see, veneration also is a clear-cut and one-sided condition only when there is a certain negation of it; if that is not conscious, then it is somewhere else, somebody else has to do it. So they should be conscious that somewhere that veneration is compensated for or contradicted, and if they don't realize that, they are apt to make a statue, an idol, which falls upon them in the moment when their veneration peters out.

> Ye say, ye believe in Zarathustra? But of what account is Zarathustra! Ye are my believers: but of what account are all believers?
> Ye had not yet sought yourselves: then did ye find me.

You see, as long as I am unconscious of the fact that a criminal or a fool is myself too, I find you the criminal and the fool. My consciousness is only really integrated when I know the same in myself—when I can say, yes, I find you an animal, and this is myself. Then I have really extended consciousness. One finds many parallels to this particular idea in Eastern texts.

> So do all believers; therefore all belief is of so little account.

This is again to be sent to the address of late Christianity where people always talk about believing. Either you know a thing and so you don't need to believe it, or you don't know it and then why should you believe it? People say that you ought to believe in God, or that such and such a thing has been sent by God. But you don't—you belive that Mr. Smith sent it. And you don't think the brick which fell off the roof because there was a strong wind was sent by God, so you cannot believe it. The church teaches that you should make a special effort to believe that God has his hands in your life somewhere; but you haven't noticed it so why the devil should you believe it? You should resolutely say, "Only if I see it do I believe it: I have quite a good explanation why the thing went wrong: it can also be explained by the stupidity of man and myself." So it is much better to assume that you haven't the faintest idea of what God is doing and don't even know that he *is*, unless you have an experience where you cannot help seeing the hand of God in it. But the church doesn't risk waiting for that. That can always be anticipated. It is wise to say that everything is done by God in order to cover up the fact that nobody knows whether he does anything. Most parsons don't really believe that, of course not; but they say they do because it is the only possibility for them. They can only live in their superstructure of believing something. But the ordinary man can afford to be objective about it and say that as far as he can see, God is inefficient. And so he lives on that hypothesis until he meets God, and then he doesn't need to believe it. For instance, if I meet a rhino and he tosses me into the air, I don't need to believe it—I know it is a fact. So we can do without believing; that is the most reasonable thing. Otherwise you make God responsible for all sorts of nonsense and simply blindfold yourself. If you reckon up what pious people say God has done in the course of a year, it is appalling: he has caused automobile accidents, killed people, destroyed crops, damaged cattle and human beings and made himself an awful nuisance. And then one should be grateful! So you see, when Zarathustra makes little of believers, it is a gesture to late Christianity.

> Now do I bid you lose me and find yourselves; and only when ye have all denied me, will I return unto you.
> Verily, with other eyes, my brethren, shall I then seek my lost ones; with another love shall I then love you.
> And once again shall ye have become friends unto me, and children of one hope: then will I be with you for the third time, to celebrate the great noontide with you.

This is of course Christian symbolism; it is the *parousia*,[13] the return of Christ and the new reconciliation, the communion with the Lamb; it is the apocalyptic vision where everything is fulfilled, when Christ will set up a kingdom of heaven on earth and there will be eternal communion with him. But this is also dangerously sentimental, dangerously near to the perfectly good Christian ideas. Inasmuch as the Christian ideas are really mythological they are absolutely true, but they are no longer quite mythological. They are already disintegrated to a certain extent and so they have lost the right taste and are no longer good. We are tired of that phraseology; we have heard it every Sunday in church. So the words have changed but the meaning is the same; the great noontide is the midday meal, and if one takes the words and supposes that this Christian analogy of the communion is only apparent, one gets the real message. Then one comes to "the great noontide when man is in the middle of his course between animal and Superman"—then he celebrates that communion with Zarathustra—with the self. This is psychological, for in the middle of their way, Dante's adventure happens to certain people, if not consciously, then at least unconsciously. Then they feel the touch of the self.

> And it is the great noontide, when man is in the middle of his course between animal and Superman, and celebrating his advance to the evening as his highest hope: for it is the advance to a new morning.

[13] *Parousia*: the Divine Presence.

The animal is the unconscious existence, the merely biological, personal ego existence, and the evening is the problem of individuation, the becoming of the self or the Superman; and this is not the going down to the evening, but is the advance to a new morning, which means the idea of rebirth in the self or to the self.

At such time will the down-goer bless himself, that he should be an over-goer; and the sun of his knowledge will be at noontide.

That is of course the same idea.

"Dead are all the Gods: now do we desire the Superman to live."—Let this be our final will at the great noontide!

So, in the first part of life when there is nothing but animal purpose, unconsciousness, and ego existence, the gods are projected: they are outside because they are not integrated. Then comes the noontide where the gods will be integrated in man; he will recognize them as projections. But then he has lost the gods and there is the danger of inflation, of identification with the image of the divine, and then he has to realize the Superman. The Superman would be the superconsciousness and this is now the problem. What is this superconsciousness that has integrated even those psychological facts which formerly were projected as gods? What happens then to consciousness and what will that Superman be? That is the drama which will be enacted in the next part of *Zarathustra*.

LECTURE V

19 February 1936

Prof. Jung:
Here is a question by Miss Hannah: "I was very much interested in what you said last time about the present state of things (Germany, etc.) being caused by 'the idea of the self spreading by mental contagion.' I would like very much to understand better how this works. Is it because the idea is so much easier to grasp intellectually than to apply to the physical being, and once touched, even intellectually, the whole process must take place elsewhere? Could one almost say that a whole people, even a whole world, are caught in the parts, left in the unconscious, of the vast idea which Nietzsche fettered to the earth on its intellectual side?"

I am afraid I wouldn't be able to explain the strange fact of this mental contagion in such terms. You know, Nietzsche's idea of the self, as presented in the figure of the Superman, has in itself a peculiar effect: namely, he identifies with Zarathustra, and Zarathustra is that Superman as he appeared to him, so Nietzsche is also identical with the Superman. Now, that is already a cause for contagion, for if you identify with an idea then that thing has happened to you and you are caught by it. For instance, if a person when angry *says* he is in a very bad mood today, you are perfectly satisfied—you understand that people can be in a bad mood and are not infected by it. But if he doesn't say so, if he is really in a bad mood and caught by it, then he makes you angry. It is infectious and you are caught too. If he declares his condition you know he is human, not merely a beast, because he is able to inform you that he is human, so you can deal with that fellow: you can still talk to him. But if he doesn't acknowledge it, he is a beast and will bite, and then you are highly irritated and keep away. And so whenever you are caught by the unconscious, be it in the form of a mood or an idea, you are influenced. Therefore if Nietzsche had said, "Ladies and Gentlemen, here is the idea of the self, but I am not that self," you might see that it was a very interesting idea, but very few people would listen—otherwise they could have listened to it long ago—because it is not infectious. But if somebody says, "I *am* the self, I am the Super-man," you get excited; either you think he is a damned fool to say such a thing, just crazy, and get excited, because you have to do with a lu-natic. Or you say, "Isn't it grand? That is the self, he *is* the fellow." So those people always have either a positive or a negative following, but people who are balanced in their minds have no following because bal-ance causes no mental contagion; it may cause conviction but never persuasion.

Now, as Zarathustra is the Superman, the inference is that Nietzsche is the Superman, because on account of the identification, it is difficult to make a difference between them. For instance, when he says, "I love you, you are my brethren," you wonder who is speaking. Zarathustra is not the writer—he has no pen—but is a ghost. He lived about two thousand, seven hundred years ago, but it might be his spirit that ap-pears and speaks through Nietzsche. Then you know that Nietzsche became insane, and many passages in this book are a bit morbid, so you get very much the impression of the identity; and as soon as there is morbidity you are afraid. One often hears, "Don't read *Zarathustra* be-cause those who have read it have grown morbid or gone mad; that stuff has a bad influence." Others say the book is a revelation and Nietzsche the great prophet of the age—they are caught that way. You see, there is practically no social fool under the sun who cannot have a following; when he steps out into the street and says he is the great man of the time with a new message for the world, a certain number may think he is just crazy, but some will be convinced that he really is the fellow. He only has to shout and make a noise in order to have an audience. People who suffer from such an identification usually shout, which clearly shows that they are not above their own material, but are really caught by it. And they want to be caught because they want to catch others; because they are caught, they want to catch, just as drug fiends always want to catch other people because they are caught them-selves. So they cultivate a certain style which shows that they are caught; they know unconsciously that when they are caught they catch. The primitive medicine man, for instance, must prove to his audience that he is caught because that carries, that infects the whole tribe. And whoever is out to infect or to catch will shout and behave like a lunatic. He will demonstrate his unfree condition because he thereby catches—such people have a great following. In Nietzsche the idea of the self appears in a very tangible form, and he is visibly caught by it; and that will spread, have influence, convey contagion, either in a positive or a negative sense. He will arouse no end of resistances naturally, but his enemies who resist him are really his followers, because they cannot turn their eyes away from the phenomenon he offers to the world. Others are positively persuaded by him and will themselves seek the Superman, or at least transform themselves into forefathers of the Superman, humbly enough, in the hope that in three or four generations one of their sons or daughters will produce a Superman.

That is the way I explain this mental contagion through an idea which is not completely detached from the man in whom it originated. Of course I don't mean that Zarathustra is really the starting point for the idea of the self, because for many thousands of years this idea seems to have been lurking behind the screen of historical events. In the East it appeared much earlier than here, but we see it at work in Master Eckhardt, it approached closer in later philosophy, and in Nietzsche it broke through in a sort of *ekstasis*. Now, it is tangible, near. And because it is not completely detached from man, it has these peculiar effects. It is still in the unconscious, so the unconscious is activated; people nowadays are gripped by an unrest which they do not understand, so they spread their excitement. That is happening actually in Germany, and has happened in Russia: everybody is infecting everybody else with unrest, with a peculiarly vibrating unconscious—and there must be a reason for all that. It is as if something had gotten into man's unconscious and were stirring there, causing infectious excitement. Even the most ridiculous notions have their following; all sorts of mental epidemics—bigger or smaller—are swaying our civilized world. And it is perfectly natural; we have often spoken before of the causality or the aetiology of this phenomenon. It corresponds to the decay of Christianity, the form in which one lived securely; and the more those metaphysical convictions fade or vanish, the more the energy invested in those forms drops below the threshold of consciousness. There are comparatively few people nowadays who think in metaphysical terms; that is of the past: all that libido has disappeared into the unconscious. That utter *belief* in Christ and God and heaven, the libido which built the cathedrals of the Middle Ages, has gone into other forms. We have now big hotels, skyscrapers, enormous armies, and such things. The idea of God which was the supreme reality of the Middle Ages has been replaced by Einstein's theory of relativity and there are only about a dozen people in the world who understand that. (I don't know whether it functions in them as God: I never heard of that.) And all the other people are empty.

No wonder, then, that all that libido in the unconscious begins to stir and causes a phenomenon like Nietzsche's *Zarathustra*. This book begins, practically, with the statement that God is dead, but you can see throughout the book that Nietzsche never gets rid of him; for God is the unknown partner, the real partner of man. Unnamed and not visible, he is still there. That is the cause of this great excitement, the enormous dithyrambic enthusiasm which bursts out of Nietzsche; that is the fact which forever has been called God. In any former times they would have said a god possessed him and was speaking out of him. In Nietzsche the god for the time being is Zarathustra. You can name God what you like but he always appears in the fire. In the Old Testament he appears in the flaming bush, which is simply the dithyrambic enthusiasm of God breaking out anew in ecstasy; he was then called "Jahveh" and here it is "Zarathustra" but it is the same thing. And there is one of the causes of this infection. Now of course, many people believe that the only good is to be gripped and excited and infectious, and that everybody ought to be caught in the infection; and since that is so, I cannot say it is wrong. I don't know whether it is wrong or right—it is just a fact. But I don't share their conviction. I think it is indecent—perhaps I am quite wrong in my conviction. (I also cannot say whether that is right or wrong.) But it doesn't matter to me: I have it and this is a fact too.

Mrs. Sigg: You spoke about shouting, and Nietzsche had this symptom in his illness; when his mother wrote to the doctor she said that her son had a habit of shouting and it frightened her. She said he didn't seem to suffer. He smiled rather.

Prof. Jung: Perhaps it had a pleasant effect upon him. Well now, we will go on to the second part of *Zarathustra*. We should celebrate this moment—that we have gotten as far as this! You remember at the end of Part I, as in the beginning, Nietzsche declares that God is dead. "Dead are all the Gods: now do we desire the Superman to live." Here we have the psychology clearly; the gods are dead and now let us call for the Superman, the man who is more than the ordinary man as we know him. You see, that is not very far from the Christian idea of the Son of Man. Christ is man, so he is Superman, the God-man; the idea has not evolved very far. Then Nietzsche advises his disciples not to run after him or identify with him, or follow him and so avoid themselves. They rather should become his enemies in order to find themselves; he says it is better that he shut up and give them a chance. Also there is a certain secret tendency behind it: namely, would it not be time to manifest, to find the Superman? And the best means to find or create the Superman is always to put yourself to a test, to go into your own solitude, to strengthen yourself, in order to find out whether you are by chance the Superman. That is what people do who want to become holy or saints. These are the tendencies which lead to the second part; we shall now see what befell Zarathustra when he went into his solitude. This chapter is called "The Child with the Mirror."

> After this Zarathustra returned again into the mountains to the solitude of his cave, and withdrew himself from men, waiting like a sower who hath scattered his seed. His soul, however, became impatient and full of longing for those whom he loved: because he had still much to give them. For this is hardest of all: to close the open hand out of love, and keep modest as a giver.

From this passage we can see one of his particular difficulties: he needed an audience very badly. For, to have an audience is agreeable—it always proves something to you—while if you are all alone you lose your self-esteem. It is as if you became smaller and smaller and finally are a mere speck in an awfully extended cosmos, and then you either develop megalomania or become a nothingness. Therefore it is advisable to have a certain audience, if merely for the sake of demonstrating that you know who you are, that you become something definite, that you are just as ordinary as other people, and that you are living in your body. You lose all these considerations when you are alone with yourself. Now, he particularly suffers from the fact that he cannot give, and he feels very much that he should deliver his message.

> Thus passed with the lonesome one months and years; his wisdom meanwhile increased, and caused him pain by its abundance.
> One morning, however, he awoke ere the rosy dawn, and having meditated long on his couch, at last spake thus to his heart:
> Why did I startle in my dream, so that I awoke? Did not a child come to me, carrying a mirror?
> "O Zarathustra"—said the child unto me—"look at thyself in the mirror!"
> But when I looked into the mirror, I shrieked, and my heart throbbed: for not myself did I see therein, but a devil's grimace and derision.
> Verily, all too well do I understand the dream's portent and monition: my *doctrine* is in danger; tares want to be called wheat!
> Mine enemies have grown powerful and have disfigured the likeness of my doctrine, so that my dearest ones have to blush for the gifts that I gave them.

What about this piece of dream interpretation?

Mrs. Sigg: It is most awful extraversion, that he thinks only of his doctrine.

Prof. Jung: Oh not necessarily, that is generally human; it is what everybody does if he has a doctrine at all. You see, nobody in his sound senses would take such a dream to himself, unless he knew about analytical psychology. Of course, then he would feel under a certain obligation to think, "Damn it, what does it mean that this mirror puts such a face on me?" But an ordinary unsophisticated human being not affected by psychology would leap to the conclusion that somebody else must have painted him black. For the bad things are always somewhere else: I am very good, I have not a devil's face. But the dream means exactly that. He has a devil's face because he mirrors himself in the mind of a child. Since children and fools tell the truth, he must look like that. This is the simple and straightforward meaning of the dream. I am quite convinced that he really had this dream just then; it would be most likely to happen to him when he was withdrawing. And there was a real interruption between these two parts of Zarathustra, in which he withdrew from that rushing river of creation where one is filled with the noise and the turmoil of the waves. Then one comes to oneself, everything is quiet, and then it is most likely that one sees one's own face. This is exceedingly apt symbolism; the mirror is the intellect or the mind, and the child carrying the mirror means of course the child's mind, the simple mind, so one cannot avoid the conclusion that the child has told the truth through its magic mirror. Now, what does it mean when he sees his face like that of the devil?

Prof. Reichstein: Is it not here again an answer to the statement that all the gods are dead? And then of course the first thing that appears would be the devil.

Prof. Jung: Inasmuch as Zarathustra is God the reverse side of him is then necessarily a devil. We must also ask *who* is speaking of the gods? If it were an Eastern man, of course we could not assume that there must necessarily be a devil because the Eastern Gods are neither good nor bad, but both good *and* bad; they appear in two ways, the benevolent and the wrathful aspects. That is particularly clear in the Tibetan gods of the Mahayana; but all the Hindu gods have their different aspects and there is no fuss about it. It is quite evident that the good and benevolent goddess Kali is the most bloodthirsty monster on the other side and that the life-giver, the fertilizing God Shiva, is also the God of utter destruction. That makes no difference to the paradoxical mind of the East. But to the Western mind with its peculiar categorical character, it makes all the difference in the world; to say God is the devil or the devil is God is considered blasphemous or sacrilegious. Yet if there is such a universal being as the deity, it needs must be more complete than man; and since man is a peculiar union of good and bad qualities, then all the more so the universal being. A very famous German Protestant[1] says in one of his books that God can only be good, thereby putting a frightful restriction on God; it is as if in the organization of the welfare of humanity, he were depriving God of half his power. How can he rule the world if he is only good? And it is quite wrong to say that all the evil is just for the good; one can say just as well that all good is for the evil. Therefore, it is more to the point to say things are both good and evil; and you can be doubtful whether they are as favorable as all that, because everything tends more to evil than to good.

Nietzsche would not talk of the devil so openly, however, because that is not popular. But if God is only good, who is producing all the evil in the world? So the omnipotence of God is obviously divided—he has to halve it with the devil. It would be much more to the point to assume that the all-powerful deity was superior to good and evil—"beyond good and evil" as Nietzsche claims for the Superman. Such an all-powerful being could even handle the evil; to handle the good is no art but to handle evil is difficult. Plato expresses this in his parable of the man in a chariot driving two horses; one is good-tempered and white, the other black and evil-tempered, and the charioteer has all the trouble in the world to manage it.[2] That is the good man who does not know how to handle evil; good people are singularly incapable of handling evil. So if God is only good, he is of course ignorant in reference to evil. There he could not put up any show.

Prof. Fierz: You said that something must have happened between Part I and Part II, and in the history of his life I find that the day on which the first part of *Zarathustra* was finished, Wagner died, and Nietzsche found that significant. I think the mirror showed him also his bad side because one knows how enthusiastic he had been about Wagner, and this trouble might have to do with the fact of his death on that day. I remember that once when he was playing Wagner he wept a whole day. So there was a split in his mind, and there might be some connection with the terrible loss of Wagner who of course was a great man, with all his faults.

Prof. Jung: Yes, there is no doubt that this friendship was a most im-

[1] This theologian is Gogarten. See above, 5 Dec. 1934, n. 4.
[2] See the *Phaedrus*, 246-55. The horses and charioteer represent aspects of the psyche.

portant factor in his life, because Wagner represented very clearly his feeling side; and the fact that Wagner died just at the moment when he finished *Zarathustra* could easily be considered as a fateful event. For with *Zarathustra* Nietzsche really put the seal on his life; *Zarathustra* was his fatality—then he came definitely to the other side. Therefore, it is so important that this chapter begins with the very helpful hint from the unconscious that he might have a careful look at his other side where he really looks like a devil. But then he makes the awful mistake of thinking that somebody has attacked his doctrine, instead of being naive and assuming that he ought to see the devil in himself. You see, that would of course have put an entirely different light upon many things he had experienced, including his relation to Wagner. If he had been one of the ordinary good Christian hermits, he would probably have thought that the devil had put an awful face upon him in order to tempt him, and he might have drawn the same conclusion that it was a *diabolica fraus*, a devil's cheat; and he would have tried to chase away that devil, projecting his dark side then, not into an anonymous crowd of enemies but into a definitely existing devil. While an Eastern philosopher would probably have smiled at it and drawn the conclusion that he had been very good and that this was his other aspect, he would have said: "I am neither this nor that—this is all illusion." Now, the psychological conclusion is of course not exactly like the Eastern. It would be too cheap for us to say, "I have been very good and I am of course also very bad: I am the fellow who is indifferent to such situations." That would not go because good and evil are real powers, and if you forget for a moment that they are real, you are in the devil's kitchen: you simply lose the identity with yourself.

I don't know in how far the Eastern philosopher is allowed to lose his identity with the human being. I think it is allowed because they never really lose sight of the human being. Laotze might say that he could be superior to a human being, that that was right and this was left, that was light and this was dark—and that he was neither of these. When he in his great wisdom withdrew from his business—he was the librarian of one of the kings of China—and settled down on the Western slope of the mountain, he took a dancing girl with him. So much was he in his reality, he never got away from the fact of his ordinary, very humble humanity. We would think, "How disreputable!" But that piece of humanity was so natural that he did not bother; the human side was so much taken care of that he could disidentify himself from the human being. Only inasmuch as we live the human being, can we disidentify; inasmuch as we cannot accept good and evil, or have illusions about good and evil, we cannot detach. Therefore the true superiority is to be in the conflict and acknowledge the good and evil. That is far superior to the attitude in which one imagines oneself to be above it by merely saying so. There are such people. They say this is all illusion, neither this nor that, and lift themselves up until they feel "six thousand feet above good and evil" like the Superman; yet they suffer several hells. I am quite certain that old Laotze did not suffer; perhaps the girl was ugly with him at times and then he suffered a reasonable amount, but he took that as all in the day's work, you know. You can read such remarks in the Tao-Te-King. So according to my idea, Zarathustra would have been wise if he had looked at that devil's face and drawn another conclusion, instead of the funny conclusion that somebody had blackened his wonderful white doctrine. That is now the reason for his making a new decision.

> Lost are my friends; the hour hath come for me to seek my lost ones!—

So the logic is: Oh, I see I have a very black face, those very bad people have blackened it, they are against my doctrine, therefore I must run away to my friends, to my audience, in order to escape the ugly aspect of my other side. Very human!

> With these words Zarathustra started up, not however like a person in anguish seeking relief, but rather like a seer and a singer whom the spirit inspireth. With amazement did his eagle and serpent gaze upon him. . . .

I am certain they were amazed. You see, they are the instincts: the eagle is the spiritual instinct and the serpent the chthonic instinct; and they would certainly be flabbergasted when they saw that conclusion because they are all for the friendly neighborhood of the black and white face. They hate such conclusions as Zarathustra has drawn here.

> for a coming bliss overspread his countenance like a rosy dawn.

Where does this bliss come from so suddenly after that rather depressing vision?

Mrs. Adler: Because he believes that he can escape it.

Prof. Jung: Well, he was very satisfied with the idea that he could get away from it. But anybody who can find out who his devil is, is very grateful. That is one reason why we enjoy detective stories or reading long reports of a crime. It is also the reason the old Greeks enjoyed the drama. *He* is the criminal, I have not done it; and see what the consequences are: *he* got it in the neck! And then they go home and eat a good dinner. Somebody else has done it; happily enough we are quite human and civil people to whom such things never happen. Then for a week they are quite all right and the next Sunday they go again to the theater and again are purified. That is the releasing cathartic effect of the theater. Now how do you suppose Zarathustra comes to the idea that it is just his doctrine which has been attacked or reviled? He might have thought that somebody had said something evil about himself.

Mrs. Jung: Was he not identified with his doctrine?

Miss Wolff: He *is* the doctrine and doesn't exist outside his doctrine. He has no personal existence.

Prof. Jung: Well, that is one of the important reasons: he is his doctrine. Zarathustra is the Logos, and the message is the Logos, and the Logos is personified. He is the spirit. So when he thinks that his doctrine is blackened somehow, he could say just as well that *he* is attacked. But here is again a sort of trap. This is again a case where Nietzsche is identical with Zarathustra, and therefore there is that difference between Zarathustra-Nietzsche and the doctrine. If he would leave the whole thing in Zarathustra, Zarathustra would be the Logos, the doctrine, and then to the man, Nietzsche, it could be indifferent whether anybody reviled the spirit or not, because the spirit is strong enough to take care of itself. He could say, "If those people cannot accept this message, if they revile the spirit, they won't have the delights of the spirit; they deny themselves all that beauty, all that enlightenment, and if they prefer to move in darkness and torture themselves, leave them to their devices." You see, your truth must be so good that you can enjoy it and pity those who are fools enough not to see it. For instance, if you know what a blessing it is that you have plenty of water to wash every day, and how well you feel when you have had your bath, and that there are people who think one should not wash, that it is dangerous to take baths, you think this is perfectly all right. If they feel well that way, let them cherish their filth and their fleas: you have nothing against it, though you feel better with your own way of living. It is exactly the same with the spirit.

You see, the idea that it is a punishable offence to revile the spirit has been invented by those who believed in but did not enjoy the spirit. Perhaps they were believers of a certain truth but really doubted it. Either you know a thing and then you don't need to believe it, or you don't know it and one can doubt it then just as well. So when somebody doubts the truth which you believe, he is an offender because he has given you a bad example; you are offended because instantly the doubt can spring up in yourself too. There is danger that you may doubt that which you believe; therefore, kill those people who doubt and thus you remove doubt. That is the psychology of the church: heretics must be wiped out. They have the wrong idea and cause the church to doubt its own stuff. And that is still the psychology of those pious people who think it is terrible if one says there is no God or something of the sort, one should not say such things. One *ought* to believe, ought to *try* to believe. This is, according to my humble idea, all wrong because it leads to very bad consequences. If I force myself to believe something or want to believe something, I become exceedingly intolerant; I don't like anybody who reviles my beloved ideas because I make such an effort to believe them. Whereas if you know a thing, you can enjoy it. If you know that twice two are four, you enjoy the fact because it is true. And if somebody else says he is not sure—perhaps it is five or six, you say, "Have a good time with it." It doesn't offend you because you think you are looking at a poor fool denying something which is obvious. My Somali boys still believe that the earth is a flat disc with the sun circling over it and an angel carrying it below the disc over to the other side. Well, leave those people to their nice ideas; I am not offended that they don't believe that the earth is a globe, because I *know* the earth is a globe. So if you know of God, you are not offended if people say there is no such thing: you simply laugh; while if you only *believe* him, you are offended and must avenge yourself upon the disbelievers, because you might disbelieve just as well.

So inasmuch as Nietzsche is identical with Zarathustra, he is identical with the message, yet he feels very different; he is a man, a human being, and then there is the message. But inasmuch as he is Zarathustra he *is* identical with that message and anybody who reviles the message reviles himself, Zarathustra-Nietzsche. If Nietzsche could see that Zarathustra was identical with the message, and that he, Nietzsche, was not identical with Zarathustra, he could let it go and he would not be offended, but if he merely believes it, he naturally must be offended. This funny idea that he dreams he has a black devil's face because somebody has reviled his theory, is a very human conclusion, but it can only happen when somebody is identical with the message which is entrusted to him.

Mrs. Sigg: There seems to be a connection with the chapter before, because Zarathustra's chief teaching was that the physician had to heal himself, that he should see himself with his own eyes and make himself whole. So I think neither Zarathustra nor Nietzsche had made themselves whole.

Prof. Jung: Well, the purpose of that ritual kind of solitude was to make himself strong, whole, but the first elucidating thing that happens is used as a pretext to run away, to go down and preach the Evangel.[3]

Mrs. Jung: I wonder whether Zarathustra should not really go into the world. He says himself that he is longing for men, and also it is very comfortable to sit on a mountain and just leave his doctrine to itself. So it might be a very good instinct, some sort of realization, which calls him back to his work.

Prof. Jung: Yes, that is perfectly true; a message makes no point if it remains hidden: it ought to be told. But it must be delivered as such; the message and the man should not be identical. For if he identifies with it, it will spread—he will cause a mental epidemic, and that is the very devil. Then it will be collective, all on a low level, and such things happen as the mob rising in Alexandria. They begin to burn heretics and all that; it is simply a destruction of perfectly decent values. You see, message or no message, when Zarathustra or Nietzsche—we should always say Zarathustra-Nietzsche—has such a dream, then according to common sense he should really consider it, should ask himself, "How, how is it that I appear before the people like Moses, with a face radiant like the sun, when behind that mask I have a devil's face?" That is not so simple. That should be considered first, and naturally if Zarathustra-Nietzsche could realize that his face is also black, it would help him to disidentify. He could then make a difference between himself and Zarathustra. Of course it would injure his effect, but the effect would be poisonous anyhow, because he would not create conviction, but only persuasion and mental contagion; and then he would not have real disciples. He would have sucklings, bambinos, because all people are inclined to be sucklings.

Miss Wolff: There is a doubt in the previous chapter where he says his friends should be ashamed of him and that perhaps he has betrayed them, but he doesn't mean this seriously. He says, "Only when ye have all denied me, will I return unto you. Verily, with other eyes, my brethren, shall I then seek my lost ones; with another love shall I then love you." He gives them the benefit of the doubt but he doesn't really want them to do it. Because it belongs to his archetype, he says here that he is denied. He lives that archetype, but when it comes to himself, of course he cannot see it.

Prof. Jung: Well, the desperate thing is that the figure of Zarathustra

[3] Here Jung's repetition of a story is omitted.

is just as it should be until it comes to the moment when Nietzsche identifies with it, and then it is distorted. You see, the name Zarathustra denotes a savior; Zarathustra was a savior, the great teacher, just as good as Christ or Mani or Mohammed or any of the great prophets. But if a human being identifies with that figure, there is an admixture of human psychology, and it is due to this mixture with human imperfection that the face of Zarathustra appears like the face of a devil in the mirror. For the spirit in itself has not the face of a devil. The spirit itself has no shadow, because it is a principle. You cannot say Yang is black in itself, it is just not black; the black spot simply means the possibility of transforming into Yin; but as long as there is Yang, it is Yang, it is positive. But if a human being identifies with the Yang (or with the Yin), it brings in a creation which is both Yang and Yin and then the Yang is no longer pure. It has then a human psychology. The spirit has no human psychology—it is not human; therefore he calls the spirit divine, as Yang is divine. The Chinese don't even personify it. We have that peculiar tendency of personifying everything since the days of ancient Greece. This light which is now shining out of him like the rising sun is a sort of *ekstasis*. This *is* the spirit. He is now like Moses who came down from the mountain with his face so luminous and shining that they could not stand the light of it: he had to cover it because his face was like Jahve.

> What hath happened unto me, mine animals?—said Zarathustra. Am I not transformed? Hath not bliss come unto me like a whirlwind?
>
> Foolish is my happiness, and foolish things will it speak: it is still too young—so have patience with it.

He is here like the new born sun, the Horus child that is young in the morning.[4] And there is already a hint at the great wind which will play a role later; you see, the sun is at the same time wind and sun. Do you know a mythological connection between the wind and sun?

Mr. Allemann: Would it be in the Mithraic liturgy where the winds come from the sun?

Prof. Jung: Yes, and there is also an old connection in the fact that the morning wind comes when the sun rises; this experience has prob-

[4] On the four sons of Horus, see CW 12, par. 314, fig. 192. For the mandala and the four Evangelists, see CW 12, par. 101, fig. 62. As with sun gods generally, Horus of the East is represented first as youthful and then "as an aged man tottering down the west" (James Breasted, *Development of Religion and Thought in Ancient Egypt* [New York and London, 1912], p. 10).

ably connected the sun with the wind, the sun as the spiritual father and the wind as the emanation of the father. So the idea is that the wind, the *pneuma*, descends from the sun. God was often compared to the sun, of course. Also there was the Neoplatonist idea that the animus or the spirit of man descends from the sun and thus comes into existence; and when a man dies this animus is gathered up by the moon, a female principle, and transmitted to the sun. In Manichaean mythology—or one could call it their dogma—it was expressed in this way: The spirits of the dead are received by the moon which thereby increases until it is quite full and then it begins to approach the sun. It comes nearer and nearer and finally pours all the souls back into the sun. When the moon is quite close to the sun it is completely empty, and then it appears again on the other side slowly increasing, sucking up souls from the earth in order to bring them back to the sun; and from the sun they migrate over into the pillar of life or of souls, which apparently carries them back to the origin of life, to the divine father. This idea of the pillar of life occurs in *She*, though I don't know how it got there. Then in medieval representations of the Immaculate Conception, the spirit descends as wind: the *pneuma* comes down from the Father into the womb of Mary; and the curious fact is that the Greek word *pneuma* has taken on its specific meaning only since Christianity. Before that time and contemporary with it, *pneuma* referred wholly to the wind. So in that passage in the Bible: "The wind (or the spirit) bloweth where it listeth"—the Greek text says the wind blows. Yet it also means the spirit; it is ambiguous, sometimes it is called one and sometimes the other.[5] Another example which I have published is the lunatic who thought that the movement of the phallus of the sun was the origin of the movement of the wind.[6] Now in this case the rising sun is also identical with the wind that comes from the sun, which is perfectly understandable inasmuch as Zarathustra is the spirit; that is the way in which the spirit should behave. Also it is the spirit-child, the Horus-child of the early morning; Horus is not only the rising sun, but also the rising sun as the illumination of the mystery. Therefore, of course, having more the form of the so-called Harpocrates, who until rather late was a mystery god. He appears in alchemistic literature transformed into Harforetus.[7]

[5] John 3:8. *Pneuma:* wind, and more particularly, breath—hence spirit.
[6] See above, 14 Nov. 1934, n. 2, on the phallus of the sun.
[7] *Harpocrates* was the Graecised form of *Horus* the Mystery God of the Egyptians. See Mead*, p. 233. Later, the Latin *Harforetus* was used.

Wounded am I by my happiness: all sufferers shall be physicians unto me!

What is this?

Mrs. Adler: He is wounded by his dream, not by his happiness.

Prof. Jung: No, we must take it as it is here; you see, it is quite right when he says, "Foolish is my happiness." It *is* foolish, because the immediate manifestation of the spirit when it is still a sort of wind causes phenomena like the miracle of Pentecost, when people thought the disciples were full of sweet wine, drunk and babbling nonsense. That is the ecstatic *glossolalia*, the speaking in tongues. And this "Wounded am I by my happiness" must be taken in the same way, it really means wounded here. Now where would that wound come from? There is a definite example. When is the message told—when is the deliverer of the message fulfilled?

Prof. Fierz: When Christ died.

Prof. Jung: Yes, it is the wound in the side of Christ. You see, Christ's mission was fulfilled when he died for it on the cross; his death was really the seal upon the message. If Christ by some good luck had escaped that fate of crucifixion, of course it would not have been a complete mystery—he need not exactly die perhaps but he must be wounded. Where have we this motive in another case where something important was done for mankind?

Prof. Fierz: Prometheus.

Prof. Jung: Yes, he brought the fire from the gods. They chained him to the rock in the Caucasus where the eagle ate out his liver. Now another example.

Mrs. Baynes: Amfortas.

Prof. Jung: Well, the Amfortas story is complicated—a lot of things come in which we cannot unravel here; but the wound of Christ really influenced that story.[8]

Mrs. Jung: Wotan.

Prof. Jung: Ah yes, Wotan for nine nights was hanging on the tree, moved by the wind and "wounded by a spear, dedicated to Odin, I myself to myself." And what happened after he descended from the tree—after the suspension?

[8] Amfortas, head of the knights of the Grail (the vessel Jesus employed at the Last Supper), suffered a grave wound when captured by a sorcerer. He was healed when Parsifal, Lohengrin's father, touched the wound with his spear. See *The Poetic Edda*, tr. Henry Adams Bellows (New York, 1923). In March of 1936, Jung published an article on Wotan in which he related the Germanic neo-paganism to Wotan (or Othin, Odin), and to Nietzsche. CW 10, pars. 371-99.

Mrs. Jung: He invented the runes.

Prof. Jung: Yes, and that is the magic writing which meant to those barbarous people the dawn of civilization; he brought the light of civilization to the earth: that was the message of the spirit. So the wound has a very profound meaning. One sees it best in the Prometheus myth perhaps. It is a sort of disruption of the order of the world, as if wisdom or knowledge had been originally a part of the great divine world, in an organic connection with all things existing, as if everything worked then according to rules which never were spoken. And then a revelation takes place: a certain wisdom or knowledge comes to consciousness and then it is no longer in the organic structure of the world. It is just as if there were a hole somewhere, as if something had been taken out of the eternal structure and pulled into space, into visibility, concretization; or it is as if the heavens were splitting and an important piece torn out of its connections. You see, as long as you function unconsciously, things apparently go smoothly and everything is in its place until you make a discovery—when you pull something out of the unconscious you cause a wound. Becoming conscious is of course a sacrilege against nature; it is as if you had robbed the unconscious of something. So when the spirit comes forth bringing something out of the eternal structure of the world, then the spirit itself, being that piece of the world which now enters visibility, is wounded. The spirit is the wound and the message. It is the one that reveals and the one that is revealed, the stealer and the stolen property; and it is at the same time the God that has—one could almost say—sinned against himself, wounded himself in order to bring the light. That God deprived himself of his divinity by sending his Son to the earth to redeem us is the same idea; he caused pain to himself, underwent the symbolic torture in order to give light to man. That all expresses the inevitability of the process and its autonomy when something is revealed or becomes conscious to us. It is not exactly our merit, but is our suffering rather; we suffer it, it simply happens. And it is the tragedy of a God, who is not human; therefore it is expressed in such mythological forms. On the one side it is the glad tidings. the *euangelion* that is brought to man, and that is what Nietzsche calls "my happiness." But just that is on the other side the wound, or it causes the wound, so he says, "Wounded am I by my happiness: all sufferers shall be physicians unto me." This means that all who suffer by the revelation will be a consolation to his suffering, just as if the suffering Christian martyrs were physicians to God, as if it were a consolation to the sacrificed God that they took over his suffering. They healed him by accepting his suffering, thus the great merit in their death or torture or martyrdom.

Mrs. Baumann: I don't quite understand the connection, because he is not conscious of this dream before.

Prof. Jung: Oh heavens, you must not mix it up with Nietzsche. The dream belongs to Nietzsche very clearly inasmuch as he is identifying with Zarathustra; but this bit here is Zarathustra and not Nietzsche because it is a divine mystery expressed as it always has been expressed in old religions. Therefore, we mentioned Wotan and Prometheus and Christ. It is the mystery—or call it the psychology of the creative act—and that has nothing to do with Nietzsche.

Mrs. Baumann: Yes, but the two animals were amazed. Are they Zarathustra's or Nietzsche's instincts?

Prof. Jung: They are not Zarathustra's instincts; it is again human that these principles connect in man, not in the spirit. The spirit is the eagle, the Yang principle, and the serpent is the Yin principle; and the animals are amazed at what Zarathustra-Nietzsche is doing. I quite understand that one gets mixed up, but in order to analyse Zarathustra you must understand how to ride your horses, and not only horses but dragons. You must always keep in mind that the two are constantly interchanging, playing into each other: namely, the psychology of the suffering ordinary man Nietzsche, and the psychology of the spirit. Of course we in our immense foolishness always imagine that the spirit has a personal psychology. It is just as if one were assuming that there was no other chemistry but that of the cooking pot, that chemistry is what one cooks in the kitchen, to eat. There is the psychology of the spirit, and a psychology of the instincts, and there is also a personal psychology. The problem here is that Nietzsche is not an ideally analysed person—and not even an ordinarily analysed person is free from that peculiar crisscross of personal tendencies. If Nietzsche were analysed—as a man like Nietzsche could be[9]—he would show two sides: here the suffering neurotic Nietzsche, and there the psychology of the spirit, his particular mythological drama. But as it is, the divine drama and man's ordinary suffering are completely mixed and they distort each other, so naturally we are confused when we look at that tangle and try to decipher the contradictions. In order to have a clear picture, you must hold the thesis and antithesis ever before your eyes, the two things that constantly work into each other or influence each other and then try to separate them. But it is really very difficult.

---

[9] Jung here visualizes Nietzsche as an analysand. He once wrote that he himself had been well prepared for psychiatry by the author of *Zarathustra*. See CW 7, par. 199.

LECTURE VI

26 February 1936

Prof. Jung:

There was some confusion last time, due to that most bewildering fact of Nietzsche's identity with Zarathustra; it was just another difficult moment in the neck-breaking enterprise we have embarked upon in attempting to analyse *Zarathustra*. You see, one really cannot deal with such a fact; one has to dissolve it in order to cope with it. One has exactly the same difficulty when a real individual is identical with an archetypal figure. For a woman to deal with a man who is identical with his anima is well-nigh impossible. And for a man it is most confusing to talk to an animus-possessed woman; he thinks that she must be a woman because she looks like one anatomically, but when she opens her mouth he discovers that it is a man who is talking and feeling, and then he is all upside down. Of course, this is only one possibility: a man may be identical with the wise old man for instance, or a woman may be identical with the earth mother—and that is perfectly awful because one doesn't know whether one should fall down on one's knees or take the next taxi to a lunatic asylum. So in dealing with a man who is identical with Zarathustra, one doesn't know to what one is talking, and whatever one says is wrong, naturally, because one rests entirely upon the understanding that one can dissolve this union, that Nietzsche is one thing and Zarathustra another and that the two coincide. Sometimes Nietzsche is talking, sometimes Zarathustra, and when the text says "I," God knows which "I" it is. I must tell you again that excellent story of Schopenhauer. He was once taking a walk in the public gardens in Frankfurt, very busy with his problem, so he paid no attention to his path and stepped into a flower bed. There he stayed, thinking hard, till the gardener came along and said: "What are you doing there in the flower bed? Who are you?" And Schopenhauer said: "Exactly, that is what I don't know!" It is very difficult at times to make out who one is.

So, in talking about Zarathustra-Nietzsche, we have all the time that

857

interplay of man and God, or man and spirit in the real meaning of the word; sometimes I am referring to the spirit and sometimes to the man. And whatever is true for the spirit is not true for the man and vice versa. No wonder, then, that one gets mixed up. Therefore, the only thing to do in a moment of distress when you are completely at sea, is to assume that you have not understood, rather than that the world is all wrong; probably you have lost the thread and whatever I say would be utterly wrong from the other point of view. And I am in the same predicament, of course, in that nothing I say can apply to both. So you had better assume my hypothesis that Nietzsche and Zarathustra are really two different things; then there is a chance of dealing with them. Otherwise one is in the same unfortunate position that one is in with an anima-possessed man; one gets a peculiar feeling with such double people that whatever one says is always beside the mark.

We got as far last time as this outburst of Zarathustra, and looked at from the standpoint of the man Nietzsche, of course the conclusion that he ought to go back to mankind is all wrong. But this is exactly what on the other side the spirit has to do. To merely believe in the spirit doesn't help, because you are then assuming something that is not; the spirit must be convincing. God has to manifest himself if we are to know him. Otherwise, what is the use of believing in him? The spirit is only convincing when it *is*; when it is, it works. Then it blows as the wind blows; therefore it is named breath, *spiritus*, *animus*, or *pneuma*, wind. But if you don't feel the wind, you are perfectly justified in stating that you don't feel it. If there is no movement of the air, it is much better to say that this is a dark time in which the spirit doesn't move, so one has to be satisfied in *believing* in the spirit; but you cannot go on forever just believing that which you never perceive. When you come to a country without wind, where it is apparently non-existent, it is much safer to assume that there is no wind because that is the average truth. Only when the wind begins to blow and the waters to rush forth, is it convincing. The spirit is essentially movement. As soon as the spirit is at a standstill you fall back on belief, and that is a sad substitute for the spirit.

> My impatient love overfloweth in streams,—down towards sunrise and sunset. Out of silent mountains and storms of affliction, rusheth my soul into the valleys.

This verse is an exact description of the movement of the spirit, and this is Zarathustra's proper style, but for Nietzsche it is an inflation; when he consists of air, or water, he is no longer human. It is altogether too wonderful: to explode with all that love is impossible. If a man comes to you saying that his love overfloweth in streams down towards the sunrise and sunset, that out of silent mountains and storms of affliction he is streaming up against you with a thousand tons of water, what can you do with him? How can you adapt to that? Such impossible stuff means that there is something impossible in the man: he is really two; if it is your personal conviction that the fellow himself is talking like that, your natural reaction will be to telephone the psychiatric clinic.

> Too long have I longed and looked into the distance. Too long hath solitude possessed me: thus have I unlearned to keep silence.

Well, if this is Zarathustra speaking, it is perfectly all right; that is the suffering, the affliction of the spirit. No wind was blowing for centuries perhaps and the adventurous spirit of movement had to remain silent, unable to blow and whistle.

> Utterance have I become altogether, and the brawling of a brook from high rocks: downward into the valleys will I hurl my speech.

This is exactly what the wind does, falling down from the high mountains into the valleys.

> And let the stream of my love sweep into unfrequented channels! How should a stream not finally find its way to the sea?

You see, this image of a stream that finally finds its way to the sea would be the life of the spirit, it is the natural potential. If it moves at all, the spirit always moves on to the distant sea, to completion—the complete standstill; every movement is seeking the eternal tranquility of the sea.

> Forsooth, there is a lake in me, sequestered and self-sufficing; but the stream of my love beareth this along with it, down—to the sea!
>
> New paths do I tread, a new speech cometh unto me; tired have I become—like all creators—of the old tongues. No longer will my spirit walk on worn-out soles.
>
> Too slowly runneth all speaking for me:—into thy chariot, O storm, do I leap! And even thee will I whip with my spite!

That is again very high-sounding. You have probably noticed that in the last verse, slowly the man comes in, with the identification of man and spirit, and that causes this statement that he wants to become the

859

whip of the storm, as if the storm, or the spirit, were his riding horse. He cannot identify the storm; therefore—as always happens—since one cannot be below God one must be above God. This is quoted from a speech made by our Swiss poet Gottfried Keller at a dinner to celebrate the twenty-fifth anniversary of a friend of his youth. He said, "My dear friends, our friend who is celebrating his anniversary belongs to those theologians who are, happily enough, not above but below God." You see, that was a great truth; since you cannot be on a level with God, you are therefore either below or above him. If you are below God he is the great stream, but if you are above him he is your riding horse and then you are a mighty fellow. As soon as you identify with God you needs must transcend him because God is a stream; and you are not the air or the rushing waters, but are just a definite form called human, so you can only personify god in yourself. Then you are on top, in the saddle, and can even use the whip; you can command God and give him the spurs so that he moves a bit quicker. A pretty dangerous enterprise. You see, this is the way to the catastrophic consequences of inflation.

Like a cry and an huzza will I traverse wide seas, till I find the Happy Isles where my friends sojourn;—
And mine enemies amongst them! How I now love every one unto whom I may but speak! Even mine enemies pertain to my bliss.

Here we come to something rather cryptic—that he wants to traverse wide seas. *Wie ein Schrei und ein Jauchzen will ich über weite Meere hinfahren.* This is like the shrieking wind, the mistral for instance, and this is the symbol which Nietzsche is forever using; in other parts of *Zarathustra* he identifies with the wind that blows over lands and seas, of course always with the goal of the spirit, those blessed islands of eternal peace where his friends and also his enemies sojourn. Now what about these Happy Isles? They are another aspect of the sea of course.

Prof. Fierz: Would they be *die glückliche Inseln*, or *l'Ile de Cythère?*

Miss Hannah: Tennyson's Lotus Eaters?

Prof. Jung: Yes, and other South Sea Islands, like Ganguin's Tahiti, but there is a much better example, a famous case.

Mrs. Baumann: Atlantis.

Prof. Jung: Of course, the big island that sank into the ocean with a whole civilization that people are still talking about.

Miss Wolff: But Atlantis was not an island—it was supposed to be a continent.

Prof. Jung: Oh, it doesn't matter—one can call Australia an island or a continent. Of course it matters a lot whether you call Mars "Mars"; it is marvelous that people have discovered what the names of the stars are!

Mrs. Baumann: Could one not also mention Happy Neurosis Island?

Prof. Jung: Well yes, but that is not a generally known island. It is a very ancient idea that there are happy islands out in the West, outside the gate of the ocean or the pillars of Hercules. In Egypt we have the Isles of the Great Green, the ocean, which was also the underworld, the land of the dead. And the Western land in the Gilgamesh epic is the place of the dead where people dwell in eternal bliss forever. So the Happy Isles would be the land of the dead, and the movement of the spirit is making for that underground existence, like the way of the sun Osiris that goes under the sea and comes upon the Isles of the Great Green; therefore Osiris as the judge of the underworld was always painted a blueish green, the color of the sea.

Mrs. Jung: Could he not mean here merely the world and human beings? He has been in solitude and now he is longing for human beings, so the world might seem to him like a paradise.

Prof. Jung: Exactly, if you speak in terms of Nietzsche, but we are now on the side of the spirit, and inasmuch as it is Zarathustra, he speaks his truth; the wind blows out over the sea until it reaches the Happy Isles, for as the movement of all rivers is from above to below, so the movement of the spirit seeks finally the great tranquillity, the Great Green of the underworld. Now, when we come to the man Nietzsche we find him naturally in this idea of "where my friends sojourn." Everybody will one day go down to the Isles of the Great Green whether happy or not; and here he says definitely his friends as well as his enemies will be there. Here the man Nietzsche would identify with the spirit and traverse the seas to reach those Happy Isles where he would find friends, for heaven's sake—human beings, even enemies, somebody to talk to! Nietzsche was so forlorn; all his life he was isolated, so he was only too eager to find an audience to talk to. And his books were read by relatively few people, who were shocked by their peculiar character; as you see, they are by no means easy reading. When a man writes such stuff he naturally feels that he will not be understood, for he has the feeling within of what it is that he produces, and it takes him into a rarified atmosphere which is more than six thousand feet above good and evil. You know, Nietzsche always took as symbolic the fact that the Engadine was at an altitude of six thousand feet. So of course, he would feel tremendously isolated when he thought of his old friends in Basel, Professors Overbeck and Jakob Burkhardt and so on. I wish I could show you old man Jakob Burkhardt as I saw him practically every day, walking near the Cathedral coming from the University library. And Zarathustra!—you could not imagine anything more different than those two, Zarathustra full of modern history, and this gentleman who could have lived just as well in 1670. You see, that loneliness belongs to Nietzsche, not to the spirit; the spirit is not sentimental. Though, mind you, if you believe in the spirit it can be *anything*, because you can project anything into it; then the spirit *can* be sentimental—with blue eyes and flowing locks and a beard. But the spirit is really a tremendous adventure—cruel, inexorable, inhuman. Just now one hears many complaints of this peculiarly inhuman quality of the spirit of adventure and experience; the thing that is riding through the forests in Germany is by no means human or very compassionate. It is a great wind, passionate, and all things will tremble.

Mrs. Baumann: There is one sentence where that is shown very clearly: "With these words Zarathustra started up, not however like a person gasping for air." Why should he suddenly say "gasping for air"?

Prof. Jung: In my translation it is "like a person in anguish seeking relief."[1]

Mrs. Baumann: It is Nietzsche that is gasping.

Prof. Jung: Well no, he is not gasping, that is just the trouble; he *should* stifle in trying to identify with the spirit, but he doesn't. He dissolves into it right away.

Mrs. Baumann: But he wouldn't mention it at all if he didn't have something the matter.

Prof. Jung: That is perfectly true; it is an indirect admission that one *should* have felt like that. For instance, "lost are my friends" is a terrible statement really, and then there was that vision of the devil's face in the mirror which might have caused anxiety to any normal person, and to him it did not. There he was completely identified with Zarathustra. You see, it doesn't matter to the spirit what its face may be; it *can* have a terrible face. When the Gospel says God is spirit, it means that he can be very terrible; the spirit is an elementary movement, a tremendous outburst in man, and it can be infernal and cruel. I don't imagine, for instance, that those prophets of the Old Testament who were filled with the spirit of God were particularly lovely people—there is evi-

---

[1] Hollingdale*: "With these words Zarathustra sprang up—not, however, as if gasping for air, but rather like a sea monster whom the spirit has moved."

dence for the contrary—yet one cannot deny that they were filled with the spirit. So it is perfectly true, as you say, that Nietzsche the human being should have been filled with anxiety. He should have been stifled, suppressed, because the spirit was getting the better of him. But he identified with the spirit instead of realizing what the very weak human suffering creature feels when the spirit is taking possession of that frail thing which can so easily break. When people are attacked by the spirit, they may break just as well; there are many cases of schizophrenia where, after what is called a religious experience, they just explode; they cannot stand it, it is a very dangerous thing. But the point is that he does not realize it. Therefore, I said it was quite understandable that the eagle and the serpent should look at him in amazement; they are his instincts and they surely are startled. They would have interfered if they had not been dumb animals. They would have said, "Now look out!"

Prof. Reichstein: Can you call that an anima reaction when he says that he feels like a whip to the storm?

Prof. Jung: Well, not directly because there is no evidence for the feminine nature of that particular image. I should say it simply shows that he is identical with the storm and since he cannot be *à niveau,*[2] or the same as the storm, he will transcend it, and then he is on top of the storm and can use the whip on it.

Prof. Reichstein: But it comes out of emotion.

Prof. Jung: That is perfectly true; if he is overcome he is in the feminine role. You remember we have encountered before certain places in the text where Nietzsche uses words as if he were a woman, *sich putzen* for instance: a man wants to make himself beautiful for his friend exactly as if he were a woman. There it was quite obvious that he was transformed into his anima by identification, by being overcome by his unconscious. And here we must theoretically at least conclude that he is in the role of femininity. I remember the case of a lunatic, a house-painter who had a religious experience. The voice of God told him that he no longer had a man's name; from now on his name was Mary—he was really the mother of God. Then he, like a true prophet, said, "But how, oh God, is it possible that I should be Mary, since I am made like a man?" And God said, "Oh never mind, that can be mended." So in order to look like a woman, that man tried to amputate his external genitals, and was then brought to the lunatic asylum. That is a case of complete transformation by identification with

---

[2] *A niveau:* level with.

the spirit. But you see when he heard the voice of God he would not have accepted it if he had not already been in a feminine condition. If he had been a man, he would have said, "I, Mary! My name is so-and-so—what damned nonsense are you talking?" That would have been the reaction of a man, but no, he instantly felt flattered, very great, that God was talking to him, and at once exploded. A religious experience has that insinuating character: it is a sort of temptation like the temptation of Christ in the desert, when God appeared to him in the disguise of the devil and insinuated certain things. Christ was man enough to say it was the devil in order to hold his own; otherwise he would have been transformed into Mary or another lady and would have followed the devil, the spirit. He probably would have fallen down from the roof of the temple. This is all very paradoxical, yet things do happen in that way. It is not very clear here that a feminine element comes in unless it is in this word *Bosheit* which is translated by "spite." That is one of Nietzsche's habitual terms, and it is a rather disagreeable word; it always arouses my anima because there is some feminine element in it. Think of a man riding a horse who uses the whip with spite. That is unthinkable, and it is unthinkable of a real woman, a human being; only an anima could do that.

Miss Wolff: I think Prof. Reichstein was thinking of that chapter where it says when you go to women don't forget the whip.

Prof. Reichstein: No, I thought this was from his point of view a trial; he tried to get connection with people and as he could not get it directly, his anima now tries to get it through his teaching.

Prof. Jung: You mean he wants to force himself upon people?

Prof. Reichstein: Yes.

Prof. Jung: Well, it would come to that, and therefore the anima would be the whip that forces him to ride the spirit. Yes, you could explain it like that theoretically. That is perfectly correct. He naturally would have to identify through his anima; it could not be done otherwise. Well now,

> And when I want to mount my wildest horse, then doth my spear always help me up best; it is my foot's ever ready servant:—
> The spear which I hurl at mine enemies! How grateful am I to mine enemies that I may at last hurl it!

What about this symbolism? Isn't it a funny idea that he now questions how to get upon that horse? Apparently he was already on it and now here is the spear that is to help him up; there must be some difficulty in getting into the saddle.

Prof. Fierz: Nietzsche was certainly no rider.

Mrs. Sigg: Yes, he was in the artillery—he liked to ride; he hurt himself once riding a very wild horse.

Prof. Jung: But in the war he was not with the active troops.

Mrs. Sigg: He was a Swiss and was not allowed to be a soldier in the war.

Miss Hughes: Is it not possible that the spear is his leading function?

Prof. Jung: That is true, and it is most interesting that he needs his superior function to climb onto that horse. The spear is like a sword, a dagger, or some such instrument, and it is a symbol for the intellect on account of its piercing, discriminating, dissecting character. So this passage means that he gets onto the horse by the aid of his intellect. How is that possible? Is that the regular way?

Miss Hannah: Well, he just leaves his body entirely behind; he identifies with his intellect and then he can ride with the wind.

Prof. Jung: Yes, but that is a bit too symbolical. You see, it is obviously by the assumption of the intellect that one identifies: that is simply Nietzsche's experience. And now that peculiar adventurous movement of the spirit, the intellect, will question this function about it. It will pass a judgment on what is happening to Nietzsche. The intellect will say: "That is *your* mind, you are now in such a movement"—and then there you are in the saddle. Just as to some one having a religious experience, feeling the presence of God, the intellect might say, "Well, that is yourself. You did not know that you were so big a fellow. This feeling of amplitude is what you did not realize"—and there is the wrong conclusion: already you are on top of God. Of course another intellect might say, "Now don't identify; this is a gift—the grace of God that you are able to do a thing in such a way." There the intellect would help to disidentify, but it may also say just the opposite: "*You* have done it, *you* are the fellow." Now, the more you identify with a function, the less you suffer from your own critique, and the more of course you suffer from the critique of others. If you are identified with a function you are helped by the function to a further identification. A successful tenor, for instance, will be the biggest man in the world because his voice reaches the highest, so he is on the top of the world. He has that typical megalomania from which most tenors suffer, his surroundings naturally helping him in that belief. But the superior function will always do that, not only the intellect; it will put your achievement or whatever happens to you, down to that leading function, the best side with which one is identical—providing that one has no knowledge of the existence of other functions.

Now there is still a passage in the text to which I would like to call your attention; namely, "Forsooth, there is a lake in me, sequestered and self-sufficing; but the stream of my love beareth this along with it, down—to the sea!" Here something is formulated which bears out practically what I said about the actual situation. What is the lake?

Mr. Allemann: The self.

Prof. Jung: Well, we can only say that there is water, a lake, which wouldn't necessarily flow down, but this stream of love carries it down; so the lake is carried away by the stream as if it were part of it. And you see, this is just the situation—this is again the man Nietzsche. There is something in him like a lake, and this is carried away by the stream of the spirit. Now, why he should be compared to that lake is of course a special question. Mr. Allemann said the lake was the self, and the self is often compared to a lake of peace, or to the ocean. There are certain smaller lakes in Germany, in the Eiffel, called the Eyes of the Sea, and the island is another symbol of the self; you see, the individual self would be an isle or a separate unit of the great collective unconscious. But do you think the stream of love should carry the lake away? Is that as it should be?

Mrs. Crowley: No.

Prof. Jung: No, it is remarkable rather, for what is the use of a lake if it is carried right away? There is no point in a lake if it simply dissolves in the fury of the stream. So when a man is dissolved in that great stream of the spirit, he is no longer himself: he is identical with the spirit and his individual existence is wiped out. Now we are still concerned with that symbol of the spear.

Mrs. Crowley: Would it not have something to do with what you referred to last week in connection with the wound? Because he is wounded, might it not also have some such connotation?

Prof. Jung: Well, a wound presupposes something that wounds, and he says he is wounded by his happiness. The happiness is the consequence of his identification with the spirit, more properly the identification with the spirit by way of the intellect, so by that *détour* it is of course the spear by which he is wounded. That leads us to the Amfortas problem, and also to the idea of the suffering god. Christ suffered on the cross; he was the human being that was wounded by the overwhelming fact of the spirit, which carried him away and killed his humanity. Of course we worship that fact, but not all of us worship it. There is—at least we must suppose so—somewhere a compensating truth for the one-sided worship of the spirit, and that is also indicated here. We admire or worship the phenomenon of the spirit because we are taught to do so; we assume that it is something marvelous, grand. And if we can trust the words of Nietzsche we are also led to assume that it is a very wonderful experience to be identical with the spirit, in spite of all sorts of indications that it is not such a particularly happy event—that he is wounded by his own happiness, for instance, and that he hurls his spear against his enemies, and is grateful that he has enemies, someone upon whom he can inflict the wound again. You see, that shows a thing from which one always suffers—one is always led to inflict the wound upon others. So people who are caught or overcome by the power of the spirit seem to have the tendency to do the same to others; as they have been overcome and wounded so they will overcome and wound, because they are not themselves, because they are filled with the spirit. They are inhuman or supermen, whatever you like to call it; at all events they are no longer in a human frame and behave as if they were the spirit itself. This is obviously a process which has a very marvelous side. It is most insinuating and really very wonderful to be like a wild river rushing into the wide plains inundating everything and enjoying the play. But on the other side there is any amount of destruction linked up with it, so one can assume that this phenomenon of the spirit is a one-sided thing, and that the unconscious mind has foreseen some compensating truth which shows in the symbolism of the Grail and in similar symbolism of the unconscious. Perhaps we shall find some hints in *Zarathustra*, but I have no great hope of it.

> Too great hath been the tension of my cloud: 'twixt laughters of lightnings will I cast hail-showers into the depths.
> Violently will my breast then heave; violently will it blow its storm over the mountains: thus cometh its assuagement.
> Verily, like a storm cometh my happiness, and my freedom! But mine enemies shall think *the evil one* roareth over their heads.

Here a certain parallel becomes unavoidable. What is that evil one roaring over their heads?

Mrs. Sigg: Wotan.

Prof. Jung: Yes, it is Wotan's host roaring through the forest and here we have the symbolism: Wotan's spear and the evil one at the same time, for Wotan the wild hunter becomes later on the devil. Already in the formula of conversion, in the adjuration of the pagan gods, the Germans in the time of Charlemagne were obliged to declare that they would give up Wotan as a devil. Wotan and Erda and the others are really like devils, and so the later medieval idea that Wotan was identical with the devil came into existence.

Miss Wolff: Does it not also explain his dream of the devil's face in a more synthetic way?

Prof. Jung: That is true. The dream of the devil's face when Zarathustra showed his other side becomes more understandable now—he is the devil himself.

> Yea, ye also, my friends, will be alarmed by my wild wisdom; and perhaps ye will flee therefrom, along with mine enemies.

This is another manifestation of that peculiar Wotan effect which is so incredible. Yet it is a fact that old Wotan has to a certain extent come to life again; one hears of it either directly or indirectly, and if anybody had predicted such a fact twenty years ago, it would have been thought utterly impossible. It has become a fact to the extent that the attitude of the ruling party in Germany is really against the church; they are trying to subjugate the church and to translate, as it were, the terminology of the church into a sort of pagan belief. That idea of Pagan Christianity or the German faith is of course nothing else than the nationalization of God; they then have a specific national God, Wotan for the German as Jahveh was for the Jew. That is quite inevitable. And it is understandable that in the face of such events even friends might be alarmed. One *is* alarmed! I have quite a number of German friends and I must say I am alarmed by the fact that they are so gripped.

Mrs. Sigg: I think if we asked the Germans about Wotan they would sometimes answer that the *Asen* were also there, and that makes it milder.

Prof. Jung: Well, it means nothing else. It means that the myth is *en marche*, old Wotan is going strong again; you might even include Alberich and those other demons.[3] That thing lives.

Mrs. Sigg: I think if one reads *The Anti-Christ* of Nietzsche[4] and realizes that all the youth of Germany used to read his books during the war—Nietzsche's books were sent to them in the trenches—one is not astonished.

Prof. Jung: Not astonished, but it is nevertheless most remarkable psychologically. And you cannot put it down to Nietzsche only. It has always been admitted that Wagner did a lot along that line too: he

---

[3] Alberich was the elf-king whose cloak of invisibility was worn in battle by Siegfried. The Asa gods were ruled over by Wotan.

[4] *The Anti-Christ* was written in the last year of Nietzsche's sanity, but not published until 1895.

868

made use of that mythology—and his music is most insinuating. It caused a sort of journalistic Germanic movement. They played with old names long before the war: there were jokes in *Simplissimus*[5] about the very ordinary civilians who came together and drank out of horns with antlers on their heads—such things.

Ah, that I knew how to lure you back with shepherds' flutes! Ah, that my lioness wisdom would learn to roar softly! And much have we already learned with one another!

My wild wisdom became pregnant on the lonesome mountains; on the rough stones did she bear the youngest of her young,

Now runneth she foolishly in the arid wilderness, and seeketh and seeketh the soft sward—mine old, wild wisdom!

On the soft sward of your hearts, my friends!—on your love, would she fain couch her dearest one!—

Thus spake Zarathustra.

Here we learn more about his wisdom, and that is of course the other side of the figure of Wotan, who is a romantic god as well. He is the god of oracles, of secret knowledge, of sorcery, and he is also the equivalent of Hermes *psychopompos*. And you remember he has, like Osiris, only one eye; the other eye is sacrificed to the underworld. Therefore, he is an exceedingly apt symbol for our modern world in which the unconscious really comes to the foreground like a river, and forces us to turn one eye inward upon it, in order that we may be adapted to that side also; we feel now that the greatest enemy is threatening us, not from without but from within. So on account of all his qualities, Wotan expresses the spirit of the time to an extent which is uncanny, and that wisdom or knowledge is really wild—it is nature's wisdom. Wotan is not the God of civilized beings but a condition of nature. He brings the experience of nature and its abyss, and this is of course as Zarathustra says, a wisdom rather like that of a lioness, a wild animal. Therefore, anybody who teaches this wisdom would do well to have a flute, like Orpheus, to tame the wild beasts, in order that his friends may not be too much alarmed. The roar of a lioness cannot be soft and friendly, but is most menacing, and this wild wisdom, this wild mind of nature, causes misunderstandings and panic. Human beings will be terrified— the lioness will create an arid wilderness around herself. So she probably seeks in vain that soft sward to couch herself and her young upon. This is very much like the man Nietzsche who hopes that he can place

---

[5] *Simplicissimus* was a popular satirical, weekly magazine, published in Munich.

his child upon the love of his friends, but nobody is particularly ready to accept the young of a wild animal of prey. Well, that is just the conflict in Nietzsche's case, but with the exception of Wagner, he was the first one to realize the events of the future and to give voice to the unconscious that was about to manifest; and he realized more or less that it would be a message that was not welcome.

Mrs. Baynes: Goetz takes Wotan as a symbol of the new integration of the psyche.[6] But, if I understand you, you would consider that not correct psychologically because he is too much on the natural side?

Prof. Jung: He is just not an integration, but a disintegration. You see, the storm does not cause integration, but destroys whatever allows itself to be destroyed. It is simply the movement after a long tension or standstill, like waters that break loose after long accumulation. This will happen in different periods of history when things have reached a certain one-sidedness. Then suddenly the whole thing will crash down, in a sort of revolutionary outburst of energy that has been too tightened up, put under too much pressure; the steam begins to sizzle out somewhere or the whole boiler explodes, and that is Wotan.

Mrs. Baynes: But inasmuch as he carried for the Germans the symbol of the *Wal-Vater,*[7] is he not also that side, that form?

Prof. Jung: No, that wandering is without visible goal because it is the wandering of nature, of natural movement.

Mrs. Sigg: But is not Wotan also the inventor of the rune, a new way of expressing himself? And we heard in one poem by Goetz that the other side of Wotan was more the wise man.

Prof. Jung: There is that other side, but first the destruction is most visible; and since Wotan is a historical figure we cannot hope that it is a progression. I am convinced that behind it something else follows, but it won't be Wotan. It cannot be.

Miss Hughes: Doesn't he mention in the second stage of his *Metamorphoses*: "To create itself freedom for new creating"? That is again the lion which he mentions previous to that, so it would be the destructive element in order that new values might come in the wake of it.

Prof. Jung: Yes, but first it must be the lion which was forever the destroying animal.

---

[6] Goetz's *Das Reich ohne Raum* (Potsdam, 1919), a novel. Jung reports having been early struck with this book in which Goetz "saw the secret of coming events in Germany, in the form of a very strange vision" CW 10, par. 384. But see above, 5 June 1935, n. 10.

[7] That is, "father of the slain." He was known by a great many epithets from "Allfather" to "Long Beard."

Mrs. Jung: Would you call this wild wisdom of the lioness anima wisdom?

Prof. Jung: Or like the wisdom of the tiger; you remember the tiger is the symbol of the anima in Spitteler's *Prometheus and Epimetheus.*[8] So the lioness would be the symbol of the anima because it is nature.

Mrs. Sigg: Prometheus is accompanied by a lion and a little dog, and here Zarathustra is accompanied by a lioness and her young ones. I should like to know what the difference is.

Prof. Jung: In *Prometheus* the lion is the will to power, and the dog is the sentimentality, the weakness, the craving for love and tenderness. But one must not be too literal about these things; the real parallel is the tigress. Spitteler compares the first apparition of the anima to a tigress walking under the trees with the leaves casting shadows on her fur. That is a very suggestive passage. Now sure enough, the wisdom of the anima is wild because the anima is nature. That is the one thing in man which he cannot rule, the thing by which he is connected with nature; and if he apparently succeeds in cutting that communication, he is done for. And the animus in a woman is nature. I mean if it is in the right place: if the animus is in a woman's conscious, then of course it means opinionating, convictions, the driest, most soulless stuff you can imagine. If a man has his anima in the conscious, he has the feelings of a mother, something perfectly ridiculous, he will *schwärmen*[9] for babies and such things. There is a wonderful English book by MacDonald—I think it is called *Lilith*[10]—which you ought to read as a most gorgeous example of a man whose anima is in the conscious. The book begins with the problem of Lilith, the anima problem—Lilith of course was a demon, the first wife of Adam—and it finally ends in an orgy of babies. It is beyond words, but marvelous as a pathological manifestation: he finds an anima that produces millions of babies, eats babies and drinks them. It is something awful!

Mrs. Sigg: Wotan is not only in Germany!

Prof. Jung: No, Wotan is an international phenomenon, and he is by no means Christian, but is all over the world.

Mrs. Jung: I think it is interesting to see that, concerning the man

---

[8] Jung often cited Carl Spitteler, the only Swiss Nobel laureate for literature, but in CW 6, he dwelt at length on *Prometheus and Epimetheus: A Prose Epic* (orig. 1880-81, tr. J. F. Muirhead [London, 1931]). Spitteler denied any symbolic quality to his work, claiming that it was just straightforward fiction.

[9] Schwärmen: literally "to swarm over" like bees; to gush over or rave about.

[10] George MacDonald's *Lilith, a Visionary Novel* originally appeared in 1859 and was reissued in New York, 1954.

Nietzsche, his function of relationship is evidently all in his teaching, but it has a negative character that came out in sarcasm or spite.

Prof. Jung: Yes, one could say it *all* turns into the negative. That is not his intention. He would like to have positive relationship but he cannot; his anima twists the whole thing into just the opposite of relatedness, into destructiveness, and that won't do. He gets into a warlike attitude and becomes the enemy of mankind—hurling his spear at them. It is desperately like actual politics. Germany is again in much the same position she was in before the war, outside and inside. Hitler has written that most extraordinary book, *Mein Kampf*, for instance. Why not *My Love* or *My Peace*? Through the mouth of her leader Germany has maneuvered herself into such an unfortunate condition that everybody must believe that she wants war and that they are justified in making an iron ring round her. And Germany is again justified in defending herself against that ring, so finally she will be forced into an act of despair and say, "Oh, if we are the arch-enemy of mankind, then have it so."

Mrs. Sigg: I think it would have been pretty difficult for Hitler in prison, and after the Versailles treaty, to write a book called *My Love*. I think that would be asking too much.

Prof. Jung: Well, one might look at it from a different point of view, not always from the point of view of war. We have been talking for two thousand years about love and now, damn it, why war?

Mrs. Sigg: But he does not mean war when he says *Kampf*.

Prof. Jung: I agree that it is not meant like that but it *sounds* like that. Look at the battalions of Brown Shirts; naturally people say that means war. Then the Germans say, "By no means, this is *Arbeitsdienst*,[11] they are not carrying guns, but spades." So it is just the difference in the point of view. The book is called *Mein Kampf*, and there are many things said in it which are very difficult to swallow—all the diplomacy of the *neue Reich* for instance; the book has done a lot of harm. It would have been very much better if he had written a book called *My Peace*. If he had been an Englishman he would have written *My Love*—having not meant it at all!

[11] *Arbeitsdienst*: work service.

LECTURE VII

4 March 1936

Prof. Jung:

Before we leave this chapter about the child and the mirror, I would like to ask how you have understood the expression "my wild wisdom"? He says: "My wild wisdom became pregnant on the lonesome mountains." That is a very peculiar idea, and I wonder what you think about it.

Mrs. Crowley: I thought it was the wisdom of the collective unconscious, in the figure of the old wise man.

Prof. Jung: Ah yes, but this allusion to his wild wisdom would point to something of the old wise man that has come into the man Nietzsche himself, and then how does it look?

Mr. Allemann: It is the snake wisdom, nature's wisdom.

Miss Hughes: It is untamed wisdom.

Prof. Jung: But how does nature's wisdom look? There must be different kinds of wisdom apparently, wild and tame or domesticated wisdom.

Mrs. Sigg: An irrational wisdom.

Prof. Jung: Well yes, wisdom is understood to be irrational to a certain extent because merely rational wisdom is not very wise; science would be rational wisdom, but then one would use the word *knowledge*. (In German, to be wise and to know come from the same root, *wissen*.) But it is also not irrational; one cannot say nature is just wild, otherwise there would be no *ratio* in it, and there is.

Miss Hughes: Is it not a kind of wisdom that would carry one away in spite of oneself?

Prof. Jung: That is the way it would influence us. It is a sort of autonomous wisdom which dominates us but leaves us at times to our own devices; it is not always there, but is like a wild animal which at times one has only glimpses of, while at another time it will approach one. It is not an organized knowledge.

873

Miss Hughes: Would it be his specific feminine Eros wisdom against his typically masculine wisdom of the wise old man?

Prof. Jung: Inasmuch as he is a man, it would be the wisdom of nature, like Erda's wisdom in the Germanic myth, the wisdom of the underworld that has to do with the moon, rather.

Dr. Adler: If it is like a wild beast it would be instinctual wisdom.

Prof. Jung: Yes, but those are all formal definitions; I would like to know a bit more about the substance of this wisdom.

Mr. Baumann: It is not built up by reflection. It is a kind of *a priori* wisdom which is inherent in man like the instincts.

Prof. Jung: Yes, but I wouldn't say it was just inherent in man because it is wild; you wouldn't say of a bird that it was inherent in man. It is contained in nature—an animal or a bird or a lion or whatever it is.

Miss Hannah: It would show itself as the natural mind.

Prof. Jung: We have to reserve that term for the women; it is too characteristic, you know!

Mrs. Sigg: It might be some elementary intuition.

Prof. Jung: Yes, it can show itself in such a form.

Mrs. Crowley: It appears in a sort of Dionysian form.

Prof. Jung: It does, no doubt. When the panthers of Dionysos jump upon you, you might say a wise word—there is much wisdom in wine.

Miss Hughes: A man cannot go by the guidance of a lioness as his anima.

Prof. Jung: Heavens, he can go by the guidance of a louse even. Do you know the story of the sailor and the louse of Trafalgar? There was a lull in the battle when he felt something upon his head and a louse fell on the ground; he saw it crawling and bent down to crush it, and in that moment he just missed a cannon ball that whistled over his head. Then the sailor said thank you to the louse, and put it back on his head, adding, "But be careful, for the next time I might not recognize you again." So no animal is so small and no wisdom is so small that it might not be helpful at times. But I should like to know something about the substance. Can you name a wisdom that is within human reach—not so terribly wild, to be bought perhaps?

Mr. Baumann: Wouldn't it be the wisdom that lies in wine?

Prof. Jung: But in buying wine, you have not necessarily bought wisdom—you may have bought a monkey.

Mrs. Sigg: You might find that wisdom in a book—in the Bible for instance.

Prof. Jung: Yes, but that is chiefly religious; there might also be a worldly wisdom.

Mrs. Baynes: The *I Ching*.

Prof. Jung: Yes, the *I Ching*, or the *Tao-Te-King*, or the Upanishads, or the great philosophers: all of these contain acceptable and buyable wisdom. But that is not wild wisdom.

Mr. Allemann: It is wisdom that is not man-made.

Prof. Jung: Yes. The *Tao-Te-King*, for instance, has been formulated by Laotze; and the *I Ching* consists of formulas of King Wen and the Duke of Chou. And the Book of Wisdom in the Old Testament is ascribed to Solomon. There are also books by Master Eckhart. But wild wisdom cannot be ascribed to any one. It is not made by man, not even formulated by man. So how does it show?

Mrs. Jung: I think you might call the whole cosmos an expression of it; you might find it in nature. It is not necessarily bound to one form, but can be found everywhere.

Prof. Jung: It can be found everywhere, yes, but in what form?

Mrs. Jung: I think one finds it in the form of a feeling.

Prof. Jung: In a psychological form then. And what would that be?

Mrs. Crowley: It might be in a state of *ekstasis* since we are speaking of this particular way in *Zarathustra*. And I should also say in dreams if you can find it.

Mrs. Stutz: Or in meditation.

Prof. Jung: Oh, you can meditate, or dream, or get drunk; you can be in the mountains, or the Sahara, or the woods—and find no wisdom whatever.

Mrs. Adler: One finds it in old prophets.

Prof. Jung: Yes, and what is the characteristic of the prophet?

Miss Hannah: Intuition.

Mrs. Stutz: They hear God's voice.

Prof. Jung: And what do you call it when you hear the voice of God?

Miss Bianchi: Inspiration.

Miss Hughes: The Angel of the Lord.

Mrs. Dürler: Instinct.

Prof. Jung: It can be instinct, that is perfectly true. But I want to know the term by which you designate the form in which this wisdom comes to us.

Mrs. Fröbe-Kapteyn: Experience.

Miss Wolff: The objective unconscious.

Mr. Baumann: Is it not insight?

Prof. Jung: It can be, but that is an activity on our own part; if a wild animal crosses your path you don't say you have an insight or intuit this animal.

Mrs. Stutz: It might be a great experience in consequence of being alone with nature.

Prof. Jung: It is an experience but this doesn't designate the particular character in which it appears.

Mrs. Sigg: Revelation.

Prof. Jung: Exactly. You see the term *revelation* conveys exactly how this wild wisdom appears; it reveals itself to you. You cannot say you intuit it; you *experience* revelation. This word conveys the idea that there is a factor or an activity, one could call it a living thing at the other end of the wire that reveals its presence to you. A revelation always means a revealing will, a will to manifest which is not identical with your own will and which is not your activity. You may be overcome by it; it falls upon you. The prophetic experiences described in the Bible are very good examples of the way it happens and the character of the voice that speaks in the thunder, in the fire, everywhere—it can come out of stones. No matter where you are, the revelation can come to you when *it* chooses. The important point is that you cannot choose the partner in the game; you are not the active part, but are just the receiver, the object of the revelation. Now what does the wild wisdom teach? What is the content or the substance of revelation?

Mrs. Baynes: It often comes in the form of a command to go forth and teach. Moses was commanded to give the ten commandments, for instance.

Prof. Jung: Yes, and you find it in the prophecies of Isaiah or any other prophet. Then when you try to formulate that, to what results do you come? What, for instance, is the main point in the revelation as we know it from the Old or the New Testament?

Mrs. Baynes: It is bringing god to man.

Mr. Allemann: It gives guidance.

Prof. Jung: That is an effect upon us; it largely depends upon us. But what does it reveal?

Mr. Baumann: The will of God.

Prof. Jung: Yes, a revelation is a self-manifestation at the other end of the wire. There is a living something with a will or intention that is outside, something that conveys its own self, its own command to you: it manifests itself. That is what *revelation* means, and that is wild wisdom. Now where would Nietzsche have gotten that experience?

Mrs. Baynes: From the experience he had in the mountains.

Prof. Jung: Exactly, from the revelation he had from Zarathustra himself. Zarathustra is that wild wisdom; he embodies it, personifies it. You remember Nietzsche says: *Da wurde eins zu zwei und Zarathustra ging an mir vorbei.* Whatever Nietzsche reveals here is the revelation he has received from Zarathustra. Of course, here we get into trouble right away on account of that fact that Nietzsche is all the time identical with Zarathustra so that we never know which one is speaking; only from certain peculiarities of the text, certain thoughts and intentions and so on, can we conclude. It is as if one had to read the original text of a master, upon which in subsequent centuries several other people had tried their hand, mixing in their own intentions, so that one is saddled with the task of disentangling the presumably original text from the later additions and corrections and interpolations. So here we have to try to pull out of that entanglement what is Nietzsche's own and what has really come through revelation. Unfortunately, Nietzsche lived in a time when he could not objectify psychological events, so he thought that he himself was at the other end of the wire, that he heard his own voice. Wild wisdom, then, is really the revelation of the autonomous psychical factor at the other end of the wire, the demon or whatever you like to call it. And from the kind of revelation one can conclude as to the nature of that being at the other end. Of course we need the whole of *Zarathustra* in order to get the sum total of the message, and then from the particular kind of message we can understand what that revealing factor is, or what its qualities are.

Mrs. Sigg: I think the lioness might be at the other end of the telephone as well.

Prof. Jung: Yes, anything is possible. It might be a serpent or a bird, whatever you like; we cannot say. There is an eagle and a serpent and a lion and a camel and a child, and even the hell-hound later on.

Mr. Baumann: Didn't theology try to lift up this wild wisdom into revelation? But how does one experience such things now? We have no prophets, we don't believe in that.

Prof. Jung: But there is any amount of revelation going on all the time; plenty of people have revelations.

Mrs. Baynes: Guidance every morning!

Prof. Jung: You must not assume that revelation is always something of supreme value. The revelations of lunatics are often quite funny. So it is exceedingly difficult to make out what the wild wisdom really means. The guidance is very funny at times; I could tell you the most amazing examples which I have heard from my patients, just wild, but if you can work it out, you discover that there is great wisdom in it. I even admit that there is great wisdom in the guidance of the Oxford Movement.

Mrs. Jung: What exactly is the difference between intuition and revelation?

Prof. Jung: Well, an ordinary intuition is really one's own activity. I can set out to have an intuition and it doesn't come to me as a revelation; I can stare at a thing until something comes into my mind. I can even provoke it. An intuitive type sets out to intuit—it is very much his own activity—whereas a revelation has of course a great similarity but it appears much more as a fact outside oneself. It is true that the intuitive derives the authority for his intuition from the same source, so at times it seems to have the same autonomous character, and the more it has that character, the more it has authority of course. It is amazing how sure he is of his intuition, so certain that he can convince people of the merest possibility, a potential which might come off, or it might not. It is utterly improbable that more than 50 percent of intuitions are true because we are surrounded by a large percentage of false possibilities. You see, a potentiality can remain forever a potentiality, and it may also be a false possibility; something may *seem* to be possible yet it is not at all, although one has an intuition that it *is* already. The more intuition has an autonomous quality, the more it takes on the character of a revelation; therefore the most intuitive people behave as if they were all the time inspired. They are perfectly certain, and in consequence they fall from one hole into the other and never get anywhere. You see, what happens to them is that they assume that authority to be their own; if they did not they would be critical—then they would discuss matters with God. The prophets discussed matters first; they were disobedient because they felt there were other elements involved in it and perhaps God didn't really know whether the thing was right or not. But the moment the intuitive has an intuition, he runs away with it and therefore he falls into a hole.

Mrs. Sigg: Could one say a revelation comes from the self?

Prof. Jung: Well, whatever the phrase is, we don't know the source. We must be very careful. Yes, we could make such a theory—of the so-called self from which a revelation comes—but this is metaphysical speculation.

Mrs. Crowley: I would have thought it could start with intuition.

Prof. Jung: Of course it can have such a form, but you cannot provoke it.

Mrs. Crowley: Then I had the wrong idea of intuition. I thought that was just what could *not* be done with intuition; I thought it was autonomous.

Prof. Jung: That is just the trouble: that is what the intuitive thinks.

The more one is intuitive, the more it just comes to one, but it is one's own activity. There is a tremendous danger in intuition; the more it is differentiated, the greater the danger that it takes on that character of revelation. It is the same with the intellect; if one has a finely differentiated intellect one feels that it is almost infallible. So a philosopher once told me that thinking could never be wrong because it was right in itself.

Mrs. Crowley: I mean exactly the opposite; an intuition is so uncertain that it is no proof if it comes to you, but if it is revelation you would be absolutely convinced.

Prof. Jung: It is true that revelation has authority but the historical fact is, that even if the revelation comes to you with great authority, you may not believe it.

Mrs. Crowley: Well, you would feel more convinced, I should think, if you could possibly realize that it was revelation.

Prof. Jung: That is perfectly true: people are more convinced by a revelation than by an intuition; but it is also true that if they have a real revelation they may not believe it, while they might believe an intuition.

Mrs. Dürler: Where can you draw the line?

Prof. Jung: Yes, where can you draw the line between the very sharp intellect and error? That is just the difficulty.

Mr. Allemann: Is it not the claim of the church to be able to draw the line?

Prof. Jung: Exactly, and that is why we have such safe-guards as scientific text books or dogma. For instance, St. Ambrose said a very great word: *Omne verum a quocumque dicitur, a Spiritu Sancto est.* Everything that is true, said by whomsoever, is a gift of the Holy Ghost. Now this is very wonderful, but what is truth? Who tells you what the truth is? The church steps in and says a thing is not true and therefore it is not of the Holy Ghost.

Dr. Escher: The Apostle Peter was surely shocked at first when the command came to eat unclean meat.[1]

Prof. Jung: Yes, that was a revelation too; it is a very good example. You see, when the time had come for Christianity to be spread to the Gentiles, he had a vision that God let down a linen cloth in which were the impure animals which the orthodox Jews were forbidden to eat.

---

[1] See Acts of the Apostles, 10:11-17, for Peter's vision wherein he claimed that he never ate common or unclean beasts and was rebuked by a voice saying, "What God hath created that call not thou common."

And the voice said that what God declared to be pure could not be impure. So he had to eat it, which means that he had to assimilate the Gentiles. But he surely did not like it; he had to have the shock of such a vision in order to be shaken into accepting it. Now if St. Peter had had an intuition that such animals were not particularly impure and that it was the will of God that one should eat impure animals anyway, he would have said *he* had this intuition. *He* would have made the declaration and would have made it his own affair. It would have been an ego business, and when that is the case one is very much inclined to believe it. While if it is against you, and you have to become yourself in order to bow down to this fact, it is entirely different; then it is revelation and the true revelation is very often not believed at first. People fight against it; often they defend themselves for years against it, which of course is all against themselves, for they will be overcome in the end. But they are always inclined to believe an intuition and make an ego business of it, and then the secret power tendency creeps in and falsifies the whole thing. One would have the greatest difficulty, however, in drawing the line between what one calls an intuition and a revelation—it is very often wellnigh impossible; I don't know of one single safeguard in the world that would guarantee a clear and reliable discrimination. If God should choose to make some new revelation you can be sure that the Catholic church would step in and say it was not true, that it was an invention of the devil. It is the same in the Protestant church. God is fettered, completely lamed; he even risks being declared the devil if he says anything unconventional. So it is a most unenviable situation.

Mrs. Sigg: Did you not once quote somebody as saying that the Protestants had made a definition of God as the *ganz andere*?

Prof. Jung: Yes, Barth used that term.[2] The *ganz andere*, the totally other one, simply means the man or the voice at the other end of the wire, which is not only the opposite, because the opposite can be deduced—I know that the opposite of white must be black for instance—but the totally different. And what can that be? It can be anything.

Miss Wolff: A very good example where the church interfered is Joan of Arc; she got her revelation through the *ganz andere*, so she was pronounced a heretic for having had a conversation with the saints without the interference of the church.

Prof. Jung: Yes, and in her canonization process, they said that she had had an intuition.

[2] See above, 5 Dec. 1934, n. 9, and 2 Feb. 1936, n. 9.

Mr. Baumann: Could one not say of a certain quality of revelation that it says just another thing than one is accustomed to think?

Prof. Jung: Well, that is no more characteristic of the revelation than of intuition.

Mr. Baumann: Yes, but I was thinking of the character of the shock it gives one.

Prof. Jung: Ah well, one receives the shock from the fact that it is against one, the object thrown against one. (*Objicere* means to throw against one.) It comes with the authority of a reality, and that is characteristic for revelation. Think, for instance, of that peculiar symbolism in the Revelations of St. John where he is forced to swallow a book, causing an upset in the stomach, or that he has to swallow a live coal.[3] Or think of poor old Hosea who was a very decent chap, and the command came that he was to marry a whore.[4] He was shocked out of his wits, I presume.

Mrs. Crowley: Those all seem like evidences of a sudden conviction that worked immediately, but from what you said before a revelation has to be proved a long, long time.

Prof. Jung: But those are not sudden convictions. Hosea was not suddenly convinced, surely. And when Paul on his way to Damascus had the vision of Christ, he had to be overthrown, blinded, in order to make him believe, just because he was not convinced. Naturally out of such an experience comes a tremendous conviction, but first there is a terrible resistance against it; one cannot accept it because it is so strange.[5] I believe that the early experiences of Jeanne d'Arc were truly revelations because one cannot assume that a peasant girl in the 15th century had any kind of political aspirations; it must have been something like revelation, and though of course we don't know how it worked in her, if you were called to do something similar you would have certain qualms about it I am sure. So we can assume she had too; it must have been a pretty rough business. Now, we come to the next chapter called, "In the Happy Isles," and as usual we should make the

---

[3] "And I went unto the angel, and said unto him, 'Give me the little book.' And he said unto me, 'Take it, and eat it up; and it shall make thy belly bitter, but it shall be in thy mouth sweet as honey' " (Revelation 10:9). This echoes Ezekiel 2:8-10 and 3:1-3, but in neither place is a live coal mentioned.

[4] Hosea 1:2-3.

[5] "And as (Paul) journeyed, he came near Damascus: and suddenly there shined round about him a light from heaven: And he fell to the earth, and heard a voice saying unto him, 'Saul, Saul, why persecuteth thou me?' " (Acts of the Apostles, 9:3-4).

connection with the chapter before, "The Child with the Mirror." How does he arrive at the new picture?

Miss Wolff: There is one connection in the text. It is not a real explanation, but in the last chapter he says, "Like a cry and a huzza will I traverse wide seas, till I find the Happy Isles where my friends sojourn."

Prof. Jung: Yes, that is of course the formal connection, but we must try to find out if there is any internal connection, and for that it is necessary to get at the concentrated meaning of the chapter we have just dealt with. For instance, there is that passage "Too slowly runneth all speaking from me:—into thy chariot, O storm, do I leap! And even thee will I whip with my spite!" He was travelling with the storm, being the storm itself, and then he comes to the Happy Islands. Now what is the gist of that whole chapter? What does "The Child with the Mirror" show?

Mrs. Jung: The child suggests that his teaching is in danger and that he has to go to his friends to try to make it right again.

Prof. Jung: Yes, that is the idea in the text, but we decided that his being afraid that his doctrine was in danger, showed that he had seen his shadow aspect without realizing that that devilish image was his own face. Otherwise, he would not have arrived at the idea that his doctrine had been distorted behind his back so that he must run to his friends to protect it. Now, as far as we can see, this is a very wrong idea, inasmuch as it is the conclusion of the man. But now let us assume that this scene with the child and the mirror has not been presented to us through the man Nietzsche but is an impersonal revelation of the spirit Zarathustra. Then what about it as the conclusion of the spirit?

Mrs. Adler: Then the god also would be one-sided inasmuch as he denies his shadow.

Prof. Jung: If a god or a demon—of course in the antique sense of the word, a divine being[6]—had created a certain favorable aspect of himself in the world, and then should suddenly see his face in a most unfavorable light, would it seem right for him to run at once to do something for the general opinion people hold about him? If he were wise, if he were really benevolent, he would have to say, "Beware! My face is also like a devil's face." But these man-made gods are very reluctant to admit such aspects of their respective personalities; of course we cannot burden them with such a responsibility. The fact that there is such a story of a child holding the mirror up to his face, and that we

---

[6] *Daimonion*—as in Socrates' inner voice.

know it was a devil's grimace in it, shows that the deity really doesn't care. The deity reveals itself in its own way naively; it has this face and another face, creates this view and another view. It is only we human beings who are afraid of that other aspect and run to others to strengthen our good opinion.

There is that beautiful example of our Swiss saint, Nicolaus von der Flüe—though he is not yet a saint because the money is lacking to get him canonized.[7] They have tried for a long time, but he is still only *Beatus*. He had a terrible vision of a face full of wrath, and he was so shocked that his own face took on the imprint of it, so that people could not stand the sight of him. They ran away. That was the devil's grimace, and he tried afterwards with the greatest concentration to interpret it in the terms of the Trinity. He struggled to express his vision in a dogmatic form, even painted it on the wall of his cell. It is in the form of a mandala but with the threefold division according to the orthodox rules for the Trinity, and in the center is the face of God or Christ, a very lovely face. One sees nothing of the horror of the face in his vision, that has been completely wiped out by the influence of the church and of course also by his own mind; he was too much influenced by the church and could not stand the revelation of God in his terrible aspect. There is a copy of this painting in the church of his village, Sachseln, where his skeleton is also to be seen, and I am told that there are traces of the original painting in his cell in a little Hermitage in a valley above Sachseln.

This truth, the dual aspect of the god, is not denied in Mahayana Buddhism and Lamaism, where even the most benevolent gods are also gruesome demons. There the dark side of the gods is admitted, while to us God is the absolutely perfect being; we cannot admit that he has a wrathful aspect. The whole thing has to be molded and maneuvered until it looks right. But the fact is that the same thing which now looks quite lovely has been terrible, really shocking. The deity reveals itself as it is, then, and to model it into something else is man's work. So we must conclude that this is Nietzsche's own idea. He draws the conclusion: "Oh heavens, somebody has distorted my beautiful face probably, Zarathustra's reputation has been injured, and therefore my doctrine looks now like the devil—and that cannot be." That is a very human conclusion for anybody who mixes himself up with his revelation as if it were his own business, who is identical with his doctrine instead of accepting it as the manifestation of a deity that has

---

[7] For Nicholas von der Flüe, see above, 7 Nov. 1934, n. 5.

freedom enough to show its wrathful face just as well. You see, when Nietzsche hears that story of the child with the mirror, the sound conclusion would be: "Zarathustra looks now like a devil, so let us be careful. He is not only the living teacher of man, he is also a sort of danger, has a wrathful aspect, and may be a demon of the underworld. The East has experienced this fact so many times that they can admit it, and from it they draw a lot of wisdom. For example, Kuan-Yin is often likened, particularly in China and Japan, to the Mother Mary, the kind loving mother, yet even that beautiful being has a wrathful aspect.[8] According to Eastern wisdom it would mean that there is no virtue so great that it has not also an unconscious, opposite aspect. Generosity, for instance, creates perfect fiends, vampires, animals of prey that jump upon the gifts generosity bestows. You have not done good to your fellow beings by being just and kindly and generous, or by loving your neighbor. He will take advantage of it; you teach him to steal by offering him easy opportunities, not reckoning with the fact that your fellow being has a negative aspect. And even in your virtues, just there, you show the devil's grimace. So whenever you find a shining virtue you must always be aware of the contrary.

Miss Wolff: Is not one aspect of the chapter that Zarathustra is *relieved* by the dream? A whole source of new energy is coming up in him because of it. He is speaking in images of wild nature, compares himself to the weather, and to a lioness attacking his enemies, and all that comes from this aspect he gets of himself in the mirror. Before, he was really a bit too human.

Prof. Jung: Exactly. The dream anticipates the experience of Zarathustra like a cold wind; in his wrathful aspect he is like Wotan.

Miss Wolff: And he speaks of a lioness that will sleep on the soft sward of his friends' hearts.

Prof. Jung: Yes, all that comes to the foreground; this is really the wrathful aspect of the demon. But if you draw the wrong conclusion first, you are naturally possessed by the effect of the image. For instance, if an archetypal image comes into your dream and you interpret it wrongly, you will be possessed by the image; then you have to perform it. It simply catches you. While if you interpret it correctly, if you understand what it conveys and can look at it objectively without putting a propitious interpretation upon it, then you have a chance.

---

[8] Kuan-Yin, a Buddhist Mother Goddess, is called "the Goddess of Boundless Kindness." In an Eranos Lecture of 1934, "The Madonna as a Religious Symbol," Friedrich Heiler associated Diana, Artemis, Isis, and Shakti with Mary.

Otherwise you are possessed, and that has happened here; Zarathus-tra-Nietzsche has identified with Wotan and therefore must become the man with the spear and the horse and so on. But now, having become the cold storm that rages over land and sea seeking the Happy Isles, what about the next chapter?

Miss Hughes: Would that be his escape?

Prof. Jung: Well, it would be a sort of escape. We already mentioned that the "Happy Isles" meant the islands of bliss, something like the idea we harbor about the islands of the Pacific, a paradise where one is out of the turmoil and torment of life, where life is apparently easy and where one lives like a god. This is an age-old idea: the happy island is even a symbol of heaven, of the ghostland where spirits live in eternal bliss. So he would really be getting to the Western Land of the Gilga-mesh epic, where Uta-Napishtim lives. It is a sort of escape, but why does he make for that country?

Mrs. Sigg: There seems to be a connection here with the old Greek myth of the pregnant goddess who had to look out for a land to bring forth her child.

Prof. Jung: That was Leto.

Miss Wolff: She was persecuted by the dragon.

Prof. Jung: Yes, like the story in Revelations of the pregnant woman who was persecuted by a dragon that spat water at her to drown her and the child. Leto was cursed by Hera who made a contract with the rulers of all lands that nobody should give her hospitality; she was jealous because Leto was pregnant by Zeus. But there was an island floating around under the sea which came up out of the water just then, so it was a land where nobody was bound by that contract. Leto happened to get to this island—it is supposed to have been Delos—and Poseidon made four pillars for it to rest upon, so that it was a safe place to bring forth the child. There is of course a hint of that myth in the pregnancy of the lioness; the Happy Isles would be the protected place where she could bring forth. Now why would the lioness or the wild wisdom need such a place of shelter, where she is safe against persecution?

Mrs. Adler: She will again bring forth the bad aspect of Zarathustra because that has not been accepted. It seems to me that it is the resistance of Nietzsche or Zarathustra against the bad aspect.

Prof. Jung: That is the original reason.

Mr. Baumann: It might refer to the fact that sometimes the male lion or bear eats the young, so the lioness has to be protected from her own male, which in this case I should say was the Logos.

Miss Wolff: She has really already given birth to the young one in the last chapter where he says she has borne her young on rough stones.

Prof. Jung: She has given birth but she is now in a disagreeable situation because she has not found a sheltered place where she can nurse the young.

Miss Hughes: Inasmuch as Nietzsche has denied his other side, he is defenseless. He says here, "on your love, would she fain couch her dearest one," so she is in need of feeling.

Prof. Jung: It has to do with that, sure enough.

Mrs. Jung: As he has put the Superman in the place of God he must be afraid of the wrath of the gods.

Prof. Jung: That is true, and that links up with the story of Leto who incurred the wrath of the gods because she had an affair with Zeus. She should have known that Hera was a very jealous goddess who would see that she was persecuted by all the universe under the rule of the gods. Now, we are here confronted with the psychology of a peculiar myth. You see, Leto found that island, the place of refuge which had been under the sea, and that means that there is a place which the gods of the day really do not touch—they don't even know of its existence because it is covered by the sea. Translated into psychological language, the ruling gods of Olympus would be the gods of the day; those gods are our ideas and Olympus the seat of consciousness. And as a universal ruler the conscious rules over everything and therefore can make a contract with everything, in order not to allow anything irregular like Leto. Leto is an anima myth; she would be the illegitimate anima of Zeus, and Zeus was imprudent enough to have a child by her. This is again the story of Mary and the flight into Egypt, where they had to find shelter against the persecution of the gods of the day—represented through Herod killing the boys. The anima is the representative of the unconscious, and Zeus is the supreme lord of consciousness, so the ruling idea has created a child with the unconscious which should be sheltered and protected. The island floating in the unconscious is dead matter covered by the water, something like a spiritual earth, and that is the *prima materia* of alchemistic philosophy without which nothing can be made. Yet nobody has ever known what this primal matter is. The alchemists did not know, and nobody has found out what was really meant by it, because it is a substance in the unconscious which is needed for the incarnation of the god. And now this island coming up from below is a parallel to the child that comes from above, from heaven, and gets its substance from below. Zeus, the highest idea, descended to the earth, like the Holy Ghost coming down to Mary on earth but touching that which is below the earth, the water. From the bottom of the sea comes up the island upon which the god is seated; that is the lotus, the earth matter that has first been in the water, and on the third day after his birth Buddha stepped into the lotus and announced the law to the world. So the lotus is the seat of the god, the thing that grows from below, while the ruler, the divine form, descends from heaven. Then this matter which comes from below is based on four pillars, placed there by Poseidon, the god of the sea, who, being a partner in the game, has some point of litigation with Zeus. Zeus rules above with his thunderbolt and Poseidon rules in the sea with his trident, the equivalent of the thunderbolt. And he plays a trick on Hera by helping Leto. Now, these four pillars are the four pillars of the world, the four qualities, the four elements. The Tetraktys, the number four, is the basis of nature—and that refers now to what?

Miss Hannah: To a mandala.

Prof. Jung: Yes, the Happy Island is a mandala, the Padma, the material seat of the god, in which the god expresses himself. So the god of the underworld, or the water world, which is the collective unconscious, brings up that Happy Island upon which the god is seated; on that flower he can be nursed. You may remember, perhaps, that the German poet Hölderlin uses exactly the same image of the gods:

> Schicksallos, wie der schlafende
> Säugling, atmen die Himmlischen;
> Keusch bewahrt in bescheidener Knospe,
> Blühet ewig ihnen der Geist,
> Und die stillen Augen
> Blicken in stiller
> Ewiger Klarheit.[9]

You see, that is like the flower in the bud protected by the brown leaves, and so the birth of the spirit is sheltered against the cold north wind of the winter. That is a very beautiful parallel with the lotus, for the lotus bud grows under the water and opens when it reaches the surface; then the god is revealed. Another parallel is the idea that flowers are really the mirror images of the sun. They are matter that forms

---

[9] Friedrich Hölderlin's (1770-1843) "Hyperion's Song of Fate." The lines cited have been rendered into English prose as: "The heavenly ones breathe fatelessly, like a sleeping infant; / their spirit blooms eternally, chastely preserved in modest bud and their blissful eyes see with tranquil eternal clarity" (*The Penguin Book of German Verse* [Baltimore, 1957]). Hölderlin was a favorite poet of Nietzsche's too: they are linked as geniuses who ended in madness.

into the shape of the sun, receive the sun's image and the sun's rays and represent it. The sun of course is the god that descends into matter, fertilizing and vivifying it. That is the underlying archetypal idea here.

Mr. Baumann: There is a very interesting parallel in Christianity in the pictures of the Annunciation. Always between the angel and Mary there is a flower, usually a lily. I think it is the same archetype. By the impregnation of the Holy Ghost, the flower comes up.

Prof. Jung: Yes, and sometimes it is a bunch of flowers. It is the three roses in alchemy or the *Rosenlilie*, a rose and a lily at the same time. And the *rosa mystica* is of course a mandala; our Western idea of the *rosa mystica* is the absolute parallel to the Eastern Padma lotus. In a medieval poem there is an even closer connection; in one of his hymns to Mary the poet says that Christ has hidden himself in the flower of the sea, not in the *stella maris* but in the *flos maris*, like a water bird. That is of course the spirit, the water bird descending upon the flower that rises above the sea; and that is based upon the four pillars, the quality of four in the earth. Therefore, the earth is represented in old symbolism by a square. In China it is a square. And in the Muladhara chakra, the earth chakra, where the elephant carries the world upon its back, the yellow square is the yellow earth, and the four petals symbolize the Tetraktys, the four qualities. In this chakra according to the Tantric Yoga, the god is dormant and encoiled by the Shakti in the form of the Kundalini serpent; this is the condition of the god in the moment of his birth. Now, this being the underlying mythology, or archetypal imagery, we will see what happens in this chapter. It is obvious that the Happy Isle is needed for the birth of that child. And who is the child? Have you ever heard of a child of Zarathustra?

Mrs. Sigg: He was carrying a child under his mantle.

Prof. Jung: Yes, as if he were a woman. And who is the child of the wise old man? We have a psychological name for it.

Mrs. Baynes: The *Puer Aeternus.*

Prof. Jung: Yes, the eternal boy. That is the mythological figure that appears, historically, in the form of the Etruscan Tages, the boylike god.[10] The legend is that a peasant was plowing in the field and suddenly behind him out of the furrow sprang up a youthful god who then taught the people all sorts of arts and crafts. This is a parallel to the Eastern Babylonian idea of Johannes who came daily out of the water in the form of a fish. And it is a funny fact that the idea of the

---

[10] For Tages, see CW 5, pars. 291-92.

Tages appears in an old report in a book that is now about one hundred and twenty years old by Justinus Kerner, the report itself being much older: namely, that such a thing really happened to a peasant. He was plowing and suddenly out of the furrow came a little man with a pointed cap—the characteristic covering of the cabiri—who gave him a message. He prophesied something which I don't remember, and the peasant naively believed him. You see, that is one of the forms in which the *Puer Aeternus* can appear. Of course that *Puer Aeternus* is a specific fact; he is Christ the wise one. You remember the scene in the temple when he was a little boy; he is the God's son, the rejuvenated god, the rejuvenated father. And what is the peculiarity of Christ in comparison with the God-Father?

Miss Wolff: He is incarnated.

Prof. Jung: Exactly, and the God-Father was not. The son is the equal of the God, coexistent and coeternal, yet he is in human form, mortal as man is mortal. He is the man-begotten God. Dionysos was also worshipped as a boylike youth. And Horus is a very similar figure.

Mr. Baumann: Osiris was also human; before he was killed by Set he was supposed to be a man.

Prof. Jung: Yes, there the case is reversed; Osiris was not understood to be a god who became man, but a pious man who became a god. You know, Horus in the form of Harpocrates became a mystery god, and the legend is that as Harpocrates he was lame in the legs, which points to a peculiar disease of the gods. The powerless condition in which that child is born is comparable to the powerless, utterly miserable condition in which Christ was born, quite helpless. Of course that is so with intention. It would not befit the god to be born under favorable social conditions. To become man he must be born in human misery and in the worst of misery, as an illegitimate child. That is logical; otherwise he could never experience the misery of human life.

SPRING TERM

May / June 1936

LECTURE I

6 May 1936

Prof. Jung:
Ladies and Gentlemen: I have heard during the vacation that certain members of the seminar were impressed with the pathological side of Nietzsche shown in *Zarathustra*, and the suggestion was made that I should not go on with this dangerous stuff, that I should rather take something more normal, Goethe's fairy tales, for instance. There is a famous fairy tale by Goethe which is a typical fantasy series as we know them; it is an alchemistic story like those one encounters in old Latin texts, and this was suggested instead of the awful Nietzsche. Now if you come to the conclusion that you would prefer something so-called normal instead of this admittedly pathological Nietzsche, which has of course an unpleasant side, then you must tell me. I don't want to grate on your nerves, but you must remember that the suggestion that we should deal with *Zarathustra* came originally from the members of the seminar. I was rather doubtful, but I myself agreed to risk the analysis of *Zarathustra* chiefly because it is a very modern piece of work which has much to do with what is happening in our time; I thought it might be of great interest to look into the actual working of the unconscious mind, which has anticipated all the great political and historical events of our days. But I have to admit that Nietzsche is very involved and what he produces in *Thus Spake Zarathustra* is of a kind which stirs the unconscious of modern man to an uncanny degree, all the more because one doesn't notice the way in which it works; it works secretly and at times even in a poisonous way. So if you feel that we have had enough of the devils of *Zarathustra*, you must say so. Since we are still in a democratic country we can vote. Now who is for Nietzsche? [The great majority voted for Nietzsche.]

Well, I must speak also in favor of Goethe's fairy tale. It is in a way interesting, and I don't doubt that there are things in it which might teach us a great deal. But one point speaks against it. I studied it recently in view of the possibility of dealing with it here and I was amazed

893

at the amount of alchemistic knowledge it contained; this is not a mere hypothesis because we know that when Goethe was studying in Leipzig he read a great deal about alchemy, and that is something which we do not encounter in Nietzsche. Nietzsche read very little because his eyes were bad, and most of his material was drawn out of his own unconscious and not out of contemporary or historical literature. Whereas Goethe read a great deal and particularly things with which you would be very little acquainted. Until about two years ago I also would not have been able to give a satisfactory interpretation of that fairy tale because I had not then read the Latin alchemistic tracts. Of course I can now say something about it, but I am afraid I should have to give you an almost complete picture of the work done in medieval philosophy, what medieval philosophy tried to accomplish, which I could not possibly expect you to know; you would not be in a position to value those attempts because it needs a very special knowledge. So looked at from this particular angle the task would not be easy. I am afraid I would have to say things which would go right into the air, simply because you would not have the necessary basis or the necessary form in which to receive those allusions. You know, there is a very particular language in alchemy and we would get rather far away from the present time.

You must not forget that Goethe died more than a hundred years ago; he lived in the end of the second half of the 18th century, and despite all his pre-vision he was a man of the Middle Ages who really lived and thought and felt in the mind and the spirit of the Middle Ages; one sees it from this fairy tale very clearly. Of course, Goethe's greatest fairy tale is *Faust*, and *Faust* is also an alchemistic mystery story. I don't know whether there is any commentary in existence which has come anywhere near an understanding of the enormous alchemistic contribution to *Faust*; Goethe had read a great deal. Now Nietzsche has nothing of that medieval spirit; he is very much the man of the 19th century, completely severed from medieval tradition, and so he takes his material directly from the unconscious. Of course he tries to formulate it sometimes, to twist it into the form of the 19th century, and naturally he then exhibits all the disadvantages of the mind of that time, a mind which had been uprooted. If he had had the continuity of culture which Goethe possessed through his connection with alchemistic philosophy, it surely would have helped him tremendously to formulate his ideas. But it sometimes needs a complete destruction and a complete separation from historical continuity in order to be able to envisage something new.

You see, in *Faust* the solution is absolutely medieval: Faust knows completion only when he arrives in heaven. Whereas Nietzsche never arrives in heaven; he seeks his solution in the here-and-now, and that is the modern point of view. He tries not to be metaphysical, which is very much the spirit of our time; we try not to be metaphysical, at least in the sense of that word as defined by the medieval mind. While Goethe's is still the medieval mind, he tries to find the medicine of immortality. Nietzsche of course cannot get away from certain eternal truths but consciously at least he is not seeking that elixir of life. Therefore, *Zarathustra* is in a way a document of our time, and it surely has much to do with our own psychological condition. I quite understand that it may have very bad effects, I myself often felt when I was plowing through the text that it had disagreeable effects upon me. There are passages which I intensely dislike and they really are irritating. But when you plow through your own psychology you also come across certain irritating places. So when I am irritated in those places in *Zarathustra* I say, well, here is a sore spot or an open wound. I take note of it, and then I know where the trouble is. I would advise you to take it in the same way, and then I think we can get safely through. You see, when we can stand *Zarathustra* we can stand a part of our modern world, particularly our European world; we feel it here very immediately.

We stopped last term at the chapter about the Happy Isles. We are now at a critical point in *Zarathustra*. You remember in the chapter before, "The Child with the Mirror," we encountered old Wotan, and we discovered that Zarathustra was there becoming more or less identical with Wotan; he was filled with that peculiar spirit. We talked at length about the psychology of Wotan then, and I must ask the new members of the seminar to read the last report in order to get the continuity. But I quite realize that it will be a bit difficult and therefore I will try to indicate a little the development of thought we have hitherto traced in *Zarathustra*. You remember in the last chapter, "The Child with the Mirror," we encountered also the lioness that gave birth to a cub. The first appearance of the lion is in chapter 1, "The Three Metamorphoses," and in order to see where we are now, we had best have recourse to that chapter, where Zarathustra says.

> Three metamorphoses of the spirit do I designate to you: how the spirit becometh a camel, the camel a lion, and the lion at last a child.

Then in the chapter about the child with the mirror he says, "Too great hath been the tension of my cloud: 'twixt laughters of lightnings will I cast hail-showers into the depths." Now that tension in the cloud is the state of pregnancy of the lioness. You see, the thunderstorm is a natural catastrophe; it is an analogy to the lioness that is pregnant with young and about to bring forth. The tension of the cloud, which is a well-known speech metaphor in *Zarathustra*, always denotes a state of pregnancy. And that is the mental pregnancy of the camel that carries the heavy load: the camel transforms into a lion that then brings forth. So we are now at the point where the third metamorphosis begins. The lion brings forth young, but it is not a child. It is a so-called animal pre-stage; that is a symbolic mechanism which we encounter very often in dreams.

For instance, if you dream of a certain animal, whatever it does is an anticipation of what is prepared in your instincts, just as what the animus figure does is always an anticipation; so animals mean unconscious movements or tendencies towards what you are going to do, or what is going to happen to you. You see, in the actual functioning of the psyche, it does not matter whether you do a thing or whether it happens to you; whether it reaches you from without or happens within, fate moves through yourself and outside circumstances equally. It is as if outside circumstances were simply projections of your own psychological structure. Of course subjectively it matters a lot, but psychologically it does not matter whether you are the cause of the misfortune or whether the misfortune comes to you. In either case you are miserable and that is all that counts; you are the victim whether it is a self-inflicted misery or whether the world has inflicted it upon you. If the animal appears in the dream, you cannot say whether it is an objective or a subjective tendency, whether it will come from within or without. It is hovering about you and something is going to happen to you, or you are going to do something. If the latter, you will surely be moved, for it happens to you from within exactly as if it had happened from without. And the reason why we have psychology is to make conscious that instinctive motive or that moving cause in the instincts, because by making it conscious you can keep it at a certain distance, or modify it; you may be able to bend or mitigate it—give it a human form. Or you can avoid perhaps the destructive effects if the thing happens from without; but when things take that course—when they happen from without—you are unable to mitigate them very much: you cannot change circumstances to any great extent. Then you are helpless, the victim. Of course you can also do very little when things happen in a merely instinctive form. If you are unconscious of it, you are swept off your feet as if by a motor car; you cannot stand up against it. Only by being conscious have you a fair chance to do something for or against it.

Now the transformation of the camel into the lion has happened in the chapters before and we did not notice how it happened. That the camel means a state of pregnancy, that it carries the heavy load, was to be seen in that first chapter:

> Many heavy things are there for the spirit, the strong load-bearing spirit in which reverence dwelleth: for the heavy and the heaviest longeth its strength.
>
> "What is heavy?" so asketh the load-bearing spirit; then kneeleth it down like the camel, and wanteth to be well laden.

That is a pregnant spirit or a mind. The German word *Geist* has that double meaning of spirit and mind, one never can make a difference, so it can be understood here just as well as mind. And that load-bearing mind is a pregnant mind. He has taken up the whole load, is pregnant with the whole problem of his time; and in carrying that problem, under the influence of that pregnancy, the mind changes into the form of the lion. In other words, out of the suppression by the load develops a spirit of freedom and independence and liberty, the spirit of the animal of prey. You can easily understand such a transformation; if you have been oppressed by a certain load for a long time, wild rebellious instincts begin to break out in you because you hate to carry it. So the lion is the law-breaker. Just as to the primitive man the lion is the law-breaker, the great nuisance, dangerous to human beings and to animals, that breaks into the Kraal at night and fetches the bull out of the herd: he is the destructive instinct. And mythologically the lion has that same quality as the symbol of the hottest month of the year. It is the sign of the *domicilium solis*, the symbol for the time immediately after the summer solstice when, in those countries where the zodiac originated, all the vegetation is parched and burnt by the sun; its devouring heat destroys whatever nature has built up before. The lion, then, is a destructive, law-breaking animal that develops out of the spirit that is weighed down by the load of the great problems of the time. Just as Zarathustra declares that God is dead and becomes a god himself, so the lion shakes off his fetters and burdens and begins to break laws. But by destroying the spirit of the camel he becomes the pregnant animal himself. That is not for long, however; the lion seldom symbolizes the carrying animal because it is naturally the law-breaking instinct, but it does here immediately produce young, so we see in a glimpse that we are just crossing from the second metamorphosis to the third, from the lion to the child as was foretold in the beginning of *Zarathustra*.

Now, I am not at all convinced that when Nietzsche wrote about the three metamorphoses, he foresaw that later on he would come back to it as it were, or that he intended *Zarathustra* to have such an inner structure; in that case, I think he would have shown more signs of it. It just happens in this way, and this is the way in which the unconscious development always takes place; namely, it has its own structure and its own laws, so the anticipation in the beginning really comes off in the subsequent text. That change in the spirit when the camel has come to an end and the lion begins, is also shown in the apparition of Wotan, who is also a law-breaking spirit—the spirit that appears when the load of the past is shaken off or the spirit that makes one shake off the load of the past. It is an absolutely detached free spirit that appears here and there with no continuity whatever, a wanderer with no obligations, whose sole purpose is to arouse life and trouble and strife and misunderstanding. Wotan is also the great sorcerer, and he is a spirit of enthusiasm, of ecstasy; therefore he has very much in common with Dionysos.

If you have any knowledge of Greek religion, you know that there was the same difficulty when the Greeks were confronted with the task of integrating that Dionysian spirit; first, there was some trouble over the Delphic oracle and they finally settled that claim in such a way that Dionysos became a shareholder in Delphi having equal rights with Apollo. They were fifty-fifty and so it worked; in that way they could arrange themselves with that Dionysian spirit without upsetting Olympus, and Zeus remained on top. But Wotan is a different proposition: he is not alone but all the others are of a somewhat different character—Loki, for instance, and such fellows. Yet Wotan is the supreme god. There is no Zeus above him and therefore he is an uncontrolled factor; he doesn't appear in a nicely governed house like Olympus where Hera was always looking out that Zeus didn't raise Cain too much. So Dionysos could be assimilated while Wotan is an unassimilated element. He is the spirit of the lion, and out of that spirit the child is born—for the time being only a lion cub, something absolutely undefined which needs development and care. So no wonder that we come now to the motive of the Happy Isles. We said at the end of last term that the idea of the Happy Isles is often connected with the idea of birth. You probably know some examples.

Mrs. Crowley: Apollo.

Prof. Jung: Apollo himself was born on an island because his mother

Leto was persecuted by Hera; this was one of those domestic cases of Olympus. She was the sweetheart of old Zeus and Hera was awfully jealous and had made a contract with everybody on earth not to give harbor to her. But finally poor Leto reached that island which had been submerged in the ocean and which happened to come to the surface just then, and there she gave birth to the child. And Poseidon—always a bit on the wrong side you know—was very favorable and made four pillars by which the island was rooted fast to the ground of the ocean, so Leto had a nice bed for her child by the god. Now, the four points created for the birth of the god is very clearly a mandala, and it is absolutely necessary that the god have such a safe place, because his birth is always a bit incommoded by rationalists like old Herod who killed hundreds of boys in order to reach the right one. Then there are other cases: there is a very nice one in the New Testament, a bit more obscure but very typical.

Mrs. Crowley: Do you mean Christ's birth?

Prof. Jung: Yes, that would be just what we were speaking of. They had to make for Egypt—Egypt was their happy island—and that was all on account of Herod who was somewhat upset by the birth of the God. But there is another case in the New Testament, in Revelations.

Mrs. Bennett: Do you mean the star-woman who had to go into the wilderness to give birth?

Prof. Jung: Yes, the star-woman gave birth to a son. And then we go right into Greek mythology; the old python from Delphi was after her—she was like Leto, like the birth of Apollo; a dragon went after her and spat a huge river in order to drown her and the child. That shows at the same time the danger of the divine birth. How would you define that?

Mrs. Baynes: The whole of the past rises against the new, trying to swallow it back again.

Prof. Jung: Exactly, and in what form does the past appear?

Mrs. Baynes: As a monster.

Prof. Jung: Yes, and what does that denote psychologically? How is the past represented in us?

Mrs. Baynes: It is the resistance in the unconscious.

Prof. Jung: Yes, the collective unconscious is the storehouse of the past, so it has that historical aspect; the collective unconscious is the swallowing dragon. We find that in the first chapter of the three metamorphoses, where Zarathustra says:

"Thou-shalt," lieth in its path, sparkling with gold—a scale-covered beast; and on every scale glittereth golden, "thou-shalt."

899

You see, this is the law of the past, exactly the same weight of tradition which St. Paul refers to when he says the law has been overcome and a higher law has been given unto us.[1]

The values of a thousand years glitter on those scales, and thus speaketh the mightiest of all dragons: "All the values of things—glitter on me.

All values have already been created, and all created values—do I represent. Verily, there shall be no 'I will' any more." Thus speaketh the dragon.

The dragon represents the historical mind, or the historical fact of our consciousness, and this is naturally in opposition to all human creations; therefore it needs a lion to destroy it. And why is it just the dragon that is such a very usual symbol for the unconscious?

Miss Hannah: You mean more than the whale?

Prof. Jung: Well, the dragon to the *consensus gentium* is a better example for the unconscious than the whale; the whale is only a local celebrity while the dragon is an absolutely universal representative in time as well as space. It is even represented where there are none: we have seen whales but we have never seen a dragon. The dragon is an age-old archetype handed down I suppose from the age when man and dragons lived at the same time—when man lived with saurians and bad saurians at that.

Mrs. von Roques: Is it because it consists of several different parts, wings and so on?

Prof. Jung: That shows the mythological character of the beast, but why is it just a dragon? It is very important in trying to understand a dream with a dragon or a snake or some other saurian-like animal, that you know what it means. Then you can localize things.

Mrs. Baumann: On account of its sympathetic nervous system?

Prof. Jung: Other animals have that.

Mrs. Crowley: Does he really not represent all the unassimilated forces of the unconscious that are such a power against one?

Prof. Jung: Oh yes, but what would it be if it were a worm?

Mrs. Crowley: Then it could be overcome.

Prof. Jung: But it might be like an octopus. No, the dragon, as well as the snake or the salamander, or even the frog, are representations of that part of the psyche which is immediately below our higher animal

---

[1] St. Paul: "For the law of the spirit of life in Christ Jesus has set you free from the law of sin and of death" (Romans 8:2).

psyche. The psyche of monkeys is not in the dragon. The dragon is supposed to be a cold-blooded animal. It has a long tail and scales, and on account of the fact that it has no warm blood, it represents the inhuman, cold-blooded part of our psychology. In many saurians the great intumescence of nervous matter is not even in the brain, which is exceedingly small, but in the lower part of the spinal cord. So the dragon shows that it is a matter of that part of the unconscious which is strongly identical with the body, *including* naturally the sympathetic system. But the sympathetic system has its proper symbols, it is symbolized by invertebrate animals, not only the cold-blooded ones—spiders and other insects, and crabs and the octopus are all symbols for the sympathetic system. These are by no means arbitrary interpretations therefore; they are all based upon experience. You know very well why I say that the dragon or the snake has to do with the spinal system, and why the spider, for instance, has to do with the sympathetic system; you see, the unconscious does not choose those symbols with a complete ignorance of zoology. They are born out of the very substance which you also find in those animals. We contain nature, are part of it; animals are not only in text books, but are living things with which we are in contact. Probably in our remote ancestry we have gone through those stages and therefore the imprints are still to be found in us. As certainly as we have a sympathetic rope-ladder system within ourselves, have we to do with insects and worms or any such invertebrate animals.

So the dragon represents not only a human past—say the laws and convictions of a thousand years ago, those of warm-blooded animals— the dragon goes back much further. And the real power we encounter in those old laws is not *their* power, but the power that has been fettered by them; the laws of five thousand years ago, primitive moral laws or primitive religious convictions, would have absolutely no power and no interest for us if they were standing by themselves, but they are still the fetters round the ankles or the necks of dragons, and *they* give them their weight. These very old destructive instincts in man were caught by the old symbolic forms, and inasmuch as these forms still seem to play a role in us, it is due to the fact that they are still in their place, still fettering those old instincts, but unconsciously. For instance, Christianity, which has become unconscious to so many people, is still doing its duty; we are unconscious of its way of doing it but it is still working, still a power over the old dragon. But naturally the further you get away from the history or the continuity of consciousness, the more you forget the purpose of certain religious convictions and of certain laws.

And the more your interest is withdrawn from such forms, the more they are weakened, till the moment comes when they no longer function, and then the dragon breaks loose.

But there are conditions, as we learn from *Zarathustra*, where that old dragon really has to be disturbed, where we must have a lion to destroy old forms in order to give a new form to old instincts and a new protection against old dangers. And that of course is the case here; the dragon ought to be fought by the lion. You see, all the old values that served the purpose of fettering the dragons became identical with the dragon, because we no longer see what those values meant. For instance, we don't understand why God should be a trinity—that conveys nothing to us—yet it was an exceedingly important concept once. It needs now a long dissertation to explain why it was absolutely important that Arianism, the idea that Jesus was not of the same substance as God, should not win out; he must be God and man at the same time completely, and not only God-like. These questions are strange to us; even theologians now avoid speaking too definitely about them. But they have a very definite psychological meaning, and people once fought and killed each other for this or that most abstruse dogma, for the *homoousia* for instance, which meant that God and man were *equal* in substance, or the *homoiousia* which meant that they were *similar* in substance. It was as if those people knew what they were about; of course they could not know as we can from this distance, but they knew it was all-important and that was enough. I understand these things now in such a way that I think I understand why they had to fight each other, why the question had to be decided in favor of *homoiousia*. It was of absolutely indispensable psychological importance. Of course I cannot explain this to you now; you must be satisfied with the fact that those old forms like the Trinity have had their functional meaning, and that it is a loss to get away from them and forget about them. You don't understand why certain doors are locked because you don't know what is behind them, but destroy those doors and you will discover the dragon behind them; you will even think that the doors are identical with this dragon that is your enemy.

You see, when Nietzsche destroys God, he then becomes identical with the idea that people have no god. But a god is a very definite psychological fact; it is the strongest thing to which man always succumbs, whatever it is. If you deny the existence of such a thing it simply takes you by the neck from behind. If you deny the fact that you are hungry, for instance, and go without eating, hunger will overcome you and you will faint; hunger will prove to be the stronger. Also a psychological fact will get you from behind, most certainly. But you can only do that most foolish thing—deny a psychological fact—when you have gone too far away from a real knowledge of the human soul. If you knew what reality that fact possesses which has been called God, you would know that you could not possibly get away from it. But you have lost sight of it; you don't know what that thing means and so it gets at you unconsciously, and then without knowing it you are transformed into God almighty, as happened to Nietzsche. It got into him to such an extent that he went crazy and signed his letters "the dismembered Zagreus," or "Christ Dionysos," because he became identical with the God he had eliminated. You see, inasmuch as we have eliminated God to a great extent, it is just as if we were all denying the fact that we were hungry, but then we begin to eat each other; we get so hungry that a catastrophe will follow: appetites will be developed in us which we would not have if these psychological factors were in the right place. But we now think that the progress of thought and the development of the human mind is hampered by the existence of such old prejudices, and we destroy those old forms because we think that we are gods and can do without them, that they were mere hindrances. There, of course, is the great danger of any creation: it destroys something which should not be destroyed, and out of that develop most catastrophic consequences, as in Nietzsche's case. Now, that child or that cub born of the lioness expresses what idea?

Mrs. Baynes: The Superman.

Prof. Jung: Of course, and the idea of the Superman is perfectly nice, a thing one can reasonably discuss, but in Nietzsche's case it is very complicated through his identification with the deity—the Superman takes the place of the deity. So since God is dead, that child who is born would be the birth of the god in animal form, which means the birth of the god in the unconscious; and whatever the leading idea of that human consciousness may be, below which such a birth takes place, it will be inflated by the admixture of the archetype, with the idea of the deity. Since the Superman assumes the place of a god, Nietzsche will himself be in the place of God. Now we will begin the next chapter.

> The figs fall from the trees, they are good and sweet; and in falling the red skins of them break. A north wind am I to ripe figs.

His identity with the north wind is of course the identity with Wotan, and that phenomenon is preparatory to bringing out whatever is ready, whatever is already mature. Wotan is a phenomenon like Dionysos who is also a god of vegetation; it means a sort of enthusiastic or

ecstatic condition in which those things which are already in the unconscious reach the daylight.

> Thus, like figs, do these doctrines fall for you, my friends: im-
> bibe now their juice and their sweet substance! It is autumn all
> around, and clear sky, and afternoon.
> Lo, what fulness is around us! And out of the midst of super-
> abundance, it is delightful to look out upon distant seas.
> Once did people say God, when they looked out upon distant
> seas; now, however, have I taught you to say, Superman.

Here we have the whole weakness of the argument—that people will
go on calling upon God when they look out upon distant seas. They
will say, "God, how wonderful!" just as the primitive Polynesians when
they hear a gramophone say, "Mulungu," meaning, "Is it not great!"
Whenever we are really astonished or overcome by something, whatever it is, either in a positive or a negative way, we exclaim, "God!" And
we swear by God; even people who do not believe in God swear and say
"God damn you!" A Frenchman says, "Oh, mon Dieu" on the slightest
provocation, and a German says, "Ach Gott, lass mich in Ruhe," or
something of the sort. Any Italian workman cries, "Per Dio" even
when he is in a club of atheists or those Bolshevist clubs that try to kill
God. It is so much in our language. You will never find a single individual who says, "Oh Superman, what a fool you are!"—nobody will
ever swear by the Superman. So God is a natural phenomenon; it is the
word that designates the thing that makes me. You see, the word *God*
has nothing to do with good; it comes from the root meaning "to be-
get." He is the begetter of things, the creator, the maker of things. Anything that makes me, anything that creates my actual mood, or anything that is greater or stronger than myself—that is like my father—
that is called "God." When I am overcome by emotion, it is positively a
god, and that is what people have always called "God," a god of wrath,
or a god of joy, or a god of love, for instance. They have understood
emotions as personalities in themselves. Instead of getting angry, the
demon of anger, an evil spirit, has entered my system, and makes me—
creates me—into an angry form, and therefore he is a god. And that
will be so forever as long as people are overcome by emotions, as long
as they are not free.

Now Zarathustra, who is in a way the anticipation of the Superman,
is overcome by all sorts of events: he gets angry, he weeps, he is the
prey of his emotions exactly like Nietzsche. Later, there is a very classical passage where you can see what happens when one thinks one is

doing a thing which one is really not doing: when one thinks one is the creator of things, one is the victim of things. So this primitive phenomenon which people call "God" is merely a statement of an overwhelming fact; there are parts of my psychical system which overwhelm me at times. And since times immemorial, man has used such a figure of speech. Of course there are certain idiots who have thought my conception of God was nothing but a human emotion; those are the idiots who think they know what an emotion is. Now, I am not among them. I only know a *phenomenon* called "emotion," but I could not tell you what it is because I don't know what a psyche is—I have no idea what it is. So when I say that phenomenon is called "God" I don't give a definition of God. I give a definition of that word and I leave it to him to manifest as he will; if he chooses to manifest through the worst sin that is his affair. But those idiots who speak of emotion think they know what it is, or when I speak of the psyche they think they know what that is. Ask a physicist what matter is. This is a hair-raising question. So you never can really suppress the psychological fact of God through teaching the Superman, but it is of course a different question when it comes to the interpretation of Nietzsche's concept of the Superman.

The definition we have made out as the probable or true one is that he really means the psychological concept of the self, but he makes the mistake of identifying with that idea; so the Superman becomes a sort of person within one's reach more or less—that can be reached, say, in several generations. You will see in the continuation of the text that though you may not now be able to create a Superman, your great-grandson will perhaps be the Superman. Now, inasmuch as the Superman is another term for the self, it is possible that the idea of a deity can transmigrate into another form, because the fact of God has been called by all names in all times. There are, one could say, millions of names and formulations for the fact of God, so why not the self, quite easily? You know that has already been done in the philosophy of the Upanishads and the Tantric philosophy for instance; they had that formulation long ago. And the Christian conception of the Kingdom of Heaven within yourself contains all the symbolism of the self: the fortified city, the precious pearl, the stone, or the gold—there are plenty of symbols for the self. It is also in Greek philosophy; Empedocles, for example, had the conception that the all-round being, the *sphairos*, was the *eudaimonéstatos theós*, the most blissful God.[2] Well, I

---

[2] In fragment 28, Empedocles of Acragas (fl. c. 450 B.C.) wrote, "But he [God] is equal

think it must be rendered something like that: it must be one that is filled with the most blissful spirit and all-round like the Platonic primordial being, which is also the idea of the self. So there are on all sides possibilities of identifying the idea of the divine factor with the self of man. If you want to go a bit deeper into the definition of the self you must look up the literature; I should advise you, for instance, to read the *Eranos* of 1934 where Prof. Hauer has a very interesting article about the symbols of the self in the Upanishads and the Tantric philosophy.[3]

Inasmuch, then, as you don't identify the idea of the self with the person, with the subject, the ego man, it can be named a god just as well—that would be quite permissible—and it is quite apt to receive the substance of the divine factor. I think this is the most valuable kernel in Nietzsche's teaching, and it is the message to our time, in that it contains the doctrine of individuation, namely: that it is the duty of our time to help to create the Superman, to prepare the way of the Superman. But the moment you identify with the possible Superman or think that your grandson might be the Superman, you fall into the same trap that Nietzsche fell into—that he identifies with an intuition. That is dangerous. If you can keep clear of that trap, it is really the answer of the whole psychological development throughout the Middle Ages. It is the logical development out of Protestantism, for instance, inasmuch as Protestantism has deprived the church of its authority.

You see, the authority of the church is the authority of the dogma, and the authority of the dogma signifies or expresses the absolute authority of the divine factor, for the divine factor is then deprived of its subjectivity. If you destroy the absolute authority of the church, the dogma, as Protestantism has done, you allow interpretations; and then naturally God becomes very relative to your interpretation. Then you can say God is absolutely outside of yourself and you can pass judgment on him: he has no authority any longer. You know that you hold one point of view and other people hold another; inasmuch as God is no longer guaranteed by the indisputable dogma of the church, he is *à votre disposition*;[4] then you can model him, say things about him, like the

---

in all directions to himself and altogether eternal, a rounded sphere enjoying a circular solitude" (Freeman*).

[3] The Eranos lectures in 1934 centered around the theme, "Symbolism and Spiritual Guidance in the East and the West." Professor J. W. Hauer of Tübingen University gave a paper entitled "Symbols and Experience of the Self in Indo-Aryan Mysticism."

[4] "To your own way of thinking."

famous modern Protestant Gogarten who says God can only be good.[5] He thinks he is saying something awfully nice about God but that is blasphemous. He deprives God of his possibilities. He leaves him no choice. Think of the marvelous things you can do when you are also bad!

When you take the sayings of the Bible as the absolute authority, the word of God, it is just as if you were prohibiting a writer from publishing anything else. For two thousand years God has been under the censorship of the priests. He could not publish a new book, he could do nothing, because he had said in the Bible what he had to say and nothing could ever be changed. That is a catastrophe because it is an encroachment upon divine rights, and moreover it is absolutely unpsychological inasmuch as the divine factor changes. Inasmuch as the divine factor does *not* change, God remains the same and then the holy book is the absolute authority, the truth, because it catches the unconscious facts and expresses them. You need nothing else—then it is absolute. But the moment man changes, or the moment God changes, his truth is no longer his truth—it does not express him—and the authority of the hitherto prevailing notions comes to an end. Then there will be a Protestant revolution, as was actually the case. One can say that towards the end of the 15th century, God changed noticeably, or man changed noticeably. You see the two must always be together; yet they are two, and you cannot say who changes first. If you are a pious individual you will say God has changed, and if you are a worldly individual you will say man has changed and in order to suit man God was forced to say something new. But it doesn't matter which is older, the egg or the hen: the change came about and the old truth was no longer a truth.

So all that truth that made the church, that made the dogma, that made finally the eternally valid quality of the notion of God—all that has collapsed and is to be found nowhere apparently. But nothing can get lost; all that authority is in the unconscious, and of course then you have it in your own body and you become all-important. Then you begin to believe in individualism and such things, and the time of the great individuals begins. That was in about the 16th century, we have certain confessions from those days which are highly interesting, the famous confession of Agrippa von Nettesheim, for instance, which I once quoted in my little biographical article about Paracelsus.[6] That

[5] For Gogarten, see above, 5 Dec. 1934, n. 4.

[6] This article (CW 15, pars. 1-17) began as a 1929 lecture given in the medieval phy-

was such an individualistic confession by a man for whom authority had completely collapsed, so that he himself became the authority: he was then identical with the absolutely divine uncertainty, with the creative uncertainty. If you know a bit about medieval psychology you will be able to substantiate what I say—it was a most interesting time then, a tremendous time. A certain megalomania that you find then in people is the God that came into man, and naturally in the first moment it had a great effect upon him. He became very enthusiastic and the kingdom of heaven descended upon earth; but then instantly came all the consequences of such an inflation. You know, after the Lutheran revolution immediately followed war, the terrible revolt of the peasants; it was an entirely mystical psychological movement but it was utterly destructive and of course it caused Luther to restrict his innovations considerably. Then came Protestantism, and there you see the interesting phenomenon that it has split up into about four hundred denominations, so its authority has gone utterly. In Switzerland, for instance, practically every parson preaches his own gospel and it is not interesting at all. It is very personal, with no synthesis, no continuity; it is all subjectified and there is not a trace of a church left. And that is so practically everywhere, except in countries like England where there is a very strong tradition, but even there Protestantism is split up into all sorts of sects and denominations. Only the Catholic church has kept the absolute form which guarantees the identity of God.

The ultimate outcome of that development will be that everybody will preach his own gospel. If preachers will preach to themselves there will be exceedingly useful monologues because everybody will then tell himself what is the matter with himself. Today they still tell other people what is the matter with them—they go on projecting. Of course there are always fools enough who believe it, and it is probably all right because everybody makes mistakes, so it works quite well. When you develop consistently as a true Protestant, of course you have to preach because God is in you, but do preach to yourself and then you are really on the way to the self. Do what Nietzsche admonishes you to do, be a camel, load yourself and then preach to yourself. I would say, don't even write such a book as *Zarathustra*; that is a concession we must

sician's home at Einsiedeln, Switzerland. See also CW 15, pars. 18-43, and CW 13, pars. 145-238. As characteristic of those times, Jung cites the motto of Agrippa von Nettesheim's book, *De incertitodine et vanitate scientiarium* (On Uncertain and Vain Science), 1527: Agrippa spares no man, / he contemns, knows, knows not, weakens, laughs, / Waxes wroth, reviles, carps at all things, / being, himself philosopher, demon, hero, god and all things (CW 15, par. 9).

allow to Mr. Nietzsche as a gifted writer, but it would have been ever so much better for him if he had preached it to himself. Of course if that moment should arrive, one would be absolutely alone. In all the millions of years before God created man, he had only his own society; if he talked at all he probably talked to himself. That is expressed in the Upanishads as a particularly lonesome condition in which the creator found himself. Therefore, he had to create an object and he created the world, the reason for the world was: that he might have an audience. So if we should arrive at the condition of being our own audience, preaching to ourselves, we would be in a way small gods isolated in the universe, all-important because we would be our only object, but at the same time quite miserable because we would be so alone.

Many serious Protestants are probably isolated on account of that: the whole responsibility of the world rests upon them and they are alone with it. If they repent, there is nobody to give them absolution; they depend perhaps upon the grace of God, but that conception of a god is very unsafe because they *have* to believe it. When you ask how they arrive at the idea of God, they say one must believe it. But why should I believe such a thing? Well, the word of God says so. But Paul did not believe in that kind of God at all; he persecuted the Christians, until on his way to Damascus he experienced God and then he knew. That was *pistis*, the Greek word which means loyalty and confidence—it has nothing to do with believing. He trusted the fact that he had experienced something, because he had that experience he knew, and then he did not need to believe. So when our parsons say you ought to believe, it is a mere confession of bankruptcy; either you know a thing and then you don't need to believe it, or you don't know it and then why should you believe it? That whole question, therefore, is linked up with the experience of the divine intercession; without that experience there is no need to believe. Belief is good for the herd instinct. Then you can make a community song together; you can sing, "We all believe!"—and that makes what we call a church or a community. And there ceases the problem.

The problem with which Nietzsche is concerned cannot be even touched by people who are singing the community song, because they don't need to bother with it—they remain a remnant of the Catholic church. They did not develop as Protestants, but remained historical derelicts of the original Christian church. But if they develop further as Protestants they will necessarily come to the tremendous problem to which Nietzsche came, namely, to the idea of the Superman, to the idea of the thing in man that takes the place of the God that has been hitherto valid; they will then be concerned with what that is and what they should be in order to be able to deal with the terrible danger of inflation. When one begins to preach to oneself, then, one is in danger of megalomania, or of being utterly crushed by an overwhelming feeling of inferiority. You find both in modern man; on the one side, feelings of inferiority, and on the other side, a conviction of himself, an impertinent self-assertion or foolish megalomania. And you find those two things also in Zarathustra.

LECTURE II

13 May 1936

Prof. Jung:
Now we will go on with our text:

> God is a conjecture: but I do not wish your conjecturing to reach
> beyond your creating will.

We have often encountered the idea that God is a conjecture. It was a peculiar prejudice of that time, the second part of the 19th century, when people began to flirt with a sort of hypothesis which in antiquity was known as euhemerism. This term comes from the name of the Greek philosopher Euhemerus who had the idea that the gods were once human beings, that Zeus, for instance, had been a king or a powerful man like Heracles, and that afterwards people thought they were gods—legend made gods of them. So all the other gods who populated Olympus were supposed to have been remarkable historical figures that had become legendary, and Osiris also had been just a man. One finds practically the same idea in Carlyle's famous book, *Heroes and Hero Worship*; he sympathizes with such euhemeristic views.[1] It is an attempt at rationalizing the existence of the concept of gods. Now in the later part of the century, they began to think that God or the gods were not even euhemeristic persons, but that the conception really dated from nowhere, that it was a mere invention which always had been made, a sort of hypothesis entirely man-made.

You know, the whole 19th century was a time when people became aware of what man was doing. When some idea passed through a man's head, when he found himself talking or thinking, he became aware that *he* was thinking it, and then he assumed that *he* was the maker of his thinking. And that looking-upon-what-he-was-doing was called "psychology"; psychology was understood to be a science of hu-

---

[1] Thomas Carlyle (1795-1881), Scots essayist and historian. His best-known book, published in 1841, presents a theory of the hero with examples drawn from history.

man behavior, a science of consciousness exclusively. When something, an event, took place in man, the assumption was that he was the doer of that event or that process—of course only inasmuch as his so-called psychology was concerned. If he developed a cancer or suffered from typhoid fever, it was not supposed that he had made up his mind to suffer from those diseases, because it was obvious that such things *happened* to him. But when it was a matter of ideas or mental conditions he was made more or less responsible for the fact unless he was just crazy. It was assumed that one did not make a psychosis; a psychosis happened to one, like typhoid fever, from certain causes. But in the beginning of the century, in the time of the first alienists—the alienist is an invention of that century—one still believed that people made even a psychosis, that they brought a psychosis upon themselves by a misdemeanor, by certain bad customs or habits, by bad management or immorality and so on. There is a famous German textbook of those days which is entirely built upon that hypothesis that people are the makers of their insanity,[2] which is about the same as assuming them to be the makers of their own typhoid fever. But we are not yet so far as to assume that our psychology, our mind, the mental processes with which we identify, happen to us; that still seems to be a most adventurous idea. Yet as soon as the mind is a bit crazy, we are inclined to be human enough to think that it happened. For instance, when you become acquainted with the extraordinary ideas of Nietzsche, you say, "Oh, that is insanity. He was forced to say such things. It is a "symptom." But to him it was not so; that was what he *wanted*, it was his will to say such things. It would of course have been ever so much better for him if he had been able to see that those things were happening to him; then he could have asked himself what they really meant and who was behind the screen making him say them. Then he would have been able to detach from Zarathustra. But he couldn't because he assumed that he was the maker of Zarathustra. His unconscious behaved very fairly to him: it made him see that he and Zarathustra were two. His famous words are, *Da wurde eins zu zwei und Zarathustra ging an mir vor-*

---

[2] Although Richard von Krafft-Ebing might not have agreed to this characterization, his *Text-book of Insanity based on Clinical Observations* (tr. C. G. Chaddock, Philadelphia, 1904; orig. Stuttgart, 1879) was much the most popular work in its field for many years. Elsewhere Jung told of happening upon this work when he was trying to decide upon his own medical specialization and was having a "violent reaction" to it because its author spoke of the "subjective character" of psychiatric textbooks, and of psychoses as diseases of personality. Jung knew on the moment where his destiny lay. See *MDR*, pp. 108-9/ 111.

bei. He paid no attention, however, because he thought that whatever man is or whatever he has done, *he* has done it, that the ego emanates such things based on its own proper will, that it is the creative will of the ego to bring them about. And naturally, when one makes such an assumption, one has to take all the responsibility for the whole procedure on oneself. Then *I* am the maker of God. I am the maker of Zarathustra. I am quite alone. I am the creator of my own world—nothing is happening to me because whatever is, is myself. Nietzsche is absolutely in the position of the creator of a world. A god could say, "I am the world. In every bit of the world I am—whatever happens is myself. I am doing it. I am every kind of foolishness, every crime, every joy, every beauty. I am everything and there is nothing outside."

You see, this identification with God is the trap into which the later part of the 19th century eventually fell, because they did not see how much did happen to the mind. And mind you, in spite of the fact that science had already evolved so far that they did not take it as a particular sign of immorality when a man became mentally ill: it was a misfortune. His father had been perhaps a drinker, or suffered from syphilis; and if there had been epileptics in the family, it was quite natural that a case of the same nature should occur, that children should be born with weak brains and might possibly become insane. That was the beginning of a newer and truer conception. One must go only a bit further to get rid of all that 19th-century prejudice, and then we would not consider ourselves exclusively responsible for what we think or do: we would know that things really happen to us. We are not free, not creative centers who probably will create supermen. We are very poor. Our free will is very limited. We are so dependent upon our surroundings, our education, our parents, because we are born with certain archetypes, or with certain disturbances.

And as we cannot make an insane person responsible for his insanity, so we cannot make Nietzsche responsible for the fact that he thought he could make or undo God, or that he could make the Superman or Zarathustra. He could not avoid thinking like that, first of all because of his time—he was under the same prejudice. He could not avoid thinking he produced Zarathustra, though he himself chose that name of the old prophet in order to denote the fact that Zarathustra had existed long before there was a Nietzsche. The archetype of the wise old man has existed since times immemorial; you find it everywhere and it is by no means Nietzsche's creation. Yet he thought he could create such things. So he participated in the attitude of his time that had not developed enough along the lines of objective consciousness.

We in the 20th century begin now to extend an objective scientific point of view into the sphere of the so-called normal functioning of the mind; and we begin to understand that our mental processes are occurrences or events to a much higher degree than has ever been thought before. And if you can join in such a conviction you have the possibility—which proves to be an exceedingly useful one—of detaching from such figures. You can assume that they have life of their own and that they make themselves; and that you come in simply in the way of a perceiving eye, or that you suffer from it exactly as you suffer from the effect of a bad inheritance. You see, when there is epilepsy in your family you might inherit epilepsy or at least a trace of it in your character, showing in emotionalism perhaps or in peculiar dreams, and naturally you are inclined to think you have surely made those dreams or emotions and that you are very bad. Then you discover it is all inheritance, so how can you avoid it? You found yourself in a body which has such-and-such disadvantages, as you found yourself with such-and-such a brain which has its bad or good dispositions. You see, if you don't identify with your vices, you have no chance to identify with your virtues; as little as we are our inherited virtues are we our inherited vices. But if we don't identify, we have a chance to discover what this poor ego is and we can learn how to deal with the inherited factors of our mind. Then we have a chance to gain freedom. As long as you assume that you are making the weather, what can you do? You will try in vain to make good weather and you never will succeed, and because you are all the time angry at yourself for making rain, you never will invent an umbrella. You will suffer from those hellish feelings of inferiority instead of inventing a good umbrella. So inasmuch as Nietzsche assumed that God was a conjecture, it is quite logical when he says, "But I do not wish your conjecturing to reach beyond your creating will." In other words, you must not make conjectures which you are unable to fulfil because, he continues,

> Could ye *create* a God?—Then, I pray you, be silent about all Gods! But ye could well create the Superman.

Of course you cannot create a God, so why conjecture a God? This is of course based upon the assumption that such things only exist because man creates them. But if you leave open the possibility that God exists without man's invention, this whole argument is naturally futile because man has nothing to do with it; God is or is not: he is beyond man's reach. Sure enough, the idea of God or God's image is very much influenced by the disposition of man in time and space, by his temperament and so on, but it is a universal fact that everywhere we encounter certain ideas which are equivalents of this basic experience of man: namely, that outside his own will, or beside his own will, there is still another will, whatever that is. For instance, if he tries to be nice, he finds he is cross; if he wants to say something good, he says something bad; if he wants to tell the truth, he lies. He is constantly interfered with by something which is not his own will. In this experience, he is as if possessed by ghosts or evil influences—or by God, the ultimate receptacle, one could say, of all the magic crossing of man's individual purposes. Now, this basic experience is not an invention of man, but simply a fact, a fact that is every day under your nose; and if you want to see how it came about that people called it finally "God," study the life of the primitives.

Or study only the cases right under your eyes. For instance, suppose you have something to do with a very temperamental person who easily becomes emotional and angry, and flies into one of his fits when you say something awkward. Then you say to him, "But now look here, you are beside yourself; be yourself, be reasonable. I cannot understand what devil has gotten into you that makes you talk such foolish stuff." You treat that person as if he had been alienated from himself, as if a strange being had taken possession of him. If you are living under primitive circumstances and using the terminology that is provided by your surroundings, you say, "Oh well, at times a bad spirit goes into that man," and then you must try to eliminate it or wait until it has vanished and the man comes back to normality. A primitive explains an ordinary fit of emotion as a magic fact; if you study the history of religions and carefully analyse what is at the back of all these ideas, you see it is a psychological non-ego that has an influence on man. So if you are quite careful and really scientific you see that God is that which we have always observed; namely, that will which interferes with our own will, a tendency which crosses our own tendency, a thing clearly psychical as our consciousness is psychical. Of the very same nature perhaps, showing traces of intelligence and reason or cunning—all sorts of human qualities—being obviously something like a psychical thing, like man; but not exactly like man because it is so cunning and devilish, or benign and benevolent, as man is not.

So certain peculiar non-human qualities or habits have always been attributed to that other will and it was imagined as not quite human in appearance—a helpful animal for instance, a doctor-animal, or a man endowed with extraordinary witchcraft, a sort of superman, either half animal below or half animal above. Those were the very first symbols for the deity. And in history, even in the most advanced forms of the Christian religion, you find such ideas; Christ is symbolized as the lamb, and the Paraclete, the Comforter, the dove; God himself came down in the form of the dove in the baptismal mystery of Christ. And the Evangelists are still symbolized as half animals or complete animals. Angels are bird men, or only heads with two wings underneath and the body somehow gone. These are all monstrous ideas of divine beings, exceedingly primitive but quite apt as expressions of the peculiar non-human nature of those psychological events which cross our own ego-will.

Now, if Nietzsche had thought like that he would have asked about this figure which he must call "Zarathustra." He could have given him any other name but he chose "Zarathustra." Of course he had a rational explanation for it, but if he had lived in our time, he most certainly would have asked himself what it meant. He would have said, "Here appears a figure; have I made it? Did I premeditate it? Did I set out with the decision to create a figure called 'Zarathustra'?" Then he would have come to the conclusion that he never had dreamt of doing such a thing—it just happened. And he could not have avoided the discovery that here something had happened: *I* have not created it, it has created itself definitely; it is a magic experience, therefore I give it a name. I give it a form even. Perhaps that figure talks, perhaps it has life of its own, for I have not invented it: it made itself. And then he would have landed with the conviction: if Zarathustra can come to life again, why not God? Is Zarathustra in any way different from a conception of God? Not at all. God has been understood to be a conception of the wise old man, and if any demon or hero can come into life again, why not God? So he would have discovered this tremendous error of his age, the idea that God was invented by man.

God never was invented, it was always an occurrence, a psychological experience—and mind you, it is still the same experience today. But in the 19th century the conditions were particularly unfavorable because they labored under that fact of having assumptions about God.

You see, things cannot be left unregulated. Particularly must they be defined when it comes to making a state or an institution like the church; and since God is an object of worship, something definite must be said about him. So the sayings of Jesus were used, for example that God was good, really the best thing in the world, and that he was a loving father. Now, all these sayings are perfectly true, but there is also the standpoint of the Old Testament, the fear of God. You cannot have the New Testament without the Old. The New Testament was the Jewish reformation of the Old Testament: it was Jewish Protestantism. The Jews were absolutely under the standpoint of the fear of God and law-abiding behavior, and therefore the reformer had to insist that God was not *only* to be feared. It was obvious from many passages and psalms that God was not only a law-giver and a policeman to punish the trespasser on the spot, but was also a loving father and really meant to be benevolent. He was exceedingly wise and kind and would give them everything they wanted. This Jewish Protestantism was then detached, and it was even a necessity to detach it, for the Gentiles to whom this Evangel was preached had no idea of a wrathful God. Their idea of a God was a beautiful and terrible force of nature with a personal psychology, and no moral purposes connected with it whatever.

You see, Zeus was a completely amoral proposition. He was a free lance even in his days, and there was nothing very respectable about Olympus or other heathen pantheons. There was no law to be observed, and there was no idea of good and bad: naturally the gods were very bad people too. If anyone behaved badly he was supposed to be possessed by Mars or something like that, or perhaps he had an affair with Venus and was caught by the husband. And all this *chronique scandaleuse* of Olympus proved that this was the condition of the world, the nature in which man lived. The Jewish standpoint was morality, obedience, the observance of the law; and the wrathful God was revengeful. Of course the Greek gods were also sometimes revengeful, but it was just bad moods, and there was no idea of a morally perfect God. Zeus was director of Olympus, but he was responsible to the great board of directors of the world, the *moîra*, an invisible influence, the *Société Anonyme* of Olympus,[3] so even Zeus could not do what he wanted. He was merely the appointed director and the *moîra* was above him.[4] So the gods were a restricted lot in a way, sort of superior hypertrophic human beings, representing aptly the human dispositions into which man is born.

The Jewish God was an entirely different thing. There was no judge above him in Israel. He was supreme. One sees that superiority in the Book of Job where he is betting with the devil over a man's soul; just for the sake of the experience he destroyed the herds and women and

---

[3] *Société Anonyme*: a corporation—indeed, a "faceless corporation."

[4] *Moîra*: destiny, though in Homeric times Moîrai were goddesses who could be blamed for misfortune.

children and slaves of the good man Job. He afflicted him with every pest under the sun in order to give a fair trial to the devil; and then God won out and gave everything back to Job. It was a very ruthless joke such as a feudal lord might play on his subject. But that is a very serious thing: it means that he is fate itself, a completely arbitrary fate that makes laws. Provided one obeys, one has a certain chance, but otherwise no chance whatever: there is only utter destruction. This is a very true picture of the world but in a horrible aspect, which of course has much to do with the history of that particular people who developed such an idea of God. The history of the Jewish tribes is full of blood and destruction. New excavations have shown that even in those times when they seemed to flourish, Egyptian kings were ruling over that country, and you can be sure the Jewish colonies did not feel particularly good under a strange ruler; so they saw God as just that, a tyrant who issued laws, and if they did not obey they were in hell.

Now, under the influence of the times, that Jewish emigration into Egypt, with the possibility of joining in the life of a civilization where there were human laws—there was a large colony in Alexandria for instance—brought about a great change which can be seen in the wisdom of "Proverbs" and "Ecclesiastes" quite particularly. And then in the Jewish Reformation called Christianity. There the benevolent, benign side of God was insisted upon and the old idea of the law was abolished to a great extent. When that religion was taught to the Gentiles they necessarily had to detach the New Testament from the Old. This was done with very great care because the message had to be grafted upon an entirely different proposition or premise: namely, the premise of the dear old *Société Anonyme* of Olympus; all those beautiful and amusing and ridiculous figures had to be answered by a different kind of system. It was then that the syncretistic, Hellenistic Christianity came into existence. You know, what we call the Catholic church in our days is chiefly a codification or a solidification of Hellenistic syncretism, a syncretism of a very high order, where one finds all sorts of primitive, pagan remnants. *Syncretism* means growing together. It is like conglomeration. Conglomerate material consists of many different things which have come together and solidified, and syncretism is very much the same, a mixture of many things made into one. Hellenistic syncretism would be the age beginning about 200/300 years B.C. and lasting until the third or fourth century A.D. All the religions and philosophies of the Near East and the West grew together then and formed an entirely new mental atmosphere.

The different aspects of God then became specified, codified, dogmatized, because it was absolutely imperative that God should be a fitting being for the center of a Christian cult; he had to be the good father, and then there must also be a lot of talk about the devil. That Christian concept of the devil is not in the Jewish religion; of course there were evil powers but God himself was a yea and a nay. He was also the God of wrath; since their main religious emotion was the fear of God, they didn't need so much the concept of a devil. With Christianity came the split into pairs of opposites, so they had to invent a devil because that aspect, the evil experience of God, did exist and had to be formulated. But by that codification or dogmatization a prejudice was formed: God had to be something definite and he became apparently something quite one-sided, to whom bad jokes, for instance, could not be attributed; yet fate is full of very cruel jokes. They could not possibly assume that God was making a nuisance of the world, or dancing a world, or drunk with the world. All those conceptions had to be excluded, and so God got poorer and poorer and became one definite thing.

Naturally, the reaction had to come once people said such an image was man-made. Mind you, the image is not the thing; the experience of God is always there. It is the most frequent experience of man, but through that whole development in the past centuries it has become the rarest experience. There are people who go through the world and say they never experience God; they don't know what it is. But it is the simplest thing. When you go out of the room and tumble over the threshold, you say damn it, because there has been a bad spirit in the room who put up a leg for you to fall over: that is the original experience of something that happens to you which you did not want. Fate is crossing you every day. We ourselves are always doing just the things we don't want to do. And who is doing it? Well, that is the other being, and if you follow it up—if you carefully examine what that being means that is crossing your line—you will see something. But we never can see far: we explain everything by itself. In this case we fell over the threshold and in that case over a chair, and a threshold is never a chair, and that we fell over both doesn't matter. Or we tell a lie and say it is just this particular lie, and the next day it is another one. That is the way we cut up things. We cut up the experience of God all the time, so naturally we never experience God; we only experience certain little facts which mean nothing. They mean nothing because we put no meaning into them. It is as if you were reading a long string of letters only, and naturally it sounds crazy, but put them together and you read "In the Happy Isles," for instance, and that means something.

But that is the way we read our psychology, or the psychology of the deity: the thing that like lightning comes in between, that crosses our intentions. Read it consistently and you will see marvelous things. That is what we do in analytical psychology—we read not just the letters, but we try to put them together. For example, a few nights ago you dreamt so and so, the next night you dreamt of a railway, the night after of a battalion of infantry, and last night you dreamt that you had given birth to a child. Each night you have had dreams and you say they have nothing to do with each other. Now I advise you to write all those letters together in their natural sequence and then study this sequence; you will see something remarkable: that it is a continuous text. You will discover something about the psychology of that non-ego, discover why people have called it a "God" or a "demon"—whatever you prefer. Because this *is* a continuation, it makes sense; it is not merely a heap of elements which have nothing to do with each other.

Well now, God is a conjecture inasmuch as his image has become a dogmatized codified form, and as I said, this fact is the reason why such an idea had to be finally upset. Life itself could not tolerate any longer such a blasphemous restriction of the powers or the possibilities of the psychical phenomenon that is ultimately called "God." This psychical development was itself instinctively working up to a moment when the dogmatized image had to be destroyed. And Nietzsche comes out of a time whose feature was the overthrow of that image. But of course, as always happens, one goes too far and then suffers the consequences—in that case, the assumption that God didn't exist when man said he didn't exist. Just as there are people now who assume there is no unconscious because they say there is none. This is of course childish, but as there are still many infantile people, such infantile judgments are often repeated and even believed. If you have a certain amount of ordinary intelligence, you know that this is all bunk: you cannot do away with a thing by saying it is not; the phenomenon still exists no matter what you say about it. Now, when the assumption is made that God does not exist because he is said to be merely an invention, which is like assuming that there is no unconscious because you say there is none, then a very peculiar thing occurs: namely, something crosses your will. And what can you say? You cannot pretend that you yourself have crossed your will; you have not. It is crossed by something else. Then how can you explain that fact—I mean, if you think philosophically? Of course if you think practically—which means not thinking at all—you have not to explain it. Then you can let it go and say it is merely accidental; you don't make it an object of philosophy or of science. Then of course you haven't the task of explaining anything, but simply refuse to think. That is perfectly feasible of course; millions of people live without thinking. You can live without thinking if you happen to be that kind of person—that is the question. But if you happen to be a person who cannot live without thinking, what can you think about it? For if you say there is nothing that interferes, there is no unconscious—in other words there is no God, no non-ego psyche—then how can you explain things?

Mr. Allemann: You either become responsible for everything, or you have to invent something.

Prof. Jung: Well, people are very clever. To be responsible for everything is awkward. That is pretty big, and there are very humble natures who don't like to be responsible, so what do they assume?

Mrs. Naeff: They make others responsible.

Prof. Jung: Naturally, they simply transfer that responsibility to others; then all the others are responsible and they praise themselves for being humble and always the victims. That is the so-called "feeling of inferiority" explanation, and the other is the "megalomania" explanation. Or the result may be, if a man has really a consistent mind in that respect and is firmly convinced that there is no such thing as an interfering will, that he will ultimately land with a paranoia; he will be quite certain of the fact that he has done such things but that persecutors arrange such traps for him and are secretly working against him. He will say it is the Freemasons or the Jesuits or the Nazis or Communist spies. You see, those are the euhemeristic explanations which ultimately lead into a sort of paranoia.

Now, when Nietzsche explains that God is a conjecture and that one should not make a conjecture which one cannot create, it means that it is an unrealizable hypothesis. He is then saying that God does not exist; since man has never made a God, and only assumes that there is a God, therefore God is not. There is nothing that is against our wishing or willing, there is no interference; if there is interference, it would be due to something wrong in other people and something ought to be done about it. Nietzsche was not a man who would project his psychology upon others; of course there is some evidence in *Zarathustra* of his exteriorizing some of his own psychology, but it is not so important. It is very important to him to be responsible; if things are imperfect they should be made perfect. Therefore, make a Superman; make the man that you really should be, the man who makes true that theory that God is not: namely, that man whose will is never crossed, to whom everything is possible. You see, this is by no means a very original idea:

921

you hear this kind of talk in a Protestant sermon; it is a most Protestant notion that you should be the one whom you wish to be—or rather, do *not* wish because it is immoral to wish for anything. You might wish for something agreeable and anything agreeable is immoral; you must always wish for something disagreeable. So since the Superman is not agreeable, it is a moral task; you ought to, you should, and damn you if you don't pray for it every Sunday. You see, this idea of the Superman is a derivative of that very Protestant idea.

Protestantism talks a lot, of course, about the grace of God, that you can do nothing without it, yet you are whipped into the belief that you must obey the law God has made. Therefore, every true Protestant has a Jewish anima who preaches the Old Testament, so he is not even a Christian, but a good old Jew. As of course the real Jews have a Christian anima, for you cannot do without the two points of view; you cannot fear God only, but also must love him. So there is no Jew without that Christian complex as there is no good Protestant without a Jewish complex; they are exceedingly like each other, only one is the inside of the glove and the other the outside. The Protestant belief in the grace of God is balanced on the other side by a careful observation of the law. Therefore the real god of Protestant communities is respectability, as you see in America and elsewhere. That means observance of the laws, a lower point of view which has nothing to do with Christian love. It is Christian fear. You see, this attempt of the Protestant to force himself into an ideal form is really disbelief in the grace of God, for if he really believes in that, he will gladly assume that in his time God will do the right thing for him; and if he is not perfect today, well, it is a bit in the interests of God that he does something in that line, that he gives him some of his grace, in order that the sinner of today becomes something better in the future. But the real Protestant practically does not believe that. He believes that he has to make himself into a good being, and that he will do it—that it is his responsibility only.

We have a wonderful poem in this country which characterizes the spirit of the Protestant in a very beautiful way. It shows his two-fold morality. It is a popular version of a certain church hymn; one verse is in high German and in between is a commentary in the Swiss patois which contradicts the meaning of the verse. Unfortunately it is in dialect, but I will try to translate it: "Whoever trusts in God and has nothing himself, whoever puts his hope in God and is doing nothing, such a one God must sustain in a miraculous way. Otherwise things won't work at all." That is exactly the Protestant point of view; everything is made dependent upon one's own morality, one's own responsibility;

there is no absolution and at the same time one believes in the grace of God.

Miss N. Taylor: Do you know that Scotch story about the faith which moves mountains? There was an old lady who prayed for a great mound before her house to be removed, and when she went down next morning and found the mound still there, she said, "I thought as much!"

Prof. Jung: That is very good. So those two things really exclude each other. This tremendous amount of moral responsibility that is heaped upon the Protestant forces him to an exaggerated and extravagant belief or hope in his own ability; he hopes and wishes to be able to create that marvelous being which he is expected to be. The text simply continues this idea.

> Not perhaps ye yourselves, my brethren! But into fathers and forefathers of the Superman could ye transform yourselves: and let that be your best creating!

Prepare yourself, you may not attain to the kingdom of heaven, but your sons or grandsons eventually will reach heaven. You see, that is in the best Protestant form: what I did not accomplish, I shall burden my son with; he will do it. For always underneath is that idea: Christ will take care of the business. If there is a conflict in me, I will hand it over to Christ and he will run away with it into the desert and take it away from me. We have large religious movements in our days where that happens. This is born out of the misery and real need of the Protestant conscience which must find a way out, so those people who take it seriously must invent the idea of the scapegoat that is sent out into the desert to deal with their own sins, and they take Christ as the scapegoat. They burden him since he is the crucified, deified scapegoat. These people simply cannot stand the moral stress any longer; they repress their own responsibility and call it Christ's and there they leave it. But then they are no longer human; they have lost their sin, the black stuff, which is spiritually fertile earth.

The idea of a sacrificial scapegoat is all right: the divine representative who takes over the role of the sacrificed; that is an idea which works psychologically as long as one is a member of an institution, or in a community in full participation with all the others. Then it doesn't matter who is carrying the burden, preferably the priest, or an animal sacrifice, or a criminal who represents the God or the king. It doesn't matter who is chosen in that community to carry the sin, because he is the whole community and the whole community is himself. This is a collective emotion which is exceedingly strange to us; we can hardly imagine it now—it is utterly primitive. Of course when you work your-self up into a dervish-like state, you are in a vibrating emotion, in an ecstatic condition, and everybody else is the same; so it doesn't matter *who* is struck, you or anybody else. Then you can tear your skin, cut your throat, or the priest may come and cut your throat and sacrifice you. It is all one: you yourself do not exist. It needs such an emotion and such a oneness to make the idea of the scapegoat work at all; now-adays it would not work because our consciousness is really too individ-ual. Though we see very peculiar things; think of the 6th of May en-thusiasm in Germany!⁵ I cannot appreciate how far that goes, but I assume, when consciousness is not particularly strong and there is much collective fear, that under certain conditions the people are again united in a sort of *ekstasis*. All that shouting and the rhythm, the music and brass bands and the marching together, produce a collective ecstasy which expresses itself in that extraordinary faith in the leader. The leader is then the scapegoat: they make him responsible. He rep-resents every one, so there is a *participation*, which is of course some-thing like a primitive collective religious phenomenon. The whole thing is probably a religious phenomenon; the politics are only talk.

Mrs. Volkhardt: There was a woman in Germany who wanted very much to meet the Führer and one day she had that chance. She said: "*Heil, mein Führer*," and then he talked to her and was so very nice that she suddenly fainted away. And this same thing has happened to others.

Prof. Jung: Well, it is a peculiar reaction—we must leave it at that. Well now, the idea of the Superman who was to be created by man was very much helped by the ideas of Darwin, which were modern in those days. Of course Darwin doesn't suggest that a Superman could be pro-duced at will; he simply shows the possibility of the transformation of a species, say from ape to man. But then at once the question is raised, if the ape has developed to man, what can man develop into? Man may go on and produce a being superior to the actual man. And then the Protestant ideal leaps in and says: That is what you *ought* to do. You see, if there was a Protestant ape, he might once on a Sunday morning say, "Now I really ought to produce man"—which is exactly what Nietzsche is proposing to do here, of course not in one generation: he

---

⁵ The 6th of May enthusiasm: whatever that was, it did not get reported in the *London Times*. Perhaps a Nazi demonstration, or some response to Mussolini's campaign against Addis Ababa. Italy would announce the annexation of Ethiopia on 9 May 1936.

gives it at least three generations. If we had put the argument under his nose in this way, he would naturally have seen all that; but this argument, as we explain it, never would have affected Nietzsche because his real motive was religious. That Superman idea is entirely symbolic. Yet if one could have suggested to him that it was a symbolic idea, that he naturally couldn't assume that in a few generations he would produce a man superior to ourselves, he would have denied it, because it was equally dark or impossible for him to accept the existence of a symbolic Superman. For a symbolic Superman is a psychological Superman, simply a superior consciousness. You see, that would not have suited him in the least.

So when we say that by his concept of the Superman Nietzsche meant the self, it is a mere assumption and not even a valid one; he did not mean the self as we understand that concept. He meant what he said, a superior man, even physically different, a beautiful man, a sound man such as one ought to be, and that idea has of course nothing to do with the self. We know quite well that no man can ever become the self; the self is an entirely different order of things. So if we try to render Nietzsche's idea, we should not use that term. Nevertheless, when he speaks of the Superman, it rings like something which does not merely mean the man of tomorrow whose tail is a bit shorter or whose ears are no longer pointed, a man who looks like a Greek god or something of the sort. He also means a man who is greater than man, a super-man. It sounds like something because it is a symbol, and it is a symbol because it is not explained; if you should try to explain it, you would meet all the contradictions which were in Nietzsche's time and which were also in him. You see, the Superman is really a god who has been killed, declared to be dead, and then naturally he appears again in an overwhelming desire for salvation; that means the birth of the Superman. There is the god again. So the word *Superman* sounded like "God" to the good Christians; it was a word pregnant with emotions, desires, hopes, highest meaning. And when we analyse it in a dry and critical way, we surely do not do justice to that conception. But we belong to a time after Nietzsche. We know of symbols and we have an idea of psychology, and to us it cannot mean the same.

LECTURE III

20 May 1936

Prof. Jung:

I hope you realize that "The Happy Isles," is a very intricate chapter, difficult and profound. It contains problems of the greatest importance, and I must confess I feel a bit hesitant in commenting upon it because it leads us into depths which are difficult to deal with. You remember we got as far as that paragraph where he speaks of the possibility of our being at least the great grandfathers of the Superman. He continues,

> God is a conjecture: but I should like your conjecturing restricted to the conceivable.
>
> Could ye *conceive* a God?—But let this mean Will to Truth unto you, that everything be transformed into the humanly conceivable, the humanly visible, the humanly sensible! Your own discernment shall ye follow out to the end!

We are already acquainted with the fact that Nietzsche takes God as a human conjecture that is not even very commendable, and he also declares God to be dead. Here we see a deeper reason for this particular attitude. It is less a concession to the spirit of his age than a concession, one could say, to his own honesty; he doesn't care to make a conjecture which goes beyond the reach of man. This attitude was prepared by Kant; as you know, Kant has shown in an irrefutable way that one cannot make metaphysical assumptions.[1] The spirit of the age influenced Nietzsche to a great extent nevertheless in his assumption that God was a human conjecture; one could hold just as well that he was an expe-

---

[1] Kant showed rather that we cannot have knowledge of the noumenal world, that is, of things before they have been subjected to the categories of human understanding. Although he believed it was necessary to assume freedom of the will, immortality of the soul, and the existence of God, he maintained that any "proof" of such metaphysical assertions lands one in an antilogism, wherein an equally good counterproof can be advanced.

rience. Kant left it open: he clearly saw that his intellectual or philosophical criticism was just philosophical criticism and he did not touch upon the field of experience, particularly the experience of things which cannot be submitted to theological criticism. You see, he lived at a time when to assume or even to explain the world through the existence of God was taken for granted. It was *the* truth. It was considered quite reasonable then to think in such a way.

As late as the 18th century practically every scientific book began with the creation of the world by God, the six days' work. It was absolutely certain, with no discussion, that God had created the world and still maintained the functioning of the world. But in the time of Nietzsche that former immediate certainty was lost sight of, so Nietzsche's saying that God is a conjecture is not only a concession to the spirit of his time, but is also the conscientiousness of the critical philosopher which does not allow him to assume more than he can prove, or more than is within the human scope. To assume, like the dogmatic Christian formulation, that God is the infinite or eternal one, or that he has any such quality, is an absolutely man-made assumption, and an honest man will never make any statement which reaches beyond the limits of the human mind. It is as if you promised to pay somebody one million francs after two hundred years; naturally in two hundred years you will no longer exist, and moreover you never will have such a sum at your disposal, so you have overreached yourself. An honest and responsible thinker therefore will restrain himself and refrain from making such assumptions. The fallacy is of course the assumption that God is only a conjecture, for he might be an experience, but the recognition of that possibility had completely disappeared, certainly from the field of Nietzsche's vision. You see, the assumption that the conception of God is really man-made is, as an assumption, perfectly all right—nobody can contradict it, just as a blind belief in the dogma cannot be discussed philosophically. So he asks, "Could ye conceive a God?" No, you cannot; you cannot conceive of something that is outside of human reach. By saying a thing is infinite you have not created infinity, but have created a mere word. Therefore Nietzsche says that it is the will to truth in man which forbids him to invent something which is not humanly conceivable, and that this attitude should be the regulation of one's thought, in order that one may never assume more than one can produce. Then he says.

And what ye have called the world shall but be created by you:
. . .

Also concerning the nature of the world you must not make any assumptions that overreach human limits; you must have the courage to create a world which is admittedly man-made and anthropomorphous. In other words you must admit the anthropomorphous quality of *all* conceptions. Now, this is an attitude which we meet every day, because we are still inclined to assume that our scientific truth is something more than man-made, that it has a certain objectivity, and is not relative only. But as a matter of fact, whatever we touch or experience is within the scope of our psychology. If I should say such a thing to a professor of philosophy he would kill me on the spot, because that means doing away with his assumption that his thinking is beyond psychology. But the universal image of the world *is* a psychological fact or feature, though it is influenced, I admit, by something beyond our psychology. What that is we don't know. There the physicist has the last word: he will inform us that it consists of atoms and peculiar things within the atoms, but that hypothesis is constantly changing, and there we have clearly come to a certain end. If he goes a bit further he begins to speculate, then he falls into the mind, and presumably he falls right into the collective unconscious, where he discovers the psychologist already at work. The speculative modern physicist will surely come into very close contact with the psychologist, and as a matter of fact he already has.[2]

So Nietzsche, in his great passion for truth, is really carrying on the best Kantian tradition, but of course he is also a child of his time when the prevalent misconception was that God was a conjecture or a concept and not an experience.

> And how would ye endure life without that hope, ye discerning ones? Neither in the inconceivable could ye have been born, nor in the irrational.
>
> But that I may reveal my heart entirely unto you, my friends: if there were God, how could I endure it to be no God! Therefore there are no Gods.

Well, the main idea here is that if there *were* a thing like God, it would be catastrophic for man, because he would be deprived of all his highest aspirations and hopes by being hopelessly anticipated; the perfect being would be there already. There would already be the most com-

[2] Both Jung and the Swiss physicist and Nobel laureate Wolfgang Pauli contributed essays to *The Interpretation of Nature and the Psyche*, tr. R.F.C. Hull and P. Silz (New York, 1955).

plete action or performance, and what is the use of seeking or trying to produce something great if it is already in existence? Why bother about it? Moreover, you might have a chance perhaps of communicating with that supreme being and receiving from him something to which you could not add; so you could only wish that he were not there in order to become supreme yourself. If somebody is already in the place you were hoping to occupy, either you must do away with him, or you desist and resign, having lost all hope of producing anything worth while. And so he says: "*if* there were Gods, how could I endure it to be no God! *Therefore* there are no Gods." Therefore there *shall* be no Gods, for if he were anticipated he would lose all his hopes. Now, he himself feels that this is not a valid conclusion—that because he could not stand having somebody on top of him, there were therefore no gods. It is indeed *hybris*, it goes too far. But looked at from the standpoint of Nietzsche, as well as from the standpoint of history, where God suffers from the human definition that he is the *summum bonum* for instance, such a definition makes of God a human conjecture which is really quite blasphemous. If you assume that God is the *summum bonum*, then what about the *infimum malum*?[3] You cannot say a thing is supremely good only, but must also establish the lowest evil, for what is light without shadow? What is high without low? You deprive the deity of its omnipotence and its universality by depriving it of the dark quality of the world. To ascribe infinite evil to man and all the good to God would make man much too important: he would be as big as God, because light and absence of light are equal, they belong together in order to make the whole. So his conception of God leads him necessarily into such conclusions, but as far as the premise goes his conclusion is right: God as he has been conceived by the preceding centuries is a conjecture, quite clearly. And nobody assumes that God is an immediate experience.

In the Christian church they talk so much of the necessity of believing in God that one really becomes doubtful whether God can *be* an experience. You see, if we have the experience, we don't need to believe. So the Greek word *pistis*, which means confidence, loyalty, is not at all what we understand by believing; it means the loyalty to the fact of the experience. The classical example is Paul who, perhaps at the worst moment in his life, on his way to persecute the Christians in Damascus, was thrown down by that experience of God. Then he knew it, and that

---

[3] Jung, firmly convinced of the dialectic of opposites, argues that the highest good must be offset by the lowest evil.

he had *pistis* means that he stuck to that experience and didn't go away from that fact. All the belief in the world doesn't make it; in believing it might be possible one experiences nothing. Of course one might call it *grace* if one is able to believe that such an experience is possible; if for a whole lifetime one is deprived of the experience of God, one deserves that grace at least. But without an experience of God one has really no right to make the effort to believe—it leads nowhere; one had better just say that one is deprived of it. Now naturally, when one draws a conclusion upon such an insufficient premise, one has a somewhat unsafe feeling, and Nietzsche shows that *sentiment d'incertitude* in the next sentence:

Yea, I have drawn the conclusion; . . .

and then comes the very interesting statement:

now, however, doth it draw me.

Now can you explain that? What has happened here?

Prof. Fierz: He is in his own trap.

Prof. Jung: Obviously. He can draw the conclusion that gods cannot exist, but now that conclusion is stronger than he. He is trapped. How is that?

Dr. Escher: It has become autonomous energy.

Prof. Jung: Well, you could say that this conclusion that there were no gods suddenly had assumed an autonomous quality, as if it had been invested with autonomous energy. It is like an obsession; this idea is now stronger than himself, beyond him. He is the victim of it. That always happens when you make a wrong assumption concerning something true and vital: it then assumes an autonomous character. You can see that very beautifully in the case of a compulsion neurosis; those people assume that there is no moral law, that they can behave like real devils in an absolutely irresponsible, ruthless way, and that it doesn't matter. Or sometimes people who might appear to be fairly normal, think they can do something definitely immoral, and inasmuch as it is not known by the public it is of no consequence. In fact, it is a widespread idea that only inasmuch as it bothers other people does it matter, that you can even commit murder if nobody knows. But as a matter of fact it does matter.

I remember the case of a woman who committed a murder about twenty years ago and she was completely destroyed. It was very cleverly done; she was a very intelligent woman, a doctor, who could cover up her tracks marvelously, and she could not understand why she was destroyed since nobody knew. She quite forgot that *she* knew, and that she was a whole nation or perhaps more. You see, there was no nation on earth that would give her hospitality; her unconscious made a contract with the whole world to give her no shelter. She forgot that her ego is not her totality; it is not the self. It would not matter that her ego knew, but there was somebody else in her, the thing that is much greater than herself that said: you have committed murder; there is no place for you in the whole world because the whole world knows it. For we are the whole world in ourselves; not in the ego, mind you—our ego is in ourselves as if it were in a great continent or the whole universe. Her universe accused her of murder and she was executed; she was in an eternal prison wherever she was, so that every human being was removed from her. She could only deal with animals in the end. She came to me when her dog got lame, then she had to confess it to the world, so she confessed it to me. I did not even ask her name; it was an anonymous business.

Now, that is what happened to Nietzsche; he was dealing with a situation that he didn't understand. He started with the assumption that God was a conjecture which one can handle; he drew that conclusion, and then it handled him. He said there could be no such thing as God, and then the self, the unconscious, said, "Now you are in my hands; because you deny my existence, you are my victim." This is a most decisive moment in the whole drama of *Zarathustra*. He will be drawn by that unknown factor, and you will see in the further chapters—if we ever get to them—testimony which shows very clearly how the thing which was denied was working in him. This place explains Nietzsche's life after writing *Zarathustra*, his tragic fate.

> God is a conjecture: but who could drink all the bitterness of this conjecture without dying? Shall his faith be taken from the creating one, and from the eagle his flights into eagle-heights?

How do you understand this verse? What about the bitterness of this conjecture?

Mrs. Crowley: Well, he has already confessed that it would be perfectly hopeless if there were a God, as that would prevent man from being creative.

Prof. Jung: Yes, he could not be creative because everything was already created. If we are permeated with the idea that the most valuable and important things are eternal, why create? It is perfectly foolish. Now, do you assume that there are people who experience the bitterness of that anticipation?

931

Mr. Allemann: I think every invention has been anticipated by somebody else.

Prof. Jung: Ah yes, naturally this priority business plays a tremendous role in life. It is a catastrophe when one is anticipated, but we are talking now of spiritual experience, when God anticipates man. Where do you see that?

Dr. Harding: You might see it in a son's relation to his father; when the father has done everything and experienced everything, the son can find nothing for himself.

Prof. Jung: Yes, but that is within the ordinary facts of life. Nietzsche's situation is a bit more involved. You see, he cannot stand the idea of God, because God would anticipate the creative man Nietzsche to such an extent that he could not make the creative effort. Now my question is, are there situations when one cannot make a creative effort because one is anticipated by God or whatever God may mean?

Miss Hannah: The Roman church does that to all its people; it stops them because it explains everything to them.

Prof. Jung: "To be born Catholic means to be stillborn!" That is not my invention, that is Thomas More's.[4] But that is also within the human scope because they don't assume that the Catholic church is God.

Mr. Martin: The man that is obsessed by the idea that cause and effect create the whole world, as some physicists are, might be deprived of creative power.

Prof. Jung: Yes, inasmuch as he collides with the spiritual fact, the experience of God, but in most scientists their attitude doesn't become a spiritual problem because they have compartmental psychology; in one drawer is science, and in another the political club to which they belong, and so on: things never touch each other. Well, it is a rather difficult question. You know if you have an intense contact with the collective unconscious, you are so much impressed by the eternal images that you are sucked under and never reappear. That is the safest way to sterilize a man completely; it kills him for the world, he simply disappears. Therefore people who are touched by the collective unconscious under pathological circumstances, lose the creative faculty, as it happened to Nietzsche himself. And it can happen in minor degrees to other people; under the influence of the specific experience of the collective unconscious they are quite lamed; floods of possibilities and images sway over them and they cannot grasp them; they can no

---

4 Thomas More (1478-1535), author of *Utopia* (1516), was martyred by Henry VIII.

longer lift a finger. They become absolutely helpless. They don't know where to tackle it because there is too much. They are in a world which is so full of possibilities that they don't know whether to seize any of them, for even when they try to fish something out of the endless sea, in the next moment it is dissolved again and they have lost their grip completely. This is the great danger of the collective unconscious and it is also in a way the great danger of mysticism.

But we don't know exactly whether it is ultimately a danger; looked at from our human point of view, naturally blindfolded more or less by the prejudices of our age, we would call it paralysis, sterilization. The man disappeared—but who knows? Perhaps it is the right thing; perhaps it is what should have happened. For instance, there were the times when all those thousands disappeared in the Libyan and Syrian deserts; they vanished into monasteries, hermitages, etc., and they and their contemporaries thought that was just right. We call it a danger because we believe that things should be manufactured and made visible, but there are other worlds. When a man vanishes into Yoga in the East, we say he is lost to the world—what is the use of being a fakir? But they think it a great merit *not* to live here, to disappear to a certain extent at least, and to complete the great disappearance is considered the height of perfection in Buddhism. So the appreciation of this factor varies a great deal. You see, that is being anticipated. In the collective unconscious you discover the identity of different times for instance, that things have been practically always the same; you begin to see that though symbols vary a great deal, *plus ça change, plus ça reste la même chose.*[5] The basic thoughts are eternal, they never change. So why should you do anything about it? Why invent? Or why should you translate them into the language of this time? You can disappear into them without ever saying a word about them. But the fact is of course that externally, to your surroundings, to your world, you are lost. When the experience of God comes to you you may be taken away, you may die. The "great bitterness" is that you have to divorce yourself from this so-called beautiful world, this human world, nature, etc., and then the faith is taken from the creating one and the flight from the

---

[5] Nietzsche's "eternal return of the same" goes even beyond "The more things change, the more they stay the same." Nietzsche considered his joyful embrace of the idea that in the infinity of time there must be an exact replication of events to be the strongest possible affirmative attitude toward life, a complete renunciation of Schopenhauer's pessimism. Since on Jung's typology of functions, it is the intuitive above all who dreads repetition, Nietzsche's delight in the necessity of the "eternal return" may be regarded as a sacrifice of his superior function.

eagle. So Nietzsche thinks it is better to assume that God is a thought. He says,

> God is a thought—it maketh all the straight crooked, and all that standeth reel. What? Time would be gone, and all the perishable would be but a lie?

Exactly, that is so. The more you are absorbed into the deity the more the ups and downs of this world become unimportant or relative, and if you get entirely into the other side, they don't exist; then this side is all illusion. And that is exactly the purpose of Buddhism as you know, and of the Christian mystics.

> To think this is giddiness and vertigo to human limbs, and even vomiting to the stomach; verily, the reeling sickness do I call it, to conjecture such a thing.

So his confession is entirely in favor of this world and nothing else; he hates the idea of spiritualism or any metaphysical aspiration—naturally under the prejudice of his time that there is only a yea *or* a nay, and not a yea *and* a nay.

> Evil do I call it and misanthropic: all that teaching about the one, and the plenum [fullness], and the unmoved, and the sufficient, [this should be translated self-sufficient] and the imperishable.

Those are qualities of the deity and he thinks it is evil to even talk about or to teach such things. That is of course very much in contradiction to the Christian teaching as we know it. You see, our late Protestantism has taught among many other things a sort of very active Christianity that is little in tune with the eschatological attitude of early Christianity. Nietzsche being the son of a parson naturally had some idea about that teaching, and under those conditions it is quite understandable that he sympathizes with the standpoint and the reality of the world rather than with that peculiar backworldliness of which he occasionally speaks. He says here,

> All the imperishable—that's but a simile, and the poets lie too much.

All perishable things are nothing but similes, Goethe says in the last part of *Faust*; and here Nietzsche says all imperishable things are but a simile—just the other way round. "And the poets lie too much!" You see he takes it that they lie when they hold that the perishable things are more or less symbolic expressions of a real existence, of a real substance. Now, this is a very great problem really, and a great conflict for people who take their life as a serious proposition. Where is the truth? Is my life really only symbolic? Is it completely anticipated? Should I make particular efforts to build railway bridges, or make engines or cannons, or write books? Or should I worship the unmovable, the eternal, the fullness, the pleroma, and become rigid or petrified? Well, Nietzsche decides for this world, and I think with some justification, because we really must remain within the human scope.

For how else could we decide about our life? We have to be human, and we cannot know better than to be human and to fulfil that law which is given unto us; we must assume that the law under which we are born is that of the human being, and what else can we live but human life? We have to live, to fulfil human life, exactly as a flower has to live the flower's life, the life of that species. What would you say about a horse that affected to be a cow? Or a dog that affected to be a canary bird? A dog is a good dog when he is a dog, and man is a good man when he is a man. And it is quite obvious that if we live at all, we must live in this world here and now; our law is that we live here and now and nowhere else, and that we don't cast illegitimate glances on things which are not; otherwise the dog is affecting to be a bird. He would be disobedient. The marvelous thing about the animal is that it is the most pious thing that exists—with the exception of the plant, which is still more pious because it is rooted in the ground and must accept its fate. It cannot jump away. An animal can at least cheat fate by running away. And a man can cheat life like anything by his devilish cunning; by his cunning he has done in the whole of creation practically, the whole of nature; we are most immoral beings in that we always try *not* to fulfil the law into which we are born.

Naturally we are saddled with the very great problem of human consciousness, which could not exist if we did not discriminate between ourselves and nature. To fulfil the law of nature completely we must have ego consciousness, and for that we must be able to do something which amounts to disobedience; we only exist when we can do something that is against the law. Many people have to commit immoral acts in order to feel that they are free. A child that is never disobedient never *becomes*. It is always dependent upon the parents, in absolute participation with the mother or the father, and pulls the wool over their eyes and over its own also. For a child always has the temptation to do just what it should not do—and that must be; otherwise it has no feeling of its own existence. So a certain amount of immorality and dis-

obedience is absolutely necessary for the existence of ego consciousness; the ego is something apart. This is of course contained in the
legend of paradise; the first parents had to commit that sin in order to
become conscious; otherwise they would have been no different from
animals—which means from God. You see, animals and plants are absolutely identical with God. And so man would be if only he were not
conscious. But since consciousness is in him as a germ at least, it is his
own decision. Culture, for instance, is only an extension of the development of consciousness and that is surely his task. He has to develop
consciousness, even if he becomes like that prehistoric giant stag that
simply became extinct because his horns grew too marvelously complicated, or like the mammoth whose tusks curled inward till they were of
no use any longer. So man may kill himself by an overdeveloped consciousness; it has already become a nuisance.

Therefore we try with all our might to compensate it, to reestablish
the connection with God, that he may protect us against our disobedience. Yet it is also a will, a law, that has been given to us, that we should
fulfil to the utmost the demands of consciousness. For example, we
have the Gnostic interpretation that the serpent in Paradise was the
son of the spiritual God who really tried to help man from the state of
anoia, unconsciousness, and to give him *ennoia*, consciousness. And we
find the same idea in the pagan Hermetic philosophy in the *Krater*, the
mixing jar, the famous vase of Hermes that was made by God after the
creation; after he had created human beings in a state of *anoia*, he
made that marvelous vessel, filled it with *nous*, and sent it down to the
earth in order that those many human beings who felt the need of increasing consciousness could dip themselves in that mixing jar, and
there attain to *ennoia*. That is the origin probably of the Grail, for instance, and it appears also in alchemistic philosophy; this idea was
widespread quite outside of biblical tradition. Now this necessity to develop consciousness doesn't allow us to obey the law completely, to fulfil the will of God in nature; disobedience is the only means by which
we can separate consciousness from unconscious participation. So
every step foward is a Promethean sin without which there is no development; we cannot be creative *and* good, but can only be creative and
pay the price for it. We would not be able to be creative, or to fulfil that
absolute necessity of becoming conscious if we remained within the law
in which we are born: we needs must be disobedient.

You see, people even go so far as to assume that there is no such
thing as God or as the law and that we are not at all bad and disobedient; that on the contrary we are marvelous, creative fellows, like little

gods going forth to create, and that it is a ridiculous, humiliating superstition to assume otherwise. There they make the fatal mistake: man *is* disobedient inasmuch as his life cannot be that of a plant or an animal. Inasmuch as he has to become conscious, he has to be disobedient and therefore he is guilty—that is inherited sin. It is a psychological truth because ego separateness is indispensable for the growth of human consciousness, and that cannot be attained without disobedience. This is a sad fact but it is so, and it is much better to assume that guilt and to declare oneself tragically responsible for it. Then we understand when we suffer for the development of consciousness; we know we have to pay a heavy price for it. As long as we keep the feeling of an obligation as if we were guilty, as if we were in debt, our attitude is correct; then we are in the right connection with these peculiar spiritual facts.

Now, it is quite clear that Nietzsche's point of view is a complete and unmitigated belief in nature, in the natural life of man in the here and now. To him every glance backwards is a sin, so he says,

> But of time and of becoming shall the best similes speak: a praise shall they be, and a justification of all perishableness!

This explains his position fully, and from a psychological point of view of course one must add that this is a very onesided standpoint. That it shall be most complete, most natural, is surely one aspect of human life, but it is not the whole thing; there is another will behind or beside it and Nietzsche himself is the very best example of it. He thought *he* was drawing the conclusion but it was that other will which was drawing him. That is a consideration which should not be forgotten.

> Creating—that is the great salvation from suffering, and life's alleviation. But for the creator to appear, suffering itself is needed, and much transformation.

This is the creating which would be anticipated by a God-creator, and this creation, according to Nietzsche, could not live if God did exist because it would be anticipated. So his tendency is to take away the supposed creative faculty of the creator and attribute it to man, to declare that it is really man's creativeness and not God's. Now, that is justifiable inasmuch as the human ego cannot live without creativeness; it proves its existence by inventing something, by doing something on its own, out of the ordinary—by living dangerously for instance, doing the things of which one is afraid, which only a human being will do. Animals refrain from doing things they are afraid of, while man quite naturally asserts the divine quality of his ego by doing just the things he is afraid of. That is so very much against nature that it is the strongest evidence of the autonomous existence of the ego and of the freedom of the human will. So it is quite understandable when Nietzsche emphasizes the creator in man. He clearly sees, with such an emphasis on the ego and its will power, that consciousness cannot come into existence without suffering, that suffering is of course detachment from nature, from unconsciousness, from the animal and the plant. The utter isolation of man in his conscious world becomes his prison. In our consciousness we are peculiarly separated from nature; it is a prison with glass walls. We see through the glass, see the things outside, yet we have no interchange, no participation with them; we can say, "Yes, this is a snake, this is a bear," but the snake is no longer our sister and the bear is no longer our brother. They ought to be our near relatives; we ought to have a spiritual relation to our relatives on this earth, but consciousness has divorced us completely from them and from many other things, not only from the totemic relation to animals.

Now, that is suffering, sure enough, and it is a transformation; therefore the process of becoming conscious has always been seen and understood as an analogy to empirical transformation processes, like the snake shedding its skin, the tadpole transforming into the frog, the caterpillar transforming from the pupal state into the butterfly. Then there was the transformation that man produced in the form of chemical inventions—for instance, in dyeing things so that they have another appearance, in cooking, in cutting things up and putting them together again. In alchemy, the transformation was shown in the form of chemical procedures. In the hero myth, the hero is swallowed by the dragon or the great whale and then kills the beast from within and comes back to daylight again. The rebirth rituals and all those similes that have been made by man are to express the attainment of a transformation of consciousness, a widening out and emphasizing of the ego in a sort of transfiguration. In the Mithraic or in the Isis mysteries a man who was transformed into Helios and worshipped as such surely did not take it as an increase of his higher self. It happened to his ego; he was now simply conscious of another order of things. In that peculiar transformation which was brought about in the mysteries—as we know from certain confessions—man knew himself to be an imperishable being. He had a new life; he knew himself in a new order of things, but it was a new ego. His ego consciousness was widened out.

Yea, much bitter dying must there be in your life, ye creators!
Thus are ye advocates and justifiers of all perishableness.

938

You see, this clearly points to the fact that you cannot believe in things that are worldly and perishable if you have not given up that connection or participation out of which you were born. You are born out of the collective unconscious, and your consciousness begins to function in your lifetime. You had been alive already for a few years as a mere existence, as an object, and then in about three or four years, sometimes even later, consciousness began to function, a certain consciousness came into existence. Some people attain to a state of consciousness only at puberty, and there are people who never attain to it, but live an accidental life where the ego appears in many different phases and they never have any control over it. They cannot sum it up. You see that in primitive life; therefore experience means so little to them. They go through things but there is no continuity, no *pistis*, nothing. The continuity of the ego is not yet established; they are only objective psychological phenomena. They live but they don't know that they live: *it* lives. They happen to be conscious of acts, of conditions with something like an ego in it, but that ego matters precious little. It decides nothing, chooses nothing, is simply a witness. But on a higher level of civilization the ego is in it and responsibly in it; it chooses, it decides, it avoids, it seeks, it shows a definite will toward something and sees life as its own doing. This is of course an entirely different proposition from the original form in which we lived.

Anybody now who cannot separate himself completely from that objective type of psychological life where the ego is a mere witness, cannot attain to a complete ego consciousness because he is all the time a victim or an appendix to objective processes that happen. He finds himself in the wake of events, and that always—under more or less civilized conditions at least—leads to a neurosis. When people complain that whenever they try to do this or that, they have an attack of such-and-such a nature, it means that a complex comes in between. And they cannot deal with it, it deals with *them*, just as here Nietzsche says he drew a conclusion and then it drew him. It was an appendix; he was in the wake of it. That is the case in any neurotic condition: part of the psychology is not detached from the original background. When Freud speaks of the early infantile fixation, it is merely the fixation to the psychical background; all his talk about incest is not personal, but is the mythology of all races, the images of the collective unconscious.[6]

[6] Freud, greatly impressed with Edward Burnett Tylor's claim (in *Primitive Culture*) that incest is a universal taboo, gave in *Totem and Taboo* (1913) his account of the primordial struggle of the father and his sons for possession of the mother. This work was, in a

These things are still there and one is still connected with them. That is the world from which one has to cut oneself loose, and it is a ruthless, almost blasphemous act. Nietzsche himself feels it; in another place he says it is a sort of sacrilegious act to detach oneself from that marvelous paradise.

Christianity rightly understood is exceedingly severe on that point; Christ himself gave ruthless advice. What did he say to the young man when he wanted to bury his father? "Let the dead bury the dead." And what did he say to his own mother when she reminded him that the wine was nearly gone and he must do something about it? "Woman, what have I to do with thee?"[7] She is completely swept aside. Now think of a Jewish boy sweeping his mother out of the way! That is unheard of. You see, those are symbolic gestures, hints as to Christ's attitude toward the detachment from the past. People were to become like unto children, but they were not to *remain* children as theologians want to make us believe. There is nothing sentimental about it, and that is what Nietzsche means here. You cannot be creative and sentimental about your aunt at the same time.

For the creator himself to be the new-born child, he must also be willing to be the child-bearer, and endure the pangs of the child-bearer.

You see, that creating will in man, which is so much linked up with his ego, is the father and the mother of the ego, for your creative will creates yourself; you create a new consciousness, a new ego is born. It is a new generation of the ego one could say, a pregnancy and a birth, and that act of creation must be repeated. To keep life as ego consciousness you must give birth to yourself repeatedly. The ego, the wider and higher state of consciousness, is first unconscious—that is the pregnancy; and then something happens. You hurt yourself against something or you have a tremendous emotion from within, and at that moment a new light comes to you and your consciousness is widened. It is true that thus far man can be creative; thus far he is a little god. Therefore, Goethe calls him the little god of this world, for he *can* produce a man of wider consciousness, and he can do it to a certain extent at will. You can build up your consciousness, increase it at will, study, read: you are entirely free to have certain experiences. This is the justifica-

sense, Freud's rebuttal of Jung's *Wandlungen und Symbole der Libido* (1912), intentionally hastening and widening the split between the two men which became final in July 1914.

7 Matthew 8:22 and John 2:4.

tion of Nietzsche's idea that man could create the Superman, perhaps not in his own existence but in a future existence. Therefore we believe in education, in mental and spiritual development, in everything man can do, for he really can do something. But he will do nothing, nothing at all, if he leaves it to somebody else; if we do anything we have to do it in the here-and-now, and we will not do it in the here-and-now if we are not convinced that this is the important place and the important time and that we have to do it here. One cannot say, "Oh well, God has not granted me certain things so I hope and expect that my children will do them," and then goad them on to a certain goal in order that they may fulfil what God has not allowed me to fulfil. I should say, "I have not done it, and my son and daughter are different people, so why should they fulfil what I have not done?" I must be satisfied with the fact that I have not done it. Of course I can repent or be glad over it, but I should stick to the fact that I have not done it, and not assume that it was God who bestowed his grace upon me to do or not to do it. This is the only argument which saves you from passing on your expectations to your children and naturally spoiling their lives by your own choice. That is a perpetuated selfishness.

> Verily, through a hundred souls went I my way, and through a hundred cradles and birth-throes. Many a farewell have I taken; I know the heart-breaking last hours.

Here he is simply describing a series of transformations of consciousness. You see, from the beginning, our individual consciousness only lives by a continuous series of pregnancies and births, a continuous series of transformations; and one can say that the belief in reincarnation of other races is merely a projection of the fact of the transformation of consciousness. You know, inasmuch as our consciousness is not only our own accomplishment, since we are born with the faculty of having a certain intensity or a certain width of consciousness, we owe gratitude to our ancestors. We repeat the life of our ancestors as we grow up; the child begins with an animal-like condition and repeats all the animal stages in the development of consciousness until it reaches what is called the modern level of consciousness. And naturally we can feel all those transformations as former lives just as well, because they were former lives; in former times people have repeated that development untold millions of times and naturally we have the deposit, the *engrammata* of all that. Our mind was not made today. It was not a *tabula rasa* when we were born; we have even in its physical structure a brain in which all the former developments have been described or molded. Therefore we have quite legitimately that feeling of having gone through many lives and endured their experiences, even the heart-breaking last hours, innumerable times.

But so willeth it my creating Will, my fate. Or, to tell you it more candidly: just such a fate—willeth my Will.

That is, this creative ego-will is responsible for its fate; we are the makers of fate, the makers of our lives. And we should think like that; if we doubt it, we don't put out our strength, our whole force. It is just the misfortune of so many neurotic people, that they cannot pull themselves together and have such a conviction, because they know of course that every human goal, every ideal, is futile. It is eternal and so it doesn't matter what they do in time about it. What is the use of it? It doesn't even matter whether they have lived or not. But from this standpoint it is all important that we live; since our life is the only one we can experience, it surely must be lived, and our highest will should be to live it to the utmost; otherwise it never has been. Now, whenever Nietzsche makes an extreme statement, as we have seen before when he drew a very bold conclusion, he then realizes the other side; so he now says:

All *feeling* suffereth in me, and is in prison: but my *willing* ever cometh to me as mine emancipator and comforter.

Here we meet a very important conflict. You see, that will to exist, or to develop, that will to the Superman, is a sort of concentration of willpower and energy, almost a spasm. It is everything heaped up—but what about the feeling? Now, what does Nietzsche call feeling? He obviously means a certain human pathos, a human sensitiveness which does not agree with that most heroic ideal of creating a suffering ego—a Superman, in Nietzsche's language. Feeling obviously wants something else. Now of course, you can accuse feeling of being cowardly or conservative or lazy or stupid, but that doesn't do away with its existence. That feeling does exist too, and it might be a very important determinant in your behavior.

Willing emancipateth: that is the true doctrine of will and emancipation—so teacheth you Zarathustra.

Well, he teaches a complete detachment from the past, a complete abolition of any tie that might fetter you. But the feeling represents that tie. The feeling suffers, doesn't want to be detached, only lives when the connection is kept, when you are not so hellishly heroic and super-manish. So there are such doubts on Nietzsche's mind when he writes that, "Now what about it? I am creating, I am emancipating myself, I am going to create the Superman"—but here is that awkward feeling.

> No longer willing, and no longer valuing, and no longer creating! Ah, that the great debility may ever be far from me!

To him it is a debility because it makes him doubt whether that creativeness is right, whether it leads anywhere and whether it can be sustained; therefore he must of course preach an emphatic sermon to himself in order to make himself believe in his own idea.

> And also in discerning do I feel only my will's procreation and evolving delight; and if there be innocence in my knowledge, it is because there is will to procreation in it.
> Away from God and Gods did this will allure me; what would there be to create if there were—Gods!

This is a repetition of his standpoint, of course.

> But to man doth it ever impel me anew, my fervent creative will; thus impelleth it the hammer to the stone.
> Ah, ye men, within the stone slumbereth an image for me, the image of my visions! Ah, that it should slumber in the hardest, ugliest stone!

Here we come to one of those deeply symbolic passages in *Zarathustra*. The sudden manifestation of feeling indicates that somewhere there is a doubt in his mind; something is harking back that is not completely detached from the past. Yet it is perfectly obvious to him that man should look forward, should detach from the past with no exception. You see, when you are quite at one with yourself about a certain necessity, you often observe that something in you is hanging back. It doesn't join in, but looks back to just those things which you think you ought to avoid, or which you have overcome. Yet something is looking back as if you still were there. You also have *such* dreams; you have changed the type of your life, you live a new life, and then in dreams the former life appears just as if it had never been changed. Or you have certain resentments or emotions which you cannot harmonize with your actual convictions. Well, they simply come from the former mind, from the former type of living, which in spite of all overcoming and conjecturing still exists. That is on account of the indubitable fact that consciousness is a surface phenomenon; our ego consciousness is absolutely on the surface. No matter how important it is or how important we make it, it is a surface consciousness, and below, it has this indissoluble historical connection with the past from which we cannot get away. And we are forever in danger of falling into the past and being cut off. If we could cut off our own head, we would be detached from the past because our body is history; we make the great changes of consciousness only in the head. The whole thing below is not changed at all. If we live another type of life, it is only up in the head. Behind our consciousness is the whole collective unconscious which lives down in the body, and that is eternally caught in the past: we cannot change it. You can only detach your head, like John the Baptist; you live in your head perhaps but the other part Salome has cut off. That is of course the anima business.

So while Nietzsche is talking great words, the anima behind his back begins to stir and causes feeling. She says, "Yes, go ahead like that, but wait until I show my hand!" Here it shows a little, and he instantly collapses and asks what the world will be if we cannot produce the Superman. If there should be gods, what would we be?—and so on. Instantly, the doubt comes up and lames him completely, so he must preach to himself with increased fervor the great sermon of the Superman. And now he discovers an entirely new idea. You see, he comes to the idea of the stone in the passage: "But to man doth it ever impel me anew, my fervent creative will; thus impelleth it the hammer to the stone."[8] That is, when he is going to create, his firmly creative will hurts itself against an obstacle: it is like the hammer beating against the stone. Then the new idea occurs that a wonderful image is sleeping in the stone; within the stone there is something that is alive, but is dormant. Now where have we encountered such a picture?

Mrs. Sigg: Pygmalion?

Prof. Jung: Well, there he gives the soul to the stone; it is not living in the stone.

Mrs. von Roques: It is the first man, who only had to be awakened.

Prof. Reichstein: It is the Gnostic idea where the soul is sleeping in prison.

Prof. Jung: Yes, and that has to do with the philosopher's stone.

Prof. Fierz: But why is it the ugliest stone?

Prof. Jung: Oh well, that is in the myth. The philosopher's stone is the thing that has been rejected, the thing you find ejected in the road; you tread it under your feet or you find it on the dung heaps cast away,

---

[8] Cf. Nietzsche's *Twilight of the Idols: or How to Philosophize With a Hammer* (Leipzig, 1889). His title was a play on Wagner's *Twilight of the Gods*.

944

vilis et vilissimus, cheap and the cheapest. Also it is unsightly, makes no impression, like the description in Isaiah of the Messiah: "He hath no form nor comeliness; and when we shall see him, there is no beauty that we should desire him."[9] But this idea of the stone is by no means of Christian origin. It has a very pagan origin; it is really an archetypal idea. And here Nietzsche has an intuition that the material out of which the Superman will be formed is the thing that is ugly, cheap, of no use whatever, just the thing he has thrown away—which of course is the past and all the values of the past. That thing which has been rejected is the raw material; out of the stone rejected by the builders must he work that precious image. In other words, just out of the anima, out of that feeling that seems to be a mere nuisance, a mere hindrance—to his creative will.

[9] Of the Messiah in Isaiah 53:1-2.

LECTURE IV
27 May 1936

Prof. Jung:
Mrs. Crowley asks the following question: "Last week in connection with the verse beginning 'So willeth my creating will,' you said that the creative ego-will was responsible for its fate, or we should think so. Yet you have again and again emphasized that the ego-will should be realized as the partner in the act of creation, which is a process taking place within the individual. My impression of the chapter was that Zarathustra was identifying with the *activity* of *creating*. And I would like to ask if the attitude toward creation is necessarily different in a man's case from that of a woman."

Well, one could not say that it was necessarily different. *Creative will* is a term used by Nietzsche and he identifies entirely with it. Of course when one experiences it, it seems to be one's own will, yet as a matter of fact one is the exponent of it, its representative or implement. The creative will is utterly impersonal; therefore it so very often works against the vital interests of the individual. It may kill him or at least expose him to all sorts of risks and dangers, and may destroy not only one but several human lives: it is like a demon. And it is the same in a woman's case; the creative urge is a fact beyond sex, so I could not imagine that a woman would have an entirely different attitude to it; one could say it was a natural condition to which human beings must have very much the same attitude, whether a man or a woman. It could be compared to an elementary event like a thunderstorm; if there is any choice left at all, the attitude will be either an umbrella or a raincoat; if it is a matter of creation, if the creative will is serious one simply has to be careful, and the sex doesn't matter.

Mrs. Crowley: But in "The Happy Isles" he speaks definitely as if he were identifying; he says: "But so willeth it my creating Will, my fate. Or, to tell you it more candidly: just such a fate—willeth my Will." It seems in that chapter as if he were very much identifying with the

946

power, the activity of creation. And that seems to be an opposition to what you have so often said.

Prof. Jung: But that he identifies so entirely is just the trouble; no one in their sound senses can possibly identify with the creative power because it is something inhuman, it is superhuman or infra-human. You cannot *be* the creative will. It is because Nietzsche identified with Zarathustra that he had an inflation.

Mrs. Crowley: But I thought you said that we must consider that it is *our* creative will.

Prof. Jung: Not *ours.* You see there is the trap. If you acquire the creative will, it means that *you* are acquired. It is like that story in an old-fashioned play which Freud quoted in one of his books: A commander is in charge of a fortress where the garrison consists of old veterans; you hear the fight going on and suddenly one of the men shouts: "Colonel, I have made a prisoner." And the colonel shouts back: "Bring him here." Then the man says: "He won't let me!" So when Nietzsche says: "So willeth it my creating Will, my fate," who can say that he is identical with his fate? One can speak of *amor fati* in the sense of accepting it—since it is so, what can one do? One accepts it and calls it one's fate. But to say one's fate is one's own creation, is *hybris*; that is an inflation because it is not true. You see, in order to be able to choose your own fate, you must be able to understand it, to hold it, but you can't; you don't know what the ultimate constituents of your fate may be. You are not God and you are not a super-consciousness that contains all the necessary elements to explain your fate. With our conscious mind, we only know the smallest part of the elements that make up fate, so we cannot identify with it. If we know enough, if we have enough self-critique, we can only accept it. And that acceptance means in religious language, I submit to the will of God and his incomprehensible decisions. But that is not identifying, that is submitting, and Nietzsche does not submit, he identifies.

Well, we came to the end of that passage: "Ah, ye men, within the stone slumbereth an image for me, the image of my visions! Ah, that it should slumber in the hardest, ugliest stone!" I mentioned the analogy with Alchemy and I only want to add that this metaphor does of course on the surface remind one of Pygmalion, that famous sculptor. As you know, he made a beautiful statue which through the grace of the gods came to life, and since it was a woman, Galatea, he lived with her—she became real.[1] Now, one generally finds this feeling in artists; it looks to

[1] In Ovid's story, Pygmalion, disillusioned with the women of the world, carved his

them as if the material with which they work, contained life. For instance, I read once in a French book or paper, that somebody had sent round a questionnaire to literary people and artists, inquiring about the conditions of their creative work. And one writer said that the aspect of an empty white space of paper has the character of a charm—it exhales a sort of voluptuous attraction. He wanted to do something to it, to fill it with his pen; in that empty stuff, in those sheets, there was a magnetic charm which drew him and pulled him out so that his substance flowed into the paper: then he could write. Of course it is a sort of sex allegory one could say, as in the case of Pygmalion, but that doesn't mean that it comes out of sex. It rather means that the creative instinct is so strong that even sex is pulled into it and made serviceable. And so the sensuous beauty of color attracts the creative fantasy of the painter, or the sensuous quality of the clay or the stone attracts the creative fantasy of the sculptor. One sees that particularly in antique art.

I once saw a striking contrast in the use made of material in Florence. I saw first in the Boboli gardens the two wonderful figures of the barbarians—you remember perhaps those antique stone statues. They are made of stone, *consist* of stone, represent the *spirit* of stone: you feel that stone has had the word! Then I went to the tombs of the Medici and saw what Michelangelo did to stone; there the stone has been brought to a super-life. It makes gestures which stone never would make; it is hysterical and exaggerated. The difference was amazing. Or go further to a man like Houdon and you see that the stone becomes absolutely acrobatic. There is the same difference between the Norman and Gothic styles. In the Gothic frame of mind stone behaves like a plant, not like a normal stone, while the Norman style is completely suggested by the stone. The stone speaks. Also an antique Egyptian temple is a most marvelous example of what stone can say; the Greek temple already plays tricks with stone, but the Egyptian temple is made of stone. It grows out of stone—the temple of Abu Simbel, for example, is amazing in that respect. Then in those cave temples in India one sees again the thing man brings into stone. He takes it into his hands and makes it jump, fills it with an uncanny sort of life which destroys the peculiar spirit of the stone. And in my opinion it is always to the detriment of art when matter has no say in the game of the artist. The quality of the matter is exceedingly important—it is all-important. For instance, I think it makes a tremendous difference whether one

own woman out of ivory, named her Galatea, and fell in love with her. Venus granted his prayer to make her live (*Metamorphoses* X).

paints with chemical colors or with so-called natural colors. All that fuss medieval painters made about the preparation of their backgrounds or the making and mixing of their colors had a great advantage. No modern artist has ever brought out anything like the colors which those old masters produced. If one studies an old picture, one feels directly that the color speaks, the color has its own life, but with a modern artist it is most questionable whether the color has a life of its own. It is all made by man, made in Germany or anywhere else, and one feels it. So the projection into matter is not only a very important but an indispensable quality of art.

Now when Nietzsche speaks of the projection into the stone, that an image is lying dormant in the stone, it is a bit more than a mere mythological metaphor—Pygmalion or some such legend. A whole chapter of psychology one could say, is behind this projection. Therefore I mentioned the alchemistic analogy where matter, the stone, was the thing which contained the mysterious life—the more important as an analogy because the early centuries up to the 18th were filled with that idea. Our ancestors have lived in that alchemistic idea; to the mind of the past, matter was filled with a peculiar spirit. In my lecture in the Psychological Club about the philosophy of the stone, I read one of the earliest texts of Greek alchemy. In the beginning it said, "Go down to the bank of the Nile and there thou shalt find a stone which contains a ghost—there you shall find a stone in which a spirit is lying dormant.[2] Now this was the fundamental theme for sixteen or seventeen hundred years of most important thinking. Alchemistic philosophy is quite unknown in our days because we can no longer understand its paradoxical character, and though it was so important in the Middle Ages, yet in a history of medieval philosophy you find practically nothing about it. It should really concern us very much more than it does because one of the most powerful monuments in the literature of the world, not only of Germany, is Goethe's *Faust*, and Faust is the last great alchemistic allegory. It is filled with most important alchemistic thought and parallels.

So it is no wonder that Nietzsche, who is very much in the situation of a medieval alchemist, pulls up an image which belongs essentially to alchemy. If Nietzsche had lived at a time between the 15th and 18th centuries, I would say that he most certainly would have been an alche-

[2] In CW 11, par. 151, Jung says that this formula was "attributed by Zosimos to the legendary Ostanes." Then, in par. 355, he cites Zosimos' interpretation of "the stone"— that is, the philosopher's stone—as quicksilver.

mistic philosopher. For to him the official dogma, the official transmutation accomplished in the Mass for instance, the transubstantiation which is of course the alchemistic mystery *par excellence,* did not hold truth, did not hold life. Otherwise he would have been a perfectly contented Catholic; he would not have worried. But that meant nothing to him; he came to the conclusion that the church didn't give him the spiritual life which he really expected or needed, so he would quite naturally seek something that would produce life.

But invariably those old philosophers went down to the bank of the Nile to seek the stone which held the ghost; that is, they sought it in the projection. For when the spirit of life has vanished from a system of thought or from the holy rites—when the church obviously doesn't contain it any more—you must find it elsewhere. Since you don't possess it yet feel the need of its presence, well, you can only find it where it is projected; you find that unconscious component of your nature projected either in another human being or in a thing or in a system. And you find it just there where you feel it. The alchemists felt it in matter, and the whole purpose of their philosophy was to find out the technique, one could say, or those methods by which they could extract the spirit they no longer possessed and which was not granted them by the church. They felt that the church spoke a great deal about spirit and performed rites similar to their own by which the transubstantiation should take place, yet nothing came of it. They did not feel redeemed, and so they went in for their peculiar practices. Now, Nietzsche was naturally in the same condition but since he lived in the 19th century when Hermetic philosophy was a matter of derision, he could not go back to that. He was entirely unacquainted with it, yet his unconscious, containing all the traces of ancestral thought, brought up such material. So when such a symbol occurs in *Zarathustra* we must cock our ears and seek the historical antecedents, because they only can explain why he uses that figure of speech in such an important place. That it is an important place we see from the subsequent text. He continues,

> Now rageth my hammer ruthlessly against its prison.

This word *raging* expresses a great deal of emotion; he tries to deal with this imprisoned image by a sort of rage.

> From the stone fly the fragments: what's that to me?

You see, it is a highly emotional condition and he tries to get at it by hammer and tongs, *cum ira et vehementia.* This is a quotation from an alchemistic philosopher of the 6th century A.D., Morienus Romanus, who in giving instruction to his disciple, tells him he never can attain to the great art by wrath and vehemence, but can only get at it *per gratiam Dei*, by the grace of God, because it is a *donum Spiritus Sancti*, the gift of the holy ghost.

I will complete it. . . .

But the Hermetic philosopher says only those elected from eternity are able to produce the miracle of the transubstantiation. The accomplishment of the great work is only possible, *Deo adjuvante*, if God assists. An interesting conversation has been reported between Morienus Romanus and Hali, a prince of Egypt. Hali asked why Morienus did not live in a monastery like the Christian monks at that time. And Morienus said, "It is true that in the monasteries there is more peace, and in solitude there is more pain and labor. But since the avenue to quietude is very narrow, nobody can attain to it without affliction of the soul. What you sow, you harvest; if little, you harvest little. The monks have good monasteries and peace but they arrive nowhere, they remain static. While if they risk loneliness they attain to quietude because the goal is reached only through the affliction of the soul."[3]

And now we come to the important statement in which Nietzsche explains why he is so emotional and why he wants so much to get at that image:

for a shadow came unto me—the stillest and lightest of all things once came unto me!

The beauty of the Superman came unto me as a shadow. Ah, my brethren! Of what account now are—the Gods to me!—

That is what came to him instead of the lost God; God is dead but he reappears in the idea of the Superman, and the Superman is the stillest and lightest of all things. Now, that description coincides in a very remarkable way with sayings of the ancients. I remember now particularly Athanasias, Archbishop of Alexandria, the biographer of St. Antony of Egypt, who wrote in about the third century. He speaks about the manifold tribulations of the mourning ones in the desert, the

---

[3] The name is usually given as Kalid (or Khalid) ibn Yazid (d. c. 704), credited with introducing alchemy to the Islamic world. Morienus Romanus is thought to have been a Greek Christian monk. In CW 12, par. 386, Jung cites a long passage in which Morienus is giving instruction to Kalid, an Omayyad prince. The dialogues of these two are discussed by R. P. Multhauf in his introduction to *Alchemy and the Occult* (New Haven, 1968), vol. 1, p. xi.

Christian anchorites, and describes how they are tempted by the devil and the tricks the devil plays on them. He says the devil even occasionally reads the Bible to them or sings hymns so that they think he is a pious one, but as he comes with a great noise singing psalms or preaching sermons, they should know that this must be the devil. It cannot be the Holy Ghost, for that is a stillness; when everything is quite still then they can be sure it is the Holy Ghost. Nietzsche uses here language which shows something one could call the essential experience, and we can see from it what the Superman really means to him; it is the manifestation of God in man, God born out of man, and that is the mystery of transmutation or of transubstantiation: namely, God born and generated in the flesh.[4]

You see, it was that mystery which made St. Augustine, who was surely a very good Christian, insist upon a thought which is very pagan and quite alchemistic; he says that the Virgin Mary is verily the earth, and that that is a proof that Christ is born from the earth.[5] St. Augustine even speaks of the earth that is not yet fecundated by the spring rains. But that was a time when the spirit still lived, when it was connected with the nature of things, while in our days spirit and earth have become entirely divided. Even in the Catholic church you would never hear that Mother Mary was the earth and that Christ was born from the earth. People would remain as stupid as before, and it would mean nothing to them if a parson of today should repeat St. Augustine's speech. But it means a whole lot because we have now a psychological equivalent. The old idea of the earth to us means the body; the savior is born from this body. To find out how the savior could be produced from the earth in a miraculous way is the alchemistic quest, for to them the philosopher's stone, the gold, or the child was really the savior. They *called* it the savior.

We have here in Zürich the so-called *Codex Rhenovacensis*, an alchemistic codex which came from the library of a monastery; it was written probably sometime in the 15th century, but it might be older than that. There it is openly said that the stone is the savior, and the whole alchemical procedure is expressed in the analogy of the Song of Songs, which is really a beautiful and most sensuous oriental love song. Arabic and Syrian parallels of exactly the same character have been found;

---

[4] Athanasias (292?-373), Greek Archbishop of Alexandria, insisted that the members of the Trinity were all of the one essence (*homoousion*, not just *homoiousion*), which became official doctrine in the Nicene Creed. Compare, "All the Buddhas are one in essence" (Paul Carus, *The Gospel of Buddha* [Chicago and London, 1915], p. 259).

[5] See above, 12 Feb. 1936, n. 6.

they were sort of wedding songs which were always of a typically sensuous character and if possible, obscene. You know, the Song of Songs
is in parts quite obscene, but the obscenity then had not the evil connotation which it has now. The obscenities in antique cults had a sort
of fertilizing power; it was sometimes believed that such allusions had
a favorable influence on the crops. One finds that in the *Aischrologia* of
Eleusis, where the rich ladies of Athens after a very good meal with
wine started making obscene jokes, because it was supposed to have a
favorable effect on the crops of the next season. Mother Earth likes to
hear such jokes, it makes her smile, she brings forth rich crops, helped
along by such allusions.[6] Now have you any question before we leave
this chapter?

Mr. Martin: Why does it come as a shadow?

Prof. Jung: Well, we mustn't be deceived by the word; our use of the
term *shadow* has a very different meaning, but here it means unsubstantial like a shadow. Of course, Nietzsche's idea of the Superman,
which I would express by the term of *the self*, would naturally appear
first under the cloak of the shadow, using the word this time as a psychological term. It appears in what has been rejected. The *lapis philosophorum*, the stone of greatest price, is at the same time the corner-
stone first rejected by the builders; also the matter out of which the
stone is made or in which the precious stone is found is what is trodden
underfoot or thrown onto dung heaps, cast out in the road. So psychologically it means that the thing which we think the least of, that part
of ourselves which we repress perhaps the most, or which we despise,
is just the part which contains the mystery. The test is: when you can
accept yourself in your totality, then you have brought together the
four elements—all the parts of yourself have come together from the
four corners of the earth. There again the unconscious uses symbolism
which is found in early Christian literature, in the *Shepherd of Hermas*,[7]
written in the middle of the second century: men come from the four
corners of the world each bringing a stone which instantly melts into
the building of an enormous tower made without joints. This is the
building of the church, but it is at the same time the idea of the self
which consists of many inherited units, so that it is even compared with
a handful of grain or gravel or pieces of iron or of gold; all that multitude of units is brought together in order to build the self.

[6] A woman named Baubo ("belly") would perform obscene dances to make Demeter
laugh. See C. Kerényi's *Eleusis*, tr. Ralph Manheim (Princeton, B.S. LXV 1967).

[7] See above, 13 June 1934, n. 21.

Now as long as things are in the state called by the alchemists *materia prima*, primal matter, it is dark and objectionable; nobody is convinced that the self will come from such a thing and therefore they don't find it. Psychologically it means of course that the mystery always begins in our inferior function, that is the place where new life, regeneration, is to be found. For we cannot finish perfect bodies, as the ancients say, we must work on imperfect bodies because only what is imperfect can be brought to perfection; a perfect thing can only be corrupted. This is perfectly obvious, so it cannot be done with the superior differentiated function. A very good, well-trained mind is the sterile field where nothing grows because it is finished. So you must take that which is most repressed by the mind, the feeling. And there you find the original chaos, a disorderly heap of possibilities which are not worked upon yet and which ought to be brought together through a peculiar kind of handling. You know we say psychologically that the inferior function, in this case the feeling, is contaminated with the collective unconscious; therefore it is disseminated all over the field of the collective unconscious and therefore it is mythological. So when you try to bring it up, a lot of archaic fantasies appear, the whole thing is unwieldy and utterly mistakeable; you easily take it for something poisonous or wrong or mad on account of that mixture of unconscious material. You reject it altogether therefore; no decent individual would have anything to do with an inferior function because it is stupid nonsense, immoral—it is everything bad under the sun. Yet it is the only thing that contains life, the only thing that contains also the fun of living. A differentiated function is no longer vital, you know what you can do with it and it bores you, it no longer yields the spark of life.

So a moment comes when people get sick of whatever they do and throw everything out of the window. Of course they are called the damnedest fools for they are just the people who have had a great success in the world, and then they disappear, take to the wood life as they do in India, and there they live in an entirely different style. They live in their inferior function because that contains the life. So you see the new experience naturally appears from the side where there was dark chaos before, such a chaos that we prefer to know nothing of it; if we have ever encountered it we have tried not to see it. Now usually, as long as things are in a normal condition, this side remains invisible, and one should imagine that one is up against such a problem when one is not; this is a thing which cannot be aped—one should not try to imitate or feel into it when one is not there. If one is there, one knows it; one does not need to ask. If not, one had better not dabble in

954

things which are most dangerous and poisonous. Well, that is the manifestation of the self under the cloak of the shadow. But I think here it is more the idea of an unsubstantial image, as unsubstantial as a shadow, also a foreshadowing, an anticipation. The beauty of the Superman appears to Nietzsche as a sort of anticipation, a shadow that falls upon his consciousness. Now, this is very genuine, one of the most genuine things in *Zarathustra*.

The title of the next chapter in German is *Von den Mitleidigen* which in my English translation is called "The Pitiful." This is a bit mistaken, according to my idea; I would rather say "The Compassionate."[8] Now as usual we have to ask ourselves by what bridge the transition is made from the former chapter to the new one. I must say to the new members that I have explained *Zarathustra* as a series of images; if you look through the index of course nobody can see at the first glance that all those different titles form a sequence, but it is really an irrational sequence like the sequences people develop when they do the actual work in analysis. One could easily look at *Zarathustra* as a work which had originated in analysis; it is an involuntary analysis, but things have happened very much as they happen in a practical analysis—of course not of the ordinary kind, but in the synthetical stage where the fundamental attempt is to synthesize the transmuted individual. First the patient is taken to pieces, which can be done by the Adlerian or Freudian or any other way of analysis, and that may be perfectly sufficient from a therapeutic point of view. That is, the ordinary symptoms may be brought to disappear, and that can be indifferent to a doctor, naturally, whether a man goes on to a spiritual development or another kind of life. In the one case the doctor breathes on a symptom and it disappears by suggestion or something like that; or it can be done by analysis, and the patient says, "Oh, is that so? Very glad to know it. Thanks, goodbye."

But in the other case, something more is needed, and such cases are usually characterized by an intense transference. They want to break away, to say goodbye and be reasonable, but the unconscious says, "No, you are now going to be unreasonable and fall in love," which is of course all bunk—it is all crazy stuff, and they themselves think so, perhaps. But their unconscious without pity holds them to the transference because something else is demanded or expected of them, some further development. And that development goes beyond that mere taking-apart stage, which is quite rational and explicable, to a synthetic

[8] Kaufmann* translated this title, "The Pitying."

955

process which, if observed and carefully taken down, appears as a series of images or pictures—or you can make chapters of it. For dreams are chapters; if you put down your dreams carefully from night to night and understand them, you can see that they are chapters of a long text. It is a process which moves in a circle if you do nothing about it. You can see that with insane people where the conscious is absolutely unable to accept what the unconscious produces, and in that case the unconscious process simply makes a circle, as an animal has its usual way where it always circulates; deer or hares or any other wild animals move like that when they are pasturing. And that is so with us inasmuch as the conscious is divorced from the unconscious. But the moment the conscious peeps into the unconscious and the line of communication is established between the two spheres of life, the unconscious no longer moves in mere circles, but in a spiral. It moves in a circle till the moment when it would join the former tracks again, and then it finds itself a bit above. So it imitates what form of life?

Mrs. Baumann: Plant life.

Prof. Jung: Yes, that is the origin of the symbol of the tree, or the plant, or the growth of the flower. Now, in Nietzsche's case it is not a going round in a circle, not a blind working of nature. There is an eye that sees it; his consciousness looks into the process and so hinders it from being a mere circle. It is a spiral which is moving up to a certain goal. And that process is dramatic: Nietzsche's *Zarathustra* is a drama really. *Faust* is very much the same in that respect. It is also an unconscious process, a drama which moves up to a definite goal. So *Zarathustra* is the making of something, or the making for something, and each chapter is connected with the preceding one in a more or less invisible way. For instance, it is not at all evident how one arrives from "The Happy Isles" at "The Compassionate"—that is dark. But if you carefully study the end of a chapter and compare it with the subsequent title, you discover how he arrives at the particular theme of the next chapter. But the transition is utterly irrational just as it happens in human life. You see, historical events usually develop as nobody has foreseen; something always comes along which nobody foresaw, because we think in straight lines, by certain rules. Now we are moving in that direction and will arrive in such-and-such a place at such-and-such a time. But that is all wrong, because life moves like a serpent in an irrational way; always when you go to the left, soon you will go to the right, and when you say Yea you will soon say Nay. It is irrational, but it is so nevertheless. So we are now confronted with the problem, why does he call the next chapter "The Compassionate"?

Mrs. Sigg: In the end of the last chapter, he speaks of the beautiful Superman, and then by contrast he sees again how miserable man really is. Nietzsche always finds compassion a very bad quality in human beings; he thinks it is a wrong Christian attitude which doesn't help to create the Superman.

Prof. Jung: So you take it that the vision of the beauty of the Superman really accounts for the vision of the misery of man: since man is really quite miserable, to talk of the beauty of the Superman is too much anticipation, too much optimism. There is truth in what you say but I have not the feeling that it fits completely. For instance, in the first sentence he says, "Walketh he not amongst us as if amongst animals?" Now what is the difference between the human being and the animal?

Mrs. Crowley: I thought, replying to your first question, it was that in the last chapter on the Happy Isles he is emphasizing the fact of being the creator, and in this chapter the animals come. It refers here to the idea of his being among animals: they are the thing created. That is the opposite again, the *enantiodromia.*

Prof. Jung: You mean that he would identify with the animals?

Mrs. Crowley: Or be like the animals in that he is just an ordinary thing that is created.

Prof. Jung: But he is here very much in contrast to animals. We had better read the first part,

> My friends, there hath arisen a satire on your friend: "Behold Zarathustra! Walketh he not amongst us as if amongst animals?"
>
> But it is better said in this wise: "The discerning one walketh amongst men as amongst animals."
>
> Man himself is to the discerning one: the animal with red cheeks.
>
> How hath that happened unto him? Is it not because he hath had to be ashamed too oft?

You see, that has to be taken into account.

Dr. Harding: Is it not that the feeling in the former chapter was said to be in prison, and when the feeling comes up as over against his willing, he feels compassionate towards feeling; but on the other hand he wants to go on with his willing. It is the feeling that makes man different from the animal, is it not?

Prof. Jung: Well, if you try to feel into the vision at the end of the preceding chapter, what it might mean to him to have that vision of the Superman, to hold that secret, you see that it gives him a very unique

957

position. That is a realization which emphasizes his solitude, his lone-liness, and naturally he will be led to compare with other people who have not had it. Such a vision always separates people from their fellow beings. I have quoted quite a number of examples. For instance, our Swiss saint Nicholas von der Flüe had such a vision, and people ran away when they saw him. They could not stand the sight of his face— it was too hellish. Now that vision *is* an experience of the divine pres-ence and naturally he will look around afterwards to see where he is. You see, that mocking remark that is made, that satire, is really a mock-ing remark he makes to himself. Am I not now a man, a human being that walks among animals? He cannot help comparing himself to his human surroundings and naturally the reaction is compassion—par-ticularly so because we know by inference and through some knowl-edge of psychology that the Superman locked in the stone is the infe-rior function. That is feeling and sensation in his case, and that leads him immediately to the reality in which he lives. He is very clearly an intuitive thinker and by means of his differentiated functions he is able to discern.

But the vision is an entirely different process which comes from within or from below, from the regions of the undifferentiated func-tions. The feeling will naturally produce a feeling condition when it comes to the daylight and sensation will produce a reality, so he will surely be led to his reality. It is as if he had said, "Now we have seen the supernatural beauty of the Superman," and then the feeling and sen-sation react and instantly he sees that he is amongst animals. For Zar-athustra, mind you, is the living Superman, within him, with all his beauty; and he came to him as a shadow, a sort of anticipation, to show him what human beings are. And you can be sure it is a very negative picture because the inferior function is not positive. An intuitive thinker has negative sensation and negative feeling, and it surely doesn't sound like a very nice feeling when he begins the chapter about compassion with the statement that he is walking amongst animals. To be addressed as animals, one would say, was a bit rough on his sur-roundings. And when he says, "The discerning one walketh amongst men *as* amongst animals," this shows very clearly that the vision has taught him a lesson: he discerns something very clearly. What would that be? What is an act of discernment? What does it increase or aug-ment?

Mrs. Crowley: Consciousness.

Prof. Jung: Yes, the discerning one is the conscious one. His vision of the Superman was so substantial obviously, in that he realized the possibility of a higher, more extended state of consciousness. It meant an increase of consciousness. Therefore he calls himself the discerning one; namely, the one who is conscious over against the blind and unconscious crowd. Expressed in antique language it would be *ennoia* in contradistinction to *anoia*. The one is the conscious man, redeemed, transmuted; and the other is unredeemed, black, dark, with no immortal soul. The one is *quasi modo genitus*, as if newborn, and the other is in an animal-like condition. The Catholic church makes a very serious difference there. They even have the dogma that children who die before being baptized, no matter how innocent they are—a newborn child cannot be sinful—are nevertheless deprived of the presence and vision of God. And what are they going to do with those unredeemed little souls? They must throw them into the wastepaper basket because they are not even fit for hell; or they may have somewhere a melting pot so they go back into the laboratory where new souls are made. But they are deprived of the vision of God as if they were sinners, only they are not submitted to eternal torture in hell. Now, the vision of the beauty of the Superman has an effect which you can observe very often in people who have had it or assume that they have had it: namely, they are easily inflated or inclined to be inflated, and look down upon the ignorant, animal-like crowd that is blind and unconscious. You see, the beginning of this chapter shows very clearly the attitude or the state of consciousness of such people. The Gnostics in the times of early Christianity had that sort of imagination or inflation about themselves, and you remember that St. Paul makes a remark about them. He uses the very word for inflation in the German text: *Viel Wissen blähet auf,* "Much knowledge is inflation."

Miss Hannah: It is "puffeth up" in English.

Prof. Jung: "Puffeth up" is quite good. That is substantial and would describe the inflation they must have observed in those days. It must have been a very common phenomenon since Paul refers to it. Then the third paragraph, "Man himself is to the discerning one: the animal with red cheeks," shows very clearly how far the discerning one is above the ordinary man. "How hath that happened unto him? Is it not because he hath had to be ashamed too oft?" Well, naturally one has to be ashamed of one's companions when they behave like animals—this is a typical experience. He continues now,

> Oh my friends! Thus speaketh the discerning one: shame, shame, shame—that is the history of man!
>
> And on that account doth the noble one enjoin upon himself

959

not to abash: bashfulness doth he enjoin on himself in presence of all sufferers.

What does that mean?

Mrs. Sigg: I should say that it was just Nietzsche's problem. He was himself ashamed of the animal part of his nature; on account of his early Christian training he could not see any God-likeness in the animal. He could not connect God and animal as you do, for instance. And this is just a hint; the beauty of the Superman comes to him as shadow, which implies that there is a dark animal side to the Superman.

Prof. Jung: Yes, that is true. The end of the tragic *peripetie*, the drama of Zarathustra, is really that he cannot accept the shadow, cannot accept the ugliest man, and so loses the connection with the body altogether. And that is surely in his case due to his early Protestant education which did not help him to accept the animal; he was really ashamed of his lower man and could not integrate him. You see, this shame or feeling of awkwardness which he experiences in the presence of sufferers is of course very exaggerated. It is a typical sort of hysterical exaggeration, but it makes it clear that he simply cannot stand seeing that inferior man, cannot stand the sight of his own inferiority. It is a sort of aesthetical offense to see how far man is from a Superman. And of course all that brought back to him how far *he* is inferior, how far *he* is from the Superman; therefore he is so particularly priggish and prudish with the imperfection or the defectiveness of man. There is also something primitive in it—in being shy of suffering or hesitant in dealing with suffering people. You see, primitives always assume that people who suffer from disease, or who are maimed, who suffer from malformation of the body, are very unfavorable. They are unlucky, and therefore one should have nothing to do with them. One should keep away from such people because they bring their unlucky mana into one's house. We still have such ideas. For instance, a general who has lost a battle is no longer considered fit. He has lost his prestige even if he wins the next. He is like a captain who has lost his ship and will never have another: he is unlucky so one can have nothing to do with him. That point of view is in Nietzsche aestheticized and exaggerated.

Verily, I like them not, the merciful ones, whose bliss is in their pity: too destitute are they of bashfulness.

If I must be pitiful, I dislike to be called so; and if I be so, it is preferably at a distance.

960

Preferably also do I shroud my head, and flee, before being recognized: and thus do I bid you do, my friends!

You see, here he is really getting terribly exaggerated about it and
whenever he, or people in general, become so particularly exaggerated about certain statements, there is always more behind than meets
the eye. You know, it seems to be a particularly ticklish problem to
show the feeling of compassion. And what is the conclusion you would
draw from such a priggish attitude?

Miss Hannah: That he is still frightfully caught by the church attitude.

Prof. Jung: That is perfectly good as a historical explanation, and it
would probably be true in his case because he is a parson's son and had
too much of that kind of talk pumped into his veins. But we must also
take into account that the man Nietzsche was then pretty far from the
Christian church; he had gone a long way, and we must give credit to
his accomplishments. So when he still goes on being so priggish, what
must we conclude?

Dr. Harding: Has it not to do with his own sickness, and that he was
in exile?

Prof. Jung: That is it. It is as if he were foreseeing what was going to
happen to him; *he* is the man who had to be taken care of for about
twelve years, absolutely *à la merci* of his surroundings. He was so particular about it because he felt that this thing was on him, and he would
not see it. He would not have it, but tried to be heroic about it, while
already he suffered from terrible migraines. He had to take drugs for
sleeplessness, and had very bad days and weeks when he could not
work; he wrote the most pitiful letters to his sister and friends about it.
So he was very much a man who appealed to compassion, and moreover he lived on compassion. He had no money and earned none, and
it was the good will of certain people in Basel that guaranteed a pension for him to live on. I happen to know a rich old lady who contributed to Nietzsche's life when he was writing *Zarathustra.* So that is the
reason why he is so particular about compassion. And one might well
be like that; one cannot be a great hero and identify with the Superman with that bad conscience in the background. It is then not solid
ground, but is a bit slippery.

May my destiny ever lead unafflicted ones like you across my
path, and those with whom I *may* have hope and repast and honey
in common!

He has that desire to be concerned if possible with unafflicted ones because he is afflicted enough himself, so naturally he has then a claim to be fastidious with his friends. You know, when people say, "Oh, I cannot stand those people, they are too neurotic, too psychopathic"—or something of the sort, you know why it grates on their nerves. If you cannot stand certain people you can draw your conclusion and are probably not far from the truth.

> Verily, I have done this and that for the afflicted: but something better did I always seem to do when I had learned to enjoy myself better.

Learn it!

> Since humanity came into being, man hath enjoyed himself too little: that alone, my brethren, is our original sin!

Exactly, if one only knew how! That is the great problem. How can you enjoy yourself? Do you know? Once a certain alienist sent a questionnaire round among the Swiss alienists asking for a definition of happiness; he was not exactly a happy man and he wanted to know from all those people who were supposed to understand something about psychology what the secret of happiness was, how to make it, so that he could make a sackful of happiness for himself. Now what would you have answered? How can you learn to enjoy yourself?

Miss Hannah: By not trying to be anything but what you just are.

Prof. Jung: That is the very first step but that does not mean that you can really enjoy yourself. I would say: Be enjoyable and then you will enjoy yourself. You cannot enjoy yourself if you are not enjoyable. People think they should enjoy something but the thing itself does not produce pleasure or pain; it is indifferent, it only matters how you take it. For instance, if there is a very excellent wine and you don't like wine, how does it help you? You must be able to enjoy it. The question is, how can you make yourself enjoy?

Mrs. Sigg: In Nietzsche's case it would be very much more possible if he could develop his inferior functions, feeling and sensation.

Prof. Jung: Exactly, in his case it is very clear; without feeling and sensation how can he enjoy his life, his world, or anybody else? You need a pretty decent kind of feeling to be able to enjoy a thing. You see, it must come to you, enjoyment is something that comes really by the grace of God, and if you are not naive, if you are not simple like a primitive in your inferior function, you cannot enjoy, that is perfectly obvious; you must still have that immediate freshness of a child or an animal. So the more you accept your undifferentiated functions, the more you are likely to be able to enjoy something; to enjoy with the freshness of the child is the best joy, and it is something exceedingly simple. If you are sophisticated you cannot really enjoy, it is not naive, but is at the expense of somebody else; you enjoy it, for instance, when somebody falls into a trap you have laid, but somebody pays for your pleasure; that is what I would call a sophisticated pleasure. *Die schönste Freude ist die Schadenfreude* is a German statement—enjoying that somebody else has fallen into a hole which you have prepared. But a real enjoyment is not at the expense of anybody; it lives by itself, and this is only to be had by simplicity and modesty, if you are satisfied with what you have to provide. And you get it naturally from the inferior functions because they contain life, while the upper functions are so extracted and distilled already that they can only imitate a sort of enjoyment inasmuch as it is at the expense of somebody else—somebody else has to step in and pay for it.

And when we learn better to enjoy ourselves, then do we unlearn best to give pain unto others, and to contrive pain.

It is perfectly true that we really do enjoy ourselves too little and therefore take a particular pleasure in torturing other people. For instance, children who are cruel to animals or to their fellows are always children who are tortured at home by the parents; and the parents torture them because they themselves are tortured, either by themselves or the grandparents. If the grandparents are dead the parents continue their bad education and torture themselves: they think it is their duty, to do something disagreeable to themselves is their idea of morality. And inasmuch as they have such barbarous beliefs they pass on to their children that unnatural cruelty, and then the child tortures animals or nurses or fellow beings. People always hand on what they get, so what children do is a sort of indicator of what parents do to the children. Of course it is all done unconsciously. That is typical Protestantism, that is inherited sin; they hand on these things to the following generation and then they of course hand them on too. Nietzsche knew a great deal of that, that is perfectly certain. If people would only enjoy themselves they would not hand on so much cruelty; then they would not enjoy disagreeable things and would avoid doing them. Then they could say that they were very immoral but they would be responsibly immoral; they would have a sort of moral inferiority but they would have a legitimate punishment, and they would not hand on the punishment for what they had omitted to do. But inasmuch as they have a sense of duty and call it morality, they think they must hand that on, and the follow-ing generations are punished in the same way.

> Therefore do I wash the hand that hath helped the sufferer; therefore do I wipe also my soul.

This is perfectly true under the assumption that the suffering is really a self-inflicted misery coming from the same premises under which Nietzsche himself suffered, that peculiar Protestant psychology.

> For in seeing the sufferer suffering—thereof was I ashamed on account of his shame; and in helping him, sorely did I wound his pride.

You see, that is only when Nietzsche assumes that the other sufferer is in exactly the same sophisticated condition as himself, but that is not true. There he is complicated by sophistication, is trying to play the role of the hero. If a man is trying to identify with a heroic figure while he is really in misery, naturally he is very sensitive and it is quite deli-cate to deal with him at all, for his misery contradicts him. It shows that he is inferior, yet by his attitude he wants to make us believe that he is a great hero, that his suffering is completely overcome. Then we must help him to hide his own misery, but it is a lie and then your hands get dirty and you must wash them, and it is quite right that you are ashamed in such a case. But if you are dealing with real suffering, it is a different matter; to feel that you must wash your hands after touch-ing real suffering is only possible when you yourself are in a state of misery which you do not want to acknowledge.

> Great obligations do not make grateful, but revengeful; and when a small kindness is not forgotten, it becometh a gnawing worm.

LECTURE V

3 June 1936

Prof. Jung:

Here is a question by Dr. Harding: "Can you take up in further detail the section in the chapter on the Compassionate Ones where Nietzsche speaks of man as the animal with red cheeks? The interpretation given at the last seminar that he was ashamed on account of the unconsciousness of his fellow man does not seem adequate to me. Is there not an analogy with the story of Eden where we are told that when Adam and Eve had eaten of the tree of knowledge they were ashamed before God of their nakedness, which had never bothered them before? And perhaps—who knows?—they may have been ashamed of their clothes before the other animals? In fact, does not consciousness itself carry its own burden of guilt because the discerning one can no longer act with the complete rightness of unconscious instinct?"

Well, you have answered your question yourself, practically. That shame is of course a very typical reaction; it is a primitive reaction which clearly shows the distance that exists between the ego consciousness and the original unconsciousness of mere instinct. As long as man is in a merely instinctive animal condition, there is absolutely no ground for shame, no possibility of shame even, but with the coming of the ego consciousness, he feels apart from the animal kingdom and the original paradise of unconsciousness, and then naturally he is inclined to have feelings of inferiority. The beginning of consciousness is characterized by feelings of inferiority, and also by megalomania. The old prophets and philosophers say nothing is greater than man, but on the other side nothing is more miserable than man, for the ego consciousness is only a little spark of light in an immense darkness. Yet it is the light, and if you pile up a thousand darknesses you don't get a spark of light, you don't make consciousness. Consciousness is the sun in the great darkness of the world. Man is just a little lantern in the world of darkness, and as soon as you have a certain amount of ego

965

consciousness, naturally you are isolated and become self-conscious—you can't help it—and naturally you no longer possess the absolute simplicity of nature: you are no longer naive. It is a great art and a great difficulty to become like unto a child again—or better still, like unto an animal; to become like an animal is then the supreme ideal.

When you have built up your consciousness to a decent degree, you become so separated from nature that you feel it to be a disadvantage; you feel that you have fallen from grace. This is of course the expulsion from paradise. Then life becomes ego misery and lawlessness and you must create artificial laws in order to develop a feeling of obedience. Having ego consciousness means that you have a certain amount of disposable willpower, which of course means arbitrary feelings and decisions, disobedience of natural laws and so on; and that gives you a terrible feeling of being lost, cursed, isolated, and wrong altogether. And of course this causes feelings of shame. Compare your state of innocence with the innocence of a little child and you have ground for shame; and compared with an animal you are nowhere. So the dawn of consciousness was naturally a tremendous problem to man; he had to invent a new law-abiding world of obedience, the careful observance of rules; instead of the herd or the natural animal state, he had to invent an artificial state. He has now succeeded in making of the state a tremendous monster, such as nature probably never would have tolerated, but he had to do it in order to compensate that *sentiment d'incomplétude, d'insuffisance*. For we should not live instinctively any longer. We had to invent machines and law books and morals in order to give mankind a feeling of being in order, of being in a decent condition—something similar to paradise where the animals knew how to behave with each other. You see, the great world seems to be a self-regulating orderliness, an organism that moves and lives in a more or less decent way. The catastrophes are not too great or too many. There are not too many diseases—only a decent amount to kill off enough animals. But we know that we can break out at any time and destroy as no volcano and no epidemic ever destroyed, and we chiefly injure our own species; we would not dream of making an international war against flies or microbes or against whales or elephants—it isn't worthwhile—but it is worthwhile when it is against man. That is so much against nature that on the other side, man seeks to protect himself by complicated machines, states, and contracts which he cannot observe. So this first reaction of shame symbolizes the moment when man felt his tragic difference from paradise, his original condition.

Yet that original condition was also not a very happy one. The primitive man did not feel his unconscious condition to be very satisfactory. He tried to get away from it. Of course we have the idea that the original condition was a wonderful paradise, but as a matter of actual fact man has always tried to move away from that unconsciousness. All his many ceremonies were attempts to create a more conscious condition, and any new positive acquisition in the field of consciousness was praised as a great asset, a great accomplishment. Prometheus stealing the fire from the immortal gods has become a savior of mankind, and man's greatest triumph was that God himself incarnated in man in order to illumine the world; that was a tremendous increase of consciousness. But every increase of consciousness means a further separation from the original animal-like condition, and I don't know where it will end: it is really a tragic problem. We have to discover more consciousness, to extend consciousness, and the more it is extended the more we get away from the original condition.

The body is the original animal condition; we are all animals in the body, and so we should have animal psychology in order to be able to live in it. Yes, if we had no body then we could live with contracts and marvelous laws which everybody could observe and a marvelous morality which everybody could easily fulfil. But since we have a body it is indispensable that we exist also as an animal, and each time we invent a new increase of consciousness we have to put a new link in the chain that binds us to the animal, till finally it will become so long that complications will surely ensue. For when the chain between man and animal has grown so long that we lose sight of the animal, anything can happen in between, the chain will snarl up somewhere. That has happened already and therefore we doctors have to find in a conscious individual the place where the chain begins; we have to go back to find out where it has been caught or what has happened to the animal at the other end of the line. Then we have to shorten it perhaps, or disentangle it, in order to improve the relationship between the consciousness that went too far ahead and the animal left behind. This figure of the chain is not my own invention. I found it the other day in a book by an old alchemistic doctor, as the so-called symbol of Avicenna;[1] the alchemists were mostly doctors and they developed their peculiar kind of psychology by means of very apt symbols. This one consists of an eagle flying high in the air, and from his body falls a chain which is attached to a toad creeping along on the earth. The eagle of course represents the air, the spirit, and in alchemy it had a very particular meaning. The

---

[1] Avicenna (980-1037), Islamic physician and philosopher, interpreter of Aristotle.

eagle would remind any alchemist of the phoenix, the self-renewing god, an Egyptian inheritance.

Now we will go on to the next question. Mr. Martin says: "In last week's Seminar you referred to the difficulty the old hermits experienced in distinguishing between the working of the Devil and of the Holy Ghost. Does not a very similar difficulty arise in analytical psychology? How is it possible in practice to distinguish between 'archetypal invasion' (of which Zarathustra is an example), and the appearance of the 'releasing symbol' which is the essential feature of the transcendent function? How is one to know whether one should use a long spoon in dealing with the visitant, or whether one should trust its leading? Again, is the origin of these two great manifestations of the unconscious the same in both cases? The archetype is a very characteristic form of action or situation, experienced many times before in the history of humanity and prehumanity, which becomes activated. Is the releasing symbol similarly a piece of human experience, floated into consciousness by the regressive libido; or is it more likely (judging by its general nature) to be an answer given by the self to the problem with which the individual is struggling?"

I am very glad that Mr. Martin has taken the trouble to ask this question. It is true that the difficulties the old monks and Christian philosophers experienced, when they tried to distinguish the *influxus diabolicus* from the working of the Holy Ghost, is a very fundamental problem. I gave you an example in the way Athanasias dealt with it, but I admit of course that his criterion—that the Holy Ghost comes in the stillness after great noise and confusion—is rather vague. It was probably of service in those days, but we would not now be able to use such a definition since we have no longer the same experience. Those people lived entirely alone for many years under most primitive conditions, generally in the desert, so they naturally had hallucinations. That happens very easily when one is quite alone. But we live in the crowded cities, and even in the country it is the same, only one is then usually invaded not by archetypes but by human beings, who are usually visible so one is able to deal with them. You see, that is all within the human scope; you can deal with them, can say *they* are guilty or wrong. But archetypes are much worse than human beings; you cannot put the blame on them because they are not visible and they have the most disagreeable quality of appearing in your own guise. They are somewhat of your own substance, so you feel how futile that would be. While if you blame human beings, you feel that you have done something quite useful: you have gotten rid of your own inferiority. Now *they* have to be inferior and damn them if they are not. Human beings are of great use as scapegoats. So we have no experiences that would compare in any way with the experiences of those lonely birds in the Libyan desert.

If you have experienced loneliness in nature for any stretch of time, you know how easily one begins to hallucinate—one hears one's name called for instance, or one feels presences or hears footsteps. And those Christian hermits in the year 100/150 would experience just marvels: the air would be full of uncanny noises, not only voices and visions. Athanasias tells of the most amazing things that happened to them. In Flaubert's *La Tentation de St. Antoine*, you get a fairly good picture of the turmoil in a primitive hermit's hut or cave.[2] Now, over against that *turba*, that confusion and turmoil, the criterion of Athanasias, the stillness of the Holy Ghost, would of course be most convincing. If the air has been filled with ten thousand devils and unclean existences, when all that has vanished and the whole thing collapses, the great stillness that came after, and the purity of the air, would give them the feeling of being redeemed. They would be sure that this was now the Holy Ghost even when they did not hear the Bible read in the next compartment; they were presumably very glad to be rid of the noise of the holy words. So for that time, that is a perfectly satisfactory argument, but we are living under entirely different circumstances and must have of course an entirely different criterion. We must have first of all the archetypal experience and there the trouble begins.

According to my experience, it is usually exceedingly difficult for the ordinary man to grasp at all what that means, because we are living so much in our personal psychology, in personal relations, in personal projections—we are so linked and cemented with human society—that we cannot perceive or conceive of anything impersonal. I experience the most unholy trouble when I try to say a word about the objectivity of our psychology: it is not popular. But now let us assume that people are quite ready to have archetypal experiences, that it really happens to them to perceive something of the objective workings of the unconscious, and let us assume that it *is* so—which is not quite self-evident—then that ancient question is put again: is it the powers of the air, of the water, of the earth, of the fire—in other words, is it an elementary power? Or is it the Holy Ghost? Now, inasmuch as it is evident that an

[2] Gustave Flaubert (1821-1880) described in his *Temptation of St. Anthony* (1874) how the credulous saint, faced with a world of contrary evidence, insisted, "We must believe in the Scriptures. . . . Leave it to the Church." St. Anthony or Athanasius (et al.) reported on the Christian hermits of the desert in *The Paradise* [or *Garden*] *of the Holy Fathers*.

archetype is operating—which in itself means nothing more than that nature is operating—this is neither good nor bad. It can be quite demoniacal and it can be quite good—generous and marvelous. It is morally indifferent. It is like a tree full of fruit: the tree lets the fruit fall and you pick it up and say how good the tree is. But the next year it has no fruit at all; you might die of starvation under that tree: it is just nature. And thus the archetypes are simply the functioning of natural elements of the unconscious, neither good nor bad. Inasmuch as we need nature, we need the life of the archetypes—it is indispensable. But though you need water for your life, you can also be drowned in a surplus of water; you need the sun yet the sun can scorch you to death; you need fire yet you can be destroyed by fire. So the archetypes naturally work both good and evil, and it all depends upon your skill whether you can manage to navigate through the many elementary dangers of nature.

Therefore, you so often have the ship as a symbol: even religions are called ships or vehicles. You remember the Christian allegory where Christ is at the tiller of the church, and in German the word *Schiff* means the nave of the church—the church is a ship. It is the same in the East, the Hinayana and the Mahayana, the little and the great vessel, designate the two forms of Buddhism. A religious system is like a safe form, a body of teaching, of principles, of advice and so on, which is destined to help man to navigate over the troubled waters of the unconscious. It is a human contrivance to protect one against the dangers of real life. There is no real life without archetypal experiences. The ordinary life is two-dimensional—it consists of pieces of paper—but the real life consists of three dimensions, and if it doesn't it is not real life, but is a provisional life. We are always exposed to the operations of nature and therefore we are always in need of a system of thought, or laws, or prescriptions—a sort of wisdom that would help us to navigate on the sea of the unconscious. And it is chiefly the skill of man that creates such a system. Not that *he* can bring it together; to say this is *his* skill is of course an insufficient statement: I am using there the ordinary language. People usually assume that they are the inventors of such things, that Moses is the inventor of the law, for instance—and even Christ is understood to be a sort of moral philosopher who had very good ideas, like Socrates; and the prophets in the Old Testament were really people who were just bothered with the fate of their nation and tried to help people by good advice.

But this is a sort of euhemerism which of course doesn't explain the facts; the real facts are that all these methods that make the ship are not inventions, but are revelations; it is a revealed truth or a perceived truth which has been thought before man has thought. Before I had that thought it had already been thought, and I merely happened to perceive it once in time; it has been there since eternity, is always there, has always lived, and I just happened in a certain moment to perceive it. Then of course I myself might get an inflation; if one touches upon such a thought, that happens. A fiery chariot comes from heaven and carries you away and you think you have invented an automobile; but wait until it comes to a standstill and you find that *you* have invented no fiery chariot because you are absolutely done for. So these things have been thought by an invisible thinker—we don't know where they come from. But I should call this the "Holy Ghost": that gives the helpful thought, personified in many forms in many times, for instance, as Oannes, the teacher who daily comes out of the sea according to the old Babylonian idea; or the boy Tages who comes out of the furrow the peasant has plowed and teaches the people useful things, how to protect themselves against all sorts of evils;[3] or it is the *Puer Aeternus* in Roman antiquity; or any other helpful god who reveals the truth. All these different personifications are always one and the same thing, the revelation of the thought that existed before man had the thought; and inasmuch as this thought is helpful, inasmuch as it reconciles a vital need of man to the absolute conditions of the archetypes, one could usefully say, "This is the Holy Ghost."

The Holy Ghost creates that symbol, that situation, or that idea or impulse, which is a happy solution of the postulates of the archetypes on the one side, and the vital needs of man on the other side. Then blind dark nature is again reconciled with the monocularity of man, his one-sided consciousness, and then the tragic gap between man's graceless consciousness and the dark abundance of the unconscious is for once shut again by the intervention of that thinker of helpful thoughts, a real Paraclete. That would be my definition of the function which has been personified in Christian antiquity as the "Holy Ghost." I would not know any better: it is a function that is just as friendly as it is inimical, to man as well as to archetypes. Sometimes the Holy Ghost is apparently quite against the vital needs of man as he imagines them; at another time it is against obvious nature, or it is for absolutely nothing but the demands of nature which we would call immoral. Yet the Holy Ghost insists upon it, and can bring it about because it is a superior thought. And when man has intelligence enough, good will enough,

[3] See CW 5, pars. 291-92.

instinct enough, to be able to perceive the superior power which at bottom is helpful, he has to submit—then he *can* submit. But if it is *nothing but* an archetype, then this is simply an elementary condition to which you can submit if you want to, to which you don't need to submit—provided always that it is not the working of the Holy Ghost. You see, the Holy Ghost "speaks to your condition"; this is a most excellent term of the Society of Friends which I learned from Mr. Martin. When a thing speaks to your condition, it means that it has gone home, it has hit the nail on the head, it clicks, it constellates something in you. The Holy Ghost is exactly that thing which speaks to your condition: you feel it all over and therefore there is no hesitation, no resistance.

If you try to resist, you create an artificial neurosis. That is most helpful, a very useful experience which I recommend. I hope you will have the experience once of being commanded by the Holy Ghost and disobeying the command. Then you see how it starts, and when you find it awkward and decide you better come round and obey the Holy Ghost, you see how it collapses. So the Holy Ghost is like a devil and can fill the air with devils if you don't obey, but the moment you obey, all the spooks collapse. You can have all the experiences of those hermits in the desert. What are a thousand years? Just nothing. You can have those experiences again if you expose yourself to those conditions. Then you can see how a neurosis or a psychosis is made and you can see how one heals it. Of course the indispensable condition is that you have an archetypal experience, and to have that means that you have surrendered to life. If your life has not three dimensions, if you don't live in the body, if you live on the two-dimensional plane in the paper world that is flat and printed, as if you were only living your biography, then you are nowhere. You don't see the archetypal world, but live like a pressed flower in the pages of a book, a mere memory of yourself.

Most people live like that in our time, an entirely artificial two-dimensional existence, and therefore they have no archetypal experience; for instance, a personal psychology, like that of Adler or Freud or any other educational experiment, is all two-dimensional. Of course you can say with great plausibility, "one ought to," "one should," and think you have done something, as when you move a letter on a flat page you think you have done something. Yes, you have created a new paragraph but of course nobody takes heed of it; as soon as you are exposed to real life you know that the whole system collapses as a perfectly flimsy house of cards.

So if I seem to avoid speaking of the Holy Ghost, it is not that I dis-

miss that idea entirely, but that we are living in this two-dimensional
world where people are not up to archetypal experiences and therefore, instead of that language of the real life, one can only use the language of the two-dimensional paper life. All that is utterly invalid in
the real life where one has archetypal experiences; then one talks of
the Holy Ghost quite certainly, as one talks of God, for this world has
nothing to do with the perfectly artificial world of consciousness which
is a sort of laboratory, or a rose-garden, or a chicken farm carefully
fenced in. There, nothing happens inside of the enclosure which you
have not made to happen; anything that happens unforeseen is a misfortune, and of course under human conditions you can always accuse
the neighbor of having done it. But if you live in a world where there
is no neighbor but the eternal deity, you cannot blame a neighbor.
Then you know that your neighbors are ghosts, archetypes, the elements of life. You cannot complain of neighbors when you are in a boat
on the sea—there are no neighbors: you are then in an archetypal condition.

Mr. Allemann: But don't you even then put the blame on the neighbors?

Prof. Jung: Ah yes, that is true; you can say the devil brought you into
such a situation if it is evident. But that is only good in a human court;
the whole archetypal world rocks with laughter when you accuse the
devil. That doesn't help you at all.

Mrs. Jung: Do you mean by "archetypal experience" a *conscious* archetypal experience? For when one has an archetypal experience one
doesn't necessarily recognize it as being such.

Prof. Jung: Exactly, that is the artificiality of our conscious world. It
is like assuming that this room, in which there are doors and windows
leading to the outer world, possesses no such doors and windows; or
like turning our backs on them and imagining that this is the whole
world. You see, that is the prejudice, the hubris of consciousness—the
assumption that we are in a perfectly reasonable world where everything can be regulated by laws. We don't recognize the fact that just
outside is a sea that can break in over our continent and drown our
whole civilization. As long as we turn our eyes to the center of the room
we are blissfully unaware of the fact that there is any archetypal situation whatever: we don't collide with the elemental world outside. As a
matter of fact, the whole room is, as it were, suspended in an elementary world, as our consciousness is suspended in a world of monsters,
but we simply won't see it; and when these monsters at times peep in
or make a noise, we explan it by indigestion or something of the sort.

We rationalize it, or if we cannot rationalize it we say it is a miracle which we don't understand—we refuse to understand. You see, this magic circle or this magic enclosure of consciousness is such a triumph—it has given man such security in a way—that he naturally tries to believe in it and to shield it against doubts. Moreover, we ought to shield it, ought to build that enclosure because the progress of consciousness is instinctual; we have to shield it in order to increase consciousness, and in doing that we increase it knowingly, knowing the danger of isolation. So it is as if we were building the most marvelous walls and dams, and then open the floodgates and let the water in, just that. For the soil of our consciousness dries up and becomes sterile if we don't let in the flood of the archetypes; if we don't expose the soil to the influence of the elements, nothing grows, nothing happens: we simply dry up. We are always a bit between the devil and the deep sea, and therefore we always need the intervention of the Holy Ghost to tell us how to reconcile the most irrational and the most paradoxical. For man is a terror in that respect, the highest principle on the one side and a perfect beast on the other. Now how do you reconcile the two? That is the conflict of Faust and Wagner, and Faust says to Wagner:

> Du bist dir nur des einen Triebs bewusst,
> O lernen nie den anderen kennen.[4]

Wagner is the typical representative of the two-dimensional world.

Mrs. Baynes: There is a point that I would like to ask, pursuing Mrs. Jung's question. Is it not true that each period of time has to find afresh its relationship to the experience of the archetype? For instance, the hermits could not be said to be conscious of the experience as we define consciousness.

Prof. Jung: No, they could not. They lived in a different time and under entirely different conditions, so their experience is necessarily different from ours. You can see the transition through the ages. It is a most interesting process, which of course I could not elucidate without very careful preparation.

Mrs. Baynes: Don't we have to say, then, that not only must we have a communication from the Holy Ghost, but we must *say* that there is a communication? That is, we must have an attitude between ourselves and the communication before we can say we are at the level of this period of consciousness. For instance, take the Wotan archetype which is apparently going round the world today; many people are experienc-

---

[4] "You are conscious of but one drive, / Oh, never seek to know the other."

ing that archetype but we cannot say that they are *consciously* experiencing it because they are in it. But if we are to be on the modern niveau, we have to be able to say, "This is an archetype."

Prof. Jung: Yes, one postulates a certain difference of ego consciousness from the archetypal *Ergriffenheit*.[5] You see, it is a matter here of a sort of periodicity: namely, it is like the mental or psychological evolution of an individual in our time of conflict and confusion, a time of inundation. Say you have been very one-sided and lived in a two-dimensional world only, behind walls, thinking that you were perfectly safe; then suddenly the sea breaks in: you are inundated by an archetypal world and you are in complete confusion. Then out of that confusion suddenly arises a reconciling symbol—we cannot say "the" in spite of the fact that is is always the same—it is *an* archetypal symbol or *a* reconciling symbol which unites the vital need of man with the archetypal conditions. So you have made a step forward in consciousness, have reached a higher level; therefore it is of course a transcendent function because you transcended from one level to another. It is as if you had crossed the great flood, the inundation, or the great river, and arrived on the other bank, and so you have transcended the obstacle. Now in that new condition you will fortify yourself again, will build new walls; for a very long time you will live on the experience of this spiritual intervention that has given you the reconciling symbol. You will take it as a final and definite manifestation of the deity perhaps if you are religious and have *pistis*, loyalty to your experience. And that is the way it should be even if you have to stay on that level to the end of your days, as so many people do. This intervention is rare; we have very few such experiences. To have a revelation of a reconciling symbol doesn't happen a dozen times in an individual lifetime.

Well now, if it is a question of the whole of mankind, then once in the course of centuries people fall into great confusion. They are flooded, and a reconciling symbol is revealed which now becomes the truth, the new basis of consciousness; the German term *Weltanschauung* expresses it.[6] It becomes a new *pistis*, a new faith, and it will be fortified by walls. It will be defended. And it will work as long as the walls stand. Then suddenly the walls break and a flood comes and we have a new condition in which a new symbol should be revealed, or where the revelation of a symbol may be hoped for. Of course we cannot make it be-

[5] *Ergriffenheit*: emotion.
[6] See CW 16, pars. 175-91, for Jung's address, "Psychotherapy and a Philosophy of Life."

cause it is not our thought, but is the thought of the invisible thinker that is waiting its time. When the condition of man is such that we have no more force to resist or oppose with our ideals—the old ideals are the worst enemies of the new—and if our resistance is utterly gone, then the manifestation of the new symbol can take place. And then the evolution goes on as it always has gone on. Is that clear?

Mrs. Baynes: Well, I think it boils down to my wanting to know whether or not the transcending function requires conscious perception in order for it to consummate itself.

Prof. Jung: Of course. You see, as long as you don't know what you are suffering from, you are not having an archetypal experience. If you are on a ship that is sinking and go on playing poker in the smoking room without noticing that your feet are getting wet and that the whole thing is going down, you never experience the catastrophe—you are dead before you notice anything. It is absolutely necessary that you make the experience conscious, that you know you are up against an elementary situation. That is of course the very first condition. Yet to apperceive the situation is not the only task for consciousness. There is still more: you have to hold your own, to fight for your own existence in the flood. If you simply go under, knowing that you are going under, you have not dealt with the situation. You have to swim, to use every means possible to defend your own against the flood—you must wrestle with those archetypes—and only when you are really up against it to the last breath, only then, the revelation may take place. But you cannot foresee how it is possible, so you have to show fight, to hold your own. Usually when archetypes come in, people just collapse—they are utterly afraid, completely gone. Then you can only take the broom and clean up the whole mess, or somebody has to hold them to enable them to stand up against it at all. Well, they did not understand that an archetypal manifestation is of immense elemental power, so the shock is all the greater. If a person who has never had an archetypal dream suddenly has one, how he jumps! It is amazing. Now we have another question to deal with: "Will you explain what you mean when you speak of archaic elements in the self?"

We have already dealt with this question in the Seminar, but of course it is not too much to go over the ground again because it is a very important and disturbing problem. You see, archetypes *mean* archaic elements because they are forms of psychical life which have an eternal existence. They have existed since times immemorial and will continue to exist in an indefinite future. And they always retain the character which we call "archaic" (*arche* means beginning or principle). They

976

date from the primeval state of things and are those forms of life which operate with the greatest frequency and regularity. From the functional point of view, one could describe them as a system or a functional unit which contains the picture of the conflict, the danger, the risk—and also the solution of it. That is the typical aspect of the archetype, and therefore it is helpful in many ways: namely, as a preexisting solution of certain average conflicts. I mean certain elemental conflicts or differences, like the archetype of the crossing of the ford for example. The archetypal situation is always beset with all sorts of dangers, such as being devoured by the dragon or swallowed by the great fish, and the hero is always doing something in order to get out of the danger, either combatting it or liberating himself when caught. This is the narrow pass, or the two rocks that clash together, or the mouth of the monster, and so on. Now, these archetypes make up the so-called archaic elements of the self.

The self is by definition the totality of all psychical facts and contents. It consists on one side of our ego consciousness that is included in the unconscious like a smaller circle in a greater one. So the self is not only an unconscious fact, but also a conscious fact: the ego is the visibility of the self. Of course, in the ego the self only becomes dimly visible, but you get under favorable conditions a fair idea of it through the ego—not a very true picture, yet it is an attempt. You see, it is as if the self were trying to manifest in space and time, but since it consists of so many elements that have neither space nor time qualities, it cannot bring them altogether into space and time. And those efforts of the self to manifest in the empirical world result in man: he is the result of the attempt. So much of the self remains outside, it doesn't enter this three-dimensional empirical world. The self consists, then, of the most recent acquisitions of the ego consciousness and on the other side, of the archaic material. The self is a fact of nature and always appears as such in immediate experiences, in dreams and visions, and so on; it is the spirit in the stone, the great secret which has to be worked out, to be extracted from nature, because it is buried in nature herself. It is also most dangerous, just as dangerous as an archetypal invasion because it contains *all* the archetypes: one could say an archetypal experience was the experience of the self. It is like a personification of nature and of anything that can be experienced in nature, including what we call God.

Therefore the term *self* is often mixed up with the idea of God. I would not do that. I would say that the term *self* should be reserved for that sphere which is within the reach of human experience, and we should be very careful not to use the word *God* too often. As we use it, it borders on impertinence; it is unlawful to use such a concept too often. The experience of the self is so marvelous and so complete that one is of course tempted to use the conception of God to express it. I think it is better not to, because the self has the peculiar quality of being specific yet universal. It is a restricted universality or a universal restrictedness, a paradox; so it is a relatively universal being and therefore doesn't deserve to be called "God." You could think of it as an intermediary, or a hierarchy of every-widening-out figures of the self *till* one arrives at the conception of a deity. So we should reserve that term *God* for a remote deity that is supposed to be the absolute unity of all singularities. The self would be the preceding stage, a being that is more than man and that definitely manifests; that is the thinker of our thoughts, the doer of our deeds, the maker of our lives, yet it is still within the reach of human experience. And that thing consists of archaic elements, of all the doubtful things with which we have to struggle. For we *have* to struggle with the self. The self is not *apparently* inimical. It is *really* inimical—and it is also of course the opposite. It is not only our best friend, but also our worst enemy; because it doesn't see, it is as if not conscious of time and space conditions. We must say to the self, "Now don't be blind; for heaven's sake be reasonable. I shall do my best to find a place for you in this world, but you don't know the conditions. You don't know what military service means or tax collectors or reputations. You have no idea of life in time and space. So if you want me to do something for you, if you want me to help you to manifest, you must be reasonable and wait. You should not storm at me. If you kill me, where are your feet?"[7] That is what *I* (the ego) am.

The self makes terrible demands and really can demand too much. For it is the next manifestation of the unconscious creator that created the world in a marvelous dream. He tried for many millions of years to produce something that had consciousness, something like a human being. He tried frogs first, a thing that has two arms and two legs and no tail, but it was coldblooded so it didn't work. Then he drew the conclusion that it must have warm blood, that apparently only the warmth of blood succeeds in producing intensity of consciousness and a refined brain. First he tried to make the skeleton outside the body and found it was no good, and then he made it inside the body. That is the way the thing worked: he kept on for millions of years trying to produce this effect. But that does not show very much forethought. It is

---

[7] See above, 27 June 1934, n. 11, for Silesius and Rilke.

just a blind experimenting: you feel that blind urge which wants to come into existence, and it is beautiful and cunning and evil as nature is. And you are the pioneer of that urge, the seeing and the hearing head and the clever hands with which you should make form, make space and existence for that thing which wants to become. That urge is always behind you, always forcing you on quite blindly, and when it becomes too bad you simply say, "Be reasonable, you overrun me. What is the use of it?" But you can only say *that*. If you lie and try to cheat the blind creator then woe unto you. It is like the play of the water that always finds a hole through which it runs out. So the builder of a dam says, "That is a devil of a river: it always finds the place in the foundations where the stones are a bit weak and undermines it—why not the place where the stones are good?" No, exactly, that is the cunning of nature; wherever the weak spot lies, wherever you try to deceive the creative deity, there you will be undermined. It doesn't help you to cheat, it doesn't help you to say, "No, it is impossible." It is only impossible when the argument is watertight; then if it is really impossible, that argument will be heard.

For Tao is of the nature of the water: it always finds the deepest places and will of course undermine the weak spot; no cheating possible, you undermine yourself by wrong statements. So you must always be very careful to consider your situation before you say, "It is really too much, I cannot do it." Otherwise it simply washes the ground from under your feet and you suddenly slip down. You should have tried first, and if it is really impossible you must say so. Then it will be heard: that is the archetypal moment in which the intervention of the Holy Ghost takes place. Then your building with the powers of nature creates such an affinity between the archetypal world and your miserable attempt at consciousness that you become one again with the archetypal world, and that is the divine moment of the revelation.

So you can say everything of the self; you can say it is a devil, a god, nothing but nature. It is your worst vice, or your strongest conviction, or your greatest virtue. It is just everything—the totality. You can even say it is the Holy Ghost. It is the victory of the divine life in the turmoil of space and time. The success is that it could manifest in space and time, that it could break through into existence and appear to the world; and whenever you suffer or enjoy such a victory you have succeeded in giving wider space to the existence of the self. I know nothing truer than that fact that something wants to live, to exist, to unfold: the tiger wants to be a tiger, the flower wants to be a flower, and the snake, a snake, and man, a man. They all want to exist and to appear.

And we want to increase our consciousness. Whether we know it or not doesn't matter. If we can produce the success of life by the aid of the divine intercession, we have fulfilled the purpose of our existence. Of course we can speculate about it—why it *should* be so—but we shall never know why it is so. Yet I think it is useful to have the right ideas, and I call an idea *right* or *true* when it is helpful: that is the only criterion.

For instance, how can you know whether a certain fruit is good or poisonous? You eat it and then you will see; if it is good and nourishing, if it doesn't poison you, that is what I call *true*. And in the same way, if a truth feeds me when I eat it, I say this is a good truth. If I don't know whether I should assume the human soul to be immortal, I simply take it in: I eat immortality, and see what the influence is on my digestion. If it is a bad influence I spit it out and will never eat it again; if it has the right effect upon my nervous and mental system I assume that is the right way. And so we can assume a lot of things inasmuch as they agree with our functioning. If they agree with life they are just as good as truth. Perhaps you don't know whether the body needs salt, so you abstain from eating it and there are bad consequences—you suffer from the absence of salt; whether you know why doesn't matter: the absence of salt is enough and you will be injured. So when a certain truth is absent, you will suffer and be miserable, and if it can be accepted and agrees with your system, it is good stuff. That is my only criterion; if it agrees, it works. You see, we are allowed to—even have to—speculate about certain things: why there should be such a fuss about the consciousness of man, for instance. Why should there be that urge that man should become conscious? It is a pre-conscious urge; once man was entirely unconscious, and then he was forced into consciousness, a most tragic enterprise. It would be much better if he stopped increasing consciousness because that means more machines, more tragedy, a greater distance from nature; but we go on. We are forced by the thing that thinks before us, that wills before us, so we assume that the deity demands the consciousness of man.

Yet if we look on his works which we can observe through millions of years in the study of paleontology and anthropology, we see that the whole thing has gone on in an irregular way. It never had much system in spite of being exceedingly clever, so we assume that the creation was no systematic attempt, but was just dabbling and experimenting and finally falling right, more or less. That is the conclusion that comes and stuns us. If one knows anything about natural science, one can see what an incomplete attempt the creation turned out to be. It was, for

instance, quite clever that water reached its greatest density at four degrees centigrade above zero; if it had not been so, our rivers and lakes
and seas would be filled with ice that never melted, and the climate of
the earth would be intolerably cold. And if it were not so, *our* creation
at least would not have been possible.

Now under those conditions we are allowed to make the speculation
that because the creator is blind he needs a seeing consciousness, and
therefore he finally made man who was the great discovery. He could
say something. He could become conscious that he lived in a space of
three dimensions. The creator has made a time-space cage; he split off
the fourth dimension from space and the three remaining formed a
marvelous cage in which things could be separated. And when time
was added, the different conditions which evolved in space could be
extended in the time dimension. There is extension in space and extension in time, so one could see things clearly, one could discriminate—and that is the possibility of consciousness. If there is no difference, no consciousness is possible. Consciousness means
discrimination. That people could say, "This is this, and that is that,"
has been the greatest discovery. So man became exceedingly important.

But it was not just man. He was the carrier of that most precious consciousness and the urge to become conscious became a passion because
it was very much in demand. Then through the revelation of the Christian symbolism, we learned the most important fact that the deity had
found a means in the human psyche to be reborn, to be born through
man. That is the message, the great symbolic teaching; and that of
course increases the conscious psyche of man to an extraordinary degree. It becomes the divine cradle, the womb, the sacred vase in which
the deity itself will be locked in, carried and born. This is really an *euangelion.* So we have to look at this whole question of consciousness, of
the human mind and so on, from an entirely new point of view.

Now that is of course all speculation, but I tell you it is perfectly good
for my system and it might be for yours too, inasmuch as you can make
such a speculation and inasmuch as you can observe how that thing
grows in you. Otherwise it means nothing, and it would be a mere theft
if you stole my words and ran away with them. But if you observe
something that seems to be the real substance, that grows—when you
yourself find it—not only in one place but in many places, then you can
eat it and it will feed you. If I just tell you a story about that plant, you
have only eaten my words and you remain empty: you know that you
have potatoes in America but you have seen none here. But if you find

potatoes somewhere, you know this is the plant that can be eaten and that they are very nourishing. This is my standpoint for speculations. Well, we got a bit away from the original problem of the archaic contents, but we cannot settle such a question without taking into account other aspects of the problem.

Mrs. Sigg: It seems as if all that you have said has brought us just to our chapter, because the absence of this truth which you have now explained about the self was the cause of all Nietzsche's suffering. He could not believe in a God. The God that was taught to Nietzsche had no archaic element in him. There was no chance—he was not allowed—to discuss things with God because that was not the Protestant standpoint. He was in a very difficult position: he felt the urge and could not help himself.

Prof. Jung: He could only rage against himself, which he tried not to do.

Mrs. Sigg: But if he had had this conception of the self?

Prof. Jung: Oh yes, I hope that this food would have been good for him, but he obviously did not get at the real potatoes.

LECTURE VI

10 June 1936

Prof. Jung:

We have a very difficult question by Dr. Harding—we are getting deeply into speculative metaphysics, "Last time you spoke of the ego as being the visibility of the self."

Well—before going further—you remember that this is a psychological statement. The psychological definition of "the self" is "the totality of the psychical processes," whatever that means; at all events the sum total of the unconscious and the conscious contents and processes would be the psychological definition of "the self." Now of course, anybody is allowed to treat the idea of the self from the standpoint of what one calls, in modern German philosophy, existential philosophy; that is, you can deal with it as being actually in existence instead of as a mere concept. But in psychology the self is a scientific concept with no assumption as to its metaphysical existence. We don't deal with it as an existence and we don't postulate an existence, but merely form a scientific psychological concept which expresses that totality, the nature of which we are ignorant of. We know far too little about it because we have only a certain amount of knowledge of our conscious processes and contents and an exceedingly restricted knowledge of the unconscious processes—otherwise one would not call them unconscious. So the unconscious is essentially unknown, and if a thing consists of a more or less known part and a more or less unknown part, its existence is surely a most obscure one. Scientifically, then, one must be exceedingly careful in making assumptions about the nature of that mostly unknown quantity. Of course you can speculate about it: you can assume, for instance, that the manifestations of that total psyche issue from a definite metaphysical existence. That is a perfectly sound conclusion, but you must admit in that case that you are moving in the speculative sphere of metaphysics, that you are then thinking more or less mythologically. That is also sound; it is legitimate to think mythologically, and if you give the proper chance to the self-manifestation

983

of that kind of thinking, it is psychological material which can be submitted to historical or philosophical or theological comparison. But it is admittedly not a scientific statement. We must be quite clear about this point before we discuss this very interesting question.

Now I will read the rest of the question. "We think of the self as being a manifestation of the Holy Spirit. The Holy Spirit is one and indivisible. Are we to think of the self as likewise *one*—the same in everyone? When, for instance, we dimly see the likeness of the self in certain people do we see the same thing in each, modified only by the ego development; or is it more likely that the self is different in different people? That, as it were, the Holy Spirit has been split up by coming into manifestation in time and space? You spoke of the self as being the nearest to us of the heavenly hierarchy which leads up to God, the Infinite and Infinitely Remote. Should we then think of each 'self' on the ascending planes as being more and more inclusive, more and more general, until, to use the Buddhist phrase, it reaches the selfhood of God, which must include all the 'selves' as manifested in different people?"

This is an entirely speculative question. In reference to the statement that we think of the self as being a manifestation of the Holy Spirit, I must say that I don't dare to think like that; in thinking about the phenomenology of the self, I cannot recognize any trace or any quality in that manifestation which would justify me in assuming that there is anything behind it which I could designate as the Holy Spirit—nothing that is a definite image of our Christian mythology, I mean. Spirit is also a definite psychological phenomenon, or we would not have such a word to designate it. So to arrive at an understanding of what the Holy Spirit psychologically consists of, we have to examine the phenomenology of what our language calls spirit, quite apart from the concept of its holiness. The spirit is a peculiar condition, or a quality, of psychological contents. We have certain contents which derive from the data of our senses, from the material physical world, and over against those we have contents which we qualify as spiritual or belonging to the spirit. Now, they are apparently of an immaterial origin, of an ideational or ideal origin that may derive from archetypes. But the very nature of that spiritual origin is just as obscure to us as the so-called material origin. We do not know what matter is: *matter* is the term for an idea used in physics which formulates the presumable nature of things; and so spirit is a peculiar quality or idea of something which is immaterial and in *its* essence perfectly unknown.

Now, we would use the word *holy* in a case where there is a mana aspect, where the situation has a fascinating, numinous or tremendous character. You know, Otto makes those three differentiations, *numinosum, tremendum* and *fascinosum*, as the three peculiar qualities of what one would call "holy," "sacred," "taboo," or "mana."[1] The mana concept is very useful because it contains all those aspects. So when the immaterial nature of a psychological content has a mana quality, we would call it "holy," and we would call that kind of form or quality a manifestation of the Holy Spirit. For instance, if an alchemist succeeded in having a wonderful vision in his retort, if a great enlightenment took place and he had the feeling that he was making progress in his work, he would say it was the *donum spiritus sancti*, the gift of the Holy Ghost. Because he was overwhelmed by the impression of an agency, a significance, a meaningfulness in what he was doing, he was forced to assume or recognize in it the work of the Holy Spirit. So the Holy Spirit is a formulation of certain phenomena which have nothing to do with the self directly, though you may naturally connect the two and say that wherever the self manifests, you have the feeling of the holy presence, of the *donum spiritus sancti*.

In the Christian legend, for instance, we have evidence of such enlightenment; and that feeling of being redeemed, of conversion—the vision of Christ, for instance—can be explained as parts, or as manifestations, of the process of individuation, Christ being the symbol of the self. The vision of Christ would be the perception of the self in a projected form naturally, and one could say this was at the same time a manifestation of the Holy Spirit inasmuch as it is an *overwhelming* spiritual experience. The vision and understanding of the old Hermetic philosophers led to the idea of the *circulus quadratus*, the squared circle, and the marvelous Golden Flower of Chinese philosophy, and the philosophical gold, and the cube which is the philosopher's stone— all are similar symbols.[2] These can be called symbols of individuation or of the self, and the finding of them, or their coming up, their self-revelation, appeared to the Hermetic philosophers as a *donum spiritus*

[1] Rudolf Otto (1868-1937) in *The Idea of the Holy* (1917) coined the term *numinum* (which Jung seized upon) to describe a feeling of awe and wonder beyond the goodness of what is holy. *Tremendum* was his word for the feeling of a gentle tide, a strange excitement, sometimes mounting to frenzy in the presence of mystery. *Fascinosum* named the uniquely attractive, over-abounding attraction of holiness.

[2] Jung often pointed to the interchangeability of alchemical gold and the philosopher's stone. Richard Wilhelm reproduced a golden mandala (squared circle) in *The Secret of the Golden Flower* (German original, 1929), a book for which Jung wrote a foreword and psychological commentary. CW 13, pars. 1-84.

sancti, the gift of the Holy Ghost. Therefore they say that nobody can arrive at a solution of their art unless God assists, *Deo adjuvante*, or only *per gratiam Dei*, through the grace of God. In that way you can unite the two things, but you could not say that the self is a manifestation of the Holy Spirit, because, if I understand Dr. Harding rightly, that would mean that the Holy Ghost is prior to the self. From the phenomenology of the symbols of the self we have no justification for that assumption; the only thing we can establish safely is that the empirical perception of the self-revelation has the character of a *mana experience* and therefore this could be called the Holy Spirit: there the two things come together. Moreover one should not omit mentioning that the Christian dogma makes a very clear distinction between the aspect of the Son and the Holy Spirit. The latter is the *divine breath* and not a *person*. It is the life breath that flows from the Father into the Son.

You see, spirit to me is not an experience which I could substantiate in any way; it is a quality, like matter. Matter is a quality of an existence which is absolutely psychical. For our only reality is psyche, there is no other reality; all we say of other realities are attributes of psychological contents. Now, Dr. Harding says the Holy Spirit is one and indivisible; yet it is part of the Trinity and thus only One inasmuch as it is God. The self, on the other hand, is *per definitionem* really one and indivisible; therefore, it is called historically "the Monad" and is therefore like Christ, the *Monogenes* the *Unigenitus*, etc. It is one by definition because we call the totality of the psychological or psychical events "the self" and that must necessarily be one. Also the concept of *energy* is one by definition because you cannot say there are many different energies; there are many different powers but only *one energy*. So the idea of the self includes the idea of oneness because the sum of many things must be one. But it consists of many units: the actual empirical phenomenology of the self consists of a heap of innumerable units, some of which we call hereditary, the Mendelian units.

Now, as the self is *one* in every individual, we are more or less led to the question, whether that self is perhaps also *one in several or many individuals*, in other words that the same self that manifests in one individual could manifest in quite a number of individuals. You see, that question is empirically possible because of the existence of the collective unconscious which is not an individual acquisition. It has an *a priori* existence; we are born *with* the collective unconscious, *in* the collective unconscious. It is prior to any conscious function in man. Moreover it has peculiar qualities which we have often mentioned, the telepathic qualities, which seem to prove its oneness. The more you are in the collective unconscious the more you are undivided from other individuals. The oneness of the collective unconscious is the reason of *participation mystique*; primitives live in a peculiar oneness of psychical functioning. They are like fishes in one and the same pond—as we also are to a remarkable degree. We have of course thousands of facts to prove that sameness, but the telepathic phenomena in particular prove an extraordinary relativity of space and—almost *more* interesting—of time. You see, you can say about the phenomena of space, "Oh well, these things were coexistent. The radio now teaches us that we can hear somebody speaking in Shanghai at this moment with no trouble; and if that is physically possible, it might be psychically possible just as well." But that you should today hear somebody talking, not in Shanghai but here in Zürich in the year 1980, is unheard of because there is no coexistence. Of course, such things don't happen and if anybody says they do we would say that he suffered from hallucinations. But there is such a thing as prevision in time. Things can be more or less accurately foreseen; and if that is possible it means a relativity of time, so there would be a relativity of time as well as of space.

These doubts are not exactly my own: modern physicists have their notions in that respect and are just about to discover these peculiar psychological facts, which are so impressive that I always say that our psyche is an existence that is only to a certain extent included in the categories of time and space. It is partly outside, or it could not have perceptions of non-space and non-time. Now, if it is true that our time and space are relative, then the psyche, being capable of manifesting beyond time and space—at least its part in the collective unconscious— is beyond individual isolation; and if that is the case, more than one individual could be contained in that same self. Then it would be like this very simple example which I often use: Suppose our space were two-dimensional, flat like this table. Now if I rest the five fingers of my hand on this flat surface, it appears as only five finger tips. They are quite separate, simply spots on the plane of the two-dimensional space, so you can say they are all isolated and have nothing to do with each other. But erect a vertical upon your two-dimensional space, and up in the third dimension you will discover that those are simply the fingers of a hand which is one, but which manifests as five. You see, it is quite possible that our collective unconscious is just the evidence for the transcendent oneness of the self; since we know that the collective unconscious exists over an extraordinary area, covering practically the whole of humanity, we could call it the self of humanity. It is one and the same thing everywhere and we are included in it. Then we have dreams, and the material of the unconscious in general, as well as the results of active imagination, give a certain amount of evidence for the fact that the self can contain several individuals; also that there is not only one self empirically but many selves, to an indefinite extent.

For instance, those old hierarchies like the one of Dionysius the Areopagite, father of scholastic philosophy,[3] or the ideas of the Gnostics, or of Paul, all point to the same idea: namely, that the world has a peculiar hierarchic structure, that different groups of people are presided over, as it were, by one angel, and that those angels are again in groups and presided over by archangels—and so on, up to the throne of God. You find such representations quite often in the Middle Ages where the heavenly hierarchies were represented even in the form of mandalas. Now, these are simply self-representations of the unconscious structure, and inasmuch as we attribute existence to these things, we are allowed to speculate about them, say in the form of the Christian or the Gnostic ideas. One finds the same thing in India, an absolute *consensus gentium*, only there the thinking goes the other way round: instead of starting from the isolated empirical fact, it always starts from the abstract metaphysical unit. They start from the idea of the one indivisible being that splits up into the millions of forms of Maya, but it is of course the same whether you consider it from this end or that. There are very interesting definitions: The *Hiranyagarbha*, the golden germ or the golden child, is the first germ of the manifesting Brahman, and *Hiranyagarbha* is defined as the accumulated collective soul that includes all individual souls. It is the self of selves of selves of selves. *Hiranyagarbha* is the absolute equivalent of the philosophic egg, or the philosopher's stone, or the *circulus quadratus*, or the Golden Flower. It is not the result of something but the beginning of everything, the one mind that starts all other minds. So, as Dr. Harding says, one can use the Buddhistic phrase: *Hiranyagarbha is* the selfhood of God. The self then becomes simply a designation or the specification for the appearance or existence, because a thing that has no appearance whatever has no existence. Existence can only *be* inasmuch as it is specific. Therefore, inasmuch as Brahman comes into existence out of his latent potentiality, he becomes *Hiranyagarbha*, the golden germ, the stone, or the egg, or the first shoot, or the first lightning.

---

[3] The pseudo-Dionysius, whose Neoplatonic/Christian works probably appeared at the end of the fifth century, was long confused with Dionysius the Areopagite, an Athenian convert of St. Paul. For Jung, the former is important as the most forthright denier of the reality of evil. Obviously neither Dionysius bore any resemblance to the Greek god Nietzsche honored.

Well now, we finally go back to Nietzsche. The last verse we read was, "Great obligations do not make grateful, but revengeful; and when a small kindness is not forgotten, it becometh a gnawing worm." He continues,

> "Be shy in accepting! Distinguish by accepting!"—thus do I advise those who have naught to bestow.
>
> I, however, am a bestower: willingly do I bestow as friend to friends. Strangers, however, and the poor, may pluck for themselves the fruit from my tree: thus doth it cause less shame.

Now what does he advocate here? Has anybody a shrewd intuition about it? What should the poor do? You see, if he gives, they must be ashamed, and *he* is also ashamed, as he later on says. And if he doesn't give and they cannot ask, what remains for them?

Mr. Allemann: To take, to steal.

Prof. Jung: Of course.

> Beggars, however, one should entirely do away with!

Yes, that is wonderful.

> Verily, it annoyeth one to give unto them, and it annoyeth one not to give unto them.
>
> And likewise sinners and bad consciences!

What does he want to do here? What is his great redeeming effort?

Miss Taylor: He wants people to live according to their own law and not to reproach themselves.

Prof. Jung: Ah yes, that is very nicely said, but it might be their own law that they are such beggars, and he says that one should do away with them.

Mrs. Jung: He wants to do away with disagreeable feelings.

Prof. Jung: Yes, he wants to do away with all the evil in the world, with all these very sorry existences, and since they of course would strongly protest against such an attempt to wipe them out of existence with the metaphysical broom, the whole thing boils down to the fact that he wants to get rid of his own disagreeable feelings when he meets the misery of the world. Therefore do away with the imperfection of the world and the problem is settled. That shows his psychology: he has an inferior feeling and naturally that is projected—any inferior function is always projected—and so he is particularly affected by the misery of the world. You think he is suffering from compassion, while as a matter of fact he would much prefer to get rid of everything which causes that disagreeable compassion. He hates everything that reminds him of the existence of his own inferiority—which is to be expected.

> Believe me, my friends: the sting of conscience teacheth one to sting.

If one could wipe out bad conscience, what a blessing! But alas, it is not to be wiped out, and the more it stings, the more *one* stings. Only one that is tortured tortures; anybody in a healthy state of well-being never tortures, except perhaps by his unconsciousness. That is a very important principle of education; for instance, children who are torturers have always to be carefully examined to find out whether they are not tortured by a most wonderful education at home.

> The worst things, however, are the petty thoughts. Verily, better to have done evilly than to have thought pettily!

I only want to point out here how, in such passages, Nietzsche deals with the petty things—the small, incomplete, imperfect things. He always has a tendency to wipe them out, and through the whole development of *Zarathustra*, these small things slowly accumulate until in the end they reach a definite form in a special figure. Do you know what that is?

Mrs. Crowley: The ugliest man.

Prof. Jung: Yes, and he is then in the end condemned to hell wholesale.

> To be sure, ye say: "The delight in petty evils spareth one many a great evil deed." But here one should not wish to be sparing.

Meaning that if you can satisfy yourself with a greater number of small petty sins, you can slip through the net, can muddle along. But if you commit one substantial sin or crime, it cries aloud; you are detected, revealed, and you can no longer say, "Nothing has happened, I am quite all right, I slipped through, I have not been caught by the police." So he is all for the honorableness or honesty, of taking the definite stand.

> Like a boil is the evil deed: it itcheth and irritateth and breaketh forth—it speaketh honourably.
>
> "Behold, I am disease," saith the evil deed: that is its honourableness.

But like infection is the petty thought: it creepeth, and hideth, and wanteth to be nowhere—until the whole body is decayed and withered by the petty infection.

You see, that is exactly what happened to him: he is of course in favor of the great things, even the great crimes, and he tries to be as evil as possible by uttering all sorts of blasphemies. But as a human being he was quite harmless, incapable of committing anything very bad; he could only fall into the traps of fate, like his syphilitic infection. He made a mistake in that he heaped up the petty things by repressing them, and did not give them the right place. He did not see that any great evil is an accumulation of thousands of small ones, and that very often a very terrible thing has happened because small things have been heaped up. It would have been very much better if those people had muddled along in the ordinary way instead of piling up those petty evils till they resulted in a great explosion and great damage. Also if one heaps up petty evils by repression, they work indirectly: whatever you repress, whatever you don't recognize in yourself, is nevertheless alive. It is constellated outside of you; it works in your surroundings and influences other people. Of course you are blissfully unconscious of those effects, but the other people get the noseful.

To him however, who is possessed of a devil, I would whisper this word in the ear: "Better for thee to rear up thy devil! Even for thee there is still a path to greatness!"—

Well, that needs no comment.

Ah, my brethren! One knoweth a little too much about every one! And many a one becometh transparent to us, but still we can by no means penetrate him.

It is difficult to live among men because silence is so difficult.

And not to him who is offensive to us are we most unfair, but to him who doth not concern us at all.

If, however, thou hast a suffering friend, then be a resting-place for his suffering; like a hard bed, however, a camp-bed; thus wilt thou serve him best.

And if a friend doeth thee wrong, then say: "I forgive thee what thou hast done unto me; and thou hast done it unto thyself, however—how could I forgive that!"

Thus speaketh all great love: it surpasseth even forgiveness and pity.

This is an important passage. You see, the unforgiveable thing is what thou hast done unto thyself. He formulates it in such a particularly drastic way over against the Christian prejudice of loving your neighbor and damning yourself. Of course, that is not the Christian form, but that is the way it is applied: anybody who loves himself is considered to be something along the line of a criminal, yet of course the original meaning of that saying was that it is self-evident that you love yourself, but not that you love your neighbor. We have twisted this very important truth; we base ourselves entirely upon the idea that we should love our neighbor, that it is unfair to hate him but quite fair to hate oneself. You expose yourself to the worst mistakes and misinterpretation if you say you love yourself; it is even quite unsound to pay any attention to yourself. The "know thyself" of Plato became extremely unpopular in our late Christianity, so "as thyself" has become inaudible and "love thy neighbor" is declared by the loud speakers of all movements.[4] Of course, over against that mistake in favor of the herd that is kept in monasteries and churches and so on, the individual has disappeared completely. He has become a pathological nuisance, the contents of a neurosis. Nietzsche sees that very clearly and puts a very high premium upon that consideration of oneself which sees that one can commit sins against oneself. This thought of Nietzsche is of course to us a very important psychological consideration, but we have evidence that already in the first or second centuries it was a current idea.

For instance I have already quoted the *logia* of Christ from the Oxyrhynchus papyrus, and then there is the famous second letter of Clemens, where a very similar idea is expressed. Also, the philosopher Karpokrates who lived around 140 A.D. interpreted the Sermon on the Mount on the subjective stage. The original text is: "If thou bringest thy gift to the altar, and there rememberest that thy brother hath fought against thee; leave there thy gift before the altar, and go thy way; first be reconciled to thy brother, and then come and offer thy gift." But Karpokrates read that in the following way: "If thou bringest thy gift to the altar and there rememberest that thou hast aught against thyself, leave then thy gift and go thy way; be reconciled to thyself and then come and offer thy gift." And he says that the brother whom you blame or whom you vilify is yourself.[5] You see, this was a most impor-

---

[4] Or, of course, long before Plato, or Socrates, as the prevailing commandment at Delphi.

[5] For the logia of Christ that says God is present even with a single individual, see p. 217, 217n above. For Karpocrates, see above, 13 June 34, n. 13.

tant teaching but unfortunately it was against the politics of the church. The church would not allow that care for yourself. It interfered with the magic institution of the church and its power of intervention. The church has always defended its magic prerogative of bestowing the grace of the sacraments, the sacred food of immortality, in the rite of the Holy Communion; nobody can reach immortal life or a state of redemption without partaking of the communion, which means of course that the church is indispensable. The individual can get nowhere without the church. So, having instituted the church, God can do practically nothing in an individual, for the church would then be meaningless. The individual is nothing, only a herd particle, and of course that brings about, in the course of centuries, an extraordinary collective psychology. Of course it had to be like that—it was unavoidable—yet we have to recognize the fact that there are people who are more or less individuals, who simply don't allow any church to interfere with their particular feelings or with their particular deities. They consider it an entirely private and exclusively individual affair. And such people of course listen to these voices of the past, like Karpokrates or the sayings of Jesus in the Oxyrhynchus papyrus, etc., knowing that they have a lot of evidence in history and numbers of passages in the New Testament in their favor.

Nietzsche also takes a very lenient point of view in reference to the poor. You know, that famous parable about the unjust steward contains this very Nietzschean point of view. This other side of the early teaching is very unpopular within the walls of the church: you hardly ever hear a sermon preached about the unjust steward. It is particularly difficult for our peculiar mentality, but it contains a precious piece of Nietzschean morality. It is in the 16th chapter of Luke. A steward had neglected the estates of his master, and when the master heard that he had been unreliable and had wasted his goods, he called for him and said:

How is it that I hear this of thee? Give an account of thy stewardship, for thou mayest be no longer steward.

Then the steward said within himself, What shall I do? for my lord taketh away from me the stewardship: I cannot dig; to beg I am ashamed.

I am resolved what to do, that, when I am put out of the stewardship, they may receive me into their houses.

So he called every one of his lord's debtors unto him, and said unto the first, How much owest thou unto my lord?

> And he said, An hundred measures of oil. And he said unto him, Take thy bill and sit down quickly and write it fifty.

You see, he is cutting down the obligations. Then when the Lord had considered the bill which the steward presented to him, he

> commended the unjust steward, because he had done wisely: for the children of this world are in their generation wiser than the children of light.
> And I say unto you, Make to yourselves friends of the mammon of unrighteousness; that, when ye fail, they may receive you into everlasting habitations.

And now he continues:

> He that is faithful in that which is least is faithful also in much: and he that is unjust in the least is unjust also in much.
> If therefore ye have not been faithful in the unrighteous mammon, who will commit to your trust the true riches?[6]

You see, this extraordinary paradox is just running on like water and oil; of course oil and water never mix but here they run on together. Now, what idea did the Lord have in his mind when he commended his unjust steward? We must assume of course that the Lord in this case is God, and the steward is man who is trusted with the goods of the Lord and has done very badly. And we must also assume that the Lord is not a fool, but sees quite clearly how inefficient and unreliable man has been. Yet here the Lord behaves as if he were a blind bat, as if he had been entirely deceived by the unjust steward. That we cannot assume, so what then?

Miss Hannah: He is pleased that he has succeeded in keeping himself together, in getting those other people to support him.

Prof. Jung: Well, if you compare the next part of the text, the way it runs on, you get a very peculiar feeling. For in what has that unjust steward really succeeded? Only in saving his face. You see, it *looked* all right, so that the Lord was only too glad that he could say, "Oh yes, that is all right, you are a very nice fellow; you have saved your face, you have muddled through. It would have been terribly awkward if I had detected you and had to accuse you publicly to show what a bad steward I have." So he has not only saved his own face but also the face of the Lord, and the Lord is quite grateful to him. Now isn't that extraordinary? The Lord is glad that mortal man has just muddled through.

---

[6] Luke 16:1-11.

994

But that is really the best we can do, mind you. This shows that the Lord is merely a loving father who knows that his child cannot be good, so if the child does not collapse when it has committed a sin, if the bad steward is not a pale criminal, if he saves his face afterwards and if he is clever, then the Lord is quite satisfied that the vessel he has made is not entirely broken. Of course, that it is a very bad vessel has to be admitted, but it held together and that is all the Lord can expect. You know, it really was a very poor work on the part of the creator—there is a bit of Gnosticism here—to have made such a poor steward, to have made such an inefficient vessel as man to deal with the powers of darkness and chaos. He does the best he can—he couldn't do any better— so if he only saves his face and his existence and holds the whole thing together, that is enough. And live by all means, hang on, and if you are clever enough to make friends with the representatives of capitalism, never mind—that enables you to live. Now, all this is exceedingly bad. The only other possibility of an explanation would be that we assume that the Lord is an idiot who doesn't see that the steward is a cheat. But this is not only bad, it is also idiotic, which makes it worse; the one thing is bad *and* idiotic, and the other is bad *but* it makes sense.

Mrs. Jung: Is it not possible that it is a mistake because it is in contradiction to all other teachings?

Prof. Jung: Yes, it is quite possible that there is a gap here, but unfortunately the text does run on like that, and my idea is that if it had been understood really, it would have been wiped out as other passages were wiped out. You remember that famous passage in the Oxyrhynchus papyrus: "Whenever there are two they are not without God, and wherever there is one alone I say I am with him," and then in the New Testament this is made of it: "For where two or three are gathered together in my name, there am I in the midst of them." You see, the church had already been formed, so if there were one alone, he would be with the devil, just the opposite of the saying in the Oxyrhynchus papyrus that the Lord is then with him. These texts have probably undergone some changes, all the more because in those first centuries they were considered to be merely good literature and not necessarily holy; only at the end of the second century, or later even, was the character of holy revelation attributed to them, and that was only after they had been purified by very clever clergy. My conclusion is that they must have overlooked this, as they did not understand it. The greater part of the Gnostic texts have been badly mutilated or quite destroyed by the church, but the intelligence of the fragments that are left is astonishing.

It is perhaps to the failure in understanding that we owe certain fragments of the Gnosis which give us a most precious insight—the fragments, for instance, where Christ says, "He who is near me is near the fire, and he who is far from me is far from the kingdom."[7] That is extraordinarily revealing. Or when he says to the man who offends against the sabbath: "If thou knowest what thou art doing thou art blessed, if thou knowest not then thou art cursed."[8] That is also a bit of the Gnostic morality which has, of course, been cleared out of the canonical text. We only know of these fragments because the Fathers of the church quoted them as being particularly foolish or blasphemous, not understanding what they really meant. It is a wonderful piece of good luck that the Oxyrhynchus papyrus was discovered. It throws an extraordinary light upon the history of the evangelical texts. This passage, "If thou knowest what thou art doing thou art blest," is surely a piece of that kind of morality. And it is surely a formula which would help philosophers and educated people to live; since they could not be as naive as the masses, they had to have such a formula, otherwise they would not have become Christian. For instance, the saying of Karpokrates that you cannot be redeemed from a sin you have not committed, is absolute truth, but what does that imply? Those are problems you simply do not find in the writings of the Fathers or in the New Testament except by mistake, and this might be such a mistake.

Now Nietzsche, in reaction against the exclusively extraverted valuation of morality, insists upon the subjective importance, or the importance of the self as an objective fact. That is, if you cut out yourself, if you only identify with your love, not minding what you are, then you can be anything and one doesn't know at all what your love is worth. For your love is worth just what *you are*. You see, that is entirely excluded when the first part: "Love your neighbor" is insisted upon, forgetting all about "as thyself"; in that case the self remains in the dark and can be whatever it pleases. You forget entirely that the love used is from that particular self and if that self is obscured you never know what the love is worth. Love is not something in itself, but is the love of a specific individual, so we want to know who the individual is and whether he really consists of 90 percent pure gold or 90 percent pure nonsense.

This passage, "Thus speakest all great love: it surpasseth even forgiveness and pity," is also an important hint. In our prejudiced age,

7 See above, 30 Jan. 1935, n. 3.
8 See above, 8 May 1935, n. 7.

our late Christianity, we only must say the word *love*, assuming that it is something very wonderful, and nobody asks *who* loves, who is doing the loving. But that is what we really want to know, because love is nothing in itself. It is always a special human being who loves and the love is worth just as much as that individual. People think that they can apply love with no understanding, think love is only an emotional condition, a sort of feeling. Yes, it is a feeling, but what is the value of the feeling if it is not coupled with a real understanding? For instance in the Middle Ages, they coined the formula *amor et visio Dei*, which means "love and the vision of God," *vision* meaning recognition, understanding, the understanding that Paul also meant, which we only reach through thinking. So when you make of love a mere feeling, the second part of it is lacking, and with such a love you might hurt yourself against a human being who doesn't feel that in the least as love. He simply feels you with your ridiculous love as thoroughly autoerotic, because the understanding is lacking; with love must be coupled understanding and feeling. For the Christian concept of love is a universal concept, like the concept of freedom for instance, which is an idea. Therefore, great love as Nietzsche understands it, contains also true understanding, and true understanding knows that love is not a thing-in-itself. It is not an activity that is hovering in space somewhere which can be fetched down by anybody. Love is my own doing and it has just as much worth as I have and not a penny more.

> One should hold fast one's heart; for when one letteth it go, how quickly doth one's head run away!

Exactly, one cannot be in an emotional condition only.

> Ah, where in the world have there been greater follies than with the pitiful? And what in the world hath caused more suffering than the follies of the pitiful?
> Woe unto all loving ones who have not an elevation which is above pity! [That means insight.]
> "Thus spake the devil unto me, once on a time: 'Even God hath his hell: it is his love for man.' "

Yes, that is very good.

> And lately, did I hear him say these words: "God is dead: of his pity for man hath God died."

How is this paralleled?
Miss Hannah: By the crucifixion.

Prof. Jung: Yes, God's incarnation in Christ, and that he really died a human death on the cross is the act of supreme pity. Now, the death of Christ is a very important question, it was a problem in the early church. There was a famous controversy between the Ebionites and the Doketes. The Doketes said it was the *man* Jesus who died on the cross, and not the god. Do you know how they arrived at that idea?

Mr. Allemann: They said that he only became the Christus when he was baptized by John and that the spirit of the Christus was taken out of him before his death.

Prof. Jung: Yes, the idea was that Jesus was an ordinary man as long as he was not initiated by John the Baptizer; in the baptism the Christus in the form of the Holy Ghost descended upon him. And the Christus departed from him when he sweated blood in the Garden before his crucifixion. He could not have been crucified if the god had remained in him, and that the god left him in the Garden was the reason for his despair, the evidence being that he called out, "My God, my God, why hast thou forsaken me?" This is a perfectly good and interesting point of view and played a great role in the early church, but it was declared to be an awful heresy. That hypothesis was made to avoid the shocking idea that God could undergo a miserable human death: they simply could not stand the idea of a god undergoing such a punishment. Now, if we take that as a symptom, it would seem as if something in man in those days resisted that awful idea that the god could be so utterly extinguished. There was a sort of instinct against it. Yet we must consider that on the other side this conflict was overcome by the majority of the people in the assumption that God *had* undergone that death, that he was there to the last moment.

The idea that Christ is *homoousios*, of both human and divine nature, is of course the orthodox point of view, over against the Arian heresy that he is *homoiousios*, only *similar* in substance to the deity and not completely divine. The standpoint that Christ as God really underwent the human death won out, and if you translate that into psychological language it means that the god, the active background of our unconscious, undergoes completely the fate of man and cannot be excluded from it. That emphasizes of course the extraordinary importance of human life; we cannot say this is all illusion, that it is the divine substance in us that passes through millions of incarnations and is always outside of us. No, it undergoes the actual suffering of life, undergoes all our misery. The god enters and is present in all our misery—he is in no way different from it; as we are absolutely imbued with the misery of life and identical with it to a certain extent, so also is the god, and that means the god can die. So we would arrive at the conclusion that when man died the god also died and was buried. Then something very peculiar must have happened. The gods had always been above and immortal; they never came down to earth. Sometimes they took on an earthly form, had perhaps an illegitimate son on earth, but this time the son was the god himself. Now, that symbolizes a certain mental condition where the unconscious is completely identical with the conscious of man, and then that concept, that image of God, goes underground. That is of course a complete revelation: it is the pouring of the *influxus divinus* into the world. It is the light that shines into the darkness, as John says,[9] and it is contained in the darkness from now on, buried in the world, buried in the flesh even. This thought is continued in alchemy. That is the interesting thing.

[9] "And the light shineth in darkness; and the darkness comprehended it not" (John 1:5).

LECTURE VII

17 June 1936

Prof. Jung:

We stopped last time at the paragraphs: "Thus spake the devil unto me, once on a time: 'Even God hath his hell: it is his love for man.' And lately did I hear him say these words: 'God is dead: of his pity for man hath God died.' " Now why does he say the devil whispered such things in his ear? Doesn't it look like a funny concession? He also seems to have certain doubtful moments. Looked at from a Christian point of view it makes sense, but looked at from the Zarathustrian point of view it makes no sense—so we must conclude that it is really a concession to his own Christianity. For to say that even God hath his hell means that God is in hell, which is a blasphemous idea; and therefore a Christian would naturally be forced to say the devil had insinuated it. So Nietzsche still cannot help yielding at times to his Christian background. I make use of this as a piece of evidence for my thesis that Nietzsche is the ordinary historical man, the traditional Christian, and his peculiar standpoint in *Zarathustra* is just due to the fact that he is possessed by the archetype of Zarathustra that naturally would speak an entirely different language. At times, the man Nietzsche appears as if coming out of clouds, and at another time he disappears utterly, and then it is not a human being speaking but an eternal image, an archetype called "Zarathustra." That is happening here of course when he says God is dead, which is a blasphemous assertion and an offence to the ears of a Christian, so he needs must say it is the devil speaking. Now we have already spoken of the fact that it was out of his pity for man that God underwent his incarnation and died; the divinity or the deity made an association with matter, and matter, according to Zarathustra's statement, caught him. Now we will go on.

So be ye warned against pity: *from thence* there cometh unto men a heavy cloud! Verily, I understand weather-signs!

Now to what on earth—or in heaven—does he allude here?

Mrs. Sigg: I think if people only have pity and love for their neighbors and not for themselves, there must come a catastrophe because they have neglected themselves too much.

Prof. Jung: Yes, that is very much Nietzsche's idea and that is perfectly true. You see, to speak in the style of Zarathustra, that God took pity on man cost him his life; he went out of his own position, he transformed, and was caught. So if man does the same, if he allows himself to indulge in his pity, he will be caught. His interest in himself will be taken away from him. It will be invested in other people, and he himself will be left high and dry, completely deprived of that precious creative substance which he should have given to himself. Many people prefer compassion. It is so much nicer to be compassionate to other people than to themselves, and so much easier because they then keep on top; other people are to be pitied, other people are poor worms that ought to be helped, and they are saviors. That is very nice; it feeds that unquenchable thirst of man to be on top. It is a wonderful narcotic for the human soul. Everybody disapproves of the idea of compassion for oneself; they interpret it as self-indulgence and vice. And it is very disagreeable to be compassionate with that most imperfect man in yourself who is in hell, so you had better turn your attention on your neighbor; there are many weeds in your own garden, so go to your neighbor's and weed out his. Now his compassion, this projected kind of interest, Nietzsche takes to be a very serious danger: *"from thence there yet cometh unto men a heavy cloud!"* What could that cloud be? What is this tremendous innuendo? You see, Zarathustra tries to convince his audience of the fact that God is dead, that the Superman ought to be created, and that in order to create him, you are no longer allowed to waste your compassion on your fellow beings, but must give it to yourselves. And then you run into this thunderstorm.

Miss Hannah: It is one's own inferiority, the whole black substance of which one is made.

Prof. Jung: Well, it is of course understood that if you give compassion to yourself you give it to the inferior being in yourself.

Miss Hannah: All your emotions are caught in that and they will come up as a sort of thunderstorm against you.

Prof. Jung: Yes, that would be a perfectly suitable explanation. If you give your compassion to yourself, if you are interested in the imperfect man in yourself, naturally you bring up a monster—all the darkness that is in man, all that with which man is cursed forever, without the grace of God or the compassion of Christ and his work of salvation. Naturally, you run into that terrific cataclysm which man has within him, that eternal skeleton in the cupboard, of which he is always afraid. In the end, Nietzsche himself runs up against this thunder-cloud: it is a question whether he shall accept the ugliest man in himself. This is the terrible danger, but why does his unconscious produce the idea of such a danger here? And mind you, it doesn't sound like an individual danger only, but like a collective danger.

Mrs. Crowley: Like a prophecy.

Mrs. Sigg: It is quite natural; formerly people gave all beauty to the gods, and Nietzsche gave all beauty to Zarathustra, so there was little left for himself.

Prof. Jung: Yes, but assume that it is for the possibility of creating the Superman that you give your compassion to the imperfect man. Now if you bring up the imperfect man, it is a collective danger, and what is that?

Miss Hannah: Is it not the danger of madness?

Prof. Jung: Well, opinions are quite divided about this point, as you know. It might be madness but not necessarily. Otherwise everybody who gives compassion to himself would be in danger of madness.

Miss Hannah: All those crazy emotions come up.

Prof. Jung: And when it is a collective phenomenon, what happens then?

Miss Hannah: Well, Germany.

Prof. Jung: I would not say just Germany. We have some good examples in past centuries.

Mrs. Sigg: One remembers Edgar Jung who wrote *Die Herrschaft der Minderwertigen* (The Dominion of the Inferior Ones).[1] Sometimes inferior elements gain power and influence.

Prof. Jung: Well, it would mean bringing up the inferior strata of a nation, the inferior psychology. Do you know of such cases already in history?

Miss Hannah: The French Revolution.

Prof. Jung: Yes, and there is a parallel there with the actual words of Zarathustra.

Dr. Harding: They said that God was dead and they enthroned a new deity called *la Déesse Raison.*

---

[1] Edgar Jung (1894-1934), *Die Herrschaft der Minderwertigen* (Berlin, 1930).

Prof. Jung: Yes, *la Déesse Raison* was enthroned in Notre Dame.[2] Then there is another case, a little further back in history.

Mrs. Jung: The revolution of the slaves in antiquity?

Prof. Jung: Yes, but that was not so much linked up with a religious upheaval; of course there were religious ideas in it, but it was economic to a great extent. It was not clear for instance that Spartacus dethroned the gods; he simply wanted to overthrow slavery. But there was a particularly good example.

Mrs. Sigg: The revolution of the peasants.

Prof. Jung: Yes. The Reformation was of course a destruction of the authority of the church, and then instantly followed that upheaval of the peasants, for when such ideas reach the collective inferior man they have the most destructive effect. The actual mob consists of cave men. The idea that every man has the same value might be a great metaphysical truth, yet in this space-and-time world it is the most tremendous illusion; nature is thoroughly aristocratic and it is the wildest mistake to assume that every man is equal. That is simply not true. Anybody in his sound senses must know that the mob is just mob. It is inferior, consisting of inferior types of the human species. If they have immortal souls at all then it is God's business, not ours; we can leave it to him to deal with their immortal souls which are presumably far away, as far away as they are in animals. I am quite inclined to attribute immortal souls to animals; they are just as dignified as the inferior man. That we should deal with the inferior man on our own terms is all wrong. To treat the inferior man as you would treat a superior man is cruel; worse than cruel, it is nonsensical, idiotic.

But that is what we do with all our democratic ideas, and as time goes on we shall see that those democratic institutions don't work since there is a fundamental psychological mistake there. Christianity has done it: we owe it to Christianity that all men are equal and dignified and such nonsense, that God looks at all men in the same way. Well, he seems to bestow his grace on everybody in an absolutely indiscriminate way, but that is not to be taken very seriously, because such an indiscriminate handing out of the goods of heaven and earth does not speak for a particularly foreseeing origin. Also, if that were so, we could say, "Since God knows better, since he planned the whole show, why should we lift a finger? No use." Moreover, it is simply blasphemous to preach of the all-foreseeing and omnipotent deity and it pre-

---

[2] "The Goddess of Reason"; see above, 6 June 1934, n. 7.

pares the way for atheism, because no reasonable man can believe that the government of the world is wise. It is not, but chaotic, rather. That is what we see and experience, and man would make no sense whatever if he were ruled by a god who knew all about his predestined fate. What about our ethics or our intelligence?

Now, what Nietzsche foresees here is just this dark thunder-cloud that is coming up over the horizon when one gives compassion to oneself. That is, if you make a general truth of it, if you still have the missionary in you, the Christian preacher who tells everybody what is good for them, you most certainly will arouse a thunder-cloud; you will arouse the inferior man in nations as well as in yourself. And you will not be able to accept him because you have brought him up by missionary attempts, in a collective way that is. You preach it to a whole crowd. You publish a book, and so you preach it to yourself too as one of the crowd; the inferior man comes up in the form of the ugliest man and of course it is not acceptable. But if you don't preach it to the crowd, if you keep it for yourself as an entirely individual and personal affair, well, you bring up the inferior man in yourself but in a manageable form, not as a political or social experiment. You can then remain in the political form or form of society in which you find yourself, and you can excuse yourself as an individual experiment for which you are awfully sorry. You *must* be sorry for yourself; compassion means to be sorry for somebody, but if you bring it up with a brass band as Nietzsche does, you cannot accept that monster; he invited him up with flags and fifes and drums and so he has to show him back into hell.

But attend also to this word: All great love is above all its pity: for it seeketh—to create what is loved!

He says that all that compassion—and this is surely Zarathustra speaking, not the ordinary man Nietzsche—is something you can put aside, because the object of your love, the purpose of your love, is to be created. Now what are we doing really? We say nobody loves us, or I am loved, somebody loves me, but no one speaks of the absolute necessity of creating what one loves—that one has to create the thing that loves and is loved. We have no responsibility in that respect; we take love like the weather or a gold mine or a fruit tree which we don't own but from which we can pick fruit, and nobody thinks of such a thing as creating that which loves us or that we love. But Zarathustra holds that this is the absolute condition under which the Superman can be created; to create the Superman we must create that thing which is the essence of love, which gives love and is loved. We cannot take it for granted that love is something we just get somewhere. It must be produced. So it is a thing which has to be created because it doesn't yet exist. Now this is a very profound idea and perhaps I am not able to make it any clearer. He continues this same argument in the next verse when he says,

"Myself do I offer unto my love, *and my neighbour as myself*"—

You see, he understands by love a creative impulse which has no pity, which creates its object, creates its purpose, and seeks an end which is perhaps against man or even does away with him, an end which does not consider the personal man. The personal man might be subservient to it or he might be just run over. That is creative love as he understands it, and that is the condition by which the Superman is made. Therefore, he says:

Such is the language of all creators.
All creators, however, are hard.

Well, perhaps you will think over this matter and in the meantime we will go on to the next chapter called "The Priests." And how is it that we come now to priests?

Mr. Allemann: Because he had been preaching himself.

Prof. Jung: Yes, he has been preaching surely, and that is an approach to the priest, but that is not quite enough.

Mrs. Crowley: In the very beginning of the chapter he was trying to distinguish between the two kinds of consciousness, the separation from the animal man and the extension of consciousness, trying to realize the two and to find some sort of bridge between them. Then all this development of the idea of love comes in, and now these priests. The bridge is the idea of love. Probably he needs an enormous amount of compassion to be able to swallow the priests.

Dr. Harding: The priests are professionally compassionate ones.

Prof. Jung: Yes, that is perfectly true.

Mrs. Crowley: But are they not just the ones who project, instead of finding the inferior man in themselves? And he projected that into others.

Prof. Jung: But why does he need to talk about them? He has settled that completely and now he writes a whole chapter about them.

Dr. Harding: He was a parson's son and the priest would be his shadow.

Prof. Jung: Well, he has much to say about them, sure enough.

Mrs. Baumann: It seems to me there is another bridge: after the creator, priests must always follow, in order to dogmatize.

Prof. Jung: Yes, and moreover towards the end of the chapter Zarathustra comes very much to the foreground with his extraordinary idea of creative love, meaning the Superman. And Nietzsche gets an intuition of an imminent danger, of that thunder-cloud: namely, the possibility of the revolution of the inferior man or the impossibility of accepting the ugliest man. That means very serious trouble and it is a very serious hindrance to the creation of the Superman, because the superior thing can be created only if it is built upon the inferior. The inferior must be accepted in order to build the superior; otherwise it is as if you were trying to build a house suspended in the air, or a roof having no foundation. First, you must go into the ground and into the dirt: you must make your hands dirty, or there is no foundation to build upon. You must not be afraid of the dirt; one has to accept the ugliest man if one wants to create. Creation means inferiority which you have to swallow; only through that can you create something new and better. Now, feeling that he has run up against a very serious obstacle, Nietzsche discovers—it becomes inevitable—that there are forms or ways that man has used before in such a situation; the collective unconscious knows that in the course of man's history, written or unwritten, this situation has repeated itself numberless times, and therefore man has elaborated certain forms for dealing with collective danger, one of the most powerful means being the church. And the church lives through the activity of the priests, men who devote themselves to the conservation of order, of tradition, of a certain amount of culture even. They take care of the moral laws, of the metaphysical need of man, in order to keep him well ensconced within a form.

This is a very important item, it is by no means to be carelessly dismissed, because there is nothing to put in its place. What are you going to put in the place of the church? What is *Nietzsche*, for instance, going to put in the place of the church? Is the inferior man of this day, not to speak of even the superior educated man of his own day, capable of understanding his ideas? We have to ride a very fast horse in order to understand what he means; it is tremendously high stuff and needs an extraordinary experience of life, or intuition, in order to understand what he is driving at. It is hellishly difficult. Does he really assume that the ordinary man is capable of understanding such a thing? He might use the word *Superman* but what does that mean to him? There is nothing for the ordinary man in it, for the ordinary man needs something visible, something tangible: words, rites; and then he must see that everybody is in it before it is valid. The inferior man is exceedingly mistrustful. He does not trust the thing that is in small houses, in a few individuals, but believes in great gatherings, in a great number of statistics. For instance, if somebody tells him that in the United States there are so many millions who believe in such-and-such a thing, he will try to believe it too—then it is right. His argument is that many people are doing the same. And in the church many people are doing the same thing. The church says, "I am many—many people believe in me." In the Protestant church they do likewise—at least they make a desperate attempt to do so, talking about their fifty million Protestants. You know, in the Stockholm ecumenical conference[3] they also tried to say they were many, to make the inferior man believe, in that way, that they were good and beautiful and true: their only argument for their particular truth is that many believe in it or have been there. So Nietzsche runs up against this terrible problem, what to do with the collective inferior man—and here is the church. It is a big problem, as one sees in the way he speaks. There is a sort of hush. Now he says,

> And one day Zarathustra made a sign to his disciples and spake these words unto them:
> "Here are priests: but although they are mine enemies pass them quietly and with sleeping swords!"

That is perfectly clear. He hushes up the presence of those priests, and he keeps his weapons on him.

> "Even among them there are heroes; many of them have suffered too much—so they want to make others suffer.
> Bad enemies are they: nothing is more revengeful than their meekness. And readily doth he soil himself who toucheth them."

You see he is beginning to boil.

> "But my blood is related to theirs: [Yes, his father was a clergyman.] and I want withall to see my blood honoured in theirs."—
> And when they had passed, a pain attacked Zarathustra; but not long had he struggled with the pain, when he began to speak thus:
> It moveth my heart for those priests. They also go against my taste; but that is the smallest matter unto me, since I am among men.

Among men who are generally of bad taste, that is.

---

[3] The Stockholm ecumenical conference of August 1925, of some 600 representatives of 37 countries, was one of the forerunners of the establishment of the World Council of Churches in 1948.

But I suffer and have suffered with them: prisoners are they unto me, and stigmatized ones. He whom they call Saviour put them in fetters:—

Here you have it. He cannot help recognizing the extraordinary importance of priests and the church. He is not the ordinary iconoclast; he can see that there is something behind it, yet he is too much of a priest to be able to stand another priest. They never can stand one another. They quite agree that it is a mighty good thing to have spiritual purposes, but they must be of their own church; other churches are all wrong, worse than the worst sinner, unforgiveable. They even deny that they exist. For instance, when I suggest to certain theologians that Buddhism is also a perfectly decent religion, they say, "Oh, we are not concerned with Buddhism." They are only concerned with the spiritual attempt of their own church. But that must be so: if a church is not intolerant it doesn't exist. It needs must be intolerant in order to have definite form, for that is what the inferior man demands. It is always a sign of inferiority to demand the absolute truth. The superior man is quite satisfied that the supreme state of life is doubt of truth, where it is always a question whether it *is* a truth. A finished truth is dead. There is no chance of development, so the best thing is half a truth— or just doubt. In that case, you are sure that whatever you know is in a state of transformation, and only a thing that changes is alive. A living truth changes. If it is static, if it doesn't change, it is dead.

But doubt is not good for the churches and it is very bad for the inferior man. The inferior man cannot stand uncertainty concerning his truth, and he is only really happy when many people believe in that same truth. He wants to go to sleep in the church, to have a safe bed in which to sleep unquestioningly; otherwise, he has no peace and then he cannot trust and believe what the priests tell him to believe. That is the psychology of the inferior man. The church is made for the inferior man and inasmuch as we are all inferior we need a church: it is a very good thing. So the wise man will never disturb it. He will say, "Thank God that we have a church, for it would be a terrible hell if all those animals got loose." You see, the church could also be described as a spiritual stable for superior animals with a good shepherd—of course the good shepherd symbolized the Lord. We are all sheep, and there are probably wolves and even bulls, but at all events he knows what is good for them. That he gives them good pastures is what the sheep expect of the shepherd; that is their legitimate expectation. So good shepherds really must know what is good for other people; and they must be very grateful, for since they are sheep they cannot do any better. Therefore the church considered from all aspects is an absolutely desirable thing, and the more Catholic and authoritative, the better for the inferior man.

But naturally what is good for the inferior man is bad for the superior man. The superior man, the creative man, who does not find his satisfaction in peace and in confidence and belief, cannot be satisfied with the church. The church is hell to him, a prison. Any kind of belief is just hell because he must create, and if he is fettered by convictions, by the eternal truth or something of the sort, he is not only miserable, but he suffocates, he dies. And then of course he thinks the church is wrong, forgetting entirely that the church is perhaps 90 percent right, even in himself. I mean that up to his neck he is Catholic, and moreover pagan, because that far he is historical—only a little bit of his existence reaches beyond. It is on account of that bit of existence beyond that he fights the church: he reviles and blames it, or tries to dissolve it if possible. This conflict is going on in the beginning of the chapter. First Nietzsche has to recognize the importance and the inevitableness of the church, and then he boils over and goes against it because he cannot stand his own inferior man, the presence of the sheep in himself. He cannot stand the smell of the stable. But since he himself smells of the stable, it would be better to recognize it and admit that he is one of the sheep.

Mrs. Jung: I think that whenever he makes such extreme statements as in the last passages, his unconscious reacts. He was himself speaking like a priest.

Prof. Jung: You understand that this part where he is boiling over is the reaction against the priestlike attitude before? Yes, that is true. The end of this chapter, the priestlike attitude, leads us to the chapter about the priests. Now, I called your attention to this very interesting passage where he says, "Myself do I offer unto my love, and my neighbour as myself." You see, this is the sacrifice in the Mass when the priest offers up himself and the community to the love of Christ, but that is in order to produce the miracle of transubstantiation. And originally a human sacrifice was offered to produce the miracle of rebirth, of increase, fecundity, etc. It sounds like an age-old sacrificial formula, "Myself do I offer unto my love." Instead of love, put the equivalent, "God," and you have it: "Myself do I offer unto my God and my neighbor as myself." That is about what the priest says in the Mass.

Then Zarathustra says here, "He whom they call Saviour put them in fetters." The priests as representatives of the church are of course in the same enclosure, the same prison, as the sheep. The shepherd makes no sense without the sheep: they have to stay together, believe in the same system. They are simply two different aspects of one and the same thing. So a priest who is not fettered makes no sense. As soon as we discover that the priest himself does not believe in the dogmas of his church, he has no value; one becomes doubtful and suspects him of hypocrisy, of being rather a cheat. Therefore, the Catholic church had to be a bit "large" in that respect. They had to give the priests more chance, or they would not have been able to deal with the more educated members of the church. They cannot insist upon certain dogmas being taken too literally, but say, "Of course you must believe in this. It is the dogma of the church, so for the sake of good form you have to admit it, but naturally it is quite understandable that you think otherwise. It is, however, much better for the church that you make no row about it since the church exists for the more or less feebleminded people or the people who are feeble in their faith; you may protest against certain dogmas, but keep quiet about it since the church is the house built for the poor and it should not be disturbed. You would not upset the minds of your own children by strange ideas or doubts, so be careful what you say."

That is almost literally what a very competent Jesuit told me. This standpoint becomes necessary as soon as the church has to deal with the more sophisticated members of human society. For instance, a papal ambassador, an excellent conversationalist, once had a very lively conversation with a certain lady at a diplomatic dinner, and he made the remark, "As you know from Zola's *Rome* . . ."[4] She made a mental note of that and at the next opportunity said to him, "I want to ask Your Eminence whether Zola is not on the Index?" "Ah yes, of course, but not for you or for me." This is a most dangerous standpoint, yet it is quite understandable. *Quod licet Jovi, non licet bovi,* "What is allowed to Jupiter is not allowed to an ox." That is a fact, and whoever observes such a truth is wise. He allows for the different needs of men and for different mental spheres. And he mitigates the lot of the people who are fettered because they must be. They *need* to be prisoners and are much more unhappy if they have not their regular food. If you send sheep out into the open and don't care for them, they will soon be dispersed and killed—the wolves will eat them. But keep them in the stable and they have peace: somebody is looking after them, and that is

[4] After Emile Zola and his wife paid a visit to Rome he published his book *Fécondité* (Fertility) (Paris, 1896) to great acclaim.

what the inferior man wants. So the Savior, who is understood to be a liberator, has made a prison, a sort of big hospital for mental diseases, a psychotherapeutic institution in which people are kept and treated and fed. For as long as the truth of the church is valid, it does nourish those people: they are fed. You must not forget that the dogma of the church expresses the truth. It is a symbolic formula that is good for an inferior level of understanding where things can only be understood when they are projected.

And if you read these symbols on a subjective level, and translate them into more psychological language, you see at once that they make sense—that they are even most extraordinarily profound ideas and useful to meditate upon. The mystery of the Trinity for instance is immensely profound, expressing the most basic facts of our unconscious mind; therefore it is quite understandable that it played such a great role.[5] So we cannot dismiss those church dogmas as perfectly useless or nonsensical. They are carefully elaborated expressions that have certain effects on the unconscious, and inasmuch as the church is capable of formulating such things, it has a catching power. The church walls hold. They are tight. People live in peace inside those walls and are fed by the right kind of dogma, a dogma which really expresses the unconscious facts as they are.

That is the secret of the life of the church, the explanation of the fact that the truly Catholic nations have far fewer problems than we have. If one talks of this stuff in Italy or in Spain, nobody understands a word; when I speak about the collective unconscious in Paris they think I am talking mysticism. Why? Because, they say, it is religion, and not psychology. That religion could be psychology has not dawned upon them. They may be atheists but you know what an atheist is: simply a man who is outside instead of inside the church walls. Instead of saying, yes, I believe that you exist, he stands outside of the house and says, no, I don't believe that you are God. That is the only difference: an atheist is just as Catholic as those within the walls. So they cannot understand of what modern psychology is talking, because this whole world of problems, the symbols we are dealing with, is for them still within the walls of the church, safely walled in. There it is, all codified; every problem has been dealt with by the Fathers of the church and by that whole tradition of learning and wisdom of which the church consists. Now this is a great asset. It makes life decidedly simpler and safer and it saves one from a great deal of worry. Well, of course even a

[5] Jung here repeats his exposition of *homoousia* and *homoiousia*.

Catholic is worried, as we are worried, but not exactly in the same way; in contradistinction to us they are kept in that living water of the church. They are the little fishes in the piscina, the lambs in the herd. Well, now comes the French Revolution, the enlightenment, with Nietzsche:

> In fetters of false values and fatuous words! Oh, that some one would save them from their Saviour!
> On an isle they once thought they had landed, when the sea tossed them about; but behold, it was a slumbering monster!

Of course as soon as you are outside of the church walls, a fish on dry land, you say, "How terrible that those poor fishes inside are all drowning in the water—they must be suffocating," and you don't see that you yourselves, thrown out on the dry land, are the ones who are really left to perdition. Nietzsche cannot convince one of the tremendous advantages of being outside the walls of the church if one is threatened by the madhouse; it should be realized that it is a miserable condition not to be in the lap of the herd, not to be in the warm stables, not to be taken care of by a loving mother church or a loving father who guides one like a good shepherd. And those people who are outside—apparently, at least—try to create the same sort of thing in their own family. They make the family their abode and they create no end of trouble. They create a society for instance, or a sect with a noble purpose, making that society responsible for their spiritual welfare. For they still want a church; they have all their tentacles outside of themselves to fasten on somewhere, to adhere to something. If they are not in a church, they cling to the arms of father and mother and brothers and sisters and God knows what—cling to the walls of the family like an octopus and expect spiritual peace. Or they marry and then it must be the husband or the wife who is wrong, or if they are members of a society the society is wrong, not producing that which they expect. They have not yet learned that when they are outside of the church, away from the lap of the loving mother, they are fishes on dry land and that they must provide for themselves, if they don't prefer to die.

That is what comes to the man who is outside the church: he has to learn to feed himself, with no longer a mother to push the spoon into his mouth. There is no human being who can provide what is provided by the church. The church provides for all that naturally; inasmuch as you are a member of the church you get the *panis super substantialis*; in partaking of the communion, you receive the spiritual food and are spiritually transformed. Do you think that any father or mother or godmother or aunt or any book can produce the miracle of transubstantiation? If you yourself can provide for it, then you are the whole mystery of the church: you *are* the transubstantiation. If you understand that, you can have the spiritual food every day; then you know what it costs and you understand what the church costs and what the church means. Well, that is usually a side of the problem which people don't reckon with: they come out of the church in the same state of infantility with which they went in, sheeplike and collective, simply bound to their surroundings and the people with whom they are in contact, always expecting from other people what they should expect from themselves. They don't see that they should provide for themselves.

Unfortunately enough, it is the common fate; even the atheist who is always shouting up to God, "I don't believe that you exist!"—even such a man is already on the way to lose the church entirely. You see, as long as you can be a member of an atheist club or something of the sort, you are not really outside of the church. It is still in view, within your reach—with one leap you are inside; you only have to confess and repent and you are inside again. But you must not look at the church from the outside if you want to live in it. Being inside the church you must not think of inferior and superior people: such considerations don't happen in the church; there you live in the original paradise-like state where all the people are like loving little sheep. Of course there are bad people outside, but you believe that the people in the church are really good. That is a clear-cut situation: all the people inside are right and the people outside are all wrong. That gives a clarity and a simplicity of life which is remarkable and beautiful. Of course, we are so far outside of such a psychology that we are even convinced that those people who live in the country beyond the frontier are not necessarily all devils. But the primitive man believes that they are all devils on the other side of the river and when he sees one he kills him right away as if he were a poisonous snake.

As long as you can feel like that, you have a firmness and a unity in your own tribe which is marvelous, because nothing welds people so much together as vice, a common wrong-doing. If you can do something collectively to your neighbor you are in a marvelous state. In the church therefore, it is part of their life to fight their enemies. For instance, when the church was threatened with falling to pieces, they put up those stakes in Spain and burned a hundred thousand heretics, and that was good for the church. They had done away with that beast outside, and so they felt well inside. At the time of the Reformation a great part of the Christian church was blown up and that wound has never been healed; Protestantism is a festering wound in the body of the church, the wound in the body of Christ which has been infected and suppurating ever since. So when you are outside of the church you will naturally reach that stage in which Nietzsche is here; then you see the church as an island of refuge, which turns out to be Sinbad's monster: they made a fire upon its back, it felt the pain of it and plunged into the water, and they were all drowned.[6]

False values and fatuous words: . . .

That is what people think and it is just stupid, nothing else. Anybody who has thought critically and scientifically about the dogma of the church cannot say those are fatuous words, as little as the teaching of Buddha or Mohammed are fatuous words or false values. They are true values—right as long as they work. But they only work under certain conditions. So in the comparative science of religion one must always ask about the country, the conditions, and the kind of people to which it belongs; then you understand why they have that particular teaching, and you can draw conclusions from the teaching as to the nature of the people to whom it is preached. Which religion preaches love? Christian love was preached to those who needed it, who didn't have it; they were cruel power devils and therefore they believed in love. The Persians were always known in antiquity to have been dirty swine, and therefore they have the cleanest, purest religion—they *needed* that kind of religion.

So every dogma, every form of religion, is a tremendous problem; if one is intelligent enough perhaps one can understand, but if not, one simply should admit that one is too stupid to understand such profound things and so had better leave them alone—rather than to malign them. If we declare that such things are false values or fatuous words, we are rejecting the ugliest man in ourselves; the inferior man believes that is the food of eternal life. And if we take his food away and throw him out of the house, we have expelled ourselves from our own home and don't know how it has happened; we uproot ourselves by reviling the truth in which the inferior man believes and in which he is rooted. Mind you, we cannot undo historical traditions: whatever is in history is in history forever, in the safe womb of eternity which no mortal ever can reach. It is there and it always will be there. So you

---

[6] Sinbad and his sailor companions landed on a small island which, when they built a fire, discovered itself to be an enormous whale and then plunged into the sea. Some interpreters have likened parts of *The Arabian Nights* to the *Odyssey*.

never can do away with the fact that you have been, say, Catholic, or anything else; you have a history that is always with you, so be careful not to deny it. It is then as if you had appendicitis and couldn't be operated on; you have appendicitis all right but you have no appendix, and if the appendix doesn't exist it cannot be cut out. You see, you are at a frightful disadvantage. For instance, if one of your devils is wrong in your unconscious, and you don't believe in your historical psyche, then you have no devils. But then what about it? What is the trouble? They may say your glands have gone wrong and give you injections, and then the devils laugh, because that is just in their scheme. It is in their interest to make us believe that they don't exist, for then they can work in the dark, and all the safer because we have scoffed at them. Now he talks like a man of the 18th century:

> these are the worst monsters for mortals—[*Ecrasez l'infâme*, Voltaire said.[7]] long slumbereth and waiteth the fate that is in them.
> But at last it cometh and awaketh and devoureth and engulfeth whatever hath built tabernacles upon it.
> Oh, just look at those tabernacles which those priests have built themselves! Churches, they call their sweet-smelling caves!

This is now the ordinary misunderstanding when somebody is devoting his life to a cause. Then all the people who don't understand the cause, who have no feeling for a cause or who never heard of causes, think that such a person is simply doing it for his own pleasure, or sacrificing his life for his own ambition. Think of the existence of an ordinary priest! Is he living his miserable life simply in his own interest? That is not possible. Those people are to be taken seriously: they really sacrifice their lives, live lonely lives for the sake of the cause. If that were not so, the church would most certainly not exist; it makes the power of the Catholic church that the priests in general live miserable lives, that they accept such a pitiful lot. If you ever have looked into such a life you will be impressed with its misery, tolerated and carried for the cause. And that works.

> Oh, that falsified light, that mustified air! Where the soul—may not fly aloft to its height!

Naturally if anyone is cursed or blessed with the creative instinct, he cannot stay at home, but such a one must know that when he leaves his

---

[7] In a letter to Alembert, 28 November 1762, Voltaire wrote, "Whatever you do, crush the infamous thing . . . and love those who love you." Nietzsche's last lines in *Ecce Homo* are: "Ecrasez l'infame. Have I been understood? Dionysos against the Crucified."

paternal home he is the lost son who has to live in the wilderness. And then he must not revile the paternal home or he will be suspected of what?

Miss Wolff: Envy.

Prof. Jung: Naturally. He wants to return home to the fleshpots of Egypt, to the security of the church; there is really a secret desire, a longing, to return to the spiritual community in the church. What else is it when Nietzsche, for instance, thought of a *Kultur* monastery? He thought our civilization was threatened and that we should found monasteries again for those people who try to maintain the level of civilization. Graf Keyserling had the same idea, and I had to ask him whether he really thought that he would stay with other people in a monastery.[8]

> But so enjoineth their belief: "On your knees, up the stair, ye sinners!"

He thoroughly misunderstands the necessity of discipline in such a body as the church. Of course he belongs to that age; this was written in the eighties of the past century and that was pretty close still to the French Revolution, and for those days it was a vital necessity that such things should be said. One cannot turn back the wheel of history, it simply had to go this way. It had to be that those people who were no longer in the church made a clean cut from the church, that they separated definitely from the possibility of regression. For if you make a regression when you are once outside, it is a really bad regression with all its awful consequences—and then it is wise to say the whole thing was a mistake. If you know that you are going out into the wilderness when you leave the church, it is right and good that you should be a hero, but don't go back on that. If you then say, "But this is a wilderness!"—and go home again, that is of course no merit. It is simply cowardice, and you deserve to be thrown into the cellar of the church, and deserve to be buried. Therefore, people who regress under such conditions are not well off.[9]

Of course it doesn't always happen like that. There are certain Protestants for whom it is much better to go back to Catholicism, because they were not meant to continue their spiritual development. There is a long stretch along which one can wander; you may begin, say, with the very high Anglican conception, and then you can wander forward

---

[8] For Keyserling, see above, 2 May 1934, n. 22.

[9] Jung now repeats his account of how Angelus Silesius regressed.

through the centuries till you come to some modern form of Protestantism, and you die, having gone through all the stages of Protestant history. But if you can continue your voyage, you arrive at the last summit where you are confronted with God alone. Well, then you have, for instance, Karl Barth with whom you can die, or you can easily die in the meantime without having covered the whole *parcours*.[10] But there are people who have more speed, and they rush through the last stage of the drama and get beyond Karl Barth even; then of course they fall completely outside the Christian temple, even outside the precincts, and land in the wilderness. That is the fate which has become a collective problem nowadays. But Nietzsche is still bound to fight the church and its concept of God. Otherwise, he could wish the church many happy returns and be quite glad that the whole concern was flourishing and that he had nothing to do with it—glad that they would take care of that part of the world which he could not take care of.

They called God that which opposed and afflicted them; and verily, there was much hero-spirit in their worship!
And they knew not how to love their God otherwise than by nailing men to the cross!

Again this humanity idea, against cruelty and so on, not knowing that he himself is nailed to the cross. People who have been brought up in the church have not been trained to open their eyes and see; they were only allowed to see it projected. They should have been taught that *they* are nailed upon the cross, and shown *where* they are nailed on the cross. No parson ever has done that—of course not. He would break up the walls of the church, but if you are out of the church, you have a chance to see in how far you are nailed to the cross. But Nietzsche is still too much fascinated: he does not see it, but thinks that is only found inside the church and that outside everything is O.K. But he is not satisfied with all the beauties outside; he has to look back and curse about the things he sees there. The thing he does not see is that he is nailed to the cross.

As corpses they thought to live; in black draped they their corpses; even in their talk do I still feel the evil flavour of charnel-houses.
And he who liveth nigh unto them liveth nigh unto black pools, wherein the toad singeth his song with sweet gravity.
Better songs would they have to sing, for me to believe in their

[10] *Parcours*: route, trip.

Saviour: more like saved ones would his disciples have to appear unto me!

Naked, would I like to see them: for beauty alone should preach penitence. But whom would that disguised affliction convince!

Verily, their Saviours themselves came not from freedom and freedom's seventh heaven! Verily, they themselves never trod the carpets of knowledge!

Of defects did the spirit of those Saviours consist; but into every defect had they put their illusion, their stop-gap, which they called God.

This is also the collective misunderstanding which doesn't give to those values which have lived for so long the credit of having attained a living meaning and fulfilling a positive function. It is the regrettable short-sightedness of enlightenment. They never take the trouble to probe into these things and see whether they really work. It is only the lack of knowledge which accounts for such peculiar illusions in judgment, and we see it projected in this passage: "Verily, they themselves never trod the carpets of knowledge!" They had more knowledge than he of the inside structure and the spiritual meaning of the dogma.

LECTURE VIII

24 June 1936

Prof. Jung:

I have here two questions that are very different in form, yet they have to do practically with one and the same thing. Miss Hannah says, "I should be very grateful if you would say some more about the last three verses of chapter 25, 'The Compassionate.' As Shakespeare asks, 'What is love?' could one say that, partly at any rate, it is the urge towards creating a whole human being, towards individuation? Is not 'my neighbor as myself' rather an optimistic remark, because can we love till we have created 'what is loved' in ourselves?"

You refer to the verses: "But attend also to this word: All great love is above all its pity: for it seeketh—to create what is loved! 'Myself do I offer unto my love, and my neighbour as myself'—such is the language of all creators. All creators, however, are hard." Well, you mean that individuation is the real goal of love and that is not possible without seeking to create that which is loved. It boils down to the fact that you must love yourself in order to create yourself. Is that what you mean?

Miss Hannah: Yes, except that I want to know what love is.

Prof. Jung: Well, what *is* love? It naturally comes to that question, and that cannot be easily answered. What is truth? You know that is the famous question of Pilate. Now "Love thy neighbor as thyself" is really a very profound formula; of course a more extraverted mood insists upon the neighbor, and a more introverted mood insists upon yourself, and both are legitimate. For you never can get to yourself without loving your neighbor—that is indispensable; you never would arrive at yourself if you were isolated on top of Mt. Everest, because you never would have a chance to know yourself. You would have no means of comparison and could only make a difference between yourself and the wind and the clouds, the sun and the stars, the ice and the moon. And if you lose yourself in the crowd, in the whole of humanity, you also never arrive at yourself; just as you can get lost in your isolation, you can also get lost in utter abandonment to the crowd. So whoever

1019

insists upon loving his neighbor cannot do it without loving himself to a certain extent. To fall into the extraverted principle and follow the object and forget about yourself, is just like going into the wilderness and losing humanity. We always make the mistake of becoming victims of the pairs of opposites. Therefore, we are only right in following the prescription, "Love thy neighbor as thyself," when we are also entitled to say, "Love thyself as thy neighbor." If you are bold enough to love your neighbor, then you must be just enough to apply that love to yourself, whatever that love may be.

It is most questionable what love is. There is something which people call "love" but which nobody would feel like love if it were applied to them. Love can be anything between the worst stupidity and a great virtue, and only God can say whether it is perfectly pure gold. Usually it is not; it is a sliding scale of values. Surely no human love is 100 percent pure gold. There is always a possibility of criticizing what people call "love"; an uncertain amount of selfishness is included in it. There is no absolutely unselfish love. Even a mother's devotion and love for her child is selfish, full of black substance, with only a little surplus which you can call ideal love. Take a little away and you have an equal amount of black and white, and if you take a little more white away the black overwhelms the white. Then you realize that the whole thing can be explained as instinctiveness, falsehood, selfishness, egotism, and unconsciousness. As soon as the white is drowned in the black substance, then you call everything black because you see everything from the black side. In the next chapter Nietzsche explains even virtue, which is generally admitted to be something right and good, as selfishness, in a way. For instance, you can take all the moral virtues as cunning; if you are nice to people, if you apparently love them, it is practical wisdom because you then avoid enemies. It is very practical not to outrage people: to create less hostility is preferable. To be honest is preferable to being dishonest because you otherwise land in jail. And so on—everything can be explained in that way. Does that settle your question?

Miss Hannah: Yes, as much as it can be.

Miss Wolff: I think Miss Hannah asked, if I understand rightly, whether one should not individuate first before one can really love, and I should say that one cannot individuate without relating.

Miss Hannah: I meant, is individuation not a pre-stage before we can love? Does not real love to other people as well as to yourself always aim at that wholeness?

Prof. Jung: Well yes, both things aim at wholeness; in the one case there is more emphasis on oneself, and in the other case on the one you love.

Miss Hannah: Well, one always will project.

Prof. Jung: But it is not a projection when we assume that other people do exist—I think you are then on the way to Mount Everest. Now here is another question which deals with something similar: Dr. Neumann asks whether Zarathustra's negative attitude in reference to the mob is not really the rejection of the inferior function, or "the ugliest man," to use Nietzsche's term. Well, it *was* the mob that created the *Déesse Raison* of the French Revolution in opposition to the church, which means that the mob there emphasized the importance of human consciousness, one of the highest virtues of human consciousness being surely human reason. In that case, then, the mob would have been the creator of a high human ideal in contrast to the church that doesn't insist and cannot insist upon human reason; it insists instead upon the divine mind and the irrational language of the symbol. So one should recognize an extraordinary creativeness, a productivity, in the collective man, and this collective activity would be the manifestation of the blind or unconscious creator. And it would be that divine and blind creator that brings about the question and the answer of a new creation—that emphasis laid upon human reason for instance. The human individual was put into the foreground and also the overwhelming importance of consciousness. Those are two points which surely play a great role in modern psychology, and also in Nietzsche's *Zarathustra*. So the growth of the individual, the problem of individuation, depends upon the inferior function, and thus upon the mob in the last resort.

Now, it is surely true that our inferior function has all the qualities of mob psychology: it is our own mob, but in that mob is the creative will. The creative will always begins in the depths and never starts at the top. One could say that the seed really grows on the philosophical tree, and then it falls down to the ground into the mob; the mob surely is the fertile earth or the incubator or the dung heap upon which the creation grows. For the seed is not the tree and the seed doesn't *make* the tree unless there is the black earth: the black substance is needed in order to create something in reality. So, as the alchemists said, even the gold must be planted in the earth like the seed of a plant. It is indispensable that consciousness and the unconscious come together, that the superior or differentiated function comes together with the inferior or undifferentiated function, that the individual comes together with the crowd, with collectivity. Without that clash or synthesis, there is no new creation; nothing gets on its own feet unless it is created in such a way. The seeds can remain for a long time without growing if circumstances are unfavorable; certain ideas can hover over mankind for thousands of years, and they never take root because there is no soil. The soil is needed: one could even say the most important creative impulses come out of the soil. It is as if it were contributing the power of growth; at all events, it provides all the necessary substance for the further development of the seed.

Now, that is very much the same question as: love thy neighbor as thyself, or love thyself as thy neighbor. If you understand your inferior function, you understand the collective lower man, because your inferior function is exceedingly collective. It is unconscious, archaic, with all the vices and all the virtues of the collective man; therefore it is always projected. The mob is merely an accumulation of archaic individuals, yet it is a true analogy to your inferior function. That is the reason why we have such a resistance against the inferior function; we have the feeling of being soiled—even our feeling of cleanliness is against it. We don't want to be mixed up with that kind of psychology. There *is* something dangerous about it: it can overwhelm the conscious existence of the individual. Yet if you don't expose your conscious personality to the danger of being overwhelmed, you never grow. So Nietzsche's aristocratic attitude has a tendency to travel to Mount Everest and to get frozen to death there because he leaves the neighborhood of the fertile black fields where he could grow his wheat. It even looks in many passages of *Zarathustra* exactly as if he were not meant to take root, as if he were really taken away from the earth by a strong wind.

Then Dr. Neumann asks whether the church, by catching the mob through her forms, doesn't suppress the creative will which can manifest in the mob. The creative will is blind, so it can be just as destructive as constructive; in some phases a mob is utterly destructive—as a stampeding herd of cattle is most decidedly destructive—and it must either be killed or put in prison. So for a certain length of time, a church or any other organization is absolutely necessary, because it keeps that unruly mob-creator at bay. For it can create all sorts of nuisances like diseases and microbes and vermin—every nuisance under the sun—and we are only too glad if we can keep away from those humble creatures of our Lord. Then naturally, at other times, the prison or the stable is no longer satisfactory. For instance, if the herd has grown and there are too much head of cattle, then the moral demands must be lowered, because the greater the crowd, the more immoral and archaic it is; so the church is then forced to a certain reformation in the negative sense. Not for the better elements but for the worse elements it is forced to proclaim certain moral laws adapted to the low nature of the collective man.

There is a remarkable example of that in the encyclical of the Pope concerning the Christian marriage.[1] It is a terrible piece of morality. It deals with love and marriage from an entirely biological point of view, and concerning the personal and human relation of man and woman there is not a word. It is a document that makes me shudder when I read it. Here is Christian marriage as presented to the lowest strata of the population; if archaic man can maintain such a marriage it means that he can accomplish something, but for a man of better quality, such a marriage would be most regrettable—any sin would be better. It is a marriage of unconscious, half-animal creatures. The man of the crowd is no better than an amoral half-wit; he is a sort of monkey or a bull or something like that, and an institution which deals with such a man must have the right kinds of walls and gates, which are just coarse enough. So the church in her positive function is meant to be on a relatively low level in order to answer the needs of the undeveloped primitive and archaic man whom she contains. That of course is most unfavorable for creative development and then the church is in danger of becoming a heavy weight, which is what Dr. Neumann obviously means. It then suppresses the better elements because the archaic man is most conservative, always looking back to the past, doing everything as his ancestors have done it. He is lazy: nothing new ever will be invented because anything his parents have not done is insane—black magic. Better to do everything in the old-fashioned way and not bother about creating anything new. That suffocates life, so the better elements of the mob will strive for something different and the institution will squash them.

Now, that is obviously not desirable and there comes in the importance of the revolutionist who doesn't bother about the mob, who says the mob is just cattle, and that he, the revolutionist, is human and will create something which will perhaps destroy the useful walls of the stable so that wolves can break into the herd and ravage it. Naturally it is the tragedy of all human accomplishments that a time comes when they are no longer good, no longer sufficient, and when it is more or less true that Voltaire's *écrasez l'infâme* must be applied—a time like the French Revolution when the ultimate power of the church was practi-

[1] This is *Casti Connubii*, an Encylical Letter of Pope Pius XI, 31 Dec. 1930.

cally destroyed. The Reformation upset the church very badly, for Protestantism has no safe walls; there are a few spiritual walls left of the old fortress but they are not strong enough to be a protection against the creation of new ideas.

Mrs. Jung: In the lecture he gave last year at Ascona, Prof. Buonaiuti said that the exercises of the Jesuits systematically destroyed the imagination.[2] That would not only concern the mob, as Jesuits have superior minds usually.

Prof. Jung: Yes, that is perfectly true. On the few occasions that I have had to treat Catholics who were still *pratiquants* in the church, I found that they all suffered from a most remarkable extinction of fantasy—they had the greatest trouble about it. It was almost impossible to get them to realize a fantasy simply because they had gone through the Jesuit training, the exercises that systematically destroy the imagination. Of course one must say that it *is* a dangerous thing to nurse the imagination. It is dangerous in a patient, and it is even dangerous to ourselves, because you never know what will come out of it. Eventually you bring up the thing you fear the most, mob psychology, which is indispensable for individuation. When you go through such an experience, you know it is a quest in which you may be killed. Even the alchemists said that some perished in their work and I well believe it: it is dangerous, no joke. The Catholic church killed imagination on purpose, knowing very well what they were doing: they wanted to uproot the danger of spiritual revolution which would upset the safety of the church. And the church *is* a safeguard; therefore I would never encourage people who find their peace safely ensconced in the church to bring up their fantasies. I would even advise a Protestant to go back into the lap of the Catholic church if he finds his peace there, even if his whole spiritual life should be completely destroyed. For the spiritual life that he could afford would not be good enough, would be too feeble, too dependent; such people would fall helpless victims to their unconscious. People have a certain instinct in that respect—they feel how far they can go before striking a high explosive; they have dreams of high tension wires that should not be touched, or dynamite or strong poison or dangerous animals or a volcano that might explode. Then one has to warn people and take them a safe distance away from the source of danger, from the place where they touch that high ten-

---

[2] Ernesto Buonaiuti (1880-1946), a former priest and a frequent contributor at the Eranos seminars, gave a paper in 1935 on "The Exercises of St. Ignatius Loyola." Jung addressed this topic in CW 11, pars. 937-40.

sion wire which would overwhelm them. So the quest is quite a dangerous thing and many people are a thousand times better off in an institution. Therefore, one doesn't dare to disturb such an institution even if it suffocates creative imagination, even if it is a challenge to the will of the creator. For it is a blind creator, a creator that can work just as much evil as good, but as long as the walls hold one should not destroy them.

One has, in our time, chance enough to escape from such a spiritual prison, and I think that if there should be a strong enough movement in the mob to upset the church, they would have a tendency to create a new church—and they would have the *ability* to create it also. You see, there is no intelligence that can create a new church except the blind creativeness of the mob; the mob can create a new church as no intelligent fellow ever could. For to create a church you must be blind: you cannot have too much intelligence or consciousness. It is something utterly irrational. The only power on earth that can make a church is the mob. So when the mob succeeds in breaking through the walls, the mob itself will soon after make a church, and a church that is perhaps worse than before—it may be a state, for instance. We have no theocracy but we have the state. You know, to an intelligent individual the state is an abstract idea. He never assumes that it is a living being, but the mob is idiotic enough to believe that it *is* a living being and that it must have supreme power, so they make a church of it. For example, the actual organized state of Russia, even the actual Germany or Italy, is a church really, a religious affair; and the laws within that church are far more fatal than the laws of the Catholic church. The church is much more tolerant: you can sin against the rules and laws of the Catholic church with far less danger for you can repent and then the case is settled *en amitié*. But if you commit the least offense in one of those states, you will wake up in prison for twenty years. Of course, in the beginning of Christianity it was the same: it destroyed no end of values. The ways of the primitive church were much severer and more intolerant than later on. Only when the church was threatened with extinction in the 15th century was it again so intolerant; then heretics were burned and tortured but it was in order to save its own existence, for the mob is a tremendous danger to the church. We will continue:

> Verily, their Saviours themselves came not from freedom and freedom's seventh heaven! Verily, they themselves never trod the carpets of knowledge!

This is of course spoken *après le coup*, after those saviors had passed, having shown what they meant; they were the exponents of the creative mob and so they came not from freedom as was seen afterwards, and surely not from freedom's seventh heaven. For any mob movement, any creation by the mob, is undesirable because they can do no more than create a new prison. It may be a new safety but it is also a new prison, and very often of such an intolerant nature that a whole generation, the representatives of a highly developed civilization, is simply wiped out of existence. The intelligence of Rome and Greece, for instance, was swept into oblivion. Very lately, however, I discovered that New Platonist and Pythagorean philosophers still survived in 1050 in Baghdad under the Caliphs. They even experienced a late blossoming then; we owe to them the existence of the so-called *Corpus Hermeticum*.[3]

Mr. Allemann: Then you would call Christ or Buddha exponents of mob psychology?

Prof. Jung: It would be wrong to say "mob psychology," but they were surely exponents of the creative will that was coming up from the depths. It was not without meaning that Christ was crucified between two thieves, and that his first disciples were fishermen and such people: there were very few educated people among them. He moved in the lowest strata of the population and he answered to the expectation and need of the ordinary man, the recognition of immortality and all that. He came at the end of a very special spiritual development, culminating in the Ptolemaic civilization, when the Osiris became the Osiris of every *better* man: the ordinary man had no Osiris because he had no decent burial. Then with Christ there was an Osiris for everybody and that simply uprooted the whole of antique civilization. Therefore, Nietzsche very correctly said that Christianity was a revolt of the slaves in the moral realm. He hated Christianity, and surely the morale of slaves is not freedom: it means a new prison. Antiquity did not know the spiritual prison of the Middle Ages; such a condition never existed before in the world's history.

We now begin to lament about the complete destruction of political freedom in three countries surrounding Switzerland. And it is most probable that our freedom of political opinion and whatever we appreciate in our liberalism, our democracies, and so on, is on the decline; it is quite possible that even our freedom of research, our freedom of thought, will be greatly curtailed. For instance, Austria was

---

[3] See above, 30 Oct. 1935, n. 9.

such a nice, tolerant country where you could do everything that was "not allowed," and now you have to be very careful with your tongue. When you look back, you can see the negative side of Christian history if you put yourself before Christ. Suppose you imagine, for instance, that you have been a small citizen in one of the big towns of antiquity, or a freed man who has been delivered from his slavery, perhaps one of those very educated people who were given freedom by the law or by a benevolent proprietor—then came the Evangel. But not to the upper classes necessarily. Just as our new message of salvation means nothing good to us, not at all freedom, though it means a lot to certain people. To the half-educated middle-class German, for instance, it is a marvelous thing to be able to walk about with drums and flags on Sundays and wear a uniform—wonderful to have the Rhineland again. But that is mob psychology.

You see, that is what is going to happen when the mob comes to the top, and since their gospel this time is a worldly one, we don't know what the future holds in store for us. As the creator can invent tapeworms he can invent a worldly gospel just as well; he may say that men like Mussolini or Stalin or Hitler are holy people whom we ought to worship. The early Christians denied the Caesar; they didn't want to participate in sacrifices to a Roman Caesar because they only believed in an invisible Lord. That was another kind of prison, but it didn't injure them so much as when they were put in fetters or thrown into the arena, and some imaginative people could see more in it than in a Roman Caesar. But now times are changing; bring an old Roman back to Rome today and he will say this is the very stuff. There he sees the lictors who whip you if you walk on the wrong side, and there is the Caesar, and he finds temples where they worship all kinds of gods—one is Peter and one is Paul and another is Anthony—and they have a pontiff as they did in the time of the old gods. He recognizes the whole show: it is exactly as it was two thousand years ago.

That will come again if we believe in the state. Why not? Of course we don't sacrifice cattle nowadays, but sacrifice in another way; we have to pay, and so heavily that we can no longer even buy books to read something decent. And we have to parade with flags and a brass band in honor of the Caesar. That is what is actually happening, and that might be—I hope not—the new gospel with all the *isms* and flags and brass bands; we have the sacrifice to Caesarism, the absolute authority of the state, and we have a law which is no law because it is liable to change by an uncontrollable authority on top. In the same way they tried to bring about the infallibility of the Pope in the church, but they have it now in worldly respects too; there is no ultimate law, only an indefinite authority which is of course arbitrary. There is no absolute law in Russia nor in Germany nor in Italy; the law can be altered by personal authority, a Caesar or a leader. That seems to be the new gospel. I don't know how long it will last, but it has all the qualities of a new style, not to say of a new religion. And that is the way the antique man felt Christianity, I am quite certain. He would say, "Is that your new religion?" As I would have said, had I been an educated individual of Alexandria and had seen the Christian mob there when they tore a nice woman named Hypatia limb from limb: "Is *that* what you call Christian love and civilization?" Yes, that is what they called Christian religion and what subsequent centuries have always called Christian civilization. So they will believe in a God-State instead of the God-Anthropos, but a God-State is just as invisible, just as abstract, as the former God. He does seem to be visible in his temples however; all the biggest things now are quite worldly buildings; the passion of the mob is for great masses,—well, as it was before. Now we will continue:

> Of defects did the spirit of those Saviours consist; but into every defect had they put their illusion, their stop-gap, which they called God.

This is said about the past but one can also say it about the present time. In the place of an illusion they put the concept *State*; that is their stop-gap.

> In their pity was their spirit drowned; and when they swelled and o'erswelled with pity, there always floated to the surface a great folly.
> Eagerly and with shouts drove they their flock over their footbridge; as if there were but one foot-bridge to the future!

What do we read in the newspapers?

> Verily, those shepherds also were still of the flock.
> Small spirits and spacious souls had those shepherds: but, my brethren, what small domains have even the most spacious souls hitherto been!
> Characters of blood did they write on the way they went, and their folly taught that truth is proved by blood.

What do we hear nowadays?

> But blood is the very worst witness to truth; blood tainteth the purest teaching, and turneth it into delusion and hatred of heart.

> And when a person goeth through fire for his teaching—what
> doth that prove!

Oh, that proves a lot to a middle-class intelligence.

> It is more, verily, when out of one's own burning cometh one's
> own teaching!
> Sultry heart and cold head; where these meet, there ariseth the
> blusterer, the "Saviour."

Now what does this last sentence mean?

Mrs. Crowley: It is the coming together of the opposites.

Prof. Jung: Yes, quite certainly, because the mob psychology
Nietzsche is envisaging here, he understands chiefly as a sultry heart
and no head whatever; and one could say that the result of that development was nothing but head with no heart at all, not even a sultry
one. But with the coming up of the inferior function, the heart is filled
with that sultry emotion. That is a good term to designate the quality
of the inferior function; it is sultry like a coming thunderstorm, and
the real head is the cold detached superiority of the developed, differentiated function. "Differentiated" means aristocratic, different, independent, and that is the quality of the aristocratic superior function.
"Where these meet, there ariseth the blusterer, the 'Saviour.' " Now
what does "the blusterer" mean? A *Brausewind* is proverbial; that
would mean a young fellow full of all sorts of fantasies and so on.

Mrs. Baynes: A wind-bag?

Prof. Jung: No, more dynamic. It would be not exactly a storm, but a
wind strong enough to be dynamic and jocose at the same time, playing
with dry leaves and pieces of paper and carrying off people's hats.

Mrs. Baynes: A whirlwind?

Prof. Jung: Yes, a sudden whirlwind is the best rendering of the
Nietzschean term *Brausewind*. Those among you who have read *Das
grüne Gesicht* by Meyrink will remember perhaps that the same phenomenon is found there.[4] It is something like a whirlwind catching up
dust, but it is not dust. *Chidr*, the Green Face, is the whirlwind, and the
dust consists of a swarm of ants. That figure is the center of Meyrink's
story, and he shows how Chidr works in ordinary human circumstances, how he comes in as a sort of sorcerer. The whole thing is a
manifestation of the collective unconscious, the way the collective unconscious breaks into an ordinary human existence, the way it transforms and influences human existence. Then in the end there is a
great catastrophe, a storm which devastates the whole town; and at the

---

[4] Gustav Meyrink's novel was published in 1916. See above, 13 March 1935, n. 7.

very end this whirlwind catches up a swarm of ants, the swarm of ants being the mob. Chidr is a whirl of mob psychology that carries people off to a distance like a swarm of ants.

The *Brausewind*, then, is this catastrophic wind that breaks into social existence. Whenever the opposites meet, whenever a cold layer of air touches a warm layer of air there is most probably movement, there will be a cyclone, or a wandering whirlwind; one sees those wandering columns of water on the ocean, and in the desert one sees columns of dust. That is the simile for the peculiar collective movement by which people are seized, *ergriffen*. Here and there spouts of air gather up dust that moves and dies down, and then in another place it starts up again, like the little whirls of water on the sea or on our lakes when the Föhn is coming. And that is so in human society when the Föhnwind begins to blow.[5] Since it shows in very different places one doesn't connect these phenomena, but it is one and the same wind really. Of course when it is in the desert it gathers up sand, and in the garden it gathers up leaves, and in a library it gathers up papers in heaps, and in crowds it gathers up hats, so each time one thinks it is something different; but it is always the same meteorological phenomenon: when opposites meet there is a whirlwind. That is the manifestation of the spirit in its most original form.

So a savior is one who seizes, the *Ergreifer* who catches people like objects and whirls them into a form which lasts as long as the whirlwind lasts, and then the thing collapses and something new must come. That is the great wind described in the Pentecostal miracle, because there two worlds were clashing together, the world of the slaves and the world of the highly differentiated mind. You see, the teaching Christ received through his teacher, John the Baptist, must have been the ripe fruit of the time; otherwise it could not have been so in tune with the surroundings, with all the great problems of the time. And it is also absolutely out of the question that one man alone could have invented it in his own lifetime without making use of an enormous tradition. Christ draws very freely from the Old Testament and from other sources which are to us more or less unknown, partially because the early church did not care for any ideas previous to Christ. It was in her interest to have a body of writing that fell from heaven, with no heathen material. It should be quite obvious that God himself was the author of that stock of books, so that nobody would be able to do any better. Any such institution must found itself upon an unquestionable

[5] *Föhnwind*: Swiss-German for Sirocco.

authority. So already in the early church nothing was known about the things that had happened before; they were soon buried in oblivion.

But we have evidence that John must have belonged to a certain religious movement, current in those days, which must have been something like the Essenes, also called the Therapeuts, who were chiefly occupied in healing the sick and interpreting dreams. They were sort of *directeurs de conscience* for rich people at the courts, and we have evidence that they were called in in cases of particularly ticklish dreams. When the Tetrarchos of Palestine had a disagreeable dream that was too hot for the court interpreters, they called in a doctor from abroad, an Essene, to tell the old man about it because they were afraid for their heads. The Essenes had great authority, as if they belonged to a feared body of medicine men. Then we know from Philo Judaeus of Alexandria[6] that monasteries existed in those days and that there were considerable settlements on the Dead Sea and in Egypt, and they naturally had a body of teaching. There are still disciples of John in the neighborhood of Basra and Kut-el-Amara in Mesopotamia; they have a collection of sacred books, one of them has been translated recently, the Mandaean Book of John.[7] The Mandaeans were disciples of John and they were Gnostics. Peculiarly enough, the Gnostic Evangel is also called the Evangel of St. John; this is obscure, but since it was written only at the beginning of the second century, it is possible that the name of John covers the Gnostic side of Christian origins; on the one side, he was decidedly an orthodox Jew and on the other side he must have received the Gnostic teaching. Paul also had been a Gnostic, a disciple of a Jewish Gnostic, the Rabbi Gamaliel the elder;[8] and we have definite evidence in his writings of a Gnostic education: he uses Gnostic terms, particularly in the Epistle to the Ephesians.

So we are almost forced to assume that Christ received Gnostic teaching and some of his sayings—like the parable of the Unjust Steward which we recently mentioned, and particularly the so-called "Sayings of Jesus" which are not contained in the New Testament—are closely related to Gnosticism. Also those Evangels which were not accepted by the church, and therefore mostly destroyed, contained Gnostic teaching; we can substantiate this from the knowledge of the fragments which we still possess, the Gospel of the Egyptians, for in-

---

[6] For Philo Judaeus, see above, 16 May 1934, n. 6.

[7] For the Mandaean Book of John, see Mead*.

[8] Paul wrote, "I am a Jew born in Tarsus of Cilicia . . . educated under Gamaliel" (Acts of the Apostles 22:3). Gamaliel was a doctor of laws, a prominent Pharisee, and in Jewish tradition was counted as one of the first of the seven great rabbis.

stance, and among the Apocrypha of the New Testament, the Acts of St. Thomas, where the Holy Ghost is called *Sophia* and where she is the blessed mother. So already in its origins, Christianity was so closely surrounded by Gnostic and by Alexandrian wisdom that it is more than probable that Christ received a Gnostic initiation and possessed a rather profound understanding of the human soul and the peculiarities of spiritual development. One could say that he himself was the ripe fruit of antiquity; he gathered up in himself the essence of the wisdom of the Near East, contained the juice of Egypt and of Greece, and came together with the mob. And that caused a great whirlwind which moved masses and formed them, which brought about that form which we call Christianity. Now Nietzsche continues,

> Greater ones, verily, have there been, and higher-born ones, than those whom the people call Saviours, those rapturous blusterers!

And who are those greater ones who have been more than saviors? To whom does he refer?

Mrs. Fierz: The wise old man. There would be a sort of difference, he makes the opposition between the figure of the wise old man and what one calls a savior.

Prof. Jung: Yes, "Greater ones, verily, have there been."

> And by still greater ones than any of the Saviours must ye be saved, my brethren, if ye would find the way to freedom!
> Never yet hath there been a Superman.

Now who are these greater ones?

Miss Hannah: The self?

Prof. Jung: Well yes, but the greater selves would mean greater personalities, so who could those greater people be?

Mrs. Fierz: People who have been initiated.

Prof. Jung: But who initiated them? Don't you think of a famous name here?

Mrs. Adler: Doesn't this mean the differentiation between Nietzsche and Zarathustra?

Prof. Jung: Of course it refers to Zarathustra, but Zarathustra himself was the founder of the Persian religion; he was a savior too, and therefore there must be a greater one than Zarathustra.

Mr. Allemann: Hermes.

Prof. Jung: Of course, the thrice-greatest Hermes who was greater than any prophet, Hermes Trismegistus.[9] Now, we cannot assume that Nietzsche knew much about that figure, and if he had, he would have made little of it because it did not fit into his system. Yet that man or that personality whom he calls "Zarathustra" is a derivative of old Hermes, the thrice-greatest. What he calls "Zarathustra" is his companion, his Poimandres, the Poimen that teaches him: that is his initiator, his Johannes. You know, Oannes is the Babylonian form of the Greek Johannes, and he is the one who in the form of a fish comes out of the sea daily and teaches people wisdom and civilization and every good thing under the sun. No mob psychology there. Hermes the thrice-greatest is the aristocrat of aristocrats. Now, Nietzsche knows nothing of him; he calls him simply "Zarathustra," but he has the right idea, that Zarathustra, or whatever that Poimandres is called, is a Savior greater than the old Zarathustra. He is greater than great, greater than the greatest saviors, the father of prophets, the father or the grandfather of saviors even in that he never has been visible. Tot is the Egyptian equivalent of Hermes. He is also a mystery god. Hermes was the teacher of all wisdom, but a wisdom which is not for the mob, a wisdom which when it touches the mob causes a conflagration or a whirlwind; it is the thing that has to be kept secret. It is "secret knowledge."

In the dialogue between Christ and John in the Mandaean Book of John, Christ is called "Jeshu ben Mirjam," the deceiver, and John reproaches him for having betrayed the secret wisdom to the people. But Christ defends himself very aptly; he pointed out his good works, that he had made the lame walk and the blind see. And the dialogue never comes to a definite solution, so it is open to doubt whether John was right or Christ. John's argument is that if this beautiful truth is given to the inept, they will only destroy it, will make something bad or ugly of it, so one should conceal it. And Christ shows what he has done with that truth. Even if this dialogue is fictitious it is at least something that might have happened. Perhaps the only bit of evidence in the New Testament is where John sends his disciples to Christ to ask him whether he is really the Son of God; that would be the doubt. He might have said just as well, "Are *you* chosen to hand out these precious secrets to the mob? Will you let that evil herd invade our beautiful garden so that whole areas of our garden are destroyed?" A very great question, it is difficult to decide whether the moment has come when the precious fruit of a past civilization should be handed over to the

[9] *Thrice Greatest Hermes*, ed. and trans. G.R.S. Mead, 3 vols (London, 1949).

herd. You see, that has once to be: the pearls have to be cast before the swine eventually, since the swine are also human. You may try to save the pearls but once the moment will come and a man will appear who will hand them over to the herd; that great wind will come when it cannot wait any longer.

SPRING TERM

May / June 1937

LECTURE I

5 May 1937

Prof. Jung:

Ladies and Gentlemen: Our last seminar dealt with the 26th chapter of Zarathustra, the chapter about the priests, but before we go on I want to make a few remarks for the benefit of those who have not been here before. *Zarathustra* is a very ticklish subject, but it was the wish of certain members of our seminar that I should deal with it. I felt rather hesitant because it is a pretty ambitious task. I admit it is highly interesting psychological material, but it is long and for certain reasons it is exceedingly difficult to deal with. Of course the fact that it is difficult is no reason against dealing with it; on the contrary, a difficult case is always very much more interesting than a simple and easy one. *Zarathustra* is Nietzsche's most significant work. He expresses in it something which is really himself and his own peculiar problem. His most productive years were the eighties of the past century and in many ways he is the child of his time, yet he is also the forerunner of times that have come since and of times that are still to come.

One could say that the stratification of our population was historical; there are certain people living who should not live yet. They are anachronistic. They anticipate the future. Then there are some who belong to our age; but many don't belong to our age at all, but should have lived at the time of our parents and grandparents. Then there are still many who belong to the Middle Ages, and others to remote times, even to the cave dwellers; one sees them on the street and in the trains, and one meets occasionally a funny old cave dweller who really ought not to live any longer. It is on account of this fact that certain problems of the time become the conscious problems of many people, while other people living at the same time are not touched by them, at least not directly. So Nietzsche at his time was a man of the future; his peculiar psychology was that of a man who might have lived today, after the great catastrophe of the world war. Therefore it is of quite particular

1037

interest to us to delve into it, since it is in many ways the pyschology of our own days.

You know, *Zarathustra* is more than a mere title: the figure of Zarathustra is in a way Nietzsche himself; that is, Nietzsche identifies to a great extent with the figure of Zarathustra, despite the fact that he himself said that "one became two" when Zarathustra first appeared to him, showing that he felt that figure as distinct from himself. Yet having no psychological concepts, it did not become a problem to him; since his general philosophical attitude was exceedingly aesthetical, he took it more or less as a metaphorical figure and identified with it. Now, this is an event of consequence: namely, it makes a great deal of difference with what one identifies, and Nietzsche was not fully aware with what he identified. He did not realize that his declaration, "God is dead," meant something which he did not quite grasp; to him the existence of God was an opinion or a kind of intellectual conviction, so one only needed to say God was not and then he was not. But in reality God is not an opinion. God is a psychological fact that happens to people.

The idea of God originated with the experience of the *numinosum*. It was a psychical experience, with moments when man felt overcome. Rudolf Otto has designated this moment in his *Psychology of Religion* as the *numinosum*, which is derived from the Latin *numen*, meaning hint, or sign.[1] It comes from the old experience that in antiquity, when a man had to direct a prayer to the statue of the god, he stepped upon a stone that was erected at its side to enable people to shout their prayer into the ear so that the god would hear them; and then he stared at the image until the god nodded his head or opened or shut his eyes or answered in some way. You see, this was an abbreviated method of active imagination, concentrating upon the image until it moved;[2] in that moment the god gave a hint, his assent or his denial or any other indication, and that is the *numinosum*. Now, this is clearly a psychical fact, and Nietzsche, not knowing of psychology at all—though he was really a great psychologist—behaved with that concept of God as if it were purely an intellectual concept and thought that if he said God was dead, then God didn't exist. But the psychological fact remains and then the question is in what form that fact will appear again.

In this case, it appeared again in Nietzsche's own dissociation:

[1] On Otto, see above, 10 June 1936, n. 1.

[2] Barbara Hannah, a member of the seminar, was to write a book on this subject: *Encounters with the Soul: Active Imagination* (Boston, 1981).

namely, when Zarathustra came up in him he clearly felt that it was not one but two, and he said so, yet since there was nothing inside beyond himself—or if there were, it would be himself—he had of course to say that Zarathustra *was* himself, he was identical. And so he was identical with the fact of the *numinosum*: he had to become a *numinosum*. That means he had an inflation, was filled with air, was *tremendous!*—and we shall soon come to a chapter where he will betray this fact, speaking of the wind with which he is filled. Moreover, when a definite image has been reduced to apparent nothingness, it is just as if the *pneuma*, what we call "spirit," were also reduced to its primeval form which is just air. You see, when you have the experience of the deity, the *numinosum*, and you have an image of it, you can say this is the experience of the spirit; but when you reduce it and deny its existence, you are simply filled with air. Then it may even lead you into a neurosis where you have all the symptoms of being suffocated; or instead of having spirit, the abdomen may be filled with air literally. Spirit is also the source of inspiration and of enthusiasm, because it is a welling-up; the German word *Geist* is a volcanic eruption, a geyser. That aspect of the spirit is the reason why alcohol, for instance, is called spirit: alcohol is the reduced form of spirit. Therefore many people, lacking spirit, take to drink. They fill themselves with alcohol; I have seen many a case of that sort. It is typical for men, though women do it too.

Now, Nietzsche's book is a confession of this condition and its peculiar problems. You know that we have, or at least have a sort of reminiscence of, what one might call a medieval or primitive world, in which the *numinosum* is outside of ourselves. I don't need to go into that. But you are probably not quite aware of that world where the *numinosum* is inside you, of *our* world where the *numinosum* is experienced as a psychological fact. The very word shows that we declare the deity as our experience and nothing but our experience; though we may deny that it is a real experience and think it a psychological occurrence that happens only to certain people. That of course produces a new kind of world, a world without a deity, without a spirit, a world in which we are the only living things, practically. Of course it is then questionable in how far we are really living, because we are so deeply convinced that we move through space just as any other object moves through space, that we see no particular difference; there is only a huge space through which things move, and since we cannot indicate any particular sense, we renounce the idea of formulating any sense in the whole thing. You see, that is a perfectly new, very peculiar world; we have never before experienced how it feels when the *numinosum* is identical with ourselves, how it is when we are the *numinosa*. That is a new problem, and it puts us right in front of an entirely new task: namely, how one should behave if one is a *numinosum*, how it is when *we* are gods or something near to that—in other words how it would be if we were supermen. For Zarathustra is the Superman already in existence in Nietzsche; he himself feels at times as if he were already the Superman.

This book leads us right into that kind of problem. It tells us at length what the inner events are, how one feels with reference to other people, to values, how everything changes its aspect. For instance, Nietzsche himself speaks of the destruction or the *Umwertung aller Werte*, the transformation of all values; naturally all values become different when you are a god, when you are something you never were before. If you are so big, then all other things become small. It is as if you were the size of a skyscraper, when of course your relation to the remaining world would be exceedingly clumsy; you wouldn't be able to enter your own house even, and so nothing would work. Now, we are here in the midst of a discussion of actual, existing values. For instance, the last chapter we dealt with had to do with the new relation to the fact of the priests, what the priests would mean to somebody who has an inflation or who is a *numinosum* himself, or how priests look in the eyes of the deity. We know quite well how the deity looks in the eyes of the priesthood, but we do not know how the priesthood looks in the eyes of the god. But we can get a pretty shrewd idea from reading that chapter.

And now we come to the chapter called "The Virtuous." Here again the question is, how does the deity look at the virtuous? How do they look in its eyes? Of course, the experiment is not quite pure, as you will realize, because we often fall upon facts which show us very clearly that Nietzsche is behind Zarathustra, that Nietzsche has an inflation and that the deity is therefore in a somewhat awkward position. If the deity finds itself to be identical with Mr. Nietzsche, naturally the space is a bit cramped, so even the judgment of God becomes a bit cramped. In such cases we have to refer to Nietzsche's biography and to the limitations of his time, since he is a child of his time. But in the better parts of his text, it is a good thing to keep in mind that not Nietzsche speaks but the deity, and it is obviously not a dogmatic deity but the deity as a psychological fact.

You see, the deity as a psychological fact is presumably not at all what churches or creeds have made of it. Certain Protestants, a Protestant theologian for instance, will assure one that God is bound to be only good, and then one must always ask why they say so. It might be because it is true that this psychological factor representing God is really nothing but good, but it also might be because they are afraid that he might *not* be good. They might say it as a sort of apotropaic gesture, in order to protect themselves, or to force or propitiate the deity. As we say to somebody who is threatening to become angry, "Now be patient—you are really quite patient," in order to make him believe that he *is* patient. So it is quite possible that we implore God to be good in order that he shall be good, that we refuse to believe that he can be bad, hoping that he will be convinced and will really be good.

That is by no means blasphemy; I have the authority of the Catholic church behind me. Or one need only go back as far as the German reformer Luther, who recognized that God was not always good; unlike the modern theologians he allowed for a *Deus absconditus*, a concealed or veiled god that is a receptacle for all the evil deeds, all the terrible things which happen in the world. We cannot conceive that a good God would be responsible for all that nonsense. It is absolutely in the hands of the All-powerful to make man a good vessel, but he preferred to make him a very imperfect vessel. He preferred to rouse all sorts of extraordinary sins in the world that were beyond the power of man to cope with and made the work of man entirely nonsensical. So, since we cannot assume that it is all for the good of man, we say it is the work of the devil, but the very existence of the devil is an exception to the omnipotence of God. When I was a boy I asked my father why there was a devil in the world since God was all-powerful, and my father said that God had granted the devil a certain time in which to do his work in order to test people. "But," I said, "if a man makes pots and wants to test whether they are good, he doesn't need a devil, he can do it himself." We still have in the Lord's prayer "lead us not into temptation," and one of my daughters said a good God would know better than to lead people into temptation, and I had nothing to say against that. So you see when the deity speaks in Nietzsche it might say very shocking things. That explains why there are so many shocking things in *Zarathustra*. Well now, the new chapter begins.

> With thunder and heavenly fireworks one must speak to indolent and somnolent senses.

If you keep in mind that God is speaking, this is almost like the psychology of old Jahve that spoke with thunder and lightening and created so much disorder in the world.

But beauty's voice speaketh gently: it appealeth only to the most awakened souls.

Gently vibrated and laughed unto me to-day my buckler; it was beauty's holy laughing and thrilling.

At you, ye virtuous ones, laughed my beauty to-day. And thus came its voice unto me: "They want—to be paid besides!"

Zarathustra very clearly hints at the fact that most people prefer to be virtuous because it pays, and so their virtue is not quite creditable—it serves a purpose, one is very often only good in the expectation that everybody will say "Isn't that nice?"—and so we shall be rewarded.

Ye want to be paid besides, ye virtuous ones! Ye want reward for virtue, and heaven for earth, and eternity for your to-day?

And know ye upbraid me for teaching that there is no reward-giver, nor paymaster? And verily, I do not even teach that virtue is its own reward.

Ah! this is my sorrow: into the basis of things have reward and punishment been insinuated—and now even into the basis of your souls, ye virtuous ones!

Well, the idea is that if the deity doesn't exist, there is no pay-master, nobody there to pay us at the end of our lives for all our virtues. If a virtue means a reward at all, it must be its own. This idea of the suitableness of virtue, the obvious value, almost the commercial value of virtue, pleases Nietzsche very much, so he indulges in it a little, and that explains the peculiar style of the next sentence:

But like the snout of the boar shall my word grub up the basis of your souls; a ploughshare will I be called by you.

You see, virtue is always a difficult thing because there wouldn't be any virtue if there were not a need, so you can expect to find something below it; virtue is often a cloak that covers up something else. If anybody insists too much upon truth or honesty or frankness, for instance, you may be sure that something is hidden behind it; just because there is a tendency to lie, to conceal, they talk a great deal about frankness: *Qui s'excuse s'accuse.* That is, I am afraid, the characteristics of many virtues, and when you have discovered it, it gives you, of course, a certain unholy pleasure to dig up all the things that are hidden; you have discovered that they are all locked doors and naturally your curiosity is aroused—you want to find out what is behind them. Of course, what you find is not always quite harmless: you may find dirt even. And in digging up dirt you are quite close to the pig and so the boar comes in, and therefore all sorts of wrong metaphors present themselves to Nietzsche—like needing the snout of the boar in order to dig up evil-smelling secrets. This sort of interest makes Nietzsche almost an analyst. Here, then, is a small restriction of the voice of God, at least I think that the man, the "all too human" of Nietzsche, has played a certain role in this.

> All the secrets of your heart shall be brought to light; and when ye lie in the sun, grubbed up and broken, then will also your falsehood be separated from your truth.
>
> For this is your truth: ye are *too pure* for the filth of the words: vengeance, punishment, recompense, retribution.
>
> Ye love your virtue as a mother loveth her child; but when did one hear of a mother wanting to be paid for her love?

Here again the "all too human" plays a trick. I have heard of mothers wanting to be paid for their love only too often. Nietzsche had not because he was a man with very developed intuition and intellect, but his feeling developed slowly. He had not his own feeling really. Such men always have mothers' feelings, continue their mothers' feelings; there is plenty of evidence in his biography for this fact. And mothers' feelings have never been subjected to a close analysis, at all events not when a man has them; he believes in mothers' feelings, and that his mother-feeling is pure and all-powerful and wonderful—and naturally never expects to be paid for. But inasmuch as there are forms of mother love that quite decidedly wait for payment, it is just as certain that the mother feeling in a man waits for the reward.

> It is your dearest Self, your virtue. The ring's thirst is in you: to reach itself again struggleth every ring, and turneth itself.

I will read you the German text here, this English rendering being not quite sufficient: *Es ist euer Liebstes selbst, eure Tugend. Des Ringes Durst ist in euch: sich selber wieder zu erreichen, dazu ringt und dreht sich jeder Ring.*[3] What does that mean? We have encountered this kind of language before.

Mrs. Crowley: Is he not referring to the return?

Prof. Jung: Yes, the ring of the eternal return. That is Nietzsche's

---

[3] Kaufmann's rendition reads: "Your virtue is what is dearest to you. The twist of the ring lives in you: every ring strives and turns to reach itself in you again" (Kaufmann*, p. 206).

conception of immortality. You see, to him the number of possibilities in the universe was restricted. You do not find that in this book. Nietzsche's idea of the Eternal Recurrence is in a posthumous publication by Horneffer, consisting of fragments from the manuscripts in the Nietzsche archives.[4] There Nietzsche dealt with the idea that the number of possibilities in the universe was restricted and therefore it was unavoidable that in the course of infinite spaces of time, the same thing would return, and then everything would be again as it was. That idea filled him with an extraordinary enthusiasm. I cannot quite understand it but that doesn't matter. It belongs with this symbolism of the ring, the ring of rings, the ring of Eternal Recurrence. Now, this ring is the idea of totality and it is the idea of individuation naturally, an individuation symbol. It means the absolute completeness of the self, and you will see that this is confirmed in the text.

In my edition of the English text there is a mistake. In the sentence, "It is your dearest Self, your virtue," *self* should not be written with a capital S—that is wrong. Nietzsche does not mean there *the* Self, he means, "it is even your dearest." That would be the literal translation of *euer Liebstes selbst*, and not "your dearest *Self*."[5] I have the original German edition where it is a small letter. To say it is the *Selbst* is of course an entirely new interpretation, and probably that apparent mistake came in through the fact that a few paragraphs further down you find the sentence that your virtue is your Self and not an outward thing. But this was suggested presumably by the sentence we are actually dealing with; namely, first he merely wanted to say that your virtue was the dearest thing to you, the thing you cherish or love the most, and then *that* suggested the idea of the Self, which is proved by the way this is printed in the first edition. You see, the fact which he tries to express here, that virtue is the thing you love the most, means that the intensity of your love is the virtue, and there he takes the word *virtue* in its antique sense. In German, it is *Tugend*, which has to do with *Tüchtigkeit*, but that also meant originally something that was efficient, like the Latin word *virtus* which had the meaning of "quality" or "power." For instance, a physical body or a chemical body had *virtus*. Opium has a *virtus dormitiva*, which means it has the quality of a narcotic. *Virtus* is a dynamic quality. So he means the very fact that you love the most, or

[4] A year after Nietzsche's death, Ernst and August Horneffer and Peter Gast (Nietzsche's most faithful disciple and correspondent) edited vol. XV of the *Werke*, "Studies and Fragments," which they titled *Will to Power* (Leipzig, 1901). See WP.

[5] In this book, the practice of the editors of the CW has been followed, of using the lower case *s* in *self* for Jung's distinctive concept.

that you love intensely, is the virtue: namely, that is the powerful or the efficient in you.

That he really meant this is borne out by the next sentence: the thirst of the ring is in you. Thirst is the dynamic element and that is the value, or the virtue. With the ring comes in the idea of totality, which is always connected with the idea of duration, of immortality, the eternal return. That is substantiated by the fact that the actual psychological experience of totality, which is a religious experience, always expressed or formulated as the experience of God, has the quality of immortality, the quality of eternal duration. That is confirmed also by the *consensus gentium*; you find the evidence in the literature of the whole world. There is that element of duration, either limited to the duration beyond death, or the immediate feeling of divine eternity. So this sentence would show that Nietzsche amplifies his dynamic concept of virtue and says it is really the most powerful, the most intense, the most efficient thing in you. And this is the thirst of the ring; namely, your highest virtue is your expectation or desire, the thirst for the ring. Or it may also be the thirst of the ring in you, or of that experience in you to become real. This is the virtue, and from this, naturally, to the self is only a step. Therefore he says in the next sentence, "to reach itself again struggleth every ring, and turneth itself." In other words, in the circular movement, in the rotation of the ring, is expressed the dynamic intensity which is the virtue. Now this circular movement of the ring is naturally round the center, so this is the famous *circumambulatio*, namely, the concentration upon the central point is the virtue, and that is Nietzsche's idea. This desire is not temporal, but eternal, of eternal duration. It is immortality. So you have practically in a nutshell here the whole symbology of individuation. Then, still amplifying that idea, he continues,

> And like the star that goeth out, so is every work of your virtue: ever is its light on its way and travelling—and when will it cease to be on its way?

This is again a bit difficult. The idea is that virtue is the ring, and that is eternal power, cosmic. It is a sort of galactic system which is also a great circle, or it is the circulation or rotation of a planet round the sun. So he comes to the idea of the star. The ring is the star and therefore every act of virtue is starlike; or it might be like a shooting star, or like a star that will become extinct, because an act of virtue will cease to be. But no, says Nietzsche, because there is a feeling of eternal duration; virtue is such a power that it can never be extinct. Therefore, it is like a star in that, though it may become extinct, yet on account of the infiniteness of space the light travels on. Whether he is able to see it depends upon the observer; if he is near, it will cease to be, but if he is at an infinite distance from the star it will shine eternally. You know, there are many stars in our universe that are extinct but we still see them. Too short a time has elapsed—the light needs perhaps a million years to come here—so if a star has only been extinct ten thousand years, it might take a million more years before we could become aware that it no longer existed. You see, Nietzsche quite naturally uses here the simile or metaphor of the planets or the galactic circle, which is forever the expression of eternal duration, now as in antiquity. For instance, you may remember in the so-called Mithraic liturgy by Dieterich, the confession of the *mystes*, the initiant, when he became aware of the presence of the planetary gods: "I am a star like yourself, who travels on the same way with you."[6] That is, he himself was starlike through the fact that he had the virtue, the eternal power of the ring. Now Nietzsche applies his insight to man, saying,

> Thus is the light of your virtue still on its way, even when its work is done. Be it forgotten and dead, still its ray of light liveth and travelleth.
> That your virtue is your Self, and not an outward thing, a skin or a cloak; that is the truth from the basis of your souls, ye virtuous ones!—

This is one of the two most important thoughts, or *the* most important thought in the whole chapter. Here he plainly says, your virtue is your Self, with a capital *S*. In German it is, *Dass eure Tugend euer Selbst sei, und nicht ein Fremdes, eine Haut, eine Bemäntelung*. The German word *fremd* means "alien." I should insist upon that translation instead of "outward" because in the old formulations of the Middle Ages, in the so-called Hermetic philosophy, where we have the nearest analogies to these ideas, one always finds that term, *nihil alienum*: nothing alien should be in the composition of the most important thing, the philosopher's stone, which is the symbol of the self. They always insisted that the stone was one thing and nothing alien should be put into it; therefore, one should keep the hermetic vase well shut, hermetically sealed. You see, that term comes from their idea that nothing could come in that was alien to the primal matter out of which the stone was made. So

---

[6] *Eine Mithrasliturgie* (Leipzig, 1905; 2nd edn., 1910), by Albrecht Dieterich, was a work very important to Jung.

when Nietzsche says, "and not an alien skin or a cloak," he means pretty much the same: namely, your virtue is only a virtue inasmuch as it is the self, understood here as a dynamic entity, a dynamic existence.

Now, of course, this is difficult to understand if you try to realize what it really conveys, and Nietzsche goes no further into it here. It is his intuitive style to just allude to things; one sees how he arrives at it—his words suggest such ideas to him very often. For instance, "It is even your dearest" and then the accent is merely changed and it means, "It is your dearest *Self*," which suggests this idea—merely alluding to it and then leaving it, to return to it again later on. It is as if he himself had not a full realization of what it really meant, which comes from the fact that he, Nietzsche, is not speaking out of his conscious mind: Zarathustra rules his hand that writes. Zarathustra is like a river that flows through him, and Nietzsche is merely the means by which Zarathustra speaks. Sometimes the means is not good—too narrow, cramped, not quite pure—and then the manifestation of Zarathustra is also cramped or contaminated or even falsified; then sometimes, inasmuch as the instrument works well, it is the absolute truth. But Nietzsche's conscious ego participates in it only intuitively. He just catches that your virtue is your self, and though he can write it, yet he has no time and no complete realization of it, and so he goes on. One often sees in *Zarathustra* that the most important ideas are just alluded to and then left. If he were really a philosopher, which he is not, he would stick at it. He never would get away from this place, but would forever turn round this one sentence: "Your virtue is your Self." What does that mean? It means a world. Who is there who really understands it? And what does it mean practically? It is a statement that would need years, a whole lifetime, to realize fully. But one thing is perfectly clear: it is not an outward thing, or an alien thing, not a thing which is taught or imitated or obeyed or followed or suggested. It is not an attitude you take on like a skin or a cloak, or a way of doing. It is just your self. It means, *be* yourself and you are virtue.

You see, to explain such a thing fully, one needs to know a great deal about the history of human thought. What is that self? Naturally, common sense reality would say: *self*—that is, myself. And what is myself? The ego, I myself. And you are completely mistaken. That is why people call Nietzsche an individualist or an egotist. But it is perfectly clear that he is two, Nietzsche and Zarathustra. Nietzsche is "I," his ego, and the self is presumably Zarathustra; we have often seen in the former chapters that Zarathustra is really in the place of, or represents, the self. Zarathustra, being the archetypal image of the old wise man naturally contains the self, as in all cases where that figure becomes a psychological experience. As the anima in a man's case contains the Self. The anima is something different from the ego. If one identifies with the anima, one is in trouble, neurotic, a sack full of moods, a most unaccountable being, most unreliable—everything wrong under the sun. So if you should say, "I am my Self," you would be neurotic, as Nietzsche was as a matter of fact, because he identified with Zarathustra. He would better say, "I am not the self, I am not Zarathustra." As you should say, "My virtue is not myself"—it is just not ego, but something impersonal. It is the power of the self. Our psychological definition of the self is the totality, the ego with its indefinite fringe of unconscious that makes the totality. We don't know how far the unconsciousness reaches, but at all events the ego, as a center of consciousness, is a smaller circle within a wider circle or indefinite extension. We only know where the center is, but we don't know where the circumference is.

Now peculiarly enough, this is the old formulation, usually attributed to St. Augustine, that God is a circle whose center is everywhere and whose circumference is nowhere. But I found recently in Hermetic literature that this saying is attributed to a Hermetic oracle. I don't, however, know the authority for this tradition; it is stated by an Italian humanist and I have had no chance yet to look up his authority. But usually, when the alchemists quoted from the Christian Fathers, they quoted correctly, and they made use of them very often. So if they had been convinced that St. Augustine was the authority for that metaphor they would surely have said so because they liked to quote the Fathers. In the Middle Ages it was always a recommendation; it meant: we are received, we are well spoken of, we are in good company. Naturally they had always a bit of inferiority feeling with reference to the church, so they even talked a lot of patristic language and used patristic metaphors in order to increase the authority for their statements. So when they definitely state that formulation to be of Hermetic origin and quote a so-called Hermetic oracle which is perfectly unknown to me, there might be something in it. I would not go so far as to say that St. Augustine borrowed it from any known Hermetic tradition—there is no such image to be found there as far as my knowledge goes—but there are numbers of Hermetic quotations from texts of which we have no evidence, because they have been lost. Therefore there is the possibility that that statement is authentic. It is also possible that it was a new invention, for the circle is an archetypal image that can occur anywhere without a direct tradition. For instance, you find it used very beautifully in Emerson's essays, in that chapter called "Circles." Of course he was aware of St. Augustine—he quoted him—yet the use he made of it is not at all what St. Augustine would have made, which shows that it was a living archetypal fact in Emerson's case.[7]

Well now, it is perfectly certain that what Nietzsche means is that virtue is nothing that can be taught or given or acquired; virtue is what you are, your strength. And your strength is of course a metaphor again, for only conditionally is it your strength: it is the strength to which you belong, in which you are included. You see, this is the embarrassed formula of a mind that has stated that God is dead, because every mind of a former epoch would have said we were included in God, that our virtue was the strength of God and nothing else. But since God is dead and non-existent now, you must invent clumsy formulas, must say this is a strength to which I belong, which manifests psychologically. And then naturally you are in the devil's kitchen because that strength which manifests in you might be a very bad emotion or a very bad desire, so that the whole world would say, "How immoral, how disgusting!" A good Christian might say your belly was apparently your God, because your greatest emotion lay in eating and drinking. Or the most powerful thing in certain people is their fear for their reputation, their respectability; and then their respectability is their greatest strength, their greatest virtue, their God. Or they may have a foolish conviction. Or in a drug fiend, the desire for drugs is the strongest thing in his life; that is his virtue according to the definition, the power within him which cannot be overcome.

You see, all this agrees with our definition of God; as that psychological fact which is not necessarily good, it also can be destructive. But in admitting that, we are in line with all religions of all times, with the sole exception of very late Protestantism. For instance, to illustrate my allusion to the Catholic church, Basilius the Great, one of the old Fathers of the church, and St. Ambrose, St. Augustine's teacher, belonging also to the fourth century, used the rhinoceros as an analogy of God. They said that God was like a rhinoceros because of his great strength. That is the origin of the legend of the unicorn in the lap of the virgin,

---

[7] Emerson's essay begins: "The eye is the first circle; the horizon it forms is the second; and throughout nature this primary figure is repeated without end. It is the highest emblem in the cipher of the world. St. Augustine described the nature of God as a circle whose centre was everywhere and its circumference nowhere." But Emerson makes no citation, and Jung is perhaps right in suspecting that the idea had a source other than Augustine. Surprisingly, Emerson was a particular favorite of Nietzsche. "Jung and Transcendentalism" has been discussed by Edward Edinger in *Spring* (1965), pp. 77ff., and by William McGuire in *Spring* (1971), pp. 136-40.

as a symbol of the Holy Ghost and the immaculate conception.[8] One finds that symbolism on many ancient tapestries; and the unicorn was also wounded in the side by the spear, so he represented Christ in the form of the Holy Ghost—the Holy Ghost having there the form of the wild untameable Jahveh, the God of the Old Testament. Then in the Catholic Church, since the time of Albert the Great,[9] they had the teaching that God, before he had a son, was of a very excitable temperament, very wrathful. He caused great disorder in the world until he found his peace in the womb of the Virgin, literally captivated by love. Then he transformed. He became the loving father of a son.

So you see, that kind of teaching in the Catholic church shows that they admit that God was not always good, but was first wild and unruly. We have plenty of evidence for that in the Old Testament. For instance, in that passage where Job, speaking about his afflictions caused through the decree of Jahveh, tells his friends that there is no ruler or lord above him in Israel. Therefore nobody could say whether it was good or bad, nobody could condemn Jahveh for playing evil tricks on a man. Of course, if a powerful lord, who had some miserable serfs that entirely depended upon his grace, should make a bet with the devil as to which of them could best lead the poor fellows astray, we would think it a pretty bad joke. But that is what happened: God gave the devil a chance to tease the old man Job, to frighten him out of everything he had, to kill any number of cattle and human beings, to deprive the poor man of his ordinary life, just in order to test him. God in his omniscience could easily have known beforehand how the experiment would turn out. Well, I am just alluding to some of the amplifications of that statement that your virtue is your self. It is something to think about. Now Nietzsche continues,

> But sure enough there are those to whom virtue meaneth writhing under the lash: and ye have hearkened too much unto their crying!

---

[8] St. Basil, or Basileus (330?-379), the great Bishop of Caesarea, is one of the many theologians whom Jung berates for denying any evil at all to God (see CW 9 i, pars. 81-85). St. Ambrose (340?-397) was Bishop of Milan. In CW 11, par. 408, Jung also cites Nicolas Caussin, a 17th-century Jesuit, as likening Jahweh to an angry rhinoceros or unicorn until, "overcome" by the love of a pure virgin, he was changed in her lap into a God of Love.

[9] Albert of Bollstadt lived in the 13th century. He was both an Aristotelian and a remarkably empirical natural scientist. He would surely have been shocked at any such account of Mary.

The following passages we can deal with very quickly. They contain important psychological statements so it is very worthwhile to hear them but they need no particular commentary.

> And others are there who call virtue the slothfulness of their vices; and when once their hatred and jealousy relax the limbs, their "justice" becometh lively and rubbeth its sleepy eyes.
>
> And others are there who are drawn downwards: their devils draw them. but the more they sink, the more ardently gloweth their eye, and the longing for their God. [A particularly juicy statement]
>
> Ah! their crying also hath reached your ears, ye virtuous ones: "What I am *not*, that, that is God to me, and virtue!"
>
> And others are there who go along heavily and creakingly, like carts taking stones downhill: they talk much of dignity and virtue—this drag they call virtue!
>
> And others are there who are like eight-day clocks when wound up; they tick, and want people to call ticking—virtue.
>
> Verily, in those have I mine amusement: wherever I find such clocks I shall wind them up with my mockery, and they shall even whirr thereby!
>
> And others are proud of their modicum of righteousness, and for the sake of it do violence to things: so that the world is drowned in their unrighteousness.
>
> Ah! how ineptly cometh the word "virtue" out of their mouth! And when they say: "I am just," it always soundeth like: "I am just—revenged!"

This is a play on words in German, with a little local peculiarity. It sounds like this: *Ich bin gerecht* (I am righteous). But Nietzsche came from Basel and there it sounds exactly like *geracht*, "revenged." That is what he heard there, I am sure.

> With their virtues they want to scratch out the eyes of their enemies; and they elevate themselves only that they may lower others.

Or by lowering others they elevate themselves!

> And again there are those who sit in their swamp, and speak thus from among the bulrushes: "Virtue—that is to sit quietly in the swamp.
>
> We bite no one, and go out of the way of him who would bite; and in all matters we have the opinion that is given us."

And again there are those who love attitudes, and think that virtue is a sort of attitude.

Their knees continually adore, and their hands are eulogies of virtue, but their heart knoweth naught thereof.

And again there are those who regard it as virtue to say: "Virtue is necessary"; but after all they believe only that policemen are necessary.

And many a one who cannot see men's loftiness, calleth it virtue to see their baseness far too well: thus calleth he his evil eye virtue.—

And some want to be edified and raised up, and call it virtue: and others want to be cast down—and likewise call it virtue.

And thus do almost all think that they participate in virtue; and at least every one claimeth to be an authority on "good" and "evil."

But Zarathustra came not to say unto all those liars and fools: "What do *ye* know of virtue! What *could* ye know of virtue!"—

But that ye, my friends, might become weary of the old words which ye have learned from the fools and liars:

That ye might become weary of the words "reward," "retribution," "punishment," "righteous vengeance."—

That ye might become weary of saying: "That an action is good is because it is unselfish."

Most mistakable—if you make the mistake of mixing up the self with the ego.

Ah! my friends! That *your* very Self be in your action, as the mother is in the child: let that be *your* formula of virtue!

Now how do you understand this; "As the mother is in the child"? Surely the child is in the mother.

Mrs. Sigg: It might be that Nietzsche thinks that a real human being is in the self, and the self is the mother for the human being.

Prof. Jung: Yes, that is right. You see, here we have the idea of the ring, the wider circle that contains the smaller, like a mother, a child. And our action is virtuous inasmuch as the wider circle can be expressed within or by means of the smaller circle: namely, inasmuch as the hypothetical invisible self manifests in our actions. In other words, inasmuch as we can allow the unconscious to flow in us, so that whatever we do always contains a certain amount of the unconscious. When a thing is fully conscious, we can be sure that we have excluded the unconscious, and have excluded the indefinite extension of psychical matter which is always there. We ought, on the contrary, to include the unconscious, but since we are unconscious of it, how is it possible? Therefore, we can only allow that action which has to be; if we do that, Nietzsche would call it virtuous. Then it has strength. But it must be clear, if the unconscious flows in with our action and with our behavior, that *we assume responsibility*. Otherwise it would not be expressed, but would simply be an event that occurred, and it would occur just as well to fishes or plants. It would have no merit; it only becomes ethical inasmuch as we know. If you know that a certain amount of unconsciousness, which means a certain amount of risk, comes in, and you stand for it, you assume responsibility: insofar is your action virtuous or ethical.

> Verily, I have taken from you a hundred formulae and your virtue's favourite playthings; and now ye upbraid me, as children upbraid.

Well, he has taken away all the hundreds and hundreds of prescriptions or criteria by which one can say this is good and that is bad, and this should be and that should not be. Naturally, if you say you are virtuous inasmuch as you have virtue, and you have virtue inasmuch as you allow that strength to which you belong to manifest through you, then it is exceedingly simple, something which you see everywhere. That is the way in which a tree builds itself up, it is the way in which an animal lives and we ourselves *would* live if we only were not conscious. But since we are conscious we think about it, understand that certain things are very difficult or even very dangerous, and then we begin to be careful, to avoid. So our morality is the practical wisdom of life. Try to be impolite, or immoral, and see what will happen; you will wind up in jail perhaps, which is not pleasant. You can injure yourself in many ways. Or you may say that something is not good, but just wise. For instance, if you are nice to your enemies, it is pretty clever because you avoid further scraps; if you are polite you don't offend and that is also a good thing, good in the same sense as the primitive chief understood it when he said to the missionary: "It is good when I take the wives of my neighbor chief, and it is bad when he takes mine." You see, there is no difference; it is entirely a utilitarian point of view.

But to be able to submit to the strength which is in us, that is virtue. You see, it is even more virtuous than when you say you submit to the strength of God. That sounds like something that is in a way very nice. You have a form, can even justify yourself apparently, particularly when that strength of God coincides with what is said in books, or with what the priests say, or public opinion says. For instance, if you raise a fund for certain charitable purposes and put all your energy into it, if you call it the will of God and say you are obeying his strength, everybody will pat you on the back and call it nice and virtuous. But it might be the other way round. It might be that the old god of Hosea would repeat himself—you know he was terribly indiscreet there, saying Hosea should marry the whore, and he did. If Bishop So-and-So were to marry a Paris cocotte it would be pretty shocking, yet there are no safeguards against such possibilities, absolutely none. You can see that in history. Inasmuch as it is eternal truth it may repeat itself at any time—that is the strength. Hosea could say it was the command of the Lord and there was no gainsaying it. But where are you if you say it is the command of the self? You are an egotist, you are excusing yourself. What is the self? It is yourself and there is no excuse whatever. So you are absolutely in the frying pan. That is what you come to when you say God is dead: you have no excuse any longer. But there we are—we have lost every authority for what we do. Now the chapter ends with this pretty ironic remark:

> But the same wave shall bring them new playthings, and spread before them new speckled shells!
> Thus will they be comforted; and like them shall ye also, my friends, have your comforting—and new speckled shells!

If you think that the god in Zarathustra is speaking like that it is exceedingly doubtful, very ambiguous; if you think Nietzsche has played with it, it is harmless and does not mean too much. But it might be that God himself has such a way of expressing himself, and then it would look almost as if he were playing with man and that is coldblooded. You will hear something about it in the next chapter.

LECTURE II

12 May 1937

Prof. Jung:

Here is a question by Miss Hannah, "You said last time that when the spirit was denied, it sometimes reappeared as actual air in the abdomen. You have often said that whereas the East begins in *muladhara* and works *up*, the West begins in the head and works *down*. Would the air be in the abdomen because when 'God is dead,' we have to work right down the centers and can only re-find him when we reach *muladhara*, or can this occur at any center?"

This is a pretty complicated question. Miss Hannah tries to express this problem in Nietzsche in the language of the Tantric Yoga but I cannot possibly go into the explanation of the Tantric chakras so I must answer rather fragmentarily. It is perfectly true that all Eastern thought-forms start from the *muladhara* region, which means that they come up from the unconscious: the Eastern mind is always in connection with the natural instinctive facts of life. But in the West we are cut off from the instincts. Our mind works out of the air—starts in the head and looks down upon the natural facts; so, instead of growing up like a plant out of the bosom of the earth, one can say the Western mind begins in the head and works down towards the earth. You can see that in our way of approaching the unconscious. So many people, particularly those who have no idea of the unconscious, speak of the *Unterbewusstsein*, the subconscious, a consciousness below the conscious; we always think of it as being somewhere below the surface. At all events *we* are on top, we are above. For instance, take water as a simile of the unconscious; but we are not in the water, we are on the surface, we look down into the water, with the unconscious always below. While in the East it is understood that the unconscious is above and the conscious of man is below because it comes out of the earth. Therefore, it is characteristic for China that the dragon is in heaven; the dragon there is a favorable and heavenly and brilliant figure, a figure of light. With us it is just the opposite: the dragon is unfavorable, humid, dark.

1055

It lives in caves and is lord of fords and rivers and springs; also it represents the lower centers of the brain and the spinal cord and we assume that we are on top of those so-called lower centers. Not so the East. The East starts from the lower centers; the instinctive truths are absolutely indisputable there. But we even dispute their right to existence; to us mind is something air-like that is always on top and allows us to look down upon the instinctive world.

So one can say that when the essence of spirit, which in Christian language is called "God," is dead, then surely it can only reappear in the lower centers. For instance, church people say that you are lost if you don't belive in God—you are on your way to hell—and to a certain extent that is perfectly true, because the moment the spiritual essence is denied, it simply comes up from below but in the form of a disturbance, as if the stomach were disturbed, for instance, or as if a bad instinct were stirred up. You see, the rising of the lower strata of the population and the destruction of the hierarchies—the destruction of *values*—are symptoms of decentralization; all that is the consequence of the undermining or hollowing out of the spiritual principle, or of identifying it with the mind. Klages makes the same mistake in his philosophy: he identifies intellect with the spirit.[1] But intellect is a human business while the spirit is no human business; it is a principle which we do not make. It makes us, it seizes us. And spirit is by no means an enemy of life; it is a dynamic condition, like anything.

Now, the fact is that when you deny that principle, it simply comes up from the other side, so it may manifest itself in the abdomen. For certain people it is quite enough to discover *manipura*. They are perfectly satisfied with the presence of that divine principle when they meet their emotions, so a part of our analysis simply consists in the making conscious of the emotions, and that may be enough. In other cases, you have to go further down into the collective unconscious, to *svadhisthana*, the water-region. But even that will not be enough in all cases; there are others that have to go right down to *muladhara*, and that gets them into reality; it is no longer mere theory, *theoria*, looking at things, being impressed by things, but becomes doing, actual deeds, actual life. That of course is concrete, completely practical, and that only will be convincing. For instance, Paul had every chance to know what Christianity was, but it was not enough until he was struck to the ground—till he was struck with blindness—that it happened to him in reality.

---

[1] For Klages, see above, 23 May 1934, n. 5.

I remember a woman whom I advised against an operation because her case was really nothing but hysteria. But her husband was a doctor himself and said that was nonsense, so she had twice a laparotomy and found there was nothing.[2] Then they thought it must be a sort of tuberculosis and she had to spend about two years in the mountains. Nine years later she came to me again, having had her belly cut open twice and having spent all that money and time. But then her sons were threatened by tuberculosis and she had a dream in which she was made responsible for their illness: the dream said she had caused their death, she had killed her two boys. Then she believed, but it needed that fact, and that is *muladhara*. I once treated a very distinguished lady—she was so distinguished that she could only speak in a very high voice, as people do who want to demonstrate how high they are—and I told her if she went on like that something would happen to her. I saw it coming: she was heading for a rape. I told her plainly but she would not believe me. Then when I had been away about eight days on my vacation it happened, naturally, and happily enough she was rescued in time with two broken ribs and a broken cartilage of the larynx. It needed something like that to make her sit up, otherwise she never would have paid any attention to what one told her. But people who have quick perceptions and can draw conclusions only need to touch the sphere of *manipura* and it is enough. Now we will go on to the next chapter, "The Rabble."

Life is a well of delight; but where the rabble also drink, there all fountains are poisoned.

We must always keep in mind that when Nietzsche talks about the pitiful, or the priests, or the rabble, he means a thing which is particularly disturbing to himself; namely, a thing that is in himself and therefore particularly irritating. You see, we curse those things the most which are the closest to ourselves; the most irritating qualities are our own. If a thing is absolutely strange to us, if it really doesn't touch us on the raw, we are just astonished, perhaps only mildly astonished, and we do not understand, don't even find the necessary words to revile it. But when it is our own fault we become loquacious and dispose of a flow of attributes and criticism to blame or revile that particular thing. So when Nietzsche talks of the rabble, he means the rabble in himself; that gives him the necessary emotion, and sure enough everybody contains rabble. A certain percentage of humanity *consists* of rabble, and since

---

[2] A laparotomy is the surgical removal of a portion of the abdominal wall.

we are all part of that humanity we contain probably the same percentage. Now, we would not mention this fact, would prefer not to know of it, as long as the rabble is not what we call constellated; but the moment we rise a bit too high, the moment we become too distinguished, instantly the rabble becomes important and we begin to revile it. Nietzsche, inflated by his identification with Zarathustra, is of course too high, too distinguished, too wonderful; and then the rabble becomes important and he has to repress it. He finds now very strong words: the simile he uses is the "well of delight" poisoned by the presence of the rabble; that means the rabble in himself poisons *his* well of life, as it naturally would.

If you identify with the distinguished figure, all the minor qualities have no place in that image, but are excluded, and they will heap up and cover the fountain of life, which is of course the unconscious. Out of the unconscious flows the well of life, and what you don't accept in yourself naturally falls back into that well and poisons it; when you don't recognize certain facts, they form a layer in the unconscious through which the water of life must come up, and it will be poisoned by all those things you have left down below. If they are accepted in your conscious life, then they are mixed with other more valuable and cleaner substances, and the odious qualities of the lower functions disappear more or less. They only form little shadows here and there, sort of spice for the good things. But by excluding them, you cause them to heap up and they become entirely evil substances; for a thing to become poisonous, you only need to repress it. If you carefully sterilize everything that you do, you make an extract of the impurity and leave it at the bottom, and once the water of life is poisoned, it doesn't need much to make everything wrong. You see this in the next image he uses.

To everything cleanly am I well disposed; . . .

Here you have it: things must be clean or they are not accepted. He has to clean things in order to be able to accept anything. But nothing is quite clean; in everything there is the admixture of the earth, in everything imperfection. So if you prefer to accept only the perfect things, all imperfections will fall to the bottom; below your choice of most perfect things there will be a heap of imperfection.

but I hate to see the grinning mouths and the thirst of the unclean.

Exactly. Somewhere impurity heaps up and that forms these grinning mouths.

They cast their eye down into the fountain: . . .

If he looks down into the well, of course he sees it; therefore he says,

and now glanceth up to me their odious smile out of the fountain.
The holy water have they poisoned with their lustfulness; and when they called their filthy dreams delight, then poisoned they also the words.

Now who has the filthiest dreams?

Mrs. Fierz: The virtuous ones.

Prof. Jung: Naturally. The saints have the filthiest dreams. That is a fact unfortunately. For instance, St. Augustine said he thanked God that he did not make him responsible for his dreams. He does not say what they were and I have always been curious to know—they must have been pretty strong.[3] You see, that was a time when there was no analysis, but there are particularly good reports of such dreams—in Flaubert's *La Tentation de St. Antoine*, for instance. This is a very juicy bit of saint psychology, and, mind you, whatever Flaubert wrote was always based upon very careful study. Also we have a contemporary account by the holy Athanasius in which he described such visions.[4] Of course those people who make such a sport of holiness must heap up impurity somewhere, and at times it just crashes down upon them— they get swamped by it—while if they had accepted it in small parcels, it would not come in big lumps. So what Nietzsche describes here is the perception of the fact that below his consciousness, in the inferior mental functions, is a lot of filth, and he projects it into people who to him are human rabble.

You see, we should be very grateful that there is such a thing as human rabble. They are inferior and I am not inferior; thank heaven that I have found people who are inferior—now I know where the inferiority lies. Therefore people are so tremendously interested in believing bad things. They hardly ever believe good things, that would be awkward. They can hardly stand believing that anybody is better than they, because it means that *they* should be better. But if they know that

[3] The many dreams St. Augustine reports in his writing are scarcely "filthy," but he took them seriously, and at least some as premonitory.

[4] Athanasius' visions were reported in *The Book of Paradise*, ed. E. A. Wallis-Budge. See below, 2 June 1937, n. 2.

other people are worse than they are, they should feel it almost as a duty to be grateful to them. They should say, "Thank heaven you are bad, for now I feel better, since I am not weighed down by the terrific task of *doing* better. You are worse, thank you. Stay where you are and then I know where the evil is, thank God, and I am all right." That explains why wives are often quite satisfied with the low moral state of the husband—that he drinks for instance—for then, quite against their will and with no effort, they are always on the good side and are never as bad as the husband. But if one takes the trouble to cure the husband, it gets uncanny; the wife tries to persuade him to drink again because she will then have a much better conscience. Or in treating a couple, if the man is badly neurotic and one happens to cure him, one can safely predict that the wife will then have a neurosis and a bad one. You see, she has always been on top. Of course she has suffered terribly and one had to pity her, sure enough. Her lot was by no means enviable. But in that case one would think when the husband was cured that happiness could begin. Not at all. Then the wife becomes neurotic. Hitherto, she was in good shape only because he was in bad shape. I don't say that this is always so, but it is very often so.

Indignant becometh the flame when they put their damp hearts to the fire; the spirit itself bubbleth and smoketh when the rabble approach the fire.
Mawkish and over-mellow becometh the fruit in their hands: unsteady, and withered at the top, doth their look make the fruit-tree.
And many a one who hath turned away from life, hath only turned away from the rabble: he hated to share with them fountain, flame and fruit.

That is very much Nietzsche's fate: he was extraordinarily intolerant of the ordinary man. He was easily hurt and could not stand banality at all, with the result that he was always isolated; he was a terribly lonely figure because he could not stand the ordinary man in himself. He tried to get away from his own banality, and anybody who tries to escape his own banality has no access to human life at all, but is completely cut off from his tribe. You see, mankind is a terribly banal fact, and inasmuch as you possess banal qualities you have a connection. In your virtues and attainments there is no connection—there your strength lies, you can stand alone; you need inferiority to have connection. If you deny your inferiority, you deny the bridge to humanity, lose your chance. That was exactly Nietzsche's case.

> And many a one who hath gone into the wilderness and suffered thirst with beasts of prey, disliked only to sit at the cistern with filthy camel-driver.
>
> And many a one who hath come along as a destroyer, and as a hailstorm to all cornfields, wanted merely to put his foot into the jaws of the rabble, and thus stop their throat.

This is again Nietzsche; you see, he is always identical with Zarathustra. He often compares himself to a destroyer or to a natural catastrophe like a hailstorm, always most destructive, of course, because he felt his new idea like purifying wind or a great revolution. But he never felt that what he imagined himself to be for the world, he most certainly was to himself because he was part of mankind; and whoever means a hailstorm to cornfields is in the first place a hailstorm to his own cornfields. Now, here he uses a very peculiar metaphor: namely, "to put his foot into the jaws of the rabble." This is an extraordinary figure of speech and those who have been in the former seminars know that whenever Nietzsche uses an image of bad taste, there is something symbolic behind it. The idea is that he puts his foot into the mouth of a monster, presumably choking it. Does that remind you of another figure? It comes later on but we have spoken of it before.

Mrs. Baumann: The snake that went into the shepherd's mouth that he could not swallow?

Prof. Jung: Yes, the snake that crept into his mouth while he was asleep. He should have swallowed it, but Zarathustra advised him to bite off his head and to spit it out. And what does that mean?

Miss Hannah: That he refuses his instinctive life.

Prof. Jung: Yes, the snake is the dragon, the representative of the lower centers of the brain and the spinal cord. It is that coldblooded animal that has no connection, no rapport, with man, symbolizing the part of our psychology which is utterly strange to ourselves, which we never can understand, at which we shudder and are afraid. People often have an instinctive fear of snakes, just as monkeys or horses have. Now, since he refused that thing, symbolizing all the lower parts of his mental functions, *la partie inférieure de ses fonctions*, they personified and came to him in the form of a snake that wanted to enter him.

Peculiarly enough, the snake is at the same time a religious symbol in the mysteries of Sabazios. The initiation consisted in the swallowing of the snake—of course not literally: they perhaps patted it or kissed it. The Christian Ophites celebrated their communion with a real snake on the altar, but in the mysteries of Sabazios they had a golden serpent that was pushed in under the chin—instead of into the mouth—and passed down under the vestments and taken out below again; it was then assumed that the God had entered the initiant and impregnated him with the divine germ, and they called him *entheos.* The serpent symbolizes the god that enters man in order to fill him with the god, to make him the mother of God, and the pulling out from below means the birth, of course.[5] That was like the antique rite of adoption. The mother who wished to adopt a son or a daughter had to hide the child under her skirts, even if it was a grown-up. And then he was pulled out from under them, and she had to give her breast to the adopted child to denote that it was her suckling. Then after such ceremonies they were nourished with milk and so on, as in the rebirth mysteries in antiquity.

Now we are here reminded of that symbol. Where it is a matter of the rabble, of that inferior part of his psychology, we surely encounter the same idea but in the reversed form: namely, he—or his foot at least—is in the position of the snake. As the snake entered the throat of the shepherd, so his foot enters the throat of the rabble. He is here very clearly identical with Zarathustra who is divine, a humanized form of God, and he has to behave as if he were the god himself, the snake. Of course it doesn't mean to choke the rabble but to fertilize, to impregnate the rabble, to enter the rabble so that the connection would take place between the inferior and the superior parts of himself. Being the superior part, he has to assume the role of the snake and enter the throat of the rabble, or dive down into the well in order that the powers which are above shall be mixed with the powers below. This is of course in order to vivify the dormant inferior layers, or to make the upper layers, the spiritual powers, real. For the spirit that does not appear in the flesh is a wind that is gone in no time: the wind must enter matter for it to be real. The spirit is nothing if it doesn't descend into matter, as matter is utterly dead if it is not vivified by the spirit. So he uses a very similar symbol here to express what should be. But this symbol is suggested by his resentment; he hates the rabble but in that very hatred the positive symbol appears. He continues,

---

[5] In CW 5, par. 530, and 530n, Jung cites Clement of Alexandria as the source of his information about the Sabazios snake mysteries. In CW 12, par. 184, Jung says, "Among the Ophites, Christ was the serpent," and goes on to compare this symbolism to that of Kundalini yoga. The Ophites were an early, possibly pre-Christian, Gnostic sect, who held that man and the universe alike were generated by the conjunction of serpent and egg.

And it is not the mouthful which hath most choked me, to know that life itself requireth enmity and death and torture–crosses:—
But I asked once, and suffocated almost with my question: What? is the rabble also *necessary* for life?

Here we have it!

Are poisoned fountains necessary, and stinking fires, and filthy dreams, and maggots in the bread of life?

He has a rich choice of words to revile the inferior functions!

Not my hatred, but my loathing gnawed hungrily at my life! Ah, ofttimes became I weary of spirit, when I found even the rabble spiritual!

This shows how touchy he is. Being a breath of air, a spirit, naturally he is terribly offended by the coarseness of matter, reality, he cannot stand the sight of spirit that has become flesh. Well, one can sympathize with him I must say!

And on the rulers turned I my back, when I saw what they now call ruling: to traffic and bargain for power—with the rabble!

That he should be expected to deal with his inferior functions is quite out of the question; it cannot be done.

Amongst peoples of a strange language did I dwell, . . .

This refers to the long time he lived in Italy. He ran away from his people and his country in order not to be mixed up with the rabble.

with stopped ears: so that the language of their trafficking might remain strange unto me, and their bargaining for power.
And holding my nose, I went morosely through all yesterdays and to-days: verily, badly smell all yesterdays and to-days of the scribbling rabble!

That is most specific; those are his colleagues.

Like a cripple become deaf, and blind, and dumb—thus I have lived long; that I might not live with the power-rabble, the scribe-rabble, and the pleasure-rabble.

This means that he could not help seeing himself to a certain extent as having a power instinct. Of course the whole of *Zarathustra* is a power drive. That is the power-rabble, and to be a famous writer is the scribe-rabble, and the pleasure-rabble—well, pleasure to a great extent was impossible to him, particularly all the qualities of love were more or less taboo on account of the syphilitic infection which he contracted when he was twenty-three.

Toilsomely did my spirit mount stairs, and cautiously; alms of delight were its refreshment; on the staff did life creep along with the blind one.

He could not accept his lower man, so he had to climb stairs.

What hath happened unto me? How have I freed myself from loathing?

He has not freed himself from loathing, but obviously here, while he was writing, he has somehow transcended his loathing.

Who hath rejuvenated mine eye? How have I flown to the height where no rabble any longer sit at the wells?

Here he is taken *in flagranti*. We have seen that he has not overcome his loathing; his mouth was full of objections and revilements a second ago, and now we suddenly discover that he is beyond, that he has climbed above it.

Did my loathing itself create for me wings and fountain-divining powers? Verily, to the loftiest height had I to fly, to find again the well of delight!

While he was realizing how low down the rabble was, he began to develop wings and to fly; he identified completely with Zarathustra, Zarathustra being the great bird, the wise man. You know the wise man is always represented with wings—the wise Hermes had wings, for instance, and in India the swan could almost be called the title of the wise man. It was always understood that a man who had attained the highest wisdom could fly, transport himself to any place. That was the criterion of perfect wisdom, the height of yoga practice and all that. So for him to say that he has created wings proves he is now completely identical with the spirit Zarathustra. Then of course he can believe that he has found the well, because the superior human wisdom of an unconscious figure like Zarathustra of course knows the well: that figure is the well itself, as a matter of fact. And then comes the *ekstasis*:

Oh, I have found it, my brethren! Here on the loftiest height bubbleth up for me the well of delight! And there is a life at whose waters none of the rabble drink with me!

You see, Zarathustra, being the concretized form or the personification of the principle of the spirit, has an energy of its own, a life of its own. And the spirit is a fountain because the spirit is essentially life. Therefore if you can identify with a spirit completely and disidentify from your own body, as has been tried in many forms of yoga, you can release the fountain of the spirit. Of course you are then no longer human; you have become dehumanized—are above the earth, are a ghost yourself—and of course you have to pay the cost. It has forever been the aspiration of mankind to fly like a bird, to become a wind, a breath; and it can be done, but it is paid for by the loss of the body, or the loss of humanity, which is the same thing. And now on the height of the *ekstasis*—you see *ekstasis* really means stepping outside of oneself—he suddenly realizes something and he says:

> Almost too violently dost thou flow for me, thou fountain of delight! And often emptiest thou the goblet again, in wanting to fill it!

> And yet must I learn to approach thee more modestly: far too violently doth my heart still flow towards thee:—

It is far too violent. That is the danger, because the identification with the spirit always causes a condition in which the mental function, which is bound up with the brain-matter, takes on such an intensity that it burns up matter. Man is burned up by such an intensity and then there is a great danger. That is exactly what happened to Nietzsche: he burned himself up in Zarathustra. He was a living flame that burned himself up, the result being the overstraining of the brain and a breakdown of the nervous system.

Now, I have a feeling here that the concept of the spirit may not be understood, and it would be in this connection particularly important that our ideas about it should agree. You see, this concept has been used so often and in such a way that most people think they know what they are talking about when they use the term *spirit*, but as a matter of fact they usually do not. We have a tendency to identify it with intellect, though the word *spirit* doesn't denote intellect at all. Of course in English there is a certain difference, but in German there is no difference at all, because the word *Geist* which Nietzsche uses, is used absolutely indiscriminately for intellect, mind, and spirit. German is a very strange language, it is very primitive in that respect; even its most fundamental concepts are still an ensemble of facts, a peculiarity which you would find in practically no other language except perhaps Chinese, or Russian which I don't know. I don't know Chinese either but I have a certain idea of Chinese characters and of their extraordinary many-sided possibilities of interpretation, and they surely form the nearest analogy to the German language. German is, peculiarly enough, the language most incapable of expressing anything definite. The Germans make frantic efforts to be accurate on account of their feeling of inferiority that their language never expresses a thing definitely. Now this is for a certain kind of philosophy most awkward; for psychology, however, it is priceless, and for *real* philosophy it is also invaluable. You see, I understand by "real philosophy" a kind of thinking which expresses the understanding of life—that is real philosophy to me. But what one ordinarily calls "philosophy" at universities is an intellectual affair—like the theory of cognition, for instance. For that purpose, German has no value whatever: it is far too living. It is the spirit of the language to be connected with things, to be the life of things.

For instance, it is most characteristic that what you call reality, the German calls *Wirklichkeit*; there you see the difference. *Reality* comes from the Latin *res*, a thing, a static something, while the German *Wirklichkeit* implies that this thing *is*, only as long as it works. As Mr. Dooley, that man on the *New York Times*, said, "A truth is a truth as long as it works." So this book is a book as long as it works. That is the German idea; their concept of reality is most relative. It is a thing, *wirklich*, inasmuch as it works, *wirken*. There is a sort of dynamic, transitory moment and that is reality. This shows the spirit of the language most clearly. And so the German concept of *Geist* has all sorts of aspects, and it contains traces of the original history of that concept of course, as the word *spirit* does also. The spirit is *spiritus*, meaning breath; it is the breath that comes out of a man's mouth. It is the soul, his life, because he breathes as long as he lives, and when the last breath has left the body the soul has gone too, the man is dead. But *Geist* is not breath. *Geist* is a geyser, something that wells up like boiling water, like steam hissing up, or like the foam fizzling when you open a champagne bottle; that is *Geist*. So *Geist* is the alcohol in the wine, or the carbonic acid, the flavor, the *parfum* that develops from the wine, what we call the flower of the wine; while spirit is liquid air, breath, a gaseous liquid, aquatic, but more or less static. Therefore when Nietzsche speaks of *Geist*, he really means intensity, a dynamic outburst; and wherever he characterizes the nature of Zarathustra—when he calls him a whirlwind, or a hailstorm, or a thunderstorm, or the lightning—then that is *Geist*, the intensity. The original phenomenon of the spirit is a seizure, one could say; one is seized by violent emotion for instance, and then you say a spirit has entered you, you are possessed. Also, *Geist* has the meaning of the English word *ghost*, and in *ghost* you have the original sense because *ghost* is related to *aghast*: there is the emotional link. The idea of outburst is always linked up with that word *Geist*, the idea of an extraordinary intensity.

One is also continually baffled by the use of the word *spirit* or *spiritus* in the alchemical concept. For instance, they say, "If thou dost not succeed in making the body a spirit, thou hast not accomplished the work." You see, in that case it would mean originally, inasmuch as the procedure was chemical, "If thou hast not succeeded in making the body, a metal, into an oxide, thou hast not succeeded in accomplishing the work." That is, the oxide is a volatile substance. If mercury is boiled, it always ascends and becomes a condensation again in those parts of the retort that are cooler; and then they say that the mercury in the state of boiling is the body, and the vapor of mercury, which ascends and transcends, is the spirit. When substances are heated, they usually oxidize or change their quality, and that change of quality was understood as what they called "sublimation"; it was like becoming a different being. You see, certain bodies change so much through oxidation that a naive person could not possibly recognize the relationship; therefore those old chemists thought that they produced new bodies, and the new body, caused by heating up the former body, was the spirit, a *spiritus*. But they used this word *spirit* absolutely indiscriminately even in their mystical texts, where they also talked about making the body a *pneuma*. Now *pneuma* is a wind, a volatile compound, a changeable compound, or it is really the spirit—I mean the spirit in its metaphysical or philosophical or religious sense—and you simply are unable to make sure which they meant. Presumably they meant that the spirit—what we now call "spirit" or what the Bible calls "spirit"—is a subtle body. You don't get away from that; it is just a subtle body. So you can make a spirit out of matter, can de-materialize—what they call "subtilize" matter to such an extent that it becomes a spirit, not a disembodied spirit but a spirit that is a subtle body.

Now, since this subtle body was made by heat, they assumed that through the fire they imparted fire-substance to the body so that it became partially like fire, and "fire" was another symbol for the soul. In Heraclitus you find a passage where it says that the noblest soul is the essence of fire—it is of the most intense radiation and splendor and quite dry—and therefore he says it is death to a spirit, or a soul, to become water. He also says that souls of alcoholics turn to water; they become water-logged or humid and they die.[6] So the idea was that the

---

[6] Heraclitus often contrasted noble fire with ignoble wetness; e.g., "It is delight, or

real spirit, the essence of life, of the soul, was fire. And by giving fire to substances they assumed that they became half spiritual, or subtle bodies. The fire means, of course, intensity, so if you submit to intensity, say to an intense emotion, you would change into a subtle body. Therefore, to subtilize or sublimate a man, you must expose him to the fire; first he must be cleansed from impurity by the ablution with water, and then exposed to the fire.

That idea is older than Christianity and you remember that saying in the New Testament: "I indeed baptize you with water unto repentance: but he that cometh after me is mightier than I, whose shoes I am not worthy to bear: he shall baptize you with the Holy Ghost, and with fire." You find that saying already in alchemistic texts of the first century—the famous text of Komarios for instance[7]—and these are all connected with pre-Christian traditions; and though we have no evidence, the texts being no longer extant, we know the names of people who were great authorities on these matters in the first or second centuries B.C. And, as I said, we have authentic texts from the first century, where we find those ideas. When a man is subjected to a great emotion, it means that he is subjected to the fire, and the contact with the fire can give him the nature of a subtle body; the fire can subtilize him, or it may destroy him. This idea is expressed also in the non-canonical saying of Jesus: "He who is near to me is near to the fire; and he who is far from me is far from the kingdom." For he is the fire, the greatest intensity, and whoever touches upon this intensity is subtilized, made pneumatic, made into a volatile body.

Now, the more Nietzsche becomes intense, the more he is identical with the flame Zarathustra; and the more he exposes himself to that fire, the more he becomes volatile, the more his body is burned up. The alchemists say that all the superfluities must be burned up and therefore the action of the fire must be strong; not so strong at first in order not to burn up too much, but later on in the process the fire must be increased, become more intense, and then all superfluities are burned away. Then one becomes subtilized; then one is a subtle body, a spirit.

Mr. Baumann: It seems to me that the German word *Geist* is best characterized as a thing that moves by itself and can move other things; and

---

rather death, to become wet." and "Fire . . . will judge and seize upon all things" (Freeman*, fragments 74, 66).

[7] Matthew 3:11. The fullest description of how, for Komarios, baptism may be in both of the opposites, fire and water, comes in CW 14, pars. 316-17. Komarios, or Comarius, was a first-century alchemist.

the opposite, the *Materie* has the characteristic of something that does not move. You can use *Materie* in German for physical substances or you can use it for intellectual or abstract concepts, which you handle, as for instance the lecturer treats the subject of his lecture. So *Geist* means an active power, or a dynamic power.

Prof. Jung: Yes. Well, I wanted to speak of this in order that you may understand his peculiar metaphoric language, for in the next passage he says,

> My heart on which my summer burneth, my short, hot, melancholy, over-happy summer: how my summer heart longeth for thy coolness!

You see, that is an accurate description of the process Nietzsche is undergoing; as he approaches the identification with Zarathustra, the living flame, he begins to blossom. That is the spring, and then comes the summer, the greatest heat, but alas, it is a short, hot summer and the end is calcination or what the alchemists call incineration. Then one becomes ashes, burned up, and that is the end—I mean the end of the ordinary banal man. Nietzsche burns up the lower man, the anatomical or physiological man, and he becomes a spirit. I have often said the he was *plus papal que le Pape*, more Christian than a Christian; one could call him the last real Christian. He is led straight back through the identification with the spirit and he doesn't realize it. And here we have the tragic fore-feeling we occasionally meet in *Zarathustra*: my short, melancholy summer. He knows this is transitory. This intensity is never to be reached again and it is a fatal injury.

> Past, the lingering distress of my spring! Past, the wickedness of my snowflakes in June! Summer have I become entirely, and summer noontide!
>
> A summer on the loftiest height, with cold fountains and blissful stillness. . . .

Prof. Jung: To what does his insistence upon the noontide refer?

Mrs. Baumann: The middle of life.

Prof. Jung: Yes, we shall come later on to this noontide idea; it is that point of indifference when things are in the balance between the rising and the falling, the idea of the middle of life. Now how old was he when he wrote this part of *Zarathustra*? It was written in 1881.

Mrs. Sigg: He was born in 1844.

Prof. Jung: So he was then thirty-seven; it was exactly the time. The real process begins before, just when the clock strikes thirty-six one could say, but of course one notices nothing. At thirty-seven there is a chance to realize it, that is noontide—that short time—and afterwards an early autumn comes.

oh come, my friends, that the stillness may become more blissful.

He longs for the coolness, he is so hot. Now the coolness is the contrary, and this cold which suddenly breaks into the heat occurs everywhere, practically, in *Zarathustra*. Often Nietzsche uses metaphors that are of bad taste even, but this idea that the pairs of opposites would touch each other is always present in his mind, not in the form of conjunction, but in the form of *enantiodromia*, the idea that things would suddenly run over into the contrary. Now the whole of *Zarathustra* was written in three weeks practically, not of course in one stretch but in three parts, each in a week. So you can see the intensity of that process; you can imagine what an extraordinary intensity must have been in that brain to enable him to produce such a thing. That was the summer and the extreme heat and the subtilization. Now Nietzsche continues:

For this is *our* height and our home: too high and steep do we here dwell for all uncleanly ones and their thirst.

He said before, "too violently," and here it is "too high and steep"—but for the others, the impure ones.

Cast but your pure eyes into the well of my delight, my friends! How could it become turbid thereby! It shall laugh back to you with *its* purity.

You see, this is instead of what he said before—that the rabble had cast an evil eye on the fountain and poisoned it. And from the height he has now reached, he says, cast your pure eyes into that well of life. Life is of course to Nietzsche almost synonymous with delight. Now, if you can see the fountain of life as something absolutely pure, you must be inhumanly pure yourself. To anybody who is not so extraordinarily pure, the fountain of life is never quite pure, but is always a bit turbid. You know, other people have had an entirely different idea, like St. Augustine, who said we were born between feces and urine.[8] That was the Christian point of view, to denote the extreme inferiority of our nature. We would be completely lost if nothing had been done for us. We are conceived and born in impurity and have to undergo the purifica-

---

[8] This is yet another saying often attributed to St. Augustine, but untraced.

tion process by ablution and fire and so on. Therefore we must be sub-limated, and here Nietzsche assumes that we have been, have reached the top, and therefore we see everything as absolutely pure. I don't doubt, if you can identify with the spirit, that you can see life as abso-lutely pure, but for man it is another question. Since man is not spirit, since man is also body, this fountain of life must have pretty much the same nature; and since he doesn't consist of 100 percent pure gold we must admit that the fountain also is not 100 percent pure gold, but produces a lot of inferior substances, which would explain why things are as imperfect as they are. Well now,

On the tree of the future build we our nest; . . .

He again uses an extraordinary metaphor, pretty daring I should say. Why does the tree come in suddenly?

Mrs. Crowley: The tree is also a sort of fountain of life.

Prof. Jung: In that it pushes up, or wells up? Yes, but that is a bit far-fetched.

Miss Hannah: Is the tree not always a symbol of the impersonal life? Doesn't he identify with the impersonal life?

Prof. Jung: Well, the tree is a symbol of spiritual development, and spiritual evolution is different from animal evolution. Animal evolu-tion would be the development of the body, and spirit is always under-stood to be a sort of secondary growth on the process of the body be-cause it burns up the body, extracts the life, in order to reach its intensity. It is most exhausting because it uses up a man's substance. You see, the tree is a plant, and it symbolizes a strange development entirely different from animal life, like the development which we call spiritual, which is always felt as most peculiar, an almost parasitic kind of development. The spiritual development in Nietzsche's case de-stroyed his brain. The brain is needed and his brain was burned up, so he is a sort of transformation symbol. As a tree extracts mineral sub-stances from the earth, the spirit transforms the coarse body, or the coarseness of matter, into the subtlety of organic matter. The tree rep-resents, then, a sort of sublimation. It grows from below up into the air above, has its roots in the earth as if it were part of the earth, and ex-tends roots again into the kingdom of air; and so the spirit of devel-opment rises out of the material, animal man and grows into a differ-ent region above. Therefore the tree has forever been a symbol of spiritual value or philosophical development, like the tree of knowl-edge in Paradise for instance, or the philosophical tree, the *arbor phi-losophorum*, the tree with the immortal fruits—a Hermetic symbol—

also the world tree in the Edda. And there you find the connection with the spring: below the tree Yggdrasil is a well.[9]

Remark: In fairy tales there is very often a tree beside the well. If a princess gets lost, she is usually found near the tree or under a tree by a well.

Prof. Jung: That is true. The tree takes its life, one could say, out of the well, a transformation of earth and water; and at more advanced levels of civilization it represents the spiritual development. You see that again in the legend of the tree of knowledge in Genesis, because upon the tree of life was the serpent that persuaded the first parents to become conscious. The serpent thought it might be better for man to know all about it, but Jahveh was not quite of the same idea, so he did not allow them to eat of that fruit. Now Nietzsche says, on the tree of the future—the spiritual anticipation of the future—we build our nests, as if we were birds. As the wise man is always a bird, and Nietzsche has become Zarathustra, he says, "I have wings. I am a bird. I make my nest on that marvelous Yoga tree, the tree of knowledge, the *arbor philosophorum.*" Now, who else had his nest in the branches of a marvelous tree? You know that is also an important religious myth.

Mr. Allemann: The Phoenix. And on Yggdrasil, it is an eagle.

Prof. Jung: Yes, the Phoenix, the symbol of renewal and rebirth.

Miss Welsh: And Ra.

Prof. Jung: Yes, there are many such myths. Mithras is often represented with wings, being born out of the top of the tree, which is of course rather the idea of Ra, building his own nest and rising like a falcon in the morning. So that again shows a complete identification with the spirit.

Eagles shall bring us lone ones food in their beaks!

Where does this image come from?

Mrs. Sigg: From Elijah.

Prof. Jung: Yes, from the Old Testament—the Protestant comes out in Nietzsche again. It is a raven that brings the food to Elijah but of course it is much more distinguished to have an eagle—a raven would not quite do. So he is in the place of Elijah the prophet; Zarathustra is a prophet as good as any.

Mrs. Sigg: I think Elijah had also to do with fire and flame—

---

[9] Jung wrote extensively about tree symbolism. See especially his essay "The Philosophical Tree" in CW 13, pars. 304-82. For Yggdrasil, see above, 17 Oct. 1934, nn. 6 and 9.

Nietzsche with the fire and the thunderstorm, and Elijah with the chariot of fire.

Prof. Jung: Yes, he also had such insight that he burned up—he went in the fiery chariot to heaven. That is like the death of Heraclitus who burned himself up—he disappeared in fire. You find the same motive in *Faust* three times. The first was the *Knabe Lenker*, the boy charioteer, the second Homunculus; the third was Euphorion, who disappeared in a flash of light, burning up in too great an intensity.[10]

Mr. Baumann: In a Seminar several years ago there was a very interesting alchemistic picture which symbolized that process. At the base was man and two lions, and the paws were cut off. Then comes the process of burning up, and above is a tree with many birds.

Prof. Jung: Yes, the tree full of birds is a regular alchemistic symbol, and they are very often eagles. You know the eagle is the bird of light, the cousin of the Phoenix, while the raven is the black bird and symbolizes darkness. So the alchemistic matter of *materia* in the state of darkness, a parallel to the human soul in the state of darkness, is called *caput corvi*, the head of the raven—like the head of Osiris, lost in the dark waters when he was dismembered by Set—and later on it becomes a golden head. Therefore, in a Greek text the alchemists called themselves children of the gold head, *caput aureum*, the *caput corvi* that became gold, shining like the sun.[11] Now we will finish this chapter.

> Verily, no food of which the impure could be fellow-partakers! Fire, would they think they devoured, and burn their mouths!
>
> Verily, no abodes do we here keep ready for the impure! An ice-cave to their bodies would our happiness be, and to their spirits!

Of course that ice cave is meant for his own body. Ice always conveys the idea of no innervation, no warmth, no life, the death of the bodily man.

> And as strong winds will we live above them, neighbours to the eagles, neighbours to the snow, neighbours to the sun: thus live the strong winds. [Complete identification with the spiritual principle again.]

[10] Elijah, told by the Lord to hide by the brook Cherith, for "I have commanded the raven to provide for you there" (I Kings 17:2-4). For Elijah in "a chariot of fire" see II Kings 2:11. Heraclitus was naturally supposed to die by fire, to which he attributed such importance. In *Faust*, Part Two, the king's renewal fails three times: the boy charioteer, Homunculus, and Euphorion, all go up in smoke. See CW 12, par. 243.

[11] Jung has several accounts of the *caput corvi*, or head of the raven, in CW 14; see, for instance, pars. 724, 772.

And like a wind will I one day blow amongst them, and with my spirit, take the breath from their spirit: thus willeth my future.

Verily, a strong wind is Zarathustra to all low places; and this counsel counselleth he to his enemies, and to whatever spitteth and speweth: "Take care not to spit *against* the wind!"—

Now he is Wotan, the wind god—that is perfectly clear—and now look out, don't spit against the wind, it is not wise; if the wind blows from a certain direction, don't resist it, it is dangerous. You see, that is what happens.

LECTURE III

19 May 1937

Prof. Jung:

Here is a picture from the Jain sect in India, representing a perfect saint who turns into a plant. Mr. Baumann brought it to us as an example of spiritual development being represented by the plant, which we were talking about last week. We are now coming to the chapter called "The Tarantulas." The chapter before was entitled "The Rabble." Now how do we get from that to the idea of tarantulas?

Miss Hannah: In the last chapter he entirely identified with the wind, the spirit; and the spider is very often the symbol of the mother complex. Having gotten into the masculine entirely, he had to get free.

Prof. Jung: Ah, you think of the wind as being entirely masculine. Have you justification for that?

Miss Hannah: No. Perhaps I got mixed up with the Logos.

Prof. Jung: But there would be an argument in favor of your idea. What did we say about the wind last time?

Mrs. Fierz: That the wind was Wotan.

Prof. Jung: Naturally. Wotan is the wind god *par excellence* and since Nietzsche was expressing himself in a German *milieu*, you can be sure that he got something of Wotan: that is in the German substance as you know. So he naturally takes on a very masculine character, though to the antique understanding the wind was not so certainly masculine. And what evidence have we for this?

Mrs. Baumann: Sophia.

Prof. Jung: Yes, Sophia as wisdom is the personification of the Holy Ghost, and the Holy Ghost has been understood as the mother of God; in the first and second centuries there were numbers of Christians who believed that Mary the mother of God was really a sort of allegory and Sophia was the real mother, the Holy Ghost. For instance, in the Acts of St. Thomas there is a hymn in which is the invocation: "Oh come, Holy Ghost our mother." Then in Hebrew the word for *pneuma* is *ruach*, meaning spirit as well as wind, and it is used as a *femininum* just as often as a *masculinum*—there is evidence for both in the texts of the Old Testament. Do you know the origin of this peculiar fact that there is uncertainty about the sex of the spirit?

Miss Hannah: That it is hermaphroditic—above sex.

Prof. Jung: Yes, but where does that hermaphroditic element come from?

Prof. Reichstein: Because the masculine part of the spirit would be the conscious part, and the unconscious part is feminine.

Prof. Jung: Ah, if you take it psychologically, that is sure, inasmuch as men have thought it. With women it would naturally be the other way round. Men had these thoughts first, and since they were contents of initiation rites, clan or tribal teaching, of course they took on a masculine form first psychologically. But we have historical evidence for these hermaphroditic ideas: namely, it is a very universal idea that the creator of the world was a hermaphroditic being. Almost every mythology contained this idea of the original being—that it created itself by means of itself, being both father and mother. And you remember in Plato's *Timaeus*, the first human beings were round with four arms and four legs, and they also were hermaphrodites; that is the so-called Platonic man.[1] Therefore, this concept of the wind, or the spirit, is uncertain in its character: it can be either masculine or feminine. And there are other ideas of the same sort, the idea of the soul being partially masculine and partially feminine, for example. So it is chiefly the fact that Nietzsche was a German that made him have such a masculine conception of the wind: the archetype Wotan was in his blood. Now it is true that any kind of spider—the idea of the spider's web and all that—has much to do with something feminine, and why would that now be constellated?

Prof. Reichstein: I think that the opposition between fire and water would mean here again the compensatory principle. In the chapter before, about the rabble, Zarathustra is on the side of the fire—too much so—and the rabble would be on the side of the water. He suppressed that side and therefore it comes up now in a negative form; the tarantulas would be a negative form of this suppressed principle.

Prof. Jung: That is an important idea too; the tarantula is a sort of

---

[1] A slip. Jung often correctly cites this story, attributed in the *Symposium* to Aristophanes. The round creatures were split into two by gods, again concerned with human usurpation of their power—and now men and women go about looking for their other half. In the Timaeus (36 B.C.) we are told of God's making a compound of soul and body, forming two lengths as a letter X and then bending each leg around on itself to form a circle, which, set in motion, became the circle of the same and the circle of the other.

compensation just because we had the identification with the masculine element, the wind, before, which always leads to an inflation of the individual. Then instantly there is a reaction of a compensatory nature, so a female element now comes up represented by the tarantula. Now I will read the first sentence,

> Lo, this is the tarantula's den! Would'st thou see the tarantula itself? Here hangeth its web: touch this, so that it may tremble.

You know, the tarantula is found in southeastern Europe; it lives in a hole in a rock or in the ground, and it is pretty poisonous, though its sting actually kills only small animals. The legend is that anybody poisoned by a tarantula goes raving mad and is seized by an uncontrollable desire to dance, but I think that idea simply comes from the fact that the people who had been poisoned were forced to dance, which was quite reasonable, in order to induce a heavy perspiration and give the poison a chance to get out of the body. Now the image here is this animal in the den or the cave, and the web by means of which it catches its prey. That is very important symbolism. What would it represent really?

Mrs. Sigg: The tarantula might also represent the rabble in a deeper layer, in the animal kingdom.

Prof. Jung: That is presumably true, for when Zarathustra uses an image like the rabble, he usually goes on enlarging upon that subject; he goes deeper and deeper into the image, one could say—a sort of amplification. The rabble appears as an underlying stratum of a very negative quality, and since that stratum is nearer to earth, the wind or the spirit, which is above, senses a particular danger lurking there. Of course to one who is in the earth there is no danger, because this is the mother from which he draws his nourishment, but to one who is dwelling in the air the earth is a great danger—it threatens to make him heavy. Inasmuch as he approaches the earth, he is filled with the spirit of heaviness and will sink down to the earth, a sort of descent of the spirit into the earth. Naturally the spirit is afraid to have its nature changed by that contact. Therefore so many people are afraid of the earth, like the intuitive who is always in the air, never touching the ground, unable to take root anywhere.

Of course intuitives *wish* to make roots, but inasmuch as they try they naturally come into contact with the earth and are infected by it, and the earth makes them heavy. It catches them and becomes a cage, a prison for them. You know, whenever an intuitive type has created a situation for himself he instantly gets sick of it and must escape again because it threatens to become real. To the intuitive, only the things that are not yet are real; the moment they take on form and *become*, he is done for, caught by his own creation. Then he is confronted by the thing that has turned static, that no longer moves, that has ceased to be a possibility; to him it ceases to be reality when it doesn't walk away with him. If he builds a house, as soon as it is finished he must leave it because it is unreal, only a fact. To the sensation type on the contrary a possibility doesn't exist; he lives in a house that is made—that is real— and as long as that house exists there is reality; the moment it ceases to be he has lost his reality and cannot foresee any other possibility; to him it is poisonous to think that anything could change, therefore he will resist any change as long as possible. While the intuitive is of just the other calibre: if anything threatens to become static, it must be instantly destroyed. He prefers to destroy his own nest as soon as it is built in order not to be the victim of it.

Now, you can be sure that nowhere else is Nietzsche so intuitive as in *Zarathustra*, so we are likely to meet here any amount of intuitive psychology. And if he is confronted with the lower strata of the human personality, it would mean to him static reality trying to pull him down, and this secret pull that he feels seems to be the worst danger. Therefore he symbolizes it by the tarantula, of which people have a kind of legendary fear. A tarantula is far less dangerous than a venomous snake for instance, but people make a great story about it, a sort of metaphor. I am quite sure that Nietzsche never saw a tarantula—that is clear from his text. Now the next sentence:

> There cometh the tarantula willingly: Welcome, tarantula! Black on thy back is thy triangle and symbol; and I know also what is in thy soul.

The tarantula to my knowledge has a yellowish back with black stripes, but no such thing as a triangle.

Prof. Reichstein: The triangle would be a sexual symbol probably because the triangle is always a one-sided symbol, and here it is probably a feminine symbol.

Prof. Jung: Yes, but first we must be clear that the tarantula really has no triangle on its back. There is, however, a spider that has a different design on its back. What spider is that?

Mrs. Sigg: The *Kreuzspinne*.

Prof. Jung: Yes, I don't know the English name. It is a big spider which one very often sees here. It is of a well-known species and it has an unmistakable cross with equal branches on its back. That is the spider with the symbol you see, and Nietzsche simply equips the tarantula with the triangle, presumably because he never has seen one. And even if he had, he never would have seen anything of the sort, because being an intuitive he wouldn't care to see it. It is enough that the spider *might* have something symbolic on its back, whether it is so in reality or not doesn't matter. If it has any pedagogic meaning he would say the spider *had* to have a symbol, and if it has none, well, in future it will have one. Now here he surely attributes to it the symbol of the triangle, the triangle and the symbol being presumably the same—we are not sure, however—he may mean that besides the triangle there is another symbol. The only hint we have is the triangle, but that is important because it was surely known to Nietzsche that there was a spider with a cross on its back. His idea undoubtedly comes from that fact, and therefore he would have been naturally prepared to speak of it—but no, it *must* be a triangle, which of course is not to be seen on the real tarantula nor on the *Kreuzspinne*.[2]

Now we arrive at the idea Prof. Reichstein has alluded to, that the triangle is a one-sided symbol and always has been used as such.[3] For instance, in alchemy they make much use of the triangle in this form: $\triangle$ and that form: $\triangledown$ the first meaning the flame or the fire, and the second meaning water. And fire and water are typical representatives of the opposites. You find this symbolism on the frontispiece of the *Songe de Poliphile* in the union of the teardrop and the flame, called in their interpretation the fires of passions and the tears of repentance.[4] That was an attempt at the union of opposites: namely, a process of life looked at from a static point of view. This is always necessary for the creation of a symbol, because it is only a symbol when it expresses opposites; otherwise it has no meaning. It must be an idea superior to any definite one-sided philosophical or intellectual concept. Now, the triangle in the first place—and when Nietzsche uses it, it cannot very well mean anything else—is the idea of the Christian Trinity which is always represented as a triangle, as you know. And the triangle is a one-sided principle inasmuch as the evil is lacking in that symbol; therefore it doesn't comprehend

---

[2] The common garden spider, *Araneus diadematus*, has long been thought significant because of its white cross. The European tarantula does have a small triangle on its back.

[3] Strictly speaking, Jung meant a symbol lacking the one side that would represent wholeness.

[4] For *The Dream of Poliphilo*, see above, 12 Dec. 1934, n. 6. In CW 12, fig. 33 represents Poliphilo surrounded by nymphs, as reprinted from Beroalde de Verville, *Le Songe de Poliphile* (1600).

the real meaning of the world, only one side of the universal substance. Then where is hell, where is the shadow? The world cannot consist of light only, so it is clearly one-sided.

Dr. James: It is only masculine.

Prof. Jung: Yes, it consists of three masculine entities. Now where is the female? Our world consists very tangibly of man and woman, but the divine world apparently is a society of men exclusively. That one-sidedness was felt in the Middle Ages tremendously; it was realized but it was simply impossible to bring about a reformation by which the female element could be introduced into the Trinity. The Catholic church had the power: the pope could introduce the feminine principle, but not into the Trinity, for it would then be a quaternion. You find that conflict between three and four throughout the Middle Ages in all forms and it really goes back to the fact of that quite insurmountable problem of introducing the feminine element into the Trinity. For the female meant darkness and evil—hell and woman were practically the same. You see, that simply comes from the fact that woman *is* associated with darkness, as the female element has always been in China for instance, and old China has of course a very much more balanced view of the world than we have in the West, including the Near East which is as unbalanced as we are.

You know, we are an unbalanced race, so our nervous system is very inferior in a way; we are highly gifted, both wind- and flame-like, but we have little earth. Therefore we are chiefly bandits, warriors, pirates, and madmen. That is the characteristic of the West as may be seen in the expressions of our faces. Study the faces of other races and you will see the difference: we have all the characteristics of more or less mad people. It is perfectly obvious—I have seen it—and that is what those other people think *au fond*. We are deeply sensitive and touchy and susceptible, we cannot stand pain and are highly excitable. We are like sort of geniuses with a great number of insupportable character traits. This is sad but so it is, and it probably accounts for the fact that we have such a one-sided idea of the deity. For an unbalanced condition always harbors a feeling of inferiority; any one-sided person has a feeling of inferiority, a feeling that he has deviated. Naturally he has deviated from nature and that gives a feeling of inferiority. The white man is chiefly characterized by an indefinite megalomania coupled with the feeling of inferiority: that is the thing which pushes us on and on. We must know everything, always in search of our lost divinity, which we can have only as long as we are in tune with nature. So even our most cherished trinity, the essence of the highest imaginable qualities, is coupled with and compensated by the idea of a devil.

There is no such thing as a devil in classical Chinese philosophy; there it is a matter of two opposites which are the agencies of the world, Yang and Yin, and as Yang is bright and dry and fiery, everything on the positive side, so Yin is everything on the other side, and Yin is the female. That is the inevitable association, darkness and femininity. We have no such point of view since we are hopelessly one-sided, so if we think straight and logically, we arrive at the conclusion that woman and hell are identical.[5] You see, if woman were only the female element, the Catholic church could easily introduce her into the dogmatic heaven, but that woman has a tail which leads straight to hell, so she would carry hell into heaven. You have probably read those visions of the old poet Guillaume de Digulleville where he describes his vision of heaven.[6] There is God on his throne as the king of heaven, and with him his consort, Mrs. Queen, who is also sitting on a decent throne, but it doesn't consist of pure flaming gold. It is of rock crystal of a brownish color, showing that she carried the mineral up to heaven—of course in a diaphanous form, yet some color, the brown of the earth, was adhering and went up to heaven too. That was the idea of a very sublime earth which Mary brought up to heaven. It is not a dogmatic idea, but it is a very valid assumption in the Catholic church that Mary is the only mortal being who has been united with the body immediately after her death, a thing which happens to other mortals only on the day of judgment. Then we all unite with our bodies—of course the subtle body, not the gross body, but containing a reasonable amount of physical atoms, presumably a bit gaseous but having weight: it is materially substantial. But Mary had that chance of being the only one to be united with her body immediately after her death, and so she carried up the earth principle. On account of that, however, she is not one of the saints and she is not divine. That is just a fact and there is nothing to be done about it, for if they made her a goddess there would be trouble—she would bring in darkness. As it is, she fills the position of mother of mercy and is particularly approachable to very bad sinners,

[5] The difference, as Jung often shows, is that in Taoism, Yin, though dark, is not any less benign (or powerful) than Yang.

[6] Guillaume is discussed in CW 11, pars. 116-25, where Jung identifies him as a Norman poet and a monastic priest of the 14th century who described paradise as consisting of forty-nine rotating spheres.

having a special understanding of that rabble, naturally a rabble which is beginning to repent of its quality.

Now we surely make no mistake in assuming that the underlying idea of that triangle is the Christian Trinity, but on the back of the tarantula it clearly represents the evil principle of the earth. Before going into that, however, I should call your attention to the fact that any insect or animal that has no spinal cord, only a sympathetic nervous system, represents the same thing in man: namely, that psychology which is more linked up with the *plexus solaris* or with the sympathetic system than with the spinal cord and the brain. There must be such a bridge, because the function of the intestines, for instance, closely depends upon conscious processes, things that presumably happen in the brain. A very conscious trouble can disturb the function of the intestines, and on the other side the state of the intestines can affect the mind; in studying the anatomy of the nervous system one sees that there are any number of bridges by which these enervations can reach this side or the other. So it is certain that the sympathetic system has a sort of psyche; it can harbor contents that perhaps become in time conscious contents. And as a matter of fact, in all cases, practically, where it is a matter of the repression of certain contents, or the retention of contents in the unconscious, we see disturbances of the intestines, particularly in hysteria. The very name *hysteria* comes from this fact: *hysteros* is the uterus that was supposed to be chiefly the cause of hysteria. Of course that is a wrong causality. It is a mere symptom of the fact that there is a disturbance in the unconscious causing trouble on this side and on the other side, in the body as well as in the mind.

The tarantula, therefore, would represent the sympathetic system, and usually when one approaches one's inferior function, no matter what it is, one reaches there this sphere of the sympathetic system. It is always a sort of descent, because the differentiated function is up in the head, the conscious is linked up with the grey matter, whether it is sensation or anything else, and the inferior function is always more connected with the body. When, therefore, Nietzsche is confronted with the unconscious he is confronted with his inferior function. His main function is surely intuition, which would be up above, connected with the brain, with consciousness, and that is in opposition to the things below, namely, the three other functions, a trinity. He was strictly identical with *one* function. Sure enough, Nietzsche in the time when he wrote *Zarathustra* was absolutely identical with intuition, using only that function, to the very exhaustion of his brain. *Zarathustra* created a peculiar disturbance in his brain: it really brought about his final insanity on account of the extraordinary strain to which it was subjected.

Now, this was an ideal situation for the constellation of the lower trinity, the trinity of the functions in the unconscious—in the first place sensation, being *la fonction du réel*, as opposed to the function of intuition, and the auxiliary functions thinking and feeling, which are both to a great extent also unconscious. I called your attention in the last chapter to the fact that Nietzsche as an intuitive simply touches upon a thing and off he goes. He does not dwell upon the subject, though in the long run one can say he really does dwell upon it by amplification. But he doesn't deal with things in a logical way, going into the intellectual process of elucidation; he just catches such an intuition on the wing and leaves it, going round and round and amplifying, so that in the end we get a complete picture but by intuitive means, not by logical means. For instance, he does not arrive at the tarantula by logical means, not at all; otherwise he would have much to say about what he writes here, but we hear not a word. We can only catch at his birds, or flies, or sparks, and from the ensemble of all these isolated bits we get a complete picture.

Mrs. Sigg: Is there not hidden magic in the idea that this tarantula is the vessel of all evil, a kind of devil?

Prof. Jung: Naturally.

Mrs. Sigg: I mean that there is a triangle and a cross because they both have magic influence on the devil. For instance, if you think of the cross on the *Kreuzspinne* . . .

Prof. Jung: But unfortunately we have no such thing as a cross here. *I* spoke of that; we must keep to the text. We have only that triangle which has never been used as an apotropaic sign. The Christian apotropaic sign is the cross—that is the interesting point—while the triangle is a symbol used in churches but never as an apotropaic charm. It is as if they did not trust that triangle but trusted the four, a finesse which could be substantiated by many psychological arguments. Now, it is pretty certain, when the triangle is made the symbol of the best things, the *summum bonum*, that there is also a triangle on the other side. Of course dogmatically there is no such thing: we have no triangle of the devil. He is coupled with his grandmother, not with the mother; that is of course colloquial, a sort of joke, but it might show an attempt at an infernal sort of dogma.

Prof. Reichstein: The devil has very often a kind of fork with three prongs like the trident of Neptune.

Prof. Jung: I remember it with two prongs but the other is quite possible. As a matter of fact, Neptune in early Christianity was occasionally used as a sort of symbol, meaning the devil. I have a vase, presumably dating from the first century, on which are represented the three forms of the union of man and woman. In the first a man and woman are standing opposite one another, and the man holds a mandrake (the German *Alraun*) which is a love charm, and behind his back is a shadow, to indicate that a demon has of course insinuated that magic: that is the union through a magic charm. Then on the other side is the representation of a pagan marriage, which was regarded as being sinful, and there the man holds a fork with three points, a trident, the Neptune symbol. And in the center is represented the Christian union of man and woman; there a vertical fish is between them and they touch hands through the fish, that is the *matrimonium in Christi*, the marriage in Christ. You know, the Christian marriage is not a union of man and woman exclusively, but is a union with Christ between. Of course our modern marriage is no longer a union in Christ, and that is a mistake. The immediate union of man and woman is too dangerous: there must be a mediation, whatever it is. Therefore the Catholic church maintains very wisely the power of interference; the priest is always between, representing the church, the body of Christ in between a married couple. And since we no longer have any such thing in our very marvelous civilization, we have invented as a remedy these damned analysts who are mixed up with I don't know how many marriages. We poor analysts have all the trouble in the world.

Mr. Baumann: I have just found in this book pictures of the three-pointed trident.

Prof. Jung: Yes, and one of the members of our Seminar has called my attention to the fact that in Dante's *Divine Comedy* the devil is represented with three heads; this is only a memory—unfortunately we have not discovered a copy of the book in the library to prove it—but I think it is true that when the devil at the bottom of hell is sticking in the ice, he has three heads that devour the sinners. In Christian language, that would be the infernal trinity, which is clearly hinted at in this triangle on the back of the tarantula. You see, that triangle joined to the upper triangle of the trinity would make the quadrangulum or the quaternion. These two triangles together form a square which would make the four; and this is that eternal problem, the three and the four. You will find a number of contributions to this problem in my essay in the last Eranos *Jahrbuch*, *Erlösungsvorstellungen in der Alchemie*; also in my essay in the *Jahrbuch* of 1935, *Traumsymbole des Individuationsprozesses*.[7] The triangles can also be joined in a different way, namely: and then you have the so-called David's shield, the Jewish symbol which is often used in Christian churches but as a symbol of Jahveh. This is a different solution of the problems of opposites, into which I don't want to go now. We must say a bit more about this spider symbol; we have looked at its negative aspect but there is another aspect: nothing is ever so negative that it has not also a positive aspect.

Mr. Baumann: I think the earthly quality is a positive aspect, and that it carries the trinity. The trinity cannot exist by itself, it must have a foundation.

Prof. Jung: Yes, the idea of Hermetic philosophy is that the three, the trinity, are represented by three bodies. They call them *sol, luna,* and *mercurius*—gold, silver, and mercury—and they are represented as three snakes joined together by their tails, a unit in themselves but with three heads, three persons in one. This is the dogmatic form of the trinity *contained* in a vessel, in the *vas Hermeticus*, and the vessel was number four. It is a well-known alchemistic symbol and would bear out what Mr. Baumann says, that the fourth may be a basis, or a base, as the earth can be a basis for water, earth, and fire; they rest upon the earth. You see, that is a formula for bringing those four together. But in the Christian psychology the fourth is the devil, and how can you bring the good and evil together? The thing is impossible: that moral valuation creates such a split that you cannot bring those opposites together, but are always forced to be one-sided.

Prof. Reichstein: There is a story that the spider was created by the kiss of the devil; the devil kissed a woman and the spider was created. Then afterwards it became beneficial from the moment it was imprisoned in a wooden box.

Prof. Jung: Yes, I can recommend that story. It was in my mind: you have anticipated me. Jeremias Gotthelf was a Swiss writer of the 19th century who wrote very popular things, and among them was this highly symbolic story, astonishingly enough, which contains an attempt at a solution. He was a parson and naturally he was bothered by that question.[8] The evil was brought on by the kiss of the devil, so the

---

[7] "Dream Symbols of the Individuation Process" was revised and expanded as "Individual Dream Symbolism in Relation to Alchemy" in CW 12.

[8] Jeremias Gotthelf, the pseudonym of Albert Bitzins, was the author of *The Black Spider*, tr. H. M. Waldon (London, 1954).

black spider was created and increased in numbers till it threatened to destroy everything, and then the evil was conjured away by putting the spider into a box, catching that spider in form, in a sort of *vas Hermeticus* (you know, we still speak of a hermetically sealed vessel), which is a vessel that must not be opened. Whatever is inside should be kept in such a way that it cannot escape. If the vessel is opened, the whole process is destroyed and evil is created. It is like the stories of thunderstorms caught in a box or a jar and the trouble it makes if somebody opens it.

Mr. Baumann: The Greek form was the box of Pandora.

Prof. Jung: Yes, this is a general symbol: you find it also in the writing of Apollonius of Tyana where this magic was attributed to Brahmanic priests.[9] They were supposed to have a particular jar or amphora containing the bad and the good weather, mighty catastrophes all sealed up in a jar. It is the motive of the magic vessel or the magic room in which something is contained that is quite beneficial, or at least does no harm, as long as it is not opened or touched. The moment the taboo is lifted, immediately there is a great catastrophe. Now, these motives and stories lead us to the positive aspect of the tarantula: we learn that this thing can be beneficial under certain conditions. In Christian language, then, if the devil is properly bottled up or caught or chained, he is useful; he has even a beneficient influence. So if the Catholic church could find a suitable formula in which to catch the devil, it might be a great asset, but hitherto nothing safe enough has been found. Today the situation is that God has allowed the devil to play his pranks on the earth, but after an indefinite lapse of time he will do something about it, which of course amounts to a certain impotence on the part of the good principle.

So the problem is a bit shelved in Christianity. It is not as openly discussed as in Manichaeism, where half the world belonged to the devil, and it was touch and go for the good god whether he escaped final destruction. Therefore mankind had to put their weight to help god to extricate the stuff of light from the power of the devil, Ahriman. Their teaching is that one should be careful every day and in every way to increase the sum of the light atoms, not only by *doing* the right things, but by eating only those fruits which consist of sun—particularly melons because they are like the sun—and by avoiding all dark foods containing too much of the heaviness of matter, causing passions and such

[9] Apollonius of Tyana was an obscure, solitary, alchemical wanderer. See CW 14, pars. 164-65.

things. Thus, the number of light particles in the body is increased and when one dies, one carries the millions of light atoms up into the big pillar of light which leads up to the heavens and the god of light. They had the interesting idea that the souls that carry those light atoms were gathered up by the moon until it became full. Then that full moon gradually poured all the souls into the sun, approaching nearer and nearer till it was quite empty when it touched the sun, and so had become the new moon again. Then it left the sun and began collecting souls once more. You see, they connected their astronomical observations with the moral problems of the world. In modern Christianity the problem is a bit repressed; we are just slightly hysterical, but, as I say, nothing is so bad that it would not contain something good, and there is a positive aspect to that tarantula. Now what would the very positive aspect be?

Miss Hannah: It is also very often a symbol for the self.

Prof. Jung: Yes. There are dreams, for instance, where the spider appears as a jewel, perhaps a sapphire, a blue resplendent gem in the center of the web which is made of golden threads. And people make pictures like that, not knowing of course what they mean. This is the symbol of the self but in a certain condition: namely, in the condition of complete unconsciousness. One could not have such a dream or make such a picture if one knew anything about its meaning, for then it becomes an object of conscious thinking, and the unconscious doesn't heap up attributes any longer—unless one makes somewhere a big mistake in one's conception of such an image. One might come across such a spider in cases that are not in actual analysis, or at the beginning of it, but never unless the person is completely unconscious of what that symbol could mean. Now, its positive aspect is that there is a central being somewhere that has spread its golden web throughout the world to catch the souls of man. Often, however, it is projected in its negative aspect onto the analyst who is then seen as a spider catching people, getting them under his influence and sucking them dry, but this is merely the negative aspect of a very positive thing. You see people of the so-called tarantula quality who preach equality (we come to this in our text presently—it is of course Nietzsche's way of putting the concept of collectivity). Those people who preach that collectivism of equal units are the ones who are afraid of the action of the spider. They feel that the spider, or the analyst, is preaching of individuation, that a hostile power is seeking them, enveloping them as a spider does. They fear that they may get stuck or caught in something, and they necessarily think that this is absolutely wrong, that they should be free.

But people lose their real freedom when they really succeed in believing in collectivism and equality. Then they are caught in their equality and there is no possibility of any differentiation any longer. It is as if all the water were in one lake where nothing moved, where there was a complete lack of potential. Now, this positive aspect of the spider of course is a symbol, but inasmuch as that symbol is a triangle it doesn't fit of course, because a triangle just means one-sidedness, while individuation means everything else but one-sidedness—it means completeness. Therefore individuation is represented by a circle and a square. You know, that medieval problem of the *quadratura circuli*, the squaring of the circle, is very important—it is really the problem of individuation. There is a famous book by Michael Majer in which he describes the whole alchemical process as the squaring of the circle, meaning the completion.[10] It is an attempt at the solution of the Christian problem; those people were really concerned with that question. But the church cannot cope with it. They have postponed it: for them it is still in the lap of God. Now, we are not concerned just here with the positive aspect of the tarantula, we shall see what Nietzsche has to say about it later. First he only sees the negative aspect.

> Revenge is in thy soul: wherever thou bitest, there ariseth black-scab; with revenge, thy poison maketh the soul giddy!

This of course refers to the tarantula dance, the madness caused by the tarantula. You see, that idea suggests something one very often encounters when people approach their inferior function; they have attacks of vertigo or nausea for instance, because the unconscious brings a peculiar sort of motion, as if the earth were moving under their feet, or as if they were on the deck of a ship rolling in a heavy swell. They get a kind of seasickness; they develop such symptoms actually. It simply means that their former basis, or their imagined basis, has gone—certain values which they thought to be basic are no longer there—so they become doubtful and suspended in a sort of indefinite atmosphere with no ground under their feet, always afraid of falling down. And of course the thing that is waiting for them underneath is the jaws of hell, or the depth of the water, or a profound darkness, or a monster—or they may call it madness. And mind you, it *is* madness to fall out of one's conscious world into an unconscious condition. Insanity means just that, being overcome by an invasion of the unconscious.

---

[10] Michael Maier (or Majer) writes on squaring the circle, which is to say individuation, in *Scutinium chymicum* (Frankfort-on-Main, 1687).

Consciousness is swept over by unconscious contents in which all orientation is lost. The ego then becomes a sort of fish swimming in a sea among other fishes, and of course fishes don't know who they are, don't even know the name of their own species. We know that we belong to the species of *homo sapiens* and the fishes do not, and when we fall into the fish species, we lose our identity and might be anything else.

That is the state of insane people: they don't know whether things are true or not, take an illusion for granted as an overwhelming fact. If they hear voices, they are quite convinced that they hear those voices; and if they go into the street and discover the sun is double, or that people have skulls instead of heads, this is a fact to them. They don't doubt it because it is too overwhelmingly clear. So there is absolutely nothing within their disposition to defend them against such realities. One cannot help being convinced by what one hears and sees. That simply comes from the fact that in a moment when the conscious is invaded by the unconscious, the energic value of consciousness is depotentiated, and then one is no longer up to the contents of one's psyche. We have not learned to behave like fishes, to swim in that flood. If you have learned to swim, then you get through: you can *stand* being suspended in water without getting seasick and losing your head. So people who possess a certain psychological insight have always a better prognosis when they become insane: the more the psychological insight, the better the prognosis. Of course certain people who have a latent psychosis just go insane and there is nothing to be done about it. But if they have acquired a certain amount of psychology, there is a chance that they can swim; they recognize something in that flow and may be able to get out of it again. While people who are rigid, without any psychological insight whatever—who are utterly unable to see themselves under another aspect than the one they are accustomed to—such people simply explode, fly into splinters, and they never return. It is as if the knowledge of psychology were making our brain more elastic, as if our brain box were becoming elastic so that it can contain more contents and vary its forms, while those people with rigid convictions are like a sort of box made of stiff boards which can only contain so much, and if the thing that wants to enter the brain box is too big for it, then the whole thing blows up. In such cases an attack of insanity often begins with a pistol shot in the head, or the feeling that something has broken or snapped. You see, a board has split; they cannot shut the lid because the thing that came in was too big.

Therefore in treating such cases, we always have to look out for enlarging the vessel, the mental horizon, and making it ready to receive any amount and any size, so that it will not explode with the inpouring contents of the unconscious. To use that simile of the fish, one should equip people to dive; the diver is equipped and doesn't get drowned. This fear of madness is always associated with the inferior function, so when Nietzsche approaches the problem of the earth and of evil, he naturally will realize that fear, all the more so as ultimately he was not inclined to accept the inferior man. The question as to whether he can finally accept the inferior man comes later on—and he cannot, he refuses him, and that of course breaks his head. Our shadow is the last thing that has to be put on top of everything, and that is the thing we cannot swallow; we can swallow anything else, but not our own shadow because it makes us doubt our good qualities. We can assume that the world is bad and that other people are bad and that everything is going to hell as long as we are sure that *we* are on the right side; but if *we* are no longer sure, it is too much. Now Nietzsche continues,

> Thus do I speak unto you in parable, ye who make the soul giddy, ye preachers of *equality*! Tarantulas are ye unto me, and secretly revengeful ones!

This is interesting. If anybody should have the impertinence to tell him that he is like other people, that all people are practically the same, it would be fatal. Why is that such a danger?

Mrs. Fierz: It touches upon his Wotan inflation and would make it burst.

Prof. Jung: Exactly, it would break his bubble. Being identical with Zarathustra, who is also Wotan, he is half divine and above humanity. Inasmuch as Zarathustra is a spirit, he deserves to be above humanity, but if Nietzsche identifies with him, it will come to the daylight that he is like everybody else. And that is the shadow. In the shadow we are exactly like everybody; in the night all cats are grey—there is no difference. So if you cannot stand living in the shadow or seeing yourself in the shadow, seeing your equality with everybody, you are forced to live in the light; and the sun fails at times: every night the sun goes under, and then you must have artificial light. Many people develop a symptom out of that: they must have the light on or within reach, in order to be able to make a light when the darkness comes. That means: hold onto consciousness for heaven's sake; don't get away from your distinction, from your knowledge of yourself as a separate being; don't fall into what equality or you are put out. And you *are* put out; you become a fish in the sea, just one in a huge swarm of herrings. But that is exactly the thing one ought to be able to stand, because it is an eternal truth that all human beings belong to *homo sapiens*, that they all came from a particular kind of quite good monkeys, no one particularly different from the other. So from a certain superior point of view, human beings are practically the same. This is a truth and it should not be a deadly poison; but he even reviles that point of view as a spirit of revenge. How on earth does he get the idea that this is a spirit of revenge?

Miss Hannah: Because he is projecting the whole thing entirely on the inferior man. He sees the whole thing as a jealousy of the inferior man who wants to destroy his own superiority.

Prof. Jung: Well, as soon as you assume that you are the god, you gravely offend the inferior man, and naturally he has a psychology like yourself. If you are offended you feel revengeful, and the inferior man is full of the spirit of revenge. So when that fellow contacts the superior man, he will get at him and say, "Now I've got you, now I will show you who I am." That is human psychology. The inferior man will come back with a vengeance as soon as he has a chance. Nietzsche says, "revenge is in thy soul," and so it is. He will be badly beaten, having been identical with the gods.

> But I will soon bring your hiding-places to the light: therefore do I laugh in your face my laughter of the height.

There you have it: he is above, they are below, and he projects the inferior man into a sort of imaginary preacher of equality and begins to give him a lecture.

> Therefore do I tear at your web, that your range may lure you out of your den of lies, and that your revenge may leap forth from behind your word "justice."
>
> Because, *for man to be redeemed from revenge*—that is for me the bridge to the highest hope, and a rainbow after long storms.

Naturally, if the shadow could be redeemed from its spirit of revenge, there would be a chance of reunion and that would be a rainbow bridge; that is the thing to be hoped for—that he could accept his inferior side. But then of course he must *behave* with his shadow, must not offend his shadow by reviling it, and he must not project it, declaring, "This is not myself, thank God I am not like him." That is the pharisaical point of view. You see, Nietzsche forgets again and again that most important fact, that he gains nothing by reviling others. You must know where *you* are guilty and then you can do something about it;

while if the other one is guilty, what can you do about it? We should realize the possibility of guilt or evil in ourselves. If we can realize that, we have gained a part of our shadow and we have added to our completeness.

But if we are forced to live under circumstances where too many other people do the wrong things, they take too much out of us. They deprive us of the possibility of doing them and of realizing our shadow.

LECTURE IV

26 May 1937

Prof. Jung:

My attention has just been called to a passage in the part we have already dealt with: "Because, for man to be redeemed from revenge—that is for me the bridge to the highest hope, and a rainbow after long storms." Mrs. Sigg suggests that this might remind us of that stunt played by Jahveh on the sinful world, when he sent the great flood and drowned all the sinners, and then afterwards made a rainbow to show that he was reconciled, or at peace with himself, and wouldn't do it again. Perhaps you have seen *Green Pastures*—there we saw that Jahveh was really quite sorry and kept on thinking of other means.[1] Well, I am sure that archetypal image of the great flood is behind this particular passage, but I would not attach too much importance to it.

Then there is a question by Mrs. Scott-Maxwell, "At the end of your last lecture you spoke of the marriage in Christ, with the hands through the fish. Then I understood you to say man and woman cannot meet directly without trouble resulting. Will you please tell us why you feel this to be so?"

The chief reason is that, as an analyst, I am usually confronted with this most amazing fact, that when man and woman meet, some trouble results. It is generally true that the relationship between man and woman is not simple. But I quite understand that such a bold statement is irritating since we are all perfectly convinced that this should not be so; as you know, we chiefly think the things we like to think and dislike to think such irritating truths as trouble arising from love or friendship. Naturally we dislike such statements, yet if we look at the world objectively, we must ask ourselves why such an important religion as Christianity invented particular rites or particular ideas round marriage; and not only Christianity: we have plenty of evidence that

[1] Marc Connelly's *Green Pastures*, a popular folk play, a light-hearted Black conception of heaven. See CW 10, pars. 16ff.

this has happened in exactly the same way in other quarters at other times and in other civilizations. Every important phase of human life, or important decisions, are always surrounded by all sorts of magic because they are threatened by certain dangers; there are always risks connected with them. And anything so particularly important as the relationship between man and woman, perhaps the greatest intensity nature has ever invented, is so full of spiritual dangers, perils of the soul, that man always felt the need of particular magic, apotropaic means to make sure that the thing worked—since it is just as possible that it won't work, or will work for a while and then turn into the opposite. So if you study the relation between man and woman with unbiased eyes—trying to refrain from thinking as you like, and forcing yourself to think according to what you really observe—you will see that there is usually a great deal of trouble.

That is the reason why I made this statement and it is also the quite obvious reason why Christianity tried to put something in between, some cotton wool or something of the sort, in order to mitigate the impact of those two forces, mutually attractive yet very opposite in character. It obviously needs some additional ideas, or auxiliary conceptions and figures, in order to make the thing go. If it were quite simple, as we always prefer to think—that it should be the simplest thing in the world to embrace each other—then there would be no trouble. But it is not so simple apparently, only we are too stupid to see why it should be so difficult. If we were just a bit more intelligent we would see that such a situation would naturally be full of spikes; it couldn't be anything else. Of course we are always taught how simple it is, "just simple love, you know"—all the world talks in that foolish style—but when you come to it you are in hot water, and then of course the doctors or the lawyers or the priests can look after the job. It is not simple, but exceedingly complicated and full of risks. Therefore, since time immemorial, man has surrounded it by all sorts of magic in order to prevent the very probable troubles of the soul resulting from such a relationship. If you realize what it means that a woman represents the Yin and the man the Yang, then you know enough; it is a pair of opposites, and whenever you try to unite a pair of opposites in your own character, you realize how difficult it is, almost impossible: you cannot see how they *could* be united. And so when they are there in reality it is like water and fire, like vinegar and oil; you must mix them together to make a decent salad—but it *might* be a salad, you know!

Well now, this chapter about the tarantulas is peculiarly important because it deals with ideas that have a particular bearing on our time.

This is obviously a time of big collective movements, collective ideals, and we hear on all sides and in all sorts of variations the sermon of equality, or the manifestation of a will to equality, that should become henceforth the nature of virtue, as he now says:

"And 'Will to Equality'—that itself shall henceforth be the name of virtue; and against all that hath power will we raise an outcry!"
Ye preachers of equality, the tyrant-frenzy of impotence crieth thus in you for "equality": your most secret tyrant-longings disguise themselves thus in virtue-words!

You see, Nietzsche clearly shows here an understanding of the compensatory or contrasting nature of any such attempt. I mean, the attempt at equality consists of, or is based upon, a secret tyrant-longing: if I cannot be king, then we shall all be kings so that everybody has his share of the kingdom. Of course equality under such conditions looks very wonderful, but since everybody is a king nobody wants to submit. It is a kingdom without subjects where everybody fights everybody. So it soon ends either with a real tyrant or in a perfectly anarchic condition.

Mrs. Fierz: In the Persian religion there is the idea that when the reign of Ahriman comes, all the mountains will be made into one plain and there will be one king.

Prof. Jung: Yes, that is a good idea. So it is.

Fretted conceit and suppressed envy—perhaps your fathers' conceit and envy: in you break they forth as flame and frenzy of vengeance.
What the father hath hid cometh out in the son; and oft have I found the son the father's revealed secret.

This is a very remarkable psychological insight, such as one often finds in *Zarathustra*. Nietzsche was a great psychologist[2] and his key was the idea of the hidden contrast, so he even looked at this aspect in the relation of father and son. He obviously has that experience particularly in mind because, being the son of a clergyman, he was himself the father's unrevealed secret.

Mrs. Sigg: His father really looked very problematic; one is astonished when one sees his photograph.

---

[2] Nietzsche of course thought so too, but that it was not what passes in Academe for psychology is indicated by Nietzsche's saying that the only psychologist from whom he had anything to learn was Dostoevsky. See *Twilight*, "Expeditions of an Untimely Man," p. 45.

Prof. Jung: I remember, but of course I know nothing of the father's possible psychology. I am myself, however, a parson's son, and I have seen many children of theologians, and I can refer to one important fact. Once I sent round a questionnaire asking whether people would prefer to go to a doctor with their complexes, or to the clergy, and among those who answered, the children of parsons—all, with no exception—said they would never go to a parson, but would prefer to go to a doctor. Now, that means something, and there are sort of proverbs about sons of parsons which bear out what Nietzsche says. Of course there are many exceptions to such a rule, particularly in former times when there were several generations of parsons and they didn't disturb each other at all: the son revealed no secret whatsoever, he just repeated the father.

Miss Hannah: Did the doctors' children all want to go to the parson?

Prof. Jung: No, they did not, not at all, although that was really the case with my father. He was the son of a doctor, a professor of medicine, and my father became a parson, but he was the only one. You see, the doctor's profession is not so provocative as a clergyman's; you can imagine all sorts of things about a doctor, and it is true that many doctors are very peculiar people. If you know the history of the profession you realize that all sorts of people are in it, while for the clergy it is far more critical. Our Swiss poet Gottfried Keller once said that there are those who are below God, and then there are the others who are above him.[3] Those are the children of Satan, wolves in sheep's clothing, because they use the relationship to God as a personal title and know everything about God. They compensate by a pious attitude for their moral inferiority. But the others really are saints by vocation. That is also true of doctors; one finds most decent characters and most indecent characters, but when a profession is based upon such particular qualities as the vocation of the priest or the parson must be, then things come to a head and the pairs of opposites are badly split. It is a tremendous thing for a man to assume that he is a priest and carries the mana. That is exceedingly provocative to the unconscious. Such people are liable to be subjected to the worst temptations. Therefore, the worst dreams are those of the saints, as we were saying last week; they are most assailed by the devil because they most provoke the devil. By the conscious assumption or by the fact that they are really decent, saintly people, they are a provocation to all the black powers, and of course they have to pay the price for their saintliness.

---

[3] For Gottfried Keller, see above, 16 Oct. 1935, n. 3.

You know the story of the man who had no wish. There was once a very pious man who did not consider himself to be a saint, but by chance he was a saint though he didn't know it. So his merit was all the greater and of course God could not help noticing him. One time when they were having a particular celebration in heaven and God was considering the people who had merit, giving them orders and decorations, he said to Gabriel, "Well, I suppose we ought to do something for Mr. So-and-So, he is really a saint. Go down and tell him that I want to grant him his most important wish." So Gabriel went down and told the saint who he was and that God would grant him his wish. And that man being a saint had no wish. "But surely you must have a wish, everybody has a wish, God in his omniscience knows that you have a wish," said Gabriel. But the man was conscious of none. So Gabriel went back and told God who said, "That is awkward, he should have a wish. Go back and tell him he must have one." And so Gabriel went back again and said it was the command of God that he should have a wish, *any* bad wish, and the only wish that man could possibly think of was to have just one look into the soul of a real saint. Gabriel asked him if he couldn't think of something else, but no, that was his only interest. Then Gabriel flew back and said to God, "This is a terrible man. He only wants to look into the soul of a real saint; what can we do about it?" "That is impossible," said God, "one cannot grant that." But Gabriel said since he had promised to fulfill his wish he would have to do it, and God said, "Of course I cannot go back on my promise. Let him have his look." So the angel again went down and led the man to a real acknowledged saint, and the man took one look into the soul of that saint and went instantly crazy. Therefore we shall never know how the soul of a saint looks. That is a very psychological story which I use as a sort of medicine for all those who cannot put their minds at peace about their inner contrasts.

Now it is surely a great truth that under certain favorable or unfavorable conditions, the son reveals the father's secret. Of course that is true for both parents—he can reveal the secret of his mother just as well. It is quite astonishing sometimes to find in what a peculiar way the secret comes to the daylight; it really explains much in a human life which cannot be explained otherwise. The secrets of the parents have the most extraordinary influence upon the lives of the children, and nothing in the world will prevent the children from being influenced. We can only try to live our lives as reasonably, as normally, or as humanly as possible, but even then we cannot help having secrets, secrets which we don't know ourselves. Those are the true secrets and they may be the most influential. So we can prevent that influence only in as much as our life is in our hands; and our life is only to a very small extent in our hands because we are only partly conscious. We can pump out of that sea of the unconscious I don't know how many gallons of water, yet it is never exhausted. We always hand on a secret, and whatever creeps out in our children will be a revelation of that thing of which we were quite ignorant. Of course inasmuch as we know of this mechanism, we are under an obligation to do something about it, but beyond that there is still enough which is secret to build up a life or destroy it. We can only say that the further our consciousness extends, the more our responsibility increases, the more we have to consider.

And since too great an amount of such responsibilities will make our lives a perfect hell, we cannot carry more than a certain amount. We soon reach a point where we have to dismiss our responsibility, where we have to admit with seeing eyes that we cannot be responsible. It would lead too far; we simply could not live any longer. It would be necessary to be conscious of every step we take, to give an account of everything we think, because it all might contain a former secret which would be influential in spoiling the lives of the next generation. A certain side of that secret consists in the inheritance of the body; our bodies are not perfect: every body contains so many inferiorities, so many degenerated functions, and we hand that on if we have children. That is also a responsibility, yet only in very bad cases would it prevent us from producing them. For instance, somebody might have a most unlucky face, or certain signs of degeneration, the gland system might be wrong, yet those people have children though they must take it for granted that they are affected by that fact just as badly as by certain psychological secrets. Of course one should try to be as sound as possible in body as well as mind, but inasmuch as we cannot reach beyond our own limits, one has to take it for granted that we hand on some trouble. People who are too much impressed by that fact become quite pessimistic, which accounts for such ascetic movements as in early Christianity for instance, when it was thought that the best thing would be to bring the world to a standstill, that eternal curse, by not having children at all. And Schopenhauer says our compassion with all living things should prevent us from continuing this terrible illusion of the world: look into the mirror of the intellect and you see your terrible face; deny it, and bring the whole thing to a standstill. Of course that would be going a bit too far for the average man, and the average man carries the life. Now, Nietzsche goes on talking about these people, the preachers of equality.

1098

Inspired ones they resemble: but it is not the heart that inspireth them—but vengeance.

We would say *ressentiment*, that is the word really.[4]

And when they become subtle and cold, it is not spirit, but envy, that maketh them so.

That is a great truth, you can see it everywhere in all our collective movements, inside and outside.

Their jealousy leadeth them also into thinker's paths; and this is the sign of their jealousy—they always go too far: [Far too one-sided!] so that their fatigue hath at last to go to sleep on the snow.

Now how do you understand this peculiar image, that finally they take their rest in the snow from all that effort of one-sidedness?

Mrs. Sigg: Nietzsche in the beginning of *Zarathustra* always speaks of climbing too high and therefore he was himself in the snow.

Prof. Jung: Yes, that metaphor occurs very frequently in *Zarathustra*, climbing very high, reaching the snows of ice-cold mind or intellect. And how would that work out practically? What happens to a person who is fanatically one-sided? Why does he get into the snow? Why not into hot water?

Prof. Reichstein: He loses connection with the other side. Pure thinking is meant here and loss of the feeling function.

Prof. Jung: Yes, with a fanatical one-sidedness you lose your connection with the human being, with the warm living thing which is always a mixture of everything. You create a sort of sterile field in which nothing is contained but that one thing you have in mind. All one-sidedness leads into the desert, or to a desert island, or to something as sterile as snow, which contains no life, but kills life or keeps it in a static condition. In Nietzsche's case, it is usually the snow and the cold, because his one-sidedness would be inclined to create abstract thought or an abstract kingdom of ideas, and that is traditionally cold. The mind or the intellect, when too one-sided, is too much separated from the opposite function feeling, and then one winds up in a perfectly cold condition. Later on, he comes back to the ice and snow. In the end of *Zarathustra* there are passages where it is obvious that he has reached the glacier and lost his connection with humanity altogether.

[4] For *ressentiment*, see above, 27 Nov. 1935, n. 1.

In all their lamentations soundeth vengeance, in all their eulogies is maleficence; and being judge seemeth to them bliss.

What psychological condition is this?

Miss Wolff: A person who is speaking out of resentment.

Prof. Jung: Yes, but that shows itself in a certain way; he describes
here that condition: "and being judge seemeth to them bliss."

Miss Wolff: Because they can always blame others.

Prof. Jung: Exactly. It is a state of complete projection. They project
their own contents into others and judge them there. So this one-sidedness naturally leads into an unconsciousness of one's own condition,
which is then of course projected. Anything unconscious that lives with
us is invariably projected; you only have to wait until you find your *bête
noire* that contains your other side. Probably you have it already, but
sometimes you find a still better one, and then that is particularly satisfactory. So if people are inclined to get tremendously excited and
judge the things that other people do, it means that they are one-sided,
unconscious of themselves in a certain respect. You see, they are really
offended by evil-doers as if they themselves were the evil-doers. They
feel shocked by the evil deed in such a personal way because it is as if
they themselves had committed it. Therefore their resentment. They
are touched by it, they have done it, and as they cannot stand themselves doing such tempting things, they blame others for doing
them—upbraid them for having committed those sins which are so terribly alluring to themselves. So on the one side that resentment is a sort
of jealousy, and on the other side it is the shock that you receive when
you see yourself doing something which you don't want to stand for,
something you would probably call immoral, a thing you would never
do. When you talk about other people doing those things which you
naturally never do, then we know enough about you.

But thus do I counsel you, my friends: distrust all in whom the
impulse to punish is powerful!

There you get it.

They are people of bad race and lineage; out of their counte-
nances peer the hangman and the sleuth-hound.

Distrust all those who talk much of their justice! Verily, in their
souls not only honey is lacking.

And when they call themselves "the good and just," forget not,
that for them to be Pharisees, nothing is lacking but—power!

I cannot add to that.

My friends, I will not be mixed up and confounded with others.

That is a bit dangerous!

There are those who preach my doctrine of life, and are at the same time preachers of equality, and tarantulas.

Now who are those who preach "my doctrine of life"—obviously Zarathustra's doctrine—and at the same time are preachers of equality? That is very cryptic. Has anyone a hunch?

Mrs. Jung: Does it not refer to the ideas of Marx, or communism, which came after Nietzsche?

Prof. Jung: Yes, but they did not come after Nietzsche; he knew of them very well. He refers here to a certain materialistic philosophy of those days. Max Stirner, for instance, is a forerunner of Nietzsche's and would belong to those preachers of equality—communistic equality, political and social equality.[5] Also the idea of democracy was very young then—I mean our modern idea of it, not the old. The old democracy was like our Swiss democracy, the oldest democracy in the world, and it was by no means what we would call a democracy now. It was an oligarchy, which is quite *different*. Our modern ideas of democracy belong entirely to the 19th-century children of the French Revolution, and that was really a serious attempt at equality. But you know that many people are by no means convinced that democracy means equality. Therefore we have still better equality movements and that was perfectly conscious to Nietzsche. Connected with those new political ideas was a certain libertinism, the reaction against moral traditions and moral laws. They began to experiment in free love, for instance, and those ideas play a role in *Zarathustra*. That devaluation of established values, the complete reversal of values which Zarathustra often preaches, has been mixed up with this parallel movement, and he wants to make sure here that he is not of the same conviction, that there is only a more or less superficial similarity. They *seem* to preach his doctrine of life according to his ideas, but they are at the same time preachers of equality, and *his* idea is that there is no equality, that man is not equal. He is absolutely individual, though he tries to produce a greater freedom of life, less dependence upon tradition, a liberation from moral and social fetters, destruction of authority hitherto indisputable—exactly as in those other political collective movements they preached of equality.

---

[5] It is not certain that Nietzsche had read him, but Stirner (i.e., Johann Schmidt, 1806-1856), author of *The Ego and His Own* (1884), anticipated Nietzsche in attacking religion and defending materialism and egoism.

That they speak in favour of life, though they sit in their den,
these poison-spiders, and withdrawn from life—is because they
would thereby do injury.
To those would they thereby do injury who have power at present: for with those the preaching of death is still most at home.

Here it is quite clear that he really means those collective movements
which were the forerunners of our existing political movements, and
he explains that as a reaction against those actually in power who still
believed in the preaching of death, meaning the union of kings and
governments with the churches and other authorities and historical
prejudices.

Were it otherwise, then would the tarantulas teach otherwise:
and they themselves were formerly the best-world-maligners and
heretic-burners.

That is perfectly true, the burning of heretics was a collective movement. Of course it seems to have been started by the church, but it was
really a collective movement which began with a faint attempt at a very
dangerous reformation, not only in Germanic countries but in Italy as
well. One exponent was St. Francis. He was a heretic, and only by the
great diplomatic cunning of Bonifazio VIII could he be smuggled into
the church.[6] There were plenty of others for whom that could not be
managed and they had to be burned or excommunicated. There was a
wide-spread movement of the spirit—Meister Eckhart is an example,
and the Brethren of the Free Spirit, or the liberated spirit, who had
absolutely communistic ideas and a wonderful way of dealing with capitalism. They said everything should be spent—offered or sacrificed
they called it—so they attacked people, a traveler perhaps, as if they
were bandits, and took his money, always using the phrase *transmittere
in aeternitatem*. They said, "We must do away with these worldly goods
and send them into eternity; they must be spent, wasted, and then
money will have no value any longer and we shall all be equal." That
was a colleective movement in the Germanic countries in the 13th century, part of the movement which brought about the great *autos-da-fé*,
the reaction of the church. This movement meant liberation of unruly

---

[6] It is not clear what Jung had in mind by "heretic" or "brought into the church." Francis (1182?-1226) was a wealthy, somewhat impetuous youth until certain visions of 1205
were responsible for his conversion. Shortly thereafter the rules proposed for his new
order were approved by Innocent III, and two years after Francis' death he was canonized by Gregory IX. Boniface VIII, born eight years after Francis' death, was assigned
by Dante to hell.

spiritual powers, and they were liberated not only in the Brethren of the Free Spirit or, in the Spanish heretics, but even amongst the clergy themselves—Torquemada was the worst of the doubters.[7] Objections were raised in their own dreams, and in order to quench them they burned the heretics; otherwise *they* would have had the ideas. So they said, "Thank you, God, that you do not make me responsible for my dreams. That other man has confessed such convictions and therefore we are going to burn him." It was a collective movement and Nietzsche is perfectly right when he says there were tarantulas in other times, but they simply took on another form.

> With these preachers of equality will I not be mixed up and confounded. For thus speaketh justice *unto me*: "Men are not equal."

Again he repeats a dangerous statement. "I thank thee God that I am not like this sinner." That is the Pharisee and he does not see it, but he sees it afterwards. "For thus speaketh justice *unto me*: 'Men are not equal.' " He should be careful not to use that word *justice*. He says men are not equal.

> And neither shall they become so!

There is the mistake. He blames the others that they are pleased to be judges and tell the boys all about it, but that is what *he* is doing. He says "they shall," when if he was careful and reasonable he would say "*I* shall."

> What would be my love to the Superman, if I spake otherwise?

You see how dangerous it is. The Superman is his main idea, and if he says such things he injures his *own* idea because the Superman doesn't bother about what he should become; otherwise he would be the ordinary preacher of values and not a Superman.

> On a thousand bridges and piers shall they throng to the future, and always shall there be more war and inequality among them: thus doth my great love make me speak!
> Inventors of figures and phantoms shall they be in their hostilities; and with those figures and phantoms shall they yet fight with each other the supreme fight.

---

[7] Tomas Torquemada (1420?-1498), the Spanish grand inquisitor. The Brethren of the Free Spirit were a group of 11th-century Christian dissidents who preached in favor of following the inner voice of the Holy Spirit in preference to the writings of the Gospels. Jung discussed this movement in CW 9 i, par. 139.

Now what does he mean by that?

Mrs. Fierz: That also sounds like a hint about the future; in the world war, for instance, they were fighting for the wrong reason, with phantoms and ghosts apparently.

Prof. Jung: Well, he doesn't need to say "they should" or "they shall"—they will do it anyhow you know, as they always do. Man cannot help inventing the most amazing reasons for beating his neighbor over the head. People go to extraordinary lengths to invent some "ism" which will allow them to spend the lives of other peoples, or to create a place for themselves. So he doesn't need to preach it. This is the way of the world: figures and phantoms are ever invented and people will forever use them as a pretext to fight each other. Sometimes one can clearly see the idea is merely invented for that purpose, and sometimes people are just caught by it. Usually the great masses are mere victims of such ideas and they fight and kill because man is fundamentally a killer. We should make no mistake about that; it is the most hellish illusion when we think otherwise. Of course it should not be and we can think whatever we like, but if we think according to what actually is, we must say he is and always has been a killer. A murderous streak is in everybody, and we have to reckon with it. Therefore, in thinking of a world, you must think of *such* a world, and not of a world in which these facts are not. If you want to think such illusions, then please try first to think how you can undo that streak, how you can eliminate the man that is, for he has to be eliminated in order to create a world where such things don't exist. The world will always be like that because it is the playground of pairs of opposites. So if things are peaceful for a while, we must just thank God because it won't last long.

> Good and evil, and rich and poor, and high and low, and all names of values: weapons shall they be, and sounding signs, that life must again and again surpass itself!

If he only would not say *shall*, or if that *shall* had not the meaning of *should*, if it is a mere *futurum*, then I agree. Those have always been the names of the pretexts and motives, and they will be the same forever, because life means building up and pulling down; it means generation and corruption. The old alchemists said: *corruptio unius est generatio alterius*, "the corruption of the one is the generation of another."

Now we are coming to a place where we reach an apex, where things turn into something else. He says,

Aloft will it build itself with columns and stairs—life itself: to re-move distances would it gaze, and out towards blissful beauties—*therefore* doth it require elevation.

And because it requireth elevation, therefore doth it require steps, and variance of steps and climbers! To rise striveth life, and in rising to surpass itself.

Just before, he said that people will always fight, that life is a conflict, a battlefield. That is a very pessimistic statement which would not fit into Nietzsche's point of view, for he is not pessimistic at all: he sees an ul-timate goal for which he is striving. So naturally he cannot leave that statement about the ultimate meaning or purpose of the world in such a form. He has to add that life wants to build itself aloft, and he uses a somewhat astonishing metaphor, "with columns and stairs." Life here becomes a sort of edifice, suddenly changing its aspect. It is no longer that up and down movement that it was before, everybody fighting against everybody; it takes on now a static aspect, the aspect of a build-ing, and the movement of life is on the stairs of that building. Also it is no longer striving to get something, to acquire or to conquer some-thing. It is rather to create a high standpoint, to gaze into the distance, as if man himself were becoming a watchman on the height of that tower, man looking out toward blissful beauties and therefore requir-ing elevation, to get to a higher point of view or, anyway to a point of view. Therefore he says steps are required and variance of steps and climbers, and of course fighting among the climbers, because the meaning of life seems to be to surpass itself. Life that doesn't overcome itself is really meaningless: it is not life; only inasmuch as life surpasses itself does it make sense. That is the way one could formulate this thought, but this is of course an extraordinary statement; it seems to be quite against everything he has said before. Now he says

And just behold, my friends! Here where the tarantula's den is, riseth aloft an ancient temple's ruins [Whoever would have thought that?]—just behold it with enlightened eyes!

Just where the cave is, the hole in the ground where the tarantula lives, just there are the ruins of a temple. It is so unexpected that it almost seems like bad taste; one cannot associate the two things at all, but it is one of Nietzsche's intuitions. Happily enough he doesn't run right away from it at once. He amplifies this vision a bit: namely, he discovers now an entirely different aspect of the tarantula. He discovers first of all that the point of view he proclaimed as belonging to the tarantula, is his own point of view—that one should make use of all moral or ethical values in order to make the fight a better one, to give some pep to the fight. To have a good feeling when you are fighting, you must be able to say you are fighting for a very good or just cause. That puts some juice into it; you must not allow any relativity of standpoint, but must be convinced that what you do is wonderful and ideal and just the right thing. Otherwise it would not pay to fight; everybody must be convinced of the entire goodness of his cause. That is what he is now preaching, and then suddenly the whole vista changes, all that turmoil appears in a static thing, as if time had come to a standstill, as if there were practically no fight, as if people were climbing only to get to the next step in the building, where the only thing they possibly can do is to reach the widest platform of the highest tower in order to have the best view. Now, what has happened here? It is one of those amazing intuitive changes in Nietzsche and the reason why he is so difficult to grasp.

Mrs. Fierz: When he said that life must always enlarge itself, it seems as if the idea of the widening of consciousness were coming in, and then that idea becomes prevailing, so the temple growing out of the tarantula's den seems to be the building of consciousness out of the unconscious.

Prof. Jung: But how would the idea of the widening out of consciousness come in?

Mrs. Fierz: Because that is life.

Prof. Jung: Oh yes, but does he say so?

Mrs. Fierz: No, it seems to slip in.

Prof. Jung: Then we must see how it slips in.

Mrs. Crowley: That would be Zarathustra's point of view because he is the self, and the other would represent the point of view of Nietzsche the man.

Prof. Jung: You are quite right. It is surely Zarathustra's point of view, but that does not help us to see how this widening of consciousness slips in.

Mrs. Crowley: Because all that wideness is being focused in a center point, and before it was spread all over the world in this idea of equality.

Prof. Jung: That is so, but we want to see how this idea of the widening of consciousness slips in.

Mr. Allemann: When he says life must surpass itself then the new birth takes place.

Prof. Jung: Exactly. To say that life shall surpass itself means that you have a standpoint outside of life, you are no longer in life. As long as you are in life you cannot imagine anything that would surpass it: life is the highest thing. He has been talking of his doctrine of life—he was entirely in the movement of life—and then suddenly it strikes him that there is a point of view outside or above it, a life that can surpass its own life. This is an element which obviously is not life, for to overcome itself it must be capable of a counter movement, and that is here represented in the static building. Those among you who have read *Das Reich ohne Raum* by Bruno Goetz, will remember the same conflict there, the conflict between the *Puer Aeternus* that is nothing but life, life in a blind spreading form, full of conflict, full of worry, full of nonsense; and over against that life is the Christian world.[8] I recommend that book to you. It was written immediately after the war and is a remarkable anticipation of the political conditions prevailing in Germany. And there you find that same peculiar conflict. First, you have the feelings of the extraordinary uprush of life symbolized by the *Puer Aeternus:* you feel that this *is* the thing, or you expect that it will now grow into something—and then the thing you discover is the Christian world, which is of course the world of ideas, entirely static, cold, rigid, a world which is simply the opposite. That is invariably so, because life is on the one side the most intense movement, the greatest intensity, and on the other side it is utterly static. Of course that is exceedingly difficult to see, but the more life becomes intense, the more there is of that up and down movement, the more you are in conflict, then the more you are squeezed out of life in a peculiar way; you begin to get outside and to look at it, and you ask yourself in the end, for God's sake what is it all about? Why all that turmoil and nonsense? What is the meaning of the whole thing? And that is the life that surpasses itself.

Mr. Layard: Can you explain what you mean by *Puer Aeternus* in this connection?

Prof. Jung: Well, I was speaking about Bruno Goetz's book, but I can give you an idea of it. You know, there is a peculiar line of demarcation going right through Europe; east of the line the archetype of the *Puer Aeternus* prevails psychologically, and west of that line the psychology of the anima. One sees the characteristic difference in the literature, the novels and *belles lettres*, also in the political aspect. For instance, that whole new movement in Germany is typical of the *Puer Aeternus*. It is a mass movement, an intense movement, and nobody can see exactly

[8] For Bruno Goetz, see above, 5 June 1935, n. 10.

what it means; there is a very mystical idea behind it, but it is chiefly life and movement and what it is all about, even the people themselves don't know. That psychology is also characterized by a peculiar relationship to woman. The woman is chiefly mother, virgin, or prostitute, but she is not a woman; while in the West the woman does exist. If you compare German literature with French or English literature, you see the difference at once. The *Puer Aeternus* has all the qualities of adolescent psychology, all that hopeful one-sidedness, that hopeful attempt. They are not yet on the other side, but this movement leads very suddenly into the static world; I don't know when that will occur but it will surely come, because after a *Puer Aeternus* phase, the static principle always comes. We can't tell how it will develop because it will be a very great thing and it might take a long time. Now the question is of course how far that *Puer Aeternus* archetype reaches. We could call it the archetype of the son versus the father. The psychology of the *Puer Aeternus* is exclusively masculine, it is a man's world. The woman's world is non-existent because woman as mother, as virgin, or as prostitute is all seen from a man's point of view.[9] In a woman's world there would be a woman, but in a man's world there is only a function, woman as a function. Does that give you the idea? I cannot go into it further now.

Mr. Baumann: I want to ask a question about the former thing we talked about, the static against the dynamic, the turmoil. Bertrand Russell writes in his book *Mysticism and Logic* that the characteristic of mysticism is the absence of protest against, or the disbelief in, the ultimate division of two hostile camps—for instance, good and evil—but that with the sense of unity is associated a feeling of infinite peace which produces, as feelings do in dreams, the whole body of mystic doctrine.[10] Now I would like to know whether that only came out because they were tortured by the turmoil, or whether this static principle is a kind of peace which is already existent in man before he started to fight—a kind of *a priori* principle—to reach this harmonious flow.

Prof. Jung: Well, the two things are always there, but in certain times of history, for a certain purpose the static principle prevails, and at other times movement prevails. For instance, let us assume you live in a time when the static principle is ruling. There you will find mystics, and the mystics themselves are then the ones who are suppressed by

---

[9] Toni Wolff, analyst and member of the seminar, was to develop a typology of women in the familiar form of opposites: Hetaira, Mother; Amazon, Medial Woman. See *Structural Forms of the Feminine Psyche* (Zurich, 1956).

[10] Bertrand Russell, *Mysticism and Logic and Other Essays* (London, 1918). Russell was much keener on logic than on anything most people would call mysticism.

the static principle, and they begin to boil, to move—with no clear ideas, but they move, they are alive. It is typical for the mystics that they *live*; their most characteristic quality is the intensity of their lives— life counts with them. They are a reaction against the static principle. But in a time when mysticism is really living, as it is now, movement prevails. We live in such a period and we are looking for a static system in which to find peace. And we are going to create one, for after a time of turmoil we are longing for rest, for sleep, even for a kind of suffo- cation after that eternal boiling and vibrating. You see, it is always a question of one-sidedness. When the static principle goes too far there will be an uprush of dynamic movement, or if you have the contrary, then that will create its compensation. That is the mechanism in this chapter: it is like a piece of life. Nietzsche himself is in the process of seeing life and suddenly it throws him out. He is suddenly standing looking at a solid static thing and he looks at it from the outside. He creates an entirely different picture, instead of the up-and-down, the to-and-fro, instead of the turmoil of the battlefield, he climbs a stair in a building. Instead of the tarantula's den it is a temple, and of course the temple he envisages is the Christian church, obviously a Gothic ca- thedral—and that is the nest of the tarantula. Now, we have not inter- preted this fully; we are now only so far as to determine that that build- ing is a static, petrified system of ideas. It is petrified spirit.

Mrs. Siggs: There seems to be a development, judging from the pic- tures he chooses—first the cave or den, then the antique temple, and now the cathedral.

Prof. Jung: Well, here it is already the Gothic cathedral, but he has not amplified the picture enough, so we had better go on and see what comes next.

> Verily, he who here towered aloft his thoughts in stone [This is petrification of the spirit.] knew as well as the wisest ones about the secret of life!

The secret of life here is that life surpasses itself and comes to the static condition. But of course one could say, if life starts in a static condition, the secret of life would be the turmoil.

> That there is struggle and inequality even in beauty, and war for power and supremacy: that doth he here teach us the plainest parable.
> How divinely do vault and arch here contrast in the struggle: how with light and shade they strive against each other, the di- vinely striving ones.—

This is a clear description of the Gothic cathedral where you really feel that life itself has become congealed—one could say it was congealed life. It is often compared to a wood or to the branches of a tree; all sorts of animals run up and down those columns and spires. It is wood that has become stone, or spirit that has become incorruptible matter, and the architecture symbolizes the struggle from which it arose. One sees the struggle itself represented in Norman art, in those manifold representations of the fight between man and monsters, particularly. In the Gothic cathedral this conflict is fully developed and fully represented in the enormous height and depth, in the light and the shadow, and in the extraordinary complication of all those architectural forms melting into each other, or fighting one another. It is also expressed in the peculiar arches built outside the church to support the walls inside; it gives one the idea of tremendous tension, of a thing that is almost bursting. When you look, for instance, in Notre Dame in Paris, at the tension of the walls inside supported by the arches, you realize how daring the whole enterprise was—to catch so much spirit in matter— and what they had to do in order to secure it. There is no such thing in the Norman cathedrals; they are really made of stone, while in the Gothic cathedrals one begins to doubt the weight of the stone. And a little later one sees the same peculiarity in sculpture. In the *cinquecento* sculpture of Michelangelo and the later men, they seemed to deny the immobility of the stone; up to that time, stone had been practically immovable, even Greek sculpture, but with Michelangelo, the stone began to move with a surplus of life which is hardly believable. It seems as if it either were not stone or as if something wrong had happened. There is too much life, the stone seems to walk away. It begins to move till the whole thing falls asunder. You see, that is what Nietzsche is describing here. He calls them the divinely striving ones that are no longer striving; they have congealed, they have come to rest.

Thus, steadfast and beautiful, let us also be enemies, my friends! Divinely will we strive against one another!

And they are static, like arches that support something. Of course they stand against each other, fight each other as it were, but they are static, no movement; a static tension is expressed. Now, such a view or such a standpoint is only possible when a man is so much in the throes of his conflict that he is simply squeezed out of it. Then he begins to laugh, as it were, and say, "What is it all about? I must have been crazy, I was too much in the conflict." You see, that will start, for instance, with the recognition that what you call good is very bad for other people, or what they call good is very bad for you. So you come to the conclusion that they are human beings too and they must have their point of view as you have yours. And then you are already out of it, already static, already *au dessus de la mêlée*.[11] Of course you can take such a standpoint illegitimately before you have gone through the turmoil, just in order to avoid the conflict; people sometimes like to play that stunt, but that has no merit and they are tempted all the time to climb down into the turmoil. But if you have gone through the turmoil, if you cannot stand you any more, if the unconscious itself spits you out, then life itself spits you out as old Jonah was spit out by the whale; and then it is legitimate that you contentedly sit on the top of life, having a look at it. Then you can congeal the pairs of opposites in a beautiful static structure. That is the real summit which Nietzsche reaches in this chapter.

> Alas! There hath the tarantula bit me myself, mine old enemy! Divinely steadfast and beautiful, it hath bit me on the finger.

He was fighting the tarantulas who were preaching death, standstill, rigidity, authority, and now the tarantula has got *him*. He is now poisoned, he himself has become the tarantula as a matter of fact.

> "Punishment must there be, and justice"—so thinketh it: "not gratuitously shall he here sing songs in honour of enmity!"

That is what the tarantula in him says,

> Yea, it hath revenged itself! And alas, now will it make my soul also dizzy with revenge.
> That I may *not* turn dizzy, however, bind me fast, my friends, to this pillar.

The poison of the tarantula is supposed to make people dizzy and to cause madness, you remember; it is not true but that is the legend. And Nietzsche, being no zoologist, believed that, so the giddiness is an attack of madness; the recognition of the other side meant a stroke of madness to him. This is only my conjecture, mind you, but we will keep this in mind as a sort of hypothesis. After this we would really expect symptoms of *ekstasis*, an invasion of the unconscious, because that whole world which he could judge and tread underfoot now takes its revenge upon him. All the tarantulas in the world will get at him, and the tarantula is the sympathetic nervous system. That means the un-

---

[11] *Au dessus de la mêlée*: above the fray.

conscious; the unconscious will get at him, so we can expect some peculiar phenomena.

Mrs. Crowley: Is there not a connection between it and the buffoon in the beginning?

Prof. Jung: It would be a parallel; the buffoon is a sort of danger. It is his madness that overtook him. Of course it is only madness inasmuch as it cannot be integrated or understood, but in the first onslaught it may cause madness—it may be just too much. You see, when you have fought against a thing your whole life, when you have been convinced that a thing is all wrong and that you are quite right, then that same thing catches you. That very same thing gets into your system, and then you may explode. Perhaps you cannot cope with it and then it gets you naturally. Now, this would be the danger if it were Nietzsche who was talking like that, but it is not exactly Nietzsche. He is identical with that figure of Zarathustra, so he is in a sort of inflation all the time, not quite in control of himself; and then of course he can easily overtake himself as he has already overtaken himself through one-sidedness. You know, his preaching has all been on the side of life, all on the side of the reversal of values, the destruction of old things, having entirely new views, reviling everybody who doesn't share life. Then suddenly that whole thing turns against him. Of course it is just the sting of the tarantula which is not supposed to be mortal; it is simply disagreeable and causes a sort of madness. So he is somewhat protected against it. He realizes the danger that he might turn giddy and begin to rave, and in order that he should not, he says,

Rather will I be a pillar-saint than a whirl of vengeance.

A pillar of the church, mind you, of the cathedral.

Verily, no cyclone or whirlwind is Zarathustra: . . .

What did we read at the end of the last chapter? "Verily, a strong wind is Zarathustra."

and if he be a dancer, he is not at all a tarantula-dancer!

No, he won't join in *that*!

LECTURE V

2 June 1937

Prof. Jung:

Here are two questions. Miss Hannah says, "I see theoretically, as Nietzsche did not accept the inferior man in himself, that this is projected and shows itself—for instance, in the fear of vengeance which occurs constantly in the tarantula chapter. But I find this extremely difficult to grasp or really understand. Would you be willing to say some more about it? Or, to put it differently, the words *vengeance* and *revenge* give me a queer feeling throughout the chapter, as if I had not really understood why there is such an insistence on this note?"

Well, it is quite obvious that the very idea of the tarantula people, as Nietzsche puts it, is a projection, one of the many aspects of the projection of the inferior man. All the chapters in which he reviles certain classes of people contain the projection of the inferior man in himself; they show very clearly that he is not capable of seeing his own shadow, because what he reviles in people is a projection of his own shadow, his own inferiority. That is the usual experience: when we criticize or revile other people it is always because we are projecting something on them. It is perfectly true that you cannot make such a projection if there is not a hook on which to hang it. Inasmuch as people have a shadow, they are always full of hooks—you always have a chance to say something unkind about them. But the fact that you get excited about certain traits or qualities proves that you yourself have them, or why should they sting you? There are certain categories of things which get your goat somehow, and then that is *your* case—that is what irritates you. So Nietzsche rejects his inferior sides in those other people; he quarrels with them and reviles them. And the tarantula is of course such an aspect of the shadow in himself.

You see, when you behave like that with your shadow, when you project it and leave it always to other people, then, since it is a definite personality and all the more so when you repress it or don't recognize it, it becomes a sort of Siamese twin bound to you by a system of communicating tubes. You are in connection with it, yet it always appears as if it were in other people. But that thing wants to be with you, to be recognized, to live your life with you. It is just like a brother or anybody else who likes to be with you; and when you simply won't allow it, naturally that personality develops resistances against you. It is irritated and becomes venomous. And every time you revile that fellow, you revile yourself, and then naturally something reacts in you as if it were your enemy. Something always reacts in you against the object of your hatred. If you despise somebody, for instance, or are hostile and attack somebody, you identify with it and develop a resentment naturally, and that is the feeling of revenge. That shadow you have reviled tries to get at you—it comes back with a vengeance. Then it looks as if you had that feeling against all those who have that shadow, but as a matter of fact it is your own shadow which has the feeling of revenge, and at any time it will come back at you. You will see how the shadow comes back at Nietzsche with a vengeance: that is the tragedy of *Zarathustra*.

Then there is a question by Mr. Allemann, "You said in the last seminar that dynamic periods were succeeded by static systems and vice versa. Is it not true that even a static period or system is really efficient only as long as the dynamism of the preceding period is still living—and that, as soon as it is entirely spent, as soon as all the energy is lacking, only the 'ruins of the temple' are remaining?

"At this point of the development, I should say that even the blackest and most fanatic tarantula would be unable to restore real life to the temple, though it would certainly succeed in making things very disagreeable and even dangerous for the unlucky beings who were still remaining in the temple.

"Is it not true that a religious system is really efficient as long as the dynamism of its outburst is still in it, even if its chaotic and orgiastic trend is slowly replaced by a static system of dogmas, and is not such a religious system at the height of its efficiency and universal acceptability, when the dynamic experience is still strong enough to hold the imagination and feeling, and the dogmatic system already subtle enough to catch the thinking and keep it working?

"As an example of a religious system at this moment of its development, I think of a few gnostic systems with their ecstatic experience on the one side and their subtle cosmogonic and eschatological speculation and terminology on the other."

I entirely agree, it is quite impossible for a static system to live if there is no *dynamis* in it. The term *reality* or *real* (derived from *res*, "thing") of course doesn't contain the idea of dynamism, but the German word *Wirklichkeit* does contain it. Inasmuch as such a static form of religion is efficient, it is *efficiens*, it is working, it is *wirklich*. So it needs the dynamism inside, and as soon as that dies down, the efficiency of the static system vanishes, crumbles away. We can observe that in our days. A static system can only come into existence, then, when there has been a dynamic outburst; only inasmuch as there is a dynamic outburst can a static system exist at all. But when a dynamic outburst loses its efficiency, it is impossible to get it back, because it has left the temple and appears now as the tarantula. And to fill the temples with tarantulas, as you say, would make the situation too uncomfortable for the people who remain inside; they can't worship in a box full of tarantulas. You know, that is proverbial: if you put a lot of spiders together in one box they will devour each other.

So a schismatic movement in a church is already the beginning of the tarantula phenomenon. The spiders then begin to show their real character. If that whole crowd, the four hundred denominations of the Protestant church, were brought back into the Catholic church, they would kill each other. That box has exploded and we have now irreconcilable units out in the world which cannot be brought back again. As Christ said, you cannot put new wine into old skins. But people always think they can—well, they don't speak of new wine, that is too dangerous, they just try to revive the old skins. For instance, there was a movement in the Protestant church to bring back the old liturgies, but those are of course old skins, and whatever there is of new wine simply doesn't go into them. As soon as there is a schism, it means really the end. You see, a static system must be totalitarian, as the church was till about 1200; the original outburst really worked and filled the whole reach of the church, and the church spread as long as that outburst kept on working. Then there was a moment of static immobility, and the schism began and has kept on working ever since. It is working in our days in the German reaction; that is the continuation of the German Reformation. It is now taking a new breath as it were, working now in the same schismatic way that it worked four hundred years ago. And what is happening in Spain is all a part of it; anarchism, communism, socialism are really religious movements, only with an *a* or an *anti*—the negation is the same—and there it is directly against the Catholic church. In Russia also it is exactly the same. Now I don't quite understand why you thought of the Gnostic systems as suitable examples; they never really developed into churches, into static systems.

Mr. Allemann: Yes, but they were religious systems and they had both sides, a very developed eschatology, very subtle terms, and on the other hand the ecstatic movement, the *dynamis*.

Prof. Jung: Absolutely, but according to my mind they came to a standstill before they really developed into a static building. By a static system I understand not only the teaching, but also the institution, and they never developed institutions. Therefore there was a really extraordinary variation in the Gnostic systems, and they are ill-defined; it is very difficult to make out which is which. But in the Catholic church it is quite different; there it worked out into dogma and ritual, into liturgies and ceremonies and buildings, and into definite symbolism, like the Greek orthodox church. Of course if the Gnostic systems had had a fair chance, they probably would have widened out into sorts of churches. For instance, Manichaeism was really a Gnostic syncretistic system, and that grew into a static system. It was a church.

Mrs. Sigg: It seems to me that Nietzsche's difficulty is that in a Christian church, the priest asks that Jehovah shall be worshipped, and even Jehovah has a tarantula quality because he is revengeful.

Prof. Jung: But that is Protestantism. Protestants are already revengeful in their conception of God, while in the Catholic church that is not the case. There God has definitely forgotten to sting, *zu stechen*.

Mrs. Sigg: But Protestantism is the church as well as Catholicism.

Prof. Jung: The Protestant conception is far more poisonous.

Mrs. Sigg: Yes, I think so too, and I think Nietzsche wants to reform this poison.

Prof. Jung: Oh yes. Of course his idea of Christianity is entirely Protestant; he had no real knowledge of the Catholic church and was not interested in it. To him it was always that foolish question of his age, whether God existed or not. You see, that is a terribly barbarous idea; one never should ask such a foolish question because the answer can never be proved. His reaction was entirely against his German Protestantism which surely contains a dogmatic conception. You can speak of a Protestant dogma, but it is not the strict and severe dogma of the Catholic church. Well now, we will continue our text. We had finished the last chapter and are coming now to "The Famous Wise Ones." By what transition does he arrive at the wise ones after the tarantulas?

Mrs. Crowley: It occurred to me that in the last chapter by the process of *enantiodromia* he stressed the conflict between the opposites. At the end of the chapter, he arrived at the image of the pillar saint, one who had in some way solved the problem by identifying with the self. Now, from that distant perspective, he looks back and down upon those socalled "wise ones," the representatives of ego-conscious reality, who—

from the angle of the saint bound to the pillar—look like inferior fauna struggling in the mud, as if he were denying his former intellectual values.

Prof. Jung: Yes, there is something in that. Has anybody else an idea about it?

Dr. James: They are "stiff-necked and artful, like the ass"; he is looking at these wise men and of course he despises them.

Prof. Jung: Yes, but that doesn't explain how he comes to the idea of the wise ones after the tarantulas.

Miss Hannah: Is it not sheer green-eyed jealousy of the people who hold the professional chairs and get the money, while he has to go out into the wilderness?

Prof. Jung: Well, in this chapter there is surely a definite resentment on account of that, but what about the tarantulas?

Miss Hannah: The tarantula has bitten him, therefore he himself represents the revenge to a certain extent now, instead of seeing it entirely outside him.

Prof. Jung: You are right. You see, the dramatic picture in the chapter before is that he himself got bitten by the tarantulas. First he reviles all those tarantula people, and then suddenly the tarantulas bite him, so the poison gets into him and there is danger that he might turn giddy. Therefore he says to bind him fast to that pillar, so that he won't go mad—dancing the tarantula dance. But the poison is in him. Now, the tarantula represents one of the many aspects of the inferior man, and if the inferior man bites him, pours his shadow into his face, it has surely gotten at him and then *he* becomes the shadow. He is filled with that poison so we may expect that he will have a new resentment to spit out, and he arrives now at the wise ones who represent the useful educators of the people—of course, according to his idea, the professors at universities or any other well-meaning and meritful leaders of the people. He himself now plays the role of the tarantula: he becomes poisonous, and his *ressentiment* is manifest even against people to whom he cannot deny a certain amount of merit.

> The people have ye served and the people's superstition—*not* the truth!—all ye famous wise ones! And just on that account did they pay you reverence.

Here you get the idea. He comes out with the somewhat venomous statement that these wise ones are reverenced only because they say what people expect of them. They don't speak the truth.

And on that account also did they tolerate your unbelief, because it was a pleasantry and a by-path for the people. Thus doth the master give free scope to his slaves, and even enjoyeth their presumptuousness.

But he who is hated by the people, as the wolf by the dogs—is the free spirit, the enemy of fetters, the non-adorer, the dweller in the woods.

Now, here he uses a number of metaphors which need some explanation. Why does he use the figures of the wolf and the dogs and the dweller in the woods as a particularly good demonstration of the free spirit?

Miss Wolff: Nietzsche apparently assumes that those wise men are really atheists; they only talk like that to make an impression on people. They still get all the benefits from living collectively, whereas he is really lonely because he does not believe in God.

Prof. Jung: But why just the wolf?

Miss Wolff: Nietzsche's ideas are dangerous, therefore collective man hates him as the dogs hate the wolf.

Prof. Jung: Yes, and now why the dweller in the woods?

Miss Wolff: Perhaps Nietzsche refers here to that chapter at the very beginning where he met the hermit.

Prof. Jung: And do you remember what we said about that dweller in the woods?

Mrs. Crowley: That he represents the past.

Prof. Jung: He represents what had retired into the unconscious; that means whatever is left over in the world, left over and not integrated in the actually existing philosophic and religious viewpoint. Now we have a lead for the interpretation of that dweller in the wood: the hermit is the tarantula. You see, when a static system begins to get feeble, a schismatic movement will ensue. Then a part of the people who were organized in the church turn against it and become tarantulas; they become poisonous. And they go out of the church into the wilderness, as it were, into the uncultivated land. They disappear into the woods. The woods are always a symbol for the unconscious, so they disappear into the unconscious where everything which is not integrated is to be found, everything which is no longer included and living within the static system. Such people or such thoughts are always considered by the people inside the system to be particularly poisonous, dangerous tarantulas. Of course Nietzsche, who is outside the system, calls the people "tarantulas" who are inside, but you must not forget that the ones inside call the one outside "the wolf." But he calls those who are inside the wolves also, because they injure each other; they are hostile to each other. So the free spirit is the wolf, the non-adorer, the dweller in the woods; and Nietzsche identifies with that so-called "free spirit," the spirit which is not organized, which is not in a static system. We can designate it quite definitely as a non-Christian spirit.

> To hunt him out of his lair—that was always called "sense of right" by the people: on him do they still hound their sharpest-toothed dogs.
> "For there the truth is, where the people are! Woe, woe to the seeking ones!"—thus hath it echoed through all time.

This is perfectly understandable. That a thing is true when most of the people believe it, is a certain standpoint. And it is a fact; as long as most people believe it, you can consider it as true. You see, if you consider it a lie you are in the hole. That is your funeral, not theirs, so you had better consider such things true because they work. You can say it is stupid and shouldn't be, but that is a sort of empty talk. It means nothing because you have absolutely no possibility of undoing the apparent error. If everybody shares that error, it is called a truth for the time being. Of course you may think differently, but then you must be careful not to say so openly if you don't want to injure yourself—and I don't see any particular point in injuring oneself on principle. One has to be careful because life wants to be lived, and that is more reasonable than fighting over a thing about which you yourself don't know exactly what to believe. Naturally for anybody with an independent mind it is most trying to see how flimsy what is generally held to be a truth may be, since one can easily see that in ten years, or even less, it will no longer be a truth. Today it is a truth, tomorrow it is no longer, but after tomorrow it will again be a truth. Of course a philosophically minded person will always ask what is truth after all. You see, things that were true two thousand years ago are not true now, but after two thousand years they will be true again.

> Your people would ye justify in their reverence: that called ye "Will to Truth," ye famous wise ones!

That is also quite obvious.

> And your heart hath always said to itself: "From the people have I come: from thence came to me also the voice of God."

Now this is a bit more serious—this is a terrifying truth really. We have all come from the people—we are the people—and if the majority say; "I am the voice of God," well then, this is a truth because it works. The majority of the people establish it, and the greater part of myself is collective, made of entirely collective stuff. The molecules of my body are chemically in no way different from the molecules of anybody else. The making of my mind is absolutely the same as everybody else's. There is only a peculiar variation of the composition, the element in myself that accounts for my so-called individuality. So to begin with, we are 99.99999 percent collective, and just a bit of unaccountable something is individual. But that is the thumbling which is the maker of things, or the grain of mustard that becomes the whole kingdom of heaven. This is a funny fact but it is so. You see, there is a definite valid standpoint that *vox populi est vox Dei*, "that the voice of the people is the voice of God." For instance, if you are convinced that humanity is a manifestation of the divine will, you must assume that the voice of humanity is a manifestation of the divine voice, and so you must own that the *consensus gentium*, the consent of the majority of human beings, establishes the truth. And it is really so: a truth is a truth as long as it works. We have no other criterion except in cases where we can experiment, but they are very few. We cannot experiment with history or geology or astronomy for example. There are few natural sciences in which we can experiment. So this standpoint that the people's voice is the voice of God, a superior overwhelming voice, is a very important psychological truth which has to be taken into consideration in every case.

You see, Nietzsche preaches that truth, but of course in an unconscious sense. He blames them for having such a view, but it would be a redeeming truth to himself if he could only accept it. For he is just the one who says that the voice of the people is nonsense, that there is only one truth and that an individual truth. He believes that his truth is the only truth. But how can anyone say his truth is the only one? Yet, that is the individualistic point of view, which leads people far afield and very often quite astray. Of course it is necessary that a person should have his own individual point of view, but he should know that he is then in terrible conflict with the *vox populi* in himself and that is what we always forget. We must never forget that our individual conviction is a sort of Promethean sin, a violence against the laws of nature that we are all fishes in one shoal and in one river; and if we are not, it is a presumption, a rebellion. And that conflict is in ourselves. But the individual thinks that the conflict is by no means in himself, and whatever individual feeling he has on account of an individual conception, he projects into others: they are against me because I have such a conception—entirely forgetting that he is against himself. If ever you discover an individual truth, you will find that you are in a conflict about it. You are contradicted by yourself and at every turn you meet an obstacle which you think other people have put in your way. Inasmuch as you make individual opinions public naturally you will meet obstacles, and then you take it as a truth that you are persecuted; you develop a sort of paranoia. Therefore whoever discovers an individual truth should discover at the same time that he is the first enemy of himself, that *he* is the one who has the strongest objection to his truth, and he should be careful not to project it or he will develop a paranoia. Now Nietzsche continues,

> Stiff-necked and artful, like the ass, have ye always been, as the advocates of the people.
> And many a powerful one who wanted to run well with the people, hath harnessed in front of his horses—a donkey, a famous wise man.

He refers here to a famous example in the history of philosophy. Hegel was the Prussian state philosopher, considered to be a famous wise one, and of course Nietzsche was well acquainted with his philosophy. Hegel was a philosopher in a definite political system; one always finds such a fellow in every political system—that is, the ass harnessed by the powers of the earth to the political cart.[1] There have been more or less modest attempts to make Nietzsche into such an ass in front of a political cart, but I should say he was an unreliable ass, not of pure blood. He would be a mule and full of tricks.

> And now, ye famous wise ones, I would have you finally throw off entirely the skin of the lion!
> The skin of the beast of prey, the speckled skin, and the dishevelled locks of the investigator, the searcher, and the conqueror!
> Ah! for me to learn to believe in your "conscientiousness," ye would first have to break your venerating will.

[1] Hegel (1770-1831), never a favorite of either Jung or Nietzsche, viewed the rational course of history as culminating in the Prussian state. See esp. *The Philosophy of History* (orig. 1837; English trans. 1860).

Well, his criticism is justified. You know, there is a German proverb: *Wess' Brot ich ess, Dess' Lied ich sing*, meaning, "If I eat the bread of some-body, I shall sing his song." Many thinkers have praised certain politi-cal conditions because they received their bread from that system; their intellectual conscientiousness was a bit suspect. Nietzsche, of course, could not be accused of such an impurity, yet he simply doesn't see that he also is manipulated by the forces of his time. Creative peo-ple often have that difficulty: they think they are the makers of them-selves, without seeing at all how they are manipulated by the necessities of the time. Like all the others, they are the megaphones or the micro-phones of powers in human society which are not realized. You see, that is most difficult: I don't know whether it is at all possible to realize the underlying powers in an actual moment of history. You remember that story of the knight who was caught by his enemies and put down into a dark dungeon, where he was kept year after year until finally he got impatient and, banging his fist upon the table, he said, "Now when are these damned Middle Ages coming to an end!" You see, he got sick of the medieval style—he was the only one who realized that he was liv-ing in the Middle Ages. That is like the Pueblo Indians who are always talking about Americans but don't know that they are living in Amer-ica. Or like the story of Columbus landing on his island: The inhabit-ants came to the sea to greet him, and he asked, "Are you the natives?" And they replied, "Yes, and are you Columbus?" He said, "Yes," and they said, "Oh well then, there is nothing to be done anymore: Amer-ica is discovered!"

Well now, Nietzsche was intelligent enough to see that certain pro-fessors were preaching the truth of a certain political system, not by virtue of their intellectual integrity, but moved by suggestions and all sorts of unconscious reasons which they had not always realized; they were probably perfectly honest people only not conscious enough to realize their ulterior motives. Some were perhaps unclean devils who consciously said things in order to please the master, or whoever was the boss on top of them, but we can give them the credit that they were mostly unconscious, as Nietzsche himself was unconscious of his lead-ing principle or whoever his boss might be. He spoke out of the spirit of his time and he didn't see it at all. One often clearly feels that he was speaking out of German Protestantism, for instance, or out of the Vic-torian age, or out of the age of materialism, but he knew it as little as the people who fought in it knew that they were fighting the famous Thirty Years War; they were living in the here and now, as we do. The more primitive civilizations felt that they were living in eternity, that they always had lived in that way and would live in that way forever. And so it was in other times of history: the time never knew itself. You see, it was just that amount of intelligence and superior criticism which helped Nietzsche to see that certain people were moved by their surroundings and unconsciously represented the voice of the people. But he assumed that he himself did not, and there he was entirely mistaken; he voiced the people perhaps more than all the others. They only voiced a very thin surface, a layer that was thinning out every day, while he voiced the future which was already there under the surface. He voiced something much deeper and more concealed than the other fellows represented, yet he was moved by unconscious motives as much and even more than the others.

> Conscientious—so call I him who goeth into God-forsaken wilderness, and hath broken his venerating heart.

So it appeared to him and of course it was also true in his life. In his time it made sense, and anybody who had reached the realization that he had reached really had to choose between the Godforsaken wilderness and a chair at the university. Conscientious as he was, he chose the wilderness. But choosing the wilderness does not always mean conscientiousness. As soon as it becomes a fashion to go to the wilderness, it is no longer conscientiousness that prompts you to go there. You can credit the first hermit that went into the desert with an extraordinary conscientiousness, but think of the tens of thousands that went after him! It was just the fashion; it became a most respectable vocation to be a hermit. They went to the desert because that was the thing one did. If it had been the fashion to go to Aix-les-Bains they would have gone there because they were respectable people.

> In the yellow sands and burnt by the sun, he doubtless peereth thirstily at the isles rich in fountains, where life reposeth under shady trees.

Now here one really can ask why in hell he should go out into the desert to be burnt by the sun and tortured by thirst, instead of living in a community of Christian beings. Well, one could ask the first Christian dwellers in the desert the same question: "Why are you going to the desert? Are you preaching to the sand and to the jackals? Is it better that you should be fed by the pious peasants in the vicinity instead of earning your own living?" I told you that story of St. Anthony when he went to the desert. He thought he was listening to the voice of the devil, but it was the voice of reason: thy devil said most reasonable things to those hermits. And here again we can ask, "Is it reasonable? Why must he torture himself?" It might be very reasonable if he lived among other people and opened their eyes. You see, there is no authority really in the Bible for a monastic life in the desert or in monasteries; it is really of another origin, before the time of Christianity. The Libyan desert and the Sinai peninsula and the region of the Dead Sea were all cultivated by such funny people living in caves and apparently doing nothing. What prompted them?

Miss Hannah: You can only get the values of the unconscious by going right into it.

Prof. Jung: But did they really seek revelation?

Miss Hannah: Did they not seek the voice of God more or less—which they could not hear for the noise of the cities?

Prof. Jung: That is true, but there is another reason.

Mr. Allemann: They wanted to get out of the way of temptation.

Prof. Jung: Yes, and that is also the reason given by the people themselves. They tried to avoid the temptations of the great cities, which must have been great. There are excellent stories about the monks of Egypt in a Coptic text called *The Paradise* of Palladius.[2] For instance, the story about the monk who had lived in the desert for twenty years and had attained absolute certainty of belief, and then he remembered having heard that an old friend had become bishop of Alexandria; and since he was advanced in age and perfectly fortified against all devilish temptations, he made up his mind to go to visit him. So he packed his bag and travelled to Alexandria, but when he arrived at the suburbs, he came to an inn, and it smelled so lovely of wine and garlic and oil that he thought, "Oh, just a sip." But he never came out of that inn: they discovered him in the depths of slime; he forgot all about his twenty years in the desert and his saintliness, and out came the pig as fresh as on the first day. That story was quoted in order to show how great was the power of the devil. You see, people might hold to their convictions against the obvious beauties of the world, but when it smelt of oil and garlic and onions and wine, you know, they were just gone. So they needed the desert as a sort of protection. Whenever people discovered something which was too much in contradiction with their surrounding conditions, they either isolated themselves, created a sort of

---

[2] Palladius, Bishop of Hellenopolis and of Aspona (d. c. 430), a devoted adherent of the controversial St. Chrysostom, wrote an account of a number of Christian ascetics and monastics who lived between A.D. 250 and 400. It has been translated by W. K. Lowther Clarke as *The Lausiac History of Palladius* (New York, 1918), and by A. Wallis-Budge as *The Paradise of Palladius.*

fence around themselves, or they left the country and their relations in order not to be tempted to another point of view. Of course they would not be tempted to such an extent if they only knew that the worst temptation was in themselves—they were their own worst temptors. When they arrived in the desert they could not get drunk, because there was nothing to drink except some rather bad water, and they could not overfeed because there was nothing much to feed on—food was scarce. But they had carried their conscientious objector with them. He was right there, and who was that?

Miss Hannah: The devil.

Prof. Jung: Of course. They were tempted by devils like anything. As I said, nobody is so gorgeously tempted as the saint; the dreams of saints are simply amazing, the performances that were shown them by the devils. Read *La Tentation de St. Antoine* by Flaubert; there you get it.[3] I could not compete with them. No patient of mine ever had such dreams. But then, I never had a saint. So Nietzsche has to remove himself on account of temptation, and the temptation only reaches him because the temptor is already in himself: he has the devil already with him. When he went to the Engadine or any other lonely place it was of course for the same purpose, to escape the temptations of the world that reached him through his own devil, whom he did not see enough.

Now, here is a metaphor, "In the yellow sands and burnt by the sun," which I mention because it is a symbol that occasionally occurs in dreams; people sometimes dream that they appear with their face badly burnt by the sun, which is obviously what Nietzsche refers to here. It is not frequent, and when I first encountered it, it vexed me very much. Then I found out that the symbol usually occurs when something that has been unconscious is exposed to consciousness, so that the light of consciousness, which is the sun of the day, burns it. When there has been too much exposure to the sun of consciousness, that dream symbol turns up. It is apt to happen when something hitherto unconscious wants to leap out into the open just as it had been concealed before in the darkness. But it should be kept in the shadow. If you allow it to manifest, if you show it to everybody, then you dream of the burnt face, so badly burnt sometimes that there are open wounds. And this symbol of the sunburn applies to Nietzsche's case because he discovered a new individual truth and exposed it; he is in a situation where he might have such a dream. We do not know what he did but at all events in his metaphorical language that image comes up.

[3] For *The Temptation of St. Anthony*, see above, 3 June 1936, n. 2.

The metaphors in our speech are made of what our dreams are made of: an apt speech metaphor may take the place of a dream. For instance, if you use a particular metaphor in a speech the evening before, you won't dream it, you have anticipated it; you can save yourself many dreams if you give expression to the unconscious in other ways. If you anticipate them by active imagination, you do not need to dream them. Now he continues,

> But his thirst doth not persuade him to become like those comfortable ones: for where there are oases, there are also idols.

The idea is quite near to him: why should one live in the desert if there are nice oases near by where one would have sufficient food and shade and water? And here we hear the reason: namely, in the oases there are always idols. The prevailing ideas are the idols to Nietzsche, and they are highly tempting and might make him deviate from his individual truth. You see, when you come out with an individual truth against the whole world, you feel how small it is, how feeble, and how easily wiped out by collectivity, while whoever follows the style and ideas of collectivity always speaks with ten thousand voices.

> Hungry, fierce, lonesome, God-foresaken: so doth lion-will wish itself.
> Free from the happiness of slaves, redeemed from Deities and adorations, fearless and fear-inspiring, grand and lonesome: so is the will of the conscientious.

Here we see the identification with the so-called free spirit; it is quite clearly an inflation that removes him from ordinary mankind.

> In the wilderness have ever dwelt the conscientious, the free spirits, as lords of the wilderness; but in the cities dwell the well-foddered, famous wise ones—the draught-beasts.

Well, we may add, not only they but also those children of the free spirit who can resist temptation, who have dealt with their own devil so that it doesn't tempt them any longer. As soon as the hermit has overcome the tempter within himself he can live among other people or idols—they don't injure him; even if he thinks the idols are fairly interesting, they won't poison him. But if one is still so feeble and collective that one cannot resist such impressions, without losing one's individual idea, of course one cannot stand life in a community.

Mr. Baumann: This problem of the idols in the oases was very important for Islam. The whole Arabic population was divided up into tribes who lived in and around the different oases, each tribe worshipping a special idol. This contributed a good deal to the many terrible fights between the tribes. To overcome their belief in the omnipotence of their own idols was a major problem to Mohammed in establishing his religion, which stopped the fighting and made that impressive unity of Islamic countries.

Prof. Jung: I don't know whether Nietzsche was aware of that particular piece of Mohammedan history. It is an interesting fact that Nietzsche was not particularly well read on account of his eyes, so when he did read, it always made a tremendous impression on him. Therefore his taste is sometimes a bit queer: he admired things which were not particularly admirable simply because he did not know anything better.⁴ So I do not think that really influenced his style here; he might rather have gleaned such an idea from his knowledge of antiquity. You know, there were famous temples in the oases.

Mr. Alleman: The temple of Jupiter Ammon, for example.

Prof. Jung: Yes, in the great oases of Egypt there were many such temples, also in Northern Africa.

For, always, do they draw, as asses—the *people's* carts!

We must keep in mind that Nietzsche is merely unconscious of the fact that he is also drawing the people's carts, but the people of the future. That is the only difference.

Not that I on that account upbraid them: but serving ones do they remain, and harnessed ones, even though they glitter in golden harness.

And often have they been good servants and worthy of their hire. For thus saith virtue: "If thou must be a servant, seek him unto whom thy service is most useful!

The spirit and virtue of thy master shall advance by thou being his servant: thus wilt thou thyself advance with his spirit and virtue!"

And verily, ye famous wise ones, ye servants of the people! Ye yourselves have advanced with the people's spirit and virtue—and the people by you! To your honor do I say it!

But the people ye remain for me, even with your virtues, the

---

⁴ Not only was Nietzsche's sight dim but his eyes were the source of debilitating headaches. Yet in affirmative moods, he would claim that not reading kept his mind clear and his energy available for thinking and writing.

people with purblind eyes—the people who know not what *spirit* is!

His conception of the spirit is of course not so peculiar to us, but it is peculiar if you consider what the spirit meant in his time. He used the word *Geist*, of course, and the *Geist* was then absolutely dead. Naturally, if you said to a theologian then, that what he designated as spirit was dead, he would not have been pleased—and he would not be pleased today—but as a matter of fact this concept of spirit has become so obnoxious that Klages wrote a volume of about seven hundred pages about the spirit being the enemy of the soul.[5] Now in no other time do you find the idea that the spirit could be the enemy of the soul; on the contrary, these two concepts have always been confounded, the words used interchangeably. What Klages understands by *Geist* is the idea which developed at the end of the 19th century; namely, intellect in the form of books, science, philosophy, and so on. But never before had *Geist* meant that; it was merely a degeneration of the meaning of the word. To Nietzsche, *spirit* meant the original thing, an intensity, a volcanic outburst, while to the scientific or rationalistic spirit of the second half of the 19th century, it was an ice-cold space in which there were things, but it was no longer life. Naturally if you understand *Geist* in this way, it is the deadliest enemy of the soul you could think of. Now here we see his conception,

> Spirit is life which itself cutteth into life: by its own torture doth it increase its own knowledge,—did ye know that before?

You see, that is his discovery. He was born and lived in an age when that death of the spirit became obvious, when the word *Geist* meant only mind, but he experienced spirit as the most intense form of life. He felt it as such because he experienced the spirit that cutteth into itself. He had had a certain *Geist* of course, a certain philosophical conception which was the religious philosophical conception of his time, and then he discovered a new spirit before. Therefore, to him it was a phenomenon of life which apparently was against life. So he would explain the hermit that seeks the desert by such a phenomenon: namely, that that man discovered a new spirit, or a new spirit was made visible by a spirit which cut into his former convictions, into his former conceptions and ideals, and forced him to leave the human community. Nietzsche discovered by the onslaught of the spirit that spirit was life itself, and life which was against life, which could overcome life. And

[5] For Klages, see above, 23 May 1934, n. 5.

from that experience he rightly concluded that the spirit is a vital power; it is not an empty, dead, ice-cold space, but is warm intense life, even hot life, most dynamic. It can cut a man loose from his community. It can even create hermits. You see, this experience is very much like the religious experiences of the early Christians, like the experience of Paul on his way to Damascus for instance, when the spirit cut into *his* life, and like many other cases of such violent forms of conversion. To those people spirit was a life force that could upset one's whole life as one had conceived of it before. It was nothing mental, nor could it be formulated by mental means. It was a sort of autonomous, divine manifestation.

So Nietzsche's definition of the spirit being life which cutteth into life is absolutely true. That is the phenomenon. But of course nobody who has not had such an experience can follow it. Even now a German philosopher writing about *Geist* would mean what they meant in the 19th century, since a definite experience of the spirit has not taken place. If it had, the people to whom it had happened would not have written about philosophy. They would rather have preferred to write something in the style of Nietzsche: they would have written a confession. Philosophy is no longer a confession, but it used to be. For instance, one of the oldest fathers of the church, Justinus Martyrus who lived about 190, called the Christianity which flourished in the times of Augustus "our philosophy."[6] It would seem quite absurd now to call it a philosophy, but in those days philosophy and religion were pretty much the same thing, an experience of the spirit. Now, Nietzsche himself had what we would call a definite religious experience, but he called it the experience of Dionysos. It was the experience of the free spirit, the spirit that was against his hitherto prevailing attitude of mind, a spirit that changed his life, that exploded him completely. You see, he was formerly a teacher of Greek and Latin in the public schools, and then a professor at the University of Basel. He was just trying to be an ordinary citizen, just an ordinary professor, and suddenly that thing seized upon him and drove him out of his previous existence. From that moment on he depended for his living upon a very small pension which he drew from the university, and contributions from nice pious rich people in Basel. Otherwise he would not have been able to live. He was the hermit to whom the peasants brought food every week so that he should not starve. So he himself has an experience at first hand of how the spirit can cut into life.

[6] For Justin Martyr, see above, 20 Nov. 1935, n. 8.

And the spirit's happiness is this: to be anointed and consecrated with tears as a sacrificial victim,—did ye know that before?

Here he tells us exactly what has happened to him. He understands his
condition as an "anointed and consecrated condition"; he has entered
as it were an ecclesiastic order, or even a kingly office, and the sacred
oil by which he has been anointed were the tears which were wept for
him—not the tears wept over him, but the tears he wept about himself
because he was the sacrificial victim.

And the blindness of the blind one, and his seeking and grop-
ing, shall yet testify to the power of the sun into which he hath
gazed,—did ye know that before?

You see, he repeats in that epic manner "Did ye know that before?" because he realizes perfectly that his conception of the spirit is entirely
new, of course not new in history but new for his age. In the first centuries of Christianity there were plenty of confessions of this kind, or
at any other time when people were moved by the spirit, but when he
was born things seemed to be established and the spirit had become an
extinct volcano. Then suddenly there was that outburst in Nietzsche
and naturally he was impressed by it and thought he was the only one
to experience it, particularly since he was identical with it. That is the
danger when people have such a spiritual experience: they become
identical with it and think they are the chosen ones, the only ones,
great reformers of the world or something of the sort.

And with mountains shall the discerning one learn to *build*! It is
a small thing for the spirit to remove mountains,—did ye know
that before?

But it is not a small thing for Mr. Nietzsche to remove a mountain, that
is the trouble.

Ye know only the sparks of the spirit: but ye do not see the anvil
which it is, and the cruelty of its hammer!

Well, it can smash your whole existence and that is exactly what we
have not realized; we have forgotten entirely that the spirit is such a
power. We call it a neurosis perhaps and deny that it has any power,
because we can say of a neurosis that it should not be, it is wrong. That
is as if, when your house burns down, you should say that the fire
should not be, as if that made it less obnoxious. But when you have to
cure a neurosis you know what it means and you don't think so little of

it; when you know what is behind it, you think more of it. So his proc-
lamation of the spirit is quite right: nobody knows what the spirit is and
what a power it is. People think that two thousand years ago human
beings were barbarous and wandered into the desert because they
were damned fools. Or on Tuesday morning at nine o'clock they sent
Mrs. Smith and Mrs. Jones into the arena to be eaten by lions and
bears, but such things don't happen any longer. That is our mistake.
They may come up at any time again; of course it may not be an arena.
It might be a machine gun or a knife or poison gas—we have plenty of
means to do away with Mrs. Smith and Mrs. Jones. We prefer other explanations, we rationalize it, but in reality it is the same thing again.
That is probably the reason why we have to learn the power of the
spirit again, of the spirit that is against us.

> Verily, ye know not the spirit's pride! But still less could ye en-
> dure the spirit's humility, should it ever want to speak!

What he means by the spirit's humility is pretty cryptic, but it has to do
with our mental pride, the pride of our reason of intellect. In comparison with our intellect the spirit has an extraordinary humility, or it
forces *us* to an extraordinary humility. Otherwise we cannot hear it.
But if you are convinced of the power of the spirit you try to hear it;
we even learn to humiliate ourselves so that we may hear it. I once had
a patient who always tried in her way to hear the spirit and this problem was presented in a most instructive dream. She had a dream which
often repeated itself and she never could remember it (it often happens that one has a dream repeatedly which one cannot quite remember), and then suddenly once she was able to. She was in a very beautiful park, the sun was shining and the birds were singing and she felt
that this was it; something was going to happen; she was becoming
aware of something. And gradually she knew that she would be able to
understand what the birds were singing. It became clearer and clearer,
and the moment was approaching when she would be able to understand it. Then suddenly she found herself holding one of those noisy
instruments children have at carnival time, and she was making such
an awful noise with it that she could not hear what the spirit birds were
singing. She preferred to make her own noise, for what the birds say is
so humble that we have to assert ourselves. So we never hear what they
say.

LECTURE VI
9 June 1937

Prof. Jung:

Here is a question by Mrs. Crowley: "Last week you said, Nietzsche was born in an age which marked the death of the Spirit, in that *Geist* had become mind, and that in opposition to that Nietzsche expressed the *dynamis* of spirit as if he were one of those megaphones of powers in human society wanting to be released. This is what is unclear to me. If Nietzsche was voicing the new *Geist*, how account for the Superman who seems to epitomize the consciousness of the 19th century with its one-sided power drive? My impression was that Nietzsche expressed the consummation of an epoch, not a beginning. If it had been a beginning, wouldn't he have had the experience of the birth of God rather than his death? I thought that was the clue to his self-destruction, that he couldn't make the bridge to the beginning, but served as a sort of grave digger for the epoch."

This goes of course to the core of the whole problem of Nietzsche's *Zarathustra*. You see, *Zarathustra* is just everything: it is like a dream in its representation of events. It expresses renewal and self-destruction, the death of a god and the birth of a god, the end of an epoch and the beginning of a new one. When an epoch comes to an end a new epoch begins. The end is a beginning: what has come to an end is reborn in the moment when it ceases to be. That is all demonstrated in *Zarathustra* and it is most bewildering. It is terribly difficult because there are so many aspects. It is exactly like a dream—a whole world of prospects—so you cannot expect cut-and-dried formulas. Whatever one says about *Zarathustra* must be contradicted, as he contradicts himself in every word, because he is an end and a beginning, an *Untergang* and an *Aufgang*. It is so paradoxical that without the help of the whole equipment of our modern psychology of the unconscious, I would not know how to deal with it. We stopped at a place where we were right in the midst of a paradox, where Zarathustra was speaking of the spirit, the *Geist*.

1132

Ye know only the sparks of the spirit: but ye do not see the anvil
which it is, and the cruelty of its hammer!

You see he tried, in his very intuitive way, to hint at the nature of the
spirit—in a few words to explain or to comment on his own view of it.
But he merely throws out some sparks about a thing which would need
a thick volume, an enormous dissertation, to make what he is trying to
say quite clear. Nietzsche is particularly aphoristic in his thinking as
you know. With the exception of his very early *Unzeitgemässige Betrach-*
tungen, practically everything he has written is aphoristic.[1] And even
Zarathustra, despite the fact that it is a continuous text, is aphoristic in
nature; it is split up into many chapters very loosely hung together,
and the chapters themselves are split up by a multitude of intuitive
sparks or hints. As I said, as soon as he has an intuition, off he is already to the next one, as if he were afraid to dwell upon one single subject, one single intuition, because it might catch him. And catch him it
most certainly would. For instance, he says spirit is the anvil. Well, if
you remain with that statement for a while you find yourself between
the hammer and the anvil and so you get a most needed explanation.
But already in the next sentence, "Verily, ye know not the spirit's
pride," he jumps away, as if it were plain that the spirit is so inaccessible, so proud, that he cannot get anywhere near it. You see, he approaches for a moment, and then immediately feels that this is too
hot—it cannot be touched—and off he goes, to speak about the spirit's
pride, and its humility, an entirely different aspect.

Of course, we must stick to such very awkward statements in order
to elucidate them. Jumping over those passages would mean being superficial, reading *Zarathustra* as everybody else reads it: just glancing at
it. It is so slippery, you slip off the subject for a moment, hesitate and
glance at the next sentence, and already you are spirited away from the
thoughts he has intuited. You know, I pointed out last time that
Nietzsche was proclaiming here a conception of *Geist* which was entirely different from the intellectual concept of the 19th century, and
we are now well on in the 20th century and still our idea of *Geist*, mind,
spirit, is very much the same. Not much has changed since, except our
collective psychology, which can be seen in the political conditions. To
know what *Geist* is, look at the collective mentality of our days; then you

[1] The *Untimely Meditations, or Thoughts Out of Season* (1873-1876). Jung would willingly
have added the still earlier *The Birth of Tragedy from the Spirit of Music* (1872), a work he
knew well and dealt with extensively in CW 6. Other works combine essays and aphorisms.

get an idea why Nietzsche says that *Geist* is anvil and hammer. Now, these are typical pairs of opposites: the anvil is the Yin part and the hammer is the Yang, the active part, and there must be something in between, but he carefully omits to say what it is. It is man. Between the hammer and the anvil is always a human being.

You see, it is a terrible conflict. Of course, we know there cannot be any spiritual manifestation, which according to Zarathustra's definition is a dynamic and *not* an intellectual manifestation. That was the mistake of the 19th century, or the magic if you like to say so. We thought we were mighty magicians and could fetter the spirit in the form of intellect and make it serviceable to our needs, but Zarathustra rightly points out that this is one of the great mistakes of the age. Such a thing as spirit never could be fettered. It is free by definition—it is a volcanic eruption and nobody has ever fettered a volcano. Now, wherever there is such a mighty phenomenon as a volcanic eruption, there is a mighty possibility of energy; and energy cannot be without pairs of opposites: a potential is needed in order to have energy. So if there is a mighty manifestation of energy you can safely assume the presence of extreme pairs of opposites, a very high mountain and a very deep valley, or a very high degree of heat and a corresponding coldness; otherwise there would not be the potential. That is what he wants to express by the idea that the spirit is an anvil and a hammer. You see, the spirit is not only a dynamic manifestation, but is at the same time a conflict. That is indispensable; without the conflict there would not be that dynamic manifestation of the spirit. The spirit, to repeat, is essentially a tremendous, dynamic manifestation, but what that is, we don't know. Just as we don't know what the state of Europe is essentially; it is a spiritual manifestation but we only see the opposite aspect and complain about the hammer and the anvil. But those are simply the pairs of opposites as in any manifestation of energy.

Now of course, the pairs of opposites in the spirit, the great conflict, is such a hot problem because here the question arises: what are these opposites? You see, Nietzsche says nothing; of course for a fraction of a second he happens to look at it and then instantly he looks away, complaining about the proud spirit that doesn't allow itself to be touched. As a matter of fact, it is too hot, or it is so magnetic, that if you touch it you are instantly caught, and then you are in between the hammer and the anvil. The pairs of opposites in any spiritual manifestation are tremendous contrasts, because you see quite accurately that this point of view is true, and you see just as accurately that the directly opposite point of view is true as well, and then naturally you are in a hole.

1134

Then there is a conflict. For inasmuch as you are caught by a conviction, entirely convicted of something, and are honest, you must say,
"Well, if *this* is true, it means something"—you see, such a thing gets a
moral rise out of you. Of course there are chess players, people with an
absolutely detached intellect, who are never roused by anything. You
can make this or that statement, and if it is the truest thing on earth it
makes no difference. They don't react to it; they have such a thick
hide, or are such a swamp inside, that it simply means nothing. But
other people have a certain temperament in that respect so to them a
truth really means something. And Nietzsche was such a man. He said
that a spark from the fire of justice fallen into the soul of a learned man
was sufficient to devour his whole life, which means: if you once understand that this is the truth, you will live by it and for it—your life
will be subject to the law of this truth.

That is all very well as long as you know that this is the only truth,
and of course we are all educated in that sense; every age has preached
to us that there is only one truth and that is a truth forever. It cannot
change. There is only that one fact. And necessarily from that conclusion all other values are at fault—lies or illusions. Then as long as we
live by a perfectly safe truth—which means a truth by which we can
really live—naturally things are quite simple. We know what we have
to do; we have a safe regulation of our lives, a moral, practical, philosophical, and religious regulation. But if you should become aware of
the fact that the contrary truth is equally true, what then? That is such
a catastrophe that nobody dares to think of the possibility. You see, if
Nietzsche would stop for a moment, remain with his statement for just
a fraction of a second, he would ask, "What is my anvil—that safe, absolutely unshakable basis of truth? And what is my hammer, which is
equally a truth but an opposite truth?" Then he would instantly be in
his conflict, the conflict of Zarathustra. He would have to say, "Well,
inasmuch as Zarathustra is my truth, what is its opposite?" And he
must admit that its opposite is equally true. If Zarathustra is the hammer, what is the anvil? Or if Zarathustra is the anvil, what is the hammer? You see, he would be swept into an overpowering conflict; it
would tear him to shreds if he should stop to touch it, so it is quite humanly comprehensible that he jumps away. It is too critical, too difficult, nobody would touch such a live wire. He explains his attitude by
saying the spirit is proud and didn't allow him to go anywhere near it,
but at the same time he says, "Still less could ye endure the spirit's humility, should it ever want to speak," which is just the opposite. Spirit is
proud, yet you could not stand its humility—which means that *he*

would not stand its humility. Now, whatever he says betrays an extraordinary pride, so that critics have always complained that Nietzsche suffered from megalomania. But he is quite aware of the fact that the spirit is also extremely humble, so humble that he can hardly stand it. And this is again a new aspect, full of conflict. I continue with Nietzsche's words,

> And never yet could ye cast your spirit into a pit of snow: . . .

We must read it: *I* could not afford to cast my spirit into a pit of snow. You see, if he should realize the humility of the spirit, it would mean dipping old Zarathustra into cold water or snow, because he is really too big. And so if Nietzsche should prick the bubble of his inflation, he would collapse till he was the size of his thumb, and that would be spirit too, the spirit being both the greatest and the smallest. The deity itself would necessarily force him to such an extraordinary maneuvre. But Nietzsche himself in his intuitive function is still under the influence of centuries of Christian education, so he is unable to stand the sight of the spirit being the greatest, the proudest, and at the same time the most humble, the greatest and the smallest, the hammer and the anvil. Therefore, he naturally jumps away again, accusing his time that they are unable to dip their spirit in the snow. Yes, then he is very careful not to let the heat rise to such an extent that it would suddenly by *enantiodromia* change into ice. But that is what has happened to him:

> ye are not hot enough for that! Thus are ye unaware, also, of the delight of its coldness.

It should be: thus *I* am unaware—that it might be very agreeable to cool down such excessive heat. The spirit is only bearable if it can be checked by its own opposite. You see, if the deity, being the greatest thing, cannot be at the same time the smallest thing, it is utterly unbearable. If the greatest heat cannot be followed by the greatest cold, then there is no energy, nothing happens. So spirit can only be alive inasmuch as it can be very hot and very cold, very proud and very humble. Now of course, the spirit is never proud and the spirit is never humble: those are human attributes. Inasmuch as we are inflated we are proud; inasmuch as we are deflated we are humble. The spirit fills us immediately with an inflation, which means an *Einblasung*, a breathing into. A balloon is an inflation, and since spirit is breath or wind, it has that effect. But an inflation only has a moral or philosophical value if it can be pricked, if you can deflate; you must be able to submit to deflation in order to see what inflated you before. In that which is coming out of you, you can see what has gone into you. Therefore it would be necessary that Nietzsche should submit to his own paradox. But being intuitive he touches it and leaves it: it is too dangerous to him. He continues in the same way his moral exhortation,

> In all respects, however, ye make too familiar with the spirit; . . .

It is really true that we have been too familiar with the spirit, making it into an intellect that was to be used like a servant. But all that familiarization of the spirit doesn't touch its real nature; we have gained something by acquiring that most useful and important human instrument, the intellect, but it has nothing to do with spirit. Of course it is only from wrestling with the spirit that we have produced the intellect at all, but the production of intelligence through the contact with the spirit has an inflating effect, for when the spirit subsided we thought we had overcome it. But it simply disappeared, because the spirit comes and goes. For instance, you resist the wind, and after a while it subsides, and then you might say you had overcome it. But the wind has simply subsided. You have learned to resist it, but you make the wrong conclusion in assuming that your faculty of resistance has done anything to the wind. No, the wind has done something to you; you have learned to stand up to it. The wind will blow again, and again your resistance will be tested, and you might be thrown down if the wind chose to become stronger than your resistance. So when we became familiar with what we thought to be spirit by calling it intellect, we made that mistake—we came to the conclusion that we really were the fellows who could deal with the spirit, that we had mastered and possessed it in the form of intellect.

> and out of wisdom have ye often made an almshouse and a hospital for bad poets.

Namely, a collection of useful sentences and principles. If anywhere a wind blows, we take a collection of useful sentences and apply one. Or we may use proverbial wisdom to get out of awkward situations, but it is not helpful to our neighbor. "A hospital for bad poets"—very good! I do not need to elucidate that.

> Ye are not eagles: [He should say, *I* am not an eagle.] thus have ye never experienced the happiness of the alarm of the spirit.

This translation is hopeless. To be alarmed means to be a bit upset or excited, while the German *Schrecken* means really "terror." The "alarm of the spirit" is poor and inadequate. The fact that this translator has chosen the word *alarm* shows how little he can imagine the nature of the spirit.[2] When a hurricane is blowing against you, particularly if you are in a boat on the open sea, you feel absolute terror, and the spirit is such an elemental phenomenon. I remember a case, a very educated man who always had much to say about the spirit, but he didn't see that one could be in any way alarmed or terrified by it—the spirit to him is something quite nice and wonderful. But that same man would be utterly shaken, get into a complete panic, if he were exposed to a more or less disreputable situation. If I should say, "Public opinion is also the spirit, and your terror of it is the terror of the spirit," he would not understand of course—it would be altogether too strange to him. Yet the fact is that the only god he was afraid of is public opinion. In other words, Mrs. Grundy is his god. You see, that is the natural truth: just where we are overcome, where we give out, that is the deity.

You know, whenever something overcomes you, when you are under an overwhelming impression, or when you are merely astonished or upset, you say, "Oh God!"—exactly as the primitives when they hear the gramophone for the first time say, "*Mulungu!*" (which means mana), and as we say, "*Gott!*" But in German, one uses that word more freely than in English. You have all sorts of circuitous paraphrases for the name of God on account of your better education, but in the German language one is more or less bound to the truth, not from any kind of sincerity or modesty but because one cannot help it—it just blurts out. So when you are overcome by excitement and wrath, you curse, and there is hardly any curse in which there is not a blasphemy. In anything that has an overwhelming effect, in any kind of affect, you experience the deity. If you are overcome by Mrs. Grundy you know where your goddess is, and if you are overcome by drink, well, God is in the alcohol of your drinks. That is a bitter truth. People do not like such a statement, but it is really the truth. So the spirit, being a dynamic manifestation, is a terror, an insurmountable affect. Now Nietzsche continues,

And he who is not a bird should not camp above abysses.

But a bird never *camps*, particularly not over an abyss. Perfect nonsense! The idea is that only a bird which is aloof and can fly away, is able to live at all above such abysses. It means the untouchable spirit. It needs an eagle with an extraordinary power of flight to stand the

---

[2] Holingdale* renders this: "You are no eagles: so neither do you know the spirit's joy in terror."

neighborhood of the spirit. And it is an aloofness—the aloofness of the intuitive type that sees the thing yet will not touch it.

> Ye seem to me lukewarm ones: but coldly floweth all deep knowledge. Ice-cold are the innermost wells of the spirit: a refreshment to hot hands and handlers.

Now again an awful translation: "handlers" is wrong.

Mrs. Baumann: In my translation it is "and to them that labour."

Prof. Jung: That also is not good. The German *Handelnden* is really not translatable. It means those that act, that are doing. The hands are the instrument of doing, so when you dream of the hands it means the doing or executing part of yourself, the way you touch things, the way you handle certain situations—all that can be expressed by the hands. If a finger is cut off, it means a restriction in your way of handling things, or a sacrifice to the peculiar spirit of things, or that you touch them with a partially sacrificed hand, that is, reverently, remembering the gods that are dwelling in them. Therefore you cannot touch a thing immediately with your bare hand and with your full power or grip, but will wear gloves; having to handle people with gloves means also a sort of restriction, or a certain care, a measure of protection. You see, all that refers to acting or to actually doing.[3]

Here we encounter again Nietzsche's very peculiar love for the metaphor of ice and snow and cold—all that contrasts with the heat. He understands the spirit chiefly as hot, like a lava flow or a fiery explosion, and the contrast would be extremely cold. That is the same as pride and humility, the pair of opposites in the spirit. The spirit as a manifestation of energy is very hot on the one side and very cold on the other. If one has an inflation, then one is only balanced if the bubble can also be pricked; if you are increased in size by inflation, you must also have the experience of decreasing to an incredibly small size. You can, of course, infect other people by inflation, can cause a sort of mental contagion; people are often inflated and they have an equally inflating influence on other people. Also the contrary is true: when a person is too small for his size he can have a deflating effect upon others. It doesn't matter whether you are too big or too small, whether you are beyond your size or so far within your own confines that you don't even touch your frontiers—either can have such an effect. So where there is inflation there is also the contrary; where there is the heat of the spirit there is also the coldness. And since it is not a human

---

[3] Hollingdale* also has "handlers," but Kaufmann* has "men of action."

phenomenon—it is just not: it is a nature phenomenon—it has not human proportions. It is too big and too small, too hot and too cold, and whoever gets into that pair of opposites is between the hammer and the anvil.

> Respectable do ye there stand, and stiff, and with straight backs, ye famous wise ones!—no strong wind or will impelleth you.

These wise ones are the people who have resisted the hurricane to such an extent that even the hurricane gave up, and then they think that they have mastered the hurricane.

> Have ye ne'er seen a sail crossing the sea, rounded and inflated, and trembling with the violence of the wind?

Here he himself uses the term *inflation*. But that ship with the inflated sails thinks that she has a very big belly—thinks that *she* is sailing, nobody else, and she doesn't think of the wind that is pushing her. Inflated people never reckon with the fact that that increase of size is really due to an inflating spirit, and of course nobody else would think that they had any particular spirit. Yet they have, otherwise they could not be inflated. Naturally, this conception of the spirit is utterly inapplicable to the Christian idea of the spirit. But if you have a conception of the spirit such as Zarathustra hints at, you can understand the true nature of inflation; there is something visibly negative in it and something very positive.

> Like the sail trembling with the violence of the spirit, doth my wisdom cross the sea—my wild wisdom!

This wild wisdom is the wisdom of nature, of the unconscious that *is* the wind, and anybody driven by the unconscious is in a state of savage natural wisdom which is not human.

> But ye servants of the people, ye famous wise ones—how *could* ye go with me!

Inasmuch as he is the wind, they naturally resist him, so there is no reconciliation between the two. But sometimes the wind is so strong that those famous wise ones are blown away like dry leaves.

Now in this chapter, Nietzsche is really reaching the point where he becomes confronted with the true nature of the spirit; and since this was for his time an entirely new discovery, he is quite justified in feeling that it is an important discovery. Yet we have seen the signs of his hesitation, his shyness in touching that thing; as usual, he just gives a hint and disappears again. That is the way in which the intuitive generally deals, not only with his problems but also with his life; he creates a situation and as soon as it is more or less established, then off he goes because it threatens to become a prison to him, so his life consists chiefly in movement, in discovering new possibilities. And that goes down into every detail, so we are not at all astonished to find Nietzsche in exactly the same condition when it comes to his confrontation with the true nature of the spirit.

You see, whenever an intuitive escapes a self-created situation, he is only apparently rid of it. That unfinished thing clings to him and will in time lame him; he carries it with him and it has a paralysing effect. For instance, he oversteps the reality of his body, time and again, and the body takes its revenge after a while: it gets out of order and makes him sick. Many intuitives are particularly troubled with all sorts of illnesses which arise chiefly from neglect. Or he may be troubled by his banal situation; always at cross purposes with his surroundings, he loses opportunities and is never settled. He never gets rooted, in spite of the fact that he has a marvelous ability to worm himself into new situations, to make friends and acquaintances and to be well spoken of for a while. Then it becomes a prison to him and he escapes—thank heaven that chance has come! And he forgets that he carries the old situation with him, but it is no longer outside of him, it is inside; and it will go on living as an unfinished thing in himself. For whatever we do and whatever we create outside, whatever we make visible in this world, is always ourselves, our own work, and when we do not finish it, we don't finish ourselves. So he carries that burden all the time with him; every unfinished situation which he has built up and left is in himself. He is an unfulfilled promise. And what he encounters in life is also himself, and that is true for everybody, not only the so-called intuitive. Whatever fate or whatever curse we meet, whatever people we come into contact with, they all represent ourselves—whatever comes to us is our own fate and so it is ourselves. If we give it up, if we betray it, we have betrayed ourselves, and whatever we split off which belongs to us, will follow and eventually overtake us. Therefore, if Nietzsche tries here to avoid the contact of the spirit, we can be sure that the spirit will catch hold of him: he will get into that out of which he thinks he has escaped. You see, this is the introduction to the next chapter. *Zarathustra* is the confession of one who has been overtaken by the spirit.

Nietzsche himself handled all that people then called spirit and still call spirit. In a most brilliant way, he wrote in the style of the best aphorists. He was brilliant in his formulation and expression, and the mind or the intellect was in his hands like a sword handled by a master. But just that turned against him. Because he handled it so brilliantly, he was convinced that it was his own mind and overlooked the fact entirely that the wind was pushing his vessel. The motor power of his craft was not himself and his ability, but was the spirit, at first invisible or only visible as if it were his own brilliant mind. Then more and more it became clear to him that it was not himself. He even felt when he wrote *Zarathustra* that Zarathustra was not himself, and therefore coined that famous formula, *Da wurde eins zu zwei und Zarathustra ging an mir vorbei.* In that formula he confessed his conviction that he and the spirit were two. In the part of *Zarathustra* which we have hitherto dealt with, he was practically identical with that spirit, but we may expect that after a while this must come to a head and then he will be confronted with that power which moves him. Here he comes very close to it; he has here the intuition of the true nature of the spirit. People with a considerable inflation are utterly unable to realize their identity with the driving force. It always needs an exaggeration of the inflation in order to explode it, and so it happened to Nietzsche.

Now in the next chapter called "The Night-Song" he realizes the nature of the spirit profoundly; he is still identical with it, but to such an extent that he begins to become aware of the inhuman or superhuman nature of the spirit, and he feels his own reaction against it. In other words, he becomes aware of the hammer and the anvil. This is a great experience: it is the apex of a long development and at the same time an end and a beginning. It is a catastrophe and it is what antiquity would have understood as a *rencontre* with the deity. Whenever that happens in *Zarathustra* his language becomes, one could say, truly divine; it has been sometimes grotesque, often brilliant and intellectual, but then it loses that quality and takes on the quality of music. That is the case here. This is the first place in *Zarathustra* where his language becomes truly musical, where it takes on a descriptive quality from the unconscious which the intellect can never produce; no matter how brilliant the mind, no matter how cunning or fitting its formulations, this kind of language is never reached. It is of course exceedingly poetic but I should say *poetic* was almost too feeble a word, because it is of such a musical quality that it expressed something of the nature of the unconscious which is untranslatable. Now, in the English or French translations you simply cannot get this, as, for instance, you cannot translate the second part of *Faust*. There is no language on God's earth which could render the second part of *Faust*—the most important part. Therefore I should like to read you the first part in German.

Mr. Baumann: May I ask a question? You said Nietzsche did realize the nature of the spirit—you used the word *realize*—and I wonder whether he was really conscious of it or not.

Prof. Jung: No, if I said *realize*, it would be too much. He approaches a realization. He is confronted here with the nature of the spirit. That is as far as he could go and that confrontation has released in him extraordinary reactions. You see, if there were no such passages in *Zarathustra* as "The Night-Song"—and others later on, of course—it would be hardly worthwhile to plow through it for the sake of the psychological enlightenment we get from his formulations, not worthwhile to take all that trouble. When I think of *Zarathustra*, it is of such chapters as "The Night-Song" because that is the substance and the immortal merit of the book.

Mrs. Baumann: Do you think that was the beginning of his tragic end, that he then came in touch with it?

Prof. Jung: Oh, the whole of *Zarathustra* is the catastrophe, you know: every chapter has something in it that is an aspect of the catastrophe.[4] Well now:

> Nacht ist es: nun reden lauter alle springenden Brunnen. Und auch meine Seele ist ein springender Brunnen.
>
> Nacht ist es: nun erst erwachen alle Lieder der Liebenden. Und auch meine Seele ist das Lied eines Liebenden.
>
> Ein Ungestilltes, Unstillbares ist in mir; das will laut werden. Eine Begierde nach Liebe ist in mir, die redet selber die Sprache der Liebe.
>
> Licht bin ich: ach, dass ich Nacht wäre! Aber dies ist meine Einsamkeit, dass ich von Licht umgürtet bin.
>
> Ach, dass ich dunkel wäre und nächtig! Wie wollte ich an den Brüsten des Lichts saugen!
>
> Und euch selber wollte ich noch segnen, ihr kleinen Funkelsterne und Leuchtwürmer droben!—und selig sein ob eurer Licht-Geschenke.
>
> Aber ich lebe in meinem eignen Lichte, ich trinke die Flammen in mich zurück, die aus mir brechen.
>
> Ich kenne das Glück des Nehmenden nicht; und oft träumte mir davon, dass Stehlen noch seliger sein müsse als Nehmen.

That is the first part, and that is the theme of the whole chapter, but from the last sentence I read, onwards, the musical style begins to dis-

---

[4] Nietzsche called this "the lovliest of all songs."

appear and the aphoristic character begins again, until the last part where he comes by *enantiodromia* to the opposite; from the light—that is the fire, the flames—he realizes the ice, and then that musical quality comes back. So I will read you that last part also:

> Oh, ihr erst seid es, ihr Dunklen, ihr Nächtigen, die ihr Wärme schafft aus Leuchtendem! Oh, ihr erst trinkt euch Milch und Labsal aus des Lichtes Eutern!
>
> Ach, Eis ist um mich, meine Hand verbrennt sich an Eisigem! Ach, Durst ist in mir, der schmachtet nach eurem Durste!
>
> Nacht ist es: ech, dass ich Licht sein muss! Und Durst nach Nachtigem! Und Einsamkeit!
>
> Nacht ist es: nun bricht wie ein Born aus mir mein Verlangen— nach Rede verlangt mich.
>
> Nacht ist es: nun reden lauter alle springenden Brunnen. Und auch meine Seele ist ein springender Brunnen.
>
> Nacht ist es: nun erwachen alle Lieder der Liebenden. Und auch meine Seele ist das Lied eines Liebenden.—
>
> Also sprach Zarathustra.

Now, it is of course almost impossible to say anything about the intellectual contents of such music. These two passages convey their own meaning. They describe the peculiar emotion of a man who experiences the spirit, its superhuman light and its cosmic coldness. You know, experiencing the spirit means at the same time its denial because it is the positive and the negative at the same time. One could say it was the light and its own overcoming, the light and the darkness in the same moment, the heat and the cold. It is the great paradox, that thing which we cannot express; we have no means whatever to express the paradox of the deity. You see, this is the overcoming effect: *he* is no longer speaking, it is the experience itself that speaks out of him; that which he experiences expresses itself, and that is beautiful. It is indisputable, inexplicable—one has only to submit to it. You can feel the nature of the experience when you allow yourself to dwell upon your own impression from such a passage; then you get a certain idea of the spirit or the deity that expressed itself in that phenomenon. And this experience teaches Nietzsche something: namely, after all the praise of the bestowing one which he has expressed in the former chapters, the praise of the one who spends, he suddenly realizes that he doesn't know the happiness of the one who receives. As soon as this realization comes to him the style changes, and at once that sort of brilliancy comes in which is characteristic of his personal gifts. So when he says

"And oft have I dreamt that stealing must be more blessed than receiving," this is again only brilliant. And that is the point where, to my feeling, the whole rhythm and poetry of the passage before comes to an end. This is also the point where he touches upon his own ego, and there we can begin our critical examination of his text.

> It is my poverty that my hand never ceaseth bestowing; it is mine envy that I see waiting eyes and the brightened nights of longing.

This shows to what extent he realizes that he has been driven by something and that he himself is poor. He is not the maker of the wind that drives his vessel, but is practically left alone by that power, so he can say:

> Oh, the misery of all bestowers! Oh, the darkening of the sun! Oh, the craving to crave! Oh, the violent hunger in satiety!
> They take from me: but do I yet touch their soul? there is a gap 'twixt giving and receiving; and the smallest gap hath finally to be bridged over.
> A hunger ariseth out of my beauty: I should like to injure those I illuminate; I should like to rob those I have gifted:—thus do I hunger for wickedness.

This is a very important statement and again a profound psychological law: namely, those people who give too much become hungry, but the hungrier they get the more they give, and the more they give, the more their giving becomes a taking. Not a real receiving because nobody gives them anything; by their giving they take, they begin to steal, to suck. They become a nuisance through their gifts because they are taking. You see, anybody who knows his own poverty should not go on giving because you cannot give more than you possess; if you give more, you take. You can receive gifts from people who are rich but not from those who are poor, for when poor people give, they take; it is a poisonous gift because they give in order to make you give. *Do ut des*, "I give that thou mayest give." Now if that giving goes on, the inner emptiness increases to such an extent that Nietzsche here begins to speak of robbing. There is such a madness, such a hunger, in him that he would even kill somebody in order to get his food. That is the result of this wonderful virtue of giving. You remember there was a mighty chapter about the virtue of giving; he made a tremendous noise about it, of course exaggerated because he already felt the hunger.

Now this realization comes to him on account of the way in which he wrote *Zarathustra*; he felt as if he were pouring out of a full vessel. *Zarathustra* flowed out of him till be became aware finally of the inner emptiness caused by it. First, he was pouring it out with the feeling that he should fill the whole world, and then no echo came back, apparently nothing has happened. He had poured out his very blood and nothing came back, and naturally he developed a tremendous hunger, a desire to be filled up again. Then he realized that his desire was just as low as his gifts were high. He had been on a very high level before and suddenly he realized that he was on a very low level. As a matter of fact, after all his giving he was a thief, a beggar, perhaps even a bandit who robs people, because he felt as if he himself had been robbed. But he had robbed himself. Now, that happens regularly with people who are, on principle, so-called altruists: they give and give and don't understand the art of receiving. You can only give legitimately inasmuch as you receive. If you don't receive , you can no longer give. If you give too much you take from your own substance, and then something in you goes down, descends to a lower level, so that finally, behind the virtue of the giving, one appears as an animal of prey. That is what he realizes here.

You see, this is an example of the humility of the spirit: inasmuch as the spirit is shining and hot like the sun, it is positive, but inasmuch as it is cold, it is negative. And inasmuch as a man is filled with the warmth of the spirit he will give, and inasmuch as he is filled with the coldness of the spirit, he will take, but not in a human way. It will be less than human. So to realize the spirit you must be able to think the one thing and the other: namely, that your thought is hot and cold and that *you* are hot and cold, that you are on the one side of god, on the other side an animal of prey. Now if the spirit cannot think that of itself—or rather, the one filled with that spirit, because the spirit is a phenomenon that doesn't think—then he has not realized the spirit. That is the pride and humility of the spirit. Usually inflated people never hesitate to realize the deity in their inflation, but they fail to realize the other side, that they are lowdown animals of prey where every value is just the reverse. So an inflation can look like grace from heaven, yet it is always the famous gift of the Danaides. It is negative, something subhuman at the same time, because it is a phenomenon which is not of human origin.[5] You see, the realization we spoke of, which did not take place when he was confronted with his own intuition, is now coming to him in the form of an immediate experience.

[5] Danaus, required by the besiegers of Argos to marry off his fifty daughters, gave each a pin with which to kill her husband on the wedding night.

The irrational type doesn't see or realize by rational feeling or think-ing—it always *happens* to him. If he can confess it, like Nietzsche, it is then of course a demonstration which has the value of a vital confes-sion; one sees how it happens, one can experience it with him. If he had had, or had tried to have, a realization through his rational func-tions, he probably would have written a philosophical essay which we most certainly would not have dealt with in our seminar because there would hardly have been any psychology in it. It might have been inter-esting to historians of philosophy, but it would not have taken on the aspect of a living experience. That is the advantage of it, but the great disadvantage is that it can destroy him, and he would never know it be-cause it just happened to him. He cannot see that the whole thing is a divine argument represented by the puppet man, that he is entirely in-strumental, the instrument of a divine thought in the general uncon-scious. So the one who has a rational gift can formulate the divine thought that is the unconscious but he acquires relatively little merit. While an irrational type involuntarily represents it and by playing the divine role, he is eventually destroyed by it—but he leaves a living ac-count. Nietzsche always reminds me of those criminals or prisoners of war who were chosen to represent the gods, in Mexico and also in Ba-bylonia. They were allowed every freedom, until the sun went down, and then they were sacrificed to the gods. In Babylonia they had the chance to escape if they could get out of town before sunset, but in Mexico there was no escape—they were simply sacrificed, but they were worshipped as the gods, they themselves being very poor devils. That is Nietzsche all over, being entirely instrumental, a figure on the chess board, giving us a living account through his confession of his ex-periences. It is an unrealized and undigested experience, but of course with all the advantages and all the virtues of an immediate and living experience.

> Withdrawing my hand when another hand already stretcheth out to it; hesitating like the cascade, which hesitateth even in its leap:—thus do I hunger for wickedness!

You see, here he expressed what I anticipated: namely, his hesitation, his shyness, his reluctance to establish an immediate contact with his experience, with human beings or with situations. He doesn't want to make roots and he is forced to pour himself out, which causes the fatal hunger.

> Such revenge doth mine abundance think of: such mischief welleth out of my lonesomeness.

My happiness in bestowing died in bestowing; my virtue became weary of itself by its abundance!

He who ever bestoweth is in danger of losing his shame; to him who ever dispenseth, the hand and heart becomes callous by very dispensing.

Mine eye no longer overfloweth for the shame of suppliants; my hand hath become too hard for the trembling of filled hands.

Whence have gone the tears of mine eye, and the down of my heart? Oh, the lonesomeness of all bestowers! Oh, the silence of all shining ones!

Many suns circle in desert space: to all that is dark do they speak with their light—but to me they are silent.

Oh, this is the hostility of light to the shining one: unpityingly doth it pursue its course.

Unfair to the shining one in its innermost heart, cold to the suns:—thus travelleth every sun.

Here he identifies with the sun, the hottest thing we know of; he is entirely identical with Yang.

Like a storm do the suns pursue their courses: that is their travelling.

As if driven by the wind, he thought, but they themselves are the source of their movement; the sun is not driven by a storm. It *is* the storm, it *is* the movement.

Their inexorable will do they follow: that is their coldness.

Here we see the fact that the sun or the suns, the fixed stars, etc., are following a mechanical principle which is utterly inhuman; therefore they are cold, despite all heat. And that is the image or the allegory of the hunger of the spirit.

Oh, ye only is it, ye dark, nightly ones, that extract warmth from the shining ones! Oh, ye only drink milk and refreshment from the light's udders!

Ah, there is ice around me; my hand burneth with the iciness!

Now he is transforming into the cold aspect of the spirit which is the other side of its inhumanity. I think we will stop here; I have already read you the last part in German. Such things must always be read in the original, just as certain passages of the Mass should not be translated.

1148

LECTURE VII

16 June 1937

Prof. Jung:

Here is a question by Miss Welsh: "Speaking of Nietzsche's intuitive way, you said, 'When an intuitive escapes from a situation because it threatens to become a prison, he only does so apparently, for the unfinished thing follows him and clings to him and may lame him; he has overstepped the body and it will take its revenge.' Will you say something about the reverse situation of the sensation type. When he gets stuck in a situation and is unwilling or unable to leave it, has something gone ahead in spite of him? Does this pull and worry at him and can this tension also cause the body to suffer?"

This is an interesting question. Of course it is not exactly on the line of *Zarathustra*, but since it is just the opposite of Nietzsche's problem it is perhaps worthwhile to say something about it. The sensation type always finds or creates a situation in which he believes: that is his reality, the thing that *is*; but the thing that is only possible is definitely unreal to him, because the function which is concerned with possibilities, intuition, is in his case the inferior function. And like every other type, the sensation type represses the inferior function because it is the opposite of the superior function and is contaminated not only with the personal unconscious but also with the collective unconscious. It is weighed down by the enormous weight of the whole unconscious world. Therefore, the sensation type will not use intuition and then it works against him, just as the intuitive type is counteracted by his inferior function, sensation.

Now the question is, what is the inferior intuition doing in such a case? Well, it creates possibilities but possibilities unknown to the consciousness of the sensation type, and it does pull and worry because this unconscious intuition creates projections. You know, when the differentiated intuitive function creates a reality from a mere possibility, it is as if it were giving substance to what is nothing but a possibility in itself. So the intuitive can create fabulous schemes and make them

1149

more or less real: he gives reality to his possibilities. Now in the case of the sensation type, where the intuitive function is inferior, the intuition does the same thing, only of course the possibilities are of a more symbolic kind, more primitive. Although it is in an inferior condition, his intuition nevertheless creates a possibility, makes it real, and projects it. You see, a seemingly real possibility cannot be only in yourself; it is always outside too. It does exist somewhere, so the inferior intuition creates a situation as if in space, a phantasy world or existence which is expensive because it drains the forces of consciousness of their energy. The sensation type will therefore suffer a certain loss of energy which escapes, or is drained off, into a sort of mythical or fabulous creation, a wonderland where the things happen which their intuition creates; and that is, as a projection, semi-substantial.

I should make it clear here that we use our libido for such a projection, and libido is energy, and energy is substantial, it has mass. That fact explains the possibility of spook phenomena, materialization and such things, which really do occur. It is an awkward fact, so people prefer to say they do not, since they would then be forced to explain them, but strangely enough, they do exist. So to a certain extent every projection is a substantial entity, and it drains the body, takes substance from the body. Therefore it is quite possible that the body in a sensation type may suffer on account of such unconscious intuitive creations. It is just as if somebody having a definite position, being a cashier, say, were unconsciously creating another business into which the money he earns is secretly flowing away; it disappears in a sort of miraculous way, and then the body begins to suffer from peculiar ailments, ghostly diseases which one often cannot explain properly. It can take all sorts of forms: if there are certain inferiorities or weaknesses in the body already, an inferior stomach or any other organ that is not quite up to the mark, the symptoms will surely begin there. If the digestion is a bit weak, it will become weaker; or if there is a little deafness, that will increase. Perhaps a rheumatic tendency might become more marked, for instance. In the case of the intuitive type, it is chiefly the intestines that suffer, and intuitives seem particularly apt to have ulcers of the stomach, while with the sensation type it seems to be more the bones or the muscle substance that is affected. And we know, in cases of materialization, that it is chiefly the large muscles which lose substance, apparently drained off in order to produce semi-material phenomena. That is my experience, but of course one should make quite specific studies about these things and I have had too much to do in my life to be an intern and work in a hospital, examining the different forms of rheumatism exclusively: that is a life work in itself. Now the next chapter is called, "The Dance-Song." How does Nietzsche arrive at this new topic after "The Night-Song"?

Mrs. Fierz: Is it not as if it had become night and that now a sort of vision or phantasy comes up from an unconscious side?

Prof. Jung: And what character would that unconscious side have in his case?

Mrs. Fierz: It would be the female side.

Prof. Jung: Yes. Zarathustra and Nietzsche being practically identical are chiefly Yang, the positive masculine principle, and we can be absolutely certain that after a relatively short time the Yang will seek the Yin, because the two opposites must operate together and the one presupposes the other. He is bound to arrive at the situation where Yang reaches its climax, and then the desire for the Yin will become obvious. In "The Night-Song" we have seen how he is thirsting and longing for the Yin principle, which is nocturnal and everything feminine, just the contrary of the fiery, hot, and shining Yang. So it is quite natural that we arrive now at "The Dance-Song":

> One evening went Zarathustra and his disciples through the forest; and when he sought for a well, lo, he lighted upon a green meadow peacefully surrounded with trees and bushes, where maidens were dancing together.

You see the fire, the Yang, seeks its own opposite, the well that quenches the thirst. And there he finds a gathering of maidens.

> As soon as the maidens recognized Zarathustra, they ceased dancing; . . .

So they were dancing before he came. Apparently in a nowhere, in an eternity, these maidens were dancing in that lovely spot, in that meadow where there is presumably a well. Now what is this? Have we ever encountered such a symbol?

Mrs. Jung: I think the well is a symbol of life, and this group of dancing girls are elves.

Dr. James: In Masefield's poem, "South and East," maidens were dancing and a man comes along.[1]

---

[1] John Masefield (1874-1967), English poet. In his ballad a young man spies on three maidens who come to a secluded spot, remove their wings, and dance. He falls in love with one of them and seeks her out in her home, which is south of the earth and east of the sun, and after a wearisome journey he succeeds in his quest and is presented with his own wings.

1151

Prof. Jung: I don't know that poem. Well, as you know, the elves form such companies, and these maidens seem to be a sort of eternally existing society; they occur everywhere and they usually dance, like the houris in paradise or the elves in the midst of the woods in the moonshine. In my German seminar on children's dreams, I have just been analysing a dream of a little boy between three and four years old, who repeatedly dreamt that the white maidens came down every night in an airship and invited him to come with them up to heaven. That motif is like one you certainly know which occurs in a famous poem of Goethe.

Mrs. Fierz: Der Erlkönig.

Prof. Jung: Yes. *Du liebes Kind, komm, geh mit mir!*[2] And some of you English people must have seen that most suggestive play by Barrie, *Mary Rose,* about the "Island that wants to be visited," where the child hears the voices of the elves who want to play with him, the Green Folk, presumably those nice maidens who seem to be always ready in the unconscious to entice lonely wanderers or children.[3] You might have encountered them also in a recent publication of mine, "Traumsymbole des Individuationsprozesses," where those nymphs are sort of dancing girls. And in the *Songe de Poliphile,* the nymphs are the first thing he meets after the ruined city. (There is a picture of them in the book.)[4] Now here we have the same symbolism. Who are these maidens and what do they mean psychologically?

Mrs. Fierz: It is a plurality of anima figures.

Prof. Jung: Exactly. You see, the anima by definition is always one that is two, but those two are identical as you will see in this chapter, though of most contradictory qualities, the yea and nay at the same time. But it is a definite person, so definite that every man who is capable of introspection can give a definite picture of his anima. I have often tested men; it needs of course an introduction to the concept and a certain amount of intelligence and introspection, but as soon as they have grasped the idea, the picture is right before their eyes. Now in this case it is not one figure but several so it must be a very particular condition of the anima. What accounts for such a multiplicity of animae? Under what condition would she be so collective?

[2] In Goethe's poem (and Schubert's song), the Erlkönig summons those whose time has arrived with "Come, dear child, go with me."

[3] James Barrie (1860-1937) was an immensely popular Scots playwright and novelist. In one of his lesser known plays, *Mary Rose* (1924), the title character, like Peter Pan, exists off and on in a world where there is no growing old and dying.

[4] For *Le Songe de Poliphile,* see above, 12 Dec. 1934, n. 6.

Mrs. Crowley: It would be a very primitive condition, inferior.

Miss Welsh: Very unconscious.

Prof. Jung: Yes, that is it. A multiplicity of anima figures is only to be met with in cases where the individual is utterly unconscious of his anima. In a man who is completely identical with the anima, you might find that plurality, but the moment he becomes conscious of that figure, she assumes a personality and is definitely one. This is in contradistinction to the animus in women, who as soon as she becomes conscious of him is definitely several. If there is a particular personality it is just that one, and there are always several others. The animus is in itself a plurality, while the anima is in itself a unit, one definite person though contradictory in aspect. So from such a symbol you can conclude that Nietzsche/Zarathustra is profoundly unconscious of the fact of the anima. Yet we cannot assume, inasmuch as Zarathustra is the typical wise old man, that he would be unconscious of the nature of the anima—that is excluded since he is always associated with the anima. The myth of Simon Magus and Helena is a typical example, and [the tale of] Faust and Gretchen is another, but not so good because she is too unconscious and he is not wise enough.[5]

Mrs. Crowley: On the other hand Krishna contained all this. Would he be so unconscious?

Prof. Jung: Utterly unconscious because he is the hero god and not the wise old man. That is the *Puer Aeternus* psychology of the heroic age where women were an indefinite multitude consisting of mothers, sisters, daughters, and prostitutes. There was no distinct woman, only a type. Therefore those Wagnerian heroes all had to do with indefinite Walkyries; there is only one definite anima, Brünnhilde, but she is chosen by her father, the wise old man. In the myth of Krishna, they are milkmaids or shepherdesses, you know,. He comes to a society of nice young girls, perfectly indistinct, all alike of course, and he chooses one who becomes his favorite, but he also married seven or eight others. Rhada is chiefly chosen to join him in the mandala dance, the *nrityia*, that circular dance which forms a mandala; Krishna and Rhada are in the center, of course representing the god and his shakti.[6] Now this is

---

[5] For Simon Magus and Helena, see above, 5 June 1935, n. 4.

[6] Jung says elsewhere that some of his women patients have preferred dancing a mandala to drawing one. "In India there is a special name for this: mandala nritya, the mandala dance. The dance figures express the same meanings as the drawings" (CW 13, par. 32). For a reproduction of a South Indian bronze, "Lord of the Dance," see Zimmer Myths, Plate 38.

a very similar situation. Zarathustra is the hero god coming to the dancing girls.

> Zarathustra, however, approached them with friendly mien and spake these words:
>
> Cease not your dancing, ye lovely maidens! No game-spoiler hath come to you with evil eye, no enemy of the maidens.
>
> God's advocate am I with the devil: he, however, is the spirit of gravity. How could I, ye light-footed ones, be hostile to divine dances? Or to maidens' feet with fine ankles?

Here the devil enters the game, and how does he come in?

Miss Hannah: It is the spirit of gravity, and that is always the piece Nietzsche doesn't accept, the ugliest man.

Prof. Jung: And what is the spirit of gravity doing?

Miss Hannah: Pulling him down.

Prof. Jung: Yes, he obviously approaches here the inferior function. He comes to his own opposite. He is threatened with sinking down into the depth of the Yin, but he makes light of it. He praises the light-footed ones who are not pulled down by the spirit of gravity, who show him how to dance above the abyss—another Nietzscheian term. But I think Zarathustra had a particular fantasy about the maidens' feet with fine ankles. Do you know where a similar passage occurs?

Mrs. Sigg: At the end of *Zarathustra*, in "Daughters of the Desert," Dudu and Suleika.[7]

Prof. Jung: Yes, there is that famous passage:

> To a dance-girl like, who, as it seemeth to me,
> Too long, and dangerously persistent,
> Always, always just on *single* leg hath stood?
> —Then forgot she thereby, as it seemeth to me,
> The *other* leg?
> For vainly I, at least,
> Did search for the amissing
> Fellow-jewel
> —Namely, the other leg—
> In the sanctified precincts,
> Nigh her very dearest, very tenderest,
> Flapping and fluttering and flickering skirting.
> Yea, if ye should, ye beauteous friendly ones,

---

[7] "Among the Daughters of the Desert," Part IV, ch. 76. The seminar stops short of this final part.

Quite take my word:
She hath, alas! *lost* it!
Hu! Hu! Hu! Hu! Hu!
It is away!
For ever away!
The other leg!
Oh, pity for that loveliest other leg!

You see, that is already the transition to his insanity: he literally got into that form of Yin, and there he became definitely insane. He produced a lot of erotic literature at which his highly respectable sister became so scandalized that she burned it up.

To be sure, I am a forest, and a night of dark trees: but he who is not afraid of my darkness will find banks full of roses under my cypresses.

That is plain.

And even the little God may he find, who is dearest to maidens:
. . .

Who is this?
Mrs. Crowley: Cupid.
Prof. Jung: Yes.

beside the well lieth he quietly, with closed eyes.

What about that?
Mrs. Fierz: It is like a fantasy of a love garden.
Prof. Jung: And where have you seen such fantasies? What style does it suggest?
Mrs. Sigg: It is rococo.
Prof. Jung: Yes, haven't you seen faded fantasies of cupids and shepherdesses in an old drawing room? In England you still find such lovely pictures, Cupid sleeping and nice shepherdesses round him tickling him—or he tickling them, the old story. But the interesting thing is that Nietzsche has such a lovely picture in mind. Where did he get that? When was Nietzsche born?
Mrs. Sigg: In 1844.
Prof. Jung: Yes, so the rococo is a bit far away, but when did his parents live?
Miss Hannah: In the time of the French Empire.
Mrs. Sigg: The Biedermeier period.

Prof. Jung: Yes, that was an interesting time in France. They made a Roman Imperial style, and in Germany it was Biedermeier, the classical epoch with its wonderful columns and little temples; the style was also in a way imperial but Hellenistic as it were.[8] It was the philo-hellenistic time, the time of the war for the liberation of Greece, when Byron fought for Greece, which was supposed to be an ideal country in every way—Greek manhood, the Greek citizen, and Greek beauty. They entirely forgot the garlic and all the dirt of Greek towns. That Greek idea was valid practically till the end of the 19th century, and we still suffer from it; it gave us an entirely wrong idea of Greek civilization.[9] Now, his parents lived then and I am pretty certain that his mother flirted with such pictures. I am sure that you would still discover them on the walls of houses in the country in which she lived, at least I can remember seeing them when I was young. They have perhaps disappeared now because they have a historical value, but in those days they were just the remnants of a foolish past.

Now, this kind of feeling-fantasy is derived from the mother, and it is typical that a man who is entirely unconscious of his anima will first—when he discovers anything of the sort—fall into his mother's feelings, the kind of feelings that have been particularly dear to the mother. So when a man with a plurality of animae discovers Yin, he will surely be the mother. As an example, I can only advise you to read the wonderful English story *Lilith*, by a man named MacDonald.[10] Lilith was Adam's first wife, a particularly evil creature because she didn't want to have children, and later on she became a sort of child-eating monster. You ought to read that novel, it is perfectly sweet, one of the most marvelous demonstrations of the feelings of a man who is wonderfully unaware of his own anima, of how his own feelings look in the whole world of Eros. This man MacDonald would also have the plurality of animae. I don't know whether there is any evidence for it in the book but at all events he developed that kind of psychology. He talks about "the girls," as his mother did: you know, "The girls don't, and I hope you won't," etc., so "the girls" remain a class by themselves, a society of girls, and that causes a plurality of animae.

[8] The term *Biedermeier* was invented by a Munich humor magazine, *Fliegende Blatter*, to describe a period style, 1815 to 1848, of shallow, realistic, or neoclassical works which were favored by the *nouveau riche*.

[9] The Greeks fought for their independence from Turkey from 1821 to 1832. Lord Byron arrived in Mesolonghi in January 1824 and by April, at age 35, was dead. Yet he was important in calling the attention of the world to this historic struggle.

[10] For George MacDonald, see 26 Feb. 1936, n. 10.

When a man becomes aware that he should function with his feelings, he will inevitably get into his mother's feeling, as a girl when she develops her mind will be strongly influenced by her father's traditional mind; in other words, the anima develops out of the mother as the animus develops out of the father. So it happens that men who have remained very young for a long time—often till an advanced age—indulge in mother's feelings, and you are never quite sure whether they are really masculine or not. Such men have never discovered what they really feel, as women who live on with an animus can never make out what they really think. They have always represented the *Encyclopedia Britannica* and what they said was marvelously correct, but just off the real thing, and what they really thought was presumably nothing. And so with men in their relationships: you never can tell what a relationship really was because it was always so covered up by the mother, by the way the mother has related. This became the model for his world and surroundings, for women and children particularly but sometimes even for his friends.

Dr. Escher: In the book *Der Landvogt von Greifensee,* all girls and women were called *die Figuren.*

Prof. Jung: Yes, that story is a representation of a society of girls with the hero in the center, but you know Gottfried Keller was just such an old boy—that is why he drank so heavily. He was an old *célibataire* and his feelings were in the mother world. He had a perfect mother complex which had to be compensated by a good deal of drink, otherwise it would have been absolutely unbearable—all those girls would have become just too much.[11] So we see that the choice of this lovely picture, Cupid lying sleeping by the well and the pretty shepherdesses round him, is a fantasy of the time just before Nietzsche was born—and also the dark trees, the cypresses, and the banks full of roses. *Rosenhänge* might mean garlands of roses, or hanging roses, or slopes covered with roses: you can imagine anything because the German word is absolutely indefinite. That also makes a picture. Do you know such a picture in the history of art.

Remark: There is one by Macquart.[12]

[11] Gottfried Keller (1819-1890), often described as the most representative of all Swiss writers, was admired by both Jung and Nietzsche. *The Governor of Greifssee* (1878), translated by Paul Bernard Thomas, is included in vol. 14 of *The German Classics of the Nineteenth and Twentieth Centuries,* ed. Kuno Francke. In this fine story, the bachelor (*célibataire*) governor stages a party for the three lost loves of his youth.

[12] Macquart? Possibly August Macke, a German painter (1877-1914) whose works ap-

Prof. Jung: Yes. Probably many of you do not know of him but I should advise you, if you ever go to Munich, just to have a look at his painting and then go away and weep. That is also very poetical you know; you find any amount of oil paintings and prints of cypresses and roses—that kind of stuff. And that is more like the fifties, sixties, seventies, so it is more the time of Nietzsche himself. Now why is that little god sleeping near the well? There must be a peculiar connection between Cupid and the well.

Dr. von Bomhard: They are the opposites, the Yin and the Yang.

Prof. Jung: No, they are very close together. The opposites are Zarathustra and the well—he is the fire and the well is the water—but Cupid and the well are sleeping beautifully together.

Mrs. Crowley: It is because the maidens are there.

Prof. Jung: Yes, you see that is just one picture, a sort of mandala: the sleeping Cupid is a little male and the well is of course the female. Nietzsche often compares woman, or the soul of woman, to a deep well over which a dragon watches on account of the treasure that is buried in it. Therefore certain women are called dragons.

Mrs. Crowley: And actually in antiquity were not statues of Aphrodite usually connected with the well?

Prof. Jung: Yes, and there are other examples. For instance, the famous Abraham's pond in Harran; that was a pond for Astarte, and it was full of carp which are the fishes of Astarte.[13] So this well can be called the Well of Astarte, the love goddess, and here is Cupid her son, the dying and resurrecting god. They form a sort of couple like Krishna and Rhada, or like Shiva and his Shakti. They belong together, but not as a pair of opposites. They may become a pair of opposites if Cupid should by any chance develop into the wise old man, but that is a long way off. Here the pair of opposites are dormant and so well fitted that they are almost one: it is one and the same mood. For instance, one could amplify that picture easily, making of Cupid a more powerful god, and Astarte would be the well, then you have it more or less. But that is the world of the creative mother goddess Astarte, and this is the world of the Yin in a dormant condition; therefore the main characteristic of that Yin world, Cupid, is represented as dormant. Zarathustra discovers him in his sleep and blames him for it:

pear in Munich, among other places; or more likely, C. Macourt (1716-1767), a German who lived for a time in London where he was mainly a portrait painter.

[13] Harran is a town in southern Turkey, the home of Abraham's family after the migration from Ur. Beside the pond, there is a mosque and a pavilion.

Verily, in broad daylight did he fall asleep, the sluggard! Had he perhaps chased butterflies too much?

To what does that refer? Why should Cupid chase butterflies?

Remark: He is not functioning as he ought; he should be doing something to those girls instead of playing like a little child.

Prof. Jung: But what are the butterflies?

Mrs. Jung: The butterfly is the psyche.

Prof. Jung: Yes, *psyche* is the Greek word for soul. Psyche, the soul, is the butterfly he is chasing—Eros and Psyche. But he forgot the girls and that is what Zarathustra means: he shouldn't go to sleep, he should be busy with the girls. Now, what does it mean that Cupid performs Eros and Psyche? How do we know what they did?

Miss Wolff: Cupid did nothing, and Psyche wanted to look at him. She was not allowed to, so she lost him through her curiosity.

Prof. Jung: Where do you find that story?

Miss Wolff: Apuleius.

Prof. Jung: Yes, in his book *The Golden Ass,* a Roman novel. You see, when he is chasing butterflies he is Amor and Psyche, and presumably Nietzsche, being a classical philologist, knew all about that. The story of Eros and Psyche is a sort of *entremets* in *The Golden Ass,* where Psyche lost Eros because she was too curious.[14]

Miss Wolff: I think the idea was that she thought he was a monster— she was a bit alarmed as to what he really was, and therefore of course she wanted to see whether he was young or not.

Mrs. Jung: There is a very beautiful picture by Segantini called *Die Liebe an der Lebensquelle.* It is a landscape of mountains with a well, a young couple and an angel. He painted it in the Engadine and Nietzsche wrote *Zarathustra* in the Engadine.

Mrs. Sigg: There are two pictures by Segantini: one is the *Lebensquelle,* and there is another where a young boy is lying quite naked in his mother's lap. Both pictures are up in the high mountains but they are different.[15]

Prof. Jung: It is interesting that Segantini should have had the same vision in the same place in Engadine. Well now, as long as Cupid is

[14] Originally, *The Transformation,* by Lucius Apuleius of Madaura, which is near the birthplace of St. Augustine (who of course hated Apuleius). This second-century work has been much discussed by Jung and Jungians, notably Erich Neumann in *Amor and Psyche: The Psychic Development of the Feminine* (New York/Princeton and London, 1956) B.S. XLVII.

[15] Giovanni Segantini, an Italian painter (1858-1899) who moved from a naturalistic to a symbolic style.

chasing butterflies, it means that it is a phenomenon which takes place entirely in the unconscious: it never reaches the surface, never reaches the woman. Cupid should mean connection, Cupid ought to reach a woman, but he doesn't—he is dormant. Therefore the maidens remain just maidens, indistinct; they don't take on any personal form, don't become complete. One sees that transition in the myth of Krishna. First he is just dancing with the maidens and they become enamored of him. Then he chooses one—well, several others too, but making at least one distinct by choosing her—and inasmuch as he doesn't choose the others they remain indistinct, nameless. That is the case with a man whose feeling is still identical with the feeling of the mother: he doesn't choose the woman, doesn't give her a name, doesn't make her distinct. To him girls are girls and there is only one woman and that is the mother. And his relationship to women is rather like the relation of a mother to so many daughters or children.

> Upbraid me not, ye beautiful dancers, when I chasten the little God somewhat! He will cry, certainly, and weep—but he is laughable even when weeping!
>
> And with tears in his eyes shall he ask you for a dance; and I myself will sing a song to his dance:
>
> A dance-song and satire on the spirit of gravity my supremest, powerfulest devil, who is said to be "lord of the world."—

You see, the advice he gives to Cupid, a sort of encouragement, is like a punishment. This is perfectly good advice: Cupid ought to be busy with the girls; but Nietzsche uses the girls for a purpose which is not legitimate—that their dance should be a mockery, a satire, of the spirit of gravity, so that the lightness of the movement should prove his superiority over the spirit of gravity. While the whole arrangement, the beautiful garden of temptation, the beautiful girls, Cupid, the well—everything suggests a going down, a sort of Venusberg,[16] or a temple of Astarte where he should touch the earth, where he should succumb to the spirit of gravity in order to compensate himself, or in order to transform himself into the opposite, into Yin. Now, this is the necessary procedure for a man whose feelings are identical with the mother; he cannot get rid of that identity, and he will never discover what a woman is, unless he succumbs to the spirit of gravity. So Zarathustra is

---

[16] Venusberg was the mountain where the goddess of love held her court. In Wagner's *Tannhäuser* (1843-45) the basic conflict is between the spiritual and sensual sides of man, the latter expressed by the shimmering Venusberg music.

making unlawful use of this situation of the girls and the Cupid, just using them for his own ends, against his supremest, most powerful devil, the spirit of gravity. Now what is this devil?

Miss Hannah: Is it not the clown that jumped over him and destroyed him?

Prof. Jung: Of course. The clown who jumped over the rope-dancer deals with dancing again: whenever the dance comes up that danger comes up too. The man who dances on the rope is the one who dances over the abyss with the danger of falling down, of utter destruction. You see, whenever Zarathustra speaks of dancing it is to keep himself suspended over the depths. There is always a dangerous situation, the immediate vicinity of destruction, death or insanity or both. In the catastrophe of the rope-dancer it was insanity as well as death, because the clown that jumped over him was practically insane. And there Nietzsche made the famous prophecy, 'Thy soul will be dead even sooner than thy body," which really becomes true in his own case. You see, he clearly realizes that the arch-devil, that factor which counteracts him the most, is the function which counteracts his intuition, the inferior functions. The inferior function is always the devil. One always feels it as destructive, the thing one is most afraid of and loathes and resists the most, but which is in a way peculiarly fascinating. We often find passages in *Zarathustra* where one sees how he is attracted by the devil, how he is longing for it, but he always tries to escape it again as if something were hindering him from going down into it, as if it would be his complete destruction. Now, do you believe that it would have been his complete destruction?

Miss Hannah: Not if he could have accepted it.

Prof. Jung: Yes, but why was he so afraid of it?

Miss Hannah: Because it seems to have been too insane a spot; he could not assimilate it.

Prof. Jung: But it is in practically everybody. It doesn't need an insane spot.

Mr. Baumann: Would it not have destroyed his creative power if he had accepted this gravity?

Prof. Jung: I don't think so, but you are on the right track; you only have to formulate it a bit differently.

Miss Hannah: If he had accepted it, he would have had to live it instead of writing it.

Prof. Jung: Well yes, but probably he would have written something different because you cannot kill the creative demon. A demon that you can kill is not the right one.

Mrs. Sigg: He would have lost the vital feeling of life if he had gone down into it.

Prof. Jung: But who would have lost it?

Miss Welsh: He would have had to disidentify with Zarathustra.

Prof. Jung: Yes, that is the point. Zarathustra is the Yang and he would be reduced to a mere germ, to a mere white spot in a sea of blackness. Any man who was identical with Zarathustra would be afraid to go under, because he would think that he would lose his life, that he would have to sacrifice his spirit. So inasmuch as one is identical with Zarathustra one keeps away from it, one tries to dance over the abyss. But one remains suspended, and then the spirit of gravity is the devil.

Miss Wolff: He doesn't realize at all what he is saying here—he should not speak of a devil. As he has got rid of God, he should have got rid of the devil too, because that is a completely Christian concept. Also that the spirit of gravity should mean the devil is a bit mad; it is earth, matter, everything real, empirical, just the thing he preaches acceptance of. But he cannot. He is still in the Christian attitude of aloofness.

Prof. Jung: Yes of course, but one should not take it too seriously when he speaks of the devil. It is perfectly true that if he denies the existence of God, he necessarily ought to deny the devil too, but when it comes to his inferior function he forgets, naturally, everything. Then there is no old superstition that would not come back. A man who is entirely convinced of the completely sterile condition of the world, that there is no miracle anywhere, no sooner touches this function than the world is full of devils and demons. I have seen the most amazing things in that respect. People who were completely rational and enlightened, when the inferior function came up were just as superstitious as any old witch—perfectly ridiculous. It is like people who laugh about religious feeling. Then something happens and they are drowned in it: the Oxford Movement comes along and they think they have discovered something. The inferior function is touched and down they go into the sheep pen. It is incredible how people can deceive themselves about such eternal truths. You see, that world of demons is still alive—it only needs a certain change in the level of your consciousness and you are deeply in it; then it is as it has always been. For instance, if I put you in a primeval forest and let you go without a compass, in an hour you are reduced to shreds, and in a few more hours the whole world of devils is true again. So the devil comes in quite handy here. He forgets all about his grand statement that God is dead and preaches the devil, and then it is perfectly true. Of course he is using a speech metaphor, but that does not change his inferior function; he is nevertheless in the hellish depths of the Yin.

And this is the song that Zarathustra sang when Cupid and the maidens danced together:
Of late did I gaze into thine eye, O Life! And into the unfathomable did I there seem to sink.

Here you have it. Now what is the eye of life? How was it indicated in the preceding symbolism?

Mrs. Crowley: The well.

Prof. Jung: Yes, you know those little blue lakes in the Eiffel, poured onto the crust of the earth, are called "the eyes of the sea," *Meeraugen.* So the well is an eye because an eye reflects the light; when you look into a deep well you see light of the sky mirrored below. And so the eye of life is really that deep well—there is life—and he felt that it was unfathomable and he seemed to sink into it.

But thou pulledst me out with a golden angle; derisively didst thou laugh when I called thee unfathomable.
"Such is the language of all fish," saidst thou; "what *they* do not fathom is unfathomable."

He is like a fish caught with a golden hook. And who is pulling him out of that well?

Mr. Allemann: The anima.

Prof. Jung: Yes, he is speaking to life as if it were a person and we soon see what person it is.

"But changeable am I only, and wild, and altogether a woman, and no virtuous one:
Though I be called by you men the 'profound one,' or the 'faithful one,' 'the eternal one,' 'the mysterious one.'
But ye men endow us always with your own virtues—alas, ye virtuous ones!"

Here it is undeniable that life, that deep well, Yin, is the woman in himself. Here he approaches what we call the inferior function and that is a woman, because the anima always represents the inferior function in a man's case. Therefore, if a man is highly virtuous he can reckon with the fact that when he meets a woman it will be his anima, who will have all those vices which counteract his virtues. She contains all that he is combatting, and—a particularly marvelous stunt of fate—he finds all the wrong qualities fascinating in her. And then he projects all his virtues into her, while he contains the corresponding vices. He is infected and has to carry now all the vices for which he had the compensation. For if you contact the unconscious you will be contaminated: you must develop the same qualities, otherwise they eat you up. When you have to do with devils you must develop devils in yourself. The mere fact that you have to do with devils creates devils within you, so please use them if they are there. Don't be horrified, they come in quite handy, only you must use them or they will use you, and then you are dissolved. But if you use them they give you the necessary protection against the devils of others, particularly in the case of anima devils. By that process you acquire all the qualities you formerly repressed and which thus had become qualities of the anima. Now if that process takes place the anima changes her quality; inasmuch as you take over those qualities, the anima has a chance to become much better. Somebody must have the devils: either the anima has them or you have them. If you have them, then the anima can wash herself and become very decent and nice because she is then on the positive side. But if you assume that you are the virtuous one, the anima is hell.

Mr. Baumann: There is a famous passage in the Koran about Moses going into the desert with a fish in his basket, and it jumps into a little brook which was running down from an oasis and took it down to the sea.[17] And Islam is like Yang, very masculine, but where is the anima?

Prof. Jung: Oh, they have a plurality of animae. You know, they have a peculiar attitude towards women: they are the houris in paradise, a society of girls, sort of girl scouts, as the Walkyries are Wotan's girl scouts.

Miss Fabisch: I think the Mohammedan woman is veiled.

Prof. Jung: Yes, that is another stunt of the anima, particularly when they are transparent veils—then it is hellish. Well now, this temptation, or the fascination of the opposite of himself, is of course teleological: it should compensate a one-sidedness. Zarathustra feels that there is a possibility of sinking down into this depth, and then suddenly an invisible fisherman with hook and rod interferes and pulls him out again. Now we really ought to explain this. We assume it is life that fishes him out of the water according to his text, but life in this case is an anima and one never heard that the anima was a fisherman. One *has* heard of

---

[17] The story of Moses and Chidr (who was symbolized by the lost fish) is in Surah 13 "The Cave," of the Koran. See "Concerning Rebirth," CW 9 i.

cases where a fisherman has caught a *nixe* in his net, so the anima might be something that was caught, but this is an unheard of abnormality.[18] How can it be that life itself fishes you out of life?—it is unthinkable. But here you must remember Nietzsche's mental condition, and you must remember also that famous *soreites syllogismos* which I made when we were talking about the first chapters of Zarathustra.[19] What was the result?

Miss Hannah: That Nietzsche and Zarathustra are identical.

Prof. Jung: Yes, and now you must only extend that equation, Nietzsche equals Zarathustra equals anima. So you never can tell for sure which is which because all three are identical. A few paragraphs further down, he says, "For thus do things stand with us three." The three are Zarathustra, Nietzsche, and the anima. Then who is the traditional fisherman?

Miss Wolff: Christ.

Mrs. Sigg: Peter.

Prof. Jung: Yes, and what do they fish?

Mrs. Sigg: Human beings.

Prof. Jung: Yes. Then what other fisherman is there?

Mrs. Jung: Orpheus.

Prof. Jung: Yes, that is true. There is a thick book by Eisler which contains all the symbolism.[20] And there is another famous fisher who is still alive.

Miss Wolff: The Pope.

Prof. Jung: Yes, and the symbolism is expressed there in his fisher ring, an antique gem representing the miraculous draught of fishes, for the Pope is the great fisher, he is the fisher king.

Mrs. Crowley: And Vishnu?

Prof. Jung: Yes, but *he* appears in the form of the fish. He develops out of a fish but that is something else, like the fish of Manu.[21] It is the same motif but we are here concerned with the symbolism of the fish-

---

[18] A *nixe*, in German folklore, is a water sprite, usually in the form of a woman or a combination of woman and fish. See CW 9 i, par. 52.

[19] See above, 27 June 1934, n. 1.

[20] Robert Eisler, *Orpheus, The Fisher* (London, 1921). See CW 9 ii, par. 147.

[21] In CW 9 ii, par. 176, Jung, citing the Shatapatha Brahmana, writes, "The fish of Manu is a saviour, identified in legend with Vishnu, who had assumed the form of a small goldfish. He begs Manu to take him home, because he was afraid of being devoured by the water monsters. He then grows mightily, fairy-tale fashion, and in the end rescues Manu from the great flood."

erman; that is a definite archetypal figure. The mystic Bakcheus, or Dionysos, is also a fisherman, for instance. Now what have all those figures in common?

Miss Hannah: They are saviors.

Miss Fabisch: Psychopompoi.

Prof. Jung: Yes, sort of *psychopompoi*, leaders of souls, the shepherds. Christ has often been represented as the good shepherd in the catacombs, and as Orpheus on the other side taming the wild animals; or as the fisher he is pulling in the net full of the souls of the faithful ones. So the representative of the spiritual power is the leader of souls, a sort of *poimandres*, the shepherd of men is the fisherman. Now in that case who would be the fisherman here?

Answer: Zarathustra.

Prof. Jung: Of course. Zarathustra himself would be the fisherman. And when Zarathustra, speaking to life, says, "Thou pulledst me out of the water," what happened in that case?

Mr. Allemann: He identifies with his own anima.

Prof. Jung: Yes, and one calls such a mechanism a projection. Zarathustra is making the projection into life or into the anima, and he assumes that she is of course fishing him out of life, that she is responsible.

Mrs. Jung: It seems to me that the fish that is pulled out of the water is not saved, but is caught.

Prof. Jung: Quite right, the fish is not saved. But you know, it is understood that all the fishes pulled in by the divine fisher are really saved. It is only the devil that advises you to say that they are caught. You should not say such heretical things!

Mrs. Jung: But I think he is actually caught by the anima; he is afraid of life and afraid of being caught by life.

Prof. Jung: Sure! He really is afraid of being caught by life, so if anything gets him out of it, he is only too glad. But the thing that gets him out of life seems to be again the anima, so he never gets entirely out of it. It is a sort of vicious circle into which Nietzsche would inevitably get, since he does not differentiate between those figures. He makes an attempt though—we are presently coming to it—he gets into such a tangle with these figures that one almost feels that he will make a difference. At all events, you see he projects here the fisherman symbol, which is hardly his own, upon life, the anima, and that is a mistake. If either of the two should fish, *he* should be the one to do it and not the anima. Now, the attributes life gives to itself, "the profound one, the

1166

faithful one, the eternal one, and the mysterious one," are all wonderful anima attributes; you find them, for instance, very beautifully in Rider Haggard's *She*.

> Thus did she laugh, the unbelievable one; but never do I believe her and her laughter, when she speaketh evil of herself.

It doesn't help very much, even if she tells an unfavorable truth about herself, because whatever she says is fascinating.

> And when I talked face to face with my wild Wisdom, she said to me angrily: "Thou willest, thou cravest, thou lovest; on that account alone dost thou *praise* life!"

This is an excellent dialogue with an anima. You see, something happens here which is like active imagination: he already begins to dissociate into his figures, substantiates his figures and confronts them face to face, has a dialogue, and now he calls life—mind you, the woman, his mysterious woman—"my wild wisdom." Now is she wisdom?

Mrs. Sigg: She is insofar as the man Nietzsche is *begehrend*—loving, wishing—because he always wanted to project that.

Prof. Jung: That is perfectly true. She tells him the truth that he praises life because he is full of longings and desires, which means that he appreciates the anima on account of his own wishes. If he really knew her he would not praise her so much. You see, you always praise the things you want—unless you just want to buy them. But usually one praises what one doesn't possess. If you did possess them, you presumably would not praise them because you would know them. What you possess is never so good as what you don't possess—the old story. Now this Wisdom (with a capital) is surely not the ordinary anima that is life. What kind of anima would it be?

Mrs. Fierz: Sophia.

Prof. Jung: That would be the highest form of anima. Sophia has always been represented as a sort of virgin, beautiful, with the highest qualities of virtue and knowledge.[22] She is a form of the anima, but it is incredible that such a figure could be meant here, because there is one that is much nearer, and *that* we see in the fact that the wise old man is combined with the anima; then the anima appears as wisdom, one could say, because of the identity, but Zarathustra is wisdom really. You see, she has not attained the highest wisdom. The teaching she

[22] For Sophia, see above, 5 June 1935, n. 6.

gives him is just not the highest wisdom, but is only a very clever re-mark, one which would be worthy of Diotima for instance, the anima of Socrates who made such apt remarks. What she had to say in that famous dialogue about the Eros sounds exactly like this passage.[23] So we must assume it is just the anima that talks here, and the aspect of wisdom is due to the identity with Zarathustra.

> Then had I almost answered indignantly and told the truth to the angry one; and one cannot answer more indignantly than when one "telleth the truth" to one's Wisdom.

To *that* kind of wisdom you see, because it is a typical anima remark. Also the whole course of events described here is very typical of such a discussion. You see, when the anima is projected on a real woman and she talks in that rather pointed way, she invariably gets a man's goat. The anima jumps out of him because that woman is talking through the animus—talking through her hat. "Thou willest, thou cravest, thou lovest," is animus. The animus always puts it onto somebody else, and moreover it is always a little beside the mark, just one inch to the wrong side. Then the man becomes possessed by his anima: he gets indignant and begins to tell the truth to this animus-anima, to the woman who talks in this style. Here it is a case of a projection because he says "And told the truth to the angry one," so *she* was indignant. But she simply made that remark out of playful malice; she is not angry at all. That is the playful way in which the anima talks. She is quite nice in her role, like the woman who plays that role and makes such remarks. She thinks she is objective, but the man gets angry and says *she* is angry. As soon as the anima gets on top, it is projected.

> For thus do things stand with us three. In my heart do I love only Life—and verily, most when I hate her!
> But that I am fond of wisdom, and often too fond, is because she remindeth me very strongly of Life!

You see the identity: he feels it as three figures but at the same time they are all one.

> She hath her eye, her laugh, and even her golden ankle-rod: am I responsible for it that both are so alike?
> And when once Life asked me: "Who is she then, this Wis-dom?"—then said I eagerly: "Ah, yes! Wisdom!"

---

[23] In Plato's *Symposium*, Socrates says he learned about Eros from Diotima, a priestess.

As if he were talking to one woman of another one!

"One thirsteth for her and is not satisfied, one looketh through veils, one graspeth through nets.

Is she beautiful? What do I know! But the oldest carps are still lured by her."

Those are the fishes in the pond of Astarte.

LECTURE VIII

23 June 1937

Prof. Jung:

Here is a question by Miss Hannah: "In speaking of the multiplicity of the dancing girls, caused by Nietzsche's unconsciousness of the anima, you alluded to the animus as being a *plurality in itself*. I would be glad to know whether this plurality persists in all stages of a woman's consciousness. Or if it is a compensation for the attitude to the outer world, which, in the higher stages of consciousness, would give way to one figure, the Poimen?"

This question refers to the peculiar fact that Nietzsche's anima was represented by a number of dancing maidens. It is a somewhat rare occurrence but I gave you other examples—the boy who dreamt of those many white maidens, for instance—and I said that a profound unconsciousness in a man of his anima would account for this multiplicity. I also mentioned the fact that the animus as a rule is a plurality, but when a woman is very unconscious, the animus is rather apt to be one, just the opposite phenomenon. The animus is then entirely identical with the father or with the traditional conception of the deity, to be split up later in the process of becoming conscious, into the ordinary empirical plurality. Now the question is whether in a later, more developed state of consciousness, the animus has the tendency to again become one. And we could also ask whether in a later state of consciousness the anima would not have the tendency to again become a plurality. Well, if consciousness could reach the same extension as the unconscious and could become a universal consciousness, then of course the animus or the anima might reach very much the same condition again. But since such a thing as an all-consciousness is absolutely excluded in a human being we cannot hope to reach such a level—though we might perhaps dream of it.

Mystics always try to get at this all-consciousness, the Yoga experts for instance; but since I have never analysed such a fellow—one who had attained to the highest conditions of enlightenment—I cannot say

1170

whether his anima ever reached the state of plurality again. Also I have never seen a woman who had reached such a state of consciousness that her animus would have become one. So I can hardly answer your question. Theoretically it is quite possible, but empirically the animus is as a rule a plurality, though it is true that there is a tendency to emphasize particularly one aspect of the animus, and that would be the Poimen, the shepherd: there you are quite right. But that never entirely supersedes the plurality because besides that Poimen, there are all sorts of other shepherds and policemen and God knows what, who are always busy creating plots and such things. And in a man's case, the oneness of the anima can be described as a sort of existent, or perhaps a prevailing figure, but there are always certain things hanging back, naturally, which accounts for the fact that the anima can be projected into numbers of very different women and even at the same time—certain aspects of the anima at least. So this oneness could only be reached if an absolutely perfect state of consciousness could be reached, a complete equivalent of the collective unconscious.[1] And since such a condition is superhuman, we cannot hope, and should not even wish to attain to such a height. It would be too inhuman.

Miss Hannah: I really meant to ask how much the plurality of the animus was a compensation for the attitude to the outer world. A woman is usually monogamous and a man polygamous. If a woman should overcome her monogamous attitude, would the animus tend to become one as the anima does in a man?

Prof. Jung: Such a thing happens empirically only under certain conditions; for instance, if there is a certain amount of homosexuality, you are apt to get an animus figure which is almost indistinguishable from an anima—it would have a very mixed sex character. Well now, we remained stuck in the chapter called, "The Dance-Song"—not that it is very much of a song, but more a rather difficult piece of psychology. You remember that the general problem we have been concerned with in these last chapters is the *enantiodromia*, or the transition from a Yang point of view to the Yin, the female aspect. And he gives here a very good description of the anima under the aspect that she really represents: namely, chaotic life, a moving, shifting kind of life, not obeying any particular rules. At least they are not very visible, but are more like occult laws. In my essay about the archetypes of the collective unconscious, you may remember that I identified the anima with life or liv-

---

[1] See CW 9 i, where such especially prominent archetypes as the Anima, the Mother, the Child, and the Trickster are extensively treated.

ing; the anima is really the archetype of life, as the old man is the archetype of the meaning of life. In the part we have just dealt with, Nietzsche describes the anima very beautifully as being essentially life. He shows in how far life has the aspects of woman, or we could turn it round and say how much the woman is an aspect of life, or represents life. For life comes to a man through the anima, in spite of the fact that he thinks it comes to him through the mind. He masters life through the mind but life *lives* in him through the anima. And the mystery in woman is that life comes to her through the spiritual form of the animus, though she assumes that it comes through the Eros. She masters life, she *does* life professionally through the Eros, but the actual life, where one is also a victim, really comes through the mind.

I realize that these things are hard to understand if one has not had certain experiences to give the necessary empirical material, and to show to what formulations apply. Nietzsche, inasmuch as he is a mind, is always apt to lose himself in the icy heights of the spirit, or in the desert of the spirit, where there is light, yet where everything else is dry or cold. If he gets too lonely in that world, he is necessarily forced to descend, and then he comes to life, but in the form of the woman, so he naturally arrives at the anima. It is always a sort of descent into those lower regions where there is warmth and emotion and also the darkness of chaotic life. You see, when he descends into the Yin, he will realize first of all the anima aspects of life, and then also the wisdom of life—the old man representing the archetype—and the meaning of life, the reflection of life in the mind. He sees now these aspects, and he also sees himself as if betwixt them: he speaks of "us three." So he makes a trinity of himself, life or the anima, and wisdom, which would be Zarathustra.

That he feels himself as a trinity comes from a certain condition which we have often mentioned. You remember a while ago, we spoke of the infernal trinity: namely, the reflection in hell of the spiritual trinity, the threefold devil. In Dante's *Inferno* he is in the form of Satan, with the three faces—whitish-yellow, red, and black. Now, since then I have found in a medieval treatise another formulation which states most clearly that there is a trinity in heaven, a trinity in man, and a trinity in hell. Nietzsche becomes aware of the trinity in hell from the fact that he feels himself as a trinity, and that feeling comes from his identity with God, the trinity in heaven. He denied the existence of the Christian deity, and so he would be apt to have first an inflation, and then, by a sort of mirror reflection, he discovers again the trinity, but a trinity in which he is included. Instead of Father, Son, and Holy ghost, it would be himself, life, and wisdom. Well now, we will continue.

"Perhaps she is wicked and false, and altogether a woman; but when she speaketh ill of herself, just then doth she seduce most."

When I had said this unto Life, then laughed she maliciously, and shut her eyes. "Of whom dost thou speak?" said she. "Perhaps of me?

And if thou wert right—is it proper to say that in such wise to my face! But now, pray, speak also of thy Wisdom!"

Ah, and now hast thou again opened thine eyes, O beloved Life! And into the unfathomable have I again seemed to sink.—

Thus sang Zarathustra. But when the dance was over and the maidens had departed, he became sad.

"The sun hath been long set," said he at last, "the meadow is damp, and from the forest cometh coolness."

The aspect of life here is alluring. It is represented by those dancing maidens and that is of course rather suspect. It is a superficial, joyous aspect of life, or an aesthetic aspect, as the analogy of Krishna and the milk-maidens is a sort of divine, playful aspect. But when that process has set in—the descent to the Yin—one is apt to come to oneself finally, and not at all to a divine aspect of life or to a sort of playful Shakti creating a world of illusions. This ring of maidens is a kind of shadowy maya, and inasmuch as Nietzsche is divine he can remain in such a world, as God can remain in the changing colors of the world, surrounded by the images of becoming and vanishing, the abundance of created figures. But inasmuch as he is human, the descent goes further: it goes right down into the isolation and singleness of man and he is quite unable to envisage the world as the gods do, as a sort of mirror reflex of himself—at least the Hindu gods do that: they don't suffer from the reality of the world because they assume that it is their own mirage. The Yogin is naturally always striving to reach a condition in which he might be able to envisage the world as his own creation, or his imagery, a self-reflection; but he can only do that—if he can do it at all—by the complete sacrifice of his human existence. He must transcend humanity in order to attain to the vision of God.

Since Nietzsche is human he cannot stand that sight eternally. He cannot keep away from his human side because he is part of that maya, a human being among human beings, not a god. He is neither below nor above humanity, and so he naturally comes to himself. It is as if he were falling through the veils of maya, not into the deity, but into himself. Naturally, when the darkness comes, when that lovely aspect of the many colors and the abundance of life has departed, then the sun sets. Consciousness goes further down into the night of the Yin, into the darkness of matter—into the prison of the body as the Gnostics would say. That the meadow is damp means that the psyche becomes humid. It was the idea of Heraclitus that the soul becomes water. It is a sort of condensation. The air gets cool in the evening and vapor becoming condensed, falls down to the ground.[2] Out of the forest, or the darkness, comes the coolness, the darkness being of course the Yin, humidity, the north side of the mountain. And one becomes that substance, a semi-liquid matter. The body is a sort of system that contains liquids, consisting of about 98 percent water. So instantly one is caught in the body, exactly as the god, when he looked down into the mirror of matter, was caught by the love of matter, and so was locked into matter forever. Therefore we can understand when he says,

> An unknown presence is about me, and gazeth thoughtfully. What! Thou livest still, Zarathustra?

One cannot feel a presence if one is God oneself, because it is then one's own presence and there is no other. If all is conscious, one knows of no presence because one is everything, so as long as one is identical with the deity there is no presence. If one feels an unknown presence it means that there is something besides oneself and then one is no longer God. So the moment Nietzsche gets into the dampness and coolness of the Yin, he is by himself, isolated, and then he is capable of feeling a presence—then he suddenly becomes aware that he is not alone. If he were God he would be alone and would never know it, but being man he is capable of feeling alone and therefore capable of feeling a presence. It is not the first time that the man Nietzsche has realized a presence but it is a rare occurrence. And now realizing that Zarathustra is the unknown presence, he asks, "What! Thou livest still, Zarathustra?"—as if Zarathustra had been dead. In a way Nietzsche lost the connection with Zarathustra in getting into the darkness of Yin. It looked as if Zarathustra were dead, or had at least been removed. Therefore this question, "Thou livest still, Zarathustra?"

> Why? Wherefore? Whereby? Whither? Where? How? Is it not folly still to live?—

---

[2] Heraclitus: "Souls also are vaporized from what is wet" (Freeman*, fragment 12).

1174

meaning that this presence, Zarathustra, could live even outside Nietzsche. You see, he was so completely identical with the spirit that he assumed Zarathustra could only exist because he, Nietzsche, existed. Then suddenly he discovers that the man Nietzsche can exist without Zarathustra and so Zarathustra should be dead, but he is not.

> Ah, my friends; the evening is it which thus interrogateth in me. Forgive me my sadness!

This sadness is depression, he is weighted down. Depression means that one had been much too high and aloof in the upper air, and the only thing that brings one down to earth into one's isolation, into being human, is depression. To become human, he needs depression. He was so inflated that it needed a heavy weight or the magnetic attraction of matter to bring him down, so he rightly says, "The evening is it which thus interrogateth in me." It is the setting of the sun, Yin, which creates that question in him.

> "Evening hath come on: forgive me that evening hath come on!"
> Thus sang Zarathustra.

As if he had to ask for forgiveness for being human! It is quite understandable that the next chapter is called "The Grave-Song." It is as if we were now continuing into the material human being, into the darkness of matter. He begins,

> "Yonder is the grave-island, the silent isle, yonder also are the graves of my youth. Thither will I carry an evergreen wreath of life."

This beginning is very symbolic. What does it mean?

Mrs. Crowley: It suggests rebirth again. He has to go down into it in order to be reborn, and he brings the evergreen wreath of life.

Prof. Jung: We haven't gotten to the rebirth; we now have to do with dying. What is the grave-island and why a silent isle?

Miss Hannah: Isn't it because he tried to cheat that spirit of gravity?

Prof. Jung: Why do you not enter upon the island, why do you all avoid the island? Are you all like Nietzsche?

Miss Welsh: It is the island of himself.

Prof. Jung: Yes, the island is a very small bit of land in the midst of the sea. An island means isolation, insulation, being one thing only. That is his loneliness: he is a lost island somewhere in the sea.

Prof. Reichstein: May I ask a question referring to the last bit of the former chapter? Could this conception be reversed—that the unknown presence would not be Zarathustra, but Zarathustra would be the one who is caught in the unknown? Then the situation would be what you mentioned first; it would be the spark of the god instead of the man Nietzsche. He says, *Ein Unbekanntes ist um mich und blickt nachdenklich. Was! Du lebst noch, Zarathustra?*[3] That would mean that the unknown one would ask Zarathustra if he were still living.

Prof. Jung: Well, the German text is: *Ein Unbekanntes ist um mich*, so he obviously personifies that unknown presence. It can only look or gaze if it is a sort of person. And the question, "What! Thou livest still?" must be—according to my idea at least—a remark made to the unknown presence that gazes so thoughtfully. Now, we know that Nietzsche has experienced Zarathustra as a sort of second presence already: *Da wurde eins zu zwei, und Zarathustra ging an mir vorbei.*[4] That describes exactly the feeling of a presence, and this is moreover a form of religious experience. (There is an interesting chapter about this experience of the unknown presence in William James' *The Varieties of Religious Experiences.*[5] This experience means: I am aware of the fact that I am not alone in this room; there is a presence and an unknown one. This is the experience of the objectivity of the psyche, an experience of the reality of the unconscious. You see, you could not have such a dissociation from the unconscious if the unconscious were nothing but an empty mirage. Such experiences would then be ridiculous illusions. But when a person has once had that experience of the presence, you never can convince him that it was not real. The fact is that it is always experienced as a most significant and important reality. Read William James.

You see, in psychology you cannot judge by your own unconscious or by your own ignorance. If a man has had a certain experience we have to take it for granted that he has had it; unless he definitely lies, we cannot say the experience was an illusion. So when Paul experienced Christ on his way to Damascus, we cannot say that was an illusion; he was obviously gripped by that experience and so it is a fact. Of course, stupid people would say that if someone had been there with a photographic apparatus, he would not have been able to photograph Christ coming down from heaven; that is the way the ordinary idiots

---

[3] This part of *Zarathustra* is translated on p. 1174 above.

[4] Again, "One becomes two and Zarathustra passes by me."

[5] "It is as if there were in the human consciousness a sense of reality, a feeling of objective presence, a perception of what we may call 'something there' . . ." (William James, *The Varieties of Religious Experience*, New York, 1902, Lecture III).

think. But it is enough that the man Paul was gripped by that experience, that is a fact. Your American humorist Mark Twain in his book about Christian Science gives a description of all their idiotic notions, and then says: "You see it is all obvious nonsense, terribly idiotic, but that is just the reason why it is so dangerous, because the greatest force on earth is mass stupidity, not mass intelligence." Stupidity is the extraordinary power and Mark Twain saw it.[6]

Just because a thing is stupid is it important, for then it appeals to many people. When we think, "Now this is the very thing," it is just *not* the thing, because millions will never see it—two or three perhaps may, but what does that mean? Of course it is very precious but what is the value of a diamond if nobody discovers it? But when a thing is tangibly idiotic, you can be sure that it is very powerful, very dangerous. You see, when we call a thing stupid, we think that we undo it, that we have overcome it somehow. Of course nothing of the sort happens; we have simply made a statement that it is very important, have advertised it, and it appeals to everybody. People think, thank heaven, here is something we can understand, and they eat it. But if we say something is very intelligent, they vanish and won't touch it. So you see, we might say that was only a subjective experience, an illusion. No, it was not an illusion. It shaped Nietzsche's life. There would be no Paul if it had not been for his experience on the way to Damascus, and probably a great part of our Christianity—we don't know how great a part—would not exist if that illusion had not happened. And when you call it an illusion you advertise it—you make that also very important—because the most important thing to man, besides his stupidity, is illusion. Nothing has been created in the world that has not first been an illusion or imagination: there is no railway, no hotel, no man-of-war that has not been imagination.

So the experience of the unknown presence is a very real thing and since Nietzsche has been identical with Zarathustra, it is absolutely necessary that when he comes to the Yin, to the opposite of the spirit Zarathustra, he must realize that he is two: Nietzsche the man, and Zarathustra, the unknown presence. Therefore I think that the unknown presence really refers to Zarathustra, for Zarathustra would gaze

---

[6] Samuel Clemens wrote to a stranger in Scotland in 1909 that Christian Science has "just the same value now that it had when Mrs. Eddy stole it from Quimby. . . . It was a tramp stealing a ride on the lightning express" (*Mark Twain's Letters*, ed. A. B. Paine, 2 vols., New York and London, 1917). The subject interested him so much that he wrote a book, *Christian Science* (New York and London, 1907). Once asked to say something about Christian Science, he responded with masterful terseness, "It's neither."

rather thoughtfully if he should see his human carrier in a state of Yin. Yin is the condition that is apt to be difficult for Yang—it may reduce Yang to that famous white spot in the black.

Miss Wolff: You could perhaps also interpret the passage as a summing up of the whole chapter: Zarathustra has met the anima under the form of life. He is fascinated by her, but he has not accepted her because she appears in this youthful and superficial aspect which he feels to be too great a contrast to himself. I would then take the whole passage after the disappearance of the girls as symbolizing Zarathustra's mood after the anima has gone away. The sun sets, evening comes, and Zarathustra feels like an old man for whom life has lost its meaning. He could just as well be dead.

Prof. Jung: But death is included in life, therefore the anima always has the death aspect.

Miss Wolff: Yes, but that doesn't come into this chapter. Life is here seen under a gay and youthful aspect, and the anima as a seductive young woman. This if of course a too superficial aspect for Zarathustra, therefore he rejects her in that form. But then the sun goes down and night comes: everything gets dark and cool. He feels sad and old, and so the unknown presence that asks Zarathustra if he still lives, I would take to personify a strange feeling within him that night and death come when the anima in that warm youthful form has gone.

Prof. Jung: Well, it is perfectly true that in Nietzsche's case this feeling comes on when the anima in the superficial aspect of the dancing girls leaves. When the sun sets, it is natural that the doubt arises whether Zarathustra still lives, because to Nietzsche life meant the dance, meant that warm and youthful aspect, *la gaya scienza*, the gay science. But the evening is another aspect of life; therefore the anima also has the death aspect. As, for instance, Rider Haggard's "She" lives in the tomb, and in Benoit's *Atlantide*, Antinea surrounds herself with the corpses of her dead lovers. Nietzsche has this doubt because he had the prejudice that life had only the beautiful superficial, gay aspect. But now he is scared because life suddenly reveals the other side, the aspect of death. And then he asks, "Thou livest still, Zarathustra?" For Zarathustra was the fellow who always enjoyed the divine, beautiful, positive aspect of life, like Krishna and the milk maidens, and in that picture of eternal bliss, there is no suggestion of death. But since Nietzsche is not God, he has to meet death; since he is not Krishna, he has to see the other aspect of life which includes death. So I think the doubt whether Zarathustra still lives really comes from a feeling which is very much the equivalent of Christ's doubt of his Father on the cross:

1178

Mein Gott, mein Gott, warum hast Du mich verlassen? That is very much the same question.

Miss Wolff: As if Nietzsche, as the son, had lost Zarathustra?

Prof. Jung: Yes, apparently he has lost him, and Zarathustra has become an unknown presence, almost uncanny. An unknown presence has usually the character of something uncanny.

Mrs. Jung: Could one not say the unknown presence is the shadow, because afterwards he comes to this island of the graves, the graves of his youth? And it would make the fourth to add to the Trinity.

Prof. Jung: That is a somewhat difficult aspect. I would not say this unknown presence was the shadow. It is more another aspect of Zarathustra, or another aspect of Wisdom. You see, Zarathustra also has the aspect of death. In the East, you remember, the deities always had two aspects, the positive and the negative; even Kwan Yin, the goddess of boundless kindness, had also a wrathful and infernal aspect. And so the archetypes have always a positive and a negative aspect. Therefore I would rather say that he suddenly sees Zarathustra in another light.

Prof. Reichstein: He says here: *Und ins Unergründliche schien ich mir wieder zu sinken.*[7] And Zarathustra would be caught in it.

Prof. Jung: Prof. Reichstein thinks that Zarathustra is like the spark of light of the Gnostics, the eternal spirit that falls down into matter and is caught in it. That is perfectly true. It just depends upon the standpoint from which one looks at it. The curse of analysing *Zarathustra* is that Nietzsche is interchangeable with Zarathustra and we have the dickens of a time to discern which is which because the two are always together. From the standpoint of Nietzsche it is an ordinary human experience—well, of course it is most unusual, but there are many parallels in literature—he is first identical with the spirit, uplifted and exalted, and then he sinks down and suddenly discovers an entirely different aspect of things. And where is his beautiful spirit, where is Zarathustra? Now from the standpoint of Zarathustra—and obviously Nietzsche speaks from the standpoint of Zarathustra— things are naturally different. Zarathustra, being the archetype of the spirit is of course not a human being belonging to three-dimensional space and consisting of matter. So be naive, take him for a spirit; he claims to be a spirit—all right, accept it. Well, a spirit has an incorporeal existence. It is in no space; it is four-dimensional. But if that thing enters matter, it comes into space, and then the eternal myth of the descent of the spirit is repeated once more. Zarathustra is linked up with

[7] "And into the unfathomable have I again seemed to sink."

the man Nietzsche; the man Nietzsche is a sort of tool or vehicle for the eternal four-dimensional spirit of Zarathustra.

And now Nietzsche undergoes a certain change: namely, he becomes aware of the other aspect of things, his sun sets, his consciousness goes into the underworld—and through Nietzsche the eternal spirit has that same experience. You know, the *Nous* of the Gnosis was attracted by his own reflection in the chaotic waters, and instantly the Physis leapt up and took him in and he dissolved in matter. Now the result of it was the creation of man, the ordinary man. The *anthropos* was the second man, who was born from that embrace. Zarathustra is something like the first man, the Adam Cadmon of the Cabalists or the Primus Adam of medieval philosophers. And we are the second Adam, one could say. As Adam was the first creation of God, so Christ is the second creation of God.[8] Zarathustra is really the *anthropos* that has been caught in Nietzsche and shares to a certain extent Nietzsche's experience. You see, we can imagine ourselves, or we can feel into Zarathustra's mind, and we are to a certain extent able to see things from his point of view. But it is very conjectural because we are not archetypes and cannot feel into archetypes enough to know exactly what has happened to Zarathustra. We can feel properly only what happens to the man Nietzsche. We can put ourselves into his situation and we can also understand what he says about Zarathustra, but what Zarathustra feels about it is divine and beyond us.

That is as if I should take you to task and say, "You have a certain complex, perhaps an inferiority complex, which is an autonomous being in you because it comes and goes when it wants and not when you want. You are in the possession of that complex. Now please tell me the story of your complex: how does it feel in you? And what does *it* feel about your experience?" You see it is exceedingly difficult, and that is the case with Zarathustra. It is perfectly obvious that Zarathustra is a superiority complex in Nietzsche, if you want to put it bluntly and without imagination. But it is most unjust to say that the god or his genius is his superiority complex. That is technical slang which is simply out of place when it comes to the real facts, though psychologically it is so of course. We can only give the phenomenology of such a complex, but to feel into it, to establish the romance of that complex, is too difficult. I have no imagination about the way elves experience the

---

[8] In the Jewish Kabbalah, Adam Cadmon is the First Man, who is complete—thus equivalent to the Jungian self—containing all the partial persons who come after. The medieval *anthropos* represents much the same idea.

world, or what any fragmentary soul knows or experiences about the world.

You may remember that story about the two elves and the Danish pastor. He had been with a sick man and was very tired, and he was going home late at night by a lonely way over the moors, when he suddenly heard faint and very beautiful music. Then he was thunderstruck to see two people walking over a place on the moors where no man could walk without drowning, and then he found they were elves and it was they who were making the music. (Elves make music, you know.) They approached him and asked who he was and where he came from and said how nice it was that he was a parson. And they were very sad that they had no immortal souls and asked him what they should do to get them. Now that good parson could not think what to do: he couldn't feel into that complex. He had not foreseen such a situation and he did not understand their psychology. But he said they must pray to God to give them souls and the only thing he could think of was the *Our Father*. So he said to repeat after him, "Our Father, who art in Heaven." And they said, "Our Father, who art not in Heaven." "No," he said, "that is wrong, you must say 'who art in Heaven.'" And again they said, "who art not in Heaven." They simply could not say it as he said it. He could not make it out. Of course not, how can a man with a soul feel into a thing that has no soul? If we could do that we would know something about the psychology of stones. I wish I could!

Now, Zarathustra is of course a superior soul, a super-intensity, and we must handle Zarathustra very carefully and reverently because it is Nietzsche's spiritual experience. You see, the questions, "Why? Wherefore? Whereby? Whither? Where? How?" are of course the questions of a man in despair. What about the spirit? What is the purpose? Why should there be such a thing? It is really "My Father, why hast thou forsaken me" and "Is it not folly still to live"? Does life make sense at all? But that is an aspect of life too, that is the chaos; it is no longer the dance, but the night life, and it is not understandable. It is darkness, the complete blackness of despair. Now sure enough, Zarathustra is touching the darkness here; inasmuch as man is affected by that darkness, the spirit that dwells near him—over or above him but contacting him—becomes acquainted with its own opposite, the darkness. There it touches matter and therefore that moment is all important. So what Prof. Reichstein says emphasizes a moment of metaphysical importance, because the question is asked from the standpoint of Zarathustra, the spirit that got into matter. And this is the moment when the spirit gets into matter. You see, that explains a good deal of the subsequent symbolism.

Mrs. Crowley: In connection with the Trinity, could it not also be the opposites, the Yin and the Yang, and the self?

Prof. Jung: Naturally. For instance, the trinity in medieval philosophy was spirit, soul, and body. The body of course refers to the Yin and the spirit to Yang, and the psyche would be in between.

Now we will go on to the next chapter, "The Grave-Song." I have already read the first paragraph. The grave-island, the silent isle, as is understandable from the general character of the preceding chapters, is a descent into Yin. The ultimate character of the Yang is the extinction into Yin because it is its opposite in character. But one cannot say it is death; it only feels like death when you come from the side of the Yang. It is rather, one could say, the vessel in which the positive activity of the Yang is contained, or it is the possibility through which the Yang can work. Therefore, the Yin can easily be identified with Shakti: it is the vessel of the creator. Or it is Maya, the building material of the world, moved by the creative point in the center, the *Shiva bindu;* that is the god from which all moving forces emanate, but they only become visible through Maya or Shakti.[9] So the Yin is an indispensable condition to real existence; without it the latent creative power of Shiva would lie dormant forever. And the Yin in itself doesn't mean death, but only a negative condition over against an active condition. But when you come from an identification with the spirit, it looks like death, as if you were buried. It becomes doubtful whether the spirit has ever lived and above all one doesn't see of what use it could be. The real essence of the spirit seems to be denied, improbable—impossible even. So naturally when Nietzsche comes to the realization of himself as a human being apart from Zarathustra, it feels to him exactly like death, or like a prison. At all events, what he realizes in the first place is what he formulates here, the grave-island or the silent isle. And what kind of psychological condition is that?

Mr. van Waveren: A state of introversion.

Prof. Jung: Yes, but when a man is on an isolated island in the sea he probably gazes out to the horizon and that would be rather an extraverted activity. Of course if he sought that island in order not to be

---

[9] Maya: Mother of the World. Shakti: spouse or female companion of the god Shiva. *Bindu* means "point," defined as in geometry to be without dimension, which is where creation begins. See CW 9 i, par. 631.

bothered by the world, he would curse every ship that came into the vicinity and would turn his back on the sea, and then you would speak of introversion. But this island has a different tone. What condition does it symbolize?

Mr. Baumann: That all human relations are cut off.

Miss Hannah: Isolation.

Prof. Jung: Yes, it is the utter stillness and solitude of the grave. A man is completely cut off on such an island. For who goes there? Only the dead that never return. So it is also an eternal prison, and he himself is a sort of ghost landing there. The psychological condition that he now becomes aware of is his absolute loneliness. Before, he was Zarathustra surrounded by imaginary disciples, talking to crowds in the marketplaces of towns. He had a mission, he represented something. His heart was full to overflowing with all that he wanted to bestow on people; he bestowed his gifts upon nations. And now he is on the island of the dead. That inflation has gone, as even the worst inflation comes to an end at times. You know, a person who has an habitual inflation will have his bad moments when he has the idea he is all wrong, but when actually for the first time he is normal, and so this is a perfectly normal moment of depression. He suddenly realizes his real isolation and falls into himself, into his human existence. Nietzsche was then presumably in Sils Maria or some such place where he didn't know a soul, where he talked to nobody or where he only talked to ghosts. He was absolutely lonely from a human point of view, and when a man under such conditions is left by the spirit, to what is he left? Well, to a sackful of bad memories, or wasps' nests or nettles in which he can sit. And all that is himself.

> Resolving thus in my heart, did I sail o'er the sea.—
> Oh, ye sights and scenes of my youth! Oh, all ye gleams of love, ye divine fleeting gleams! How could ye perish so soon for me! I think of you to-day as my dead ones.

What has happend here?

Mrs. Adler: It is a memory out of his personal unconscious.

Prof. Jung: Yes, he enters here on his personal psychology; he comes to his very personal memories. In my German lecture I showed a chart where you see that the first thing you meet when you turn into yourself is reminiscences. When you are alone things suddenly come into your mind which you had forgotten because there was too much noise, too much activity. So when you come to yourself you get to the world of thought, of memories.[10] As long as Zarathustra kept Nietzsche busy, his personal life was non-existent, but when he comes to the isolation of his own body he drops into the world of memories. The very first thing you do in an analysis, in order to learn something about yourself, is to fall into reminiscences, and sometimes for months people go on spinning the yarn of their own infantile memories down to the womb of the mother. For memories, reminiscences, are the gate, the entrance to the world within, and as soon as you open the door, out they come. So the first thing is that he sees all those sights and scenes of his youth, those divine, fleeting gleams of love that soon ceased. Here we approach a sphere of *ressentiment*. Something very bad has been done to the poor child: "I could not remain a child, unfortunately enough; bad people have wounded me!" And then up comes the *ressentiment*.

> From you, my dearest dead ones, cometh unto me a sweet savour, heart-opening and melting. Verily, it convulseth and openeth the heart of the lone seafarer.

What is this?

Mrs. Fierz: His inferior feeling.

Prof. Jung: Yes, now the feelings come up, and why inferior?

Mrs. Fierz: Because he never lived them later, when he grew up.

Prof. Jung: Exactly, so they never developed. But what is their general quality?

Mrs. Crowley: An insistence.

Miss Welsh: Emotional.

Prof. Jung: They are emotional sure enough, and what is the general quality of the emotions?

Remark: Compulsive.

Remark: They have an archetypal quality.

Miss Welsh: They possess him.

Prof. Jung: Exactly, they are possessive and they insist, they take possession of the subject as if he were a piece of property. An emotion catches you, sits upon you; you cannot get rid of it. It sits upon your neck or clings to your throat. You may say you have an emotion, but usually the emotion has you—that is the trouble. Though it is euphonious to say you have an emotion, an emotion always has the bearer. So the inferior feelings that are now coming up have an extraordinary insistence and penetration: they envelop him, encoil him completely, and he will soon be possessed by them again, which means that he has

[10] See below pp. 1197-98.

always been possessed by them. He even jumped into the world of the spirit, one could say, in order to escape the terrible clutch of the inferior function. That spiritual exaltation was because he could not get along with his inferior feeling life—it was too tough, too touchy, too insistent and penetrating—and instantly one knows that he himself remained under the feeling that he was such a poor beggar that he could be done out by that feeling on the spot. He says,

> Still am I the richest and most to be envied—I, the lonesomest one! For I have possessed you, and ye possess me still.

You see, he realizes the quality of possessiveness and he even arrives, though with protest, at the admission "And ye possess me still."

> Tell me: to whom hath there ever fallen such rosy apples from the tree as have fallen unto me?

Here he becomes euphemistic as before when he said, "I have possessed you"—I am the richest; the most wonderful rosy apples from the tree have fallen to me. He still tries to cling to the positive aspect. As Krishna sees the world, so Nietzsche, inasmuch as he is possessed by the spirit, tries to see the world in a positive aspect. So even the fact that this feeling renders him completely helpless, he tries to turn to his own advantage, as if *he* possessed his feelings, as if those experiences were rosy apples that fell from the tree for him.

> Still am I your love's heir and heritage, blooming to your memory with many-hued, wild-growing virtues, O ye dearest ones!

That is exactly like a euphemistic invocation to very wrathful gods—or to a wrathful sea, calling it a hospitable sea because it was absolutely inhospitable.

> Ah, we were made to remain nigh unto each other, ye kindly strange marvels; and not like timid birds did ye come to me and my longing—nay, but as trusting ones to a trusting one!
>
> Yea, made for faithfulness, like me, and for fond eternities, must I now name you by your faithlessness, ye divine glances and fleeting gleams: no other name have I yet learnt.

Here comes again the anima aspect of the inferior function—that the feelings have an anima aspect, or that these reminiscences or former experiences look like so many love stories, in a personification. One is really quite in doubt whether he doesn't refer to love stories. But he doesn't really: it is only the anima aspect of the world. And now he begins to complain about faithlessness; he resents the fact that they should have died so early.

> Verily, too early did ye die for me, ye fugitives. Yet did ye not flee from me, nor did I flee from you: innocent are we to each other in our faithlessness.

That means he drifted away from them and they drifted away from him.

> To kill *me*, did they strangle you, ye singing birds of my hopes!

Now his resentment comes into the open. He never says who the enemies are that have stolen the feelings. You see, he has an idea that there has been faithlessness: either his early feelings have been faithless and left him, or perhaps he will admit that he also has been faithless to them, that he got away and rescued himself in the world of spirit. But no, nothing of the kind: I am myself with my memories and former experiences, and then there was the devil that came in between and killed those lovely singing birds. "They" have strangled them. Who are "they"?

Miss Hannah: Does he project it upon his parents and everybody?

Prof. Jung: Presumably.

Prof. Reichstein: Is it not his identification with Zarathustra which killed them? He took the way of the spirit and that was the reason why he excluded all this.

Prof. Jung: That is perfectly true. He identified with the spirit in order to escape the feeling world of his inferior function, and he tries now to explain how it came about that he is no longer in touch with that former world. The idea is that they, those memories, have left him, vanished: they were faithless. And then he also might have drifted away—he admits so much. But his idea is that both were really innocent: "innocent are we to each other"—one could say even in their faithlessness. So he tries to explain this peculiar fact that he could ever have left these beautiful things; he doesn't understand how he got away from them. And this is all the world of feeling. There is no question of the spirit Zarathustra any longer. For now he has entered the darkness and it clutches his feeling first of all, his feeling memories, and now he discovers that the devil has come in between. "They" have come in between; "they" have strangled his lovely birds.

> Yea, at you, ye dearest ones, did malice ever shoot its arrows—to hit my heart!

Murderers came in between, who either shot at those lovely memories and feelings, or directly at his heart.

> And they hit it! Because ye were always my dearest, my possession and my possessedness: . . .

If he is in a positive mood, he says he possesses *them*, and if he feels low he says *he* is possessed.

> *on that account* had ye to die young, and far too early!
> At my most vulnerable point . . . What is all manslaughter in comparison with what ye have done unto me!

He is now a sort of St. Sebastian at the pillar, a complete victim of certain enemies who are shooting arrows at him.[11] That is the way in which people ordinarily explain their negative experiences of life. Their enemies are called parents or school teachers, and later on, the analyst, or the newspapers, or the Jesuits, or the Freemasons are the enemies who have destroyed their lives—or it may be the wife. It is very often women who have destroyed them, projected something which they cannot explain to themselves otherwise. Now what is this enemy really? And what has his enemy done to him—I mean, if we don't take it literally that he has been surrounded from early youth by devils? We would say there is surely something in him that has deprived him of his early world.

Mrs. Crowley: It was really his intuition I suppose.

Prof. Jung: You are quite right, in his case it would be intuition, his superior function. You see, our superior function is the devil that takes us away from the lovely things of childhood, because it is the riding animal that takes us right away into the world, that keeps us busy, and then we forget all about that lovely drama which began in our early youth. For then we become sort of professional and one-sided; we get busy, and naturally we forget about ourselves to become acquainted instead with all the possibilities of the world. And so the thing that seemed to us the most useful—and not only seems but actually *is* the most useful, the most probable thing—turns out to be the very devil when it comes to the question of the self. You see, it might be your greatest gift, and if you are very gifted in a certain way, you would be an idiot if you did not make use of that gift. But if you are identified with your superior function, it becomes in a way autonomous; the tenor becomes his voice, the violinist becomes his fiddle, the king is

---

[11] St. Sebastian, third-century Roman soldier and Christian martyr.

nothing but his crown, and the scientist or the professor nothing but his text book. Naturally, if you do not identify, you couldn't do it. You must put out your entire strength in order to produce something—your heart and your body and everything in it. Otherwise you would produce nothing. But you must know that you have to pay for it; you will be separated from yourself, will become a one-sided, cultural product that has lost its roots. We shall see next time what these treasures are that Nietzsche has left behind and is now trying to rediscover.

LECTURE IX

30 June 1937

Prof. Jung:

We had begun with "The Grave-Song" last week, and I want to go over those first paragraphs again. You remember that in these last chapters—"The Night-Song, "The Dance-Song," and "The Grave-Song"—we are concerned with Nietzsche's approach to himself. It is a sort of descent to his inferior function, and the Grave-Song is leading now to the precincts of the unconscious. As you know, the unconscious has always been—and is still—projected. Under primitive circumstances the unconscious is the ghostland, the land of the dead. It is completely projected, far more so than with us. We project the unconscious chiefly into our surroundings, into people and circumstances, and are very little concerned with the ghost land. Of course there are exceptions, but it is not an idea that would be part of the general public opinion; it is very unusual for anybody to be bothered by the ghosts of the dead. It would be rather an extraordinary case, or even pathological. People are far more inclined to accept the possibility that they suffer from a neurosis, or even from a slight psychosis; they prefer to think that they have obsessions or compulsions rather than explain their symptomatology by the presence of ghosts. So when Nietzsche approaches the unconscious, he calls it the grave-island or the silent isle in a sort of metaphoric way. He doesn't mean it too concretely. It is a metaphor but as it is not poetic language, it is also a bit more than a metaphor, and still contains something of the primitive atmosphere, something of the original aspect of an initiation or a descent to the unconscious. You see, an initiation has always to do with ghosts, and the approach to the unconscious therefore has also to do with ghosts in a more or less visible way. Sometimes it doesn't look like that at all, but in certain cases the approach to the unconscious is like a psychic phenomenon; peculiar things happen. It really looks like ghosts.

I once saw such a case. (It was published in one of my lectures but I will repeat it now.)[1] A woman, a rather hysterical individual, had gotten to a point when I felt that we should get something from the unconscious. You know, there are such situations. When people are in an impasse and one doesn't know exactly how to get them out of their difficulty, or when things are very unclear, one naturally has the feeling that now something should manifest—one should get a hint, or another factor should come into the game. That was the condition when she told me she had had a peculiar dream which she never had had before. She dreamt that she awoke in the night and noticed that the cause of her waking was that the room was filled with a strange light. First, she thought that she had left the electricity on but the bulb was not lit. The light was diffused and she didn't known exactly where it came from, but finally discovered that it issued from several places where there were sort-of accumulations of luminosity. Particularly in the curtains, which were drawn, she saw those round luminous accretions. And then she woke up, really. That was a dream, but of course it was not an ordinary one. It was a psychic phenomenon—what is called an exteriorization, whatever that is. I don't go much into the theories of these peculiar things; it was a dream, an objectivation of certain psychical things, and we have to be satisfied with this fact.

I told her then that something was on the way, because I knew from experience that when such dreams or similar facts occur, something else will soon come to the daylight. I rather expected that we would discover something that one could call psychological, but instead, the miracle with the glass happened. One morning at about seven o'clock she was wakened by a peculiar cracking and a trickling sound, and discovered that water was trickling down from the glass of water on her night table and that the whole of the rim of the glass had been split off in a perfectly clean-cut regular fashion. She called her maid to give her another glass and tried to sleep again. Suddenly she heard the same noise—the same thing had happened, and of course she got excited this time and thought it quite miraculous. She rang the bell again and the maid brought her another glass. And then the same thing happened once more. So it happened three times—three glasses were split, and all in the same regular way.

Now this is by no means the only case I have observed: I have another glass in my possession which was split in exactly the same way. It is an exteriorized phenomenon and it shows the peculiar reality of certain psychological events. Such things do happen under particular cir-

---

[1] See CW 10, par. 123.

cumstances. And, as I said, the same phenomenon can take on the aspect of ghosts or of visions. All these phenomena, which of course have been observed since time immemorial, are the reason for the idea of a really existing ghostland, and the descent into the unconscious has always been thought of as a descent into that other world, a reestablishment of the lost connections with the dead. A very good example is in Homer, where Ulysses descends into the underworld, and the blood of the sacrificed sheep makes the ghosts so real that they can speak. He has to wave them away with his sword and only allows certain ghosts to partake of the blood, that they may have substance enough to talk in an audible voice and to appear definitely.[2] All those stories in antiquity of the descent into Hades are of a similar kind; that was the old, primitive way of approaching the unconscious. And the approach to the unconscious in our days is still often characterized by such peculiar phenomena, which either happen in reality or in dreams of a very particular kind. From these dreams I got the impression that it was a matter of something far less futile or abstract than our conscious psychology; there is something there that approaches a certain substantiality.

So the analogy which Nietzsche uses here is partially a speech metaphor or a poetic image, and partially it is due to primitive reasons. The land of the dead is often an island—the island of the blessed, or the island of immortality, or the island of the graves where the dead are buried or the ghosts are supposed to live. Or it is perhaps a certain wood or a particular mountain—in Switzerland the glaciers are still haunted by the ghosts of the dead. And in the part of Africa that I saw, an especially dense growth of bamboos in the forest, the so-called bamboo-belt on Mount Elgon, was supposed to be the abode of the spirits. One really gets an extraordinary impression there. The bamboo grows very quickly and perfectly huge. The wind goes over the treetops way up above, no air can penetrate, and inside the wood it is completely still. The sound of steps is deadened by the moss and the dead leaves that cover the ground so deep that you sink in over your ankles. No birds live there so it is really soundless, and there is a sort of greenish darkness as if one were under water. The natives were scared to death of the ghosts and tried all sorts of tricks to escape being forced to go into that part of the wood. So Nietzsche's picture of the silent isle in the ocean is quite true to type, and he has to sail over the sea to reach that place where the dead live. You have probably seen the picture called

[2] *Odyssey* XI.22-33.

"The Island of the Dead" by our famous Swiss painter Böcklin; it is practically everywhere in the form of picture postal cards and such horrors.[3] Now what does he meet there? He says,

> Resolving thus in my heart, did I sail o'er the sea.—
> Oh, ye sights and scenes of my youth! Oh, all ye gleams of love, ye divine fleeting gleams! How could ye perish so soon for me! I think of you to-day as my dead ones.

You see, the shadows of Hades that are coming up to meet him are instantly explained as his personal reminiscences—of course a very modern point of view. To a more primitive man it would have been the ghosts of the past—not the shadows, the ghosts of the people who were dead—just as Ulysses meets the spirit of his mother and embraces her again. We would say, "I had a very clear memory of my mother. I saw her as she was in life." But to a more primitive mind it is the mother who appears in reality, as it were, of course in a shadowy form. You know perhaps that story of the little black boy who used to sit with the missionary by the fire in the evening. He noticed that the boy always put a bowl of rice aside and talked and answered as if he were having a discussion with somebody. So he asked him about it and the boy said: "My mother comes every evening and sits with us by the fire and I talk to her." The missionary said, "I didn't know you had a mother and moreover I see nobody here." "Of course," said the boy, "I don't see her either, but she is here. I talk to her and she answers." We would say that in the evening, sitting by the fire, we remember our dead parents or our dead friends. It is the charm of an open fire that one begins to dream and one's dreams of course take the form of reminiscences.

Now this is another aspect of the approach to the unconscious: you get caught by your reminiscences of the past and follow the lure of your reminiscences. I mentioned last week a chart that I made in my German lectures of the structure of the ego. I depicted the ego as a circle, and in the first layer of the psychic structure would be reminiscences, or the memory, the faculty of reproduction (1). Outside (5) are the famous four functions that adapt to outer reality, serving us as functions of orientation in our psychological space; and you handle these functions by your will, giving direction to them inasmuch as they are subject to your willpower. At least one function is as a rule differentiated, so that you can use it as you like, but of course the inferior

---

[3] Arnold Böcklin (1827-1901), a once popular and admired painter of mythological landscapes.

function is as if inside so that it cannot be used at will. The second of these layers round the center consists of affectivity, the source of emotions, where the unconscious begins to break in (2). The further you enter the ego, the more you lose your willpower: you cannot dominate in this inner sphere, but become more and more the victim of a strange willpower one could say, which issues from somewhere here in the center (4), a force you may call "instinct" or whatever you like—libido" or "energy"—to which you are subject. You become more and more passive.

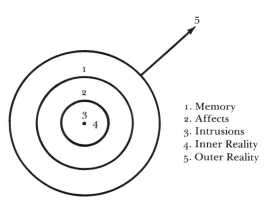

1. Memory
2. Affects
3. Intrusions
4. Inner Reality
5. Outer Reality

You see, we can rule our reminiscences to a certain extent—can order certain reminiscences to come up, for instance—and use our reproductive faculty that far. On the other hand, we largely depend on the spontaneity of our reproductive faculty to bring memories back. It often happens that they *won't* come back; you seek a name or a fact and cannot remember it, and then suddenly at another time it reproduces itself. Sometimes it is quite annoying, for it behaves like a *kobold*[4] or an elf: it is there when you don't need it, and when you need it, it is not there. So you are already annoyed by elfish interludes when it comes to your reproducing faculty, but still more when you come to affects (2).[5] You cannot produce an affect by will: it produces itself, and a real emotion is something that knocks you out of the house. You don't expect it and you have all the trouble in the world to sit on your affect, to

[4] In German folklore, a *kobold* is an underground gnome, often mischievous.

[5] In his definition of *affect* (CW 6, par. 681) Jung makes emotion its synonym, meaning a state "characterized by marked physical innervation on the one hand and a peculiar disturbance of the ideational process on the other." In contrast, for Jung, feeling is a cognitive process, that one of the four basic functions whose object is value.

control it and keep it quiet, and sometimes you are thrown from the saddle. Further in, you come to what I call intrusions, *Einbrüchen* (3), pieces of the unconscious that suddenly break into consciousness and sometimes disturb it very gravely. They come with affect and appear in the form of reminiscences.

So when Nietzsche made his *katabasis*, his descent into the unconscious, he met first his reminiscences that came with affect and carried with it the unconscious. It really *is* the unconscious and therefore he calls it the "island of the dead." This center point (4) is the ocean of the unconscious. Of course I have to represent it by a point, because I approach this central psychical fact from a world of space. In reality it would be just the reverse: outside (5) would be an immense ocean in which lies the island of consciousness; but inside it looks as if the unconscious were the little point, a tiny island in the ocean, and the ocean is also exceedingly small since it is supposed to be inside of us. Those are sort of optical illusions due to the structure of our consciousness. It is interesting to explore the way the unconscious looks from different angles. It is smaller than small yet greater than great.

> From you, my dearest dead ones, cometh unto me a sweet savour, heart-opening and melting. Verily, it convulseth and openeth the heart of the lone seafarer.

You see, Nietzsche feels or interprets the thing that is approaching him, or which he is approaching, as reminiscences of the past. But in his first statement it is as if he were travelling over the sea and came to the island of the dead. Then as soon as he is there, he reverses the picture and says the reminiscences were coming to him, so *he* would be the island and the reminiscences crowd up to him. On the one side he is in the picture of the sea, in the boat of Charon, the boat that carries the corpses over the sea to the grave island: he is the seafarer; and on the other side he is the one who had reminiscences. So he mixes up the two statements: namely, the unconscious is that tiny island which he discovers lost somewhere in the sea, and at the same time he is that island to which reminiscences are coming.

> Still am I the richest and most to be envied—I, the lonesomest one! For I have possessed you, and ye possess me still. Tell me: to whom hath there ever fallen such rosy apples from the tree as have fallen unto me?

Here also you can see the mixture of the two points of view, "I have possessed you," and "ye possess me still," which is just the reverse.

When he assumes that he is the seafarer, he is going to take possession of that island, but if he is the island, the reminiscences possess him: they are then seafarers that come up from the unconscious.

> Still am I your love's heir and heritage, blooming to your memory with many-hued, wild-growing virtues, O ye dearest ones!
>
> Ah, we were made to remain nigh unto each other, ye kindly strange marvels; and not like timid birds did ye come to me and my longing—nay, but as trusting ones to a trusting one!

He is now more in the form or the condition of the one to whom the reminiscences come. The unconscious appears first, as I said, in the form of personal reminiscences, and also—a very important point which we were discussing last week—in the form of the inferior function. The reminiscences will be colored to a great extent by the character of the inferior function. In Nietzsche's case, this inferior side is sensation-feeling because he is in the conscious chiefly intuitive, with intellect in the second place. Now, inferior sensation gives a peculiar concretistic reality to reminiscences and that probably accounts for the particularly plastic imagery. For instance, the "sweet savour" of reminiscences, and the "rosy apples" are concretistic details which show the inferior sensation. Then the feeling is obviously not only feeling proper, but sentimentality, so the feeling is not quite trustworthy in this chapter, taking it as a whole. You know, inferior feeling has always that peculiar character of sentimentality which is the brother of brutality. Sentimentality and brutality are a pair of opposites which are very close together and can instantly change from one to the other.

> Yea, made for faithfulness, like me, and for fond eternities, must I now name you by your faithlessness, ye divine glances and fleeting gleams: no other name have I yet learnt.
>
> Verily, too early did ye die for me, ye fugitives. Yet did ye not flee from me, nor did I flee from you: innocent are we to each other in our faithlessness.

These thoughts also cast an interesting light upon his relation to his inferior function, particularly to the feeling and to the memories of the past. He speaks here of faithlessness, and you remember Nietzsche's first conception of *Zarathustra* came when he was thirty-seven years old, at the time when the great change comes. That is the age when the ego purpose normally fades from life and when life itself wants to accomplish itself, when another law begins. Before that time, it is quite normal to be faithless to reminiscences, in other words—according to our diagram—it is normal to move away from the center (5) in order to apply the will to ego purposes. But in the middle of life a time comes when suddenly this inner sphere asserts its right, when we cannot decide about our fate, when things are forced upon us, and when it seems as if our own will were estranged from ourselves, so that we can hold our ego purpose only through a sort of cramped effort. If things are natural, then the will, even when applied to ego purposes, would not be exactly our own choice any longer, but would be rather a sort of command that issues from this center (4) although, by a sort of illusion, we perhaps think it to be our own purpose. But if one has a bit of introspection, one feels or sees very clearly that we don't choose—it is chosen for us. Of course that understanding becomes all the clearer when the command detaches one from the outside world and forces one to give attention to one's subjective condition.

Now, when the inferior function comes up, it forces you invariably to give attention to yourself and it detaches you from the external world, even if it looks as if the inferior function were altogether identical with the external world, and as if you were pulled out of yourself. But you will see if you follow it that you will be detached from the world, because if you come out with your inferior function, you will arouse so much misunderstanding around you, in your family or among your friends, that you will be isolated in no time. When Nietzsche speaks of faithlessness here, he alludes to the fact that for quite a while in the life he had hitherto lived, he had separated from that world of his memory, and he looked forward, away from himself. And now he suddenly realizes that that world does still exist and that it has an enormous spell for him, so he has to explain to himself that it was not faithlessness—he always loved that world—it was only fate that somehow separated him from it. It might look like faithlessness but it really was not. Now comes a new aspect:

> To kill *me*, did they strangle you, ye singing birds of my hopes!
> Yea, at you, ye dearest ones, did malice ever shoot its arrows—to hit my heart!

This is not quite easy to understand. Here he suddenly realizes that something has estranged him from his reminiscences. He suddenly feels divorced from his past——something has happened to it—yet he finds himself loving the memory of all the experiences of his past. Sure enough, in that moment of life the past is no more, it is killed. One is no longer the man of the past, because that man lived, turned away from the past and the memories, and now, you see, it is the new man who is returning to them. So the old man seems to be dead; he cannot reverse the process. Try as he would, he can no longer live in that way. Therefore he feels as if something had been killed; that sort of faithlessness really consists in the fact that his very memories, whatever constituted his former self, are dead. This is a subjective interpretation, of course; it is as if a fiend had secretly murdered his memories, so that they have become shadows. But his memories have not become shadow; he has become a shadow. You see, he has enough intuition to say, "To kill me did they strangle you," and to say that the arrows which hit them also hit him in order to kill him. So he has the intuition that he has become a shadow in a way, not his reminiscences. But he speaks as if they had been killed and that is a projection: he as his own memory, the man of the past, has been killed, because that way of functioning is no longer possible. He cannot return to it. And this is the new experience.

And they hit it! Because ye were always my dearest, my possession and my possessedness: [the two aspects again] on that account had ye to die young, and far too early!

It is not quite understandable why they had to die, but I assume it is a projection of his experiences—that he has become in a way a shadow, that he is no longer the man he used to be. Here it comes quite clearly,

At my most vulnerable point did they shoot the arrow—namely, at you, whose skin is like down—or more like the smile that dieth at a glance!

This imagery shows that his inferior feeling is exceedingly vulnerable; it is like Siegfried, who had one spot on his back which was vulnerable and that spot killed him. That is the weak spot—the reminiscences, the looking back—that is the place from which we come and to which we go, the island of the dead from which the souls come to be reborn, and to which the souls go when they are going to sleep, to wait for the next incarnation, as it were. And that is the unconscious. We come from the unconscious and we go to the unconscious, which in primitive terminology is "the ghost land." So you see, that ghost land from which we come, our origin, forms the weak spot in us. In a way like the navel which denotes the place where the original life streamed into us through the umbilical cord, it is the place which is not well defended and which will eventually kill us, the place through which death will enter again. And since this is the critical point, one tries to get away from it. One lives away from the world of memories, which is very useful and indispensable if one wants to live at all. If one is possessed by memories, one cannot adapt to new conditions.

One sees people who are forever possessed by the past, who can never adapt because they never understand the new situation: it seems to be always the old one. They cannot forget their memories; the way they adapted to their parents becomes their unforgettable model. So in order to be able to adapt, you must have that faithlessness to your memories and to all those you loved in the past, that innocent faithlessness. You have to drift away, forget what you are, and be unconscious of yourself if you want to adapt at all—up to a certain moment in your life. And then it becomes impossible to go on any longer because if you want to be yourself you cannot forget, and more and more the past comes back. For instance, it is well known that old people think a great deal about their youth. Their youthful memories often come back to a most annoying degree; they are really possessed by their memories of the past and new things don't register at all. That is a normal phenomenon. The only abnormality is when they lose the little bit of consciousness they have and talk of nothing but infantile memories.

Now, that weak or tender spot is like a young bird, easily destructible; it is exceedingly sensitive and touchy and susceptible because it is our inferiority. The memories are the place where we are still children, utterly unadapted—where we still live the past. Therefore, inasmuch as we live the past, we are at the mercy of circumstances. Moreover, when we are unadapted we are touchy, and to be touchy means to be a tyrant who tries to master circumstances by sheer violence. Unadapted people are tyrants in order to manage their lives. They bring about a sort of adaptation by suppressing everybody else; it looks as if an adaptation had been reached because circumstances are beaten down. Now Nietzsche says,

> But this word will I say unto mine enemies: What is all manslaughter in comparison with what ye have done unto me!

This shows the extraordinary vulnerability of his inferior function. When he comes to his memories, he suddenly realizes a *ressentiment* concerning his past. It looks to him as if he had been terribly suppressed by his surroundings. And when anybody feels like that, he will be exceedingly touchy and tyrannical with his surroundings, and he will be isolated on account of those impossible feelings. That was of course Nietzsche's own case, and because it was not seen enough, his statement is so hysterical one can almost hear the plaintive sentimental way in which it is said.

Worse evil did ye do unto me than all manslaughter; the irre-
trievable did ye take from me:—thus do I speak unto you, mine
enemies!

Nietzsche explains here what it is that has been taken from him. You
see, he has been killed, has become a shadow, but that is what he
doesn't know; so he assumes that his memory world has been taken
from him—all his early reminiscences of the lovely things that he loved
and enjoyed and from which he turned away for a while. And when he
comes back to them he discovers that something has happened: they
seem to be killed. He doesn't realize that he has changed and is no
longer the same man. So he feels that he has undergone an irretrieva-
ble loss, an *Unwiederbringliches*, which means something that cannot be
brought back. It has gone forever and it looks to him like murder,
manslaughter, and he thinks that enemies have done it. Of course he
is projecting a perfectly normal fact that has happened to man forever;
since he is unaware of it, he projects it.

This is a very ordinary case—many people suffer from the same illusion. From a certain time in their life onward, they believe that people have maneuvered against them, played all sorts of tricks on them.
Or they believe that something once happened that was simply fatal; it
has very bad consequences and naturally somebody else is responsible
for it. By such illusions they try to explain why they have become different, but as a matter of fact it is life itself that has made them different; they have grown into something different from what they supposed they were. Of course you must have a peculiar illusion to assume
that you can live in a different sphere of life just as well: *ubi bene ibi pa-
tria*. That means, where the circumstances are favorable, you could live
and be yourself. But in order to have such an illusion you have to forget what you are and what you have been, for what you are is what you
have been: you carry that which you have been with you everywhere.
As long as you can put a sort of layer of unconsciousness between what
you are here and what you were there, you can manage all sorts of ad-
aptations, can imagine that you are now the fellow who has made himself into such-and-such a thing. Of course you pay for that illusion by
the loss of the memory world, by the loss of that which you have been.
In reality, however, you cannot really lose it. It is always there, but it is
a skeleton in the cupboard, a thing of which you are always afraid because it will undo the thing you have built up. It will contradict it and
inexorably remind you of what you are and what you have been. When
that thing begins to manifest, if it now attracts that man who has been

in the outer world and makes him into that which he had been, then it looks as if he had been murdered. Of course since he doesn't understand that whole thing, it is again a projection. I have not been killed but my reminiscences have been killed, the beauty of my former world has been taken away, and it is a loss which can never be made good.

Now this is the ordinary neurotic unconsciousness, a typical neurotic illusion. You see, such people mind that they live at all, mind circumstances, and project all sorts of reproaches into other people. They assume that certain events have destroyed something in them instead of understanding that they have changed, have become different beings. And peculiarly enough, what they call a different being, what they think they are, they are not. They say they have never been as they are now, but that is just the thing that they have always been, only they were unconscious of it; so when they come into it, they feel it to be something different. If they were able to see it, it is *they* who have changed; nobody murdered their reminiscences but they died—the former man died. They are now ghosts and no longer what they understood to be a living being. You see, what such people understood to be a living being was that thing that lived away from itself. It was an illusionary being, a role one played, so in a way it was an artificial position which they created. For instance, a man with a good voice is that voice—he is that tenor. Then in the later part of life his voice cracks and he feels of course that the world has injured him. You see, he discovers then what he has always been before he had that voice. His voice helped him to create a perfectly artificial illusionary existence in the world. Of course that is perfectly legitimate: you must sell yourself in order to live, so you must create a position which can be handed out to the world as a sort of value which you will be paid for. But that is not yourself really. It is what you have been, and when that thing vanishes, you find yourself in a sphere that always has been, but it was always unconscious up to the moment when you returned to it again. It is an island which was always there and you have always been on it, but you never were conscious that you were there; and now, when the illusion dies—that fiction which you have held about yourself—and you come back to the island, for the first time the island becomes conscious. But it looks mighty gloomy, yet that is yourself.

Now, Nietzsche is quite unconscious about it, so this is a passage where he somehow gets my goat. It makes me uncomfortable when he speaks of the enemies and what they have done to the poor little child. Naturally I get a professional complex here and think that damned thing ought to be mended. There are certain writers whom I cannot read on account of that professional complex. Why all that fuss? It is all illusion. Now he continues in the same plaintive style.

> Slew ye not my youth's visions and dearest marvels! My playmates took ye from me, the blessed spirits! [The *Erlkönig* and his daughters.] To their memory do I deposit this wreath and this curse.
>
> This curse upon you, mine enemies! Have ye not made mine eternal short, as a tone dieth away in a cold night! Scarcely, as the twinkle of divine eyes, did it come to me—as a fleeting gleam!
>
> Thus spake once in a happy hour my purity: "Divine shall everything be to me."

That is another memory and again a very important characteristic of early memories, of the same order as the playmates who are blessed spirits. These feeling memories point to the archetypal reminiscences of which I spoke in the last Seminar. I mentioned that little boy who was fetched every night by the white maidens that came down from heaven in a zeppelin, to take him to the island that wants to be visited. They were probably the *Erlkönig*'s daughters, those wonderful spirits whose playmate he once had been. Now those are reminiscent feelings of a perfect state, a sort of paradise state; in Goethe's poem, *Die Erlkönig*, it is the archetypal images very often in dreams that anticipate death. I have dealt with such a case in one of our dream seminars, a little girl who died of an infectious disease when she was nine. She had these archetypal dreams a year and a half before she died and before there was any trace of illness—dreams that have almost nothing to do with our kind of life or reality.[6]

These early memories often have a glamor and splendor that is quite extraordinary. It is a sort of primeval world out of which the child is born when it may have lived already for many years in this world, but in the mind the child is still in that primeval world and only gradually comes out of it. And there are not a few who get eternally stuck there, and they retain all the innocence and beauty of the primeval world even if they live a kind of life which would be called immoral by everybody in his sense. But it doesn't touch them—it is merely a compensation for a basic innocence. They are still living in the archetypal images and are utterly and divinely unaware of what they live in reality. They live in the slime in reality, but in the fantasy or inner feeling they are still in the primeval world of complete innocence. Now here Nietzsche

[6] See CW 18, pars. 525-39.

refers to that innocence: one can hardly call it an early experience because it is not really an experience, but was there before there was consciousness. Before this world existed there was the divine world, and any child that comes out of that world still looks at things with divine eyes and says, "Divine shall everything be unto me." Everything has the splendor of divinity, and what things really are remains concealed for many years, sometimes for a lifetime.

I have seen quite a number of people who have never been born, who still live in that original sphere. Of course they had a most miserable life, as you can imagine, but they were always blissfully unaware of it. They were physically ill because the body naturally reacts against such mental unreality. The body has to live in this reality, and the mind is in a primeval condition. Very often one finds cases where it is a matter of a partial or a sort of fragmentary birth, when a part of the mental personality has remained in the primeval world which then forms a sort of inclusion, a sort of enclave in the conscious world. Such people are perfectly adapted and apparently normal, but they have peculiar dreams. The more normal they are, the more they are afraid of that inclusion; and the more abnormal they are, the less it frightens them. The inclusion is like an island belonging to another world which is included in their own world but in no way attached. It is something perfectly strange. One cannot say that such cases are frequent, but they are not very rare. It is a fact which is hardly ever known, however—one seldom hears of it.

Just by chance we discovered such a case in our German dream seminar and it is well worthwhile to mention it because Nietzsche is of that kind. A young man who seems to be adapted—one could not say that he was incapacitated in any way—had a dream that repeated itself from his fourth or fifth year up to his eighteenth year. He is still in the early twenties, so it is not very long ago that this thing subsided, and it is now an inclusion. The dream was always something like this: He finds himself on the surface of a planet, presumably the earth, but it is a cosmic desert, and he is afraid of something or somebody that persecutes him. He is running away when he suddenly falls into a deep shaft. He falls and he falls, and the enemy is now up above looking down through the shaft, and occasionally he gets a glimpse of that fellow who is peeping in. While he is falling into apparently a limitless depth, he sees that at the other end far below are the flames of hell. But the persecutor on top showers a rain of square tablets down upon him, and there are so many of them that they condense the air in the shaft and form a sort of *couche* or layer which prevents him from falling any further. On a ledge of rock he comes to a standstill and there he sits: the tablets obviously have rescued him. Now the fellow up above is usually the devil, or it may be the face of quite a friendly being, often the face of a god, or the dreamer's own face. He actually made some of those tablets in order to give me an idea of them: each tablet was about six centimeters square and each one contained a different design, but it was always a mandala. So the persecutor showered mandalas down upon him, sort of magic tablets, in order to protect him, and it saved him finally.

You see, he is confronted with a most unusual problem for his age: he finds himself upon the surface of an uninhabited planet, which means loneliness in space, and he doesn't possess the faculty that other people possess of creating the illusion of friendly surroundings. And because he doesn't possess that faculty he is persecuted by the thing he doesn't possess and which he ought to have. He ought to have a god and a devil and a friend and himself, and they are after him and would give him the possibility of creating the illusion of a habitable world where he can take roots and establish himself as a definite human being in friendly relations with his surroundings. Since he was born without the illusion of relationship to this world, all that faculty is still in another world and has to run after him in order to get him finally. And that friend or devil or god, or whatever it is, gets him by that multitude of mandalas which suggest wholeness, the round thing and the four square thing which mean totality; and the two finally become one to a certain extent so that the dream could disappear. It looks, you see, as if the birth had really occurred. When he was about eighteen years old he was able to detach from the primordial world, the world of fairies, which had caused him to see the earth as an uninhabitable planet. That is a vision characteristic of childhood.

I know another instance, the dream of a girl about ten or eleven years old, which also repeated itself rather often. She is in empty cosmic space, walking on something like a path, and far in the distance ahead of her, she sees a round light, which as she approaches becomes bigger and finally is an enormous globe that comes nearer and nearer, and of course she grows afraid. Then when the globe is close to her, the path bifurcates and she doesn't know whether she should go to the right or to the left, and in that moment she wakes up. It is a nightmare. This is a very typical dream of that kind: I call them cosmic dreams of childhood. They are the archetypal experiences of children with strong memories of what the Tibetans would call the Bardo life, a prenatal condition of the mind, the condition before the birth into this spatial world.[7] That shows itself first under its absolute aspect, an empty, dead world to which life is absolutely strange—particularly human life—and it explains also why man has a mind or a consciousness at all. He must have something different, not of the same kind, or he would not be conscious. He must have something which is at variance with the conditions of our space, and it is a fact that the psyche is at variance with the conditions of our space.

Now, Nietzsche's original tendency—"divine shall everything be unto me"—was an attempt to make everything divine so that it would fit in with his primeval experience, with his presupposition of a world, the archetypal world. But the world into which he was born was not archetypal: there were fatal offences against the archetypal world. To begin with, his parents were far from being anything like an *Erlkönig*. So he was soon under the necessity of inventing or remembering a counter-position against his father. He was disappointed at having such a real, human father and could not adapt to it, so his unconscious gave him very early the idea of an entirely different kind of father, Wotan. When he was fifteen years old he had his great Wotan dream. And now you see what he complains of.

> Then did ye haunt me with foul phantoms; ah, whither hath that happy hour now fled?
> "All days shall be holy unto me"—so spake once the wisdom of my youth: verily, the language of a joyous wisdom!
> But then did ye enemies steal my nights, and sold them to sleepless torture: ah, whither hath that joyous wisdom now fled?

He is complaining that his enemies—life, in other words—have haunted him with foul phantoms. That of course refers to all sorts of fantasies. He even accuses his enemies of causing him to have evil fantasies that poisoned his former experiences, all his expectation of the world as it should be—which means as he remembered it. We have already encountered the idea that everything should be divine, and it is expressed again in "All days shall be holy unto me" which was the language of joyous wisdom. Now it is the language of the Bardo life where everything was still archetypal, the language of the beautiful dreams, the beautiful memories of the prenatal past. And that his enemies steal his nights means that they steal his memories, the images of that beautiful world of the past, so all that wisdom has disappeared. The sleepless torture refers of course to his sleeplessness, and that has much to

---

[7] For *Tibetan*, see above, 10 Oct. 1934, n. 18.

do with the fact that he lost that quiet peaceful island of memories, the world within to which he ought to return in order to sleep. If he cannot return to the inner world—if that is stolen, if he is isolated, cut off by a thick layer—naturally he cannot sleep. Sleep is the brother of death and one returns to the island of death in order to sleep. But he is far away in his illusion, and the island has been stolen, so he is left to sleepless torture. He says,

> Once did I long for happy auspices: then did ye lead an owl-monster across my path, an adverse sign. Ah, whither did my tender longing then flee?

Now what is the meaning of this?

Mrs. Sigg: He had much too much wisdom and therefore his sleeplessness.

Prof. Jung: Why should there be an owl?

Mrs. Sigg: An owl is a symbol of *Weisheit.*[8] It is the symbolic bird of Pallas Athena.

Mrs. Baumann: I want to ask whether it is an owl-monster. In my translation it is a monstrous owl, which just means big.

Prof. Jung: That is wrong. It is *ein Eulen-Untier*, an owl-monster.

Prof. Reichstein: The owl is a bird that sees in the night.

Prof. Jung: Exactly. It is the bird of Pallas Athena. Because it sees in the darkness, it has an understanding of the dark things, perspicacity. But of course here the owl-monster refers to a sort of wisdom which doesn't fulfill what one would expect of wisdom: it doesn't illuminate his darkness. This owl monster is a sort of fake wisdom. Now, what is the wisdom that has been given to us to teach us the understanding of darkness?

Mrs. Sigg: Religious teaching.

Remark: Philosophy.

Prof. Jung: Well, Sophia is wisdom, and *philosophia* means the love of wisdom: a philosopher is one who loves wisdom. But what about our philosophy? Does that enlighten the darkness of the soul? Not at all. Of course Nietzsche had a philosophical education and perhaps he refers to that, but I think the fact that he had a father who was a theologian points rather to another kind of wisdom, a religious wisdom which did not fulfill its promise. It did not enlighten him about the darkness of the soul. You know, he was concerned with an archetypal memory: we have evidence of that in his life. When he was fifteen years old, he had

---

[8] *Weisheit*: wisdom.

the great Wotan dream; that archetypal experience was in him and the darkness was not explained by the religious teaching he got from his father. So the wisdom he was shown was an owl-monster that made everybody afraid. Of course a certain kind of Protestant teaching is quite apt to make people rather afraid, particularly of hell, because it is hardly a moral teaching and it doesn't let them live. It tells them that nothing is allowed, everything is forbidden.[9] So the only conclusion one can draw is that one had best cease to exist in order to escape committing a sin! The owl is an uncanny bird, it means death. You know there is a kind of owl which is called "the death owl" on account of its uncanny cries in the night, a bird of ill omen. You see, he says, "Once did I long for happy auspices" and then that owl-monster was brought up instead of something auspicious which would have enlightened him.

Mrs. Sigg: In the Wotan dream he heard that voice.[10]

Prof. Jung: It is true that he heard then a horrible cry but whether that has to do with the owl I don't know.

[9] Whereas of course Nietzsche came to believe that since God is dead, everything is allowed, nothing is forbidden. The death of God is proclaimed in *The Gay Science*, book 3, sec. 125 and in section 3 of the Prologue to *Zarathustra*.

[10] Nietzsche's sister, in N/Life (p. 18), tells of his recording a dream just after the death of their father and just before that of their young brother: "A grave suddenly opened and my father in his shroud arose out of it. He hurried into the church and in a moment or two reappeared with a small child in his arms." Compare the howling dog, remembered from his sixth year, in *Thus Spake Zarathustra*, ch. 46, "The Vision and the Enigma," part 2, and see p. 1289 below.

SPRING TERM

May / June 1938

LECTURE I

4 May 1938

Prof. Jung:

Here we are again at our old *Zarathustra*! And when I looked through the chapters we have dealt with and those we have still to deal with, I must tell you frankly, I got bored stiff, chiefly by the style. The long interruption has done no good to my enthusiasm apparently. As often before—but this time particularly—I was impressed with the unnaturalness of the style, Nietzsche's terribly exaggerated, inflated way of expressing himself. So I came to the conclusion that you have now had enough of this and that we don't need to go further into the actual detail. I think we had better do what the Germans call *Die Rosinen aus dem Kuchen picken.*

Mrs. Crowley: We say "to pick the plums out of the cake."

Prof. Jung: Yes, and so I have made a selection of such plums within the next chapters, where we get the principal ideas or the particular gems of psychology that are characteristic of *Zarathustra*. You know, in dealing with this material, we must always keep in mind, as I have emphasized time and again, that Zarathustra is not exactly Nietzsche, as Nietzsche is not exactly Zarathustra, yet the two are of course in a sort of personal union; there is an aspect of Nietzsche better called "Zarathustra," and an aspect of Zarathustra better called "Nietzsche," the personal, all-too-human man. For instance, Zarathustra suffers from any number of personal resentments which clearly belong to Nietzsche's professional existence: we cannot saddle Zarathustra with such ordinary reactions. Also much of the peculiar style is not to be put down to Zarathustra, though I should assume he would naturally prefer a somewhat hieratic style.

Zarathustra is a sort of *Geist*. That is a very ambiguous word; you can use the French word *esprit*, but the English word "spirit" does not cover it; you might say he was a genius though I am afraid that is not ambiguous *enough*—English in that respect is much too definite. But if you understand what *Geist* or *esprit* mean, you get about the size of Zarathustra.[1] Zarathustra is a more or less autonomous existence that Nietzsche clearly felt as a double, so we must assume that Zarathustra has in a way his own psychology; yet on account of that most unfortunate identification of Nietzsche with Zarathustra throughout the whole book, there is a continuous mixing of the two factors. From the standpoint of common sense or rationalism, one would naturally say, "But what is the figure of Zarathustra after all? Only a sort of metaphoric impersonation." But that point of view is not psychological; one would just miss the peculiarity of Zarathustra's character, and one would not be able to explain that manifestation. So we have to give him a certain amount of autonomy, and thus far we can call him a *Geist* or *esprit*, as if he were an extension of Nietzsche's own existence. Of course this is a logical process; one calls such a procedure an hypostasis—giving substance, extending existence, to something. This is not a metaphysical assertion, as you will understand, but merely a psychological assertion. There are indubitably psychological factors that have an autonomous existence. You feel such an existence as soon as something *gets* you, particularly if it gets your goat; then *it* gets you—you don't take it, it gets you—expressing thereby the fact that there is an autonomous factor within yourself, in that particular moment at least.

Now we will plunge in. Chapter 34 is called "Self-surpassing," *Selbstüberwindung*, and here are some passages which I should not like to omit. We will begin at the twenty-first paragraph:

Hearken now unto my word, ye wisest ones! Test it seriously, whether I have crept into the heart of life itself, and into the roots of its heart!

Wherever I found a living thing, there found I Will to Power; and even in the will of the servant found I the will to be master.

That to the stronger the weaker shall serve—thereto persuadeth he his will who would be master over a still weaker one. That delight alone he is unwilling to forego.

And as the lesser surrendereth himself to the greater that he may have delight and power over the least of all, so doth even the greatest surrender himself, and staketh—life, for the sake of power.

It is the surrender of the greatest to run risk and danger, and play dice for death.

[1] The ambiguity of *Geist* is such that it is often translated "mind," but often also "spirit"; but as Jung repeatedly explains "mind" is usually wrong and "spirit" insufficient.

And where there is sacrifice and service and love-glances, there also is the will to be master. By by-ways doth the weaker then slink into the fortress, and into the heart of the mightier one—and there stealeth power.

And this secret spake Life herself unto me. "Behold," said she, "I am that *which must ever surpass itself.*"

This is very characteristic of Nietzsche's outlook on life. He really produced the psychological power theory first, anticipating, thus, Adlerian psychology, the so-called individual psychology, though it is not individual at all, but is very collective, as one sees from the way Nietzsche states the case.[2] You know, Nietzsche had already written a large book about power psychology, so here he simply alludes to it.[3] It is quite certainly a very important truth, yet it is not the whole truth, but is *one* important aspect. A great many human reactions can be explained by the theory of power. Naturally power is inevitable: we need it. It is an instinct without which we can do nothing, so whenever a person produces anything, he is liable to be accused of a power attitude—if you want to accuse him at all, which is also a sort of power attitude.

People with a power attitude are always inclined to *accuse*, either to accuse in themselves a gesture of power, or anything suggesting such an attitude in anybody else. You see, that so-called power attitude is always expressed on the other side by feelings of inferiority; otherwise power makes no sense. It needs the power attitude to overcome the feelings of inferiority; but then the person with the power has again feelings of inferiority because of his own power attitude. So the two are always together: whoever has a power theory has feelings of inferiority, coupled with feelings of megalomania. Of course it may be realized to a certain extent, or it may be well concealed. In any case it is there.

When the power attitude is concealed, people chiefly speak of feelings of inferiority; even people with an absolutely clear power attitude insist very much on their feelings of inferiority—what modest little frightened mice they are, and how cruel people are to them—so one is perhaps quite impressed by their great modesty and inconspicuousness. But it is all a trick. Behind that is megalomania and a power atti-

---

[2] Alfred Adler (1870-1937), Freud's first important "defector," replaced the sexual drive by the power drive, though he disavowed Nietzsche as a model or even an influence. He is best known for *The Practice and Theory of Individual Psychology* (1923). On Freud vs. Adler, see CW 7, pars. 16-55.

[3] It is not clear what work Jung is thinking of here—*The Gay Science, Untimely Meditations?* As he well knew, *The Will to Power*, the most obvious book to fit the description, was compiled from a multitude of notes only after Nietzsche's death.

tude. It is a fishing for compliments: such a person laments his incompetence in order to make people say, "But you know that is not true!" It is a famous trick.

Of course other people have the declared power attitude that they are mighty bulls. I had a wonderful chance to observe that on my trip to India; and particularly on the boat coming back I studied the voices of those Indian officials, military and civil servants. I noticed that most of the men had made a sort of culture of the voice. It is remarkable. One man (he was a scientist, however) was a great boomer. I thought it sounded wonderful when he said "Good morning." One felt that it *weighed*. It was like old father Zeus getting up in the morning and saying to his gods, "Good Morning!" Then I overheard him telling another man, "Oh, I hadn't seen that fellow for twenty years, and lo and behold, he came up and asked me if I was not professor So-and-So; he didn't remember my face but he remembered my voice." And because the great boomer was booming himself, you could hear it over half the deck against the wind. At first I thought, what a mighty fellow! But it didn't take me long to see that this voice was just a big cloud, a smokescreen, and behind was a very nice, modest little man who was afraid that he would not be taken for a full-grown personality, so he cultivated the voice to make *something* big at least. Then I saw the same thing in many others on board.

You see, most of the men on military service are really overcome by the immensity of India, the immensity of their task of being the superior people who uphold or carry the Indian Empire, a great continent of over 360 million people. How can they do it? Well, they must boom it, must make a noise, and so they cultivate that voice. It is the boss that speaks, the fellow that rules twenty slaves or servants, and at least five children, and two secretaries in the office, and he must impress himself—so his voice sounds very disagreeable, bossy, tyrannical, harsh, and arrogant. But those people are really perfectly nice, very ordinary, and very small—simply inadequate to their big task. That is very typical of the English colonial civilization. None of those civil servants or military people talked naturally—except one, and he was a very distinguished man. I did not ask his name, but he obviously belonged to the nobility, and he had the style of the very good boy of the grandmother. He talked very, very softly, had learned the trick of being inconspicuous, and didn't need to boom, but you could see in his face that he actually had the power. All the others only sounded as if they had.

Now, whenever people are called upon to perform a role which is too big for the human size, they are apt to learn such tricks by which to inflate themselves—a little frog becomes like a bull—but it is really against their natural grain. So the social conditions are capable of producing that phenomenon of the too big and the too small, and create that social complex in response to the social demands. If conditions demand that they should be very big, people apparently produce a power psychology which is not really their own: they are merely the victims of their situation. Of course there are other people who are not called upon at all to develop such a psychology, yet produce it all by themselves, and those are the people who could do better than they do. Because they don't know their capacities, they don't make the effort that they really could make. They have feelings of inferiority and fall into a power attitude. Then there are the people who *can* do something. They are successful, and they are accused of having a power attitude by all those who have feelings of inferiority about their own power attitude. And there is the mistake; there the power theory comes to an end. For to be able to do a thing requires power; if one has not the power, one doesn't do it. Yet for having shown that power one will be accused of a power attitude, and that is all wrong because the power has not been used for illegitimate purposes; a person who can really do a thing is quite wrongly explained as having a power attitude. To use that power is legitimate. So the power instinct in itself is perfectly legitimate. The question is only to what ends it is applied. If it is applied to personal, illegitimate ends, one can call it a power attitude because it is merely a compensatory game. It is in order to prove that one is a big fellow: the power is used to compensate one's inferior feelings. But that forms a vicious circle. The more one has feelings of inferiority, the more one has a power attitude, and the more one has a power attitude, the more one has feelings of inferiority.

Now when Nietzsche sees the power aspect of things—and that aspect cannot be denied—he is quite right inasmuch as there is a misuse of power. But if he sees it everywhere, at the core of everything, if it has crept in as the secret of life even, if he sees it as the will to be and to create, then he makes a great mistake. Then he is blindfolded by his own complex, for he is the man who, on the one side, has feelings of inferiority, and on the other, a tremendous power complex. What was the man Nietzsche in reality? A neurotic, a poor devil who suffered from migraine and a bad digestion, and had such bad eyes that he could read very little and was forced to give up his academic career. And he couldn't marry because an early syphilitic infection blighted his whole Eros side. Of course, all that contributed to the most beautiful inferiority complex you can imagine; such a fellow is made for an inferiority complex, and will therefore build up an immense power attitude on the other side. And then he is apt to discover that complex everywhere, for complexes are also a means of understanding other people: you can assume that others have the same complex. If you know your one passion is power and assume that other people have such a passion too, you are not far from the mark. But there are people who *have* power, who have good eyes and no migraine and can swing things, and to accuse those people of "power" is perfectly ridiculous, for they create something, they are positive. Then the devil gets them naturally by another corner and that is what the power psychologist does not see.

Now of course, Nietzsche is very much on the side of the inferiority, where the only passion, the only ambition, is: how can I get to the top? How can I make a success, make an impression? So Nietzsche is here the man in the glass house who should not throw stones; he should be careful. His style is easily a power style, he is a boomer, he makes tremendous noise with his words, and what for? To make an impression, to show what he is and to make everybody believe it. So one can conclude as to the abysmal intensity of his feelings of inferiority. Well, the last sentence is,

> And this secret spake Life herself unto me: "Behold," said she, "I am that *which must ever surpass itself*."

This is a good conclusion. A power condition making a vicious circle with the feelings of inferiority is most unsatisfactory and it must surpass itself. As a matter of fact, life does surpass itself: it is always undoing itself, always creating a new day, a new generation. Well, it is always imperfect, but it is not necessarily imperfect from that power side. It must follow the law of *enantiodromia*: there must be destruction and creation, or it would not be at all. A thing that is absolutely static has no existence. It must be in a process or it would never even be perceived. Therefore a truth is only a truth as much as it changes. Now we come to the end of the chapter.

> And he who hath to be a creator in good and evil—verily, he hath first to be a destroyer, and break values in pieces.
>
> Thus doth the greatest evil pertain to the greatest good: that, however, is the creating good.—
>
> Let us *speak* thereof, ye wisest ones, even though it be bad. To be silent is worse; all suppressed truths become poisonous.

And let everything break up which—can break up by our truths! Many a house is still to be built!—

This is a variation of the other sentence "that *which must ever surpass itself.*" In other words, whatever exists must be destroyed in order to be created into something new. Of course this is also a one-sided truth, but a revolutionary truth. Nietzsche was a forerunner of our revolutionary age, and he felt very much that that was a truth of the time which should not be concealed, that many old things had become overmature and were really beginning to rot. Therefore he realized the necessity of destruction. And he was clear-sighted enough to see that in the process of life and of becoming, the pairs of opposites come together; good and evil are the classical designations, the idea that next to the best is the worst. So if a bad thing gets very bad it may transform into something good, and when a thing is too good it becomes unlikely—we say it is too good to be true, it undoes itself. This is the natural *enantiodromia*. You see, he expresses a truth here which was already said by old Heraclitus, and it is of course a passage which formulates the modern mind.[4]

Now there is nothing very important in the next chapter, "The Sublime Ones," nor in the following one, "The Land of Culture," nor in that chapter called "Immaculate Perception." ("Perception" is the wrong translation. *Erkenntnis* would mean, rather, cognition or apperception.)[5] Then, in the chapter called "Scholars," he chiefly realizes professional resentments, and in the chapter called "Poets," he chiefly realizes all his resentments when he was called a poet. Of course it is all represented in a generalized form, but is is quite obvious that they are his personal resentments. So we come now to the fortieth chapter, "Great Events," and there we will pick out something right in the beginning.

> There is an isle in the sea—not far from the Happy Isles of Zarathustra—on which a volcano ever smoketh; of which isle the people, and especially the old women amongst them, say that it is a place as a rock before the gate of the netherworld; but that through the volcano itself the narrow way leadeth downwards which conducteth to this gate.
> Now about the time that Zarathustra sojourned on the Happy

---

[4] Heraclitus wrote of each pair of opposites that the latter "having changed becomes the former, and this again having changed becomes the latter." But "God is day-night, winter-summer, war-peace, satiety-famine" (Freeman*, fragments 88, 67).

[5] Translators have not been able to resist the pun, however.

Isles, it happened that a ship anchored at the isle on which stand-eth the smoking mountain, and the crew went ashore to shoot rab-bits. About the noontide hour, however, when the captain and his men were together again, they saw suddenly a man coming to-wards them through the air, and a voice said distinctly: "It is time! It is the highest time!" But when the figure was nearest to them (it flew past quickly, however, like a shadow, in the direction of the volcano), then did they recognise with the greatest surprise that it was Zarathustra; for they had all seen him before except the cap-tain himself, and they loved him as the people love: in such wise that love and awe were combined in equal degree.

"Behold!" said the old helmsman, "there goeth Zarathustra to hell!"

About the same time that these sailors landed on the fire-isle, there was a rumour that Zarathustra had disappeared; and when his friends were asked about it, they said that he had gone on board a ship by night, without saying whither he was going.

Thus there arose some uneasiness. After three days, however, there came the story of the ship's crew in addition to this uneasi-ness—and then did all the people say that the devil had taken Zar-athustra. His disciples laughed, sure enough, at this talk; and one of them said even: "Sooner would I believe that Zarathustra hath taken the devil." But at the bottom of their hearts they were all full of anxiety and longing: so their joy was great when on the fifth day Zarathustra appeared amongst them.

Here is a bit of legend. These legendary interspersions in *Zarathustra* are always sort of happy isles, because they liberate us from the exag-gerated kind of expression and something comes through in the lan-guage of a simple tale, showing that here a truth is coming out which is truly Zarathustra. This is not Nietzsche, but conveys something which Nietzsche could not twist into his own style, or his own sermon; it is a piece of nature that breaks through. This is the other one, the old fellow that talks in parables. Therefore all parables, particularly the tale-like parables in *Zarathustra*, have an extraordinary value because they are not over-philosophized; they say what is to be said and are not twisted. You see, after his dissertation about power in these chapters we have just passed, where he creates for himself an exclusive position and criticizes his surroundings, we can almost expect a reaction from below. If one pours out a mouthful, one can be sure that something will happen to teach one the contrary. Now, the main content of this story is the descent of Zarathustra into Hades. There is the volcano and the fire underneath, the entrance to the interior of the earth, the underworld—there is even old Cerberus, the fire dog—and Zarathustra is now going down into all this. Psychologically it would mean that after all that great talk, there is an underworld and down there one has to go. But if one is so high and efficient, why not stay up there? Why bother about this descent? Yet the tale says inevitably one goes down—that is the *enantiodromia*—and when one gets down there, well, one will be burned up, one will dissolve.

Of course Nietzsche must have known—he was a classical philologist—that Empedocles, the great philosopher, had chosen that form of death for himself: he jumped into the flaming crater of Aetna. I often wonder why he did it. A Latin poet said about him that it was in order to be considered an immortal god. But in the biography of old Empedocles we get the real clue! You know, he was very popular: wherever he appeared, large crowds of people came to hear him talk, and when he left town about ten thousand people followed him to the next one where he had to talk again. I assume he was human, so what could he do? He had to find a place where the ten thousand people would not run after him, so he jumped into Aetna.[6] It had nothing to do with being an immortal god, but was just in order to have his peace. Now this story is of course also a kind of psychological tale. It may be true that the great philosopher committed suicide in order to escape his ten thousand lovely followers, but it is also a mythological motif. So after that greatness, when Nietzsche felt that he was the savior of the world, the one who tells all the boys what to do in order to get salvation, he would have to make the descent into utter destruction. But it is curious that he does not allude to Empedocles, and his story altogether has a very peculiar ring.

When I was a student I first read that passage, and it stuck in my mind. It was so funny—the noontide hour and the captain and his men—what was the matter with that ship that they go to shoot rabbits near the entrance of hell? Then slowly it came to me that when I was about eighteen, I had read a book from my grandfather's library called *Blätter aus Prévorst* by Kerner, a collection in four volumes of wonderful stories about all sorts of ghosts and phantasies and forebodings,

---

[6] That Empedocles (484-424 B.C.) jumped into Mt. Aetna's crater is reported by Diogenes Laertius in *Lives of Eminent Philosophers* bk. VIII, ch. 2, secs. 66-69. He in turn cites one Timaeus, not Plato's dialectician but a historian on whom Diogenes leans. Nietzsche often referred to Empedocles favorably, even calling him, in *The Anti-Christ*, Zarathustra's successor.

and among them I found that story.[7] It is called "An Extract of awe-inspiring import from the log of the ship 'Sphinx,' in the year 1686, in the Mediterranean." I give you the literal text.

The four captains and a merchant, Mr. Bell, went ashore on the island of Mt. Stromboli to shoot rabbits. At three o'clock they called the crew together to go aboard, when, to their inexpressible astonishment, they saw two men flying rapidly over them through the air. One was dressed in black, the other in grey. They approached them very closely, in the greatest haste; to their greatest dismay they descended amid the burning flames into the crater of the terrible volcano, Mt. Stromboli. They recognized the pair as acquaintances from London.

The absolute parallel is of course formed by the rabbits; also the noon-tide, for it was three o'clock in the afternoon when the captain and his men assembled again. It is perfectly clear that it is the same story. I then wrote to Nietzsche's sister and she told me that, as a matter of fact, somewhere between his tenth and eleventh year she and her brother had read *Blätter aus Prevorst*, which they found when nosing about in the library of *their* grandfather, Pastor Oehler. She could not remember that particular story but she said that my theory was quite possible because that book was in the library and she remembered having read such marvelous stories with Nietzsche; she had some reason for being quite certain that after his eleventh year it was out of the question, so it would have been, at the latest, in his eleventh year. Now it is most probable that Nietzsche had forgotten the story, and therefore he produces it so literally, with the funny details. One wonders what those rabbits have to do with the descent of Zarathustra: it is so foolish, but is is explained by that parallel. This is what we call cryptomnesia; secretly that memory crept up and reproduced itself. It shows how the unconscious layers of the mind work.

Then you can be sure that, as the unconscious was capable of putting over that story, it is also capable of carrying a truth against Nietzsche's consciousness, against his insight or understanding. Now, the descent into the volcano as described in the log of that ship *Sphinx* would be explained as the vision of two people who had died during the absence

[7] *The Seeress of Prevorst.* Here the compiler of the lecture notes kindly furnishes the citations: vol. IV, p. 57. Justinus Kerner's work was first published in Karlsruhe. Jung told this story about Nietzsche in his inaugural dissertation, published in Leipzig in 1902, and it is the first item in CW 1!

of the ship from England. Visions were the only sort of radio they had in those days—or perhaps clairaudience or second sight. But of course when Mr. Jones or Mr. Smith dies, it is not yet broadcast by the BBC. and it still happens in this natural way through dreams or visions. You find wonderful accounts of such cases in the *Fantasies of the Living*, a very well-substantiated collection published by the British Society of Psychical Research. And here it means that the spirit is going to die after that exaggerated self-assertion. For nothing is more killing for the spirit than when a man asserts himself to be *it*. That is most unbecoming to *l'esprit; esprit* only lives when it is impersonal. If it is personal it becomes a mere resentment and then it is no good. Then it is no longer *esprit*. You see, after that inflation it goes down and ends its life. It is really a catastrophe—not yet a catastrophe in Nietzsche's case, but it is the anticipation of one. It is exactly like a dream which tells you to look out; it is a sort of warning that hell is coming close and is already visible—a fellow is already going down over there.

You know, such stories are recorded because they are edifying. Those two gentlemen from London were big merchants and evidently they were not quite all right, because they are painted with the colors of hell which express sinfulness; one is black and the other grey, whereas they should be wearing white shirts which is court dress in heaven. Formerly at funerals I remember people would be wondering whether the dead man was entering eternal bliss or whether he was going to the bad place. I knew a nice old theologian, a professor of church history, who was an original, and also he was quite deaf. And once he went to the funeral of a man of high repute where all the friends and acquaintances were gathered in the drawing room, as was the custom, whispering to each other in hushed voices, before they went with the funeral cortège. A man was trying to say to the professor that he was so glad to know that the man had passed away so peacefully, and the professor, nodding his head, said in a loud booming voice: "Yes, yes, I know that he had no real joy in dying!"

Now this edifying aspect shows the psychological importance of such a vision and it should be pretty much the same with Nietzsche. He should ask himself, "What is going to happen now? Where have I made such a mistake? How did I get so inflated that I am now threatened with complete dissolution in fire?" Suppose that this parable had been a dream, as it might have been just as well—it functions as such in the flow of this sermon—what conclusion should we draw from it? Very clearly, Zarathustra for the time being is the superior leading personality in Nietzsche's psychology—not in his mind. Nietzsche naturally would be tremendously impressed by that figure that expressed revelation, inspiration—he even had a certain feeling of its autonomy—and now the tale says he is going to hell. The old helmsman emphasizes it, "Behold! there goeth Zarathustra to hell!" Now, I doubt whether Nietzsche was conscious at all of the example of Empedocles, but he might have been. He *must* have been aware of it, and if he had told me such a dream and I had asked him who once had jumped into a volcano, it would have come into his mind. And naturally he would have been impressed. That was a pretty dangerous enterprise—it ended Empedocles' life. And he would have realized that jumping into melting lava and poisonous gases would be a very unfavorable feeling, a gruesome death. Such a story denotes a terrible disaster really. So in Nietzsche's mood at this moment, when he realizes every thought that comes to his mind, one would expect him to feel the impact of such a danger. Now we will see what he says:

> And this is the account of Zarathustra's interview with the fire-dog:
> The earth, said he, hath a skin; and this skin hath diseases. One of these diseases, for example, is called "man."
> And another of these diseases is called "the fire-dog": concerning *him* men have greatly deceived themselves, and let themselves be deceived.
> To fathom this mystery did I go o'er the sea; and I have seen the truth naked, verily! barefooted up to the neck.
> Now do I know how it is concerning the fire-dog; and, likewise concerning all the spouting and subversive devils, of which not only old women are afraid.
> "Up with thee, fire-dog, out of thy depth!" cried I, "and confess how deep that depth is! Whence cometh that which thou snortest up?
> Thou drinkest copiously at the sea: that doth thine embittered eloquence betray! In sooth, for a dog of the depth, thou takest thy nourishment too much from the surface!
> At the most, I regard thee as the ventriloquist of the earth: and ever, when I have heard subversive and spouting devils speak, I have found them like thee: embittered, mendacious, and shallow.
> Ye understand how to roar and obscure with ashes! Ye are the

best braggarts, and have sufficiently learned the art of making
dregs boil.

Where ye are, there must always be dregs at hand, and much
that is spongy, hollow, and compressed: it wanteth to have freedom.

'Freedom' ye all roar most eagerly: but I have unlearned the belief in 'great events,' when there is much roaring and smoke about
them.

And believe me, friend Hollaballoo! The greatest events—are
not our noisiest, but our stillest hours.

Not around the inventors of new noise, but around the inventors of new values, doth the world revolve; *inaudibly* it revolveth."

This is his reaction and one must ask who is speaking here. Zarathustra has gone down into the volcano. Who then is speaking? You
see, he talks as if he were quite detached from that tale in which he was
said to have entered hell. As a matter of fact he is standing on the earth
outside and nothing is said about his having gone down to hell to come
out again. Whatever has happened, it is very clear that Nietzsche himself takes Zarathustra's place and *assumes* what Zarathustra might have
said to fire-dog. This is now very much the way Nietzsche himself
would talk. You see, in a fantasy or dream, if you put yourself at once
in the place of an awkward figure and take the word, it is because you
are getting frightened. In a nightmare, for instance, you can insist that
it is nothing but a dream in order to stop it, because you are afraid to
have it go on. Just as when something disagreeable turns up in reality,
you try to shout louder than the disagreeable impression. You make a
noise in order not to hear the truth. Or if you are afraid that something
awkward may be said, you talk all the time; not that you have anything
to say, but out of fear you are making a continuous noise. Or people
often have an extraordinary difficulty in realizing an unprejudiced
flow of fantasy, and with no exception such people are afraid of what
they may produce; therefore they stop the fantasies, or they replace
them by their own remarks. If one gives any chance to the partner, the
animus or anima may say something very disagreeable. So Nietzsche
simply jumps in, *assuming* that this is what Zarathustra would say to the
fire-dog and the spouting devils, the idea of the flames and the volcano, the original chaos that is still boiling below. And by clinging to the
ridiculous figure of the fire-dog he spins out the story, tries to make it
unimportant and light, Then that word interview, *Gespräch*, means a

very quiet sort of thing; he is assuming that Zarathustra goes down into the volcano for philosophic interview with the fire-dog, belittling man—that vermin of mankind, that skin disease of the earth; and he says the fire-dog himself is another form of the skin disease. Obviously that is a metaphysical assumption. It is instead of the devil, that old nonsense invented by man: "concerning *him* men have greatly deceived themselves and let themselves be deceived."

You know, Nietzsche was very much influenced by David Friedrich Strauss, who wrote a famous life of Christ, a very rational conception, like certain later biographies of Christ where the effort was made to explain his traditional life in terms of common sense.[8] But the point of that story is of course that it is *not* and *should* not be common sense: it makes no point if it is not miraculous. Nietzsche knows here that it may be a mystery—"to fathom this mystery, did I go o'er the sea"—but he says he has seen the naked truth about it, and those old specters and ghosts must be removed. That fire-dog is a ventriloquist of the earth, a deceiver who makes you believe the earth can speak; but you must not be so stupid as to believe that the earth has a voice: that is again the old nonsensical invention.

This is just as if one should say of the unconscious that it was merely an invention, a ventriloquist in everybody talking nonsense. It is the standpoint of that cheap rationalism of the 19th century, the same kind of psychology. As when Edison's representative was demonstrating the first phonograph at the meeting of the French Academy of Science, a physicist jumped up and took the man by the throat shouting, "You damned ventriloquist!" He was unable to assume that the apparatus had produced that voice. So whatever that hell could produce would be empty smoke and noise with nothing behind it. Of course that is quite certainly Nietzsche's attempt to belittle it, in order to save himself from it. As a matter of fact, it is one of several attacks of the unconscious; the volcano comes up and attracts Zarathustra and makes him jump into it. It is the first inkling of a danger somewhere connected with the earth. Now, in spite of having belittled the whole thing, he cannot help having another idea about it; he is unable to make so little of the earth, though it naturally should be liberated from

[8] David Friedrich Strauss (1808-1874), author of *Life of Jesus Critically Examined* (1835). In the first of his *Untimely Meditations*, Nietzsche launched a heavy attack on Strauss, with whom he shared many beliefs. It is possible that he was put up to this polemic by Wagner, who had in turn been sharply criticized by Strauss.

such foolish ideas as fire-dogs. So thirteen paragraphs further on, he says:

> And that I may also maintain the right, hear the story of another fire-dog; . . .

He invents another figure that impersonates the earth.

> he speaketh actually out of the heart of the earth.

Here he recognizes what he suppressed before.

> "Gold doth his breath exhale, and golden rain: so doth his heart desire. What are ashes and smoke and hot dregs to him!
> Laughter flitteth from him like a variegated cloud; adverse is he to thy gargling and spewing and grips in the bowels!
> The gold, however, and the laughter—these doth he take out of the heart of the earth: for, that thou mayest know it,—*the heart of the earth is of gold.*"

This extraordinary statement is a recognition that there is something about the earth—there is even a second fire-dog that betrays the secret that the heart of the earth consists of gold. This is an old mythological idea, but Nietzsche did not know it. It is also an alchemical idea that the core of the earth is gold which originated through the movement of the sun round the earth. Since the sun is identical with gold, its continual revolution round the earth has spun the gold in the center and has created its image in the heart of the earth. This is a recognition that in the unconscious, the volcano, there is not only that first fire-dog, but also something of value: a kernel of gold. And this fits in with his idea that one should become a friend of the earth again. The two streams of thought come together here: namely, the idea that the volcano is really the entrance to the interior of the earth, and his other idea that man is a son of the earth, that the earth should be acknowledged again, contrary to the Christian point of view that the flesh and everything earthly is all wrong. This is another attempt to get rid of the fatal impression of the volcano, trying to apply the thought stuff to one of his hobbies and to the earth in general, omitting entirely the catastrophical character of the picture. Now at the end of the chapter he might be satisfied with the result he has reached: he succeeded in avoiding the impact of that descent into hell, he has overcome the fire-dog, and he has realized that the heart of the earth is of gold. But then he says;

And once more Zarathustra shook his head and wondered. "What am I to think of it!" said he once more.

Apparently something has not been answered, the case is not settled.

"Why did the ghost cry: 'It is time! It is the highest time!'
For what is it then—the highest time?"—
Thus spake Zarathustra.

You see that is not answered. Why this haste? "It is highest time" means that a very short time is left. To what does this refer?

Mrs. Crowley: His own condition.

Prof. Jung: Yes. Soon after he had finished *Zarathustra* the end came, when he died before his body. This is the secret, this is the key to the meaning of that descent into hell. It was a warning: soon you will go down into dissolution. Therefore the next chapter: "The Soothsayer," is an attempt to belittle this warning voice, to say, "Oh, that is nothing but a soothsayer." Now the soothsayer says,

"—And I saw a great sadness come over mankind. The best turned weary of their works.
A doctrine appeared, a faith ran beside it: 'All is empty, all is alike, all hath been!' "

Everything has disappeared, everything has gone. This is the way a dying man might speak.

"And from all hills, there re-echoed: 'All is empty, all is alike, all hath been!'
To be sure we have harvested: but why have all our fruits become rotten and brown? What was it fell last night from the evil moon?
In vain was all our labour, poison hath our wine become, the evil eye hath singed yellow our fields and hearts.
Arid have we all become; and fire falling upon us, then do we turn dust like ashes:—yea, the fire itself have we made aweary."

That is what happens to Zarathustra in the volcano: fire falls upon him, fire swallows him. He is turned into ashes.

"All our fountains have dried up, even the sea hath receded. All the ground trieth to gape, but the depth will not swallow!
'Alas! where is there still a sea in which one could be drowned?' so soundeth our plaint—across shallow swamps."

One might of course think of a sea in which to drown if one were burning in the flames of a volcano.

"Verily, even for dying have we become too weary; now do we keep awake and live on—in sepulchres."

Thus did Zarathustra hear a soothsayer speak; and the foreboding touched his heart and transformed him. Sorrowfully did he go about and wearily; and he became like unto those of whom the soothsayer had spoken.—

Verily, said he unto his disciples, a little while, and there cometh the long twilight. Alas, how shall I preserve my light through it!

He did not.

That it may not smother in this sorrowfulness! To remoter worlds shall it be a light, and also to remotest nights!

Thus did Zarathustra go about grieved in his heart, and for three days he did not take any meat or drink: he had no rest, and lost his speech. At last it came to pass that he fell into a deep sleep. His disciples, however, sat around him in long night-watches, and waited anxiously to see if he would awake, and speak again, and recover from his affliction.

Here we have the full reaction to Zarathustra's descent, just the thing we missed in the chapter before, and this is most instructive as to the nature of Zarathustra's or Nietzsche's style. When he talks excitedly and exaggeratedly, he is covering up or repressing something, he won't look at it. He makes a noise in order not to hear the voices that come in the "stillest hour" of the night. You remember in "The Night-Song": "Tis night: now do all gushing fountains speak louder. And my soul also is a gushing fountain." In the stillness of the night, the fountain of the soul can be heard. Nietzsche spoke so exaggeratedly in order that the voices of the soul should not be heard. But here he gets the full impact of it. This is his true reaction, and here one's feeling can follow, one can sympathize.

And this is the discourse that Zarathustra spake when he awoke; his voice, however, came unto his disciples as from afar:
Hear, I pray you, the dream that I dreamed, my friends, and help me to divine its meaning!
A riddle is it still unto me, this dream; the meaning is hidden in it and encaged, and doth not yet fly above it on free pinions.
All life had I renounced, so I dreamed. [Again the idea of

death.] Night-watchman and grave-guardian had I become, aloft, in the lonely mountain-fortress of Death.

There did I guard his coffins: full stood the musty vaults of those trophies of victory. Out of glass coffins did vanquished life gaze upon me.

The odour of dust-covered eternities did I breathe: sultry and dust-covered lay my soul. And who could have aired his soul there!

Brightness of midnight was ever around me; lonesomeness cowered beside her; and as a third, death-rattle stillness, the worst of my female friends.

Keys did I carry, the rustiest of all keys; and I knew how to open with them the most creaking of all gates.

Like a bitterly angry croaking ran the sound through the long corridors when the leaves of the gate opened: ungraciously did this bird cry, unwillingly was it awakened.

But more frightful even, and more heart-strangling was it, when it again became silent and still all around, and I alone sat in that malignant silence. [That is the stillest hour of course.]

Thus did time pass with me, and slip by, . . . for as yet he knew not the interpretation thereof.

This is again an honest report, as if something like that had really happened to him. It is again a tale or a dream where one hears the impartial, unadulterated voice which has not been twisted into an exaggerated style. It is a reaction to the Hades episode, and now we are going to hear the secret: what he is watching down below. This is the real Zarathustra; he is now in hell, in the castle of death where he watches the graves in order to bring up that secret. No question of its being nonsense any longer, there is a fearful secret hidden down below, of which he *ought* to think, compensating all the hysterical noise he made up above. And now when the door flies open, one sees that it is a roaring wind, and the wind is a spirit; a merciless wind is tearing out with a thousand laughters. That is insanity very clearly—those distorted figures. Insanity is the secret, the utter destruction of his mind. One can understand why he was prostrated. Now, this wind plays a peculiar role in Nietzsche's life. There are several passages where Zarathustra is the wind, and in Nietzsche's biography there is an incident where it appears in a peculiar form. And a little later we come to the dog that howls in the night, that awful cry which belongs in the same complex of forebodings. When he was about fifteen, he already had had such an experience.[9] It is in my Wotan article, but unfortunately this passage was omitted by the publishers of the English translation because they thought it would not be met with sufficient understanding. Maybe! I don't know, but it is of course particularly important, the most interesting thing in the whole article.

He tells about taking a walk in the night with a friend, another young boy, and undoubtedly something like this happened in reality, but it is also a fantastical story, a dream. In a dark wood he heard a terrible cry issuing from a nearby lunatic asylum, which means that there already he went into the unconscious—the wood. And then, after a while, in that same dream, they almost went astray in the wood, and they met an uncanny man, the wild hunter. That was Wotan. This hunter wanted to lead them to Teutschtal, which is a real village, but it is of course also symbolic. *Teutsch* is the old form of *Deutsch*, and it was used at the time of the Romantic school to designate those people who already had the same craze about the Germanic blood which we observe now. They were called *Teutsche*, and were represented in caricature with horns and furs and such things. Suddenly, that hunter took a whistle and produced a most awful whistling, and Nietzsche in the dream lost consciousness. Then, when he recovered, he knew he had had a nightmare. Now this shrieking here, this whistling and whizzing, is the cry from the lunatic asylum. It is Wotan who gets him, the old wind god breaking forth, the god of inspiration, of madness, intoxication and wildness, the god of the Berserkers, those wild people who run amok. It is, of course, the shrieking and whistling of the wind in a storm in a nocturnal wood, the unconscious. It is the unconscious itself that breaks forth. This is very beautifully described here: doors fly open and out bursts that wind, bringing a thousand laughters. It is a horrible foreboding of his insanity, and he admits that he does not know the interpretation of this experience. Well, that is humanly understandable.

But the disciple whom he loved most arose quickly, seized Zarathustra's hand and said:
"Thy life itself interpreteth unto us this dream, O Zarathustra!
Art thou not thyself the wind with shrill whistling, which bursteth open the gates of the fortress of Death?

[9] "Wotan" first appeared in *Neue Schweitzer Rundschau* (Zurich, March 1936). It is reprinted in CW 10, pars. 371-99. In Nietzsche's sister's biography (vol. I, pp. 18-19), the story of the howling dog is told.

Art thou not thyself the coffin full of many-hued malices and angel-caricatures of life?

Verily, like a thousand peals of children's laughter cometh Zarathustra into all sepulchres, laughing at those night-watchmen and grave-guardians, and whoever else rattleth with sinister keys."

Belittling!

"With thy laughter wilt thou frighten and prostrate them: fainting and recovering will demonstrate thy power over them."

Fainting and recovering from his descent: that reminds him of what he experienced when he was a youth.

"And when the long twilight cometh and the mortal weariness, even then wilt thou not disappear from our firmament, thou advocate of life!

New stars hast thou made us see, and new nocturnal glories: verily, laughter itself hast thou spread out over us like a many-hued canopy.

Now will children's laughter ever from coffins flow; now will a strong wind ever come victoriously unto all mortal weariness: of this thou art thyself the pledge and the prophet!

Verily, *they themselves didst thou dream*, thine enemies: that was thy sorest dream.

But as thou awokest from them and camest to thyself, so shall they awaken from themselves—and come unto thee!"

This interpretation is of course a desperate attempt to twist it into a favorable statement—that he himself is Wotan. It is of course true: Zarathustra is identical with Wotan. He is also identical with the terrible paradox of the unconscious. That coffin full of laughter is the paradoxical pair of opposites that are mixed up together and form the grotesque and horrible aspects of the unconscious, where there is absolutely no order, where man has gone under completely. Naturally, if you identify with the unconscious, you are gone, because your consciousness is the only element of order. If you *keep* your consciousness in the unconscious you can establish order there, but if you lose consciousness and go under, you become identical with the unconsciousness, and then you are that coffin and the laughter. The attempt at twisting or interpreting the dream winds up, then, with the very weak statement that he has dreamt his enemies. But who is his enemy? His own unconscious—his enemy is himself. So he has dreamt himself;

that is his own case, his own insanity. The danger is always that he identifies with Zarathustra, and Zarathustra is the unconscious.

... and all the others then thronged around Zarathustra, grasped him by the hands, and tried to persuade him to leave his bed and his sadness, and return unto them.

LECTURE II

11 May 1938

Prof. Jung:
We spoke last time, in the chapter about the soothsayer, of Zarathustra's dream where Nietzsche's imminent madness was portrayed, and at the end of the dream he was still in a somewhat upset condition.

> Zarathustra, however, sat upright on his couch, with an absent look. Like one returning from long foreign sojourn did he look on his disciples, and examined their features; but still he knew them not. When, however, they raised him, and set him upon his feet, behold, all on a sudden his eye changed; he understood everything that had happened, stroked his beard, and said with a strong voice:
> "Well! this hath just its time; but see to it, my disciples, that we have a good repast, and without delay! Thus do I mean to make amends for bad dreams!"

The text describes an annihilation of consciousness. He was overwhelmed by a sort of unconscious condition. That has of course to do with the character of insanity; it is a sudden invasion, a flow of unconscious contents of an entirely different mental nature, which suppresses or alienates consciousness. So it is now as if he were coming back from a quite foreign condition—foreign because he has been unconscious of such contents before. This is another demonstration of what we have seen very often, that Nietzsche is utterly unaware of his unconscious, and only one who is so unaware can be completely overcome by it. If you are more or less aware of your unconscious contents, if the area of unconsciousness is not so great, you are never overcome. If the things which come into your consciousness are not entirely foreign, you don't feel overwhelmed and lost, don't lose your orientation. You are perhaps emotional or a bit upset, but you are not surrounded by absolutely strange impressions and views. That can only happen when you are in decided opposition to yourself, when one part is con-

1230

scious and the other utterly unconscious and therefore quite different. With all his insight, Nietzsche was peculiarly unaware of his other side. He didn't understand what it was all about. Now whenever that is the case, the conscious attitude is naturally open to criticism; one is forced to criticise a consciousness which is threatened by an unconscious opposition. because the unconscious opposition always contains the dementia of consciousness. When there is no such opposition, the unconscious can collaborate and then it has not that character of utter strangeness. So we have to be critical all the time of the conscious attitude of Nietzsche or Zarathustra.

Now in the end, he thinks of eating as a means of saving himself from the fatal impression, clinging to ordinary reality in order to escape the uncanny shadow that fell upon him. It is of particular interest to see what he is going to do next, in order to digest that intrusion, so it is quite apt that the following chapter is called "Redemption." The idea indicated in the title is perfectly clear: namely, when the unconscious is so overwhelmed, there is a feeling that one should be redeemed from such a dangerous suppressing influence. As a matter of fact a feeling of the need for redemption always appears when there is great opposition between the conscious and the unconscious. In all cases when the aims of the conscious and the unconscious are quite different, one finds that marked need for redemption. Now the text says:

> When Zarathustra went one day over the great bridge, then did the cripples and beggars surround him, and a hunchback spake thus unto him: . . .

Why does he use the symbol of the bridge here?

Mrs. Crowley: It would be that connection between the two.

Prof. Jung: Exactly. He obviously needs a bridge in order to cross the gap between the conscious and the unconscious. And what would that be psychologically?

Mr. Baumann: Usually, we say the bridge is the anima or animus.

Prof. Jung: Well yes, they can serve as a bridge, as the other pillar, the support on the other side, but we have a special term.

Miss Foote: The transcendent function.

Prof. Jung: Yes, that is by definition the functioning together of conscious and unconscious. And that such a function can be, is due to such figures as the animus and anima, because they represent the unconscious. In the myth of the Grail, for instance, Kundry is the messenger from the other side, a sort of angel in the antique sense of the word, *angelos*, the messenger. It is as if the anima were standing on the other bank and I on this bank, and we were talking to each other, deliberating about how to produce a function in between, for we must build a bridge from both sides, not from one side only. If there were no such figure at the other end, I never could build the bridge. It needs such a personification. The fact that the unconscious is personified means that it is inclined to collaborate; wherever we encounter the animus or anima it always denotes that the unconscious is inclined to form a connection with consciousness. You see, consciousness is exceedingly personal, and we happen to be the personification of consciousness and its contents: the whole world is personified in us. And when the unconscious tries to collaborate, it personifies in the counter figure.

Often we think of the animus and anima as if they were disagreeable symptoms or occurrences; they *are*, I admit, but they are also suitable teleological attempts of the unconscious to produce an access to us. Just as any symptom of any kind of disease is not only destructive but also constructive; even sickness itself, the symptomatology of illness, is on the one side destructive, but it is at the same time an attempt at healing. So when a case is particularly bothersome on account of animus or anima, one knows that there is a gap which wants to be bridged, and nature has already made the attempt to bridge it. I emphasize the existence of anima or animus because they are really products of nature, and we make use of them. There would be plenty of reasons for saying this is perfect nonsense, imagination, and so on. Of course it *is* imagination, but that is what nature produces, and if we want to cure an illness we have to use its manifestations, have to use nature in order to cure nature. It is nothing abstract: we can cure by imitating the natural ways which nature herself has invented. Since nature has invented such figures as animus and anima, it is for a purpose, and we are fools if we do not use them; that it produces such figures is a perfectly legitimate tendency in nature. So it is quite logical here for Nietzsche to speak of a bridge, because he is in need of a bridge; the situation is such that he has a most uncanny premonition of things that are still below the horizon, and he feels something ought to be done about them. His unconscious argument would be: "Well, since I contain contents which are so strange to me, I must have a connection, a communication, between those two parts of myself." And so he finds himself on that bridge and there he is instantly surrounded by cripples and beggars. Now why?

Mrs. Sigg: Because he is crippled himself; he is one-sided.

Prof. Jung: Exactly, he is very one-sided. He has a great idea about the superman, he is on the way to the superman, and sometimes it appears as if he were already the superman. But then that appears also as a compensation for the fact that he is crippled. Moreover, his encounter with the unconscious proves to him that he is wounded; a hole has been created in his system. Whoever has suffered once from an intrusion of the unconscious has at least a scar if not an open wound. His wholeness, as he understood it, the wholeness of his ego personality, had been badly damaged, for it became obvious that he was not alone; something which he did not control was in the same house with him, and that is of course wounding to the pride of the ego personality, a fatal blow to his own monarchy. So it is quite understandable that when he approaches the gulf, he meets the cripples and beggars, as would happen in a dream; for they demonstrate to him that it is really a matter of cripples and beggars, and that he is harboring them, that he is just like them and among them. And in the text, we shall see how very much he realizes that he really belongs to them.

The next part says that he should teach the cripples first; if he could teach them it would prove that his teaching really meant something, would prove that he was up to his task. That, I think, would be the "right method"; you see, that would be the ultimate proof. Whether he can influence the unconscious, whether he can assimilate the unconscious, is the criterion—whether his teaching can express the unconscious so that it flows in and collaborates with him. If he cannot, his teaching is no good. And that is the criterion for any real philosophical teaching; if it expresses the unconscious it is good, if it does not it is simply beside the mark. The same criterion can be applied to natural science or to any scientific theory. If it does not fit the facts it is no good: the test is whether it fits the facts. Now, his next arguments are not very important; he is not aware what the problems really mean and therefore he tries to play with them. For instance,

> When one taketh his hump from the hunchback, then doth one take from him his spirit—so do the people teach.

He is simply making images now; he makes a picture of those cripples, talks about externals, making more or less apt remarks about them, about the eyes of the blind man, about the lameness and other mutilations. Then he says,

> And why should not Zarathustra also learn from the people, when the people learn from Zarathustra?

Here is an inclination to listen or to take into account: this is more or less the "right method." If such figures appear in dreams or fantasies, we expect to learn something from them. And here he doubts his attitude a little, whether he should teach them—which is understandable. He might better be taught by them. But he instantly says,

It is, however, the smallest thing unto me since I have been amongst men, to see one person lacking an eye, another an ear, and a third a leg, and that others have lost the tongue, or the nose, or the head.

Minimizing it!

I see and have seen worse things, and divers things so hideous, that I should neither like to speak of all matters, nor even keep silent about some of them: namely, men who lack everything, except that they have too much of one thing—men who are nothing more than a big eye, or a big mouth, or a big belly, or something else big,—reversed cripples, I call such men.

Again, he makes little of the cripples. He has seen things very much worse. Instantly he is talking them away, so one can only assume that he is afraid of what the cripples might teach him. Then he falls into another truth, a very good remark, that there are really other cripples, positive or reversed cripples as he calls them, who would be quite complete if one organ were not overgrown. The usual cripple is of course one who has an organ lacking. And who would the other cripple be?

Miss Hannah: People who have differentiated one function at the expense of the others.

Prof. Jung: Yes, and particularly those who identify with their best function—the tenor with his voice or the painter with his brush. Of course, everybody, if he has a decent function, will most certainly be badly tempted to identify with it.

Mr. Baumann: There is even an expression, *déformation professionelle.*

Prof. Jung: Yes. You see, he makes there a perfectly good remark, but he is talking the cripples away: I have seen much worse cases than yours, you are nothing, you have no show. This is a means of self-protection, so he rather dwells on it and we are still somewhat in the dark as to why this chapter should be called "Redemption." One is curious to know why or how that redemption is to be brought about. Now, after a good deal of conversation, of more or less apt remarks about the fragmentary nature of ordinary man, he comes to the conclusion a little farther on that he himself is not quite complete. He admits that he also is human, but in a way a cripple too. You know the motif of the cripple plays quite a role in *Zarathustra*; this figure appears in different forms. Do you remember a similar figure?

Remark: The ugliest man.

Mrs. Crowley: And the clown.

Prof. Jung: Of course, and there is also the dwarf. Those figures are more or less alike and they keep on recurring. Do you know what they generally mean?

Dr. Henderson: They stand for the inferior function.

Prof. Jung: Yes, being dwarfish, clownish, foolish, mad—all that denotes the inferior function. But cripples or madmen have a different value among primitives. What is their point of view?

Mrs. Sigg: That insane people are godlike.

Mrs. Crowley: They are ghosts or spirits.

Prof. Jung: Well, they are mana people; they are what the Irish would call *fey.*

Dr. Escher: In south Italy there is the custom that if a male hunchback is passing in the street, even educated, very polite ladies go and touch him. But only a male hunchback.

Prof. Jung: That is so in France also.

Mr. Allemann: I think it is quite egotistical. They think it is a good omen, that they will have good luck after that.

Prof. Jung: Oh yes, it is for good luck—they are after the mana. I saw it once in Italy; a hunchback was in a crowd and a fellow who was passing rubbed his back a bit, which of course upset him very much. They hate it like anything. It is the same idea when people rub their hands on the tomb of St. Anthony in Padua, in order to get the mana of the saint inside. And it is exactly the same when the Central Australians rub their churingas to get the good medicine that is in them, in exchange for the bad mana inside their own systems. All crippled people, people marked by an obvious misfortune, are considered uncanny and they have magic prestige. Either they are avoided carefully, as unlucky people are usually avoided by primitives because they spread bad luck, or they are supposed to contain mana, having obviously been chosen as particular and peculiar vessels. So the gods of magic are often distorted; the figures that have to do with the secret arts, with the magic production of ore, gold, silver, etc., are typically crippled, either hunchbacks or dwarfs. Extraordinary people are always supposed to be mana because their extraordinary aspect causes emotion, and whatever causes emotion is believed to be causal, to have a causal *dynamis.* You see, primitives conclude that that which causes emotion must be strong enough to cause another emotion—that is perfectly rational, natural primitive logic—so whatever is astonishing, like a man who does not look like an ordinary man in any way, must be causally dynamic. Also women with red hair were apt to be suspected of magic among the village people; they were understood to be not quite safe because it is not ordinary to have red hair. Of course if everyone had red hair they would not be astonished and those red-haired women would not have mana.

Now, this mana aspect of crippled figures always points to the unconscious; whatever arouses emotions has touched upon the unconscious. When you get an emotional impression from something, you can be sure that you have instantly made a projection; otherwise you would not have an emotion—I mean of course an illegitimate emotion, an emotion that you cannot quite control. A controlled emotion, which is a feeling, may be without projection—for instance, when you think something is abominably ugly or despicable but are not upset to the point of losing your self-control. While if you are just caught by an uncontrolled emotion, there is quite certainly a projection, and then you have to fetch the projected contents back again into yourself.

Mrs. Sigg: I think the mana is there, and of such value, because it would really be the only way to redemption for Nietzsche. If he would keep in close contact with the cripples in himself, he would be stronger. But just because it is the only way, the emotion is therefore avoided.

Prof. Jung: Yes, you see, it is quite certain that the cripples are an aspect of the unconscious inferior function—the unconscious approaches him in that form. It was that which caused the great emotion in the dream, the anticipation of madness. In order to draw the legitimate psychological conclusion, he should say to himself, "Here is a manifestation of the unconscious. The cripples have caused this upset, now what do cripples mean to me?" Then he might realize that cripples are mana and are acquainted with the secrets of the interior of the earth. They have eyes that see in the dark, so they know things that man does not know. You see, he would then meet the situation with an entirely different attitude, with humility. He knows that one should have humility in order to meet such an uncanny crowd, yet he tries to minimize the impression, almost to ridicule this peculiar aspect of the unconscious, because he is afraid and his mind cannot think far enough.

It is very curious that Nietzsche, a highly intelligent man, had not a scientific mind. He could not accept psychological facts in a scientific way and take them for what they are. He behaved exactly like everybody else—it is nothing but a foolish dream and so on—instead of thinking philosophically about the matter of connecting B to A. A is the horrible dream he had, and whatever follows after is under that impression. Why should he deny that such a dream makes such an impression? Why should he lie to himself? But one simply takes a good meal and it is gone. Then something else turns up under very suspect circumstances, and instead of assuming, "This is one of the representatives of the other side; I must be very polite and humble because the whole future depends upon the way I deal with this figure"—instead of doing that—he minimizes those figures and talks them away. That is the most unspeakably foolish and irritating way in which he screws himself into his madness, an awful fatality. And the fatality does not consist of anything tragic or great; it consists of a lack of intelligence, the lack of a scientific and philosophical attitude. It is a sort of avoidance, a sort of impatient gesture. "It is nothing; it is just disagreeable or ridiculous"—putting himself always beyond the facts. The fact that he has had such a terrible dream has impressed him like anything, but he creates a kind of vapor of foolish thoughts, belittling what has happened, and by that he forces the situation. He creates a superficial consciousness which naturally will always be threatened by the intrusion of substantial facts that are far more dangerous. For the flimsier the conscious construction, the more easily it is exploded by contents which ordinarily would not explode consciousness. And this is flimsy consciousness; it lacks a scientific attitude. He behaves like a politician who thinks that when he opens his mouth and makes a big noise, the social problem is solved. Now the question is: what is he going to do—or to *say*, at least—about redemption? Because it is a very big problem. Can one be redeemed from that opponent, or what should be done in such a dangerous situation? And his idea is that the will is the redeemer, that by will one can even work redemption. So he applies now this principle.

> To redeem what is past, and to transform every "It was" into "Thus would I have it!"—that only do I call redemption!
> Will—so is the emancipator and joy-bringer called: thus have I taught you, my friends!

You see the idea that one could swing it by the will is a perfectly good and legitimate attempt. At least one can try. So he tries and instantly he realizes something.

But now learn this likewise: the Will itself is still a prisoner.

Now, in what is it imprisoned?

Mrs. Baumann: It is imprisoned in the past which cannot be changed.

Mrs. Adler: The past contains all those tendencies which don't go with the will.

Prof. Jung: Yes, but how does the past influence the will?

Mrs. Crowley: Because all the traditions are in the past and all the unconscious sides of the personality.

Mr. Allemann: The germs of the present and the future are in the past, and the will cannot get away from that fact.

Prof. Jung: And why cannot will deviate? You see, one can suppose that the will is free—a perfectly good hypothesis—but will could then deviate. So what is the fetter?

Dr. Henderson: The body.

Mrs. Crowley: I should say it was the unconscious.

Prof. Jung: Well, you can always will something, but the *choice* depends upon the past, upon that which already is. Will in itself could be free, but you must give it an object, and the choice of the goal is very much what you know from your experience of the past. You see, that explains his emotion about the past. He expresses himself very strongly.

"It was": thus is the Will's teeth-gnashing and lonesomest tribulation called. Impotent towards what hath been done—it is a malicious spectator of all that is past.

Not backward can the Will will; that it cannot break time and time's desire—that is the Will's lonesomest tribulation.

Willing emancipateth: what doth Willing itself devise in order to get free from its tribulation and mock at its prison?

So will depends entirely upon the past, and how can will help you if you have not superior insight, almost a sort of revelation, something beyond the ordinary needs? Your will always tries to get at the things of which you already know, for if you don't know of a thing, how can you will it? Therefore if you make will the redeeming factor, you must have inspiration or revelation, an insight beyond what you really are able to understand, or what you have hitherto understood. And who would give you that revelation? Who would give you secret knowledge?

Mrs. Fierz: The cripples.

Prof. Jung: Yes, the dwarfs know the things that are hidden. That is the reason why they come now. For whoever believes in the will, whoever wants redemption and wills to have it, needs revelation, and these little gods, dwarfs or cripples or mana people, have since time immemorial, been supposed to have the secret knowledge. But Nietzsche doesn't see that.

Now this terrible dream, and his upset, is the consequence of the descent into Hades or into the volcano. Zarathustra made that rather unexpected move, but of course if one follows up Nietzsche's thought before, one sees it was absolutely necessary that the spirit Zarathustra should go down into the interior of the earth, because earth is just what he lacks. That Zarathustra makes such a descent means that Nietzsche should understand what is going on: namely, that earth should come into his consideration, that earth is needed and whatever earth means to man. But Nietzsche is so identified with Zarathustra that it is very difficult to differentiate between the two. So that descent into the underworld is on the one side Zarathustra's philosophical problem—now what about the earth?—and on the other, Nietzsche's personal problem, to pay attention to the earth, the body. Psychologically that would mean he should pay attention to the unconscious, because the psychological side of the body *is* the unconscious, and we reach the body—psychologically, not physically—only through the unconscious. What we call the unconscious is an avenue, an access, to the body. In going to hell, Zarathustra is anticipating what Nietzsche personally ought to do, because danger is threatening from that side. He is really throwing his stone too high and there is danger of its falling back upon him.

He always tries to be above his physical existence, and that means a great strain to the body, particularly to the brain, and it also means a one-sidedness which is again injurious to the proper functioning of the brain. Therefore in order to round out his philosophical outlook, he ought to pay attention to the brain, to return to human measure, to human proportions. That dream is in itself already a symptom of the grave condition of his mind. If one takes it as an ordinary dream one could not yet say for certain that it contained unmistakable signs of organic destruction, but it contains all the signs of a mental condition which may prove to be most injurious for his physical health, including his brain. The cripples, the mutilated ones, point to the same probability: there is some doubt about his completeness. Usually, such a crippled condition is caused by an illness or by a congenital trouble, and presumably his condition is also due to some illness, either congenital or in a state of becoming, something below the threshold. So it would be most advisable if Nietzsche could relate to his unconscious in order to get that measure which would allow him to have a balanced mind, and to live without doing too much injury to his nervous system.

If Nietzsche had consulted me at that stage and had brought me that dream, I should have said, "Now this is a stiff dose. You are obviously in terrible contradiction to your own unconscious and therefore it appears in a most frightening way. You must listen very carefully and take into account all that the unconscious has to say, and you must try to adapt your conscious mind to its intimations. That doesn't mean taking it for gospel truth. The statement of the unconscious is not in itself an absolute truth, but you have to consider it, to take into account that the unconscious is against you." Of course I should advise him against all such theories as doing it by will, or being superior to it, or teaching it. I would treat him as if I had made the statement that he had a temperature of about 102, or that his heart was wrong, or that he had typhoid fever. I would say, "Go to bed at once, give in, go under with your unconscious in order to be sure of being on the spot." But instead of all this, he turns to the will as the redeeming principle—the will should liberate him from this condition. And there, as we have seen, he begins to doubt whether the will is really so free, whether the will is able to bring about that redemption. He asks towards the end of the chapter,

> Hath the Will become its own deliverer and joy-bringer? Hath it unlearned the spirit of revenge and all teeth-gnashing?
> And who hath taught it reconciliation with time, and something higher than all reconciliation?

You see, here is a grave doubt as to whether the will is really capable of freeing itself from the past enough to enable it to bring about a new condition, and he speaks of reconciliation, the reconciling of two opposite tendencies, bringing together the right and the left, the here and the there—meaning the bridge of course. Then he goes on to say,

> Something higher than all reconciliation must the Will will which is the Will to Power—: but how doth that take place? Who hath taught it also to will backwards?

In other words, how can your will influence or overcome its own condition, the fact that it can only will what you know? What will be the revelation, the vision beyond what you know, that will show the goal to the will?

1240

—But at this point in his discourse it chanced that Zarathustra suddenly paused, and looked like a person in the greatest alarm. With terror in his eyes did he gaze on his disciples; his glances pierced as with arrows their thoughts and arrear-thoughts.

Now here something has happened. When he reached the questions— How can the will be superior to itself? How can the will lead you to that which is beyond what you know?—in that moment something happened. What would that be? What impression do you get from that interlude when he ceased to speak?

Prof. Reichstein: He sees that he has the wrong idea about the will and that he has a possibility of seeing something from the unconscious which he is not able to accept.

Prof. Jung: That is right, but of what does it remind you?

Mrs. Fierz: Of the dream.

Prof. Jung: Yes, it is very much the same situation. The dream was such an interlude. It caused terror and here again an intrusion threatens, and "his glances pierced as with arrows their thoughts and arrear-thoughts." What does that mean?

Miss Hannah: He is trying to project again.

Prof. Jung: He is already doing so. It is as if his disciples appeared to him in quite a different light, as if they contained a secret. Now, under what conditions does such a thing happen?

Mr. Allemann: When somebody is insane.

Prof. Jung: Well yes, but what is actually happening in him? Why does he see his mental contents in someone else?

Mrs. Stauffacher: It is too uncomfortable for him.

Prof. Jung: Oh, if it were just not easy for him, he would have thought at once: "This is very disagreeable and therefore I don't accept it. I prefer to assume that it is in other people." But it never happens like that.

Miss Hannah: He just doesn't see it in himself.

Prof. Jung: Exactly, it is so strange that he doesn't see it in himself. You see, there is no bridge between himself and the other one who is also himself. When he sees that other one he thinks it is a stranger, presumably having to do with those people there. That is typical of an insane condition when it is a matter of something very important. You see, it is a matter here of the whole other side which compensates Nietzsche's actual consciousness, and now all that appears in other people. It is as if I were preaching to you a very one-sided, ridiculous idea, and naturally my unconscious would ask what in hell I was talking about. And then I might begin to swear at you, to try to convince you, to talk down upon you, and even to emphasize your extreme stupidity that you cannot understand. But *I* don't understand—something in me doesn't understand. So in this moment it suddenly appears to him as if his pupils were against him; they appear to him in an entirely different light. Therefore that expression of terror and the suspicious glance in his eyes, which is typical of paranoia, of the man with a persecution mania, that peculiar look of fundamental suspicion, of extreme hatred and fear of his fellow human beings, because it appears to him as if they were enemies persecuting him. He is the *persécuteur persécuté*. He is the one who runs away from himself and pursues himself, like a dog who chases his own tail; sometimes he is the tail and sometimes the dog. This is another moment of madness, because he has not succeeded in bridging the gulf. The idea of the will doesn't help at all. He himself undermines the idea of the will, and it is to be understood, for nobody can bridge the gulf between the conscious and the unconscious by sheer willpower. It is not a matter of willpower, but is a matter of submission.

But after a brief space he again laughed and said soothedly:
"It is difficult to live amongst men, because silence is so difficult—especially for a babbler."

He has caught himself again. He picks up the thread. After a moment of intense terror, he ridicules himself and laughs away the terror: nothing has happened. It is only a bit difficult to live amongst men because they are fragmentary, and he himself is a bit fragmentary, being human too. But he doesn't accept his own fragmentariness, doesn't accept the fact that he also is a cripple, or he would accept the mutilation of other people. If he could see that we are all alike, it would not be difficult to live amongst men. That he doesn't accept other people, as he himself has asserted, means that he is in contradiction with himself and then naturally he cannot live with other people "because silence is so difficult." You see, he talks too much and then he ceases because he has an idea that *he* has babbled: he has said a whole mouthful about those poor cripples. But he himself is one; and instead of accepting it, he assumes that he is the great and complete one and they are incomplete. He doesn't accept himself, doesn't accept humanity, or he could not talk like that. The right conclusion after that interlude would be: "Shut up, don't get excited about what other people do, just look at yourself and see where *you* are complete or incomplete." That would be the silence. But he had to speak, therefore the title of the book is

Thus Spake Zarathustra. And that is the case with most people: they continue to talk instead of looking quietly at themselves. Now, the end of this chapter is uninteresting, but the next one, "Manly Prudence," gives us again some valuable insight. It begins,

> Not the height, it is the declivity that is terrible!

He is beginning to realize the thoughts which had been behind the scene in the chapter before, as is usually the case.

> The declivity, where the gaze shooteth *downwards*, and the hand graspeth *upwards*. There doth the heart become giddy through its double will.
>
> Ah, friends, do ye divine also my heart's double will?
>
> This, this is *my* declivity and my danger, that my gaze shooteth towards the summit, and my hand would fain clutch and lean—on the depth!

Mark the peculiar reversal: in the sentence before, the gaze shooteth downwards and the hand graspeth upwards, and here it is just the reverse. That means that he is thoroughly double and exchangeable, a description of a complete dissociation, a complete duality.

> To man clingeth my will; [He has just said he could not live among human beings.] with chains do I bind myself to man, because I am pulled upwards to the Superman: for thither doth mine other will tend.
>
> And *therefore* do I live blindly among men, as if I knew them not: that my hand may not entirely lose belief in firmness.
>
> I know not you men: this gloom and consolation is often spread around me.

In these words he confesses his duality, the dissociation of his mental condition—between Zarathustra, who is merely a spirit, and the man Nietzsche who wants to live among human beings, wants to live *blindly* among human beings, unconsciously. That is of course the way he actually did live. It was not ideal, and that is just the reason why Nietzsche the man could not stand the onslaught of Zarathustra; he preferred to be blind when Zarathustra threatened to appear.

The rest of this chapter is not very important, so we will go now to chapter 44, "The Stillest Hour." In the last two chapters he tries to digest that onslaught of the unconscious, tries to deal with it, but with very inefficient means, so we may expect that an undigested impression will linger on and reappear. And in this chapter the impression does appear again. It begins,

> What hath happened unto me, my friends? Ye see me troubled, driven forth, unwillingly obedient, ready to go—alas, to go away from *you*!
>
> Yea, once more must Zarathustra retire to his solitude: but unjoyously this time doth the bear go back to his cave!
>
> What hath happened unto me? Who ordereth this!—Ah, mine angry mistress wisheth it so; she spake unto me. Have I ever named her name to you?
>
> Yesterday towards evening there spake unto me *my stillest hour*: that is the name of my terrible mistress.
>
> And thus did it happen—for everything must I tell you, that your heart may not harden against the suddenly departing one!
>
> Do ye know the terror of him who falleth asleep?—
>
> To the very toes he is terrified, because the ground giveth way under him, and the dream beginneth.
>
> This do I speak unto you in parable. Yesterday at the stillest hour did the ground give way under me: the dream began.
>
> The hour-hand moved on, the timepiece of my life drew breath—never did I hear such stillness around me, so that my heart was terrified.

This is very much what happened to him, a recrudescence of the impression which had not been dealt with sufficiently. In the chapter before we heard that he clung to man, that he wanted to stay and to live with man. But here he has to leave his pupils, because an unknown force, an unknown command, is calling him away. That is of course the superior will of Zarathustra calling him away from his human existence. So he asks who ordered this, and he comes to the conclusion that it was the "stillest hour." Now, mark the way he describes the "stillest hour": it is an angry mistress, obviously a "she that wants to be obeyed." That is the anima, of course, and in a still hour one hears naturally what the anima says—one hears the voices of the other side. The text now is very suggestive: it contains a threatening uncanny note.

> Then was there spoken unto me without voice; "*Thou knowest it, Zarathustra?*"

This allusion to a secret knowledge in him is most uncanny.

And I cried in terror at this whispering, and the blood left my face: but I was silent.

That is understandable because "Thou knowest it, Zarathustra?" is the fundamental question. "You know what the dream means, why don't you confess it? Why don't you give in?" When the thing comes at him so directly, it is interesting to see how he will react to it, whether he will try to veil it, or to digest and assimilate it so that it will not be so injurious. The way in which he is asked is most insinuating and threatening and therefore his tremendous reaction.

> Then was there once more spoken unto me without voice: "Thou knowest it, Zarathustra, but thou dost not speak it!"—
> And at last I answered like one defiant.

Instead of acknowledging it, he is defiant, which is of course utter weakness. The strong man says, "Damn it, that is so!" but the weak man is defiant, as if he could frighten away a whale.

> "Yea, I know it, but I will not speak it!"

This is childish obstinacy.

> Then was there again spoken unto me without voice: "Thou *wilt* not, Zarathustra? Is this true? Conceal thyself not behind thy defiance!"—

Is that not excellent advice?

> And I wept and trembled like a child and said: "Ah, I would indeed, but how can I do it! Exempt me only from this! It is beyond my power!"
> Then was there again spoken unto me without voice: "What matter about thyself, Zarathustra! Speak thy word and succumb!"

You see, he should be willing to accept even his own destruction. If he could confess it, if he could say, "Yes, that is it, and if I am meant to go under, I go under," he would have won the battle, but he was not strong enough to succumb. The anima speaks absolutely to the point, as if she were a first-rate psychotherapist!

> And I answered: "Ah, is it *my* word? Who am I? I await the worthier one; I am not worthy even to succumb by it."

An easy way to escape. Yes, you have spoken great words before, but now you pay the price. At least you must be willing to pay the price, like old Abraham when he had to sacrifice his son Isaac. He did not say, "I wait for a worthier one to sacrifice his son. I am a very modest man. It is not worthwhile to sacrifice my son. He is no good at all, take another one." That is the psychology here. He does succumb but not voluntarily; he simply crumples up and that is not submission.

Then was there again spoken unto me without voice: "What matter about thyself? Thou art not yet humble enough for me. Humility hath the hardest skin."—

The unconscious is saying this through its own personification, the anima, "You must learn humility and then you will not be injured. Humility has the hardest skin."

And I answered: "What hath not the skin of my humility endured! At the foot of my height do I dwell: how high are my summits, no one hath yet told me. But well do I know my valleys."

Then was there again spoken unto me without voice: "O Zarathustra, he who hath to remove mountains removeth also valleys and plains."—

His valleys and plains are as little important as the summits at the foot of which he imagines himself to be; and now, because he has been flippant and superficial, the anima becomes flippant. Instead of realizing that humility is now the test to prove what he can stand, he says, "What have I not endured?" But he has not endured it. And when the cripples appeared, he said he had seen much worse things—that was no news to him—belittling it and pushing it away, instead of accepting it. And then he thinks of the wonderful high summits: here comes in the idea of greatness again. That he is only at the foot of the mountain means that there are possibilities which he might fulfill in the future: he might go much higher. So the unconscious says, "What is this foolish talk about the mountains?"

And I answered: As yet hath my word not removed mountains, and what I have spoken hath not reached man. I went, indeed, unto men, but not yet have I attained unto them."

Then was there again spoken unto me without voice: "What knowest thou *thereof*! The dew falleth on the grass when the night is most silent."

This is a very cryptic remark of the anima. It is quite obvious that he now tries to dwell upon his mountain view, and that he has not quite succeeded in putting his ideas over to other men. You see, he has wriggled out of his own responsibility, the fact that it concerns himself. It is now the truth for other men—what he can do for them. That removes the trouble for himself apparently. And she asks what he knows of human beings after all. He has confessed that he didn't know them and yet he wants to teach them. He should learn about himself first. Then after this very absolute statement of the anima, "What knowest thou *thereof?*" comes the mysterious assertion: "The dew falleth on the grass when the night is most silent." You see, over against the babbling, there is a silence, which would be that "stillest hour" in which he has the chance to realize himself, to hear the voice of the unconscious. Now what about the dew that falls in the stillest hour?

Miss Hannah: It is an alchemistic symbol.

Prof. Jung: Yes, but there is also something in the Old Testament about it, where the alchemists found it originally.

Mr. Baumann: The dew of Gideon.

Prof. Jung: Yes, that was the sign from heaven. Jahveh let the dew fall to show that he was on Gideon's side. It was a miracle, a revelation. So the anima would be saying, "Now keep quiet, don't talk, particularly don't try to teach people, because in the stillest hour the revelation will come to you, as the dew came to Gideon." That is an excellent example of what the anima can do in a critical moment of life. Well, this book is full of such critical moments in Nietzsche's personal life, and you see how he passes them by.

Prof. Jung:
Here is a question by Miss Hannah, "In talking of the Will to Power in the chapter on "Self-Surpassing," you said that Nietzsche, as a man who had not succeeded in life, was necessarily always occupied with trying to make himself felt. In "The Stillest Hour," however, the utmost submission is demanded of him. It would interest me very much to know whether it lay in the realms of possibility for Nietzsche, situated as he was, to make this submission?"

Well, we are concerned here with a threatening incursion of the unconscious, and what he is going to do about it. How he is to meet that impact, or onslaught, is a rather poignant question. This was between 1880 and 1890, the time when rationalism and materialism were in full swing, when every science was even more specialized than today. The educated people, the academical people and so on, took pride in the fact that they were nothing but specialists and absolute monarchs in their own field. That is still the case, naturally, but it is no longer so popular, because the general public has become more critical in that respect, more sceptical. But in that time I don't see how Nietzsche could have accepted such a situation, how he could have met it differently. I think it was wellnigh impossible for him to have done anything else—I am unable to see any other possibility—except under one condition: *In habentibus symbolum facilior est transitus.* Quite by chance I found this interesting passage in the 16th-century Latin text of one of my old Hermetic philosophers, where he makes this cryptic statement, which means, "For those who have a symbol, the passing from one side to the other, the transmutation, is easier." In other words, those who have no symbol will find it very difficult to make the transition.[1] Of

[1] No idea is more central to Jungian thought than that of the transformative power of the symbol, for which Jung found anticipation in the mystery religions, in Christianity (thus, the cross as carried by Jesus in the passage from mortality to immortality), and in

course it sounds exactly as if he were talking about human beings; and he was talking of *beings*, but not of *human* beings—rather, of chemical substances, metals, which as you know, were often understood by the alchemists as *homunculi*, the little men of iron or copper or lead. They were the souls of chemical substances, and it was supposed that those souls or metals that had a symbol would have less difficulty in making the transition—the transmutation into another condition.

This is the condition by which any man in any time can make a transition: with the symbol he can transmute himself. Now what does that mean? I speak now, of course, of the symbol in general; the creed, for instance, is called the *symbolum*. It is the system or the symbolic formula to apply when the soul is in danger. The religious symbol is used against the perils of the soul. The symbol functions as a sort of machine, one could say, by which the libido is transformed. For a more detailed explanation of the symbol, I recommend you read my essay, "On Psychic Energy."[2] You see, by means of a symbol, such dangers can be accepted: one can submit to them, digest them. Otherwise, as in Nietzsche's case, it is a very dangerous situation: one is exposed without protection to the onslaught of the unconscious. He wiped out his symbol when he declared that God was dead. God is such a symbol, but Nietzsche had wiped out all the old dogmas. He had destroyed all the old values, so there was nothing left to defend him.

That is what people don't know: that they are exposed, naked to the unconscious when they can no longer use the old ways, particularly since nowadays they don't even understand what they mean. Who understands the meaning of the Trinity or the immaculate conception? And because they cannot understand these things rationally any longer, they obliterate them, abolish them, so they are defenseless and have to repress their unconscious. They cannot express it because it is inexpressible. It would be expressible in the dogma inasmuch as they accepted the dogma, inasmuch as they felt that the dogma lived, but that doesn't mean saying lightly, "Oh yes, I accept the dogma." For they cannot understand it; they have not even the understanding in these matters of the medieval man. He knew in a way, but his impressions or his rationalizations are absolutely meaningless to us and therefore we reject them. If we had an understanding of the symbols, we could accept them and they would work as they have always worked,

---

alchemy, wherein the search was ever for the element (e.g., mercury) that facilitates change both in matter and in the psyche.

[2] The first essay in CW 8.

but the *way* to an adequate understanding is also obliterated. And when that is gone it is gone forever; the symbols have lost their specific value.

Of course it was because those old symbols were utterly gone that Nietzsche could make the foolish statement that God is dead, which is just as if I should declare that the president of the United States is dead, that Roosevelt doesn't exist. But he does exist, and it doesn't matter to him whether or not I say he is dead. Nietzsche thought that somebody once said that God existed and that naturally, when they did not prove it, did not bring any evidence, it meant that God was not. You see, *God* is only a formulation of a natural fact—it doesn't matter what you call it, God or instinct or whatever you like. Any superior force in your psychology can be the true god, and you cannot say this fact does not exist. The fact exists as it has always existed; the psychological condition is always there and nothing is changed by calling it another name. The mere fact that Nietzsche declared God to be dead shows his attitude. He was without a symbol and so, naturally, to make the transition, to leave one condition and to enter another mental condition, would be exceedingly difficult, if not wholly impossible. In this case it was impossible.

Mrs. Sigg: It is somewhat difficult to think that Nietzsche had no symbol; I think he had two symbols, two creeds. He believed in the superman and the idea of the eternal return.

Prof. Jung: Yes, that was the *Ersatz*, the compensation.

Mrs. Sigg: But why was it not valid?

Prof. Jung: Because it was only what his mind did: his mind invented those ideas in order to compensate the onslaught of the unconscious, which came from below with such power that he tried to climb the highest mountains and be the superman. That means above man, not here, somewhere in the future, in a safe place where he could not be reached by that terrific power from below. You see, he could not accept it. It was an attempt of his consciousness, a bold invention, a bold structure, which collapsed as it always collapses. Any structure built over against the unconscious with the mind, no matter how bold, will always collapse because it has no feet, no roots. Only something that is rooted in the unconscious can live, because that is its origin. Otherwise it is like a plant which has been removed from the soil. That Nietzsche tried to build a structure *against* the unconscious, one sees everywhere—in the descent into the volcano, for instance. Instantly he makes light of it: it is twisted into a dialogue with the fire-dog and that collapses as you know. In "The Stillest Hour," the unconscious approaches him in a most uncanny and menacing way and he has no adequate answer. We are coming now to the third part and there the same thing continues: he is still trying to assimilate the onslaught of the unconscious, and in the next chapter he has to give way. He has to leave his friends and give up his life as he has lived it hitherto, has to go into solitude, in order to meet the demands of that which is coming up from the unconscious. He has not digested it at all. So I would say the superman is an invention, not a symbol.

A symbol is never an invention. It *happens* to man. You know, what we call perhaps dogmatic ideas are all very primitive facts which happened to man long before he thought them; he began to think them long after they first appeared. Our forefathers never thought about the Easter eggs, for instance, or about the Christmas tree, which were just *done*. And so the very complicated rites we observe in primitives, or in old civilizations that are relatively primitive, were never thought of to begin with. They were done, and then after a while thinkers came who asked, "Now why in hell are we doing these things?" There was a Trinity, or a triad of the gods, long before there was a dogma. There was an immaculate conception and a virgin birth before anybody speculated why Mary had to be a virgin. (The miraculous birth out of the virgin happened long before; it was not a recent process.) So for a thing to be a symbol it must be very old, most original. For instance, did the early Christians think that behind the idea of the holy communion lay that of cannibalism? We have no evidence for it, but of course it is so: that is the very primitive way of partaking in the life of the one you have conquered. When the Red Indians eat the brain or the heart of the killed enemy, that is communion, but none of the Fathers of the church ever thought of explaining the holy communion in such a way. Yet if their holy communion had not contained the old idea of cannibalism it would not have lived, would have no roots. All roots are dark.

Well now, the first chapter in the third part of *Zarathustra* is "The Wanderer." The idea is that he has quit his country and he describes climbing over the ridge of the mountain to the other side. The mountains form a divide, and then he descends again to the sea where he takes a boat. That is the old symbol of the night sea-journey, navigating on the sea of the unconscious to reach the new country, and that is the *transitus*. You know, in the ancient mysteries the *transitus* was always difficult; the hero had to undergo the transmutation by performing difficult tasks. For example, Mithras is represented on monuments as carrying the bull, meaning himself in the animal form; he had to shoulder his animal side. And the *transitus* is shown in the passing of

Christ on the cross—that is, going from life to death, carrying that symbol of the cross. In the cult of Mithras it was carrying the bull that is himself, as Christ was the cross—whatever that means. And in the cult of Attis it was the carrying of the tree, which was Attis, into the cave of the Mother. Also the so-called *athla*, the heavy work, the trials or tests which people had to undergo in the initiations, belong to the *transitus*.

There is a neolithic initiation place, a Hypogaeum, an underground temple, at Hal Safliena in Malta, where I have seen a transition place. It was very probably a mother cult. Before coming to the most sacred place in the depths of the temple, there is, one could say, a multicellular womb, a central round cave with adjoining little caves like manholes in the wall, so that a man could just creep through one of those partitions into the next cave; and then he was in the retort or bottle, or the uterus, where he had to be hatched. Incubation symbols, terracotta figures of women in the incubation sleep, have been found there. Then, before reaching the innermost place, there is a cut in the descent, about two meters deep, which was filled with water, so whoever was descending in the darkness—or perhaps it was lighted by torches—had to go through the water, to be metaphorically drowned, in order to come out on the other side. The Christian baptism was of course the same idea, part of the transmutation process, and people were literally submerged. It has degenerated now into the few drops that are administered in our existing Christian church, but formerly people were really put in the water, as if drowned. You see that is a danger, a sort of metaphorical death which one has to pass through in order to reach a new attitude, the transmutation of oneself. So the crossing of the mountain is part of the *athla*, the heavy work, and Nietzsche expresses this in the text. He has very depressing thoughts which of course make the transition particularly disagreeable. Then when he sees the sea, he says,

> Ah, this sombre, sad sea, below me! Ah, this sombre nocturnal vexation! Ah fate and sea! To you must I now *go down*!

The sea is, of course, the unconscious to which he has to descend, and it means fate also, because the unconscious is fate. There the roots are, and whatever your roots are, is what you will get. So the descent into the unconscious is a sort of fatality; one surrenders to fate, not knowing what the outcome will be, as that neolithic man who fell into the water in the darkness did not know what was going to happen next. It was perhaps a test for his courage; at all events it was disagreeable to drop into the dark, cold water, not knowing how deep it was, or whether something awful was in it. That is Nietzsche's feeling now; he knows he has to go down. He is giving way in an unexpected manner to something which he belittled and made very light of before. You see, he could have learned when he went down into the volcano, but it was too disagreeable—he could not realize it. He held onto his consciousness, which was entirely rational, and made nothing of the volcano, and then he thought it was dealt with, overcome. But now it comes again. As Faust in one place says: *In verwandelter Gestalt, Ueb' ich grimmige Gewalt* ("In another form I apply a cruel power").

> Before my highest mountain do I stand, and before my longest wandering: therefore must I first go deeper down than I ever ascended.

This is an attempt to make it acceptable, a sort of rationalization or solution. He says, "Ah well, I have to go down into this awful thing; it is unavoidable," as one might think something an awful threat to one's existence but say hopefully, "Well, *reculer pour mieux sauter!*"[3] Or as one might say, "Oh, I am just going down to the unconscious," or "I have a bad attack, simply because I am putting up the Christmas tree, but it will be very nice afterwards." In the initiations one stood all the pain in order to be redeemed; one would be illuminated or have some secret knowledge. But in reality it doesn't feel like that, but feels exactly like going down into the cold sea with all its monsters and no promise of a Christmas tree afterwards. Nietzsche promises himself that the mountain will come afterwards—that is the superstructure—and we shall see how he constructs that high mountain which is not to be overcome.

> —Deeper down into pain than I ever ascended, even into its darkest flood! So willeth my fate. Well! I am ready.

So after his helpful thought that the mountain would come afterwards, again he says, "No, you go down." That is, of course, very difficult, a big order, and a little further on he says,

> Everything as yet sleepeth, said he; even the sea sleepeth. Drowsily and strangely doth its eye gaze upon me.
> But it breatheth warmly—I feel it. And I feel also that it dreameth. It tosseth about dreamily on hard pillows.
> Hark! Hark! How it groaneth with evil recollections! Or evil expectations?

---

[3] "Step back in order to jump better."

Ah, I am sad along with thee, thou dusky monster, and angry
with myself even for thy sake.

Ah, that my hand hath not strength enough! Gladly, indeed,
would I free thee from evil dreams!—

This is a very remarkable passage. You see, he is trying to formulate
what he feels in standing upon the mountain looking down at the sea.
The aspect of the unconscious is like a dormant sea; one doesn't know
what it will be when it wakes up. For the time being, it is mysterious,
very still, like someone dreaming. But it breathes—it is alive with
dreamlike life. And the sound of the surf is described as groaning; the
sea suffers from evil recollections or perhaps from evil expectations.
That is, of course, a projection. *He* has evil recollections and even evil
expectations, as we have heard already. And now having made that
projection, instantly he is liberated from the weight of his own evil, and
he really considers curing the sea, the unconscious, of its bad dreams
and recollections. But the unconscious has no bad recollections, as the
sea has no bad recollections. That is anthropomorphic: man has bad
expectations, man suffers from his recollections, and he may have
dreams. But how could one ever imagine being able to free nature
from her world-creating dreams? Those dreams are divine, creative
thoughts—the very life of nature. The question is, of course, how he
can free himself from these evil dreams, and Nietzsche might have
drawn this conclusion if he could have afforded it. But that is pathological; he cannot afford that honesty. He is always called the most
honest philosopher, but he could not afford to be honest with himself.
Yes, in a hundred thousand minor details he was honest—he saw the
truth in other people—but when it actually happened to himself, he
could not draw correct conclusions. That he could not in this situation
shows that he either did not want to see it, or he may have been blindfolded by the idea that he was a great fellow who was writing a book
which was quite objective, not himself.

Many a writer thinks his book is not himself, that it is objective, as if
he were a god dismissing a world from his bosom: "There is a world
which goes by itself, that is not I!" In this case, however, Nietzsche
surely should have realized that the idea of curing the sea of its evil
dreams was an extraordinary assumption; it is a god-almighty likeness,
and it is even a sort of aesthetical test, which tact should have pre-
vented. But it makes an excellent paradox, makes good reading. It
sounds marvelous to say to nature, "Shall I free you from dreams?"
One is already the great mountain. It shows an extraordinary con-

temptuousness, yet that great mountain trembles with fear, and that is what he could not afford to see. It was too much. Therefore I absolutely believe he was not able to. He has a certain realization of it, however, as we can see in the next paragraph:

> And while Zarathustra thus spake, he laughed at himself with melancholy and bitterness. What! Zarathustra, said he, wilt thou even sing consolation to the sea?
>
> Ah, thou amiable fool, Zarathustra, thou too-blindly confiding one! But thus hast thou ever been: ever hast thou approached confidently all that is terrible.
>
> Every monster wouldst thou caress. [Making light of it!] A whiff of warm breath, a little soft tuft on its paw—: and immediately wert thou ready to love and lure it.

Not knowing what it was all about. You see, even that little insight was not taken seriously, but playfully, as people with an aesthetical attitude take things. It was Nietzsche himself who said, in his *Unzeitgemässige Betrachtungen*: After all, the world is an aesthetical problem.[4] But it is not, it goes right under the skin. That is what he was always trying to escape, but he did not escape it, though he tried to deny it.

Miss Hannah: Your speaking of the aesthetical attitude made me wonder whether it would have been possible for Nietzsche to have achieved submission by giving a freer rein to himself as an artist? Some passages (in "The Night Song," for instance) prove that sometimes he could be a very great artist.

Prof. Jung: He *was* a great artist, but he was also a philosopher and we expect a philosopher to think. His work ran away with him and that was his weakness. Such a thing would not have happened to Goethe, or Schiller, or Shakespeare. That was his weakness: he was a genius with a big hole in him.[5]

[4] In a sense, the principal motif of Nietzsche's essay, "Richard Wagner in Bayreuth," is that it is art, not religion or morality or politics, that addresses and in some measure solves life's problems. From the fact that art is a reflection "of a simpler world, a more rapid solution of the riddle of life—art derives its greatness and indispensability" (sec. 4). In a time when language is sick, it remains for music to provide "correct feeling, the enemy of all convention" (sec. 5) "Thoughts Out of Season," tr. Anthony M. Ludovici, in N/Complete, vol. I, part I. Or again, in *WP*, "We have art in order that we not perish from the truth" (book III, n. 822).

[5] Thomas Mann wrote, "Nietzsche inherited from Schopenhauer the proposition that life is representation alone . . .—that is, that life can be justified, only as an aesthetic phenomenon." "Nietzsche's Philosophy in the Light of Recent History," *Last Essays* (New York, 1951), p. 141.

We are now coming to the chapter, "The Vision and the Enigma." And here we come again to a story, an adventure, and, as I said, these stories in *Zarathustra* are always particularly valuable because they are events that speak objectively. When Nietzsche is talking, he twists, he transforms, he assimilates; he is always doing something to his material. While in such stories something happens to him. Therefore they are so valuable. They give an extraordinary insight into the real events, the real processes, of his unconscious. Now, he went over the mountain and on board the ship, to sail over the sea of the unconscious, to make the *transitus*.

> When it got abroad among the sailors that Zarathustra was on board the ship—for a man who came from the Happy Isles had gone on board along with him,—there was great curiosity and expectation. But Zarathustra kept silent for two days, and was cold and deaf with sadness; so that he neither answered looks nor questions. On the evening of the second day, however, he again opened his ears, though he still kept silent: for there were many curious and dangerous things to be heard on board the ship, which came from afar, and was to go still further. Zarathustra, however, was fond of all those who make distant voyages and dislike to live without danger. And behold! when listening, his own tongue was at last loosened, and the ice of his heart broke. Then did he begin to speak thus:
>
> To you, the daring venturers and adventurers, and whoever hath embarked with cunning sails upon frightful seas,—
>
> To you the enigma-intoxicated, the twilight-enjoyers, whose souls are allured by flutes to every treacherous gulf:
>
> —For ye dislike to grope at a thread with cowardly hand; and where ye can *divine*, there do ye hate to *calculate*—
>
> To you only do I tell the enigma that I *saw*—the vision of the lonesomest one.—
>
> Gloomily walked I lately in corpse-coloured twilight—gloomily and sternly, with compressed lips. Not only one sun had set for me.

In these words he describes how he enters the kingdom of gloom, the darkness of the unconscious. Or the darkness of consciousness, one had better say, and it is a very disagreeable formulation: a "corpse-coloured twilight" is not beautiful. That is the taste of death hovering about the unconscious, for the unconscious is not only a storehouse of life, but is a storehouse of death in which there are many corpses. For the past and the future are one: whatever is left over from the past still lives, and the germ of the future is living in the unconscious too. So, under a certain aspect, it is a graveyard, the inside of the tomb, and from another standpoint it is a blossoming field; it all depends upon the attitude of the one who enters it. To Zarathustra, life is all on the surface and in the sunlight—only the conscious lives—and when he enters the unconscious, he finds the graves of all the things that have died or have been. So he says "not only one sun had set for me"—but a number of suns, a number of conscious lights: enlightening, helpful ideas that give orientation, insight, and so on. All that comes and disappears and has to disappear. Otherwise, he cannot see the twilight, the darkness.

> A path which ascended daringly among boulders, an evil, lonesome path, which neither herb nor shrub any longer cheered, a mountain-path, crunched under the daring of my foot.
> Mutely marching over the scornful clinking of pebbles, trampling the stone that let it slip: thus did my foot force its way upwards.
> Upwards:—in spite of the spirit that drew it downwards, towards the abyss, the spirit of gravity, my devil and arch-enemy.

He is again embarking upon a compensatory attempt. He has gone down already, is in the gloom, in the darkness of the sea. And now here he is remembering his ascent. He describes the upward climb *against* the spirit that drew him down towards the abyss, where he actually is.

> Upwards:—although it sat upon me, half-dwarf, half-mole; paralysed, paralysing; dripping lead in mine ear, and thoughts like drops of lead into my brain.

That is the spirit of gravity. His description of it is very interesting.

> "O Zarathustra," it whispered scornfully, syllable by syllable, "thou stone of wisdom! Thou threwest thyself high, but every thrown stone must—fall!
> O Zarathustra, thou stone of wisdom, thou sling-stone, thou star-destroyer! Thyself threwest thou so high,—but every thrown stone—must fall!
> Condemned of thyself, and to thine own stoning: O Zarathustra, far indeed threwest thou thy stone—but upon *thyself* will it recoil!"

1257

You see, this is the dwarf speaking. In this passage he is really already in the kingdom of gloom, surrounded by it, like a diver or a man drowning. This is an overpowering situation which he has to combat, and he tries to bring himself back on the upper path, to remember how he felt when he was climbing up to a region of safety high above the sea. And he now transforms his actual experience into a personification, as if it were merely that spirit of gravity which is always weighing him down. This is a very peculiar twist which I should criticize in a patient's fantasy, for instance. If he were going down into the darkness of the sea, and then suddenly something seemed to happen and he was out of it, I should say, "You did not remain true to your theme; because it has beaten you or burned you, you jumped away from it into another condition." So Nietzsche really jumps out of his first mood into a different situation, where he is not going down, but going up.

You see, when you jump away from the theme in a fantasy, you aggravate the situation; when you don't accept the situation as it comes along, you make it more aggressive. Say you dream of a pursuing animal; a lion or a wild bull is after you. If you run away or try to rescue yourself into another situation, in most cases the thing gets worse. If you could face it, if you could say this *is* the situation, you have a reasonable chance that it will turn, that something will happen to make it better. For example, if you have a horrible dream and conclude, "Ah, I am very much at variance with my unconscious or my instincts, therefore I should accept this monster, this enemy," then it changes its face almost instantly. What you were deadly afraid of becomes relatively harmless; if you accept that awful lion or terrible bull, in the next dream it is a dog or a mouse and finally it disappears, merging with you perhaps in a friendly way. It is only a terrible face because you make a terrible face at it; if you don't make that face, it is quite reasonable and nice. It only persecutes you because it wants to live with you. It is a terrifying ghost because you make it into one, but if you say, "You are my friend, you belong to me, you are myself too," it merges with you, and of course you receive an effect, but it has received your effect just as well. While if you jump away, it becomes all the more aggressive—and you really only jump away because you assume that it is strange and has nothing to do with you.

Now I don't say this is an absolute rule: there is no rule without exceptions and these laws I am teaching are not laws but rules of thumb which suffer many exceptions. One exception I should like to mention, though it is treacherous and gives you a pretext for saying that a fantasy is strange and doesn't belong to you. There are cases where it *is* strange, where it really doesn't belong to you; you can dream other people's dreams, can get them through the walls. It is not usual, but you had better look out. For instance, if you are observing the series of your dreams, keeping in contact with your unconscious, and then have suddenly a very strange dream, it would be fair to assume that a strange influence had taken place. On the other hand, if you have not carefully recorded the series, you do not know. You cannot say that the dream is strange, no matter how strange you feel it to be. It is perhaps not strange at all, but is only something in you that is strange to yourself. I would say that in one hundred cases, or not even as many, you might find perhaps one or two where the strangeness is objective, where you have dreamt the dream of another person.

Mr. Baumann: I think this idea of running away from the fantasy is beautifully expressed in the *Tibetan Book of the Dead*, chiefly at the end where rebirth is coming and the dead woman is persecuted by the spirits. She tries to run away and hide in a hollow tree, and because she does that, she is reborn in a very inferior condition.

Prof. Jung: In the womb of an animal perhaps. I am glad that you mentioned the *Tibetan Book of the Dead*. There you find this drama of making things much worse through running away, making your enemy still more aggressive, still more dangerous.[6] That happens now to Zarathustra; he holds off the realization of his actual situation and then the unconscious becomes personified. This is on the one side a great danger; on the other side, it is an asset. And what would the advantage of a personification be?

Mrs. Jung: It can be discriminated better, better realized.

Mrs. Baumann: You can talk to it.

Prof. Jung: Yes, when a thing is personified it has autonomy and you can talk to it. It is like the poodle in *Faust*. Faust is concerned with the black poodle that is running in circles round him. Sometimes it seems to be an ordinary dog and sometimes it seems very uncanny, and he cannot establish any kind of rapport with the thing. When he thinks it is just an ordinary dog, he can be sure that he has made too little of it. Then it is no longer what it seemed to be, but becomes dangerous. It increases its size and suddenly the whole thing opens like a box and out comes the devil. Then Faust says, *Das also war des Pudels Kern!* ("So that was the kernel of the poodle.") The poodle then is personified—it can talk—and so the discussion with the devil begins.

Mrs. Sigg: Would not the Indian king who carried the corpse be a

[6] *Tibetan*, book 1, part 2, 11th day.

good example? He was so very patient and had not such a negative attitude as Nietzsche has to the dwarf.[7] Nietzsche says "Thou! Or I!" as if one of them must die, while the king in the Indian tale is very patient and carries the corpse, accepting it in order that the ghost shall teach him.

Prof. Jung: Yes, that is also a very good example.

Mrs. Jung: It seems to me he tries to give himself courage: he doesn't want to run away, but he is afraid; what threatened him was not something that turned into a nice comrade, but something utterly destructive.

Prof. Jung: Yes, we are coming to that. Of course he is trying to compensate. He jumps away because he is afraid and naturally he must have courage. He succeeded in personifying it in the form of a dwarf, which is very small and apparently unimportant, but again he overlooks the fact that a dwarf has cunning and is mana—a very mythological figure, something like an evil jinn. Of course he doesn't believe in devils so it seems to be nothing but a dwarf, and he calls it the spirit of gravity. But that is the eternal sloth, eternal inertia, the spirit of lead, "the man of lead" as Zosimos called him. (In astrology old Saturn, the planet, is called "the man of lead.")[8] And Democritus said that lead contains a most impertinent demon, a very angry demon indeed, and that whoever releases that demon is in great danger of becoming insane: he destroys the mind. You see, that was their experience: those Hermetic philosophers knew that dwarf, that spirit of lead, that leadlike heaviness, and they knew that you should not tickle it or make light of it because it contains an impertinent demon that causes the perils of the soul. In alchemy that meant insanity.[9] They were quite aware of it and always repeat that numbers of people could not stand it and went mad. So that universal medicine, the essence of the minerals, which

---

[7] A virtuous king was told to cut down a hanged man and bring the corpse back to the palace. He did so, but the hanged man managed to ask a complex moral question to which the king conscientiously replied, only to have his interlocutor fly back to his scaffold. This was to repeat itself twenty-four times, at which point the king is transformed. Zimmer, *The King and The Corpse: Tales of the Soul's Conquest of Evil* (Princeton, B.S. XI, 2nd edn., 1956), pp. 202-45.

[8] Jung deals with this third-century Hermetic writer in CW 13, pars. 85-86: "I am the leaden man and I submit myself to unendurable torment." This is taken to mean that lead is to be rejected.

[9] This is not the ancient Greek atomist but the pseudo-Democritus, a mystic of the first or second century A.D. In CW 13, par. 430, Jung cites the sixth-century Olympiodorus on lead as containing a demon that drives people mad.

they tried to extract, was chiefly a medicine to cure the afflictions of the soul or the mind, *afflictiones mentis.*

Dr. Escher: A good example of the autonomy of figures is *Six Characters in Search of an Author*, the play by Pirandello.[10] He puts six figures on the stage with himself and he tells them what they must do. Then they say: "You have created us but we do as we like," and they have a fight. He is furious with them but they go on doing whatever they wish. It is psychologically very interesting.

Prof. Jung: I don't know that play of Pirandello, but it is a good idea, the demonstration on the stage might give one a vivid idea of how that thing functions. It is really like that. There is the same motif in Goethe, the idea of the thing you have created taking on life of its own. It is also the Golem motif.[11]

Mr. Bash: There is another example in a tale by Edgar Allan Poe, where the hero of the story is accompanied by his double, who leads him into disgrace after disgrace. He is finally killed by the hero, but at the moment of being killed he tells the hero that it is he who has created him—the double.[12]

Prof. Jung: That would be similar, the self-created thing that becomes more powerful than the creator.

Mrs. Sigg: Is that not an illustration of what you said—that because Nietzsche doesn't accept the cripple, it comes now as a dwarf?

Prof. Jung: Yes, it is all one line.

Miss Hannah: And *The Picture of Dorian Gray* by Oscar Wilde[13] is the same.

Prof. Jung: Oh yes, it is really a very frequent occurrence that something which one assumes one has created, which one assumes to be one's own thought, is not one's thought really. One must be mighty careful of saying a thought is one's own creation. It is then as if it lived all by itself. It is quite possible, when one thinks one has created a thought, that it really grows by itself. Then there is the possibility that it *overgrows* one, and then suddenly one is up against it. That is exactly

---

[10] Luigi Pirandello's *Six Characters in Search of an Author: A Comedy in the Making* continues to attract directors and audiences by virtue of its ingenious presentation of characters who "precede" their author.

[11] By "the Golem motif," Jung means a demon with magical powers, such as Mephisto in *Faust*, which Jung interprets as a projection of unconscious contents. Gustav Meyrink in *The Golem*, a novel which Jung often cites, wrote a story of the appearance of this mysterious figure in a ghetto. See *Dream Sem.*, pp. 507-9; CW 6, par. 205; et al.

[12] In *William Wilson: A Tale* (1839), Edgar Allan Poe (1804-1849) tells of this protagonist's footsteps being dogged over many years by his non-fraternal twin.

[13] Oscar Wilde published this, his only novel, in 1891.

what has happened here. Zarathustra rejects it because he is afraid and then it comes up against him. That dwarf holds trumps of which Nietzsche knows nothing apparently and he says awful things to him: "Yes, yes, you can climb Mont Blanc and throw a stone higher than anybody has every thrown one, but it is a superstructure that has no roots and it will fall back upon you." This is again a forecast of what is going to happen—that the Superman will fall back on him; it is a stone thrown high in the air which has no basis. Nietzsche himself has no basis so how can he sustain a superman? And the stone has another interesting aspect. The dwarf calls Zarathustra, "thou stone of wisdom," and says, "Thou threwest thyself high." So Zarathustra is the stone, and the dwarf thinks he has thrown himself too high, that it is a mighty effort but in vain. For to jump into the air doesn't increase one's size, and he comes down with a crash and falls upon himself, that miserable self on the surface of the earth. You see, here is a fatal critique of the whole of *Zarathustra*. Of course we are in a fortunate situation, we can understand, but it was too close to Nietzsche: it was his own fate and he could not fully realize what it meant. Though he must have had his premonitions; otherwise he could not have written *Zarathustra*.

Mr. Baumann: I would like to point out the difference between Nietzsche's *Zarathustra* and the real Zarathustra. The real Zarathustra's religion was very spiritual, but at the same time he said that man should be a peasant, an animal.

Prof. Jung: Quite. Only the spirit can rise because the spirit is a vapor anyway, but man lives in the body and belongs to the earth. While Nietzsche's idea of the superman doesn't encourage that at all, for the idea of the Superman is to create something that is beyond man, beyond reality.

Prof. Reichstein: This situation was anticipated also in the scene of the rope-dancer.

Prof. Jung: Yes, it is one continuous line, that jumping into the air and then the fatal fall. The dwarf's terrible prophecy has an extraordinary strength because he knows the future. That is a piece of the real unconscious, it is nature—not Nietzsche. Nature speaks and gives him the right prognosis. Now he continues.

> Then was the dwarf silent; and it lasted long. The silence, however, oppressed me; and to be thus in pairs, one is verily lonesomer than when alone!
>
> I ascended, I ascended, I dreamt, I thought,—but everything

oppressed me. A sick one did I resemble, whom bad torture wea-
rieth, and a worse dream reawakeneth out of his first sleep.—

But there is something in me which I call courage: it hath hitherto slain for me every dejection. This courage at last bade me
stand still and say: "Dwarf! Thou! Or I!"—

For courage is the best slayer,—courage which attacketh: for in
every attack there is sound of triumph.

He got a fatal blow, that is quite visible, and the reaction is courage, a
"quandmême" against whatever he has realized; of course we don't
know in how far he has realized it. This is surely a very brave reaction,
this is the greatness of Nietzsche. He was a *déséquilibré* genius,[14] but it
was just his genius that he did not show cowardice in such a moment,
but had to assert himself. Now he goes on talking about courage and
he says finally in the paragraph next to the last.

Courage, however, is the best slayer, courage which attacketh: it
slayeth even death itself; for it saith: "*Was that* life? Well! Once
more!"

In such speech, however, there is much sound of triumph. He
who hath ears to hear, let him hear.

This passage shows that there is a certain realization—here is the courage that faces death—so we can assume that Nietzsche perhaps took it
as a premonition of death. Or it might be a speech metaphor, we don't
know. At all events the word *death* is here, and the conclusion is the new
idea that comes in here; we don't know when it originated in him but
it became the main idea in an essay which was posthumously published
by one of the secretaries of the Nietzsche archives. It is the idea of *die
ewige Wiederkunft*, the eternal return of all things. We have had hints
before in *Zarathustra* of the eternal return, his idea of immortality.[15]
Why should one be afraid of death since everything eternally returns?
So the onslaught of the dwarf brings out in him the idea of the eternity
of life.

[14] A *quandmene*: an "even so." *Déséquilibré*: disequilibrated.

[15] Nietzsche said that the "fundamental concept" of his *Zarathustra* was "the idea of
Eternal Recurrence, the highest formula of affirmation that can ever be attained." See
his section on *Zarathustra* in *Ecce Homo*.

LECTURE IV

25 May 1938

Prof. Jung:
We got to the second part of "The Vision and the Enigma" last time.
It begins,

> "Halt, dwarf!" said I. "Either I—or thou! I, however, am the
> stronger of the two—: thou knowest not mine abysmal thought!
> *It*—couldst thou not endure!"
>
> Then happened that which made me lighter: for the dwarf
> sprang from my shoulder, the prying sprite! And it squatted on a
> stone in front of me. There was however a gateway just where we
> halted.

You remember in the first part, the dwarf was sitting on Zarathustra's
back. That is a typical demonstration of a possession: evil spirits are always supposed to sit on the backs of their victims. Therefore certain
primitive tribes wear peculiar amulets at the back of the neck, sort of
scowling faces to protect them against the evil eye or against the spirits
that come after them. You see, spirits are often associated with the archetypal form of the shadow that follows after. The Greeks had formulation of this idea in one word meaning "the one that follows behind." Now whatever follows behind is in the sphere where we have no
eyes, no consciousness, our consciousness being closely associated with
the sense of vision. We know that from our everyday speech, when we
understand or become conscious of a thing, we say, "I see," or "It dawns
upon me." And the metaphors that we use to explain the essence of
consciousness are analogies taken from the world of light and of
seeing. When it is a matter of a feeling realization, on the other hand,
we choose our analogies from the sense of hearing. "I hear" means
something quite different from, "I see." "I hear" means that the thing
has penetrated your system more, been taken more to heart, while "I
see" need not imply that at all. For instance, the German word *Gehör*
meaning "hearing," "having an ear for a thing," is related to *gehorsam*

1264

meaning obedient, or *gehorchen*, to obey. When the Lord speaks to Samuel, and he answers, "Oh Lord, I hear," it means "I obey, I submit," but if Samuel had said, "Oh Lord, I see, yes Lord, I see what you mean," it wouldn't mean that he would necessarily be *gehorsam*, that he would submit and be obedient. It would sound almost blasphemous, preposterous. So whatever comes from behind comes from the shadow, from the darkness of the unconscious, and because you have no eyes there, and because you wear no neck amulet to ward off evil influences, that thing gets at you, possesses and obsesses you. It sits on top of you.

Therefore if a patient in analysis feels obsessed, it is the task of the analyst to dispossess him of his anima or animus, and in such a case one turns him round and says, "Now look at the thing." And in that moment it gets off him. He can objectify it. That is the reason why one should objectify unconscious figures. We make a figure of the animus and the anima, because in nature they are not visible as figures, but are invisible possessions; they occur as if they were really in one's system. The man who carries an evil spirit on his back doesn't know it, doesn't know that this thing behind is manipulating his brain and causing a peculiar expression on his face. It often happens that people who as far as they know have perfectly harmless nice thoughts, yet betray something quite different in their faces; the face is not at all in accordance with their conscious mental contents, but is in accordance with the sprite, the jinn, that is sitting on their backs. They are being unconsciously manipulated by a possessive spirit. Now, if they turn round and face that thing, then instantly it becomes objective, and therefore personified. For it is impossible to perceive an object which is not something in itself. As long as they don't turn round, as long as they are possessed, it has no form—they cannot imagine a form.

People have the greatest difficulty in understanding what one can possibly mean by an anima or an animus, because they never turn round. To make it objective is to them quite unnatural, against nature, for they prefer to act on impulse, even when admitting that they do things which are strange to themselves, which react on themselves, and which they will be sorry for. Afterwards, they don't understand how they could ever have done such a thing. Nevertheless, they go on behaving in that way, apparently thinking that possession is justified because it is quite natural. It is indeed quite natural; it is, one could say, the original condition of mankind. Man is always a bit possessed: he is necessarily possessed inasmuch as his consciousness is weak. Primitive consciousness is very frail, easily overcome; therefore primitive people are always suffering from loss of consciousness. Suddenly something jumps upon them, seizes them, and they are alienated from themselves. In a dance they easily get into an ecstatic condition in which they are no longer themselves, and knowing this, they even apply that knowledge in their rites. They induce that condition. The Central Australian aborigines say that they perform the Alcheringa rites in order to become some one that ordinarily they are not. They identify with their ancestors of the Alcheringa time, a sort of heroic age long ago, as the time of the Homeric heroes would be to us. They return to that condition, become their ancestors in the Alchuringa time, and as such they perform the rites; otherwise the rites are not valid.[1]

The Pueblo Indians have the same idea. The master of the religious ceremonies who accompanied me to the buffalo dances, told me he could not dance himself that day because he was not purified. Then he explained to me that at sunrise all the men went up on the roofs of the houses—the pueblos are built like skyscrapers, the houses piled up on top of each other, pyramid-shaped—and there they watch the sun the whole day long until evening. They turn slowly with the sun until they are in a state of complete identification with it, the sun being their ancestor, their father. Then they are the sons of the sun and as such they can dance. But if they are not reidentified with the divine ancestor, they cannot perform the rites. Or if they did, it would be merely a theatrical performance and would have no magic effects—that is what he told me. You see, that is another application of the same fact, that they know these phenomena of psychological possession so well that they even apply them for their own ritual use. This is a primitive piece of psychology which is pretty difficult for us to understand, but it shows clearly how general and normal that fact is with them.

Now of course, that all lives in us: we have the same brain, the same metabolism—our whole system is the same—and therefore we can observe the same phenomena in ourselves. Here Nietzsche, in his poetical language, blurts it out. But we express the same fact when we say to someone in a very bad mood, "What in hell has gotten into you?" or, "We will discuss this matter again tomorrow when you are yourself." That is a recognition of the fact that one is alienated by a strange possession, which in true primitive style one could symbolize here by that little demoniacal thing, the dwarf that sits upon his back. The right procedure, as I said, is to turn round and face it. You say you are pos-

[1] On alcheringa time, see Lévy-Bruhl, p. 1382, and below, 8 Feb. 1939, n. 2.

sessed, and you ask by whom, and then you get the answer. You reconstruct the figures; you try to find out what that thing is in you.

This is not my invention, but is an age-old idea. Leon Daudet has arrived at the same idea; in his book *L'Hérédo* he speaks of *auto-fécondation intérieure*, by which he understands an inner transformation caused by the reawakening of the soul of an ancestor.[2] In other words, an inner self generated in oneself, a secondary personality which can become a possessive spirit. For instance, your grandfather or your uncle may generate himself within you and become a possessive personality which for years, for the better part of your life even, supplants your own personality. Daudet thought it was a great discovery and cites certain cases which are perfectly convincing if one knows anything about it. Any case of a neurotic split personality would be an equally good example. For instance, one often hears that until he was twenty, So-and-So was a very nice boy, but he is quite different now and one doesn't know what has got into him. Or the other way round: somebody who had a very negative personality turns out very positive. And it can be a real possession, quite against the personal character; one becomes a different individual.

That comes from the original weakness of consciousness. There is so much unconscious matter outside, that consciousness can be overrun at any time and a strange complex simply takes the seat. Then what you assumed yourself to be disappears into the shadow and becomes an unconscious complex. Perhaps someone who had really a very doubtful character to begin with suddenly turns out to be a saint and dies a saint. To know what he really is, one must study his dreams or visions; that is most instructive, most interesting. The visions of St. Anthony, for example, show quite a sensuous, lascivious character, which was supplanted by a decent one.[3] Then one is in doubt as to who the real fellow may be, or what he would be like if he were not a mere conglomeration—if he were, instead, a composition, a synthesis. The original condition of a personality is an absolutely irrational conglomeration of inherited units. A part is from the grandfather on the mother's side, another from the grandfather on the father's side; the nose comes from 1750 and the ears from 1640, and so on. And it is the same with your different qualities, a certain artistic quality for instance, or a

[2] Leon Daudet published *L'Hérédo* (Paris, 1916), which Jung elsewhere called "Confused but ingenious." CW 9 i, par. 224. Interior auto-fecundation has to do with the presence in all of us of ancestral elements which occasionally manifest themselves, a variant on alcheringa time.

[3] For St. Anthony's visions, see above, 3 June 1936, n. 2.

mental quality. All that is in the family tree, but unfortunately we have not careful records of our ancestors, but only have occasional portraits or perhaps there are some letters left, or old tales, which allow us a certain insight. The grandmother may have said that one child was like her own grandmother, and so we reach back some generations. But we know nothing certainly; we are a conglomeration, not a composition, and only become a composition when the parts know about each other. And when you know about your own society of dwarfs, all the minor personalities in you—when you confront them and get the full shock of that mood—you almost lose your head over yourself: "Who in hell am I?"

That was Schopenhauer's question—I have often told you that story. He was walking in the public gardens in Frankfurt one day, lost in thought, so he strayed into a flower-bed. And the guardian rushed at him: "Hey! Get out of there! Who are you anyway?" And Schopenhauer said, "Exactly, that is what I want to know." You see, he was concerned with the identity of the ego—who *is* that fellow? Now, anybody can have that doubt; there is always the possibility of doubt, because it might be something else there—really something else. Sure enough, when you come to those split compartments in yourself, conglomerations that are not your own, you do ask yourself who you are. If St. Anthony had asked himself about his visions, naturally that would have been an awful question to him: "Am I the fellow who produces such awful stuff or am I a saint?" He would have been in profound doubt.

Athanasius, the Bishop of Alexandria wrote a collection of excellent stories about the "mourning ones," the hermits in the desert. One saint, for instance, had lived twenty years in the desert and was absolutely sure that he was watertight and could meet the world again; he felt completely detached. Then he remembered that he had an old friend who had become a bishop somewhere and he decided to pay him a visit, so he left the desert and went out into the world. And when he came to the outskirts of the town, he was passing an inn which smelt so lovely of meat and wine and garlic and so on, that he thought, well, he might try, and in he went. But he never came out. He went under completely: he ate and drank and forgot that he was a saint and lost himself in the world again. That was a fellow who had made an artificial compartment and thought he was that and nothing else.

So we should always be a little in doubt about ourselves. That is quite healthy and not primitive; a primitive would be in horrible doubt about himself if he could think at all. But *we* think; at least we assume we do, and in certain cases it is a fact that one does think and therefore there is doubt. While if someone has no doubt at all, if he has absolute conviction, absolute certainty, we can be sure there is a compartment: he is bordering on a neurosis. That is a hysterical condition; certainty is not normal. To be in doubt is a more normal condition than certainty. To confess that you doubt, to admit that you never know for certain, is the supremely human condition; for to be able to suffer the doubt, to carry the doubt, means that one is able to carry the other side. The one who is certain carries no cross. He is redeemed: you can only congratulate him and have no further discussion. He loses the human contact, redeemed from the humanity that really carries the burden. That the redeemed one is redeemed from his burden is the tragic split in any religious conviction.

Dr. Escher: There is a funny story of the inferior man in Nietzsche the wise philosopher. He had a quarrel with his tailor who brought him a frockcoat.

Prof. Jung: I remember—a most unphilosophical scene. I could tell you very similar anecdotes about Schopenhauer and Kant—human, all-too-human. Even the great philosopher is a very small man occasionally. Well, we are perfectly satisfied with the fact that Nietzsche had a shadow. So this scene with the dwarf is one of the incidents in the great drama which begins now, the coming up of the unconscious. First there was the symbol of the volcano, the descent into the volcano, and now the volcanic material is coming up. He approaches it slowly and very carefully. We have seen the attempt to minimize and to mitigate, because he is afraid it might be too much—which it was, of course, in the end. The unconscious appears here in the form of the possessive dwarf, and the very fact that he understands him to be nothing but a dwarf is minimizing the danger. So instead of asking the dwarf who he is and where he got that funny kind of power, sitting on his back and causing him to have terrible feelings (which would be the natural question) he begins to preach. He addresses the dwarf in a sort of sermon:

> "Look at this gateway! Dwarf!" I continued, "it hath two faces. Two roads come together here: these hath no one yet gone to the end of.
>
> This long lane backwards: it continueth for an eternity. And that long lane forward—that is another eternity."

Whatever he tries to convey to the dwarf here, it is clear that he handles him as if he were nothing but his own thoughts, as if he were another mood or something like that, as if it did not matter at all what the dwarf might say. That is apotropaic, a means we often apply. If you expect a rather disagreeable discussion with somebody, for instance, which you would like to ward off, you begin to talk rapidly, in order to prevent the other fellow from saying anything. We were speaking the other day of that reason for so much uninterrupted talk. And those people like to talk fluently and in a loud voice: they are so convinced that something disagreeable might be said that they think they had better start in right away and force it into a certain shape.

I remember such a case. The famous Professor Forel was an alienist here; he had formerly been the director of the Psychiatric Clinic, but later he was chiefly occupied with propaganda for total abstinence.[4] And one day he suddenly burst into our office where a number of young doctors were working and instantly assumed that of course those young devils were not total abstainers. So he buttonholed a man who happened to be a fervent member of the most orthodox Verein against alcohol—I think he was the president of it—and shouted, "You probably don't know about the awful effects of alcohol, the terrible hereditary effects" and so on. The young man took a breath and tried to reply but Forel was just going at him hammer and tongs, on and on like a torrent, till he had to stop to take breath. Then the young doctor began, "Er . . . , pardon . . ." but Forel was already on top of him. "I know what you are going to say, but it is all wrong!" Of course Forel was under the impression that everybody was contradicting him. There was naturally some criticism, so he applied that mechanism. Sometimes you have not the faintest idea what the disagreeable subject could be which you might mention, but you can be sure if people get at you in that way, that they want to prevent you from saying something disagreeable. So here Nietzsche talks the dwarf down. Now, of these two ways he says:

> "They are antithetical to one another, these roads; they directly abut on one another:—and it is here, at this gateway, that they come together. The name of the gateway is inscribed above: 'This Moment.'
> But should one follow them further—and ever further and fur-

---

[4] August Henri Forel (1848-1931) was director of the Burghöltzli before the more famous and influential Eugen Bleuler, who was Jung's superior when he went there directly after medical school. Both men were militant teetotalers. Jung said of Forel's book *The Sexual Question* (1905) that it "not only had an enormous sale but found a good many imitators" (CW 10, par. 213).

ther on, thinkest thou, dwarf, that these roads would be eternally antithetical?"—

"Everything straight lieth," murmured the dwarf, contemptuously. "All truth is crooked; time itself is a circle."

"Thou spirit of gravity!" said I wrathfully, "do not take it too lightly! Or I shall let thee squat where thou squattest, Haltfoot,— and I carried thee *high*!"

You see, he instantly tells the dwarf that it is he, Zarathustra, who is carrying him high. But the point is that the rider controls the horse, and not that the horse carries him—it is self-evident that the horse has to carry him. Zarathustra doesn't realize that in taking the part of the horse, he makes a point in his favor out of what is a clear defeat. The dwarf is triumphant: he is the rider, and he is using Zarathustra as his riding animal. Now the dwarf says here, "All truth is crooked; time itself is a circle, everything straight lieth." How does that sound to you?

Mr. Allemann: It is a natural truth.

Prof. Jung: Yes, but what is its character? Whose truth is that?

Mr. Henley: Zarathustra's.

Prof. Jung: Of course. All truth is crooked, the snake's way is the right way, every straight way lieth, time itself is a circle—the idea of the eternal return—that is the teaching of Zarathustra himself. And he calls it the "spirit of gravity," and then later he adopts just these ideas. So the dwarf is really the rider, Zarathustra's higher mind. Zarathustra behaves here like a schoolboy with a very intelligent teacher whom he cannot understand, so he calls him an old idiot. We usually say a man is stupid when we cannot understand him. In this case, Zarathustra talks as if he were on a mighty high horse in order not to recognize his defeat, but the dwarf is the higher mind which Zarathustra will come to soon after. We have already met in the text the idea of the eternal return: it was hovering over him, but he has not yet a realization of it. So what we recognize as an evil spirit has often a superior insight. Therefore we should not shout it down, but should at least give it the benefit of the doubt. We should ask, "What have you to say? What is your idea?" Usually when people make the attempt to objectify such a figure, they talk it down. They know better, just on account of that primitive fear of the overwhelming power of the unconscious. That one is unable to give such a figure the right of independent speech proves that consciousness is still too weak. It is always a sign of a strong consciousness when one can say, "Talk, I listen." The weak one will not risk giving the other one that chance, for fear that it might get on top of him.

"Observe," continued I, "This Moment! From the gateway, This Moment, there runneth a long eternal lane *backwards*: behind us lieth an eternity.

Must not whatever *can* run its course of all things, have already run along that lane? Must not whatever can happen of all things have already happened, resulted, and gone by?

And if everything have already existed, what thinkest thou, dwarf, of This Moment? Must not this gateway also—have already existed?

And are not all things closely bound together in such wise that This Moment draweth all coming things after it? Consequently—itself also?

For whatever can run its course of all things, also in this long lane outward—must it once more run!—

And this slow spider which creepeth in the moonlight, and this moonlight itself, and thou and I in this gateway whispering together, whispering of eternal things—must we not all have already existed?

—And must we not return and run in that other lane out before us, that long weird lane—must we not eternally return?"

Thus did I speak, and always more softly: for I was afraid of mine own thoughts, and arrear-thoughts. Then, suddenly did I hear a dog howl near me.

The dwarf has already said this. This is the thinking of the dwarf, "Everything straight lieth . . . all truth is crooked, time itself is a circle." This is great language, and Zarathustra assimilates it, but he dilutes it and he thinks that they are his own ideas. But the dwarf has brought up these ideas in Zarathustra. These monumental short words of wisdom come from the intestines of the world. They are like the words of Laotze, or Pythagoras, or Heraclitus—short and pregnant with meaning. Then a man, or a mind, that speaks like that is called dark, obscure. It is still assumed that Heraclitus was a somewhat confused old bird; he is called "mystical," "the dark one." But that is because everybody else felt dark when he spoke; because he was too bright, they felt the extreme darkness in their own heads. What happens here is what usually happens when people have slow understanding: by the slow process of solution and digestion it comes to their minds again and then they think they have discovered it. Then they say, "But why didn't you say so before?" Now Zarathustra, as I said, has realized here what the dwarf told him, but he realizes it as if he had thought it, and he doesn't admit any indebtedness to the dwarf, doesn't give him any credit for it. He even speaks as if the dwarf had said something quite different. But this idea of the eternal return, which to Nietzsche was most inspiring, really belongs to the spirit of gravity. The dwarf is the originator of this idea, which is perfectly paradoxical—just the thing which he reviles as the spirit of gravity is the originator of this most inspiring wisdom. This is one of the passages where one sees how little reasoning there is in this book. There is no reasoning, no thinking—it just runs away with him, flowing on. He has no standpoint against it, no critical point of view. He is the victim of a process. That is characteristic of any incursion of the unconscious: when the unconscious comes up like this, the danger is that one will be hopelessly carried off one's feet. There seems to be no coming back to a clear point of view, a clear division: this is I and that is he, this is this and that is that. It is just a torrent of mental contents with an individual present to reason about them. Here he should have seen, as any thinker would have seen without any trouble at all, that what he reviles as the spirit of gravity was the origin of the most inspiring thought.

Now he says, "Thus did I speak, and always more softly: for I was afraid of mine own thoughts, and arrear-thoughts." Well, if he is frightened by his own thoughts, why does he make them? That they are not his thoughts is just the trouble; therefore he is afraid of them. You see, one is not afraid of something one can do and undo; the potter doesn't need to be afraid of the pots he makes, because he can break them up if he dislikes them—that is in his power. But what Nietzsche calls "mine own thoughts" are just not his own thoughts, and then one can understand his fear, because those thoughts can affect him. If he only could *say* they were not his own. Why should you be afraid of anything of your own manufacture when you can change it? But he doesn't discriminate. He simply identifies with the thing and runs with the herd. You see, this is the critical moment; he cannot help admitting that he is afraid of these thoughts. In other words, he is afraid of the spirit of gravity, afraid of the thing that possesses him. But he calls it "mine own" and there is the fatal mistake. Now, in such a moment one could expect a reaction from the side of the instincts. You see, when people are threatened by the unconscious so that they are carried away by it, really afloat and really frightened, then the instinctive unconscious, the animal instincts, realizes the danger, and that is now the dog that begins to howl:

Then, suddenly did I hear a dog *howl* near me.

Had I ever heard a dog howl thus? My thoughts ran back. Yes! When I was a child, in my most distant childhood:

—Then did I hear a dog howl thus. And saw it also, with hair bristling, its head upwards, trembling in the stillest midnight, when even dogs believe in ghosts:

You see, even dogs believe in ghosts, but not he. This is an indirect admission nevertheless that the dwarf is a ghost. If he could only *say* it was a ghost! But then Mr. So-and-So would come along and say it was superstition, as if that were a criterion. You must make ghosts if there are none, otherwise you are possessed; therefore make one—or several—as quickly as you can. If it is all your own thoughts you are in hell; then they run away with you. While if you say a ghost possesses you, you can attribute certain thoughts to him and others to yourself. Then you have a standpoint. The reason why we say everything is white, or are absolutely convinced that everything is black, is in order to have a standpoint. We need to create such a standpoint because there are plenty of other thoughts in us to say that what we call white is really black. And that is possible: that what we think of as white is black at the same time is psychologically true. There are thoughts in us which tell us: what you call good is bad; what you call virtue is cowardice; what you call value is no value at all; what you call good is vice; what you praise you loathe, perhaps. That is the truth, but it is so awkward that we make a fence around ourselves and project it into other people, and then we set ourselves against other people, create archenemies. It is enemy No. 1 who says it. But that is all ourselves.

Now, since ghosts are mental factors—surely it is a psychological fact that people believe that there are ghosts—so it doesn't matter whether you can weigh them, or photograph them. That is absolutely irrelevant. If you can make a photograph of a ghost, all the better. If you cannot, it doesn't matter. If you have never observed any psychic phenomena, with materializations or anything of the sort to prove their existence, it is too bad, but that makes it all the more necessary to insist that they exist because you need them in your functioning. You have to attribute your thoughts to somebody, for if you say they are your own, you will go crazy like our friend here; you will uproot yourself entirely, because you cannot be yourself and something else at the same time. So you are forced to be one-sided, to create one-sided convictions; for practical purposes it is absolutely necessary that you should be this one person who is assumed to have such-and-such convictions. Therefore we believe in principles, knowing all the time, if we are honest enough, that we have other principles just as well and that we believe in other principles just as well. But for practical purposes we adopt a certain system of convictions.

Now in order to be able to hold to one principle you have to repress the others, and in that case they may vanish from your consciousness. Then of course they will be projected and you will feel persecuted by people who have other views, or you may persecute them—it works both ways. You will then become a conscientious objector, and all your fighting spirit will exhaust itself in conscientious objections. But that fighting spirit exists, and the very thing you fight against, you will be using in fighting for the right cause. You see, nobody wants war, but everybody goes to war because they all assume they don't want it. That is the truth. But at the same time, we play with the idea of war, because it is a wonderful sensation. Yet we do not recognize this. Therefore, we are convinced that we don't want a war, and we project it. That was true in the world war: nobody wanted it, but nobody could stop it—nobody could get in control of the situation. And the terrible part is that human beings did it. Now, if a terrible god were influencing mankind, or a dangerous devil, we could ask ourselves what we could do to propitiate him and prevent such a catastrophe. But we think there is no such thing: no devil, no god, no ruling power. If anybody wants war it is the Germans or the French, the English or the Italians. If you can find the slightest trace of a tendency to war in them, you are sure it is they who want it. We don't assume responsibility; we simply say *they* want it. While all the time nobody really wants it consciously. Probably nobody in this room wants a war consciously, and just as little do people outside in the world want it. Who then makes a war?

Well, just as we don't want a war, we are also capable of wanting it, only we don't know it. That we could wish for a war is a terrible thought, but let us assume there are too many people in the world, too great an increase in the population, so that we are too close to one another, too crowded upon each other, and finally we hate each other. Then the thoughts begin to develop: "What can we do about it? Could we not cause a conflagration? Could we not kill that whole crowd in order to get a little space?" Or suppose that life is too hard, that you don't get a job, or the job doesn't pay, or other people take it away from you. If there were fewer people life would be much easier to live than it is now. Don't you think that slowly the idea would dawn upon you that you want to kill that other fellow? Now, we must admit that in no other time have there been so many people crowded together in Europe. It is a brand new experience. Not only are we crowded in our cities, but are crowded in other ways. We know practically everything that happens in the world; it is shouted on the radio, we get it in our newspapers. If someone falls off his bicycle in Siam we get it in the post next day; we are impressed with an unheard-of misery when we hear of so many people having been drowned in China, so many starved in Siberia, so many killed in Spain, and perhaps a railway accident in Norway, and always a revolution in South America. You see, we are impressed with all the misery of the world, because the whole world is now shouting in our ears every day. We enjoy it and we don't know what it is doing to us—till finally we get the feeling that it is too much. How can one stop it? We must kill them all.

When I was in India, I talked with certain people of the Swaraj party who want Home Rule. I said, "But do you assume that you can run India with your party? Do you not realize that in no time you would have a terrible quarrel between the Mohammedans and the Hindus? They would cut each other's throats, kill each other by the hundreds of thousands." "Yes, naturally," one said, "they would." "But don't you think that is awful? They are your own people." "Oh well, for those worthless chaps to cut each other's throats is just right. We have an increase in population of 34 millions these last ten years." Now, India has always been threatened by famine; even by increasing the irrigated area, the greater part of the Indian population would be underfed. The cattle are underfed already. You see, if you wipe out all epidemics, too few people will die; therefore that awful politic idea. No politician would dare to admit such ideas here. But that is the East. There they are not hampered with such sentimentalism, such honest lies as we cultivate; they just admit it and that is right. They would have disorder and epidemic, but India has always had that and it needs it really. The Chinese population would increase to such an extent under European civilization that they couldn't possibly be fed, so when a number are drowned by one of those big rivers, that is right. All well-meaning people are terribly concerned with the fast-increasing population. What they are going to do about it? And there is no answer.

But nature will answer. We think we are good and we are, yes: we have the best of intentions, sure enough, but do you think that somewhere we are not nature, that we are different from nature? No, we are in nature and we think exactly like nature. I am not God, I don't know whether, according to the standpoint of God, there are too many people in Europe. Perhaps there must be still more, perhaps we must live like termites. But I can tell you one thing: I would not live under such a condition. I would develop a war instinct—better kill all that cra-pule—and there are plenty of people who would think like that. That is unescapable, and it is much better to know it, to know that we are really the makers of all the misfortune which war means: we ourselves heap up the ammunition, the soldiers and the cannons. If we don't do it, we are fools; of course we have to do it, but it inevitably leads to dis-aster because it denotes the will to destruction which is absolutely unes-capable. That is a terrible fact, but we should know it.

So we should say—and I should like to say—that there is a terrible demon in man that blindfolds him, that prepares awful destruction; and it would be much better if we had a temple for the god of war, where now, for instance, with all this trouble in Europe, we could say: "The god of war is restless, we must propitiate him. Let us sacrifice to the god of war." And then every country would be going to the temples of the war god to sacrifice. Perhaps it would be a human sacrifice, I don't know—something precious. They might burn up a lot of am-munition or destroy cannons for the god of war. That would help. To say that it is not we who want it would help because man could then believe in his goodness. For if you have to admit that you are doing just what you say you are not doing, you are not only a liar, but a devil—and then where is the self-esteem of man? How can he hope for a bet-ter future? We can never become anything else because we are caught in that contradiction: on the one side we want to do good and on the other we are doing the worst. How can man develop? He is forever caught in that dilemma. So you had better acknowledge the evil—what you call it doesn't matter. If there were priests who said that the god of war must be propitiated, that would be a way of protecting yourself. But of course there are no such things, so we must admit that *we* pre-pare the war, that *we* are just thirsty for blood, everybody.

Now this dog represents, as it always does, the instinct of man that accompanies him. He is a true servant of man and through the acute-ness of his senses he protects him. He has a very fine sense of smell; he scents the danger and warns him. So in this moment when Nietzsche ought to realize that there are thoughts and tendencies in man which he should not attribute to himself, the dog gives the warning. Now Nietzsche alludes to a time in his childhood when he once heard a dog howl like this. I don't know to what he refers here, but it might be to that terrible howl he heard from the lunatic asylum in the night, the dream in which Wotan appeared, that I mentioned three or four weeks ago. You see, the dog howling in the midnight, apparently at nothing, conveys the idea to Nietzsche that one ought to believe in ghosts: one should personify such thoughts and attribute them to a definite figure, because even the dog, the instinct, does that. Instinctively we say, "*I* never thought such a thing," and so we invent fiends and enemies, trying to make somebody responsible for our own inimical thoughts. While the dog naturally would suggest that it is better to say that these thoughts belong to somebody else, perhaps to a ghost.

—So that it excited my commiseration. For just then went the full moon, silent as death, a glowing globe—at rest on the flat roof, as if on some one's property:—

Thereby had the dog been terrified: for dogs believe in thieves and ghosts. And when I again heard such howling, then did it excite my commiseration once more.

What has happened here? You see, it was definitely uncanny to Nietzsche, particularly on account of the memory of that terrible scream from the lunatic asylum. So in order to combat that deep impression he again invents a rationalization: namely, it is not ghosts, but just the moon, and dogs are supposed to howl at the full moon—it means nothing. Yet if you understand it as symbolism, you come to the same conclusion. Now what about the moon?

Prof. Reichstein: He spoke some time ago of the slow spider which creeps in the moonshine; it might be connected with this.

Prof. Jung: Quite. But what is the spider then?

Prof. Reichstein: His thoughts which he doesn't admit.

Prof. Jung: Well, the spider has no cerebro-spinal system, but has only a sympathetic nervous system, which is analogous to our own sympathetic nervous system. When a thing is deeply unconscious in us it is not in the cerebro-spinal system, but the sympathetic system is disturbed on account of contents which should be further up, which should be admitted to consciousness at least. Then one dreams of such insects, or one may have a pathological fear of them. So the spider means an unconscious tendency, and the fear of the spider is the fear of poison and also the fear of its way of killing its prey. It envelops its prey, and sits on it and sucks it. It is a horrible death and it is particularly suggestive because it symbolizes a psychological fact which can happen to us, the fact that the unconscious is circulating round us. It is always somewhere in us, and we don't know where. It spins a web around one, and one is caught by it, lamed by it, and finally it sits on one and saps one's life like a vampire. It is the evil spirit that sucks one's blood. Now the moon, which is obviously associated with the spider, is a well-known symbol for what?

Mr. Allemann: Lunacy.

Prof. Jung: Yes, the moon is the light in the darkness of the night, and it is always said that moonshine is most treacherous, that it causes illusions; so since time immemorial, all states of mental alienation are associated with the moon. We still have that meaning in our language: the German word *Mondsucht,* moon sickness, is practically never used, but it is not quite obsolete. It was the old name for epilepsy and is still used by peasants. So when Nietzsche explains or rationalizes the howl of the dog by the moon, he puts his foot in it again. It would mean that the dog is afraid, not of ghosts, but of insanity.

Mrs. Sigg: In Germany people believe that if you hear a dog howling in the night it means that somebody is dying in the neighborhood.

Prof. Jung: It means the same here, as you see in what folows:

> Where was now the dwarf? And the gateway? And the spider? And all the whispering? Had I dreamt? Had I awakened? 'Twixt rugged rocks did I suddenly stand alone, dreary in the dreariest moonlight.
>
> *But there lay a man!* And there! The dog leaping, bristling, whining—now did it see me coming—then did it howl again, then did it *cry:*—had I ever heard a dog cry so for help?
>
> And verily, what I saw, the like had I never seen. A young shepherd did I see, writhing, choking, quivering with distorted countenance, and with a heavy black serpent hanging out of his mouth.
>
> Had I ever seen so much loathing and pale horror on one countenance? He had perhaps gone to sleep? Then had the serpent crawled into his throat—there had it bitten itself fast.
>
> My hand pulled at the serpent, and pulled:—in vain! I failed to pull the serpent out of his throat. Then there cried out of me: "Bite! Bite!
>
> Its head off! Bite"—so cried it out of me; my horror, my hatred, my loathing, my pity, all my good and my bad cried with one voice out of me.—
>
> Ye daring ones around me! Ye venturers and adventurers, and whoever of you have embarked with cunning sails on unexplored seas! Ye enigma-enjoyers!
>
> Solve unto me the enigma that I then beheld, interpret unto me the vision of the lonesomest one!
>
> For it was a vision and a foresight:—*what* did I then behold in parable? And *who* is it that must come some day?
>
> *Who* is the shepherd into whose throat the serpent thus crawled?

Who is the man into whose throat all the heaviest and blackest will thus crawl?

—The shepherd however bit as my cry had admonished him: he bit with a strong bite! Far away did he spit the head of the serpent—: and sprang up.—

No longer shepherd, no longer man—a transfigured being, a light-surrounded being, that *laughed!* Never on earth laughed a man as *he* laughed!

O my brethren, I heard a laughter which was no human laughter,—and now gnaweth a thirst at me, a longing that is never allayed.

My longing for that laughter gnaweth at me: oh, how can I still endure to live! And how could I endure to die at present!—

This spake Zarathustra.

LECTURE V

8 June 1938

Prof. Jung:

Last time I read to the end of the chapter "The Vision and the Enigma," but we didn't have time to deal with the famous story of the shepherd into whose mouth the snake crawled while he was asleep. You have now had a fortnight to think about it—though I admit that isn't enough—and I should like to ask if you know of a parallel—or any similar story?

Mrs. Fierz: The snake in the initiation mysteries of Sabazios?

Prof. Jung: That is a ritual and we shall come to that—just keep it in mind—but I should like to know now of a parallel story, or perhaps one that contains the contrary.

Mrs. Mellon: Jonah.

Prof. Jung: Yes, Jonah was swallowed by the whale but he didn't crawl in, the whale seized him.

Mrs. Sigg: The contrary would be the Kundalini snake.

Prof. Jung: No. You see, here the shepherd is about to swallow the snake, and the contrary would be that the snake swallows the shepherd. That is the ordinary form of the story: it is simply the hero myth, the hero that fights the dragon. This is a peculiar twisting round of that motif.

Mrs. Jung: Could one say that Christ crushing the head of the snake was a similar story?

Prof. Jung: Crushing the head is similar to biting off the head, but it is not quite the idea of swallowing it or the interpenetration of the two. The descent into hell would be a parallel if hell were represented by a dragon's belly.

Mrs. Fierz: How about the Nordic fairy tales of the snake coming out of the mouth of a sleeper, representing his soul?

Prof. Jung: The soul of a dying person—or when the soul leaves the body in a dream? Yes, that would be a sort of parallel, this being of course the reverse case. Well, as a matter of fact there are no exact par-

1281

allels as far as my knowledge goes. I cannot remember one, so I assume this is rather a contrast to the usual hero myth where the dragon—or the whale or the serpent—swallows the hero. And here for certain reasons, that motif is turned round and transformed into its opposite. Now, Mrs. Fierz has just mentioned the rites from the mysteries of Sabazius.

Mrs. Fierz: During the course of the initiation, they pulled a snake down through the dress of the initiant, as if it were passing through him.

Prof. Jung: It was not a real snake, but a golden imitation, and it was pushed in at the neck and pulled down under the robe and out again at the feet. The idea was that the snake had entered the initiant and had left his body *per via naturalis.* Then there is another example.

Mrs. Mellon: The statue of Aion in the Mithraic rituals is depicted as a lion-headed god with a snake in his mouth.

Prof. Jung: No, it is coiled round him, and the head of the snake projects forward from behind over the lion's head. That is the *deus leontocephalus,* the syncretistic symbol for Zrwanakarana, that Iranian or Zarathustrian idea of the "infinitely long duration" or the infinitely long time.[1] But that has nothing to do with this symbolism. There are other snake rituals however.

Dr. Henderson: The Hopi Indians dance with snakes in their mouths.

Prof. Jung: And what does it mean in that case?

Dr. Henderson: It is the idea of the assimilation of the ancestral mana, which the snakes are supposed to bring up from the underworld.

Prof. Jung: Yes, and the snakes actually live in clefts in the rocks and down in the ground, and there the Hopis gather them before the festival. Then in their ritual dance, they even put the snakes into their mouths. We have a picture in the Club of a Hopi snake dance, where one of them has a rattlesnake in his mouth. That is very near the symbolism here. Also keep in mind that the snake represents the chthonic mana of ancestors that have gone underground; the snakes bring it up, and taking the snakes *in* their mouths means that they are eating the mana, one could say. It is a communion with the mana, the power, left by the ancestors. It is at bottom of course a magic fertility ritual, for the purpose of increasing the fertility of the earth, as well as the fertility or the power of man. The idea is that life is strengthened by uniting

---

[1] In the Foreword of *Aion,* CW 9 ii, Jung says that the Mithraic god, represented as a human figure with lion head and a torso entwined by a serpent, symbolized the *aeon,* an immense period of time. See too the frontispiece of that volume.

oneself to those underground chthonic forces. Like the giant Antaeus in Greek mythology, who was powerful as long as he had his feet on the earth; in order to conquer him, Hercules had to lift him off the ground. So the ancient Greeks apparently had very much the same idea of the chthonic powers.

It was in Greece of course that the very interesting Eleusinian mysteries took place, though they have never been quite understood because we have no text or any other exact evidence of what happened there, the actual functioning. But we have monuments where the mystes is depicted kissing or fondling a pretty big snake, representing the earth power. There was nothing spiritual about the Eleusinian mysteries though in later times people made a fuss about them, assuming that they were very wonderful and spiritual. That was a great mistake, however; we would probably have been terribly shocked at what went on at Eleusis. It was a chthonic performance which made the collaboration of the earth with the higher man quite clear. We have evidence for that in the famous ritual celebrated by the women, the *Aischrologia*. The ladies of Athens gathered yearly in Eleusis, and there they celebrated their own mystery to which the men were not admitted. They arranged a very good dinner, plenty of food and good wine, and after dinner the priestess of Demeter, the earth mother, and the president, who was one of the noble ladies of Athens, started the ritual of the *Aischrologia*, which consisted of telling obscene jokes, smutty stories, to each other. This was supposed to be good for the fertility of the fields in the coming season. One can see how it worked: the fact that they could tell such stories, which ordinarily they would not tell, had a certain effect upon those noble ladies. It was the earth in them that was helped and since they were identical with the earth, the earth itself was helped. They naively supposed that what was good for them would also be good for the fields.

Of course we cannot understand these things now because our women are uprooted. They are no longer identical with the earth—perhaps identical with a flat but not with the earth. But one sees it under primitive circumstances. I have seen it in East Africa, though I don't know how long it will be before the missionaries succeed in destroying the original order of things. The woman there owns the *shamba*, the plantation. She is identical with her estate and has the dignity of the whole earth. She *is* the earth, has her own piece of ground, and so she makes sense. She is not up in the air, a sort of social appendix. So you see, the two apparently disconnected facts—that kissing and fondling of the snake on the one side, and the *Aischrologia* on the other—belong together, start from the same original idea: namely, the serpent represents the magic mana in the earth which has to be brought up for man to again establish communication with that fertile power, and the Aischrologia also augments the fertility of the earth. It is pretty much the same idea, expressed in another form. Then we have another parallel with the reach of Christianity, which may be a derivative of the Eleusinian mysteries.

Mrs. Sigg: In *Wandlungen und Symbole der Libido* you spoke of a Christian sect, the Ophites, that kissed the snake.[2]

Prof. Jung: You are right, but the main point in their ritual was something else.

Mr. Allemann: They let the snake crawl over the bread.

Prof. Jung: Yes, they had a basket containing the snake on the communion table, and they made it crawl over the bread they were to use in the communion, the host. They celebrated communion with the bread which had been magically endowed with power by the chthonic snake. Then it contained the proper nutritive quality, then it was right for use; it was what the Christians called the *panis immortalis*, the food of immortality. It is the same idea that the chthonic powers bring fertility, health, duration, strength, and so on.

Mr. Henley: The East Indian snake cults, where they permit themselves to be bitten by a poisonous snake, are similar.

Prof. Jung: All those rites in which snakes figure were originally fertility rites. In India one still sees temples in which snakes are crawling about. And one finds those stone nagas nearly everywhere; they are supposed to be sort of goddesses or demons that come up from the ground. The river Ganges is represented as such a naga, woman above and serpent below. Then in Mamallapuram on the East coast of India, on the bay of Bengal, is the famous rock that is carved all over and called *The Birth of the Ganga*; the naga is in a cleft of the huge boulder, and that is the source, the origin, of the heavenly river Ganges. The Ganges is the main river of India and it spreads fertility over the greater part of the country, in contradistinction to the Indus which is also a great river but flows through vast deserts. It is a peculiar fact that the west of India is far less fertile. While in the east there are no such deserts. The Ganges, or any river belonging to the same system, always flows through rice fields or cultivated places. Well now, all this material should aid us in approaching this peculiar symbolism. But there is one

[2] See CW 5, pars. 563-77 where Jung discusses the snake rituals among the Ophites. There too, he refers to this episode of *Thus Spake Zarathustra*.

other parallel which I should like to use here to help us understand the union of serpent and man. As I said, the origin of this symbol in *Zarathustra* is the swallowing of the hero by the serpent or the dragon; turned round it is the swallowing of the serpent by the hero, and if you keep both things in mind, you get a sort of interpenetration, which would be represented by a symbol which has played a very great role, and which we should remember here in dealing with this modern symbolism. What would that be?

Mrs. Fierz: There was the idea that the hero had snake eyes, that there was something of the snake in him naturally.

Prof. Jung: The hero himself has qualities of the snake. The dragon, for instance, was supposed to have an invulnerable skin, and in the Siegfried saga the hero has to bathe himself in the blood of the dragon in order to acquire the same skin. And a Nordic saga says that heroes can be recognized by the fact that they have snake eyes, that peculiar rigid, magic expression of the eyes. But there is a real symbol of interpenetration.

Mrs. Fierz: I don't know whether it is too farfetched, but the journey of the dead to the Egyptian underworld seems to me to contain a similar symbolism. Pictures of this underworld show it to be full of snakes—every door, for instance, has a snake depicted on both sides, as in *The Book of the Dead*.[3]

Prof. Jung: Well, in *The Book of the Dead* there is the eternal struggle of the sun god Ra with the great serpent Apepi. It is the daily repetition of the hero myth. Always in the seventh hour of the night the great fight begins, where Ra is depicted as a he-cat, fighting and overcoming the snake that has wound itself round the ship in which the sun god travels through the sea of the underworld. Only when the cat, or the hero, succeeds in killing the serpent, aided by the ceremonies of the priests in the temples, can the sun rise. Therefore, in the primitive hero myths, the sun rises at the moment that the hero comes out of the belly of the monster. With the first rays of the sun, consciousness again dawns from the nocturnal unconsciousness; so life is once more victorious over death and destruction, having overcome that state of being swallowed by the monster. But you see, that is only one side of it. It is the serpent swallowing the hero, not the hero swallowing the serpent, and the two belong together. We have a definite symbol for the interpenetration.

---

[3] *The Book of the Dead*, Introduction and translation by E. A. Wallis-Budge (New York, n.d.).

Miss Hannah: Is it not Christ as the serpent?

Prof. Jung: That is the hero again. The snake always means resurrection on account of shedding its skin. According to an African myth, there was no death on earth originally; death came in by mistake. People could shed their skins every year and so they were always new, rejuvenated, until once an old woman, in a distracted condition and feeble-minded, put on her old skin again and then she died. That is the way death came into the world. It is again the idea that human beings were like snakes originally: they did not die. It was a snake that brought the idea of death to Adam and Eve in Paradise. The snake was always associated with death, but death out of which new life was born. But what is that definite symbol? A great deal has been said about it lately.

Miss von Franz: The *ouroboros.*

Prof. Jung: Exactly. The tail eater, or the two animals that devour each other. In alchemy that is represented in the form of the winged dragon and the wingless dragon that devour each other, one catching the tail of the other and forming a ring. The simplest form is of course the dragon or the serpent that bites its own tail, so making the ring; the tail is the serpent and the head is as if it belonged to another animal. The same idea has also been expressed by two animals, the dog and the wolf, devouring each other, or the winged and the wingless lion, or a male and a female lion, always forming a ring, so that one cannot see which is eating which. They are eating each other; both destroy and both are destroyed. And that expresses the idea that once the hero eats the serpent and once the serpent eats the hero. You see, in these Gnostic rituals, or the ritual of Sabazios, man is superior to the serpent in a way—he makes use of the serpent. That the golden snake descends through the body of the initiant means that the initiant asserts himself against the divine element of the snake: he is then a sort of dragon that eats or overcomes the other dragon. So it is one and the same symbolism whether expressed in this form or that. In primitive myths it is usually the dragon that devours everything. Even the hero, who by sheer luck and at the last moment succeeds in destroying the monster that has eaten him, cannot overcome the monster by a frontal attack, but he is able to defend his life and destroy the monster from within by the peculiar means of making a fire in its belly. Fire is the artificial light against nature, as consciousness is the light which man has made against nature. Nature herself is unconscious and the original man is unconscious; his great achievement against nature is that he becomes conscious. And that light of consciousness against the unconsciousness of nature is expressed, for instance, by fire. Against the powers of darkness, the dangers of the night, man can make a fire which enables him to see and to protect himself. Fire is an extraordinary fact really. I often felt that when we were travelling in the wilds of Africa. The pitch dark tropical night comes on quite suddenly: it just drops down on the earth, and everything becomes quite black. And then we made a fire. That is an amazing thing, the most impressive demonstration of man's victory over nature; it was the means of the primitive hero against the power of devouring beasts, his attack against the great unconsciousness, when the light of consciousness disappeared again into the original darkness.

Now, in the alchemistic symbol of the two animals that devour each other, that peculiar functional relationship of man's conscious to the natural darkness is depicted, and it is an astonishing fact that such a symbol developed in a time when the idea of the manifest religion was that the light had definitely overcome the darkness, that evil—or the devil—had been overcome by the redeemer. In just that time, this symbol developed, where darkness and light were on the same level practically; they were even represented as functioning together in a sort of natural rhythm. Like the operation of the Chinese Yin and Yang, the transformation into each other, being conceived and born of each other, the one eating the other, and the one dying becoming the seed of itself in its own opposite. This symbol of the Taigitu expresses the idea of the essence of life, because it shows the operation of the pairs of opposites. In the heart of the darkness, the Yin, lies the seed of the light, the Yang; and in the light, the day, the Yang, lies the dark seed of the Yin again. This is often represented in the East as two fishes in that position, meaning the two sides or the two aspects of man, the conscious and the unconscious man.

Now this preparation should make us understand the situation of the shepherd and the serpent. What does it mean in the psychology of Nietzsche-Zarathustra that he suddenly discovers that shepherd in deadly embrace with the serpent? He is apparently swallowing the snake, but the snake is attacking him at the same time, penetrating him. Why such an image, or symbol, at this place? You remember in his discussion with the dwarf just before, the dwarf was already the chthonic power.

Miss Hannah: Was he not trying to escape from the chthonic, and is it not getting back at him by attacking his throat? When he met the gateway, "This Moment," he really took no notice of it, but merely asked if we do not eternally return, putting countless millions of moments on either side of it. No doubt this is an inspiring idea in itself but it seems to me to rob the moment, the here and now, of its whole importance and thereby to deny the body and the chthonic.

Prof. Jung: Well, in the actual text, he says to the dwarf, ". . . what thinkest thou, dwarf, of This Moment? Must not this gateway also— have already existed? And are not all things closely bound together in such wise that This Moment draweth all coming things after it? *Consequently*—itself also?" Here he gets hold of the important idea of the eternal return, and one can see that this is an attempt at getting out of the moment. For if you are confronted with the unique moment and regard it as merely a moment that has repeated itself a million times before and will repeat itself a million times afterwards, you naturally don't take much notice of it, as Miss Hannah says. And then you can say you are out of it. But why should he deny the uniqueness of the moment? How would it have been if he had not tried to get out of it— if he had said, yes, this *is* the unique moment, there is no eternal return?

Miss Hannah: He would have to take up his responsibilities as man in the flesh.

Prof. Jung: What would that mean?

Miss Hannah: Giving that dog a bone so that it doesn't howl.

Prof. Jung: No, we know nothing of the dog now.

Mrs. Jung: He should have realized in that moment what threatened him.

Prof. Jung: Yes, if he takes this moment that has been emphasized by both the dwarf and himself in mutual collaboration, as a unique moment, with no return, no repetition, then he would be forced to realize it completely. You see, when someone makes a sort of bold statement, you will always find certain people who say they knew it already, and then the wind is taken out of his sails: all the juice has gone, it means nothing, it is only repetition, an idea known long ago. Now such people are always hoping that the whole thing will fall flat, so that they won't have to realize it. Unfortunately it is true of many things that they have been already and will be again, and it is a sad truth that many things in human life are flat—that is also a fact. But if you see flatness only, you cease to exist—there is only an immense continuity of flatness, and that is of course not worthwhile. Why should we continue such a string of nonentities, mere repetitions? So when you hear some one asserting that what you say has long been known, you know that he has an interest that that moment should not be realized because it would be dangerous or too disagreeable. We have a proof here. He says, " 'And must we not return and run in that other lane out before us, that long weird lane—must we not eternally return?'—Thus did I speak, and always more softly: for I was afraid of mine own thoughts, and arrear-thoughts." And then the dog began to howl, which means that he talked in that way because he was afraid of his own thoughts, of what he *might* think.

So when Nietzsche says that the moment will repeat itself and has already repeated itself many a time, he makes it into a thing we are used to; it is an ordinary day, an ordinary hour, so why bother about it? And he repeats that as often as possible to himself, but always more softly because it doesn't help exactly. He asks himself: "Now why do I say that? Why do I try to make it as flat as possible?" Then the howling dog, the instinct, is the reaction against that attempt to get out of the realization. Now, those thoughts of which he is so afraid should be realized, but it is too much, he cannot do it, he is trembling in a sort of panic. That volcano is always threatening to burst out, and he is fighting on the edge against the fire which comes nearer and nearer. This idea which he invents—that one has gone through this moment many times and will go through it many times again—is the attempt of a consciousness which resists realization out of fear of what might be contained in the unique moment. If he admits that this is the unique moment, he has to realize what is in it and why it is unique.

Dr. Escher: It is the situation of the provisional life instead of keeping to the here and now.

Prof. Jung: Exactly. You see, the full realization of the here and now is a moral accomplishment which is only short of heroism: it is an almost heroic achievement. You may not believe that, but it is true. These ideas are strange to us so I speak—perhaps at boring length—about that question of realization. Our civilization is ignorant of these terms; we have no such conceptions, because we always start with the idea that our consciousness is perfect. It never occurs to us that it could be dim, or that it might develop. That notion is left to the East, where they are fully aware of the fact that our consciousness is at fault. It is true that the Eastern consciousness, when compared to our own, seems to be dim; but that is only because we see it and measure it against our own—we see it only from our side. For instance, when it comes to writing or mailing a letter at a definite time, doing a given thing at a given moment, calculating how much time is needed to go to another town, do an errand, and return by airplane in the shortest time possible, there of course our consciousness is very bright and the Eastern consciousness is exceedingly dim. To write on a letter, *inshallah*, by the grace of Allah, as they do, means if it please God the letter will arrive. But we have no such notion; we think it is the duty of our mail system to see that a letter arrives in time. It is due to man and not to God's grace. There we meet the Eastern mind where it is the dimmest. When it comes to that concept of realization, however, our consciousness is very dim indeed: very few of us know what realizati∂n is, and even the word *realize* is pretty vague. How would you define it? When would you say that some one had realized a thing? You are never sure that it is actually realized. Already in the sixth century B.C., Buddha made the extraordinary attempt to educate consciousness, to make people realize, and that has gone on until now. Zen, the most modern form of Buddhism, is nothing but the education of consciousness, the faculty of realizing things.

Here I will tell you a story from the first century after Christ, of the way a master of Zen made a pupil understand its meaning. Zen is the Japanese word for the Indian *dhyana* which means enlightenment; they have another word *satori*, and also *sambodhi*, which mean the same—illumination. A Chinese statesman, a follower of Confucius, came to the master and asked to be initiated into the mysteries of Zen, and the master consented, and added, "You know, your master Confucius once said to his disciples: 'I have told you everything, I have kept nothing back.' " And the statesman said that was true. A few days later the master and the statesman took a walk together in the hills at the time when the wild laurel was in bloom and the air was full of its perfume. Then the master said to his initiant: "Do you smell it?" And the initiant replied that he did. Then the master said: "There, I have told you everything, I have kept nothing back." And the statesman was enlightened. He realized. It broke through into consciousness. Understand that if you can!

We may be aware of the fact that our consciousness is not what it ought to be, but we are still quite naive in that respect, and so we have great trouble in understanding attempts at an increase or improvement of consciousness. We think that we need, rather, a widening out of consciousness, an increase of its contents, so we believe in reading books or in an accumulation of knowledge. We think if we only accumulate the right kind of knowledge, that will do. We always forget that everything depends upon the kind of consciousness that accumulates the knowledge. If you have an idiotic consciousness you can pile up a whole library of knowledge, but you remain nothing but an ass that carries a heavy load of books, of which you understand nothing. It is perhaps not necessary to read a book if you have a consciousness which is able to realize, a penetrating consciousness. But that idea is utterly strange. Yet it is as simple as the difference between eyes that see dimly and eyes that see accurately, or the difference between myopic eyes and eyes that see far. It is a different kind of seeing, a more penetrating, more complete seeing, and that is what consciousness would do.

It is quite obvious that Nietzsche is in an impasse with his faculty of realization. He feels the presence of these thoughts, but he is afraid and prefers not to see them. So the unconscious makes the attempt to bring them close to him, to force something upon him, and he fights a sort of losing fight against it, resisting, trying to put some shield between himself and that realization which should come. And so naturally he increases the danger. When you fight against a realization, you make it worse. Each step you make in fighting it off increases the power of that which is repressed, and finally it takes on such a form that it cannot be realized: it becomes too incompatible. But you have done it, have maneuvred it into such a corner that it took on an impossible form. Here Zarathustra fought off the realization with the effect that it got out of his hands when he talked to the dwarf—well, the dwarf is perhaps not quite human, but an elemental or something of the sort. He told him what to think, tried to take the conversation out of the dwarf's hands and to envelop him in his own mind, in order to get rid of that other thought which he is up against; and therefore he brought about the howling dog. Then there again he tried to make little of it; he couldn't help being impressed, but he made belittling remarks—that dogs see ghosts and naturally they howl when they are frightened by the full moon—hoping thereby to make the dog so unimportant and small that he could rid himself of the bad impression. He was so impressed nevertheless that suddenly he saw that the dwarf was no longer there. "Where was now the dwarf? And the gateway? And the spider? And all the whispering? Had I dreamt? Had I awakened? 'Twixt rugged rocks did I suddenly stand alone, dreary in the dreariest moonlight." So he is now very much in the position of the dog, which means he did not succeed in fighting off that bad impression: the realization is coming nearer. And now he sees the horrible picture of the shepherd and the snake. That is the concretization of his feeling about what is approaching him, and the *dramatis personae* are of course himself and the young shepherd and that thing that tries to get him.[4] Now, why just a young shepherd?

---

[4] For Jung the internal personifications of the psyche constitute its *dramatis personae*.

Prof. Reichstein: Is that not a Christian idea coming in here—Christ as the shepherd?

Prof. Jung: Maybe, but I think Christ would not be represented as a *young* shepherd; he would be, rather, a *Poimen*, the leader, the shepherd of men.

Mrs. Fierz: It reminds me of John the Baptist, the forerunner of Christ, who is often depicted as a sort of young shepherd with a staff and a fur.

Prof. Jung: Well, that represents less the shepherd than the hermit—eating wild honey and locusts and wearing a camels-wool coat. A young shepherd conveys the idea of something very innocent, like the German *Hirtenknabe*,[5] who proverbially knows nothing and always says, "Ich weiss von nichts"—the innocent child of nature, completely naive. He walks with a staff amidst little lambs on nice meadows, straying through nature playing the flute; about the most that could happen in his life would be a young shepherdess. Unfortunately, it is most descriptive of the situation here. Zarathustra is the shepherd boy, knowing of nothing, but completely innocent, and therefore the contrast is particularly horrible—that poisonous black snake attacking this innocent, lovely youth. But you see, that is a special brand of European consciousness. Like the *deutsche Michel*, whom you have seen in a white nightcap in cartoons innumerable times; he never knows anything, he is just a jackass—always misunderstood and always with a wonderful feeling of innocence.[6] That is just the primitive unconsciousness that forever feels innocent and never sees itself as the cause of anything; causes are always somewhere else but never in that fellow. He always meant the best. He is quite simple, only drinks milk and eats cheese, and he has rosy cheeks and blue eyes that never see anything black. Such a fellow stands open to such an attack sure enough, because his other side, the shadow side, his second self, is the black snake.

And that is what Nietzsche cannot realize—that to everything positive there is a negation; with everything great or grand, there is something very small. He cannot see these pairs of opposites as belonging to himself; he cannot see that he casts a shadow, represented by the horrible serpent. This is the thought which is trying to get at him, the thought he is fighting off in order to be something marvelous and great. One might say to him: "Yes, it is wonderful how well you can de-

---

[5] *Hirtenknabe*: shepherd boy.

[6] The *deutsche Michel* is a legendary *naïf*, one who unwittingly always supports law, order, and authority.

fend yourself against the realization, but I am afraid nature sees nothing wonderful in it: nature merely destroys chaps who don't realize."
Therefore the ambition of mankind, its highest aspiration, has always
been an improvement of consciousness, a development of realization—but against the most intense resistances. It almost kills people
when they are forced to come to a certain realization. All the trouble in
the work of analytical psychology comes from that resistance against
realization, that inability to realize, that absolute incapacity for being
consciously simple. People are complicated because the simple thing is
impossible for them apparently. It is in fact the most difficult thing to
be simple, the greatest art, the greatest achievement, so it might be better that we all remain very complicated and let things stay in the dark.
We always say we can't see because it is so complicated, but as a matter
of fact we are unable to see because it is so simple. Of course when
things have come to such a pass that the other side is a black snake, one
understands that there is an incompatability, that it is almost impossible to accept such a horror. Nevertheless, the two sides should come
together: one should see the other side.

So we reach the conclusion that he really should swallow that serpent
in order that the regular thing should happen. Then the eternal
rhythm of nature would fulfil itself, which is an approach to perfection. It is not an approach to perfection when one sees only white; to
see both white and black is the proper functioning. If we can see ourselves with our real values, with our real merits and demerits, that is
proper; but to see ourselves as wonderful and full of merit is no particular art, rather, just childish. The only heroic thing about it is the extraordinary size of the self-deception; one might say that it was almost
grand that a fellow could deceive himself so, that there was something
wonderful about his thinking himself a savior. But I never would say
this was a desirable accomplishment. If such a fellow plays the role of
the savior for the sake of people who cannot realize themselves, one
might say it was very decent of him, provided that he knows he is playing that role, that he does it as a performance, an educational achievement, a sort of Kultur film for educational purposes. But he must
know that he is in a Kultur film.

Now, here the whole impossibility of Nietzsche's situation is depicted. He says, "Had I ever seen so much loathing and pale horror on
one countenance?" Well, that is his own countenance and the black disgusting snake is just his other side: we can of course understand that
he is horrified. Nevertheless, it is just the thing he should accept. And
now he comes to the conclusion that the shepherd ought to bite off the

serpent's head. But the head had bitten itself fast in the sleeper's throat. The snake bit first and has such a hold that Zarathustra cannot pull it out of the shepherd's mouth. That means that they are already almost one: it needs that *tour de force* of biting off the snake's head in order to liberate the man from the serpent. Of course we must realize that if it were a poisonous snake, he would die in spite of having got rid of the serpent. I don't know whether Nietzsche thought of it as being poisonous—he doesn't say so—but one is almost forced to assume that such an awful black serpent would be poisonous. It would be a more or less unadventurous story if it were just an ordinary water snake for instance, which is an absolutely harmless animal and usually eats mice. Of course no snake would creep into the mouth of another animal— that is impossible, too—but the poison seems to belong to this picture. In that case, of course, biting off the head would not be helpful at all. You see, Nietzsche handles this case as if the snake were something loathsome which one could get rid of, with no idea of what it really is. Here he makes an attempt at realization, in saying, "For it was a vision and a foresight:—what did I then behold in parable? And who is it that must come some day? Who is the shepherd into whose throat the serpent thus crawled? Who is the man into whose throat all the heaviest and blackest will thus crawl?" But there is no question of what the serpent may be. It is interesting that he wants to know all about the shepherd without stopping for a moment to consider the serpent. The serpent is the other side and he is not interested in that other side.

Mrs. Baumann: But he says what it is—all "the heaviest and blackest."

Prof. Jung: Oh yes, but that is seen from his side. The question of the snake is not included in the realization.

Mrs. Jung: Why did you say that it was no use to bite off the head? I think it is the only thing he could do.

Prof. Jung: Oh, on account of the poison. It would be no use because the poison would be in his body. Of course, that is an assumption. Naturally to get rid of the snake he has to bite off the head. But I don't see how he can spit out the head if it is caught in his throat.

Mrs. Jung: But if the snake is dead?

Prof. Jung: The question is whether it opens its fangs, and we must assume that it does. Well, there are many little impossibilities in this picture; we can't be too accurate or meticulous about it. It is a very questionable story anyhow.

Miss Wolff: In the previous chapter, "The Wanderer," Nietzsche does point out more or less what the black snake is to him when Zarathustra says that he has to go into the deepest pain and the blackest waters of despair in order to climb to the highest mountain.

Prof. Jung: Naturally he has his ideas. He knows about the snake, but he only knows what *he* knows about it and doesn't realize the snake.

Miss Wolff: He only describes how the snake feels to him.

Prof. Jung: I pointed that out because I should like to know what that serpent really means and why it gets at him. I am not much interested in what the shepherd has to say, because the snake is the important figure in that drama. The shepherd is so far only an innocent shepherd boy—all his name betrays. But the serpent is really interesting. Moreover, we know from historical parallels that the serpent is a pretty important figure. What does it represent?

Dr. Henderson: It is a personification of all the inferior aspects of the unconscious, the underworld.

Remark: It is Satan, the devil.

Prof. Jung: In that example of the golden snake, the initiant through whom the serpent went was *entheos*, filled with the god. The serpent represents also the god. He is the *deus absconditus*, the god concealed in the darkness. When Ra is not shining in heaven he is in the underworld hidden in the coils of the snake. When you look at the god you see the snake. The god is hidden in the snake, but he is both the snake and the sun. Therefore, he is that movement, the rotation of day and night. He is the whole, a circle. So this is the dark god and the god that died, the god that Nietzsche decared to be non-existent. The god appears here as a demoniacal power in the old way—when the god appears from below he is a snake. Even the lord Jesus is a serpent, as you know from the Evangel of John; and the *agathodaimon*, the redeemer, was represented by the Christian Ophites as a serpent, so this is a healing serpent, really. Nietzsche doesn't realize it because he is so frightened by that aspect that he stops thinking.

Now after the shepherd has bitten off the head of the serpent, he is no longer the same. He went through a tremendous experience, and therefore Zarathustra says, "No longer shepherd, no longer man—a transformed being, a light-surrounded being, that laughed!" You see, that is the sunrise in a way: the shepherd got rid of his snake form but then he was "no longer man." So what is he? Either an animal or a god: that is the only possibility. One might say "superman" but between superman and god there is no difference—that is only a *façon de parler*. A transfigured being would be a god: "light-surrounded" means that he is the sun which rises after the seventh hour of the night. It is the eternal mystery happening before Zarathustra's eyes, but he doesn't realize it; he is only fascinated by that very uncanny laughter. "Never on earth laughed a man as he laughed! O my brethren, I heard a laughter which was no human laughter. . . ." Well, the gods laugh on Olympus. Or it might be that the coffin he dreamed about was spouting forth a thousand peals of laughter, the mad laughter of the madhouse. He was transfigured, so we can say that Nietzsche hears the laughter of a superhuman being, the laughter of a god that has transformed himself, that has got rid of his snake form and become the sun again. But that is not for man to imitate; he can't get rid of his snake form because he can't rise like the sun. He can participate in the events of nature, can see how the sun rises out of darkness, but if he thinks that he is the sun, he has to accept the fact that he is the snake, and he cannot be both. So this is a mystery that happens in his unconscious mind, from which we cannot detach it.

If we assume that we can take a leap into heaven and be the sun, then you may be sure our other side would be right down in hell. It would be the serpent, and it would be only a question of time until that shadow caught us. And then naturally we shall be afraid of that other aspect, of which, in our naiveté, we did not know. Nietzsche is fascinated by that performance: he says, ". . . and now gnaweth a thirst at me, a longing that is never allayed. My longing for that laughter gnaweth at me: oh, how can I still endure to live! And how could I endure to die at present!" This is his identification with the shepherd and this is the god in his positive form. We come now to what Prof. Reichstein alluded to, the good shepherd as a divine figure. The good shepherd is a famous old figure. Orpheus, for instance, is something like a shepherd; and the Poimen or the Poimandres is a shepherd, a leader of men. Also Krishna is a sort of shepherd—in India he is the figure that leads the herd of mankind. And Buddha is called "the shepherd" because he is the perfect one, the Poimen, as Christ is the Poimen of mankind. Of course, that is exactly what Zarathustra wants to be, and so that fascination, that thirst which gnawed at him, is the longing to be identical with the god. But this scene should show him that he cannot identify with the god because he would then be also the serpent, and that is what he rejects: that is the tragedy. If he could realize that he could not be the Poimen, he would be spared; then he need not be the serpent. It is like that famous dream of Hannibal before he went to Rome: he saw himself with his hosts conquering cities and fighting battles, but then he turned round and saw a huge monster crawling behind him, eating up all the countries and towns. That was his other aspect. From that dream we may conclude that in his consciousness he had a very positive idea of himself, probably a sort of savior for his own people, or for the Carthaginians at least; and he did not realize that he was also a terrible monster.[7] It is inevitably true that the savior is also the great destroyer, the god is also the black serpent. We don't realize that in our extraordinary shepherd-like naiveté, but the East knew it long ago; the East knows that the gods have a wrathful aspect, that they are not only bright light, but also abysmal darkness.

[7] For Livy's story of Hannibal's dream, see above, pp. 598, 598n.

LECTURE VI

15 June 1938

Prof. Jung:

We talked last week of that shepherd who was in danger of being penetrated by the black snake, and I find here a contribution: the dream of a young Swiss girl thirteen years old who also dreamt of a snake, but she behaved quite differently with it. She dreamt that she was on a road with many adult people, and as they were about to reach the crossroad, she became suddenly aware of a huge grey snake that was moving along beside them, looking as long as the road they were on. The snake said, follow me, but the adult people preferred to go in another direction. The girl, however, obeyed; in spite of the fact that she was afraid, she followed the snake. Of course, she didn't know how to protect herself against such a monster, but as she followed along, the snake became more and more benevolent and less and less dangerous. The way on which she was then walking was bordered by great boulders, and she saw that the way the other people were following was bordered, not by stones, but by huge scarabs. First, they were ordinary scarabs but as the people approached them, they increased in size until they were as large as human beings; she describes them as horrible animals, and she was very glad that she had not to pass them. You know, scarabs live on rotten matter: they dig into carrion in order to bury their eggs in it, or they make balls of manure to feed on and deposit their eggs in, so they are not particularly nice animals in that respect, though they look all right. If they attain human size they would be quite dangerous, naturally; those people who have chosen the other way, the way that is not parallel to the snake, would be in danger of being eaten up by them. Now what is a scarab? It is a very typical symbol, but one cannot assume that this child had any notion of its meaning.

Mr. Baumann: The scarab is male and female at the same time.

Prof. Jung: That is the old legend, but that is only one aspect. What

1298

would the scarab denote under all conditions? What is the beetle anyhow?

Mrs. Fierz: It is coldblooded.

Prof. Jung: Well, a snake is coldblooded also. No, I mean the fact that it has a sympathetic nervous system and no cerebro-spinal system. To dream of a worm would have the same meaning—they stand for the sympathetic system. Now I don't know how man knows that. I assume that it is as a wasp knows that the third dorsal ganglion of the caterpillar's sympathetic system is the motor ganglion and puts its sting just into that, so it lames the caterpillar without killing it; and then the eggs which the wasp deposits thrive on that still living caterpillar. It is the wisdom of nature itself apparently, and with that knowledge as key, one can unlock the dream. Then, you remember, the scarab was the symbol of resurrection in Egypt, the transitory form of Ra when he is invoked as Cheper or Chepra, the rising sun. Ra in the form of the Chepra is buried in the ball of dung, and then he rises as the sun. That means man in the incubation sleep, in a state of rebirth, man buried in the sympathetic system when consciousness—which is a function of the cerebro-spinal system—is entirely extinguished. So the beetle represents the state of man when there is only deep unconsciousness. Now when the dream says that those people are threatened by such animals, what would it mean?

Miss Hannah: That they are being caught by the unconscious.

Prof. Jung: Well, to be caught by the unconscious, or devoured by the unconscious, would mean what?

Miss Hannah: Madness in its worst form.

Prof. Jung: It might be madness, or it might also be a neurosis, or simply being at variance with one's unconscious, hollowed out from within, a loss of libido, a loss of intensity of life. Sure enough, people who don't follow the serpent suffer from a loss of life; they are drained from within, for the faculty of realization is lacking. It is as if the unconscious were all the time sapping their vitality, so something gets lost; they are only fragmentary. They are usually in contradiction with their unconscious; therefore circumstances are unfavorable and they become neurotic—or if it is not exactly a neurosis they are at least only half existing. The world is full of such people. Now, this child of thirteen is of course at the age when she would encounter the serpent, namely, the whole force of the instinctive being. If you choose to follow the way of fear, you are sure of experiencing the totality of life, because the snake is the mediator between the conscious and the unconscious worlds. Therefore, the snake is the symbol of the savior, the *agathodaimon*, the good daimon, the redeemer that forms the bridge between heaven and hell, or between the world and god, between the conscious and the unconscious. In the Evangel of St. John, Christ likens himself to the serpent that was raised by Moses in the desert, against the many poisonous snakes that were killing the people. That is exactly the same motif, but instead of the beetle, it was the serpent directly. If one is at variance with one's cerebro-spinal system plus the sympathetic system, it would be expressed by the poisonous snake. Many people resist not only their sympathetic system, but the cerebro-spinal system as well, and they are of course directly threatened by the serpent. The snake then becomes poisonous. There is no question of Nietzsche's being threatened by the sympathetic system, for that would be very little in comparison with his dissociation from the cerebro-spinal system. He raised himself too high, onto the point of a needle, with his idea of the superman, so he is naturally in contradiction to his human side and that forms the black snake. This dream is most typical. This is a normal child and it shows what the normal solution would be.

Now, we are not yet through with that vision of the shepherd and the snake. We tried to explain it last time from the standpoint of Nietzsche and Zarathustra. Today I should like to look at it from our own point of view. You see, it remains rather distant and perhaps more or less incomprehensible as the vision of Nietzsche's Zarathustra, but if we try to realize what such a vision could mean if it happened in our own life today, it looks somewhat different. At all events it gains in intensity and immediate importance. Nietzsche would not have had such a vision if it had not been a problem of that time and the following decades. He anticipated, through his sensitivity, a great deal of the subsequent mental development; he was assailed by the collective unconscious to such an extent that quite involuntarily he became aware of the collective unconscious that was characteristic of his time and the time that followed. Therefore, he is called a prophet, and in a way he is a prophet. He is the man who said that the next century would be one of the most warlike in human history, which was quite true, unfortunately—at least up to the present moment. And he foretold, as you know, his own end. So his life and fate, one could say, was a collective program; his life was a forecast of a certain fate for his own country. It is not exaggerated, therefore, to assume that we also might have such a dream, because we are in a way in his situation; everybody is a bit at variance with his own cerebro-spinal system.

Now, if a modern man knowing of analysis, should have such a vision, or let us say, if Nietzsche himself had known about it, what could he have done? Of course, such a speculation is like asking what the old Romans would have done if they had had gunpowder and rifles. To be sure they had no such thing and therefore it is futile to speculate about it, and so here too it is in a way futile to make such a speculation. But Nietzsche is so close to us that he might almost have had that knowledge. You see, I was a boy when he was a professor at the university. I never saw him, but I saw his friend Jakob Burckhardt very often, and also Bachofen,[1] so we were not separated by cosmic distances. Nietzsche's mind was one of the first spiritual influences I experienced. It was all brand new then, and it was the closest thing to me. So we could easily assume that he might have known what I know now. Why not? What do you think he would have done, then, if he had had analytical knowledge?

Mrs. Sigg: He could have compared the two visions. He could have asked why Zarathustra himself was bitten on the outside of his neck by this snake before, while here the shepherd is bitten inside, in his throat.

Prof. Jung: And if you compare the two, what conclusion would you come to?

Mrs. Sigg: I ask you because I do not know.

Prof. Jung: Does anybody know? You see, that is a perfectly apt argument; that is very good. The two visions, or events: Zarathustra being attacked by that snake before, and now the shepherd, are practically one and the same experience. Of course it is a variation of the same experience, but most characteristic. Have you a solution?

Mrs. Sigg: No, but there is one little point which would help perhaps—that Nietzsche meets the black snake again at the end of *Zarathustra*. He said the black snake came to die then, so I think it was something out of his early childhood that came again at the end.

Prof. Jung: We must not anticipate. That is an assumption and it would not answer our problem. But how would you understand it? What does it mean when Zarathustra is bitten externally?

Mrs. Sigg: It is not so bad as the internal bite.

Prof. Reichstein: Has not the bite of the snake in the region of the

---

[1] Johann Jakob Bachofen (1815-1887), a professor at Basel when Nietzsche was there, is remembered mainly for his *Das Mutterrecht* (Stuttgart, 1867), a work that probably influenced Jungian thought about the mother archetype. See *Myth, Religion and Mother Right: Selected Writing* (B.S. XCV, 1967). Nietzsche said of him that he was neglected by his contemporaries: "His time had not yet come. I have resigned myself to being posthumous" (*Letters*, vol. II, p. 299). Jacob Burckhardt (1819-1887) was perhaps Basel's most famous scholar.

throat something to do with the speech center? He was always preaching and he tried to put others down instead of hearing what they had to say.

Prof. Jung: I should say that was right, because Zarathustra has talked a lot since he was first bitten by the snake, and of course the throat has to do with speech. You see, a tenor who has sung a great deal, or a speaker, might be bitten in the throat, because a neurosis always reaches one in the main function. A singer would develop symptoms in his voice, and a man who is inclined to eat too much would develop his neurosis in the stomach. I once treated an infantry officer who had hysterical symptoms in his feet, while a man who uses his brain chiefly will develop a sort of neurasthenia, a headache or certain symptoms in the head. It is always the main activity which is threatened in a neurosis. Now at first, the snake did not penetrate his throat, but it attacked his neck, so we can be sure the neck is meant.

I make that clear because we are about to realize what that vision would mean in ordinary life, say to ourselves; you surely remember certain pictures of black snakes or black animals, or an indefinite sort of monster that approaches a human body; and it is of the greatest importance to make out where it attacks the person—whether he is attacked on the head or at the throat, for instance, or whether it enters the body. Also, just what form it takes is very important; it is not always a snake: sometimes it is a black bird, or a dark crocodile, or an elephant, or a mouse, or a rat, or a black panther. Of course they all mean the cerebro-spinal system, yet in each case there is an important symbolic variation, which has to be translated in a somewhat different way. It may also be black foodstuff—it is not necessarily an animal. Or just blackness alone may be emphasized and then the cerebro-spinal system is not in it. The blackness can detach itself, and in that case, it is not a matter of the sensitivity of the cerebro-spinal system but a blackness that has to do with the mind. You see, the blackness is detachable, it can go by itself, or it may be connected with the black dragon, but they are not always together.

So it is quite certainly most important that Zarathustra is attacked from the outside in the beginning—that is a hint from the unconscious: look out that you don't talk too much. The organ of speech is in the neck and there the snake will jump at him—there he will be attacked by the enemy. Sure enough, the actual text of *Zarathustra* is all talk, not writing. It should be a dialogue but it is really a monologue: all through the book he talks to an invisible audience. Yet now it is no longer Zarathustra who is attacked, but the shepherd boy who has this peculiar *rencontre* with the snake. Now, why the shepherd boy? That is the *deutsche Michel*, the youthful, blue-eyed, blond innocence. What is the relation between this figure and Zarathustra? We said last time that Zarathustra was a shepherd himself, the poimen, a leader of men; and the shepherd boy is a small leader: he is a shepherd but a shepherd of sheep. Zarathustra is the big figure and the shepherd is the small figure. And that shepherd is inside of Zarathustra. It is illuminating that Zarathustra or Nietzsche is confronted here with the small shepherd. What does that mean?

Dr. Henderson: The shepherd is the undeveloped side.

Prof. Jung: Zarathustra is the exaggerated sort of swallowing-up figure, an inflated big figure, and the other side is the simple naive shepherd, something extraordinarily small for a compensation—unimportant and very nice, an altogether too modest simplicity. Plenty of people cannot stand that simplicity and therefore they take something into the mouth which makes them explode. There are many quite simple and modest individuals who would be all right if they only could be what they are, but they think they should be something better, that they are not good enough, and then they begin to ornament themselves with feathers and I don't know what, in order to be big and wonderful. But they are quite wonderful when they are simple. You see, we have had a lot of huge talk and now out of it creeps the shepherd. Again one can say, *Das also war des Pudels Kern.*[2] In *Faust*, the poodle was swelling up like anything and there it was the devil, while here the shepherd is behind that dangerous swelling of Zarathustra, who is always walking on mountain tops six thousand feet above good and evil. Now, what would this vision convey under that aspect?

Miss Hannah: He should give up his inflation and become what he really is.

Dr. Henderson: He should live his ordinary human life, should come down to the earth.

Prof. Jung: Well yes, but to take it humanly. That is too technical. Ordinary people don't talk of inflation, nor of coming down to earth.

Mr. Allemann: Be simple and stop talking.

Prof. Jung: Exactly, just that. It would mean, "Now look here, that nice, simple thing in you is threatened—that blue-eyed, very simple (perhaps a bit dotty) individual that is simply unconscious life itself. You have overtalked yourself; you became a balloon that went up to the moon, and in the meantime your simpleton inside is going to hell.

[2] "So that was the poodle's stone."

One has to use straight, plain language in such a case. Nietzsche should have had a human feeling toward that shepherd. One doesn't get away with big talk when one has such a dream; one cannot say, "Oh, god is entering me!" It simply means: stop talking and see what happens. For if one can be simple, if one can realize such a thing, nothing can happen. The best antidote against madness is to settle down and say, "I am that little fellow and that is all there is to it. I went astray and thought I was big, but I am just that unconscious fool wandering over the surface of the earth seeking good luck somewhere." Then he would be safe, because that would be the truth. You see, that is *Hans in Glück*, or that other *dumme Hans* who has luck and finds something, the stupid fellow in the fairy tale who knows nothing and tumbles into the valley of diamonds.[3] But one only gets there by one's dumbness and not by big talk or intelligence; one gets there by stupidity, by simplicity. If one can accept that, what can happen to one? Such a fellow cannot go mad, because if madness comes alone, there is nothing on the throne. It is like the great Mara experience of Buddha. When he was attacked by the devil with his whole host, the city of Buddha was empty. He had the great simplicity to say, "What is all this talk about the great Buddha? He is not, he is a void." We wonder how he could say of himself that he was the perfect one, the accomplished one, the *Tathagata*, but that was because he knew he was a void, that he did not even exist; such a big sounding word as *Tathagata* can only be compensated by a void. If you have reached the stage where you are not even the *dumme Michel*, where you are less than the simpleton, then you can use a very big word on the other side without being attacked by the devil. But as long as you are feeling that you *are* something, the devil will attack you. So you had better doubt it. We are not *Tathagata*.

Mrs. Fierz: What is *Tathagata*?

Prof. Jung: Der Vollendete, the perfect one, the complete one. That is a term for Buddha in the original collection of sermons. Buddhism is very interesting in that respect. One might mind those exaggerated terms, as in a way one must mind it that Jesus said, "I am the way, the truth and the life"—that is terribly big; then one understands that he had to undergo the divine punishment, the crucifixion, the dismemberment. The Buddha said "I am the perfect one," but at the same time he said, "I am not"; and he himself said that, so it is possible. But the

---

[3] Hans in *Hans in Glück*, a Grimm fairy tale, is a kind of Candide. Everybody cheats him and he always congratulates himself on his good luck. The other Hans in *The Poor Miller's Boy and the Cat*, a *dumme Hans*, goes from blunder to blunder to—a wealthy wife.

one without the other is too big. It would be impossible for us because we feel that we are *something*; we don't know what, but no matter how small, it is there, so we cannot use the big words.

Now, supposing one of you had had such a vision. I should say, "Now look here, it is not so bad as long as you realize that you are a little shepherd." That is quite possible to accept; but of course it is difficult to accept that you should be attacked or killed as such. And so Nietzsche might say, "Since I am *not* old Zarathustra and I am not that legendary shepherd, since I am Professor Nietzsche of Basel University and this happens in my psychical sphere, it is not exactly my personal concern. Of course, I am afraid. I am between the hammer and the anvil. Inasmuch as I imagine I am Zarathustra I am too big, and in order to be able to stand the onslaught of such greatness I must be very simple on the other side." Then that attack the shepherd had to undergo would be terrible, but he could say he had brought it on by talking too much, and his simpleton really had to suffer, because it was owing to that unconscious simplicity that he did not realize in time that he was not his big mouth. So a tenor should realize that he is not his voice, and the painter should realize that he is not his brush, and the man with a mind should know that he is not identical with his mind, lest the gift run away with the man. For each gift is a demon that can seize a man and carry him away. Therefore in antiquity they represented the genius of a man as a winged being or even as a bird of prey that could carry away the individual, like the famous capture of Ganymede. The eagle of Zeus carried him off to the throne of the gods; he was lifted up from the soil upon which he should remain. That is a wonderful representation of the way they conceived of an enthusiasm, of the divine gift.

Now this shepherd in Nietzsche should die. It is a horrible catastrophe after identifying with Zarathustra, but if one identifies with the big figure, one dies miserably. If Nietzsche had remained the shepherd, he might have had an experience like Ganymede, but since he identified with the great figure, he has to end in the small compensatory figure, and the catastrophe is unavoidable. Inasmuch as you identify with one or the other figure, it is your catastrophe; it is not your catastrophe if you don't identify. You see, since Zarathustra is there with his great words, Nietzsche has to realize Zarathustra; he cannot afford not to listen and he cannot avoid hearing them. But he should say, "What amazing big words! That fellow has to come down somehow." If he has that attitude he will also realize an extreme simplicity against that greatness, and then he will understand that it is the gods' play on the scene of man's mind. Our mind is the scene upon which the gods perform their plays, and we don't know the beginning and we don't know the end. And it is well for man if he doesn't identify, as it is well for the actor not to identify with his role; to be Hamlet or King Lear or one of the witches forever would be most unhealthy.

Prof. Reichstein: I should like to ask about the laughter of the shepherd. It reminds me of the legend that Professor Abegg told here about the real Zarathustra, the legend that the real prophet was born, not with a cry, but with laughter.[4] There is a connection here because this is a kind of rebirth.

Prof. Jung: Of course we don't know in how far Nietzsche was informed about the legend of Zarathustra. I assume that story would be in the original form of the Bundahish[5] which was known in Nietzsche's time, and it is possible that laughter plays such a role with him just because he knew that story about the Persian founder of the religion. I don't know. But the laughter here has to do with the thousand peals of mad laughter when the coffin was split open. The shepherd went mad—that is perfectly clear. That is the inevitable outcome when one integrates one of the performers of the divine play. That is Nietzsche's madness: it explodes his brain-box. Therefore the last part, the transfigured shepherd, is so terribly tragic. You remember when Nietzsche became mad he signed his letters Dionysos Zagreus. (Zagreus was the Thracian Dionysos.) He also became Christ: he was identical with the figure of the mediator or the god. There is a book by Salin,[6] a professor in Basel, about the friendship of Nietzsche and Jakob Burkhardt, in which he quotes from one of Nietzsche's letters the statement that as a matter of fact he would much prefer to be a professor in Basel, that it was terribly awkward to have to produce a new world, but alas, since he was god, he could not avoid seeing the thing through, so he had no time to occupy himself with the ordinary affairs of man. This bears out what I said in the beginning, that by denying the existence of god, in declaring God to be dead, he himself became God; and he realized that it would have been better to have remained a professor in Basel.

Now to ask what would happen if a person who knew about psychology had to deal with such a vision is really futile because presum-

---

[4] For Emil Abegg, see above, p. 4.

[5] This story of Zarathustra's mirthful birth is told in the Bundahish, the Persian scripture which was written over the long period 226 to 640. Nietzsche once wrote, "I should actually risk an order of rank among philosophers depending on the rank of their laughter" (*BG&E*, no. 291).

[6] Edgar Salin, *Burckhardt und Nietzsche, der Briefwechsel* (Heidelberg, 1948, 2nd ed.).

ably such a person would never had had such a vision. He would not have gone so far, but would have left that road long before. As a matter of fact it is an altogether artificial assumption that he *could* get so far, because he would have realized that to be a prophet like Zarathustra was too big an order. He would have been mistrustful, or he could not have had a real knowledge of psychology. So even that assumption is impossible. But one can ask—and I think that would be a fair question—what the solution of such a problem would be if it were not expressed by such exaggerated figures and so had not come to such a head.

You see, the question was already asked when Zarathustra was first attacked by the snake. Anyone who knows something about psychology could easily have such a dream—that is within our reach. I assume our realization would begin then and there. One would ask oneself, "Why am I persecuted by that serpent?" Well, that is the personification of my cerebro-spinal system, or my system of instincts, with which I am obviously at variance, and now I have to keep still and see what it does to me, what it is when I accept it. That is the ordinary case. In the practical treatment and development of an individual, it would be the union with the instincts, the acceptance of the instincts, by which you have also to accept a specific humility. For you cannot accept your instincts without humility; if you do, you have an inflation—you are up in heaven somewhere, but in the wrong one. You can only accept them humbly, and then you remain simple. Then you have the simple human fate, the happiness and the misery of ordinary human life, and something on top, because you have accepted it. Of course people are particularly interested in that something on top, the tip you get by living the ordinary life, and I always hate to talk about it because it is not good for them to know it: then they accept life merely *because* of the tip. You have to accept a thing for better or worse, have to accept it unconditionally, even without hope. If you do it for the tip you hope for, it is no good: you have cheated yourself.

Mr. Baumann: I recently heard of two dreams of very different people, but both are good Catholics; one is a priest and the other is very much wrapped up in Semitic philosophy. The dreams are very similar and one point is that they are running at a tremendous speed with a black serpent. And they think they have to run beside the serpent, not to follow it. It is like a race.

Prof. Jung: There is a very clear interpretation of course: namely, that in consciousness they have an exceedingly static philosophy which has not changed for 1500 years practically, and the compensation is the rapid movement of a very lively cerebro-spinal system which they ought to follow. But there is a complete dissociation between the conscious and the unconscious. For instance, I am quite certain that if they had submitted this dream to a priest of the 12th or 13th century, when they were still occupied with the interpretation of dreams, that the father confessor would have told them they were forced by the devil to run along with him, that their carnal man was under the influence of the devil. The black snake would most certainly be the devil, the serpent of temptation. Of course within the last centuries the church has not taken dreams into consideration, at least not openly. (I don't know whether there are still individual priests in monasteries who do so.) But formerly it was a recognized fact that certain dreams were messages sent by God, so they had a certain dignity. Also they were aware that the demon sometimes sent dreams which were very upsetting. You see the medieval man would be upset by such a dream, but we make a wall and don't recognize that we are influenced by them. So I don't think that the men you speak of would confess such dreams now. Formerly, when a dream was an experience, they would have believed that they had had communion with a demon, or a demon had appeared to them, and they would have felt sinful. Since they had been touched by the demon they needed purification, so they naturally would have brought it up in confession. Nowadays, I assume that no Catholic would think of mentioning a dream; I have analyzed several but I never saw that they had the slightest idea that one could be responsible for one's dreams.

You remember St. Augustine said, "I thank thee Lord, that thou dost not make me responsible for my dreams." So we may conclude that he had very nice dreams indeed—well, in a saint, one must expect that. But he declared himself irresponsible—God did not make him responsible—and that is an attempt at making light of dreams in order to get out of it. Of course they could do that, knowing so very little about their meaning. Already at that time, thousands of dreams were excluded from consideration because they were supposed to be futile. Just as the primitives believe that the dreams of an ordinary man don't count at all; only the dreams of the chief or the medicine man count, and then only their big dreams. They were limited to dreams that were important, where one felt a certain responsibility. That was true in antiquity. For instance, in the middle of the first century the daughter of a Roman senator dreamt that Minerva complained to her that her temple was neglected and crumbling to pieces. So this Roman woman went to the Senate and told them the dream, and the Senate voted a certain sum for the restoration of the temple. And a certain Greek poet had a dream which repeated itself three times: A famous golden vessel had been stolen from the temple of Hermes, and they could not find the thief. Three times the poet was told by the god the name of the thief and where the vessel was hidden, so he felt responsible and announced it to the Areopagus, the equivalent of the Roman Senate, and they found that thief and the golden vessel. Such things do happen in dreams and we have no reason to believe that these are just legends. You see, they felt the responsibility. But with the beginning of Christianity, particularly in the fourth century, that began to vanish.

Mr. Henley: It seems that these things repeat themselves. Our President Roosevelt told a number of Representatives recently that he dreamed that he got out of bed and walked to a window of the White House and stood there looking out. The scene before him was the present Washington airport. Suddenly a terrible airplane crash took place. So he is going to get a new landing stage outside Washington!

Prof. Jung: But think of the Chambre de Députés in Paris: if some one should stand up and say, "Gentlemen, I must tell you that I have had a dream." They would send him to the lunatic asylum on the spot. And even in the confessional, dreams no longer play a role. Of course it is quite different when you begin to realize the meaning and the importance of dreams; then you develop the sense of psychological responsibility—an idea of it at least.

Prof. Reichstein: There are attempts in *Zarathustra* to see the snake not only from the negative side. He says it is identical with wisdom and understanding for instance, and there is a scene where the eagle was flying with the snake round its neck, which would be an attempt to reconcile them.

Prof. Jung: Yes, and he even calls the eagle and the serpent his two animals; they would be divine attributes. But the eagle and the serpent are Zarathustra's animals and when Nietzsche identifies with Zarathustra, the impossible situation arises that he is lord of the serpent and the eagle. Zeus is lord of the eagle so he is putting himself in the place of divinity; and the lord over the serpent is a chthonic god perhaps—in Christianity it would be the devil. The eagle and the serpent simply mean the union of the opposites, and Zarathustra is the lord of the thing beyond the opposites. You see, the eagle and the serpent form that symbol of the *ouroboros*, the tail-eater, and the thing beyond; the lord of the two, the figure that unites the opposites, is the god Zarathustra. The mediator or the redeemer is always the redeemer from the opposites and the outcome of the opposites, so the center of that

circle, of the *ouroboros*, is the deity. The deity has always been represented as the unchanging center of the circle, and the circle is the rotation of the universe, the extension in space that is the *ouroboros* that returns into itself. And the unchangeable, immovable center is God as static eternity, and time and space at the same time. So Zarathustra and his two animals really symbolize a deity, like Zeus with his eagle, or the Holy Ghost with a dove, or Christ with the lamb, or any number of Indian gods associated with certain animals or expressed by them.

Dr. Escher: In the Catholic church the snake is considered evil, an enemy, but in Milan in the old church of St. Ambrogio there is a huge bronze snake on a pillar in the middle of the church, just opposite a pillar that has a cross on top. It is not the *ouroboros*. It is very old and very simple.

Prof. Jung: What it is meant to be depends very much upon its age, of course. They would not represent the devil—that is certain—so it may be the old idea of Christ as the serpent. That figure, or metaphor, was frequently used by the Latin Fathers of the church. They made free use of Christ as the serpent, and it was well prepared historically in the pre-Christian mediator: the *agathodaimon* of the Hellenic-Egyptian mysteries was represented as a serpent. So if that serpent in Milan dates from the 9th to the 11th century, or even as late as the 13th century, it is quite possible that it represents Christ; if it is later it becomes doubtful. They had to be careful, naturally, on account of the infernal meaning of the serpent.

Mrs. Sigg: This answer of Zarathustra to the poisonous snake is very strange: Take back your poison, you are not yet rich enough to make a present to me. Does it mean that Zarathustra is above the savior?

Prof. Jung: Oh, that is one of those big things he has to say because he is afraid of the serpent. He assumes a higher position against the danger. We have seen that technique all along, and we shall see it again when he is up against something. He hopes to take the wind out of its sails in that way. Now the beginning of the next chapter, "Involuntary Bliss," is not very important, but at the bottom of the second page he says,

> My past burst its tomb, many pains buried alive woke up—: fully slept had they merely, concealed in corpse-clothes.
>
> So called everything unto me in signs: "It is time!" But I—heard not, until at last mine abyss moved, and my thought bit me.

Here is a confession which we have not heard before. He is referring back to his descent into the volcano with the cry, "It is time! it is highest time!" He repeats that here; at that time he would not have admitted what he is admitting now. Even when the coffin was splitting up and spouting out a thousand peals of laughter, Zarathustra was the coffin, and he was the big wind and the thousand peals of laughter—and there was no danger at all. But here we hear another tune, "My past burst its tomb." Where, then, is Zarathustra? He has entirely forgotten that the roaring, whistling wind and the uncanny coffin, which was thrown out, were all Zarathustra, his power and his greatness; he was that dangerous laughter and the overwhelming fact of the wind. And now we hear it is his past, a demon really of his past, that has burst open the tomb, and "many pains buried alive [repressed contents] woke up"—they had only slept deeply as if they were corpses. "So called everything unto me in signs: 'It is time!' " An entirely new interpretation of "It is time":—it sounds quite different. Here he himself understands it as a warning, "But I heard it not." He realizes that he had not even listened before. You see, it was too dangerous: it would have overcome him. Here he is more used to the whole situation. He begins slowly to realize that he did not listen then; the abyss had to move, the volcanic eruption had to follow, in order to call his attention to the fact that there was something behind that moved *him*. But "my thought bit me" is again an attempt at declaring his possessiveness, that the serpent is his own thought. He is trying to convey the idea that he is naturally the fellow who has such dangerous thoughts, that he makes them at will. He lets them come and he lets them disappear: he controls them. That is of course a tremendous exaggeration. The serpent is not his invention, but is a power that gets at him. Yet in the moment when he has to realize that the thing has got at *him*, that the abyss moves, that the serpent has bitten him—even then he says that he has bitten himself. He continues,

> Ah, abysmal thought, which art my thought! [Again this tragic misunderstanding.] When shall I find strength to hear thee burrowing, and no longer tremble?

But if it is his own thought, why should he tremble? When I hear an uncanny noise in the night, I call it an hallucination: something has rustled, or a paper has fallen to the floor. I combat a nocturnal fear by such rationalizations, saying it is only my nocturnal fear that produces such phenomena. Why should one tremble unless one is afraid of something which one cannot control? If there is something you do not control, you don't call it yourself. If you know the dog that is barking at you is yourself, why should you be afraid? You say, "Don't make a fuss, you are myself, why such a noise?" But you see, you are only sure that *you* know it; you are not sure that the dog knows it too. So Nietzsche is sure he knows all about it. But when the unconscious knows it, you *should* begin to tremble; then you had better say, "I am not that thing; that is against me, that is strange to me." Everybody makes the same mistake; no matter how much afraid they are, they talk about *my* thought, *my* dog.

> To my very throat throbbeth my heart when I hear thee burrowing! Thy muteness even is like to strangle me, thou abysmal mute one!

Now could one put it better? In formulating it, he confesses that this is not himself, but a strange opponent. Our foolish, almost insane prejudice is that whatever appears in our psyche is oneself, and only where it is absolutely certain that it is outside, can we admit it—as if we could only grudgingly admit the reality of the world. That is a remnant of the god-almighty-likeness of our consciousness, which naturally has always assumed—and is still assuming—that whatever is, is oneself. It is the old identity of man with his unconscious that is the world creator.

Inasmuch as you are identical with your unconscious, you are the world creator, and then you can say, "This is myself." By that technique, when you learn not only with words but with your whole head and heart, to say, "*Tat twam asi*," "That is thou," or "Thou art that," do you make the way back to the deity, and become the super-personal Atman. You can make the way back to your divine existence because that idea starts really from the condition in which you are still identical with the Unconscious, and the Unconscious is the world creator. They are absolutely identical. The Unconscious is in everything because it is projected into everything; it is not just in the brain-box, but is all over the place. You always encounter the unconscious outside. When you encounter it inside of you and say, "This is my thought," it is already approaching the psychological sphere, which means that it is partially conscious. In claiming a thought as your own, you are partially right but it is misleading, for inasmuch as it is a phenomenon it is not exactly your thought. For instance, if you say, "This is my light," it is true to a certain extent: it is in your brain and you would not see that light if you were not conscious of it. Yet you make a big mistake when you say light is nothing but what you produce: that would be denying the reality of the world. Inasmuch as you are conscious of it, it is yours, but the thing that causes you to have an idea of that which becomes what you call "light" or "sound," that is not your own; that is exactly what you do not possess, something of the great unknown outside. So when Nietzsche says, "This is my thought, that abyss is mine," it is only his inasmuch as he has a word for it, inasmuch as he makes a representation of it, but the thing itself is not his. That is a fact, and you never can call it your own fact.

Mrs. von Roques: That is what Goethe says:

> Wär nicht das Auge sonnenhaft,
> Die Sonne könnt' es nie erblicken.
> Wär nicht in uns des Gottes eigne Kraft,
> Wie könnte uns das Göttliche entzücken?[7]

Prof. Jung: Yes, and the old Latin poet, Manilius, had the same idea: it is an antique thought really.[8] Now, Indian philosophy makes use of

[7] A prose translation of Goethe's poem reads: "If the eye were not sun-like, it could not see the sun; if we did not carry within us the very power of the god, how could anything god-like delight us?" *Great German Poetry*, tr. David Luke (Harmondsworth, Middlesex, England, 1964).

[8] Jung would be thinking of some such expression of this first century Roman poet's Stoic emphasis upon cosmic sympathy as: "Who after this can doubt that a link exists

the fact that we have that primitive prejudice, that the world, inasuch as it is my thought, is really nothing else than my thought; and by saying this they make the conscious return to the original condition, to the universal Atman. They bring the world to an end, deny the existence of the world, by bringing the thought back to its source, to the Atman or the *Purusha*.

Here again would be a wonderful chance for Nietzsche to realize that one should make a difference between one's own thought and the thing that makes the thought, whatever that is, and to realize, when he is afraid, that he is not afraid of his own representations, but of the thing that causes those representations to be. You see, it is just as if you came home and found somebody in your place; you don't see who it is but you see that he is walking about in your clothes. You are not afraid of your clothes naturally, but you would be afraid of the thing that is inside your clothes. The clothing would be our thought forms, but the thing that fills the thought forms, that makes the thought forms live and act, is something of which one can be rightfully afraid, for it is really uncanny. Nietzsche expresses that here too. But nobody in those days ever really grasped this, though Schopenhauer, who was Nietzsche's master, said as much: in his philosophy the world is seen as will and representation, but he made the mistake of identifying the world with his representation.[9] He assumed that nothing would be left of the world if there were no representation of it, and that is a mistake, because the representation can be caused by that world outside. On the other hand, natural science believes exclusively in the outside world and not in the representation—the representation is nothing; it is the world outside that causes the representation to be. And so the materialistic prejudice came about that *Der Mann ist was er isst*, "Man is what he eats."[10] That prejudice makes even your mental health dependent upon physical or tangible facts.

---

between heaven and man, to whom, in its desire for earth to rise to the stars, gifts outstanding, did nature give . . . and into whom alone indeed has God come down and dwells, and seeks himself in man's seeking of him . . . ? Who could know heaven save by heaven's gift? . . . Who could discern and compass in his narrow mind the vastness of this vaulted infinite . . . had not nature endowed our minds with divine vision . . . ?" See *Astronomica*, vol. 2, pp. 105-22, tr. G. P. Goold (Cambridge, Mass. and London, 1977). Another of Jung's favorites who makes this point is Meister Eckhart; see *Meister Eckhart*, tr. R. B. Blackney, p. 172.

9 Schopenhauer's four volume masterwork is translated both as *The World as Will and Idea* and as *The World as Will and Representation*. The original was published in 1819.

10 Jacob Moleschott (1822-1893), German materialist, is today remembered exclusively for his dogmatic epigram.

Mr. Baumann: There is a very interesting Indian idea of a chain which has ten or twelve links. One of the twelve is consciousness and that is represented by a monkey because it can only imitate.

Prof. Jung: Yes, that is a Buddhist idea, the so-called *nidana* chain. There is first consciousness, then follows the becoming, from the becoming follows birth, from birth follows age and death, and from age and death follows suffering. I only mention a few, there are ten or twelve. Now if you stop the *avidya* of the beginning, there is no becoming, and if you stop the becoming there is no birth. If you stop birth there is no age and death, and if you stop age and death there is no suffering, and so on. So the whole world of suffering is abolished. Therefore Buddha says consciousness is like a monkey, a mere imitator, a sort of playful thing. That is the true Eastern point of view. Now Nietzsche continues.

> As yet have I never ventured to call thee up; it hath been enough that I have carried thee about with me! As yet have I not been strong enough for my final lion-wantonness and playfulness.

Here you get it. He is trembling with fear really and he admits that this "abysmal mute one" is formidable, but he has not ventured to call him up yet. It has been enough that he has carried him about—as if he had the ghost of a chance not to carry him! Then he says he has not been strong enough for his "lion wantonness and playfulness"—to play with that thing! But he admits that it needs the strength of a lion. Well, the lion is a very cowardly animal in reality. It is not true that he has a great heart and great courage, but let us assume that he has great courage, for Nietzsche, indirectly at least, admits that it needs a lion's heart, a lion's strength, and a lion's courage, to deal with his thought, and he doesn't see that he is just blind to that fact.

> Sufficiently formidable unto me hath thy weight ever been: . . .

As if he had the choice of not carrying that formidable weight!

> but one day shall I yet find the strength and the lion's voice which will call thee up!

But he is at the time talking as if it were nothing, as if it were his own thought and really within his reach.

> When I shall have surmounted myself therein, then will I surmount myself also in that which is greater; and a *victory* shall be the seal of my perfection!—

This peroration follows that admission from the tomb. "It is time!" Because he had not heard that, his abyss began to move and now he winds up with an anticipation of victory.

> Meanwhile do I sail along on uncertain seas; chance flattereth me, smooth-tongued chance; forward and backward do I gaze—, still see I no end.
>
> As yet hath the hour of my final struggle not come to me—or doth it come to me perhaps just now? Verily, with insidious beauty do sea and life gaze upon me round about:
>
> O afternoon of my life! O happiness before eventide! O haven upon high seas! O peace in uncertainty! How I distrust all of you!

Again a wonderful admission—that the situation is not at all trustworthy, that all the big words are very doubtful pretexts.

> Verily, distrustful am I of your insidious beauty! Like the lover am I, who distrusteth too sleek smiling.
>
> As he pusheth the best-beloved before him—tender even in severity, the jealous one—, so do I push this blissful hour before me.

You see, he has the feeling that a certain cheat is going on, that he is cheating himself in making light of certain things, and that behind the imagined beauty is something quite different. We shall see next time what that is.

LECTURE VII

22 June 1938

Prof. Jung:

I have brought that book, *Jakob Burckhardt und Nietzsche*, by Edgar Salin, which I mentioned to you last time, and I will translate literally a passage from a letter dated January 6, 1889, written to Burckhardt by Nietzsche in Turin. He says: "Alas, I would have much preferred to be a professor in Basel rather than God, but I did not dare to push my private egotism so far as to omit the creation of the world on account of that professorship. You see one has to sacrifice something,—where and how one lives." This was in the beginning of his disease and it shows how he understood his role: he really believed he had become God, or something like God, and had to create a new world, and therefore could not be an ordinary human being.[1] Now, last week we stopped in the middle of the chapter called "Involuntary Bliss" where Nietsche had that very irrational feeling of happiness. According to all expectations, he should have realized there what was threatening him, but instead, what he calls the blissful hour suddenly overcame him. He had just been asking himself, "When shall I find strength to hear thee burrowing and no longer tremble?" And the answer would be that he should screw up his courage and approach that thought which was burrowing in him. There was no reason for any particular happiness, but unexpectedly and irrationally enough, it is as if he were anticipating a final victory. He says, "When I shall have surmounted myself therein, then will I surmount myself also in that which is greater; and a victory shall be the seal of my perfection." He puts himself into the mood of one who has already overcome his fear and won that victory, while actually he leaps over the fear and gets into a sort of ecstasy of anticipation of a victory that has not even been fought for. Yet he feels

---

[1] In the months just before this letter, Nietzsche had continually expressed an uncanny bliss that permeated even the most ordinary aspects of his life, such as eating in his regular restaurant. See his letters of October and November 1988.

that this blissful hour is not quite trustworthy, that there is some cheat in it, and therefore he says, "Like the lover am I, who distrusteth too sleek smiling." And he continues:

> Away with thee, thou blissful hour! With thee hath there come to me an involuntary bliss! Ready for my severest pain do I here stand:—at the wrong time hast thou come!

Here is the insight which one would expect of him; he should be making ready for his severest pain: happiness is absolutely inappropriate. But that is due to his peculiar sort of hysterical mechanism; it is like the laughter one observes in hysterical cases: in a moment of great distress or real despair they begin to laugh. Or like the *Hexenschlaf*, the witches' sleep: when the pain of torture becomes unbearable they fall into a sort of somnambulistic condition, a state of anaesthesia—they are completely narcotized; that is one of the signs of witchcraft mentioned in the *Malleus Maleficarum*, the *Witches' Hammer*, a very famous book written in the 15th century.[2] Then he goes on:

> Away with thee, thou blissful hour! Rather harbour there—with my children! Hasten! and bless them before eventide with my happiness!
> There, already approacheth eventide: the sun sinketh. Away— my happiness!—

This is surely a decent attempt at facing the dark, dangerous thoughts.

> Thus spake Zarathustra. And he waited for his misfortune the whole night; but he waited in vain. The night remained clear and calm, and happiness itself came nigher and nigher unto him. Towards morning, however, Zarathustra laughed to his heart, and said mockingly: "Happiness runneth after me. That is because I do not run after women. Happiness, however, is a woman."

You see, this is again that element which makes light of danger, which plays with dangerous things, like that laughter which comes to him in the face of his dark thoughts. Where he should be exceedingly serious and perhaps weep, his mood simply changes; something hinders realization. He cannot control the mood. It is astonishing that in the face of the very black and dangerous thoughts such an uncontrollable mood of happiness should arise, but he can control his thoughts no better. He has no control over his unconscious whatever, and therefore

---

[2] For the *Witches' Hammer*, see above, 23 Jan. 1935, n. 9.

the situation is generally dangerous. Whether it is an unexpected happiness or a great fear, a panic, it is the same. It is an uncontrolled function and sometimes one takes the lead and sometimes the other. As I said, one often finds that condition in hysteria, when it is a matter of two sides of the character for instance, when the positive consciousness is in opposition to a sort of negative character—one can call it the shadow. That is the prevailing conflict in hysteria, and therefore the hysterical character is always trying to make a positive impression, but they cannot hold it, cannot be consistent, because after a while the other side comes up and then they spoil everything: they deny everything positive they have said before. So one of the prejudices against hysterics is that they lie, but they cannot help it; their inconsistency is the play of the opposites.

Now, if it is not a matter of two personalities, as it were, but of several or if it is a matter of a number of dissociated aspects, that is something else—that approaches schizophrenia. When different aspects of a personality become so independent of each other that they are able to manifest themselves one after the other, with no control and no inner consistency or relatedness, there is a very justifiable suspicion of a sort of schizophrenic condition. And that is the case with Nietzsche. Of course the disease which followed has been understood to be general paralysis of the insane, which is without exception a syphilitic infection of the brain. His case was not typical however. According to my idea, there is plenty of evidence that it was more a schizophrenic than a paralytic condition; probably both diseases existed in a peculiar mixture, for through the whole course of development of his disease, there were numbers of indications which would not point to the usual diagnosis of paralysis only. He often behaved very queerly and said very strange things which one is unlikely to hear from anyone with general paralysis of the insane. So he cannot control his happiness—it simply gets him—and now he gives word to it. He expresses in the following chapter, "Before Sunrise," the contents of that happiness. It begins,

> O heaven above me, thou pure, thou deep heaven! Thou abyss of light! Gazing on thee, I tremble with divine desires.
> Up to thy height to toss myself—That is my depth! In thy purity to hide myself—that is mine innocence!
> The God veileth his beauty: thus hidest thou thy stars. Thou speakest not: thus proclaimest thou thy wisdom unto me.

Something happens here which we have seen many times before: namely, he is almost unable to give a definite or a decisive value to anything outside of himself, but must take it into himself, must introject those values. We have seen that he uses that mechanism in order to belittle dangerous situations or dangerous figures. He simply says, "Oh, you are just my thought," introjecting that figure into his own system. That is, of course, absolutely against analytical principles. When the unconscious makes a careful attempt to show a figure as something outside of yourself, you had better take it as something outside of yourself.

You see, you are a whole world of things and they are all mixed in you and form a terrible sauce, a chaos. So you should be mighty glad when the unconscious chooses certain figures and consolidates them outside of yourself. Of course that may be in the form of projections, which is not recommendable. For example, perhaps you have a sort of hostile element in yourself that crosses your path now and then, or a poisonous element that destroys all your attempts at a decent adaptation, and it is so mixed up with everything else that you never can definitely lay your hand on it. Then you suddenly discover somebody whom you can really declare to be your archenemy, so you can say *this* is the fellow who has done this and that against you: you succeed in constructing your archenemy. Now, that is already an asset which makes you sit up, because you know that there is the definite danger which can injure you. Of course it is in a way quite negative because it is not true; that fellow is not really the devil, but is only your best enemy and you should give him the credit. As a human being he is just as much in the soup as you are. But inasmuch as you succeed in creating a figure, in objectifying a certain thing in yourself which you hitherto could never contact, it is an advantage.

Now, the analyst will tell you that you cannot assume Mr. So-and-So to be the arch-devil with a hand in your own soul. That is just a projection, and then of course follows the ordinary reflux of projection, till the patient gradually gets to the point of saying, "Oh very well, then *I* am the devil"—hating it like hell naturally and nothing is gained. Then the devil falls back into the sauce and instantly dissolves there. So you must prevent that. Then follows a sort of philosophical teaching— against which philosophers would kick of course. The analyst has to say, "Now look here, in spite of the fact that you say there is no terrible devil, there is at least a psychological fact which you might *call* the devil. If you should not find a devil, then you had better construct one—and quickly—before he dissolves in your own system. *Make* a devil, say there is one, and if you doubt it, suppress your doubts as much as you can. For it is just as if you were building a house because you know you need one, and then conclude that there never was a house there and destroy whatever you have started to build; so of course you never will have a house. Therefore in order to construct a devil you must be convinced that you have to construct him, that it is absolutely essential to construct that figure. Otherwise the thing dissolves in your unconscious right away and you are left in the same condition as before."

You see, patients are quite right when they say this is merely a projection, and this would be a wrong procedure were it not that I must give them a chance to *catch* the reflux in a form. I cannot tell them it is a projection without providing a vessel in which to receive the reflux. And that must be a sort of suspended image between the object and the patient; otherwise—to compare it to water—what he has projected simply flows back into himself and then the poison is all over him. So he had better objectify it in one way or another; he mustn't pour it all over the other person, nor must it flow back into himself. For people who make bad projections on other people have a very bad effect upon them. They poison them or it is as if they were darting projectiles into them. The reason why people have always talked of witchcraft is that there is such a thing as psychological projection; if your unconscious makes you project into other people, you insinuate such an atmosphere that in the end you might cause them to behave accordingly, and then they could rightly complain of being bewitched. Of course they are *not* bewitched and the one who makes the projection always complains in the end: *I* have been the ass, *I* have been the devil. The devil in the one has caused the devil in the other, so there is wrongness all over the place. Therefore if anything is wrong, take it out of its place and put it in the vessel that is between your neighbor and yourself. For the love of your neighbor, and for love of yourself, don't introject nor project it. For love of mankind, create a vessel into which you can catch all that damned poison. For it must be somewhere—it is always somewhere—and not to catch it, to say it doesn't exist, gives the best chance to any germ. To say there is no such thing as cholera is the best means to cause a world epidemic.

So you had better make an image in order to be able to put your finger on it, and to say, *this* is this thing. You can call it nothing but a figure for the development of your consciousness, for how can you develop consciousness if you don't figure things out? Do you think anyone would ever have thought of gravitation if Newton had not figured it out as a species of attraction? God knows whether it is an attraction— that is a human word—but he figured out that phenomenon. Nobody had ever figured out before why things didn't fall from below to above; nobody wondered. But Newton wondered and he figured it out: he made a vessel and did not take it for granted. So I don't take it for granted that a poison should spoil my system. I am going to do something about it. I don't take it for granted that everybody else is an angel and I a devil, or that I am an angel and everybody else a devil.

Mrs. Sigg: Would not what you said about the devil dissolving in the system be the best explanation of the poisonous black snake getting into Zarathustra? Nietzsche had given too much beauty and perfection in consolidating the figure of Zarathustra, and therefore it would be the natural consequence that he remained too poor and ugly himself.

Prof. Jung: Yes, that is inevitable. Having constructed a figure like Zarathustra he is bound to construct the counter figure; Zarathustra casts a shadow. You cannot construct a perfect figure that is nothing but pure light. It has a shadow and you are bound to create a shadow too. Therefore as soon as you have the idea of creating a good god you have to create a devil. You see, the old Jews had no idea of a devil; their devils were just funny things that hopped about in deserted villages and ruins, or made noises in the night. The real devil came along in Christianity—or earlier, in the Persian religion where you have the god of pure light, and the devil of pure darkness on the other side. It is unavoidable: if you split the opposites you cannot content yourself with light only. It is not true, as some of our modern theologians say, that evil is only a mistake of the good, or something like that; for if you say good is absolute you must say in the same breath that evil is absolute. But that is what Nietzsche did not realize. He did not see that in the wake of Zarathustra follows the grotesque parade of evil figures, dwarfs and demons and black snakes that all together make up Zarathustra's shadow. He was unable to draw conclusions, because he was unwilling to admit that they were true. He was too Christian—that was just his trouble: he was too Christian.

Mrs. Sigg: Could you not tell us something about the art of creating a real devil, because the black snake is too primitive?

Prof. Jung: That is a long story. But it is always something simple; you see, it is an act of devotion.

Mrs. Sigg: To create the devil?

Prof. Jung: Yes, it is an act of devotion. Therefore my formula: for the love of mankind and for the love of yourself—of mankind in yourself—create a devil. That is an act of devotion, I should say; you have to put something where there is nothing, for the sake of mankind.

Mrs. Baynes: Would it be too big a jump to go back to the Yale lectures and the question of the devil?[3]

Prof. Jung: No, since we are dealing with the devil.

Mrs. Baynes: Well, if you admit the devil into the quaternity, as you explained in the lecture, how should we avoid devil worship?

Prof Jung: You cannot avoid it, in a way. I call it an act of devotion, for devotion in the actual sense of the word is not what we call divine worship. It is a hair-raising fear, a giving due attention to the powers; since you give due attention to the powers of the positive gods, you have also to take into account the negative gods. In antiquity the evil was all incorporated in the gods along with the good—as, for instance, when Zeus got into fits of rage and threw about his thunderbolts. All those gods were very doubtful characters, so they did not need the devil. And Jahveh also led a very wrathful existence—well, he was generous in a way but full of moods. The most horrible picture of Jahveh is depicted in the Book of Job, where he bets with the devil as to who could play the best trick on man. Suppose I created a little child, knowing nothing, blind as man is blind in comparison to the gods, and then bet with some bad individual whether that little thing could be seduced! That is Jahveh as he is presented in the Book of Job. There was no judge above him; he was supreme. He could not be judged so whatever he did, one could only say it just happened like that—one didn't know why. He is an amoral figure and therefore of course no devil is needed; there the devil is in the deity itself. But in Christianity it is quite different. There the evil principle is split off and God is only good. I cannot go into the historical structure of Christianity here, but I spoke about the problem in my Yale lectures.

Miss Wolff: In answer to Mrs. Baynes' question one might say that she seems to overlook the fact that when the fourth principle, which in Christianity is the devil, is added to the Trinity we have an entirely different situation. The principles of good and evil are then no longer in absolute opposition, but are inter-related and influence each other, and the result is an entirely new configuration. And when there is no devil in the Christian sense anymore, there can be no devil worship either. The bewilderment we feel is perhaps due to the theological formulation of the problem. If we look at it from the side of human ex-

[3] In the Terry Lectures delivered at Yale University in 1937, Jung argued that the embodiment of evil in the figure of a devil better recognized the dark side of the world than the supposition that evil is merely the absence of good (CW 11, pars. 248, 463).

perience, from the moral aspect for instance, we know quite well that we cannot be only good, but our bad side has also to be lived somehow.

Prof. Jung: I understood Mrs. Baynes to mean that if there was an idea of a positive god and a negative god, there would be what one could call "devil worship," but I should call it a consideration: it has to do with consideration more than with obligation or devotion. To consciously take into account the existence of an evil factor would be the psychological equivalent of devil worship. Of course that is quite different from those cults that worshipped the devil under the symbol of a peacock, for instance. That was just the Christian devil, Satan, and they worshipped him because they thought he could do more for them than God. So in the 12th and 13th centuries in France, in those times of terrible plagues and wars and famines, they worshipped the devil by means of the black mass. They reverted to the devil because they said God didn't hear them any longer. He had become quite inclement and didn't accept their offerings, so they had to apply to some other factor. They began to worship the devil because, since God didn't help, they thought the devil would do better and it could not be worse. But of course it has nothing to do with all that; when you come to psychology you cannot keep on thinking in the same terms as before.

For instance, when you know you have created a figure, you naturally can't worship it as you could worship a figure which you have not created. If you grow up in the conviction that there is a good God in heaven, you can worship that good God, as a little child can worship the father who he knows does exist because he can see that god. That is a sort of childlike confidence and faith, which is no longer possible if you have begun to doubt the existence of a God—or the existence of a good God at least. So it is quite impossible to fall back into devil worship when you know that you have just barely succeeded in constructing a very poor devil—a pretty poor figure you know. It will be a poor vessel because you will be eaten away by doubt all the time you are constructing it. It is just as if you were building a house and the weather was beating it down as fast as you build it. You will have the greatest trouble in the world to create such a figure and assume it does exist, just because you yourself have created it. The only justification for the effort is that, if you don't do it, you will have it in your system. Or the poison will be in somebody else and then you will be just as badly off. But if you succeed in catching that hypothetical liquid in a vessel in between you and your enemy, things will work out much better. You will be less poisoned and the other will be less poisoned and something will have been done after all. You see, we can only conclude from the effect and the effect is wholesome. If I am on bad terms with somebody and tell him he is a devil and all wrong, how can I discuss with him? I only shout at him and beat him down. If we project our devils into each other, we are both just poor victims. But let us assume that neither of us is a devil, but a devil is there between us to whom we can talk and who will listen. Then, providing my partner can do the same, we can assume that for the love of mankind, sure enough we shall be able to understand each other. At least we have a chance. And if we cannot, we shall conclude that here the separating element is too great: we must give way to it—there must be a reason. For I am quite against forcing. For instance, if a patient has an unsurmountable resistance against me, there must be a reason, and if I cannot construct the corresponding figure, if I cannot figure it out, we give in; he goes his way and I go mine. There is no misunderstanding, no hatred, because we have both understood that there is a superior factor between us, and we must not work against such a thing. It is a case of devil-worship again, and we must give in to the separating factor.

Mr. Baumann: You have just mentioned the confidence and faith that children have in a good God. What do you think about the saying of Christ: if you are not like a little child you will not enter the kingdom of Heaven? Is that wrong?

Prof. Jung: No, that is right—but not according to the ordinary theological understanding of it. Their idea is that if you don't remain a child, if you don't develop your childlike feeling, you won't be able to enter the kingdom of heaven. But that is a downright lie. Christ said, if you do not become *like* children and "become" means that in the meantime you have become highly adult. Also you must remember that he preached to the Jews and not to the good Christians of our days, and the Jews believed in the law and in following the law. Their belief was that if the father and mother died the good son had to give them a decent burial. But Christ said unto them, "Let the dead bury their dead." And in the temple, as a boy twelve years old, he said to his own mother: What have I to do with you? What I am belongs to me, you must vanish.[4] That was against the law; the teaching of Christ was that they should give up their belief in the law, that he was the fulfiller of all laws, of all predictions. So he demanded a complete revolution, which is adult business. That is a supreme decision which cannot be

---

[4] Jesus: "Let the dead bury their dead" (Matthew 8:22). Here Jung conflates two incidents. The question was asked at the wedding at Cana (John 2:4). As a boy in the temple he said to his mother who has been anxiously searching for him, "Did you not know that I had to be in my Father's house?" (Luke 2:46-49).

made in a childlike spirit. Those people had to overcome an inevitable conflict, for it is good to behave according to the law, and it is bad not to respect the law.

For instance, when Christ spoke to that man who was working on the Sabbath in the fields: If thou knowest what thou art doing thou art blessed. Naturally the disciples must have jumped out of their skins. It is as if I should say to a criminal: If you *know* that you are a murderer, you are blessed. Of course we could not stomach such a thing. To work on the Sabbath was a mortal offence in those days. It means nothing to us naturally. If a man even on Christmas day is chopping wood perhaps, we don't consider it a mortal offence—but it looked like murder to those old Jews. So when he says we must become like children, it means: be as adult as you can, suffer that supreme conflict, that terrible collision between duty to the law, to your parents, to the whole tradition. And on the other side is the insight that the law is not the last word, that there is another word, redemption from evil. The law never gives you that; Christ gives you redemption from evil. This was a new thought. Now the decision can only be made by an adult mind, and when you have made that decision, *then* become like a little child. That is what Christ meant, not that we should become like sheep.

Mrs. Jung: The attitude of the child doesn't only consist of complete confidence; it includes also the fear of dark powers.

Prof. Jung: Oh yes, when Christ says you should become like unto children he obviously means that you should have the attitude of a child, and then we have to discover what that is. Is it a rational attitude? Is it philosophical? No, it is exceedingly simple; a child's attitude gives way to all the intimations of nature. And then we understand that apocryphal saying of Jesus: "The fowls of the air, and all beasts that are under the earth or upon the earth, and the fishes of the sea, these are they that draw you; and the Kingdom of Heaven is within you."[5] This means that the instincts then come into play. You see, these ideas began to get very difficult, because a child has implicit faith. It is not unlike an animal—therefore that saying about the animals and about the lilies in the field, for instance—and that complete confidence is an extraordinary sacrifice, almost impossible. So it is nothing simple from the standpoint of an adult being, and this demand of Christianity has forever remained unfulfilled because it cannot be fulfilled.

Mrs. Sigg: I think Prof. Zimmer has given us a most valuable contri-

---

[5] Jung is here citing an attempted restoration of the mutilated third-century *Oxyrhynchus Papyrus*. See *Apocrypha*, p. 26.

bution to the question of accepting the reverse side, in his description of the way the Indian deals with that question. It is in his book *Kunstform und Yoga in Indischen Kultbild*. There he gives a real technique.

Prof. Jung: There are many ways of dealing with this problem. I mentioned the Christian way of becoming like a child; but there are Eastern ways which are quite different, and even in our Middle Ages we had a different way. You see, the way of the child has been preached by the church, the church taking the attitude of being the father and mother, and all the others being children. The pope never had to assume that he was perhaps one of the children, nor did the cardinals. But we must not be unjust; the pope has a very simple priest as father confessor, which shows that they make it as true as possible and that even the pope is as human as possible. It is quite unjust when the Protestants accuse the pope of megalomania on account of the claim that he is invulnerable; that has only to do with his office. There is the same assumption in another field, in the claim that the church is a divine institution and therefore invulnerable. There are doubts about that however. We are not certain that it is a divine institution. That is a compromise of man, and the fact that one ought to become like a child is not fulfilled.

Mrs. von Roques: A child understands so very well; if a child is naughty he will say, "Send the naughty dog away," for instance. The child understands that there is something in him which can be sent away.

Prof. Jung: Well, there are many reasons why Christ said what he did about children, and one can go a long stretch along the road with him on that question of the child. But the theological interpretation causes trouble in the end; ultimately it becomes impossible. That is the reason why there is no *consensus gentium* about it; only a sort of school, I should say, prefers that solution. In the East, and even in Europe in the Middle Ages, they had another idea, but you know it was not very healthy to have other ideas, as today it is not very healthy.

Dr. Escher: There are historic examples of devotion to the devil as a sort of moral act, the sacrifice of the most valuable things to a cruel god. The Phoenicians and the Carthaginians threw their first-born child into the fiery mouth of the statue of Baal, hoping that he would work in their favor afterwards. Abraham was the first to turn the sacrifice of a child into the sacrifice of a ram (*Agnum pro vicario*). And sacrificing their virginity in the temple of the *Magna Mater* was supposed to bring good luck to women for the rest of their lives.

Prof. Jung: Yes, we have plenty of evidence in the old cults that there

were very gruesome deities. There was no hesitation in calling the earlier gods devils, as there was no hesitation in calling Zeus and all the
other inhabitants of Olympus devils later on, on account of the fact that
they were a peculiar mixture of good and evil. People have always
taken care just of the more dangerous gods—naturally you would pay
more attention to a dangerous god than to one from whom you would
expect something better. The primitives are shameless in that respect.
They say; "Why should we worship the great gods who never harm
mankind? They are all right. We must worship the bad spirits because
they are dangerous." You see, that makes sense and if you apply that
very negative principle to our hero Zarathustra you reach pretty much
the same conclusion. The figure of Zarathustra is practically perfect,
and the dangerous thing that causes no end of panic to Nietzsche is the
shadow, the dark Zarathustra. If Nietzsche could give more recognition, or even a sort of homage, to all that negative side of Zarathustra,
it surely would help him. For he is all the time in the greatest danger
of poisoning himself in assuming that the dangerous thoughts of that
fellow are his own thoughts; and since he makes such introjections, he
cannot help including the big figures. He has to introject Zarathustra
too and even the heavens, which of course makes quite a nice speech
metaphor but it is not healthy. One could say one was Zeus himself and
the blue sky above, and it is very wonderful, but then one must admit
that one is everything in hell underneath. The one leads inevitably into
the other. So we had better decide that we are neither this nor that; we
had better not identify with the good, for then we have not to identify
with the bad. We must construct those qualities as entities outside ourselves. *There* is good and *there* is evil. I am not good and I am not evil, I
am not the hammer and I am not the anvil. I am the thing in between
the hammer and the anvil. You see, if you are the hammer, then you
are the anvil too; you are the beater and the beaten, and then you are
on the wheel, eternally up and down.

Mrs. Sigg: In the very moment when Nietzsche wrote that letter to
Burckhardt, identifying himself with God, after the great catastrophe
in Turin, he identified with Caesar Borgia and with a lust murder.

Prof. Jung: Naturally in his disease all these things came out and it is
coming out here already—in the way he identifies with the heavens,
for instance. If I had looked over his shoulder while he was writing this
paragraph I should have said, "Now hold on, think of what you are
writing here—this is dangerous. You say that beautiful blue sky you
worship, or whatever heaven means to you, is *your* depth, and that
means it is yourself, so either heaven is very small or you are very big."

Of course that is the intuitive. He just doesn't stop to pay attention. He swallows the most amazing whales of thoughts and pays no attention at all, and if he has indigestion and headache afterwards, he wonders what has happened.

Whenever Nietzsche makes such a statement we should interfere and ask what it means, what are the implications. You see there he is too much poet and too little philosopher; he doesn't stop to question. He says that heaven is his depth and his innocence—but what then? Or in the following paragraph, ". . . thus hidest thou thy stars. Thou speakest not, thus proclaimest thou thy wisdom unto me." One would think that inasmuch as heaven is himself, he would have learned so much from heaven that *he* would not speak, thus proclaiming his wisdom—but he does speak. Of course he has to speak inasmuch as he is human, but then he is not heaven. Now, all that realization is missing here; he is driven by his intuition. He cannot wait for a realization, and so he swallows one whale after another, which naturally causes a tremendous inflation and indigestion in the end. There are realizations in the subsequent paragraphs, but they are only realizations of possibilities, intuitions, and he draws no conclusions. So that whole thing really passes by him without his realizing, and one can only say it is too bad.

Mrs. Sigg: In my translation he does not say he is heaven. He says, "To throw myself in that height, that is my depth." He doesn't identify with heaven really.

Prof. Jung: Oh, that is pretty much the same: he throws himself into the depths of the heavens, extraordinary distances, and since he couldn't jump so high, it would mean a sort of falling into abysmal depths. And he says it is *his* depth, which is perfectly true.

Mr. Allemann: Is it not the *tabula smaragdina*—the microcosm and the macrocosm?[6]

Prof. Jung: I wish it were. You see, that is a realization, but he doesn't make that realization really. He uses again this unfortunate shield that it is his own—simply introjects it and it remains a speech metaphor. You know the *tabula smaragdina* is a philosophical or metaphysical statement about the structure of the universe: "Ether above, Ether below, heaven above, heaven below, all this above, all this below—take it and be happy." But we can introject into the macrocosm just as well. We can say heaven is here and earth is below: we have all that in ourselves too. In later Hermetic philosophy it surely has been understood

---

[6] See pp. 1533-34 below.

in that way. But the trouble is that Nietzsche is inclined to take it only in the way of a speech metaphor, as his own mental phenomenon. Mind you, if he should say that this world was an illusion and the depth of the heaven was the depth of his own being, it would be true, but then he would write quite a different philosophy. He would not talk about the Superman he was going to create, he would not shout. He would be a hermit or an Indian sage or something like that. And he could not call the beauty of heaven or the superman his own; it is not his, but is outside of him. It is neither this nor that, and later on he will tell you as much. That is the trouble. It is no use defending Nietzsche here; it is a lack, a defect. Now he continues in his quasi realization.

> Mute o'er the raging sea hast thou risen for me today; thy love and thy modesty make a revelation unto my raging soul.

This is the idea of that vision of heaven which would be a remedy for the turmoils of his soul. If he could ask himself, "Why do I think of heaven? Why do I say 'my depth?' "—then he would realize that there was a part which is all peace and another part which is all turmoil, and just as he had to name the part of peace "heaven," he could name the other side, the counterpart, "hell," and it would not be himself. Otherwise he would find himself completely isolated in the world; he would be heaven and we would be something else. So he must create a form in between, which means heaven, and another which means hell—two principles, a pair of opposites, with which he is not identical. You see, the simplicity and modesty of heaven would be helpful if he could only realize it.

> In that thou camest unto me beautiful, veiled in thy beauty, in that thou spakest unto me mutely, obvious in thy wisdom:
> Oh, how could I fail to divine all the modesty of thy soul!

As he said before that heaven was his soul. This could be, "How could I fail to divine the modesty of *my* soul?" But then why not behave accordingly? Why talk? And if that is his soul, then where is the turmoil?

> We have been friends from the beginning: to us are grief, grue-someness, and ground common; even the sun is common to us.
> We do not speak to each other, because we know too much—: we keep silent to each other, we smile our knowledge to each other.
> Art thou not the light of my fire? Hast thou not the sister-soul of mine insight?

Together did we learn everything; together did we learn to as-
cend beyond ourselves to ourselves, and to smile uncloudedly:—

—Uncloudedly to smile down out of luminous eyes and out of
miles of distance, when under us constraint and purpose and guilt
steam like rain.

And wandered I alone, for *what* did my soul hunger by night
and in labyrinthine paths? And climbed I mountains, *whom* did I
ever seek, if not thee, upon mountains?

And all my wandering and mountain-climbing: a necessity was
it merely, and a makeshift of the unhandy one:—to *fly* only, wanteth mine entire will, to fly into *thee*!

It would be better to lay less emphasis upon himself and more upon
the heaven, since the heaven is decidedly a bigger thing than the individual. But if the emphasis is on the human individual, then—according to the Indian notion—the *Purusha* is more than heaven. Heaven
would be only the visible expression of the nature of the *Purusha* and
decidedly less than the *Purusha*, since the *Purusha* is the whole, the sole
and only thing. It is clear that there is no such insight, or there would
have been entirely different consequences. Then it would be a sort of
philosophical understanding, in the highest sense of the word, from
which would necessarily result a philosophical attitude. But that is exactly what does not result in his case, only a sort of ecstasy, an identification with a superior principle, a sort of godlike being—like father
Zeus who sits upon Olympus. He says, "Uncloudedly to smile down out
of luminous eyes and out of miles of distance," but that is much too big.
And he trembles at what he calls his own thoughts, but can you imagine
him being troubled by thoughts which he doesn't even know, merely
supposing that they must be evil? It is a lack of philosophical consciousness, a lack of thinking. We can well believe that he longs to fly into that
heaven, and we don't need to assume that this is an old infantile desire
to fly into the Christian heaven. Probably it was in the beginning, but
we can credit him with a more developed point of view. But it doesn't
really make much difference. It is the desire for redemption, the desire to be redeemed from turmoil. He feels in himself a clarity above
the chaos, an order against the confusion. All that is perfectly clear,
only as I said, it remains words—perhaps beautiful words—but there
is no philosophical realization.

Now, the next paragraphs contain the idea of disturbances, things
that disturb the view of heaven. After having sung that praise of
heaven he instantly feels the onslaught of the dark powers; once more

the clouds come up, and he hates the thunderstorms which veil the sight of heaven till he can no longer see it. That is the acknowledgment that there are powers in him which cloud this perfect beauty. Then at the bottom of this page, after he has spoken of the thunder, the angry drummer, he says,

> For rather will I have noise and thunders and tempest-blasts, than this discreet, doubting cat-repose; and also amongst men do I hate most of all the soft-treaders, and half-and-half ones, and the doubting, hesitating, passing clouds.

He realizes all this in himself, but it is projected into those other fools who do such things. Here he should realize that that is exactly what he is doing. By seeing things without realizing them, he talks about them and doesn't make them true because he doesn't *draw* conclusions, and so he is in the fray as the half-and-half one, the one who has seen and not seen, the one who knows and doesn't know, the one who speaks the great word and doesn't believe it. He is really reviling himself in this paragraph. Now that is the difference between the believer in words, or the fellow with a merely aesthetic attitude that is enchanted by some beauty of thought or of color or of music, and a real philosopher—by which I don't mean a professor of philosophy, who *per definitionem* is never a philosopher, because he merely talks about it and never lives it. A real philosopher draws conclusions which are valid for his life: they are not mere talk. He lives his truth. He doesn't mean a string of words, but a particular kind of life; and even if he doesn't succeed in living it, he at least means it and he *lives* it, more or less.

I have seen such individuals. They were not very wonderful specimens of humanity, but they did not think of a philosophical truth as a string of words, or something sounding clever which was printed in a book. They admitted that a truth is something you can live, and that, whether you live your life or not, the only criterion is life. They were even quite ready to admit that they had perhaps failed in such-and-such a way, or they would tell some small lies about it but they would at least feel apologetic about it and would concede so much to your criticism. I know a fellow, an Eastern philosopher, who I am quite certain plays some dirty tricks like a true Oriental, but he would say that he didn't do such things, and it would not be just a mean lie. He would lie in spite of his conviction that a truth is only a truth inasmuch as you live it. But our philosophy—heavens, it is perfectly ridiculous! To a Western professor of philosophy, no way of life has ever to do with his philosophy. That is a theory of cognition and life is a different case: it doesn't touch cognition. You see, that is our Western prejudice, our belief in words, and it seduces Nietzsche and handicaps him. We don't understand what realization means. The Eastern man says that is the main thing, and we don't even understand the problem. We say, "*what* realization?"—it means nothing to us. When you find yourself saying, "That is my depth," what do you mean? What are the implications of that thought? What are the ultimate consequences when you try to live it, to make it true? You see, we cannot realize: we are those fellows who are half-and-half, who live in between, who live something quite different from what we think and profess.

Mrs. Sigg: In these chapters, I think the wrong high tones are because Nietzsche was lifted up to those ideals by the school and the church.

Prof. Jung: Of course, that is exactly what I mean: the intellectual milieu in Germany was handed out to him by tons.

Mrs. Sigg: And therefore, to counteract that tragic inclination, forced on him by the spirit of the time, it would seem that the world really needed the word of a Swiss psychologist: Thou shalt not strive after the good and beautiful, but after your own being.

Prof. Jung: Well, unfortunately his friend Jakob Burckhardt did not tell him that the only thing to do was to keep as mum as possible. Burckhardt was an anxious soul who did not like to mix himself up in such matters. He even preferred to say he was too old and too stupid. He was too sly an old fox to put his finger into that pie.

Mrs. Sigg: But I did not mean Jakob Burckhardt.

Prof. Jung: But *I* meant him!

Mr. Allemann: Buddhists consider the aptitude for realization as necessary in order to progress on the path of knowledge, and in order to convey the meaning of "realization" they give the following example: Everybody comes into contact with illness, old age, and death, but most people simply register the fact and pass on. When Buddha came to see illness, old age, and death, he realized that to live meant to suffer and he began his search for a way out of the wheel of Samsara.

Prof. Jung: That is an excellent example. To know what the East means by realization, read the sermons of the Buddha, chiefly those from the middle collection of the Pali-canon.[7] They are quite illuminating, a most systematic education toward the utmost consciousness.

---

[7] "In Ceylon, about 80 B.C., the early Buddhistic canon was committed to writing. This corpus of sacred literature—the often cited Pali canon—is preserved, probably without much alteration to the present" (Zimmer/*Philosophies*, p. 499).

He says that whatever you do, do it consciously, know that you do it; and he even goes so far as to say that when you eat and when you drink, know it, and when you satisfy your physical needs, all the functions of your body, know it. That is realization—not for one moment to be without realization. You must always know what you do, and also *who* is doing it. And that is exactly the realization which is lacking with us. You see, nowadays the thing which is shouted into our ears all the time—and probably all over America too—is that we must take the responsibility for this or that: "There is a fellow who takes on the responsibility, he says he will do it!" That sounds, of course, wonderful; we are all waiting for such a fellow. But is nobody going to enquire who that fellow is? For instance, if your business was in a mess and a fellow came along and said to hand it over to him and he would take care of it, you would naturally say, "That is all right, but who are you?" But you might be blindfolded; if you have only the collective consciousness of actual Europe, you would be thankful and assume that this was really the fellow who would take care of it. And then you hear that the fellow is bankrupt in his own business, which he knew nothing about, and is perhaps a swindler, so how can he take over the responsibility? But we don't ask that; we are quite satisfied that somebody takes it on. Look at all the politicians! Well now, there is only one thing more to mention in this chapter. Half way down on the next page, Nietzsche says,

> "Of Hazard"—that is the oldest nobility in the world; that gave I back to all things; I emancipated them from bondage under purpose.
> This freedom and celestial serenity did I put like an azure bell above all things, when I taught that over them and through them, no "eternal Will"—willeth.
> This wantonness and folly did I put in place of that Will, when I taught that "In everything there is one thing impossible—rationality!"

This is like that very witty philosopher who said: "Nothing is quite true and even that is not quite true."[8]

> A little reason, to be sure, a germ of wisdom scattered from star to star—this leaven is mixed in all things; for the sake of folly, wisdom is mixed in all things!

[8] E. D. Decker, an obscure nineteenth-century Dutch philosopher who wrote under the name of Multatuli.

This insight we owe to Nietzsche. He is one of the first protagonists for irrationalism, a great merit considering that he lived in a time of extreme positivism and rationalism. In our days it doesn't make so much sense any longer; we have to go back fifty or sixty years to understand the full value of such a passage. He was surely the only one of his time who had the extraordinary courage to insist upon the thoroughly irrational nature of things, and also upon the feeling value of such a world. A world that was exclusively rational would be absolutely divested of all feeling values, and so we could not share it, as we cannot share the life of a machine. It is as if we were now thoroughly convinced of the fact that we are living beings, and a machine after all is not a living being but a premeditated rational device. And we feel that we are not premeditated rational devices; we feel that we are a sort of experiment, say an experiment of nature, or, to express it modestly, of hazard. Things somehow came together and finally it happened that man appeared. It was an experiment and forever remains an experiment. So we can say it is the oldest nobility in the world, that we all come from a sort of hazard, which means that there is nothing rational about it; it has nothing to do with any device.

That is a very important realization because it breaks the old traditional belief, which was almost a certainty, that we are sort of useful and intended structures and are here for a certain definite purpose. Then we are naturally in a terrible quandary when we don't see the purpose, when it looks almost as if there were none. That simply comes from our prejudice that things *au fond* are somehow rational, but that is impossible—probably a childish prejudice which still has to do with the idea that God premeditated a machine which turned out to be the world, and which works in a way like a clock. We have been infected with that point of view, but that is trust in a father, in a premeditating, exceedingly wise and clever old man who sits in his workshop and pulls the strings, having calculated the clockwork of the whole world. Inasmuch as we believe that, we are just *fils à papa*, we live provisionally. But it is absolutely necessary, if we want to get anywhere, to cut off those imaginary strings, for there *are* no strings. And that is what Nietzsche tried to do, to convey the idea that there are no such strings, no such premeditations, no such *papa à fils* that sits behind the scene and manipulates the string that leads him from the stage of the dear little child to the good, better, best. It may be, and it is even probable, that the thing is not arranged, that it is really accidental.

And here I want to remind you of those old books by Daudet, *Tar-*

tarin de Tarasçon and *Tartarin sur les Alpes*.[9] Tartarin thought that the dangers of the Alps were simply arranged by a limited company who had bought those places and arranged them to look dangerous, so he walked up the Jungfrau as if it were nothing. He knew all about it. But then he went up Mont Blanc and there he suddenly discovered that the thing was not fake. Then doubt assailed him and instantly he was in an absolutely blue funk. You see, that blue funk is what we try to prevent—we might feel lost. But only if we can feel lost, can we experience that the water also carries us; nobody learns to swim as long as he believes that he has to support his weight in the water. You must be able to trust the water, trust that the water really carries your weight, and then you can swim. That is what we have to learn from the world.

[9] Alphonse Daudet, father of Leon Daudet, *Tartarin de Tarasçon* (1877), and *Tartarin sur les Alpes* (1885). Tartarin was a genial teller of tall tales.

AUTUMN TERM

October / December 1938

LECTURE I

19 October 1938

Prof. Jung:

Ladies and Gentlemen: On the way of the "eternal return" we come back to our old *Zarathustra* once more. We will begin with the 49th chapter, "The Bedwarfing Virtue." It would be impossible to give a resumé of what has been said in the preceding chapters. As a matter of fact so much has been said that it becomes wellnigh impossible even to remember it. *Zarathustra* is such a bewildering phenomenon, there are so many diverse aspects, that one could hardly make a whole of it. Moreover, *Zarathustra* itself is not a whole; it is, rather, a river of pictures and it is difficult to make out the laws of the river, how it moves, or toward what goal it is meandering.

If you take the preceding chapter, "Before Sunrise," and now "The Bedwarfing Virtue," you cannot see exactly why the one should follow the other. You only have a sort of dull sensation that somehow it is moving correctly, somehow making sense, but nobody could say what sense. This is a very typical quality of all products of the unconscious. The unconscious contents flow out in such a seemingly chaotic river, which meanders on through nature, and only the water can tell what the next move will be. We cannot tell because we are unable to perceive the small differences in the potential, the incline of the soil, but the water knows and follows it. It seems to be a thoroughly unconscious, unpurposive movement that just follows natural gravity. It happens to begin somewhere and it happens to end somewhere. One cannot say that this makes any particular sense, as one cannot say—as was formerly said—that it is due to the wonderful foresight and grace of God that a river is near every town, another proof of the divine providence in nature. One has the uncanny impression of something inhuman, and it is impossible to speculate about it because there is absolutely no ground for speculation; one is simply impressed with the abysmal depths of the meanings of nature.

Nevertheless, one has all the time a certain feeling that somewhere there is perhaps a secret goal. Otherwise, we would never be able to concentrate upon such a book, as we could never concentrate upon the enormous problem of why the Danube is making for the Black Sea, or why the Rhine runs north. Works like *Zarathustra* are at least born out of man; it is the nature process in a human psyche. And it would be absolutely desperate if we should come to the conclusion that, where consciousness doesn't give purposes or ends, the natural functioning of the psyche necessarily leads to a merely incidental solution, that it ends in the Black Sea. For then it would not be worthwhile to speculate about the life of the psyche. Since, however, we have a certain intuition, or a feeling, of some purpose underneath, we think it worthwhile to concentrate upon such a work, and to try to find out whether there is not really a secret design in the whole thing, perhaps one which never appears clearly upon the surface, or in other words, a purpose which has never become conscious to the author himself. Now Nietzsche begins this chapter in the following way,

> When Zarathustra was again on the continent, he did not go straightway to his mountains and his cave, but made many wanderings and questionings, and ascertained this and that; so that he said of himself jestingly: "Lo, a river that floweth back unto its source in many windings!" For he wanted to learn what had taken place among men during the interval: whether they had become greater or smaller.

In his remark: "Lo, a river that floweth back into its source in many windings!" we have that meandering movement we were speaking of, and also the extraordinary idea that the river doesn't flow on to its natural end, but back to its own source. What form would the river produce by that movement?

Mrs. Schevill: The snake, winding back on itself.

Mrs. Baumann: The *ouroborus*.

Prof. Jung: Yes, the snake biting its own tail, which forms the symbol of eternity and was one of the main subjects of medieval speculation. It returns to the place where it started and so it forms something like a circle, even though the circle may be interrupted by many meanderings. So that gives us at once a symbol. And Zarathustra is himself struck by his movements; he seems bewildered that he is not going straight to his cave. He wonders about his meanderings—as he says, "wanderings and questionings," many hesitations, stumbling over this stone and that stone—and he comes to the conclusion that it is like a river which seeks its own source, not its end but its source. We don't know whether Nietzsche himself realized what that means, presumably not, because he makes nothing of it. It remains one of his ideas which he leaves there on the shore while he continues his wanderings, paying no attention to it. But later on that idea will come up again and again; this is another indication of that future thought, one of Nietzsche's most important thoughts.

Mrs. Sigg: Die ewige Wiederkunft.

Prof. Jung: Yes, the idea of the eternal return is indicated here, the idea that life, or the life of the psyche more probably, is an eternal return, a river which seeks its own source and not the goal, the end. It returns to the source, thereby producing a circular movement which brings back whatever has been. Here we can use another nice Greek term, the *apokatastasis*, which means the return of everything that has been lost, a complete restoration of whatever has been. We find that idea of the eternal return also in Christianity, in the Epistles of St. Paul, where he speaks of the mystical or metaphysical significance of Christ, and our importance in his work of redemption. He says that all creatures are sighing in fetters and expecting the revelation of the children of God, meaning that man has an importance as the savior for the whole of nature. All creation groaneth and travaileth in pain, fettered, unfree, and through the manifestation of the children of God, the whole of nature will be led back into the original state of completeness and innocence. The same idea is in the cabala of which St. Paul was a connoisseur. Who was his teacher?

Mrs. Sigg: Gamaliel.

Prof. Jung: Yes, Rabbi Gamaliel the Elder, who was a Jewish Gnostic, what was called later on a "cabalist." The old cabalistic tradition about paradise was, that when God saw that the first parents had been imprudent enough to eat of the fruits of the tree, he cast them out, and shut the gates of paradise, and since it was no longer any good, he moved paradise into the future. There you have the same idea. Paradise was the origin of life, where the four rivers arose, and he removed the origin of life into the future and made it a goal. So those rivers which issued from paradise will flow back into paradise in the future. It is a circle, the eternal return. That is probably the historical origin of the idea of the *apokatastasis*, but that life is a circle is psychologically an archetypal idea. Where have we evidence for that? Ethnologists to the foreground!—or primitive psychology, mythology!

Mrs. Fierz: I always wondered whether one could not take that way of burying people in a sitting position as symbolizing a return to the original position of the embryo in the womb.

Prof. Jung: That comes into it.

Mr. Allemann: In German mythology, after the world is destroyed, it returns again to the primordial condition.

Prof. Jung: Yes, that is the eternal return. And there is also the typical hero-myth, where the idea of the restoration of all the past is very clear. When the dragon has swallowed the hero and absolutely everything belonging to him, his brothers, his parents and grandparents, the whole tribe, herds of cattle, even the woods and fields, then the hero kills the dragon, and all that the dragon has devoured comes back as it was before. You see, the idea that everything returns as it has been would mean that time comes to an end. To express it more philosophically, if the flux of time can be done away with, then everything is, everything exists, because things only appear and disappear in time. If time is abolished, nothing disappears and nothing appears—unless it is already there and then it needs must be! So that idea of the eternal return means really the abolition of time; time would be suspended.

Now, this chapter about the bedwarfing virtue is one of the meanderings. He is now coming again to human beings and wonders about men.

And once, when he saw a row of new houses, he marvelled, and said:

"What do these houses mean? Verily, no great soul put them up as its simile!

Did perhaps a silly child take them out of its toy-box? Would that another child put them again into the box!

And these rooms and chambers—can men go out and in there? They seem to be made for silk dolls; or for dainty-eaters, who perhaps let others eat with them."

And Zarathustra stood still and meditated. At last he said sorrowfully: "There hath everything become smaller!

Everywhere do I see lower doorways: he who is of my type can still go therethrough, but—he must stoop!

Oh, when shall I arrive again at my home, where I shall no longer have to stoop—shall no longer have to stoop before the small ones!" And Zarathustra sighed, and gazed into the distance.

The same day, however, he gave his discourse on the bedwarfing virtue.

He is particularly impressed with that change in size. What has happened to Zarathustra that he suddenly becomes aware of the exceedingly small size of his contemporaries?

Mrs. Fierz: He has become bigger.

Prof. Jung: Yes, since it is not very probable that many people would change in any particular aspect, since they are practically the same as they ever were, changing perhaps in millions of years but not in a hundred years, it is very much more probable that Nietzsche the man has changed. And that would be symptomatic for what psychological condition?

Mrs. Fierz: His inflation.

Prof. Jung: Yes. Now we have long ago discussed the fact very thoroughly that Zarathustra himself is the archetypal figure of the wise old man. Therefore Nietzsche chose the name of Zarathustra, who was the founder of a religion, a great wise man. So that name should express the peculiar quality of the archetype by which Nietzsche himself is possessed. You see, anyone possessed by an archetype cannot help having all the symptoms of an inflation. For the archetype is nothing human; no archetype is properly human. The archetype itself is an exaggeration and it reaches beyond the confines of humanity. The archetype of the wise old man, for instance, is nothing but wise, and that is not human. Anyone who has any claim to wisdom is always cursed with a certain amount of foolishness. And a god is nothing but power in essence, with no drawback or qualification. Another reason why the archetypes are not quite human is that they are exceedingly old. I don't know whether one should even speak of age because they belong to the fundamental structure of our psyche. If one could ascribe any origin to the archetypes, it would be in the animal age; they reach down into an epoch where man could hardly be differentiated from the animal. And that entirely unconscious background of the archetypes gives them a quality which is decidedly inhuman. So anybody possessed by an archetype develops inhuman qualities. One could say that a man possessed by his anima was all-too-human, but all-too-human is already inhuman. You see, man is a certain optimum between all-too-human and superhuman or inhuman, so all-too-human is on the way to inhumanity. Therefore, inasmuch as Nietzsche is possessed by Zarathustra, the archetype of the wise old man, he loses human proportions and becomes uncertain about his size.

Sometimes people who are possessed by an unconscious figure—the anima or the animus or the wise old man or the great mother, for instances—become uncertain even about their own looks. I had a patient who always carried a little mirror in her pocket in order to make out what she was like, and if she didn't look in this mirror before her analytic hour, she couldn't remember. Or this inhumanity may be projected into the analyst, which explains why people have often believed that I have a wonderful white beard and blue eyes, or that I am blond at least. Many people are uncertain about their looks. They are always astonished when they look in the mirror—either shocked or they think they look quite nice perhaps, which merely shows that they are unacquainted even with themselves. And one's feeling about one's size can also be affected; one sometimes feels decidedly small for instance. We have an expression for this in our Swiss patois: we say that one feels three cheeses high, which would be about the size of a dwarf. One feels perhaps that one's size has decreased, or that one is suddenly very tall, and that is always according to the size of the possession. One is possessed by a certain thought which was originally an archetype, and if one personifies that thought or possession one arrives at an archetypal figure. To be possessed by a dwarf makes one feel small, and to be possessed by a great figure makes one stretch and grow tall, and one likes or dislikes one's looks accordingly. So what has happened here to Nietzsche is a symptom of inflation and of possession and it is a very ordinary human feeling. Nietzsche himself, the author, expresses its value to him but he projects it. Now why does he project such subjective conditions?

Remark: He doesn't realize it.

Prof. Jung: That is the point, and therefore he could project it. But why should he not realize that he is bigger? When something happens to us and we project it into other people, why don't we recognize that it is our own fact, that it belongs to us?

Mr. Allemann: Because we are not conscious of it.

Remark: Because we are possessed by it.

Prof. Jung: But why are we not conscious of it? Why are we accessible to possessions?

Miss Hannah: Because its realization is too disagreeable.

Prof. Jung: And what is so disagreeable about the feeling of being possessed? What might it produce?

Miss Hannah: It might go as far as madness.

Prof. Jung: Well yes, but I want to know how you would feel about a possession if you knew of it?

Miss Hannah: Horrid, because you don't know what is going to happen next.

Prof. Jung: Yes, it would be just as if you were sinking into your bed and then discover that somebody is already there. It is questionable whether you would like that. Or as if you were alone in your house and suddenly hear a funny noise and think someone else must be in the place too. Or as if you should climb a mountain thinking you were the very first to reach the top, and then find an old bottle there; you are anticipated, your exertion has been in vain. It is intensely disagreeable to feel that one is not master in one's own house—it is like a defeat. So when one discovers a possession there is a fear about possible events; anything may happen then. One doesn't know what that other fellow might do. He has already taken the liberty of stepping into my room through the window without asking my permission, and he might be up to any kind of trick. That is the reason why we prefer to deny the possession even if we know it. Therefore if you hear a queer noise when you think you are alone in your house, your first reaction is: it is not possible. Because it would be disagreeable to have burglars in the house, you try to deny that you have heard anything and hope it was a mouse, or the wind, or that a piece of furniture has creaked. You hope there is a perfectly natural and indifferent explanation. It is exceedingly disagreeable and uncanny to realize a possession, so we prefer to say that nothing has happened at all. If anything has happened, it has happened to the other fellow: *I* am not disagreeable at all; *you* are the disagreeable devil. *I* would be perfectly all right if *you* were not there. That is the way in which we project and that is of course what Nietzsche-Zarathustra is doing here. He doesn't realize his own inflation, but thinks that other people have become smaller. Now if you assume that all the other people become smaller, what would be your conclusion in regard to such a perception?

Mr. Allemann: I am all right and all the others are wrong.

Prof. Jung: Yes, and that gives tremendous satisfaction—*I* am the fellow. To be beyond human size gives you a great advantage over the others. Not that you are in any way supernatural, you may admit you are only the normal size, but the others are underfed and undersized. Then you are on top of the whole business. But you also might draw another more edifying conclusion if you are intellectual or have a more scientific mind, which Nietzsche decidedly has not. Or you need only have an imagination plastic enough to make a picture of such a case—that you are in a crowd of people who are all two feet high, while you have remained the ordinary size. What would a scientific consciousness say then?

Mrs. Sigg: That something is not quite right.

Prof. Jung: That is too vague. You would say it was a miracle. And a scientist might say: "It is an optical delusion; I have perhaps the wrong spectacles." Or: "*They* are human beings, and I am a human being too. Nothing has happened to me, so how do I explain this?" He would look at himself at once and thus he would discover that that projection of smallness was because he himself had decreased in size. He would discover that they were normal and he had diminished; he had projected it. This would be a very normal conclusion. And Nietzsche would inevitably come to the same conclusion if he could only apply a scientific consciousness. You see, in an inflation, you as a human being are smaller than ever before, because vis à vis the possessive spirit or whatever it is, you have lost your importance. So anyone who is possessed is really very small; his humanity has fallen below its normal size and has become a dwarf. Nietzsche himself is here a dwarf and therefore he arrives at the funny title, "The Bedwarfing Virtue." And whatever he says in this chapter will be a *ressentiment* against that thing which has bedwarfed him. He would not admit that he was dwarfed, and he doesn't see what is dwarfed—he only has the *ressentiment* from being dwarfed—and like everyone having a possession, he accuses the whole world of being against him, underrating him and making him small, which is absolutely unjust.

In the next part, Nietzsche steps down to the bedwarfed people and busies himself with a very thorough critique of their psychology. I won't read the whole text but I recommend your studying it attentively. You will see that he is moved by a strong resentment against the small people; he reviles them properly. That is of course somewhat disproportionate; he should be quite satisfied with the fact that they are now little dwarfs who are punished enough and could be passed by. But that they are already punished by fate doesn't satisfy him in the least. Why not?

Mrs. Sigg: Because he himself is so small in some parts of his being.

Mrs. Fierz: But he must always be again confronted with this fact; something in him always pushes him into a situation where he is confronted with it, so that he may get another chance.

Prof. Jung: Well, that is the typically neurotic way—it is a neurotic fact in Nietzsche. He projects that idea of smallness, which is not of course satisfactory. If it were real, he could have pity on them that fate had punished them so awfully, but something in him knows that they are not small, so he must make them smaller; therefore his projection. You see, you are not satisfied when you project, so you must help it along, because you are always threatened with the disagreeable possibility of suddenly discovering that it is only a projection. So you must defend your projection with great insistence on account of that fear lurking in the background of discovering that you are wrong. It is rather unfair that those people are so punished by God; one would think he could let it go, but no, he insists upon it. And so he goes on through several paragraphs reviling the dwarfs, which would make no sense at all if it were true. But it isn't, and therefore he has to insist upon it.

Now, when people have such a critical and resentful attitude they will of course make many mistakes in their judgments and criticisms of others, but since we are all human, naturally we always have somewhere a hook on which a projection can be hung. And a projection often hits the nail on the head—*a* nail, at least; not every nail. There is something in it, so in a certain way you can say a projection is also an organ of cognition. Of course it is wrong to make a projection, but there is that much justification, for you thereby discover the nail on which you have hung something. The coat which you have hung on that nail naturally covers the whole figure and that gives it a wrong aspect, a wrong quality, but if you take the coat off the nail, that nail remains and is true. So when someone who is increased by a projection becomes very critical of his surroundings, he will discover a number of nails which he has not noticed before and his projection will hit those nails on the head. A projection is an unjustifiable exaggeration, but the nail is not. So certain points which Nietzsche sees and criticizes are absolutely correct, and they show him to be a remarkable psychologist; he is one of the greatest psychologists that ever lived, on account of his discoveries.[1] He saw certain things very clearly and pointed them out even cruelly, but they are truths—of course disagreeable truths. If such truths are declared in a certain tone of voice, it is undermining, destructive and inhuman.

Now I will pick out some remarks which seem to me to be particularly interesting and important for our psychology. Thus, he says,

> Some of them *will*, but most of them are *willed*. Some of them are genuine, but most of them are bad actors.
>
> There are actors without knowing it amongst them, and actors without intending it, the genuine ones are always rare, especially the genuine actors.

Here he makes a very apt remark which is also characteristic of himself; in fact, if he realizes what he is saying here he really ought to see his projection. For he sees clearly that very few individuals have con-

---

[1] For Nietzsche as psychologist, see above pp. 120, 120n, 745-46. Jung's tribute to Nietzsche as psychologist is like Nietzsche's to Stendhal and Dostoevsky, and Freud's to Shakespeare and other poets.

scious intentions, or are capable of conscious decisions, of saying "I will." Most of them are willed, which means that they are the victims of their so-called will. Naturally he should turn that conclusion round and apply it to himself. He should ask himself, "Am I the one who wills, or am I perhaps willed—am I perhaps a victim? Am I a genuine actor or a bad actor?" But it is characteristic of Nietzsche throughout the book that very rarely does his judgment return to himself. We shall presently come to a place where suddenly that whole difficult tendency turns round to himself, and only with great difficulty could he ward it off and keep it in a box where it wouldn't hurt him too much. But here he shows no sign of applying it to himself; he simply harangues the others. Of course he is right in his conclusion that most people are not capable of willing; they are willed, they simply represent the living thing in themselves without deciding for or against it. Even their decisions, even their moral conflicts, are mere demonstrations of the living thing in them; they merely happen.

And it is very difficult to say to what extent we all function in that way. Nobody would dare to say that he is not a mere actor of himself, of the basic self that lives in him. We cannot tell how far we are liberated, or partially liberated, from the compulsion of the unconscious, even in our most perfect accomplishments or highest aspirations. We are perhaps the actors, the implements, the toolbox of a being greater than ourselves, greater at least in having more volume or periphery in which we are contained. This difficulty always exists because we don't know enough about the unconscious; the unconscious is that which we do not know, therefore we call it the unconscious. We cannot tell how far it reaches, and we can never say, "Here I am absolutely free," because even our freedom may be a role assigned to us which we have to play. It may be that we are all genuine actors to a certain extent, and then to another extent bad actors and even fools, who have thought the truth to be "I will." For man is most foolish when he says "I will"; that is the greatest illusion. The idea that one is a bad actor is a smaller illusion, and the idea that one is a genuine actor is the smallest illusion if it is an illusion at all.

It is curious that Nietzsche should not arrive at such conclusions, but there was a lack of knowledge, for which one cannot make him responsible. It would have helped him if he could have known a bit more about Eastern philosophy—if he had known, for instance, such a sentence as this, "One should play the role of the king, of the beggar, and of the criminal, being conscious of the gods." This is a piece of Eastern wisdom: namely, that the one who is king should be conscious of the fact that he is king only as another is a beggar, or a criminal, or a thief. It is the role he is given: he *finds* himself in a certain situation which is called "king"; another one is called "beggar," or "thief," and each one has to fulfil that role, never forgetting the gods that have assigned the role to him. This is a very superior point of view which we miss in Nietzsche altogether through a lack of consciousness of himself in a way, a lack of self-critique, never looking at himself in a reflective way, never mirroring himself in the mirror of his own understanding. He is only infatuated with himself, filled with himself, fascinated, and therefore inflated.

Of man there is little here: therefore do their women masculinise themselves. For only he who is man enough, will—*save the woman* in woman.

This is a very curious remark. If he meant by "man" the human being, it would be rather understandable, for the less one is conscious of one's own role, or the less one is conscious of oneself, the less one is human, because one is then inflated—as he is. But he obviously means man in the sense of sex, a masculine being, and therefore the conclusion that the women masculinize themselves. So he finds a sort of effeminacy in the men of his actual time; the tendency of women to masculinize themselves corresponds to the effeminization of men. Now this is a strange fact. The emanicipation of women, which began in his time, was one of the first symptoms of this tendency in women. He doesn't speak of the corresponding tendency in men—of course not—but he makes that statement, which was of course a blow in the face of his time, because those men did not imagine that they were particularly effeminate: men never assume that. But in women it became disagreeably obvious, in Mrs. Pankhurst and such people for example;[2] that whole tendency of making sort-of men out of women was particularly striking. The effeminization of men was not so obvious, but as a matter of fact there is something very peculiar about the men of today: there are very few real men. This comes from the fact, which you discover when you look at men closely and with a bit of poisonous projection, that most of them are possessed by the anima—practically all. Of course I exclude myself! And women are all slightly possessed by their

[2] Emmeline Gouldner Pankhurst (1858-1928) began her career as suffragist mildly enough, but grew increasingly ostentatious and even violent. She was jailed in 1914 after an attempt to storm Buckingham Palace, but by 1918 she had helped extend the suffrage in England to women.

ghostly friend the animus, which causes their masculine quality. Now if you mix man and woman in one individual, what do you produce?

Miss Hannah: The hermaphrodite.

Prof. Jung: Yes. So we are all consciously or unconsciously aiming at playing to a certain extent the role of the hermaphrodite; one finds marvelous examples in the ways of women at present in the world. And men do the same, *nolens volens*, but more in the moral sense. They cultivate deep voices and all kinds of masculine qualities, but their souls are like melting butter; as a rule they are entirely possessed by a very doubtful anima. That the unconscious has come up and taken possession of the conscious personality is a peculiarity of our time. I, also, came across that idea quite independently. As a student I read *Zarathustra*, and in 1914 I read it again, but I did not discover that passage. Of course my unconscious might have cast an eye on it, but I would not say that Nietzsche was responsible for that idea in me because I found it myself in the world, in human beings. I consider it a fact: Nietzsche observed correctly, according to my idea. Now what accounts for this fact of the mingling of sexes in one individual? It is the welling up and the inundation of the unconscious. The unconscious takes possession of the conscious, which ought to be a well-defined male or female; but being possessed by the unconscious, it becomes a mixed being, something of the hermaphrodite.

Mrs. Crowley: Has it to do with the extreme emphasis upon rational consciousness in our time—so that there would be a proportionate drag from the unconscious—as if we were more susceptible to its influence because of a one-sided attitude? It could also have to do with his image of the eternal return. We have a parallel in the symbol of the Yang and Yin expressing the eternal alternation of the archetypes. While Yang dominated we had the emphasis upon Logos. Now Yin brings a new code of values and naturally while the old one is disappearing, there is a conflict in the unconscious which has a very disturbing effect upon consciousness.

Prof. Jung: That is a fact, but we ought to have a reason why the unconscious comes up so close to consciousness just as consciousness is detaching itself. There must have been a reason why that did not happen long ago, for we must admit that the consciousness of man has not increased very much since the Middle Ages. We have only gained a sort of horizontal knowledge as it were, but the size of consciousness and its intensity has increased very little. Those men of the Middle Ages were capable of extraordinary concentration of mind—if you consider their works of art for instance, that assiduity, love of detail and so on. They had just as much as the men who work at the microscope in our days. Of course from a dogmatic point of view we are different but, as William James said in speaking of the natural science of our time, our temper is devout. The temper in which we live and work is the same as that of the Middle Ages only the name is different; it is no longer a spiritual subject, but is now called science.[3]

Mrs. Crowley: But then too, there was a sort of marriage of religion and science in the Middle Ages.

Prof. Jung: Yes, but what does account for the fact that now the unconscious is coming up?

Mrs. Baumann: It is because religion doesn't work any longer.

Prof. Jung: Yes, that is one the main reasons. Religion is a very apt instrument to express the unconscious. The main significance of any religion is that its forms and rites express the peculiar life of the unconscious. The relationship between religion and the unconscious is everywhere obvious: all religions are full of figures from the unconscious. Now, if you have such a system or form in which to express the unconscious, it is caught, it is expressed, it lives with you; but the moment that system is upset, the moment you lose your faith and your connection with those walls, your unconscious seeks a new expression. Then naturally it comes up as a sort of chaotic lava into your consciousness, perverting and upsetting your whole conscious system, which is one-sided sexually. A man becomes perverted by the peculiar effeminate quality of the unconscious, and a woman, by the masculine quality. Since there is no longer any form for the unconscious, it inundates the conscious. It is exactly like a system of canals which has somehow been obstructed: the water overflows into the fields and what has been dry land before becomes a swamp. Moreover, Zarathustra is a religious figure and the book is full of religious problems; even the style in which it is written is religious. It is as if all the backwash of Christianity were flowing out; Nietzsche is inundated with all that material which has no longer a place in the church or in the Christian system of symbols. James Joyce at his best is the same, only in his case it is the negation of the Catholic church and the Catholic symbols;[4] the under-

---

[3] For William James (1842-1910), science, unlike religion and his kind of philosophy, was remote, general, and above all impersonal. Though like Jung with a medical degree, he was highly critical of scientists making a religion of their dedication. See especially Lectures XIV and XX in *Varieties of Religious Experience* (London, 1902). Jung got to know James a little when he went to Massachusetts in 1909.

[4] As his protagonist said in *A Portrait of the Artist as a Young Man*, written in 1916, "I will

ground cloacae come up and empty their contents into the conscious because the canals are obstructed.

Miss Wolff: Is the ineffectiveness of the dogma not a parallel phenomenon, rather than a cause, to the overflow of the unconscious? Because we could ask further: what has happened that the Christian symbol does not contain the unconscious any longer?

Prof. Jung: Yes, that would be a further question. Why have we lost our hold on the dogma? But that leads far afield; that is a historical question which has to do with an entirely different orientation of our intellect, the discovery of the world and all that that meant. And it has to do with the necessity of a new understanding which has not been found. The old understanding was that somewhere—perhaps behind the galactic system—God was sitting on a throne and if you used your telescope you might perhaps discover him; otherwise there was no God. That is the standpoint of our immediate past, but what we ought to understand is that these figures are not somewhere in space, but are really given in ourselves. They are right here, only we do not know it. Because we thought we saw them in cosmic distances, we seek them there again. Just as astrologists speak of the stars and of the particular vibrations we get from the constellations, forgetting that, owing to the precession of the equinoxes the astrological positions differ from the astronomical positions. Nothing comes from the stars; it is all in ourselves. In these matters we have not yet made much headway, because it seems to be unspeakably difficult to make people understand the *reality of the psyche*. It is as if it didn't exist; people think it is an illusion, merely an arbitrary invention. They cannot see that in dealing with the psyche, we are dealing with *facts*. But of course not with such facts as they are commonly understood. When, for instance, Mr. X says, "God is," then it neither proves that God is or that he is not. His saying so does not produce God's existence. Therefore people say it means nothing, i.e., it is *no fact*. But the fact is, that Mr. X. believes in God quite irrespectively of the question whether other people hold that God is, or that he is not. Psychical reality is, that people believe in the idea of God or that they disbelieve in it. God is therefore a psychical fact. Neither stones nor plants nor arguments nor theologians prove God's existence; only human consciousness reveals God as a fact, because it is a fact that there is an idea of a divine being in the human mind. This is not the famous argument of Anselm of Canterbury ac-

---

not serve that in which I no longer believe whether it call itself my home, my fatherland or my church" (New York, 1964, p. 245).

cording to which the idea of the most perfect being must necessarily include its existence; otherwise it would not be perfect.[5]

Now the actual psychological circumstances, this peculiar mixture in the character of the sexes, is according to my idea an excellent point. Nietzsche saw that, and of course he could see it so clearly because he had it in himself. A projection is really like having a projector throw your psychology on the screen, so what is small inside you, what you cannot see, you can see there very large and distinct. And so with your projection upon other people; you have only to take it back and say, "That comes from here; here is the lamp and here is the film, and that is myself." Then you have understood something, and that is just what is lacking here. Nietzsche is chiefly critical because his psychology is born out of that resentment. On the one side, he has feelings of inferiority and therefore on the other side the tremendous sense of power. Wherever there are feelings of inferiority there is a power scheme afoot, because one measures things from the standpoint of power: Is he more powerful than I? Am I stronger than he? That is the psychology of feelings of inferiority. Nietzsche is the author of the *Will-to-Power*, don't forget. So naturally, since his critique is created by a resentment, his judgment is often too acid, unjust; but as I say it often hits the nail on the head. Here, for instance:

> And this hypocrisy found I worst amongst them, that even those who command feign the virtues of those who serve.
>
> "I serve, thou servest, we serve"—so chanteth here even the hypocrisy of the rulers—and alas! if the first lord be only the first servant!

To what does he refer—belonging to his time?

Mrs. Sigg: Frederick der Grosse, because he said that the king must be the first servant of the State.[6]

Prof. Jung: Yes, and closer to him, Bismarck said something very

---

[5] St. Anselm (1033-1109). His "ontological argument" is still a matter of serious debate in theological and philosophical circles.

[6] Frederick was something of an amateur scholar and given to putting his thoughts on paper on a wide variety of topics. With the help of Voltaire he wrote a book on the duties of a prince of state, *Anti-Machiavel*, which was published at The Hague in 1740. As a biographer has said about the passage Jung cites, "In truth Frederick could say he was going to be the first servant of his subjects, for no one would dispute his 'complete freedom to do right' which he claimed for serving them" (Pierre Gaxotte, *Frederick the Great* [New Haven, 1942], p. 152).

similar; "In the service of my fatherland I consume myself."[7] That was in everybody's mouth in Nietzsche's time.

Mr. Allemann: And now!

Prof. Jung: But now it is a reaction. That is why I point out these verses. That hypocritical attitude has now found its revenge or its compensation. The sentimental hypocrisy of service and devotion has of course much to do with late Christianity. In reality it was just the contrary: the Christian slogan was used to cover what was sheer will-to-power. The Victorian era created a mountain of lies. Freud was like Nietzsche in that the main importance of those men lay in their critique of their time. Nietzsche, not being a doctor, did the social part of the critique as it were; and Freud, being a doctor, saw behind the screen and showed the intricacies of the individual—he brought to light all the dirt of that side.[8] And in the following chapters there are allusions which indicate that Nietzsche also had an insight into what one could call the medical side of things. But such figures as Freud and Nietzsche would not come to the foreground—they would not exist or be seen—if their ideas did not fit into their time. Of course they may not be fully true—it is a one-sided aspect, a necessary program for the time being—and then the time comes when it is no longer necessary, when it is the greatest error, when it makes no sense at all. But in Nietzsche's time it hit the nail on the head. When one said, "I serve, thou servest, we serve," it was just a lie; but times are coming, or they are already here, when it is no longer a lie, when what has been a lie has become a bitter truth. Whole nations now chant, "I serve, thou servest, we serve," and we are close to the condition, even in the democratic countries, in which we do nothing but serve the state! Everything we do is for the state or for the community. That is no longer an awful lie, it is an awful truth.

[7] As one scholar has said of Bismarck, "He spoke the truth when, some years before leaving office, in a moment of gloom and disappointment he wrote under his portrait, Patriae inserviendo consumor." Kuno Francke, "Bismarck and a National Type," in Kuno Francke, ed., *The German Classics of the Nineteenth and Twentieth Centuries* (New York, 1914), vol. 10, p. 9.

[8] In his "Sigmund Freud in His Historical Setting," Jung dilated on his claim that "Like Nietzsche, like the Great War, and like James Joyce, his literary counterpart, Freud is an answer to the sickness of the nineteenth century" (CW 15, par. 52).

LECTURE II

26 October 1938

Prof. Jung:

I spoke last time of the *apokatastasis*, which means complete restoration, and I find here this quotation from St. Paul:[1]

> In a moment, in the twinkling of an eye, at the last trump: for the trumpet shall sound, and the dead shall be raised incorruptible, and we shall be changed.
>
> For this corruptible must put on incorruption, and this mortal must put on immortality.
>
> So when this corruptible shall have put on incorruption, and this mortal shall have put on immortality, then shall be brought to pass the saying that is written, Death is swallowed up in victory.
>
> O Death, where is thy sting? O grave, where is thy victory.

Mrs. Flower contributes this and asks if it is the Christian equivalent of the *apokatastasis*. The bodily resurrection is surely one aspect of it, and there is another which I referred to last week. Now we will continue in the second part of "The Bedwarfing Virtue":

> Ah, even upon their hypocrisy did mine eyes' curiosity alight; and well did I divine all their fly-happiness, and their buzzing around sunny window-panes.
>
> So much kindness, so much weakness do I see. So much justice and pity, so much weakness.
>
> Round, fair, and considerate are they to one another, as grains of sand are round, fair, and considerate to grains of sand.
>
> Modestly to embrace a small happiness—that do they call "submission"! and at the same time they peer modestly after a new small happiness.
>
> In their hearts they want simply one thing most of all: that no

---

[1] I Corinthians 15:52-55. *Apokatastasis*: restitution, repristination.

one hurt them. Thus do they anticipate every one's wishes and do well unto every one.

That, however, is *cowardice*, though it be called "virtue."—

I won't read it all; as you see, Nietzsche is criticizing the good and mediocre people whom he hates like the pestilence. This criticism is based upon a particular psychological fact in Nietzsche, which has to do with a particular realization: these preceding chapters and the ones following contain the slow realization of something which is now welling up in him, something which is exceedingly difficult to him. What is that fact which he is trying to cope with?

Mrs. Crowley: Is it not his own future fate?

Remark: His inferior man.

Prof. Jung: Yes, the inferior man in himself, his shadow. This began some time ago, after his terrible vision, where he was threatened by the power from below, where he already had an intuition of his potential madness and tried to escape. Of course the inferior man is not necessarily mad, but if one doesn't accept the inferior man, one is liable to become mad since the inferior man brings up the whole collective unconscious. And why is that so?

Miss Hannah: Because of the contamination.

Prof. Jung: Exactly. The inferior man, being an unconscious factor, is not isolated. Nothing in the unconscious is isolated—everything is united with everything else. It is only in our consciousness that we make discriminations, that we are able to discriminate psychical facts. The unconscious is a continuity; it is like a lake—if one taps it the whole lake flows out. The shadow is one fish in that lake, but only to us is it a definite and detachable fish. To the lake it is not, the fish is merged with the lake, it is as if dissolved in the lake. So the shadow, the inferior man, is a definite concept to the conscious, but inasmuch as it is an unconscious fact, it is dissolved in the unconscious, it is always as if it were the whole unconscious. Therefore we are again and again up against the bewildering phenomenon that the shadow—the anima or the wise man or the great mother, for instance—expresses the whole collective unconscious. Each figure, when you come to it, expresses always the whole, and it appears with the overwhelming power of the whole unconscious. Of course it is useless to talk of such experiences if you have not been through them, but if you have ever experienced one such figure you will know of what I am speaking: one figure fills you with a holy terror of the unconscious. It is usually the shadow figure and you fear it, not because it is your particular shadow but because it represents the whole collective unconscious; with the shadow you get the whole thing. Now inasmuch as you are capable of detaching the shadow from the unconscious, if you are able to make a difference between the fish and the lake, if you can catch your fish without getting the whole lake, then you have won that point. But when another fish comes up, it is a whale, the whale dragon that will swallow you:—with every new fish you catch you pull up the whole thing. So when Nietzsche is afraid of his shadow or tries to cope with it, it means that he himself, alone, has to cope with the terror of the whole collective unconscious, and that makes things unwieldy.

Now when one is possessed by the unconscious to a certain extent, when a man is possessed by his anima for instance, he has of course a very difficult time in dealing with it, so as a rule people simply cannot do it alone. One cannot isolate oneself on a high mountain and deal with the unconscious; one always needs a strong link with humanity, a human relation that will hold one down to one's human reality. Therefore, most people can only realize the unconscious inasmuch as they are in analysis, inasmuch as they have a relation to a human being who has a certain amount of understanding and tries to keep the individual down to the human size, for no sooner does one touch the unconscious than one loses one's size.

Mrs. Flower: It seems to me to be the most difficult problem—that one must learn to discriminate while surrounded by the collective unconscious. Often it seems that one will be torn limb from limb.

Prof. Jung: Naturally, it is impossible to realize the collective unconscious without being entirely dismembered or devoured, unless you have help, some strong link which fastens you down to reality so that you never forget that you are a human individual like other individuals. For as soon as you touch the collective unconscious you have an inflation—it is unavoidable—and then you soar into space, disappear into a cloud, become a being beyond human proportions. That is what happened to Nietzsche. In his solitude he tapped the unconscious and was instantly filled with the inflation of Zarathustra: he became Zarathustra. Of course he knows all the time that he is not Zarathustra—Zarathustra is a figure of speech perhaps, or a more or less aesthetic metaphor. If anybody had asked him whether he was Zarathustra he would probably have denied it. Nevertheless he handles Zarathustra—or Zarathustra handles him—as if they were one and the same. You see, he could not talk in that style, as if he were Zarathustra, without getting infected. So throughout the whole book we have had the greatest trouble on account of that constant intermingling with an archetypal figure. One is never sure whether Zarathustra is speaking, or Nietzsche—or is it his anima? This is not true, that is not true, and yet everything is true; Nietzsche is Zarathustra, he is the anima, he is the shadow, and so on. That comes from the fact that Nietzsche was alone, with nobody to understand his experiences. Also, he was perhaps not inclined to share them, so there was no human link, no human rapport, no relationship to hold him down to his reality. Oh, he was surrounded by human beings and he had friends, a few at least—there were people who took care of him—but they were in no way capable of understanding what was going on in him, and that was of course necessary.

Therefore I say, an analyst is that person who is supposed to understand what is going on in such a case. But if there had been analysts in Nietzsche's days and one had told him that he was undergoing an experience of the collective unconscious and that those were archetypal figures, he would not have found a welcome in Nietzsche. You can only talk with such a man by entering into his condition. You might say, for instance, "What happened last night? Was it black? Did it move? How interesting! Heavens, what you are going through! I will come with you, I believe in Zarathustra, let us take a flight with him." You must be duly impressed, and you must undergo the same affect that the patient undergoes; if he succumbs, you must succumb also to a certain extent. You can help only inasmuch as you suffer the same onslaught, inasmuch as you succumb—and yet hold onto reality. That is the task of the analyst; if he can hold to human reality while his patient is undergoing the experience of the collective unconscious, he is helpful. But with one leg the analyst must step into the inflation; otherwise he can do nothing. You cannot be reasonable about it, but have to undergo the affect of the experience. Naturally, Nietzsche's time was most unfavorable for such an experience. In those days there was not the slightest possibility of anyone understanding. There were plenty of individuals of course—there always are—who would go crazy with him voluntarily; every fool finds followers. There is no gifted fool who remains without a large school of equally gifted followers. But to find a man who could keep his feet on the ground and fly at the same time was too big an order.

Mrs. von Roques: But what did people think when he wrote this?

Prof. Jung: That he was crazy. I remember when *Zarathustra* came out and I know what people said, what Jakob Burckhardt said, for instance. They all thought that *Zarathustra* was the work of a madman, though they had to admit that certain things were exceedingly intelligent. But they could not cope with it, they did not understand it, because in those days they kept away from such an experience in an amazingly careful way. They lived in a sort of artificial world of nice, differentiated feelings, of nice illusions. And that is exactly what Nietzsche was criticizing. Naturally, he was undermining their cathedrals and their castles in Spain, their most cherished ideals, so to them he was not only a lunatic, but also a dangerous one. All the educated people in Basel were horrified at the spectacle, shocked out of their wits in every respect. They considered him a revolutionary, an atheist—there was nothing that was not said against him then. And at the same time they were frightened because they felt an amazing amount of truth in what he said. It needed half a century at least to prepare the world to understand what happened to Nietzsche.

Of course it is no use speculating as to what would have happened if Nietzsche had had an understanding companion. We only speculate about such matters because we know something now about the experience of the collective unconscious; what to do in such a case is to us almost a professional question. Nietzsche's case is settled, but we must understand what happens to a man without the aid of that understanding. Nietzsche is an excellent example of an isolated individual trying to cope with such an experience, and we see the typical consequences. His feet don't remain on the ground, his head swells up and he becomes a sort of balloon; one is no longer sure of his identity, whether he is a god or a demon or a devil, a ghost or a madman or a genius. Now such a man, as we have seen in the preceding seminars, is always threatened by a compensation from within. Naturally when one gets an inflation, one begins to float in the air, and the body then becomes particularly irksome or heavy—it begins to drag, often quite literally. People in that condition become aware of a heaviness somewhere, of an undue weight which pulls them down, and since they are identified with the body, they often try to strangle it. The Christian saints used to deal with the problem in that way: they mortified the body in order to get rid of its weight. Nietzsche was a man of the 19th century, and that was no longer the right way. On the contrary, he makes a great point of the body; he preaches the return to the body. But he makes such a point of it that he inflates the body; he makes it inaccessible through overrating it. It is really the shadow that bothers him; while praising the body he doesn't see that the shadow is representing the body. Then the shadow takes on extraordinary importance, and since he is no longer identical with the body it becomes a demon.

As you know, I personify the shadow: it becomes "he" or "she" because it is a person. If you don't handle the shadow as a person in such a case, you are just making a technical mistake, for the shadow *ought* to be personified in order to be discriminated. As long as you feel it as having no form or particular personality, it is always partially identical with you; in other words, you are unable to make enough difference between that object and yourself. If you call the shadow a psychological aspect or quality of the collective unconscious, it then appears in you; but when you say, this is I and that is the shadow, you personify the shadow, and so you make a clean cut between the two, between yourself and that other, and inasmuch as you can do that, you have detached the shadow from the collective unconscious. As long as you psychologize the shadow, you are keeping it in yourself. (I mean by psychologizing the shadow, your calling it a quality of yourself.) For if it is simply a quality of yourself the problem is not disentangled, the shadow is not detached from you. While if you succeed in detaching the shadow, if you can personify the shadow as an object separate from yourself, then you can take the fish from the lake. Is that clear?

Mrs. Flower: It is clear, but nonetheless difficult, since in most places people still feel as they did in Nietzsche's time.

Prof. Jung: I admit that it is a very difficult question. For the shadow jumps out of you—you may get on very bad terms with people through your shadow—and also with the collective unconscious. Since "people" means the collective unconscious, it is projected onto them. Everybody touches the fate of Zarathustra in analysis: it is the greatest problem. But when you can make that difference between the shadow and yourself you have won the game. If you think that thing is clinging to you, that it is a quality of yourself, you can never be sure that you are not crazy. If you cannot explain yourself to people, if you become too paradoxical, what difference is there between yourself and a crazy man? I always say to my patients who are such borderline cases, "As long as you can explain yourself to a reasonable individual, people cannot say you are crazy, but the moment you become too paradoxical it is finished, the rapport is cut." Therefore, I say to detach the shadow and— if you can—to personify it, which is really the sign of detachment. For instance, if you have a friend with whom you feel almost identical, so that you have every reaction in common, so that you never know which is he and which is yourself, then you don't know who *you* are; but if you can say, "That is his way and he is a person independent from myself," you know which is which, who you are and who he is. It is of course a difficult question to know in how far the shadow belongs to you, in how far you have the responsibility. For as you have the responsibility for people who belong to you, so you have a responsibility for the shadow; you cannot detach the shadow to such an extent that you can treat him like a stranger who has nothing to do with you. No, he is always there; he is the fellow who belongs. Nevertheless, there is a difference, and for the sake of the differentiation you must separate those two figures in order to understand what the shadow is and what you are.

Inasmuch as Nietzsche is identical with Zarathustra, he has the shadow problem. He could not detach the fish from the lake, and as Zarathustra overwhelms him completely at times, the shadow also overwhelms him when it comes up in the fear of insanity—which is the same as the fear of the collective unconscious. In the preceding chapters we have evidence for this. The shadow appeared as a dangerous demon and Nietzsche used every imaginable trick to defend himself against its onslaught. He belittled the shadow, he made light of him, he ridiculed him, he projected the shadow into everybody. And now in these chapters he criticizes and accuses everybody, the mediocrity of the world and of all those qualities which adhere to Nietzsche himself. For instance, he says it is the sincerest wish of all those mediocre people not to be hurt. But who was more susceptible to being hurt than Nietzsche himself?

There is a characteristic story about Nietzsche: A young man, a great admirer, attended his lectures, and once when Nietzsche was speaking about the beauty of Greece and so on, he saw that this young man became quite enthusiastic. So after the lecture he talked with him, and he said they would go to Greece together to see all that beauty. The young man couldn't help believing what Nietzsche said, and Nietzsche most presumably believed it also. And of course the young man liked the prospect, but at the same time he realized that he had not a cent in his pocket. He was a poor fellow and being Swiss he was very realistic, and thought, "The ticket costs so much to Brindisi and then so much to Athens; does the professor pay for me or have I to pay my own fare?" That is what he was thinking while Nietzsche was producing a cloud of beauty round himself. Then suddenly Nietzsche saw the crestfallen look of the young man, and he just turned away and never spoke to him again; he was deeply wounded, never realizing the reason of the young man's collapse. He only saw him twisting around, getting smaller and smaller and finally disappearing into the earth, through a feeling of nothingness which was chiefly in his pocket. That is the way Nietzsche stepped beyond reality; such a natural reaction was enough to hurt him deeply.

There you have a case: that young man represented the shadow; that mediocre little fellow whom Nietzsche always disregarded—there he was. Nietzsche could not see the real reason, because that is what never counted in his life. And we must not forget that those mediocre people he is reviling were the ones who provided for his daily life. I knew the people who supported him financially and they were exactly those good people. I knew an old lady who was a terribly good person and of course did not understand a word of what he was saying, but she was a pious soul and thought, "Poor Professor Nietzsche, he has no capital, he cannot lecture, his pension is negligible, one ought to do something for the poor man." So she sent him the money, by means of which he wrote *Zarathustra*. But he never realized it. As he never realized that in kicking against those people who sustained his life, he was kicking against himself. Well now, he goes on in the third part, the fourth paragraph:

> And when I call out: "Curse all the cowardly devils in you, that would fain whimper and fold the hands and adore"—then do they shout: "Zarathustra is godless."
>
> And especially do their teachers of submission shout this;—but precisely in their ears do I love to cry: "Yea! I am Zarathustra, the godless!"
>
> Those teachers of submission! Wherever there is aught puny, or sickly, or scabby, there do they creep like lice; and only my disgust preventeth me from cracking them.
>
> Well! This is my sermon for *their* ears: I am Zarathustra the godless, who saith: "Who is more godless than I, that I may enjoy his teaching?"
>
> I am Zarathustra the godless: where do I find mine equal? And all those are mine equals who give unto themselves their Will, and divest themselves of all submission.
>
> I am Zarathustra the godless! I cook every chance in my pot. And only when it hath been quite cooked do I welcome it as *my* food.

Here is his hybris, his *superbia*; proclaiming his godlessness, he becomes God. And this God-almighty-likeness is quite evident from which sentence?

Mrs. Fierz: "I cook every chance in my pot."

Prof. Jung: Exactly. For who can cook his chance in his own pot and make his own fate? Only the master of fate, the lord of all fate. No human being can do that. Is he in any way in control of chance? Can he assimilate chance, make it his chance? That is what *happens* to man, and he has no chance of making it *his* chance. It is as if a man who was attacked and eaten by a lion should say, "This is my lion."

Mrs. Baumann: Might I ask what the German word for *chance* is? In my translation it is *event.*

Prof. Jung: Zufall. That really means chance, and the very German *zu Fall* expresses the objectivity of the thing, namely, a thing that *mir zufällt*—it falls to me, it falls to my lot, I have nothing to do with it. For instance, if a stone falls on my head I cannot say, "Ah, my stone which I have kicked falls upon my head." A lord of all fate can say it is his stone, because he is all in all—the hunter and the hunted one, the slayer and the slain—but no human being can assert that safely. Nietzsche did, as you see, but it was not safe. So his bedwarfing criticism, his underrating of the so-called good and mediocre people, causes an underrating of his own mediocrity, of the real man in himself. In such a case one instantly lifts oneself up to too high a level, and anyone who lifts his consciousness up to such an impossible, superhuman level is threatened by a specific catastrophe. What would that be?

Remark: He would fall into the hands of the demons.

Prof. Jung: Well yes, but in what way does it show?

Mr. Allemann: He would be responsible for everything that occurs.

Prof. Jung: Yes, he would become God-almighty-like, but when a human mind becomes like God what happens to it? To remain in the simile I gave you, what happens to the fish?

Miss Foote: It is dissolved.

Prof. Jung: Yes, the fish dissolves in the lake again, the mind dissolves completely. No human mind is capable of being universal, the All. Only the mind of God is All. So when Nietzsche dissolves into the mind of God he is no longer human. Then the fish has become the lake; there is no distinctness, a complete dissolution. This is the goal of certain religious practices.

Mrs. Crowley: The Yoga.

Prof. Jung: Yes, in Yoga, the state of *samadhi* or bliss, or *dhyāna* which means a sort of *ekstasis,* ends in what the Indians call superconsciousness, or what we call the unconscious. I had great difficulty in India in translating what we understand by the collective unconscious. I had to explain myself in Sanskrit terms, which are the only philosophical terms they really understand, and I found no corresponding word. I first thought that *avidya* might do, but it doesn't do at all; *avidya* means simply darkness and absence of knowledge, so it doesn't cover the idea of the unconscious. Then I soon found out that *buddhi,* the idea of the

perfectly enlightened mind, or, still better, *samadhi* was the right term
for the dissolution of the conscious in the unconscious. As a matter of
fact a man who comes back from the void, from a not-knowing which
is positive, comes back with the feeling of knowing all; yet he cannot
bring the sea with him because he has become the fish again. And the
fish is not the sea and cannot include the sea: that remains what it always was. To go into *samadhi* means that the fish is dissolved in the
water and becomes the whole sea—it *is* the sea—and since the sea has
no form but contains all forms, it cannot be transmitted by one of the
forms, for instance, the fish.

Now among all Nietzsche's critical remarks about the mediocre, all-
too-good people, certain ones deserve our attention. I will omit the
negative remarks, though from a psychological point of view his critique is often quite valuable. He has the great merit, for instance, of
having seen that virtues are based upon vices, that each virtue has its
specific vice as a mother; also that virtue only makes sense, in a way, as
a reaction against vice, and that the necessary consequences of certain
virtues are vices. That peculiar functional interrelation between good
and evil, day and night, is a point of view of great psychological value:
it makes of Nietzsche a great psychologist. But we can only deal here
with the general tendencies, and it is quite obvious that his critique is
again a *ressentiment* which is not quite just; it is true to a certain extent,
but as a whole it really goes too far. Nevertheless, in giving free rein to
all his critical ideas, certain things come out which allow us to look
down to a deeper layer of his thought; behind his superficial critique
we can see ideas of great importance.

You know, Nietzsche often liked to think of himself as a religious reformer; not in vain did he take the name of Zarathustra to express his
historical role. He took that name, as you know, because Zarathustra
was the originator of the idea of good and evil, of the moral opposites;
it was he really who caused that great split in humanity of the moral
problem. And now Zarathustra as a Saoshyant, a new savior, has to
come back in order to heal the wound he caused. Nietzsche's idea of a
superman would be the man who was beyond that wound, who had
healed that wound. One finds this idea in the Grail mystery, in the suffering king who is to be cured by a savior; he is the Christian man who
carries that moral wound, as the Persian man was rent asunder by Zarathustra's teaching. Nietzsche's idea was that his task in the history of
the world was to cure man of that incurable wound he has suffered
from hitherto. And he was not simply playing with this idea. It was a
deep-rooted conviction in him amounting to a sort of mystical experi-

ence. This accounts for the fact that Zarathustra to him was always more than a speech metaphor; it was a more or less real figure. Therefore the famous saying: *Da wurde eins zu zwei und Zarathustra ging an mir vorbei*, which clearly expresses the visionary living nature of the Zarathustra experience.

On this basis it is quite understandable that a certain truth, important for our time and important in history, must also come to the foreground. Nietzsche was a contemporary of Richard Wagner, and it is not without meaning that Wagner occupied himself with *Parsifal*, which contains this very problem. And curiously enough it was just *Parsifal* which caused the bitterest estrangement between the two former friends. Nietzsche finally accused Wagner of having broken down before the cross, which was a bitter shaft, because in his consciousness Nietzsche could only see the so-called Christian gesture or the Christian sentimentality; he was not aware of the deeper meaning of that whole fact.[2] I am not speaking now of Wagner's opera *Parsifal*, but of the fact of the occurrence of that idea at that time. It was practically the parallel of Zarathustra: Zarathustra is the other aspect of the same thing, only expressed in entirely different terms. It is the same idea but expressed in an unhistorical milieu, in a setting which was beyond history. Zarathustra is in a way historical, but Wagner remained very much more in the tradition, using a legend which was well known and still much appreciated. And he only went back to the Middle Ages, while Nietzsche made a much further regression, going back into the 8th or 9th century B.C. to fetch his figure or analogy, his myth. But the actual ideas are very much the same—the idea of the cure of the incurable wound.

So we are quite justified in accepting most important statements in *Zarathustra* as to the nature of the cure, or as to verities which are beyond even Nietzsche's mind. As dreams can tell us things which are far more intelligent than we are, far more advanced than our actual consciousness, so even to a man like Nietzsche it may happen that his unconscious tells him things that are above his head. Then in retelling them he is apt to twist them slightly, to give them an aspect which is entirely due to the more restricted sphere of his personal consciousness, so that they appear to be, say, contemporary social criticisms. In this chapter, for instance, where he very clearly gives vent to all his re-

---

[2] Although Nietzsche had been early moved by *Parsifal*, he came to believe that "The Parsifal music has character—but a bad character . . ." (to Franz Overbeck, September 1882, Letters/Middleton).

sentment against his surroundings, there is a passage which I should not like to omit, the last verses of the third part, where he says,

"Love ever your neighbour as yourselves—but first be such as *love themselves*.

—Such as love with great love, such as love with great contempt!" Thus speaketh Zarathustra the godless.

If you read through the chapter superficially, this remark easily escapes your attention, because it seems to be in keeping with the other critical and really bedwarfing remarks. But here he says something which has a double bottom; this is a synthetic thought. Of course it sounds like one of the paradoxes Nietzsche likes so much; to love your neighbor but first to love yourself, sounds like a demonstration of *sacro egoismo*—a phrase the Italians invented when they joined the Allies in the war—but here a mistake is possible. When you love your neighbor it is understood that the neighbor is meant who is the one that is with you, in your vicinity, that you know as a definite person; and when you love yourself one would be inclined to think that Nietzsche means by "yourself" just yourself, this ego person of whom you are conscious, and in that case it is self love, it is *sacro egoismo*—or not even *sacro*—ordinary mean egoism. Nietzsche is quite capable of saying such a thing, yet Zarathustra speaks these words and Zarathustra, don't forget, is always the great figure, and quite apt to utter a great truth. In that case I should mistrust a superficial judgment. I should say those words, "love thyself," really mean the self and not the ego. Then you would say, "Inasmuch as thou lovest thy self, thou lovest thy neighbor." And I should like to add that if you are unable to love yourself in that sense, you are quite incapable of loving your neighbor. For then you love in people all of which you are conscious when loving yourself in the egotistical way; you love that which you know of yourself, but not that which you do not know. There is an old saying that one can only love what one knows—there is even an alchemistical saying that nobody can love what he doesn't know—but it is very much in keeping with the whole style of Zarathustra to love what one does not know: namely, to love on credit or on hope, on expectation, to love the unknown in man, which means the hope of the future, the expectation of future development. Then if you can love yourself as that which you are and which you are not yet, you approach the self. And such a love enables you to love your neighbor with the same attitude, to love your neighbor such as he is and such as he is not yet.

Now, Zarathustra says of that love that it means loving with great love and with great contempt. This again sounds like one of those famous paradoxes which are rather irritating, but here it makes extraordinary sense, and I am quite certain that Nietzsche himself felt that it went right down to the root of things. For this is the formula of how to deal with the shadow, of how to deal with the inferior man. It is simply impossible to love the inferior man such as he is, to do nothing but love him; you must love him with great love and also with great contempt. And that is the enormous difficulty—to bring the two things together in the one action, to love yourself and to have contempt for yourself. But there you have the formula of how to assimilate your shadow. Therefore this saying of Nietzsche is really the key to the cure of that split between the superior and the inferior man, the upper and the lower, the bright and the dark. I am absolutely convinced that this passage is one of those which Nietzsche really felt, for Nietzsche was a great genius, and it is in the deepest sense in keeping with his whole style and tendency. Unfortunately, all too often this greatness is undermined or disintegrated by love of the play of words, too much emphasis, neurotic tendencies that come in between; but all those shadows fail to hinder, time and again, a very great truth from appearing. Now immediately after this he continues,

> But why talk I, when no one hath *mine* ears! It is still an hour too early for me here.

Right away the resentment comes in again: what is the use of such profound truth? There is nobody here who listens, nobody has my ears—those big ears, the elephant ears of a god, the big ears of Buddha.

> Mine own forerunner am I among this people, mine own cockcrow in dark lanes.

It often happens that when Nietzsche comes out with a very personal resentment—which is, alas, all too understandable but very sad—he then makes a mistake in his taste. "Mine own forerunner am I among this people" goes well enough, but "mine own cockcrow in dark lanes" makes one think of a dark chickenyard where a cock crows alone—his cock. It is ridiculous. The smallness of the inferior man in Nietzsche comes in here and spoils the impression. He might have finished the chapter by: "Thus speakest Zarathustra the godless," which would have made sense, but he goes on, "Why talk I"—he returns to himself, he becomes small. That remark about loving with great love and with great contempt explains why Zarathustra is godless, and what he means really by emphasizing his godlessness. But to do that is bad taste

1367

and in our days, worse than ever, it is idiotic, which was not the case then. You see, he means that man or that being who is beyond the ordinary suffering man, the man with the great moral split; he means the superman that is capable of loving with great love and with great contempt. That is God: only God is capable of such a thing, because that is the whole. To love with great hate would be the same. He unites the opposites, reconciles them completely by that; he creates the most paradoxical being which God needs must be if he is whole. *If* he is whole—that is what one always forgets.

For instance, when the Protestant theologian says God can only be good, then what about evil? Who is evil? To say man is evil does not explain the great evil in the world; man is much too small to be the creator of all evil. There must be a god of evil as well. If you make a good god, then make a god of evil too. In the Persian religion, Ormazd is the god of good and Ahriman is the god of evil. If you have a god that can only be good, then you must have a devil that can only be bad, and this dualism, though it is a logical consequence, is insupportable. It somehow makes no sense. What about the omnipotence of God if he has to suffer the existence of a partner in the cosmic game? That question bothered me already when I was a little boy. I gave my father a bad time over this problem. I always used to say, "If God is omnipotent, why doesn't he prevent the devil from doing evil?" If our neighbor has a bad dog that bites people, the police come and fine the man. But God has a bad dog apparently, and there are no police to fine him for allowing it to bite people. Then the theologian has to say that God has permitted Satan to work for a while in order to try people. But why make people like that? Since he is a good potter he must know whether the pots he has made are good; he doesn't need to try them to know whether they will hold out. The vessel should be perfect, and if it is not, then he is not a perfect potter, and then it is a foolish game. One gets an idea of the foolish game in Job, where God bets with the devil as to who could get the best of old man Job. And the same idea is in *Faust*; of course Goethe took it from the Book of Job, but it is an impossible point of view.

You see, when you try to create the idea of a universal being, you must bring the two things into one, and that you cannot do unless you can first do it in yourself. You cannot conceive of something which you cannot conceive of in yourself. You cannot conceive of goodness if there is not goodness in yourself. You cannot conceive of beauty if there is no beauty in yourself: you must have the experience of beauty. And to conceive of a being that is both good and evil, day and night, you should have the experience of the two beings in yourself. But how can you arrive at such an experience? Only by passing through a time when you no longer project good or evil, when you no longer believe that the good is somewhere beyond the galactic system and the evil somewhere in the interior of the earth, in the eternal fire of hell, but that the good is here and the evil is here. In that way you introject the qualities you have lent to the gods. Naturally, by introjecting them you pass through a time of inflation when you are much too important. But you are important just in the fact that you are the laboratory, or even the chemical vessel, in which the solution is to be made, in which the two substances should meet.

You cannot get them together somewhere in an abstract way. You can only do it in your own life, in your own self. There the two cosmic principles come together, and if you experience the oneness of the two, the unspeakable and inexplicable oneness of darkness and light, goodness and badness, you get at last the idea of a being which is neither one nor the other. If you have had that experience of being both, the one and the other, neither one nor the other, you understand what the Indians mean by *neti-neti*, which means literally "not this nor that," as an expression of supreme wisdom, of supreme truth. You learn to detach from the qualities, being this and that, being white and black. The one who knows that he has those two sides is no longer white and no longer black. And that is exactly what Nietzsche means in his idea of a superior being beyond good and evil. It is a very great psychological intuition. Of course when you have had that experience, then you must descend the whole length of the ladder, you must come back to the reality that you are not the center of the world, that you are not the reconciling symbol for which the whole world has waited, that you are not the Messiah or a perfect person or the superman. You must come down to your own reality where you are the suffering man, the man with a wound—and the wound is as incurable as ever. It is only cured inasmuch as you have access to that consciousness which knows: I am white and I am black.

Mr. Baumann: I have sometimes experimented with making people contemplate simple geometrical designs for about a minute, and one man with a rather scholastic mind, who puts all his thoughts in the proper place in his mental system, had a vision when he contemplated the square. He had never made fantasies or drawings such as we make here, but he saw Christ in the center of the square, and in the upper right corner, Ahriman, and in the lower left corner, Ormazd. I asked him if he had had anything to do with that myth and he said no, it just came like that.

Prof. Jung: Yes, that is a revelation from the unconscious. The unconscious is several lengths ahead and told him of a problem of which he was not aware: namely, that Christ is in a way a mediator between Ormazd and Ahriman. The paradox that God descended into the imperfect body of man, that God could be included in an imperfect physical body, has given the church a lot of trouble. They had to make all sorts of hypotheses as to what that body consisted of, whether body and soul (or God) were one, or whether Christ was of two natures. So the Catholic church finally made that formula of real man and real God, a monotheistic conception which is a tremendous paradox. But we have to leave it at that. I don't know whether your man was interested in such ideas.

Mr. Baumann: No, not consciously.

Prof. Jung: I should say it was rather unlikely, for if he has been accustomed to express himself in the historical Christian terms, in terms of that conflict, concerning the nature of Christ for instance, he would not have chosen Ormazd and Ahriman to express the dilemma; that is more on the line of Nietzsche, of what we are discussing today. You see, our unconscious is really rather on the lines of Nietzsche when we allow it to work freely; it would express itself in such forms rather than on the lines of the Christian dogma, because our unconscious is in the world and not in the books about history. That fantasy absolutely formulates the idea of Christ as the superman, the man that is a paradox, both god and man. Where was God when he was in Christ? Of course inasmuch as Christ felt as a man he would exclaim, "My God, my God, why hast thou forsaken me?"—or, "Our Father, who art in heaven." But if he is God himself, he would be talking to himself as if he were his own father. That God is father and son, his own father and his own son, is again an absolutely incomprehensible paradox, but it is really a psychological truth, for man can experience being his own father and his own son.

For instance, he can quite vividly be that which he used to be; you have only to watch a regression in a patient to see the man who has been, who is the father of the future man who is quite different, who is the son. If you live in the future you are your own son or your own daughter, and if you live in the past you are the father of that son— which is really the idea of God being the father of the son in one person. That is the projection of a human experience, of an experience which is not a human thought invented by a philosopher or any such intellectual person, but a human thought which is also a highly mystical experience, a divine experience. Therefore you can say, "This is not myself, this is God." But though you know that the experience of God is your own experience, you must always add that it is not your personal experience. It is a mystical experience; you feel that it is a divine experience. It is that which enabled people formerly to say that such an experience happened either in the remote past or that it is always happening, an eternal truth in metaphysical space. The transformation of the elements, of the substance of the holy communion, is the sacrifice of Christ, and that always happens. It is outside of time. The crucifixion of Christ is a historical fact and therefore it has disappeared, but the church holds that that sacrifice is a metaphysical concept. It is a thing that happens all the time—all the time Christ is being sacrificed. So whenever the rite is repeated, with the due observance of the rules and naturally with the *character indelebilis* of the priest received through the apostolic succession, it is really the sacrifice of Christ. Therefore, when a good Catholic is on a train passing through a village where there is a church, he must cross himself. That is the greeting to the Lord that dwells in the host in the ciborium on the altar; the Lord really lives there in that house, a divine presence. It is exactly the same idea as the eternal sacrifice of Christ.

LECTURE III

2 November 1938

Prof. Jung:

I will first answer these questions as well as I can. Mr. Allemann says, "If I have not misunderstood, you said last week that 'collective unconscious' could be translated by the Sanskrit term *samadhi*. Is not *samadhi* rather the *action* of diving voluntarily into the collective unconscious or the *state* of the individual during a voluntary dissolution in, or union with, the collective unconscious? In using the simile of a lake with its contents as representing the collective unconscious, would not 'active phantasy,' *dharana* and *dhyana*, mean the actions of a man standing on the shore of the lake and looking into it, or sitting in a boat floating upon the lake, or swimming in the lake, being well aware that he is not identical with the water? He may even draw fish out of it and risk being drawn in if the fish are too big for him. But when after careful preparation he dives voluntarily into the lake and becomes one with it temporarily (with a fair chance of getting out of it again) then he is in the state of *samadhi*. Hauer translates Patanjali III/11: 'Wenn in der seelischen Welt (Chitta) die bewusste Beziehung zu jeglichem Gegenstande aufhört und das In-Eins-Gesammeltsein (Ekagrata) eintritt, so ist das die Bewusstseinschwingung, die man 'Einfaltung' (Samadhi) nennt.' "[1]

Samadhi is one of those terms which was used in the past in India, and is still used in the actual religious movements of the present time. But it is used with no very definite meaning. To think that these Indian concepts have a definite meaning is one of our Western mistakes; that is doing them an injustice. The Indian mind is peculiarly indefinite, and they try to make up for it by a lot of terms which are very difficult

---

[1] Pantanjali (2nd century B.C.) was the founder (or synthesizer) of Yoga. An English translation directly from the Sanskrit is: "When the mind has overcome and fully controlled its natural inclination to consider diverse objects, and begins to become intent upon a single one, meditation is said to be reached." *The Yoga Aphorisms of Pantanjali*, tr. William Q. Judge (New York, 1912). Judge was a theosophist.

to translate, the difficulty chiefly consisting in the fact that we give them a definite meaning which does not belong to them. And their mind is extraordinarily descriptive; they want to give a picture of a thing rather than a logical definition. But in trying to give a good description, it sounds as if they were trying to give a definite concept, and that is the cause of the most baffling misunderstandings between the Indian and the Westerner; that we give a definite meaning to a concept which is not definite in itself, which only sounds definite, brings about endless misinterpretations. The terms, *samadhi, dhyana, sahasrara*, and so on, apparently have a definite meaning but in reality they have not. Even the Indians are absolutely at sea with these concepts.

For example, there is a statue of Sri Ramakrisna in the temple of Belur Mutt, made from a photograph which was taken of him quite against his will. He is clearly in what we would call a state of *ekstasis*—a somnambulistic or hypnotic condition—and they call it *samadhi*. But at the same time they call the superconsciousness which is reached in that state *samadhi* and also *dhyana*. Of course, there are definitions in literature; in the Patanjali *Yogasutra* there is a definition, but then you find another one somewhere else. In the different schools these terms have different definitions. You can only be sure that you are not wrong when it has to do with superconsciousness; every Indian will understand you when you use the term *samadhi* in that sense, for then he instantly has a picture of a Yogin in that state of *samadhi* or *dhyana*. The word *tapas* is too classical—it would only be understood by a connoisseur of Sanskrit. Every educated Indian has a certain knowledge of Sanskrit, however; he understands many of those terms. When you compare the translation of the Patanjali *Yogasutra* made by Hauer with the one by Deussen, and with the English translation, you see at once the difficulty; they have all been put to the greatest pains to find the proper Western terms.[2] That is due to the Eastern mentality which, despite all their efforts at terminology, remains indefinite; such painstaking terminology is always a compensatory attempt to make certain of something which is not certain at all. As I said before, if you want a blade of grass or a pebble, they give you a whole landscape; "a blade of grass" means grass and it means a meadow and it is also the green surface of the earth.

Of course that conveys truth, too, and leads eventually to Chinese

[2] Jung elsewhere defined the Sanskrit word *tapas* as "self-incubation through meditation" (CW 5, par. 588f.).
It was from Paul Deussen that Nietzsche learned something of Buddhism.

concepts—the peculiar way in which the Chinese mind looks at the world as a totality for instance, where everything is in connection with everything else, where everything is contained in the same stream. While we on the other hand are content to look at things when they are singled out, extracted, or selected, we have learned to detach detail from nature. If I ask a European, even a quite uneducated man, to give me a particular pebble or leaf, he is capable of doing so without bringing in the whole landscape. But the Easterner, particularly when it is a matter of a conscientious mind, is quite incapable of giving one a piece of definite information. It is somewhat the same with learned people: you ask a learned man for some bit of information and would be perfectly satisfied with yes or no, but he will say yes-under-such-conditions, and no-under-such-conditions, and finally you don't know what it is all about. Of course for other learned individuals this is excellent information: a trained mind would get very definite information in this way, but for the ordinary mind it is less than nothing. In my many conversations with Indian philosophers, I remember that their answers seemed less like yes-under-such-and-such-conditions, and more like a yea-and-nay-but-under-no-conditions. We think it is a sort-of unnecessary clumsiness, but when you look carefully at what they give you, you see really a marvelous picture; you get a vision of the whole thing.

The best example I ever came across is the story Prof. McDougall[3] told me, of his attempt to inform himself about the concept of Tao. Now, Prof. McDougall is a man whose turn of mind would not suit the Eastern mentality, but naturally he was rather curious as to the meaning of their concepts. He therefore asked a Chinese student what he understood by Tao, expecting a clear answer in one word. For instance, the Jesuit missionaries called Tao simply "God," a translation which can be defended, yet it does not render the Chinese concept of Tao. It has also been translated as "providence," and Wilhelm called it *Sinn*, or "meaning." Those are all definite aspects of a thing which is far more indefinite and incomprehensible than any of those terms; even the concept "God" is much more definite than the concept of Tao. The Chinese student told him many things but MacDougall could not follow, and finally after many attempts the Chinaman, in spite of his politeness, got impatient, and taking him by the sleeve he led him to the

[3] William McDougall (1871-1938), British social psychologist who taught at Oxford, Harvard, and Duke. A number of his theories were unpopular in academic circles, including those which endorsed Lamarckism and psychic research. See "The Therapeutic Value of Abreaction" CW 16, pars. 255-93.

window and asked him: "What do you see out there?" The professor replied: "I see trees." "And what else?" "The wind is blowing and people are walking in the street." "And what else?" "The sky and the clouds and a streetcar." "Well, that is Tao," said the Chinaman. That gives you an idea of the way the Eastern mind works.

I owed it to this story really that I was fairly capable of following the arguments of my Indian interviewers. I kept that experience in mind and it helped me to understand their mentality. They could not understand what I meant by the "collective unconscious," any more than I could understand what they meant by "superconsciousness," until I saw that it was what happens in a state of *samadhi* or *dhyana*. *Samadhi* means to them the condition of superconsciousness. Or the Tantrist would understand if you spoke of *bodhi* or of *sahasrara* or of the *ajna* consciousness.[4] All these terms really describe what we call the collective unconscious. Of course, the very term *collective unconscious* shows how we approach the problem, as their terms show their way of approaching it. You see, these two ways depend upon what one calls reality. When they say you ought to "realize," or talk about "the realization of truth," they mean something entirely different from what we would mean. I won't go into a long and complicated philosophical definition of reality because you know what it means in the Western sense. Now in contrast to what we assume reality to be, the Indian means his own conscious realization of reality, not a tangible thing like this desk, which is reality to us. But that is Maya to the Indian—that is illusion.

Now here is another question. Miss Hannah says, "The verse: 'I am Zarathustra the godless! I cook every chance in *my* pot. And only when it hath been quite cooked do I welcome it as *my* food' still bothers me. Do these words *in themselves* necessarily imply a God-identification? Or could they mean: I take every chance (*Zufall*) that falls to my lot; I suffer its pain till the last drop is cooked in my pot, for only in this way can I digest it? The next verses make it quite clear that Nietzsche did as usual identify with God, but is not the cooking verse in itself one of those deep truths that shine through *Zarathustra*?"

Here again it is a matter of a passage which might have a double meaning. In this case I decided not to be too benevolent with Nietzsche's text, because he says "in *my* pot," "*my* food," and goes on

---

[4] *Ajna* and *sahasrara* represent the two highest chakras in the Kundalini ascent. In the *ajna* center or the "Lotus of Command," the mind is "completely free of the limitation of the senses," and in *sahasrara* one experiences "The fulfillment and dissolution of the world of sound, form, and contemplation" (Zimmer/Philosophies, pp. 515, 585). *Bodhi*: knowledge, wisdom, enlightenment.

clearly identifying with God. Therefore I took it as what it appears to be: "I am the maker of my fate; I even choose my chance and say it is my chance," rather than in the way you, with far more benevolence, would interpret it. It needs too much kindness to see this deeper meaning in it. But it is possible. Of course we are quite free to say this case looks like providence, as we can say of any chance event that it is *surely* a case of providence. The question is only, have we enough evidence to make such a statement? If not, we had better not play with such hypotheses. There is surely a fair amount of evidence in *Zarathustra* of this peculiar double aspect of things. We are now moving in chapters where we continually stumble over passages in which one meaning is apparent, and yet another is apparent also—where there are two aspects, an aspect of profound truth and an aspect of *ressentiment*, criticism, and so on. This is often the case in such products; a sort of psychological raw material was just flowing out of him, and he had no time to criticize it or to ask the material: what do you mean? That element of self-criticism is entirely lacking in *Zarathustra*. Therefore, time and again I say, if only Nietzsche had asked himself, "Why do I say this? Why is this figure coming out of me? What does it mean to me?" But those questions never come up or only indirectly; we shall presently see such a case in our text. But it merely happens to him, it is not his doing. So we are forced to apply a great deal of criticism, and when he doesn't give us enough rope to explain in a benevolent way, I don't do it. For I don't want to overdo my benevolence; otherwise I create resistances to Nietzsche in myself. You see, when you have to be too kind and patient all the time, you get quite nasty behind the screen—I would suddenly burst forth once and curse the whole of *Zarathustra* to hell.

Miss Hannah: The last thing I wanted to be was benevolent.

Prof. Jung: Yes, but here it has happened to you: you got too nice and too understanding according to my idea.

Miss Hannah: I asked because you said those words could only be used in an inflation or even megalomania and I felt I could have used them myself.

Prof. Jung: Of course you could use them if you took them out of the context and concentrated upon that verse exclusively, but in the context your interpretation becomes a bit doubtful. Now here is a question from Mrs. Jay: "Last Wednesday you touched upon the parallels between Parsifal/Zarathustra, and Wagner/Nietzsche. Could you go a little further into that? You said something about the wound of Amfortas and the spear which healed it. What is the relation to Zarathustra? Is it that both become wise through compassion?"

That is a chapter in itself; if we were to treat that question, we should be reading *Der Fall Wagner*,[5] where we get the whole problem, instead of *Zarathustra*. Also that parallel between the mystery of the Grail and the meaning of *Zarathustra* must remain a mere allusion for the time being. But it would be stretching the point considerably to assume that Nietzsche/Zarathustra and Parsifal had in common that they were both "wise through compassion." That is a point which would find no welcome in Nietzsche. In the end of *Zarathustra* he curses compassion, so he is just on the other side; that is one of the things which explains the difference between their points of view. You see, as a human being Wagner was not compassionate at all, while Nietzsche surely suffered from his great compassion for the world; therefore he curses compassion and Wagner praises it. One often sees that.

Then I find here quite a number of quotations and remarks concerning the question of the *apokatastasis*. One passage that I had in mind has not been mentioned, but of course all these passages from the Epistles of St. Paul and Revelations, which have to do with a sort of return of paradise, refer to the *apokatastasis*, the ultimate restoration of all things to God from whom they have emanated. From a perfect condition everything fell into an imperfect condition, and through the action of the savior everything will return to the state of perfection in the end. This return to perfection is the *apokatastasis*. There are plenty of passages in the New Testament where one finds that idea of the complete restoration of everything that has degenerated and become imperfect through the fall of the first man—the fall of God's creation. Of course it is an interesting question in itself that that happened. One could say that God had made things imperfect with a very definite purpose, but man's mind cannot understand that apparently—otherwise we would not have theologians. Now we will continue our text. You remember we were last speaking of that way of loving—with great love and with great contempt.

But why talk I, when no one hath mine ears! It is still an hour too early for me here.

5 Nietzsche published *The Wagner Case* in 1888. His earliest—and most benign—treatment of Wagner was the last essay in *Untimely Meditations*, "Richard Wagner in Bayreuth." *Human All-Too-Human* appeared in 1878 and 1879, a work Wagner thought indicative of a nervous breakdown on Nietzsche's part, and Nietzsche's *Contra Wagner* came out in 1895.

> Mine own forerunner am I among this people, mine own cock-crow in dark lanes.
>
> But their hour cometh! And there cometh also mine! Hourly do they become smaller, poorer, unfruitfuller,—poor herbs! poor earth!

His attitude is the same as in the chapter before, contempt of his contemporary world, despising the smaller people. This is clearly a *ressentiment* against people who cannot appreciate him. Well, it is human all-too-human—one can understand. I told you how he was received with his new ideas, so it would have been a miracle if he had not had a strong resentment against such a reaction. He goes on:

> And soon shall they stand before me like dry grass and prairie, and verily, weary of themselves—and panting for fire, more than for water!
>
> O blessed hour of the lightning! O mystery before noontide!—Running fires will I one day make of them, and heralds with flaming tongues.
>
> Herald shall they one day with flaming tongues: It cometh, it is nigh, the great noontide!
>
> Thus spake Zarathustra.

There is a good deal of Old Testament in this passage—the Lord God being the living fire that will devour the peoples. There Nietzsche is identifying with the deity like an Old Testament prophet, and the style imitates the language of the prophets. His allusion means of course that he will burn up all that chaff. But it means more than that: it means also a descent of the Holy Ghost in the form of fiery tongues, not to devour people but to turn them into heralds. So the Old Testament destruction through fire is coupled here with the Pentecostal miracle of the descent of the Holy Ghost in the form of fire that puts their tongues on fire, that gives them the gift of *glossolalia*, talking in foreign tongues. So the fire is not only destructive, it is also productive: it produces the gift of languages. This is a sort of message that fire has a double aspect, a negative one, destruction, and a positive one, that gift of the Holy Ghost. Now, fire symbolism plays no small role in dreams, so if we are allowed to treat this speech metaphor like a dream image, we must compare it with dreams in which fire occurs. That a fire has broken out in one's house, for instance, is a very usual motif. What does the fire motif mean in dreams?

Mrs. Crowley: It means a great disturbance in the unconscious.

Mrs. Fierz: An outbreak of emotion.

Prof. Jung: Yes, an emotional outburst flaming up. And an outburst of emotion is supposed to be hot. Why is that?

Miss Hannah: Because it hurts.

Prof. Jung: No, people are often not hurt at all—the other people are hurt.

Remark: It makes them warm.

Prof. Jung: Yes, when you have an emotion, the hot blood rises to your head: you get red hot in the head. Therefore violent emotions are always symbolized by fire or blood or heat. All languages are full of such metaphors on account of that physiological condition. When somebody is making you angry, you keep cool as long as you don't feel the blood rising to your head; you can handle the situation, you can calmly say, "You make me very angry." But the moment you feel that your blood is getting hot you can no longer control the situation, you flare up like a flame, you burn yourself up in violent anger. This fact is the reason for the so-called "James-Lange theory of affects."[6] They say that as long as the inciting cause does not bring about a physiological disturbance, the dilation of the blood vessels or a certain fast beating of the heart for instance, one has no affect, no emotion, but as soon as there is that physiological reaction, one gets the psychological affect as a consequence. The dilation of the blood vessels, the fast beating of the heart, is the first effect, and then follows the psychological emotion. That is really so. Of course it follows in quick succession, but it is true that it is the physiological reaction which causes the psychological affect. Fear, for instance, is caused by the heart phenomenon; after that the real panic occurs. A thing may be rather gruesome or dangerous, yet you know you can deal with it as your heart has not reacted to it; but when your heart reacts you get into a panic, the real fear, for that takes the ground from under your feet. You feel that you are gone, demoralized—you suffocate. Therefore they have made that funny-sounding theory. But it is a fact that as long as you can control the physiological sequence, you can control the situation; and when your heart begins to race, or your head gets too full of blood, you are unable to.

Now, these physiological phenomena are at the basis of such pictures. Fire symbolizes emotions and whenever you dream of fire it means a very critical situation on account of intolerable affects. To

[6] The theory arrived at independently by William James in America in 1884 and by C. G. Lange in Denmark a year later.

dream that a fire has broken out in the cellar or the attic of your house, means that in such-and-such a place in your psychology there will be a strong emotion. A fire in the attic will be in the head; you will be set on fire through certain ideas. If it is in the cellar, it will be in the abdomen and whatever the abdomen stands for; the fire will come from below. It might be sexual passion or a terrible anger or any other violent emotion based upon animal instincts. When it is in the attic, it might come from an anima or an animus insinuation. In women the fire often starts in the head; the instincts might be perfectly quiet and the whole situation normal, but the animus perhaps has a wrong conception or passes the wrong judgment, and then there is terrible confusion.

Now of course, Nietzsche is looking forward with a sort of mystical hope that this fire, the noontide, will come. He often speaks of the noontide, the great mystical hour. What does that mean?

Answer: The highest degree of heat at twelve o'clock.

Remark: The whole world suffers from the sun.

Prof. Jung: No, Nietzsche likes the sun.

Mrs. Fierz: It is the hour of Pan, of nature.

Prof. Jung: Well yes, the panic fright, the hour of ghosts in the south, and Nietzsche is playing a good deal on that note too. But that would not explain it; we cannot assume that this would apply for the whole world, and noontide for him is always a time of complete fulfilment.

Miss Wolff: It is the time when Zarathustra will be revealed to the world.

Prof. Jung: Yes. In the chapter called "Noon-tide" you will see that that is the hour of the complete revelation of Zarathustra. And what is the revelation?

Mrs. Schlegel: The coming of the superman.

Prof. Jung: Yes, Nietzsche's evangel is *Zarathustra*, the message to the world of the superman, the idea that man, this human world, should develop to the superman. What does that mean psychologically?

Mrs. Baumann: For Nietzsche himself it meant the middle of life, the change to the second half of life; therefore Zarathustra is the self, the non-ego.

Prof. Jung: You are quite right. He wrote *Zarathustra* when he was thirty-eight or thirty-nine, the midday of life; *Zarathustra* is the experience of noontide, the great transformation that takes place at 36.[7] Of course only in exceptional cases does that transformation become con-

---

[7] More commonly, Jung spoke of the beginning of the second, more reflective period of life as beginning between thirty-five and forty, normally.

scious, and then it is always a great revelation. But what does noontide really mean psychologically—and literally?

Mrs. Crowley: Would it not be the fullest point of consciousness?

Prof. Jung: Absolutely. The light of the sun is the day, and consciousness is the day of man. Consciousness coincides with the day and it is probably just as miraculous as it was to that child who asked why the sun shone only during the day. The child had not yet drawn the conclusion that the day and the sun are identical, and we have probably not yet drawn the conclusion—or we have forgotten it—that consciousness is the day, the sun, the light. Therefore when you are unconscious, in dreams, or when you are talking about consciousness, you always speak in terms of seeing; and as you can only see in the light, you use terms deriving from light. When you become conscious of something, you say, "Now it dawns upon me"—*ein Licht ging mir auf.*[8] We have plenty of such terms; if you examine the speech metaphors connected with the phenomenon of consciousness you will find that we always speak in terms of light, of seeing. When you understand or perceive something that is said to you, you say "Yes, I see." Why don't you say, "I hear," which would be more apt really? "I see," simply means "I agree with you, I take a note of it." You don't say, "I hear," because that has to do with something else that is below consciousness. In that case, you say, "I hear": Lord, I hear your command, I obey, I receive your words, not in consciousness, but a little bit below, in my heart. Hearing goes to the heart, has to do with the feeling, while seeing has to do with the eyes, the intellect, the mind.

So noontide means the perfect, complete consciousness, the totality, the very *comble* and summit of consciousness, and that of course is the superman, the man with an absolutely superior consciousness. And Zarathustra tries to teach his contemporaries to develop their consciousness, to become conscious of the moral paradox of consciousness, of the fact that you are not only a moral individual, but also on the other side a most despicable character; that you are not only generous but also miserly; that you are not only courageous but also a coward, not only white but also black. To be fully aware of that paradox, I would call the consciousness of the superman. Therefore it will be noontide when he appears, when the sun has come to its culmination. But that means at the same time the destruction of all chaff, of all those worthless people who are unable to produce that paradoxical consciousness. We would be largely included in the chaff naturally, for

---

[8] Literally, "a light goes on in me."

such a perfect consciousness is a very exceptional condition. And there Nietzsche falls down—falls down over the imperfection of man. You see, he has the same aspiration which one finds in the Yogin in India for instance, who also tries to reach that superconsciousness where one can say, not merely in words but in fact, "I am the hunter and the hunted one; I am the sacrificer and the sacrificed." That is exactly like Nietzsche's paradoxical consciousness—that you are and are not, that you are both this and that. This is such an achievement that the Indians long ago realized that no one is able to achieve such superiority without going through endless Yoga practices in all the different aspects. They even came to the conclusion that the highest degree of consciousness, the most complete absence of illusion, is only achieved at death.

You see, Nietzsche had very little knowledge of the East. The only knowledge which was available to him was Schopenhauer's philosophy, and that is not the right vehicle for Indian philosophy, since Schopenhauer only knew what one then called the "Oupnekhat," a Latin translation of a very incomplete Mohammedan collection of the Upanishads. We have now a translation from the original work, but any knowledge that people had of it then was mixed up with Buddhistic and German philosophy. When Nietzsche was a young man it impressed him very much; one realizes what it meant to him when one reads the chapter about Schopenhauer in the *Unzeitgemässige Betrachtungen*.[9] I am more or less convinced that his idea of the superman originated there, in that idea of the one who is able to hold a mirror up to the blind will, so that the blind primordial will that has created the world may be able to see its own face in the mirror of the intellect. This is very much like the Indian idea really, like the psychological education Buddha tried to give to his time, the idea of looking into the mirror of knowledge or understanding in order to destroy the error and illusion of the world. This is interminably repeated in his texts and sermons and in the Nidana chain of causes. Again and again Buddha says that coming into existence causes such-and-such desires and illusions, and that man proceeds through that chain of causes and effect, invariably ending in disease, old age, and death; and the only means to disrupt that inexorable chain of cause and effect is knowledge and understanding.

That is the very essence of Buddhism, and that became the integrating constituent of Schopenhauer's philosophy, where Nietzsche found it. He was probably unconscious of that derivation from the Buddhist

---

[9] "Schopenhauer as Educator" (1874), the third essay in *Untimely Meditations*.

conceptions in Schopenhauer, and as far as I know there are no allusions to it in literature, but psychologically that would be the real source. And Nietzsche is a man in whom one might find the strange faculty of cryptomnesia, whereby something one has read or heard makes an imprint upon one's unconscious, which is later literally reproduced. We had that famous example last term, where Zarathustra appeared on the volcanic island and was seen to descend into the flames of the volcano in order to fetch the hound of hell, Cerberus. That passage, you remember, is an almost literal quotation from a book in the library of Nietzsche's grandfather, Pastor Oehler, which he read when he was eleven years old, or before that date. I found this out from Frau Förster-Nietzsche who helped me to locate the time. I happened to have also read the book, so when I came across the passage later in *Zarathustra*, it brought up the memory of that story, particularly the detail about the rabbits. That is such a case, so it is quite possible that the figure of the superman is partially derived from the Buddhist ideas which he got from Schopenhauer,[10] and from the concept of Prajapati or the *Purusha* in that version of the *Oupnekhat*.

You see, *Purusha* is the original man, the *homo maximus*. Or if one be disinclined to assume such a derivation, the *Purusha* or the Superman or the *homo maximus* would be nevertheless an archetype. That the world has the form of a human being or a Superman is an idea which one finds in Swedenborg, and in other forms in India and in China, and it also plays a great role in alchemy; the *Purusha* is an archetypal idea.

Mrs. Crowley: I thought the Superman was a little different.

Prof. Jung: You are quite right, he is not the *Purusha* of the Upanishads. The *Purusha* is also a world creator like Prajapati, and he is a collateral concept like the Atman. Of course one can say there is all the difference in the world between the concept of the *Purusha* and the concept of the Atman, but there again one sees, from the way the Indians themselves handle this concept, that the Atman and Prajapati and the *Purusha* are practically the same. For our purposes there is no point in insisting upon the different aspects or shades of meaning of that concept; it is what we would call in psychology "the self"—namely, the totality of the conscious and the unconscious. The *Purusha* is a psychic fact, not only a psychological concept; the self is not a psychical fact, but an archetypal fact, an experience. It is the same as the idea of Christ in the Middle Ages, or the idea Christ had of himself and his

---

[10] See above, 15 June 1938, n. 9.

disciples when he said, "I am the vine and ye are the grapes." Or the same as that early iconographic representation of Christ as the zodiacal serpent carrying the twelve constellations, the signs of the zodiac, representing the twelve disciples; or carrying the twelve disciples each with a star over his head. Those are old representations, meaning the path of the zodiacal constellations through the year, with Christ as the way of the serpent or the way of the zodiac. Christ represents the Christian year containing his twelve disciples, as the zodiacal serpent contains the twelve constellations of the zodiac. He is the individual, the self, containing a group of twelve that makes the whole.

Therefore, the representation of Christ in the form of *Rex Gloriae*, the king of glory, surrounded by the four evangelists, forming a mandala. The medieval mandalas always represented Christ in that form—Christ on the throne in the center, and in the four corners the evangelists—the angel, the ox, the lion, and the eagle. That even became a beloved ornamentation in the 12th and 13th centuries; one sees it frequently on the doors of cathedrals or as an illustration in books. And that again means the great individual, the great self containing the others—they are just parts—which is exactly the idea of the universe being the *homo maximus*, everybody having his specific place in that great man. The learned people are in the head, and soldiers and men of action are in the arms, and heaven and hell are also contained in the *homo maximus*. So at the source of Schopenhauer's philosophy lies that age-old idea. Of course the idea in itself doesn't occur in Schopenhauer, but the psychology of the Upanishads by which he was affected, is coupled with that idea. The *Hiranyagarbha*, the so-called golden germ, or the golden egg, or the golden child, is another form of Prajapati. Prajapati was making *tapas*, brooding over himself, hatching himself out, and he became the *Hiranyagarbha*, the grain of gold, the golden child, which is again the symbol of the self.[11] This is, one could say, the *homo minimus*, the smallest form—that is, the germ of the *homo maximus* in every individual.

One finds this kind of development of symbolism also in Egypt: Osiris was originally the immortal part of the king; then later on, of the noble or wealthy people; and then in the time just before Christianity, Osiris began to descend into the heart of everyone: everyone had an immortal or a divine soul. And the idea of that great self born or being

---

[11] "He who is the source and origin of the gods who . . . beheld the Golden Germ (Hiranya-garbha) when he was born. May he endow us with clear intellect" (*Svetasratara Upanishad* 4.12, Hume, p. 404).

contained in everybody became an essential truth of Christianity; Christ was eaten by everybody. They ate and drank him in Holy Communion. Thus they were impregnated with Christ; Christ lived in them. That was the Osiris which comes to life in everybody. Osiris was also represented as wheat growing up from his coffin; it was his resurrection in the form of wheat. And Christ is the wheat; therefore the host has to consist of flour of wheat made from the grain which grows out of the ground. There was the same idea in the Eleusinian mysteries long before Christ appeared: in the *epopteia* the priest showed the ear of wheat as the son of the earth, with the announcement that the earth had brought forth the son, the *filius*.[12] That was an Evangel almost like the Christian Evangel, and it was connected with the hope of eternal life after death—the mysteries of Eleusis instilled that great hope. You see, it is exactly like the idea of the Holy Communion, the bread and the wine being Christ. So Christ impregnates everybody: he creates a germ in everybody that is the great self.

Christianity is another source of Nietzsche's ideas of course, but since he did not criticize his own thought, he never discovered it. His idea was that he was preaching a truth entirely different from any other. This is the same infernal mistake the church made, not in the time of Christ but later, when they got hold of the Christian message— the idea that the god had descended upon earth for the first time, that it was a new truth which had never existed before. We are still handicapped by that belief. Theology tries to make it appear that nobody ever had such ideas before, when, as a matter of fact, these ideas were known all over the world; but they have a tremendous resistance against such parallels; they find them awkward. The Catholic church is a bit more intelligent in that respect. They call any historical parallel an anticipation; they say that God has shown the truth time and again in the past, not only in the Old Testament but also in pagan religions— in the Isis and Osiris myth for instance. Since only fools could deny that analogy, the Catholic church admits it and says that God permitted the anticipation of the truth which was to come, that in a sort of indistinct, incorrect way they perceived the ultimate truth: God becoming man, God being born from the Virgin, the sacrifice, and the role of the savior.

---

[12] In his "The Meaning of the Eleusinian Mysteries," at the 1939 Eranos Conference, Walter F. Otto (1874-1958) explains this ritual in the *epopteia*, the initiation into the greater mysteries. He credits Hippolytus the Roman with the report of how the ear of wheat was displayed. The lecture appears in *The Mysteries*, Vol. 2, Papers from the Eranos Yearbook, ed. Joseph Campbell, Princeton (B.S. XXX) 1955.

So even Nietzsche's idea of the Superman is nothing new, but an age-old symbolism, and therefore I think we are quite justified in reducing this idea to its historical source. He had ample material for handling his idea from the Christian side on account of his family; and the philosophical background is also well established since he was a great admirer of Schopenhauer and very much influenced by him. These ideas had gone into him and the ultimate result was that he produced a mystery teaching very much like the mystery teachings I have mentioned, either the *Purusha* mystery in the East, or the savior mystery in the Hellenistic syncretism which includes the savior mystery in Christianity. And he uses the same kind of phantasmagoria: the ultimate fire, for instance, that will devour the chaff, destroy the people who are not ready to receive the savior and accept the message; and the inspiration and transubstantiation, as it were, of those who receive the tongues of fire from the Holy Ghost. They will announce and continue the message. He calls that the great noontide. You see, that is the day of judgment, with the great sun of justice, where there will be no night any longer. And there will be no pain, because all the evildoers will be roasting in hell or burned up, and the world with its errors and imperfections will have come to an end. That is the good old Christian idea of ultimate redemption with all the paraphernalia of the Apocalypse.

You see, the fire symbolism has that aspect too: when a fire breaks out in a house, panic is next door and panic is insanity. One sees that in practical cases when people have funny ideas and get too emotional about them, in the fear that something might happen to their reason. If you can keep them from getting into a real panic, you can often save them. For when you see how insanity starts, the stages through which people pass before they become insane, you realize that it is always panic which drives them really crazy. As long as they can look on without being too emotional about it, they are saved; it is panic that gets people into such abnormal states. So the fire here is a great revelation, but of a very different nature: it is the revelation of insanity. Now we will omit the next chapter because Nietzsche just goes on feeling his resentment against the small people and exaggerating it to such an extent that his whole nature gets sick of it. It is not himself really, it is his psychological situation that cannot stand it any longer. So something is going to happen in this chapter, "On Passing-By." He begins:

> Thus slowly wandering through many peoples and divers cities, did Zarathustra return by round-about roads to his mountains and his cave. And behold, thereby came he unawares also to the

gate of the *great city*. Here, however, a foaming fool, with extended hands, sprang forward to him and stood in his way. It was the same fool whom the people called "the ape of Zarathustra": for he had learned from him something of the expression and modulation of language, and perhaps liked also to borrow from the store of his wisdom. And the fool talked thus to Zarathustra:

Where have we met the fool before?

Mrs. Crowley: The harlequin who jumped over him.

Prof. Jung: Yes, and what was the situation exactly?

Miss Hannah: The rope-dancer came out on the rope, and the fool followed him and jumped over him. Then the first one lost his head and fell.

Prof. Jung: And who was the rope-dancer?

Remark: We said it was the shadow.

Mrs. Crowley: It was Nietzsche himself.

Prof. Jung: Yes, or one could say the inferior man of Zarathustra/ Nietzsche. Then who would the fool be?

Miss Hannah: I suppose he really was the negative side of the self.

Prof. Jung: Yes, we interpreted him as the negative aspect, an overwhelming fear of the inevitable, inexorable power of fate that was following him. That was insanity of course. For when the rope-dancer falls down to the ground, Nietzsche comforts him by saying what?

Miss Hannah: Thy soul will be dead before thy body.

Prof. Jung: Prophesying thus his own fate: his body lived on for eleven years after he had become totally crazy. Now is this the same fool? Was that fool the ape of Zarathustra?

Mrs. Fierz: One might say that Nietzsche, in the chapters we have just read, was behaving like a rope-dancer in a way, so he would be the same.

Prof. Jung: Well, it would be just a repetition of that first scene. And that is absolutely typical of the way in which the unconscious works. First, there is generally an allusion to a certain situation, and then the motif goes on and on, returning from time to time in a more definite form, a more definite application. One sees that in a series of dreams. Already in the first dreams one finds a definite symbolism, and again and again it returns, becoming more and more elaborate, more and more typical. So we have here a repetition of the first scene: namely, the rope-dancer is Nietzsche himself making little of humanity, dwarfing and reviling his contemporaries, forgetting all the time that he is one of those poor little things that live in great cities, that are human and imperfect and incapable and have every vice under the sun. Also something in him doesn't understand, and he should see it; that there is something which he cannot grasp is what excites and irritates him so much. On the one side, he is a great philosopher, a great genius, but he doesn't see that on the other side he is almost infantile.

For instance, he wrote letters to his sister calling her "my dear Lama," and such childishness shows that there is still an infant in him that has not given up the nursery language. And how could that side of his character follow the great genius? You see, Nietzsche didn't know where the idea of the superman started, nor the idea of the eternal return. To him it was a great revelation. He didn't know that those ideas had prevailed for many centuries. He didn't know that the idea of the eternal return is as old as mankind practically—historical mankind at least. He thinks he is the first man to discover them. He is like a little child with astonished eyes coming into the world of these ideas. He had a historical education as well as a mind, so he had the capacity to criticize himself, yet he never did. Because he was a child, he merely played. A child doesn't wonder why it is playing with just that doll, or where it comes from or why it has such-and-such a style; it is just that doll, and nobody else ever had such a doll or played such a game. It is his invention. Of course it may be that the idea came to the child without conscious transmission—nobody said the child had to play like that—but as a matter of fact all children play like that.

Mrs. Crowley: Would it be possible psychologically that he was mocking his contemporaries because he is feeling himself being drawn away from the world, that it was a peculiar way of detaching from it, that he feels the insanity but doesn't know what to do about it?

Prof. Jung: That is also true, it is a well-known phenomenon. This is a farewell kick. It is like the fox saying the grapes are too sour when as a matter of fact he cannot reach them. So when one is convinced that one has to give up a certain relationship, for instance, one is always tempted to make up all sorts of things about the partner to account for the detachment. That is the case with Nietzsche, and that is also the reason for his ideas of persecution. People who find it difficult to detach from humanity invent all sorts of things—that human beings are all devils who are against them, for instance—in order to explain to themselves why they draw away from them. They invent those stories because something in them wants to go away, to detach; they feel it and it needs to be explained, so they explain it by such ideas. And that is like the beginning of insanity. Nietzsche's resentment is really too much. It is pathological, so one can explain it as a preparation for the final insanity.

LECTURE IV

9 November 1938

Prof. Jung:

We began last time the 51st chapter, "On Passing-By." On his round-about way back to his cave, you remember, Zarathustra came unexpectedly to the gate of the great city. Now it is questionable what his intention was there. In the preceding chapters he has been reviling the small people that live in small houses where he has to stoop low to enter, so why does he stop at this city?

Mrs. Fierz: One might say that he was turning into the missionary now; he considers them silly, so he wants to tell them how they ought to be.

Prof. Jung: That is quite possible. But psychologically, what should we say in such a case? You see he stops there "unawares."

Mrs. Fierz: That something in him of which he is unconscious wants to go among them.

Mrs. Baumann: It seems as if he had a secret wish to get into contact with that inferior man, because here he is not reviling him; it is something secret in him that wants it.

Prof. Jung: Exactly, he is attracted. When a person reviles something very thoroughly, what conclusion may one draw?

Mrs. Crowley: That it fascinates him.

Prof. Jung: Yes. One sees that in societies for the prevention of immorality. There are the most amazing stories. I remember the case of a member of such a laudable organization: A man had made a collection of five thousand pornographic pictures, which he offered to the society to burn up; and they only accepted his very generous gift under the condition that they could first study the collection thoroughly so that everybody would know how awful people really were. So they had a meeting in which the five thousand photos were carefully examined and they were all duly shocked. People who are fascinated by immorality often join such societies. There was another wonderful case: The secretary of an international society to prevent vice suddenly disappeared, and at the same time the police caught a man they had long

1389

been looking for on account of his sexual attacks on boys in Berlin. He would not say who he was, but they discovered that the international secretary had disappeared, and he was soon identified. So the reason Zarathustra stops at this city is that he feels an unholy attraction. The city is the connection with all that rabble, the crowd of miserable non-entities that he has reviled, and yet he cannot let them go. Then the foaming fool appears. He has already turned up once in the beginning of the book, where the rope-dancer was practically killed by the fool who jumped over him on the rope. And we said last week that the rope-dancer was Nietzsche himself and that he there foretold his own fate. His frequent allusions to dancing always allude to the dancer in himself. Now what does this dancing mean really?

Mrs. Crowley: Would it have something of the same nature as the dancing spirit of Shiva?

Prof. Jung: Yes, that is the same symbol, and what does Shiva's dancing denote?

Mrs. Crowley: It is both the creative and destructive side. It is the movement of nature, the complete expression of nature.

Prof. Jung: That is aesthetical, but if you take it psychologically, what is the characteristic of the dancing Shiva?

Answer: That he is dancing on the dead.

Prof. Jung: Yes, he is often represented as dancing upon a corpse, but that is a particular case; he is then a female, a sort of Kali dancing in the form of Shiva. He looks exactly as if he were a woman. That refers to a special Kali legend. The corpse in that case is not a corpse, but is the body of Shiva himself, and she is a sort of Shakti—Shiva has many aspects. The story is that Kali was once in such a fit of rage with everybody and everything that she danced upon the corpses in the burial-ground and nobody could stop her. Finally they asked her husband Shiva to stop her, and the only way he knew was to place himself among the corpses, so she danced on him. But when her foot touched him he looked up, and she saw he was her husband, and then she instantly ceased dancing and shamefacedly hung her head; she was shocked that her foot had stepped upon her own husband. From that story you can see what mental attitude is denoted by the dancing. How would you feel if you were one of the many corpses and such a demon was dancing on you?

Mrs. Sigg: It is the same idea as when we say in German: *Ich pfeife auf alles.*[1]

---

[1] "I whistle at everybody." "I couldn't care less."

Prof. Jung: Exactly. It is most reckless, really ruthless. One would call such an attitude utterly inhuman. So the dancing Shiva is most inconsiderate; it is the cruelty and indifference of nature that destroys with no regret. He is in a dream of ecstasy and in this condition he creates and destroys worlds—a sort of playful attitude with no responsibility whatever, with no relationship even to one's own doing. And who would have such an attitude—I mean within human reach? What kind of mind or type?

Mrs. Crowley: An extremely creative type.

Prof. Jung: Not every creative mind is like that.

Mrs. Sigg: An unbalanced intuition.

Prof. Jung: Not exactly unbalanced but unchecked intuition, an intuition that roams about uncontrolled and in no relation to the human individual. When intuition is entirely playful it behaves like that. So whenever Nietzsche is dealing with particularly difficult or painful subjects, he invents dancing, and then skates over the most difficult and questionable things as if he were not concerned at all. That is what unchecked intuition does. When one has to do with such people in reality one gets something of that kind, one sees then that everything is indifferent to them really. It only matters inasmuch as it happens to be in the limelight of their own intuition, and plays a role as long as it fits in with a scheme of their own. When it no longer fits in, it doesn't matter at all. So they handle people or situations all in the same way; whatever they are focussing on is suddenly brought out as *the* thing, and the next moment there is nothing—it is all gone. Intuition goes in leaps and bounds. It settles down and bounces off in the next moment. Therefore intuitives never reap their crops; they plant their fields and then leave them behind before they are ready for the harvest. Now that dancing attitude, the intuitive attitude, is always compensated by what kind of unconscious attitude?

Mrs. Sigg: It is really despair at the root.

Prof. Jung: No, that is not a compensating attitude, that is a personal reaction perhaps.

Mrs. Sigg: I think Nietzsche danced when he was in utter depair. At the end I mean.

Prof. Jung: Oh yes, sometimes, but he was not always in despair. What is the compensating attitude to intuition, to this dancing?

Mrs. Fierz: It is sensation.

Prof. Jung: Naturally. An almost pathological relationship to reality is the compensating attitude. One can call it the spirit of gravity. Therefore intuitives develop all sorts of physical trouble, intestinal disturbances for instance, ulcers of the stomach or other really grave physical troubles. Because they overleap the body, it reacts against them. So Nietzsche leaps over the ordinary man, just those small people he has been reviling, and then the moment comes when all the smallness of that man who lives in the body overtakes him. Nietzsche is exactly like the rope-dancer, and now once more he encounters the foaming fool. You remember the passage where he complains about those small people not hearing him, but the one who doesn't hear is himself. He doesn't know that he is really reviling the small man in himself, himself as the real individual that leads a visible existence in the body. And not realizing it he leaps over himself. He says "Mine own forerunner am I among this people" and "But why talk I, when no one hath mine ears!" But as a matter of fact he doesn't hear what he says to himself; he doesn't realize that he is really preaching to his own inferior man. So he is the fool that leaps over himself, exactly the situation already described in the beginning of the book. You see, the fool is the shadow, the thing which is left behind; the rope-dancer dances ahead, and behind him is a very active shadow, identical with the inferior man, with the man who is not up to the rope-dancer, the man who is underneath, watching him dance high up in the air. All the time that Nietzsche is identifying with Zarathustra—saying a whole mouthful— he is followed by a hostile shadow that eventually will take his revenge. So this fool is an activated shadow that has become dangerous because Nietzsche disregarded him too long and too completely. Under such conditions, an unconscious figure may develop into a very dangerous opponent. Now the fool is called the ape of Zarathustra. Why an ape?

Mrs. Fierz: He is not yet man, but is still at the animal stage.

Prof. Jung: Exactly, the shadow is not only the inferior man but also the primeval man, the man with the fur, the monkey man. One calls an imitative person a monkey, for instance, as the devil was called God's ape, meaning one who is always doing the same thing apparently but in a very inferior way, a sort of bad imitation. But that is exactly what the shadow does. It is like the way your shadow behaves in the sunshine; it walks like you, it makes the same gestures, but all in a very incomplete way because it is not a body. And when the shadow gets detached from you, then watch it! I have spoken before of that wonderful film, *The Student of Prague,* where the devil lured the student's reflection out of the mirror and away from him, and then that shadow figure, the second personality of the student, began to live on his own and behaved in a correspondingly inferior way.[2] That was the

---

[2] See above, 20 June 1934, n. 11.

root of the tragedy in that story, and it is what happens here. The rope-dancer removes himself so far from the human sphere, puts himself onto such a high rope above the heads of the crowd, that he also becomes detached from his own inferior personality. So the shadow gathers in strength, and as Nietzsche moves off toward the very great figure of Zarathustra, his shadow moves backwards to the monkey man and eventually becomes a monkey, compensating thus the too great advance through the identification with Zarathustra. That is the tree which grows to heaven, whose roots, as Nietzsche himself said, must necessarily reach into hell. And that creates such a tension that soon the danger zone will be reached where the mind will break under the strain.

Dr. Frey: Should it not be the ape of Nietzsche instead of Zarathustra?

Prof. Jung: No, it is the ape of Zarathustra. Zarathustra is an archetype and therefore has the divine quality, and that is always based upon the animal. Therefore the gods are symbolized as animals—even the Holy Ghost is a bird; all the antique gods and the exotic gods are animals at the same time. The old wise man is a big ape really, which explains his peculiar fascination. The ape is naturally in possession of the wisdom of nature, like any animal or plant, but the wisdom is represented by a being that is not conscious of itself, and therefore it cannot be called wisdom. For instance, the glowworm represents the secret of making light without warmth; man doesn't know how to produce 98 percent of light with no loss of warmth, but the glowworm has the secret. If the glowworm could be transformed into a being who *knew* that he possessed the secret of making light without warmth, that would be a man with an insight and knowledge much greater than we have reached; he would be a great scientist perhaps or a great inventor, who would transform our present technique. So the old wise man, in this case Zarathustra, is the consciousness of the wisdom of the ape. It is the wisdom of nature which is nature itself, and if nature were conscious of itself, it would be a superior being of extraordinary knowledge and understanding. The glowworm is a pretty primitive animal, while an ape is a very highly developed animal, so we can assume that the wisdom embodied in the ape is of immensely greater value than that relatively unimportant secret of the glowworm.

That is the reason why primitives feel so impressed or fascinated by the animal. They say that the wisest of all animals, the most powerful and divine of all beings, is the elephant, and then comes the python or the lion, and only then comes man. Man is by no means on top of creation: the elephant is much greater, not only on account of his physical size and force but for his peculiar quality of divinity. And really the look of wisdom in a big elephant is tremendously impressive. So this ape is the ape of Zarathustra, and not of Nietzsche, who is not such a ridiculous person in himself that he could be characterized as an ape, nor does he contain the extraordinary wisdom which would need the utter foolishness of a monkey as compensation. Naturally, the monkey is never the symbol of wisdom but of foolishness, but foolishness is the necessary compensation for wisdom. As a matter of fact there is no real wisdom without foolishness. One often speaks of the wise fool. In the Middle Ages, the wise man at the king's court, the most intelligent philosopher, was the fool; with all his foolishness he could speak profound truths. And naturally the fool was a monkey, so he was allowed to imitate and make fun even of the king, as a monkey would; a monkey is the clownish representation of man in the animal kingdom. Now, that activated shadow, which only comes about through Nietzsche's identification with Zarathustra, is overtaking him again, but not in the same dangerous way as in the beginning. Why was it apparently far more dangerous in the beginning?

Mrs. Fierz: It was then a sort of vision of what would happen, and that is now slowly happening.

Prof. Jung: Yes, in the beginning Nietzsche was not confronted directly with the monkey, but with a rope-dancer, so one could take it as a warning picture: if you identify with that rope-dancer, you must be careful or the shadow will overtake you. But that is only a warning inasmuch as one *considers* it a warning; one might have a warning dream and not allow oneself to be warned by it. So Nietzsche has in a way been warned, but the tragedy is that he did not take it into account. This time it is Nietzsche who is confronted with the fool, and the case seems to be less dangerous. He apparently can cope with it, but as a matter of fact it is more dangerous, because the prophecy in the beginning is now fulfilling itself: Nietzsche is now on the rope. Therefore he meets the fool. He is now about to be leapt over, and that is exceedingly dangerous though it doesn't look so here. It is of course somewhat impressive when that foaming fool suddenly springs forward with extended hands. Nietzsche might have been shocked, but apparently he was not. He says,

> It was the same fool whom the people called "the ape of Zarathustra": for he had learned from him something of the expres-

sion and modulation of language, and perhaps liked also to borrow from the store of his wisdom.

Here is the connection with the wisdom which Zarathustra represents, and if the ape likes to borrow from the source of wisdom, it is because he simply takes from what he is; that wisdom is of his own structure. It is himself even.

And the fool talked thus to Zarathustra:
    Oh Zarathustra, here is the great city: here hast thou nothing to seek and everything to lose.
    Why wouldst thou wade through this mire? Have pity upon thy foot! Spit rather on the gate of the city, and—turn back.

Now why does the shadow talk like that?
    Mrs. Jung: Because an archetype does not belong in collectivity.
    Prof. Jung: That is one aspect, but there is another.
    Miss Hannah: Because he knows that he will see it again all outside of himself, it will be the same thing over again.
    Prof. Jung: That is it. So what is the good of going into the city? He will do the same thing again: he will revile those people, put himself onto a high rope, and then fall down again. The shadow is very helpful in telling Zarathustra not to repeat the same nonsense, not to go into the city to revile those people because he really is reviling himself. Of course it is not said in those words. That is the shortcoming of the shadow that it cannot express itself precisely, as it is the shortcoming of nature which also shows in our dreams. People complain, "Why does the dream not tell me directly? Why doesn't it say: 'Don't do this or that' or, 'You should behave in such and such a way'? Why is it so inhuman?" I am sure not one of you has not thought that about your dreams. It is a most maddening thing that dreams cannot talk straight. Certain dreams are so extraordinary, so much to the point—yet they are always ambiguous. Now why does nature behave like that?
    Miss Hannah: Because it cannot differentiate.
    Prof. Jung: Yes, the unconscious is nature, the reconciliation of pairs of opposites. It is this and that and it doesn't matter. Because it is an eternal repetition, death and birth and death and birth, on and on forever, it doesn't matter whether people live or die, doesn't matter whether they have lived already or are going to live. That is all contained in nature. And so the unconscious gives you this and that aspect of a situation. Now, if you are wise, you use it as a source of information. As I always say, one uses the compass in order to navigate, but not

1395

even the compass shows the way—it doesn't even show exactly where the north pole is, the magnetic north pole being not identical with the geographical north pole. So the compass is a very doubtful means. Provided you have definite information as to the position of the north pole you can use the compass as a valuable means of orientation. And it is the same with the unconscious: provided you know about the laws of dreams you can use them. The dream is nature and it is up to you how you use it; it never says you *ought* to, but only says: it *is* so. The unconscious shows such-and-such a reaction, but it doesn't say whether it is right or wrong, or that you should draw such-and-such conclusions; you are free to draw certain conclusions as you are free to use the compass—or not. So the fool, being the shadow, is of course not Nietzsche's consciousness, but Nietzsche/Zarathustra in his negative edition; and so also the wisdom is in its negative edition. That the fool tells him not to go into the city is just like a dream. This is merely a compensation for Nietzsche's tendency to enter the city, and since that is against the instincts, since it is utterly futile to go on repeating the same thing, the unconscious simply says, "Don't go always in the same way; you have turned to the right long enough, now go once to the left." So what the fool says is quite mistakable, and you will presently see how Nietzsche takes it. He misunderstands it completely.

Mrs. Sigg: Yet in the beginning of the book, the fool spoke rather clearly. He said to leave the town, that he only escaped the danger of the city because he was humble enough to carry the corpse. But Nietzsche did not know the meaning.

Prof. Jung: That is a very good point. It was shown to Nietzsche that he ought to carry the corpse, and he did carry it and it was a protection. I cannot remember whether we dealt with that question, but will you tell us what it means?

Mrs. Sigg: I have not yet fully understood it. I think it is like the idea of carrying the corpse in Zimmer's work, *Die Geschichte vom indischen König mit dem Leichnam.* But it is not only in Indian mythology. The same motif was used by our greatest painter, Dürer; by our greatest writer of church-hymns, Paul Gerhard; and by our greatest musician, Johann Sebastian Bach.[3] Dürer used it in his picture of the Trinity, where the King, the God-Father, carries the dead Christ in his arms; Paul Gerhard used it in one of his most beautiful hymns; and Bach in-

---

[3] For Zimmer's *The King and the Corpse, Tales of the Soul's Conquest of Evil,* see above, 18 May 1938, n. 7. Albrecht Dürer (1471-1528), German painter and engraver. Paul Gerhard (1607-1676), German poet and writer of hymns and other songs. Johann Sebastian Bach (1696-1750).

troduced several verses of this hymn into his Passion-music. And his arrangement of the old melody of the hymn is most perfect in the accompaniment of the verse which touches our problem. I think it occurs very seldom in art. But it seems to be a law for a creative person that the king in him must carry the corpse.

Prof. Jung: Yes, Professor Zimmer's interpretation of that myth was that the king had to carry a corpse as a sort of ordeal, and thereby he learned the greatest wisdom. That is a very wonderful myth, an extraordinary piece of psychology. The corpse represents the *corpus*, the body. The English word *corpse* coming from the Latin *corpus*; and the German word *Leichnam* comes from *Lîcham* (Middle High German) which also means just the body. So the protection against inflation, against possession through an archetype, is carrying the burden—instead of the corpse, just "a burden," which is a sort of abstraction. Carrying the burden is a motif from the mystery cults. It is called the *transitus*, which means going from one place to another, and at the same time bearing something; that of course is not expressed in the word *transitus* itself.

Mrs. von Roques: There is a story that the wise men enter the world in a certain town, carrying the burden of the gods—the relics the gods gave them—in a bag on their backs, and then they must find a place on the earth to live in.

Prof. Jung: The burden would be the body—the gods gave man the body.

Mr. Allemann: Is not carrying the cross the same thing?

Prof. Jung: Absolutely. And in the cult of Attis they carried the fir tree which represents Cybele herself or the god. Then in the Mithraic cult the god Mithras carried the world bull upon his shoulders. And Hercules carried the universe which Atlas had supported before. In the Christian mystery, it is the cross, a dead tree, a symbol for the mother. I quoted in *The Psychology of the Unconscious* an old English legend, a dialogue between the mother, the cross, and Mary. Mary accused the cross: "Cross, thou art the evil stepmother of my son." It is the same as the mother, the mother cross—exactly the idea which underlies the cult of Attis.[4]

Mrs. von Roques: Is Aeneas carrying the father the same?

Prof. Jung: Probably, but I don't know that that myth has ever been used as a mystery legend, whereas Mithras carrying the bull was part of the mystery teaching. I remember in this connection a dream a clergy-

---

[4] For a fuller account of this dialogue, see CW 5, pars. 412-15.

man had as a child: when he was about five years old he had the clergyman's dream. He dreamt that he was in a water-closet which was outside the house, and suddenly somebody forced him to take that whole little house upon his back. He made a drawing of it for me, saying that in reality such a house would never have such a form. And he did not see that the outline, the groundplan, of the house was like this: He had to carry that water-closet with all the contents. And that is where we are all closeted—in this corruptible body of dirt—and we have to carry it. A child five years old had that intimation from the unconscious.

Mrs. Baumann has just called my attention to the fact that the legend of the king and the corpse exists in an English translation called *The Vikram and the Vampire*.[5] And I have been asked about the corpse—why it is just a corpse. One reason is that it is based upon that linguistic connection, corpse and *corpus*, and *Leichnam* and *Lîcham*. There is a sort of identity in the very words, which comes from the fact that the body, being matter, is supposed to be dead in itself, and only living inasmuch as it is animated by Prana, the indwelling breath of life. Therefore the same word is used for the living and the dead body. That is also seen in the idea of the burden: Mithras carries a dead bull, the sacrificed bull, or he is in the act of sacrificing or killing the bull, as on the Heddernheim relief in the museum at Wiesbaden, which is reproduced in *The Psychology of the Unconscious*.[6] Then on the other side of that relief Mithras and Helios are depicted conversing about the condition of the dead bull, which is in a state of transforming into all sorts of living things.[7] In Christianity the cross is a dead body in itself, like a man with extended arms. Therefore in an early medieval representation, Christ is standing in front of the cross, not crucified. When one stands in the sunshine with arms outstretched, one casts a shadow like the cross, so there the cross represents the shadow, the dead body.

Now, what the living body represents is a great problem. Of course the historical symbolism, as far as we know it, refers to the animal. The life of the body is animal life. There is no difference in principle between the physiology of the monkey and our own physiology; we have the physiology of an animal with warm blood. Another analogy is with the plant and so with the tree. Therefore the cross of Christ is also called the tree; Christ was crucified upon the tree. And an old legend

[5] Sir Richard Burton, *Vikram and the Vampire or Tales of Hindu Devilry, from the Baital-Pachisi* (London, 1870).

[6] See CW 7.

[7] For the Heddernheim Relief, see CW 5, Pl. XL.

says that the wood for the cross was taken from the tree of paradise which was cut down and made into the two pillars, Aachim and Boas, in front of Solomon's temple. Then these were thrown away, and discovered again, and made into the cross. So Christ was sacrificed on the original tree of life, and in the *transitus* he carried it. The plant or the tree always refers to a non-animal growth or development and this would be spiritual development. The life of the body is animal life: it is instinctive, contains warm blood, and is able to move about. Then within the body is spiritual or mental development, and that is always expressed as the growth of a flower or a miraculous plant or an extraordinary tree, like the tree that grows from above, the roots in heaven and the branches down toward the earth. That is Western as well as Eastern symbolism. The famous tree of Yoga grows from above, and Ruysbroek, the Flemish mystic, uses the same symbol for the spiritual development within the Christian mysticism.[8] So in the one case the body or the corpse would mean the animal—we have to carry the sacrificed animal—and another aspect is that we have to carry our spiritual development which is also a part of nature, which has to do with nature just as much.

Then there is a further point to consider. Occasionally in my experience with patients—not only in that legend of Vikram—it is less a matter of a corpse than of the dead thing generally, a sort of preoccupation with the dead. This hangs together with the fact that the body is a sort of conglomeration of ancestral units called Mendelian units. Your face, for instance, obviously consists of certain units inherited from your family; your nose comes from an ancestor in the 18th century, and your eyes are perhaps from a relative in the 17th century. The characteristic protruding lower lip of the Spanish Habsburgs dates from the time of Maximilian; that is a Mendelian unit which occasionally appears in a very pronounced way in certain individuals. There is also an insane streak in the Spanish Habsburgs, which appeared in the 15th century and then disappeared, and then, according to the Mendelian law, it appeared again after two hundred years. Then there is an English family named Whitelock, which is characterized by the fact that most of the members, particularly the male members, have a tuft of white hair in the center of the skull; therefore they are called Whitelock. That is again a unit of a particular tenacity. So our

[8] Jan van Ruysbroek (1293-1381), Flemish mystic. See, for instance, *The Spiritual Espousals*, tr. Eric College (New York, 1953), pt. I, B, a.

whole body consists of inherited units from our father's or mother's side, from our particular clan or tribe for centuries past.

Now, each unit has also a psychical aspect, because the psyche represents the life or the living essence of the body. So the psyche of man contains all these units too in a way, a psychological representation; a certain trait of character is peculiar to the grandfather, another one to a great-great-grandfather, and so on. Just as much as the body derives from the ancestors, the psyche derives from them. It is like a sort-of puzzle, somewhat disjointed, not properly welded together to begin with, and then the mental development of the character, the development of the personality, consists in putting the puzzle together. The puzzle is represented in dreams sometimes by the motif of a swarm of small particles, little animals or flies or small fishes or particles of minerals, and those disjointed and disparate elements have to be brought together again by means of a peculiar process. This is the main theme of alchemy. It begins with the idea of totality, which is depicted as a circle. This is called "chaos," or the *massa confusa*, and it consists of all sorts of elements, a chaotic collection, but all in one mass. The task of the alchemist begins there. These particles are to be arranged by means of the squaring of the circle. The symbolic idea is to arrange the particles in a sort of crystal-like axis, which is called the quaternity, or the *quaternion*, or the *quadrangulum*, the four, and to each point a particular quality is given.

That is what we would call the differentiation of the psychological functions. You see, it is a fact that certain people start with an intuitive gift, for instance, which will become their main function, the function by means of which they adapt. A man who is born with a good brain will naturally use his intelligence to adapt; he will not use his feelings which are not then developed. And a man who is very musical will surely use his musical gift in making his career and not his philosophical faculty, which is practically non-existent. So one will use his feeling, another one his sense of reality, and so on, and each time there will be a one-sided product. The study of these one-sided human products led me to the idea of the four functions, and nowadays we think that we should have not only one differentiated function but should take into consideration that there are others, and that a real adaptation to the world needs four functions—or at least more than one. And this is something like the ideas of those old alchemists who wanted to produce out of chaos a symmetrical arrangement of the quaternity. The four quarters of the circle indicate the fire, the air, the water, and the earth regions, and when they are arranged they will make in the center the *quinta essentia*, the fifth essence; the four essences are in the corners and in the center is the fifth. That is the famous concept of the *quinta essentia*, a new unit which is also called the *rotundum*, the roundness, or the round complete thing. It is again that circle of the beginning but this circle has now the *anima mundi*, the soul of the world, which was hidden in chaos. At first all the elements were completely mixed in that round chaos, and the center was hidden; then the alchemist disentangles these elements and arranges them in a regular figure, like a crystal. That is the idea of the philosopher's stone in which the original round thing appears again, and this time it is the spiritual body, the ethereal thing, the *anima mundi*, the redeemed microcosmos.

The motif of the swarm of little fishes or other little objects is also found in alchemy, representing the disjointed elements. And it is often in children's dreams: I have dealt with such a case in one of my dream seminars at the E.T.H., a child who died unexpectedly about a year after she had produced a series of the most extraordinary dreams, practically all containing the swarm motif. There was a cosmological dream where it was clearly visible how the swarm comes into existence, or how it is synthesized, and how it is dissolved into the swarm. The Mendelian units join together physiologically as well as psychically and then disintegrate again. That anticipated her death: her psyche was loosely connected, and when something adverse happened it dissolved into these units. Now, each of those particles is a Mendelian unit inasmuch as it is living; for instance, your nose is living. You live inasmuch as these Mendelian units are living. They have souls, are endowed with psychic life, the psychic life of that ancestor; or you can call it part of an ancestral soul. So inasmuch as you are like your nose, or can concentrate upon your nose, you become at once identical with the grandfather who had your nose. If your brain happens to be exactly like that of the great-grandfather, you are identical with him, and nothing can help you there—you have to function as if you were entirely possessed by him. It is difficult, or quite impossible, to indicate the size of Mendelian units; some are bigger, some are smaller, and so you have either large areas or small areas of ancestral souls included within you. At all events, you are a collection of ancestral spirits, and the psychological problem is how to find yourself in that crowd. Somewhere you are also a spirit—somewhere you have the secret of your particular pattern.

Now, that is in this circle of chaos but you don't know where, and then you have to go through that whole procedure of the squaring of the circle in order to find out the *quinta essentia* which is the self. The alchemists said it was of a celestial blue color because it was heaven, and since it was round, globular, they called it "heaven in ourselves." That is their idea of the self. As we are contained in the heaven, so we are contained in the self, and the self is the *quinta essentia*. Now, when someone is threatened with dissolution, it is just as if these particles could not be united, as if the ancestral souls would not come together. I am telling you all this in order to explain that other aspect of the dead: it is not only the dead body, but the spirits of the dead. So if a primitive wants to become a medicine man, a superior man, he must be able to talk to the dead, must be able to reconcile them. For the dead are the makers of illnesses, causing all the trouble to the tribe; and then the medicine man is called upon because he is supposed to be able to talk to the ancestral spirits and make a compromise with them, to lay them or to integrate them properly. That is necessary for everybody in order to develop mentally and spiritually. He has to collect these spirits and make them into a whole, integrate them; and that difficult task, the integration process, is called the carrying of the corpse of the ancestors, or the burden of the ancestors.

Mrs. von Roques: There is a very clear example in an Irish myth. The hero Fionn[9] goes out with his mother. First she carries him, then after a while they change and he carries his mother, but he gradually loses parts of her until he has only her feet, and those he throws into a lake belonging to a witch. Then he enters the house of the witch and she tells him he must go and fish in the lake, and he catches two fishes which are the feet of his mother. After that, he has to cook them and they must not have any spots from a too hot fire. But they do get spots and he puts his thumb on them and burns it, and from that day, he is wise when he sucks his thumb.

Prof. Jung: That is part of such a mystery, the integration and disintegration. Being carried by the mother means being carried by the unconscious, and carrying the mother would of course mean carrying the unconscious. The mother, as the basis, the source, the origin of our being, always means the totality of the spirit world, and in carrying the mother one is doing what Christ has done; Christ carried his mother (the cross) and also his whole ancestral heaven and hell. So the past was fulfilled. Being of royal (King David's) blood, Christ had to carry the promise of the past, and in order to fulfil it he had to become king of a spiritual world. The Christian idea of the miraculous draft of fishes also means the integration of all parts into one. For instance, the Pope's

---

9 A popular favorite of Irish folktales, this is the Finn of *Finnegans Wake* which Jung read at least in part in its serial publication as *Work in Progress* (CW 15, par. 165).

ring, the Fisher Ring, is an intaglio with the miraculous draft of fishes engraved on it. The same motif is in the book of the so-called *Shepherd of Hermas* (about 15 A.D.), where the multitude is represented by people coming from the four corners of the world.[10] Each one brings a stone or is himself a stone, and they fit the stones and themselves into a tower; then instantly the stones melt together with no visible joints, which of course makes an extraordinarily strong unit. It symbolizes the construction of the church. Hermas was said to be the brother of the second bishop of Rome, and the main problem then was the construction of the church. But it is also an individuation symbol.

Mr. Baumann: There are documents about the building of the pyramids, in which it is said that the surface was built of very diverse stones—alabaster, granite, limestone, etc.—and the joints were so carefully made that not even a knife-blade could be put between.

Prof. Jung: Yes, presumably it is the same idea, the building symbolizing absolute unity, no joints left. And so the original, somewhat disjointed and unadapted Mendelian units are to be fitted together so finely and closely that they can no longer separate. If they separate in life, it means schizophrenia, the dissociation of the mind. Then there are cases where one or another of these units cannot be fitted in, and that may be the cause of a neurosis, or it may be a latent psychosis, or any other trouble. It is like a sort of inclusion. I call these cases *Einschlüsse*, which means something locked in. It is like those peculiar phenomena where a teratoma is found to contain parts of an embryo, teeth or fingers or hair or something like an eye. They are parts of an unfinished foetus which was included in the body of the twin. The same phenomena occur in mental conditions also—a second personality, a psychological twin included in the psychical organism. That may cause much trouble. We have such a case also in the dream seminar.[11]

[10] *Shepherd of Hermas*, see *Dream Sem.*, pp. 185-86, and p. 106n above.
[11] See *Dream Sem.*, p. 311.

LECTURE V

16 November 1938

Prof. Jung:

We were speaking last week about the multitude of the collective man in the unconscious of one individual, and I mentioned the idea of the medieval philosophers, that the alchemical development—which of course is a psychological development—starts from *chaos*. They understood chaos to be a multitude of fragments of units, which they represented as an assembly of the gods, like the Olympian gods, for example. In Egypt there was a small company and a large company of gods, with the peculiarity that the last of the series of the large company was always double but counted as one. This is a very strange idea which one also finds in the book by Wallis Budge, *The Gods of the Egyptians*, under the heading, "The Companies of the Gods."[1] And there is the same idea in alchemy in the uncertainty about the 3 or 4 or the 7 and 8. It is as if the last number were always double, whatever that means; I just wanted to call your attention to it. These companies represent the psychical multitude, or the multitudinous quality of the unconscious. The unconscious consists of the multitude and is therefore always represented by a crowd of collective beings. The collective unconscious is projected into the crowd, the crowd represents it, and what we call "mob psychology" is really the psychology of the unconscious. Therefore, crowd psychology is archaic psychology. This peculiarity of our unconscious was realized long ago. Those companies of the gods represented it, and in the Middle Ages it became the alchemists' idea of chaos. By that time the old idea of the assembly of the gods, the pantheon, had practically disappeared, or was reduced to a triune god.

The three were a company originally, it was really a triad, but under the influence of monotheism it was distilled or sublimated to a unity. The Trinity still contains the idea of the triad however, and it was a tre-

[1] E. T. Wallis Budge, *The Gods of the Egyptians*, 2 vols. (London, 1904).

1404

mendous difficulty for the western mind to produce the idea of three persons in one. Since nobody takes it very seriously nowadays, since nobody bothers his head about it, it has ceased to be a problem; but the moment it is taken seriously, one will be confronted with that extraordinary puzzle of making three into one. It is a sort of compromise, an attempt to give a head to the multitude of the collective unconscious. You see, the original monotheism, like Jahvehism in Israel, or the monotheism of Amenhotep IV in Egypt, was possible because it was a sort of reformation against a background of extreme polytheism. There were the gods of the Babylonians, and of the Phoenicians, for instance, and Jahveh was the god of Israel, but by no means the only one. In the course of time he had undergone the evolution which was characteristic of the Egyptian gods—practically every god in Egypt arrived at the dignity of the world creator. Sometimes it was the god of Heliopolis, at another time, of Thebes, or of any other town, and each one was supposed to be the world creator. There was a sort of antagonism amongst the priests, an ambition to make their god the only one. That was the original monotheism, but later on, in Roman and Hellenistic antiquity for instance, there were very marked attempts to create the one god; the writers of the time already began to speak of one god, quite apart from Christianity.

For example, you may remember a legend from very early times which I have quoted here before, about the sea-captain who arrived in Ostia and demanded immediate audience with the Emperor, in order to tell him very important news: As his ship was passing a certain Greek island, they heard such a tremendous clamor there in the night that they approached and found that the people were wailing and lamenting because the great god Pan had died. You know Pan was originally a very minor god, an inferior local demon of the fields, but his name suggests the Greek *tò pan* which means the All, the universe, so he became a universal god. That was a serious attempt at monotheism out of polytheism. Buddha's great reformation in India was such an attempt, against the immense crowd of two and a half million Hindu gods. Buddha reduced them all to the one figure of the Perfect One, the Buddha himself—in that case a man but with the idea of absolute perfection. You know, in Buddhism, even the gods must become human, must be born as men in order to be redeemed. A god is merely a being that lives much longer than the ordinary human being and under very much more favorable circumstances; he lives perhaps for aeons of time, yet the end will come. Even the supreme gods, the so-called Brahmas, were supposed to have their appointed time and then they also would suddenly come to an end; when their karma was fulfilled, they would die or be reborn. That is described in one of the Buddhistic texts which I have mentioned here: when the karma of the semidivine beings that surround Brahma is fulfilled, they suddenly vanish, nothing is left. So we have plenty of evidence for the idea of the multitude that becomes transformed into one supreme being.

I have brought you today some pictures of the alchemical chaos. The first is a classical representation, the frontispiece of the *Songe de Poliphile*. At the bottom of the page, chaos is in the form of a circle containing irregular fragments which are also characterized by the planetary signs. This is a company of the gods—the planetary signs, as you know,

refer to the gods. For instance, iron is the sign of Mars, tin, the sign of Jupiter, silver, the sign of the moon, and copper, the sign of Venus. Sometimes instead of these fragments, the gods are presented as a collection of minerals or metals in the subterranean cave, as if they had degenerated into terrestrial bodies.

Then I want to show you the so-called Ripley scroll. It is from the British Museum, a MS of the 16th century. In this, chaos is not a collection of fragments but it is also a dark sphere, and it is represented as the basis of the alchemical process. Out of the dark sphere of chaos, vaporous exhalations rise. It is a sort of cosmic representation, like the earth in a primordial state, still a glowing globe from which those fumes issue. Then out of this glowing vaporous globe, the whole alchemical procedure starts, and it ascends to the company of the gods above. The idea is that the fumes are spirits or breath-beings, that develop, transform, and finally reveal their nature up above as the company of the gods. And all those gods are now contributing to the vase in which the *coniunctio* takes place, out of which comes the divine being. This is the *Puer Aeternus*, or the *Rebis*, the hermaphrodite. Then another kind of *coniunctio* takes place, belonging in another system of thought, which we shall presently meet in *Zarathustra*, namely, the union with the cerebro-spinal being, the toad, snake, or lizard. That is a sort of anima which becomes united with the *Puer Aeternus* and together they make the hermaphrodite. Also there is the idea here of the *nyagrodha* tree growing from above, the roots in heaven. Out of that comes the female part of the male god. This is the unit, the *quinta essentia*, of the company of the gods, the summing up of the transformation of the company of the gods into the one being, the process beginning in the dark sphere that represents chaos. The round sphere is also often represented by the *ouroboros* that eats its own tail.

Similar representations occur in practical psychology: these symbols are repeated fairly often in the beginning of the individuation process. I will show you the original of an unconscious picture which I used to illustrate one of my Eranos lectures.[2] The patient herself is represented as grown fast to the rock—in other words, identical with the unconscious which is the earth. The boulders are egg-shaped and really mean eggs, or the seed substance that is to be transformed. The next stage is in this picture of lightning striking the earth, and instead of the

[2] Jung delivered his paper "A Study in the Process of Individuation" at the Eranos Conference of 1933. As revised and expanded it appears in CW 9 i under its original title. The two paintings, with others from the same case, are reproduced in color following p. 292.

human being there is a perfectly round incandescent sphere, like the earth in a primeval incandescent condition, split off from the surrounding chaos—a bit of chaos is now cut loose from the surrounding chaos, as on the frontispiece of the *Songe de Poliphile*. The lightning means an influence which suddenly starts the individuation process: namely, that separation of a certain area of chaos. It is as if the individual, as depicted here, had been partially buried in chaos, only the upper part of her body being detached. You see, she was singled out, a separate being with a consciousness of her own, but in the lower stories she was not at all separated from the universe, one could say. And then through this lightning she suddenly appears as a whole, a circle or a globe, separated from the *participation mystique* with chaos, or, as we would say, with the collective unconscious. She is still a piece of chaos, and every piece contains chaos, is chaos, has chaotic quality, but the further development of this series leads into a differentiation of this primordial incandescent globe.

Then here are two photographs of pictures made by another patient. In the first, one gets the impression of a terribly cut-up condition: it looks like sort-of spiders' webs. This is a state of complete chaos,

with many splits in it, and a close analysis shows that it is a dissolved human body; one can discern an eye in it, and in the original, which is larger, one can make out other organs and blood. This would point to a schizophrenic condition, but it is a liquid schizophrenia, not a congealed case—a latent psychosis, not very serious but dangerous enough. It is as if those sharp splits, like splitting wood or ice with sharp edges, might eventually cut the whole human being into fragments. Then the next state is the big snake, and here we see the close association. She herself is almost crushed in the coils of an enormous serpent. This is again chaos but in the form of the great leviathan, as chaos is often represented in alchemy by the *ouroboros*, the great dragon. That change took place practically from one day to the next. On one day in the beginning she was perfectly chaotic, and the next move was a transformation of the original chaos into the serpent of chaos. This was a great advance, for the chaos was then in a form and the splits had disappeared; that sort of dead chaos became vivified in the form of the great original serpent. In other words, the chaos lost its multitudinous quality and became, as it were, personified; it was

gathered together and shaped into one being, a representative of the cerebro-spinal system.

Physiologically it would probably mean the transition from the state of the sympathetic nervous system into the cerebro-spinal system. Anything that is in the state of the sympathetic system has the character of a multitude, and if the sympathetic system is disturbed, there are often dreams which point to the dissolution or disintegration of the body, death dreams—or it may be mental death, a certain kind of destruction of the brain having the character of a multitude. This is a particularly important symptom for the doctor in making a diagnosis or a prognosis. I have a series of children's dreams in which the multitude occurs in the form of swarms of ants or flies. I mentioned a case last week where the whole series of dreams were premonitory of the child's death, the dreams anticipated the end; she died about a year later from an acute disease. I got the dreams before the child was ill and instantly had a fatal impression, but I was not sure whether it meant schizophrenia or the dissolution of the body. One cannot always tell, but that it meant something fatal was quite clear.

Then one can sometimes conclude as to the localization of the trouble. I had another case, a man who was himself a doctor and an alienist. He had had a peculiar kind of paralytic attacks, and the diagnosis was G.P.I. (general paralysis of the insane), but there was no syphilitic infection. He himself and some of his colleagues thought it was epilepsy, or a psychogenic trouble—that there was nothing the matter with his nervous system, that he was just hysterical—and he came to me for my diagnosis. He wanted to know exactly what it was because the attacks were quite alarming. Since there were no sufficiently decisive symptoms, I asked him for his dreams, and found that he had had a very remarkable dream at a time when he was particularly worried about his illness. He dreamt of a sort of hollow place, perhaps a gorge, where there had formerly been a lake. This had left a deposit of slime in which a prehistoric animal, a mammal something like a rhino, had been caught and had become fossilized. I assumed that his dream would have to do with his condition, taking into account that he was a doctor himself of course, so I made the following argument with myself: There is something the matter with the nervous system—his symptoms did not impress me as being psychogenic at all—and the animal in the dream is a relatively low prehistoric animal, belonging to a different stage of development from the actual brain of the present time, so it must refer to the lower stratas, the ganglia below the main brain. Because these animals have a small and unimportant development of the cerebrum, only the lower part of the brain would be developed, and that localizes the seat of the disease. Now what kind of disease? Well, there was an inundation which left a deposit. What can that be? Too much water probably in one of the caves, in one of the ventricles of the brain, an inundation, an inflammation, causing this serum which contains a lot of floating fibrous material, so when the water gets low it leaves a deposit. Therefore it must be the remains of an inflammatory process which had taken place in the ventricles.

Then I enquired into his history and it turned out that shortly before this disease had begun, he had a recrudescence of an old wound he had received in the war, a compound fracture of the thigh with a very bad infection. The whole thing was cured and nothing remained, yet these symptoms began soon after. I told him my guess and he did not know of course; it was a very adventurous way to arrive at a diagnosis. But he went then to one of the great Harley Street brain specialists who said it must be the remains of an inflammation of the ventricle. Well now, in the case of that other patient, the chaos becomes personified or synthesized in the next move by the serpent, which is a low cerebro-spinal animal. A higher form would be one of these prehistoric pachyderms, a mammal with warm blood.

Now I have here two more representations where the symbolism is quite plain. They are from the *Viridarium*, a book containing a number

of symbolic pictures attributed to famous old alchemists. This collection was made by Michael Majer who dates only from the 16th century, but the picture I am showing you is attributed to Avicenna the Arab, an alchemist of the 13th century.[3] An eagle is flying above with a chain on his talons which reaches down to earth, where a toad is fastened to the other end of it. The verse that goes with it says,

> Bufonum terrenum Aquile conjunge volanti,
> In nostra cernes arte magisterium.

That means: "Connect the earthly toad with the flying eagle and thou shalt understand the secret of our art." The flying eagle can be compared to Zarathustra's eagle and the toad corresponds to his serpent, the eagle representing the spirit or the mind, or a flying thought-being that consists of breath, while the toad just hops on the earth, an utterly chthonic animal. The second picture shows the company of the planetary gods in the interior of the earth.

Now we will continue chapter 51, "On Passing-By." As you know,

[3] Michael Maier (Majer), 16th-century alchemist, was a major source of Jung's alchemical lore. Daniel Stolcius de Stolcenberg, *Viridarium Chymicum* . . . (Frankfort on Main, 1624). Avicenna, 10th-11th century, Persian philosopher, physician.

this town is a representation of the multitude; it represents the collective man in Nietzsche himself, and we have already asked what his purpose was in lingering there. Having reviled the collective man enough already, why should he care to be irritated by him again? And then the fool comes and warns him not to enter the city. This is as if Nietzsche/Zarathustra had been quite unconscious of what he was really looking for in that place and had said to himself, "Don't be a fool, you know you despise those people. Why should you enter the city? What have you lost there?" And as if that tendency, that reaction, then became personified. Now would you say that this fool was pathological or abnormal? I should say that this fool makes sense.

> Why wouldst thou wade through this mire? Have pity upon thy foot! Spit rather on the gate of the city, and—turn back!
>
> Here is the hell for anchorites' thoughts: here are great thoughts seethed alive and boiled small.
>
> Here do all great sentiments decay: here may only rattle-boned sensations rattle!
>
> Smellest thou not already the shambles and cookshops of the spirit? Steameth not this city with the fumes of slaughtered spirit?
>
> Seest thou not the souls hanging like limp dirty rags?—And they make newspapers also out of these rags!
>
> Hearest thou not how spirit hath here become a verbal game? Loathsome verbal swill doth it vomit forth!—And they make newspapers also out of this verbal swill.
>
> They hound one another, and know not whither! They inflame one another, and know not why! They tinkle with their pinchbeck, they jingle with their gold.
>
> They are cold, and seek warmth from distilled waters: they are inflamed, and seek coolness from frozen spirits; they are all sick and sore through public opinion.

You see, the fool reviles the great city; he is really reiterating the words of Zarathustra. But it is against Zarathustra's apparent tendency. We assume that he wants to differentiate himself from the collective man, to make sure that he is not like that rabble, that *canaille*, and to tell his world what one should be really. Yet instead of going home to his cave he lingers there at the gate of the city, and then the fool comes out saying just what he has been saying himself. This is pretty bewildering. Why should that fool, obviously a compensatory figure, simply repeat Zarathustra's words? Yet he seems to have a noble intention: namely, to prevent Zarathustra from stepping into that mire. Now, that is a typical example of the way certain dreams work. Do you know what I mean?

Mrs. Fierz: I don't know what you mean, but I thought that it was a sort of mirror.

Prof. Jung: Absolutely, yes.

Mrs. Fierz: And a sort of overdone mirror, but pointing it all out very sharply so that the man has a chance to see what he is doing.

Prof. Jung: That he has a chance, that is it. Those among you who are interested in dreams will inevitably come across certain dreams which rub it in; that is, dreams which seem first to work in a direction which is just the direction you are afraid of. You think, "Now, too bad," for instead of compensating, the dream says "Go on, follow that road"— painting that road in marvelous colors. You can see that in love affairs, for instance, which in every respect are absolutely wrong and destructive, but the dreams say, "Just go on, that is the right way, is it not marvelous?"—and they force people, perhaps quite against the judgment of the analyst, on an obviously wrong way because it is a destructive way. Then of course you feel that you have to do something about it, but the only thing open to you is to deny the compensation theory of dreams, to say: "Your conscious is absolutely destructive and your dreams as well"—and that is not what one calls compensation.

Now India has a very helpful idea in that respect. Their idea of the great illusion, Maya, is not mere foolishness. One might ask why the god should create the world when it is only his own illusion, but Maya has a purpose. You see, matter is Prakrti, the female counterpart of the god, the goddess that plays up to Shiva, the blind creator that doesn't know himself—or to Prajapati, another name of the creator. In the Samkhya philosophy Prakrti dances Maya to the god, repeating the process of the great illusion innumerable times so that he can understand himself in all his infinite aspects. Thus the veil of Maya is a sort of private theater in which the god can see all aspects of himself and so become conscious. The only chance for the creator god to know himself is when Prakrti is performing for him. And this is despite the fact that it is his illusion, that it is Maya and should be dissolved because illusion means suffering and suffering should be dispelled. One might say, "Stop your illusion as soon as possible, your illusion will make you suffer." Prakrti nevertheless goes on dancing Maya because the point is, not that you should not suffer, but that you should not be blind, that you should see all aspects. So the compensation is there, only it is on a much greater scale than we thought. If you have dreams that recommend the wrong way, the destructive way, it is that they have the purpose—like the dancing of Prakrti—of showing you all aspects, of giving you a full experience of your being, even the experience of your destructiveness. It is a gruesome game: there are cases which are just tragic, and you cannot interfere. Nature is awful, and I often ask myself, should one not interfere? But one cannot really, it is impossible, because fate must be fulfilled. It is apparently more important to nature that one should have consciousness, understanding, than to avoid suffering.

So that fool is now playing the helpful wrong role, he continues the arch-error of Zarathustra in reviling the collective man. A certain amount of critique is quite right—he should see and know the collective man—but no use reviling him because he is then simply reviling his own body, his earthly existence, the ordinary man who is the actual supporter of life. In his mind alone he doesn't live; it is the banal collective man who lives, the man who carries on his existence in a heated room and eats three times a day and even earns money to pay for his needs. That very ordinary creature is the supporter of life, and if Nietzsche reviles that part of himself, he scolds himself out of life, exiles himself. Then he becomes nothing but an anchorite's thoughts, which will naturally be destroyed when they come into contact with collectivity. So the fool is really making the attempt at driving Zarathustra away from the collective man, and if Zarathustra keeps on returning to the big city, it indicates a very unrealized desire, or a need, to make a contact again with the collective man, in spite of the fact that he has reviled him consciously. Now I think we can leave this fool who exaggerates and compensates Zarathustra's attitude, and see how Zarathustra reacts to his own exaggeration. It is in the middle of the next page:

> Stop this at once! called out Zarathustra, long have thy speech and thy species disgusted me!
>
> Why didst thou live so long by the swamp, that thou thyself hadst to become a frog and a toad?

The fool was talking exactly in the style of Zarathustra, and now suddenly Zarathustra turns against him—as if he, Zarathustra, had not said the same. What is happening here?

Miss Hannah: It is a case of having to meet yourself, is it not?

Prof. Jung: That is true. When you hold an exaggerated position and then encounter it objectively, either you are unable to recognize it, or you refuse it, deny it. It works in this way, I have a good example: I had an uncle who was a mechanical genius and when Edison invented the phonograph, he read about it and made one for himself. His wife was a sort of Xanthippe—though of course she had her point too, you can imagine such a man is not quite easy for a wife—and once she went for him and gave him a furious sermon. He meanwhile quietly let the phonograph take a record of it. Then the next day when she had quieted down, he said, "I must show you something funny, and turned the phonograph on. And she said: "That is not true, I never said such a thing!" She simply denied that objectivation of herself. Thus far the role of the fool has worked in the same way: the fool took over Zarathustra's own mind and objectified it, and when Zarathustra saw it, he denied it completely. And he accused the fool of having lived so long by the swamp that he had become a frog and a toad. These metaphors are quite interesting. What do they mean?

Mrs. Fierz: The swamp is the birthplace of low forms of life, and a frog or a toad is a low form of the human body.

Prof. Jung: Well, the interesting fact is that the frog or the toad is the first attempt of nature to make a being with two legs and two arms and no tail. That is the first edition of man, but it is on the level of cold-blooded animals. You see, whatever one may think from the biological side about such an analogy, that analogy has been made. It is not my invention that man comes up from the swamp—the unconscious—where all the little beasts abound, where life begins to develop from germs practically. The swamp is an exceedingly fertile place, teeming with low life; every drop in it is filled with low life, and that is an excellent image of the collective unconscious, where everything is breathing and breeding. And then up comes a primitive man, almost non-human, a very low form that is almost unacceptable. There is a certain fairy tale in that connection: A princess lost her golden ball. It fell into a well and was gone, and the frog was the only one who could dive down and get it. But she had to submit to a series of conditions which in the long run transformed the frog into a prince, the redeemer.

You see, it is very apt that the fool should be called "a frog," since he is a very primitive being, a sort of low animal that comes up from the collective unconscious. Of course he ought to be accepted by consciousness, and here again Nietzsche makes a tragic mistake: he doesn't reflect about it, doesn't try to explain that figure to himself, never stops to ask why the fool should appear and what it means. If he could only realize that the fool was repeating his own words, he would instantly draw the conclusion, "*I* have been the fool, Prakrti shows me that I am the fool." Then he would ask himself, "But why do I talk like a fool? Well, something is driving me crazy, something is at me." And

he would see that the frog, a low man, the fool who was called Zarathustra's ape, his more primitive self—that thing wanted to get at him.
Then he could ask himself, "But why does that low thing want to get at
me?"—and the answer would obviously be, "Because I am too differentiated, too high, too flimsy and airy; I have an exaggerated
mind."He might then conclude that the frog man was the bearer of the
good news; he might see that the unconscious was offering him something which would be most useful. While he is talking, the unconscious
flows in and gives him that healthy and useful symbolism, but he only
uses it as a new means of reviling a seeming opponent.

This idea that the primitive being from the collective unconscious is
a frog, we encounter again, at least in an illusion, on the Ripley scroll,
where the dragon is persecuting a small frog.[4] The frog is the being
that comes from below, and the dragon—originally the *ouroboros*—represents chaos underneath, and naturally he will try to catch the frog
and prevent its becoming the thing above. For the frog becomes the
Puer Aeternus; it will appear in the assembly of the gods. One could call
the assembly of the gods the brain, and there in the brain, in consciousness, the frog appears as the *Puer Aeternus* plus the being that comes
from above. Quite on top is a female with a salamander's tail and the
feet of a frog: it is half frog or lizard and half human. That is a typical
old representation of the anima, or the consort of the gods. In India
you see this figure in the famous rock sculpture at Mamallipuram,
where the birth of the Ganges river is represented as a goddess, female
above and serpent below. And that is the classical representation of Lilith, Adam's first wife, who is also identified with the serpent on the tree
of knowledge in paradise, the supposed devil that tells Adam and Eve
that they should eat of the fruit. And it is the same in these medieval
alchemistic pictures, which means that the female is only partially human, and partially she is a cerebro-spinal animal, half woman, half serpent, being stuck in the lower parts of the nervous system.

Now Zarathustra goes on reviling the fool:

> Floweth there not a tainted, frothy, swamp-blood in thine own
> veins, when thou hast thus learned to croak and revile?
> Why wentest thou not into the forest? Or why didst thou not till
> the ground? Is the sea not full of green islands?

He only becomes conscious of this very good advice when the reviling
is objectified.

---

[4] Sir George Ripley (c. 1415-90) was an English alchemist very often cited by Jung in
the CW.

I despise thy contempt; and when thou warnedst me—why didst thou not warn thyself?

It is really amazing that a man in his senses could write such contradictions. If he only could have stopped, waited a moment, and asked, "But what have I done? What am I doing? It is irritatingly like what one reads in the newspapers nowadays.

> Out of love alone shall my contempt and my warning bird take wing; but not out of the swamp!

He thinks he would take it if a golden eagle would come and serve it on a golden tray. But a frog out of the swamp! What is the good of something coming out of the unconscious, the swamp in oneself! That is the Christian prejudice.

> They call thee mine ape, thou foaming fool: but I call thee my grunting-pig,—by thy grunting, thou spoilest even my praise of folly.

Here he discovers that he even contains a grunting pig, a particularly bad one, a pig with its nose in the mire, a dirty, disgusting animal. But of course he doesn't realize what that means.

> What was it that first made thee grunt? Because no one sufficiently flattered thee:—therefore didst thou seat thyself beside this filth, that thou mightest have cause for much grunting.

This is a tremendous realization, really, so one could expect some humbleness. After such a recognition one could almost expect Nietzsche to take what he is saying a little more into consideration.

> That thou mightest have cause for much vengeance! For vengeance, thou vain fool, is all thy foaming; I have divined thee well!

But not himself. He sees very well where the fool is wrong but unfortunately he doesn't know that he himself is the fool.

> But thy fools'-word injureth *me* [*me* emphasized] even when thou art right! And even if Zarathustra's word were a hundred times justified, thou wouldst ever—do wrong with my word! [Because it is against him.]
>
> Thus spake Zarathustra. Then did he look on the great city and sighed, and was long silent. At last he spake thus:
>
> I loathe also this great city, and not only this fool. Here and there—there is nothing to better, nothing to worsen.

Woe to this great city—and I would that I already saw the pillar of fire in which it will be consumed!

For such pillars of fire must precede the great noontide. But this hath its time and its own fate.—

This precept, however, give I unto thee, in parting, thou fool: Where one can no longer love, there should one—*pass by*—

Thus spake Zarathustra, and passed by the fool and the great city.

So he really loved the great city: that was the reason he waited so long. But why did he revile what he loved? Exactly as he tells the fool: because they did not sufficiently flatter him. So he has feelings of vengeance, he is resentful. It is tantalizing that Nietzsche did not realize it. Now there is a peculiar metaphor in the last verse, the pillars of fire. Why *pillars* of fire?

Mrs. Sigg: It is in the Old Testament, the pillar of fire in the desert.[5]

Prof. Jung: Yes, Jahveh leading his people in the desert, in the day a pillar of cloud, in the night a pillar of fire. Jahveh is a fiery god, a devouring fire. This is a very Protestant vision, absolutely in the style of the Old Testament. It means: I wish that Jahveh's fire would fall upon the heads of the crowd, as in Sodom and Gomorrah. I wish that the pillar of fire would eat up that rabble. This would be to him the great noontide, the consuming fire of Jahveh would be the sign that the great noontide was beginning. But then he himself would be consumed of course. Because he wishes that on the ordinary collective man in himself, he wishes it on his own body; but his soul will die first just because his body is consumed. That is the fire of madness, the outburst of mad passion. As in dreams, a fire in the house always means an outburst of passion or a panic. So this fire, Jahveh's fire, is a sort of destructive panic, and it is the terrible god. The fear of God is just as important as the love of God, for he is not only a loving God, but also terrible; otherwise what would be his power? Man never appreciates what is lovely—he appreciates what he is afraid of. So the curse Nietzsche pronounces here works directly against his body, against the banal human creature in himself upon which he lives. By that curse he prepares his own downfall. He thinks that this pillar of fire precedes the great noontide, but it would be the holocaust. If that fire comes it will be a terrible conflagration. I rather insist upon these passages, because we are now exactly in the beginning of the holocaust.

[5] Exodus 13:21.

LECTURE VI

30 November 1938

Prof. Jung:
In the preceding chapter, you remember, Zarathustra had that interview with the fool who repeated practically everything Zarathustra had said. He took on Zarathustra's role for the obvious purpose of making him conscious of something. Now what was the fool intending?

Mrs. Crowley: Did we not already say, to be a mirror? It was to mirror his shadow in a sense.

Prof. Jung: Well, it is a compensation exactly as it is in dreams. Nietzsche, in his identity with Zarathustra, reviles the collective man without realizing that he is a collective man himself, so he is really reviling himself. And so he creates a gap between his consciousness and the biological fact that he is like everybody else; his stomach, his heart, his lungs are exactly like everybody's organs. The only difference between himself and the ordinary man is that his thoughts reach a bit farther and his mind is a bit richer. Of course he may criticize collective man, but to revile him amounts to a *ressentiment* against himself, creating, as I said, a tremendous gap, a split, in his own personality. Now, when one goes to the extreme in such an endeavor, one usually encounters a reaction on the part of the unconscious; one has a dream or some other experience which shows what one is doing. So this encounter with the fool could be a dream just as well; it is as if he dreamt of a madman assailing him and saying, curiously enough, exactly what Nietzsche had already said. From this we see that Nietzsche is identical with the fool—the fool is only another side or aspect of himself,—and when he shouts down the fool, it means he is shouting himself down. He even creates the fool a second time, you see, to show him what he ought to do, but he does it unconsciously, naively, without realizing that he is really correcting himself, his own views. And because it is done unconsciously, what may we expect in the subsequent chapter?

Miss Hannah: A repetition.

Prof. Jung: Yes, he goes on in the same style because he has not re-

alized the experience. No sooner is that episode dealt with than he simply goes on as before, as if nothing had happened in between. Even the
title of the next chapter, "The Apostates," shows that he is continuing
to revile his contemporaries, giving vent to all his resentment. For instance, he says in the fourth verse,

> Verily, many of them once lifted their legs like the dancer; to
> them winked the laughter of my wisdom:—then did they bethink
> themselves. Just now have I seen them bent down—to creep to the
> cross.

He is now attacking the good Christians, and that goes on all through
this chapter and the next, "The Return Home." It is hardly worthwhile to spend time on these critical remarks because they are so
clearly based on his resentment. I only want to call your attention to the
last verse, where he says,

> The grave-diggers dig for themselves diseases. Under old rub-
> bish rest bad vapours. One should not stir up the marsh. One
> should live on mountains.

Here he eventually reaches a sort of insight. He was just grave-digging
before; he dug graves for all the people he was criticizing, saying that
they should all be done away with, burned up like wood or chaff. But
he comes to the conclusion here that it is not really worthwhile to dig
graves—it is even obnoxious. In the German text it says *Die Totengräber
graben sich Krankheiten an*, which means that they have dug graves for
others so long that they even caught their diseases. A certain insight is
beginning to dawn, and therefore he says one should not stir up the
marsh: it contains too many bad vapors—one should live on the mountains instead. That is of course again the wrong conclusion. The lower
regions are perfectly ordinary and normal; they are only bad because
he makes them bad. Unfortunately enough, he has certain thoughts
which transcend the lower regions, but that doesn't mean that he is
identical with those high thoughts. In that respect he is exactly like the
tenor who thinks he is identical with his high notes; but the tenor is a
very ordinary man, and the more he identifies with his beautiful high
notes, the lower his character will be, if it is only by way of compensation. So Nietzsche's insight remains only half an insight; he doesn't
draw the right conclusions, and again he makes the attempt to lift himself up out of the marsh of other people. He says,

> With blessed nostrils do I again breathe mountain-freedom.
> Freed at last is my nose from the smell of all human hubbub!

That is his extraordinary illusion. He thinks when he is climbing up to the Engadine, filling his lungs with the wonderful mountain air, that he had gotten rid of himself. But he carries all the collective hubbub with him up to the mountains, because he himself is the ordinary man.

> With sharp breezes tickled, as with sparkling wine, sneezeth my soul—sneezeth, and shouteth self-congratulatingly: "Health to thee!"

The sneezing refers to the first sneeze of the new-born child. The primitives assume that in the moment when the child sneezes for the first time after birth, the soul enters the body. In Genesis it is said that God breathed the breath of life into the nostrils of Adam, and in that moment be became a living soul. That is the moment of sneezing. So when a negro king happens to sneeze, the whole crowd bows for about five minutes and everybody congratulates him, because it means that a new soul has entered the king; in other words, an increase of life, libido, mana, vital energy. Therefore we still say, "Health to thee" when someone sneezes, because the old archetypal idea that a new soul has entered the body when we sneeze is still alive. It is a lucky moment but also a dangerous one, for it is not sure what kind of soul it may be, so one must say "Prosit. Health, Luck to thee," hoping thereby to propitiate the moment, to make it a lucky moment. A bad ancestral soul or any bad soul may be hovering over a person, and by that good wish one tries to prevent its entrance, or to turn the bad luck into good luck. So Nietzsche understands the moment when he leaves the lower regions as a sort of rebirth of his own soul, as if a new soul has entered him.

Mrs. Baumann: In English the old-fashioned way is to say, "God bless you" when anyone sneezes.

Prof. Jung: Yes, that is the same propitiatory mantra. And you see it also denotes the moment of a change of mind apparently. He has been occupied too long with the lower people, and now he realizes that, by being their grave-digger, he might get infected by their diseases. So there is a sort of renewal. Now, what may we expect after this?

Mrs. Fierz: That the character of the new soul will become visible.

Prof. Jung: Yes, we may expect a change. We might expect that his continuous sermon about the misery and inferiority of his fellow beings would come to a definite end. Since a new soul means an increase of life, we might expect something more positive. In the last chapters he became so negative and sterile that it was even boring. The next chapter, the 54th, is called "The Three Evil Things"—which doesn't sound very hopeful, but right in the beginning something has happened to him: he has had a dream. A dream often accompanies or denotes a new situation, a new access of libido, a new increase of energy. After the sneezing it is quite proper that in the night he should have the corresponding dream, showing an entirely different situation, a change of mind, presumably for the better. Now he says,

In my dream, in my last morning-dream, I stood to-day on a promontory—beyond the world; I held a pair of scales, and *weighed* the world.

Alas, that the rosy dawn came too early to me: she glowed me awake, the jealous one! Jealous is she always of the glows of my morning-dream.

Measurable by him who hath time, weighable by a good weigher, attainable by strong pinions, divinable by divine nut-crackers: thus did my dream find the world:—

My dream, a bold sailor, half-ship, half-hurricane, silent as the butterfly, impatient as the falcon: how had it the patience and leisure to-day for world-weighing!

Did my wisdom perhaps speak secretly to it, my laughing, wide-awake day-wisdom, which mocketh at all "infinite worlds"? For it saith: "Where force is, there becometh *number* the master: it hath more force."

How confidently did my dream contemplate this finite world, not new-fangledly, not old-fangledly, not timidly, not entreatingly:—

—As if a big round apple presented itself to my hand, a ripe golden apple, with a coolly-soft, velvety skin:—thus did the world present itself unto me:—

—As if a tree nodded unto me, a broad-branched, strong willed tree, curved as a recline and a foot-stool for weary travellers: thus did the world stand on my promontory:—

—As if delicate hands carried a casket towards me—a casket open for the delectations of modest adoring eyes: thus did the world present itself before me to-day—

—Not riddle enough to scare human love from it, not solution enough to put to sleep human wisdom:—a humanly good thing was the world to me to-day, of which such bad things are said!

Our hypothesis that the sneezing was a good omen is substantiated by this beginning. He has discovered a more positive aspect, which becomes particularly obvious in the paragraph, "As a humanly good thing did it come unto me, this dream and heart-comforter!" He should have added "of which I have spoken so negatively," but that is not realized because the whole process of thought is peculiarly unconscious. There is a lack of that mirroring because Nietzsche never stands aside, looking at a thing or reflecting upon it: he is merely the process. So the whole thing happens in a sort of *clair-obscure*, in twilight, and one always misses the human reaction on his part. He is the process itself. You see, he says that the dream is a bold sailor, half ship, half hurricane; there are really three figures. But the sailor is by no means the ship and by no means the wind—that is a hybrid picture, and it is most characteristic of Nietzsche himself. The dream has again functioned as a sort of mirror, which his intellect should have provided. But if his intellect doesn't provide it, the dream will provide it. This is usually the case with people who don't think, who take a pride in blindly living, flowing on like a river with no self-reflection. Then the unconscious functions as a mirror; the dream takes over the function of the intellect.

We are usually simply unable—even if we try—to think or to realize what we live. We just live without knowing what we live, and of course it would be an almost superhuman task to realize oneself completely. The Indian philosophers are aware of this fact, far more so than we in the West. We praise a life that is just living, that is not really lived because there is no subject, but only an object to it. A life that runs away with a man seems wonderful to us. There is no subject because we only know of the will that inhibits life; we use our intellect or willpower to inhibit life. And we know very little about reflecting and mirroring life, accompanying this life. Therefore we know so little about a symbolic mentality, a symbolic mind that creates and at the same time formulates life. The East is fully aware of our peculiar incapacity for knowing what we are living, and there they insist upon *realizing*; one often hears that word out there. And then the Westerner says, "Realize what?" Well, realizing what one is, what one lives, what one does. To a stranger such talk is bewildering, but if one is able to enter a bit further into the Eastern mind, one sees what they mean, and one then profoundly realizes the fact that we do not realize enough. So any Eastern philosophy—or Yoga, rather, for it is not philosophy in the Western sense—begins with the question, "Who am I? Who are you?" That is the philosophic question *par excellence* which the Yogin asks his disciples. For the goal and the purpose of Eastern philosophy is that complete realization of the thing which lives, the thing which *is*. And they have that idea because they are aware of the fact that man's consciousness is always behind the facts; it never keeps up with the flux of life. Life is in a way too rich, too quick, to be realized fully, and they know that one only lives completely when one's mind really accompanies one's life, when one lives no more than one can reflect upon with one's thought, and when one thinks no further than one is able to live. If one could say that of oneself, it would be a guarantee that one really was living.

For what is a life or a world of which one is not aware? If there is a great treasure which nobody knows exists, it is as if there were no treasure. Schopenhauer, who was influenced by Buddhist philosophy, was practically the only one in the West to realize that the world would not exist if we did not know it existed; that is the *sine qua non* of existence. Consciousness is appreciated very little in the West; everybody talks as if the world were going to exist even beyond consciousness.[1] But we are by no means sure whether anything exists beyond consciousness. As long as America was not discovered, our world went on as if it were not there, America only began to exist when we discovered it. So it is futile to discuss the possibility of anything existing unless we know it exists.

Now, Nietzsche was in a more of less unconscious condition practically all the time that he was writing this book, and that shows itself very clearly in this hybrid image, the sailor, the ship, and the hurricane; for his dream is himself. He himself is the sailor and the ship and the hurricane: "silent as the butterfly, impatient as the falcon." The dream begins with the statement that he is standing on a promontory. Why just on a promontory? He has been on the plain in the midst of the human hubbub, in the big town where the swamp of humanity dwells, and he is now seeking solitude. I was under the impression that he had gone up to the wonderful, clear atmosphere of the Engadine, that he was breathing the pure air six thousand feet above good and evil. But it turns out that he is on a promontory, and that is usually a precipitous point of land jutting out into the sea.

---

[1] Jung, in making Schopenhauer so nearly distinctive in this respect is presumably thinking simply of those who strongly influenced Nietzsche. Other idealists like Berkeley and Hegel do not figure at all prominently in Nietzsche's (or Jung's) philosophical education. As he occasionally explains, Jung does not mean to say that the universe is merely a content of human consciousness, but rather that for the purposes of life, that which is outside of consciousness is as if it did not exist.

Mrs. Baumann: But it is not an ordinary promontory, because he is outside of the world.

Prof. Jung: You are quite right, but I should like a more definite formulation.

Mrs. Jung: In reality there is a sort of promontory on the lake of Sils, and it was a favorite spot of Nietzsche's.

Prof. Jung: That is true. Part of *Zarathustra* was conceived on a promontory in reality. His eternity song was created on the so-called Chastè, which is a little promontory jutting out into the Silsersee. There is an inscription there to commemorate it.

Mrs. Sigg: Another favorite place of Nietzsche's, the place he liked best, was the promontory of Porto Fino.

Prof. Jung: Yes, he worked on *Zarathustra* there also, and he is speaking in this passage about the sea; obviously his image does not refer to the lake of Sils but to the Mediterranean: Porto Fino is on the Riviera. So the idea of a promontory plays rather an important and very concrete role in Nietzsche's mind. But of course it is a symbol too, so what does it mean when a man arrives on a promontory?

Mrs. Schlegel: It is the end of the world.

Prof. Jung: Yes, like Finisterre or Land's End: those are promontories; he is really at the end of the world where the infinity of sea begins. And that means what psychologically?

Mr. Allemann: Where his conscious ends and the unconscious begins.

Prof. Jung: Yes, he comes to the end of conscious knowledge, conscious views, *terra firma*, and he is now vis-à-vis the infinite and indefinite sea, which has forever been a symbol of the unconscious state of mind, where new things may begin. Something may come up from the sea. For the time being, he has definitely reached an end.

Mrs. Crowley: He has really been annihilating the world.

Prof. Jung: Yes, nothing good was left in his world. Everything became negative and was trampled underfoot, and now he is at the end of his rope one could say—there is Finisterre. So he might expect a new island to appear, or that he would discover new contents. Therefore the picture of the bold sailor, the ship, and the hurricane; that image, his mental process, leads him out to the sea. Now into what further does that process lead him? In order to weigh a planet, where would he have to be?

Mrs. Baumann: Outside the world.

Prof. Jung: Of course, in space somewhere. And then how does the earth appear?

Mrs. Fierz: Like a sort of apple.

Prof. Jung: Yes, so that hurricane, or that adventure he is undergoing, now leads him not only beyond humanity but beyond the planet, in a sort of extra-mundane condition; he takes his position in space and looks down on the earth as if he were God. Where do we encounter that symbolism—where the world appears as an apple?

Miss Wolff: The *Reichsapfel.*

Prof. Jung: Yes, the apple that represents the world in the hand of the Emperor. It was not an apple really, but a golden globe which the Emperor held in his hand at the coronation, denoting that he was *in loco Dei,* that he was God's lieutenant. Therefore his head was the sun, and his crown expressed the celestial rays issuing from the sun. And the *pallium,* the coronation tunic, symbolized the firmament, decorated with stars and with the zodiacal signs. His body was covered with stars, orders, and decorations, like the old Babylonian kings and the kings of Assyria. To wear stars upon their bodies meant that they were gods. The king was a manifestation or an incarnation of the deity upon earth, so he was able to carry the earth in the hollow of his hand. Nietzsche has here unwittingly slipped into the role of the deity even, and is now weighing the earth in his hand; from that very remote standpoint he is judging the world. Where does that image—weighing the world in the scales—come from?

Answer: The Apocalypse.

Mrs. Fierz: From Egypt.

Prof. Jung: Yes, it is in Revelations, and there was an Egyptian ceremony where the heart was weighed. It is an age-old idea. In the *Book of the Dead* by Sir Wallis Budge there is a picture of the heart of the king being weighed. Only the king's heart was weighed in the beginning, and then very much later, in the Ptolemaic era, when Osiris became the personal Osiris of everybody, that chapter in the *Book of the Dead* was applicable for the funeral rites of any ordinary person. But originally it was only the king's heart which was weighed. If it was found to be righteous, he could enter eternal life, and if it was found to be worthless, it was thrown to Tefnut, the hippo-crocodile monster of the underworld that swallowed the hearts of those men whose evil deeds outweighed their good deeds. That is the picture here: Zarathustra is weighing the world as if it were the heart in order to judge its value. This is one of the clearest cases of Nietzsche's God-Almighty identification.

Now, there is a peculiar idea in these two paragraphs: "As if the big round apple presented itself to my hand, a ripe golden apple, with a coolly-soft, velvety skin:—thus did the world present itself unto me:—

As if a tree nodded unto me, a broad-branched, strong-willed tree, curved as a recline and a foot-stool for weary travellers: thus did the world stand on my promontory." This is rather interesting. It is as if he had encountered a tree growing on that promontory, with a golden apple hanging on it, and as if he had weighed that apple on the scales of his judgment. Our assumption was that he had been whirled out into space like a ship driven by a hurricane, and from the cosmic distances of space was now judging the world, since the world, seen from afar, looks the size of an apple. We were not prepared for this image of the tree on the promontory. Therefore the suspicion arises here that two pictures are mixed up and interfering. And this other image, a bold sailor, half ship and half hurricane, is perfectly nonsensical. So this is an unconscious contamination of pictures which one easily passes over in reading the text. If one thinks about it, one knows it is impossible as a picture, but in just reading it over, it sinks into one's mind without arousing any further comment because it fits somehow the peculiar condition of the images in the unconscious. What is that condition?

Miss Hannah: Contamination. There is a mixture of everything, so nothing comes up pure.

Prof. Jung: Yes, they are interchangeable; anything can be mixed with anything. Unfortunately it is impossible to have a look into the unconscious without disturbing it, for no sooner do you look than it is already disturbed. It is like trying to observe the process in the interior of the atom; in the instant of observation, a disturbance is created—by observing you produce distortion. But let us assume that you could look into the unconscious without disturbing anything: you would then see something which you could not define because everything would be mixed with everything else even to the minutest detail. It is not that certain recognizable fragments of this and that are mixing or contacting or overlapping: they are perfectly unrecognizable atoms so that you are even unable to make out to what kind of bodies they eventually will belong—unrecognizable atoms producing shapes which are impossible to follow. If a dream, for instance, comes out of that depth of the unconscious, you cannot remember it, or if by great good luck you are able to remember a detail of it, it is utterly chaotic and almost impossible to interpret. The reason why you cannot remember dreams is because the fragments of which they are composed are too small to be recognizable; you cannot say to what one fragment belongs, or what it would be if integrated with a more tangible connection. Well now, that tree standing on the promontory at the end of his consciousness is

1429

surely the idea of the world-tree upon which the sun is an apple, and the whole universe, the planets, the starry sky, just the blossoms or fruits. But this tree is standing upon *his* promontory.

Mr. Bash: Is not the idea here like the tree with the golden apples of the Hesperides on the edge of the world—that he has finished his conscious living and launches out as the souls did?

Prof. Jung: Yes, the garden of the Hesperides is in the West, at the end of the known world in antiquity; that would be this *"finis terrae"* where the tree grows. Of course the garden of the Hesperides is an application of an archetypal idea—that when you come to the end of things you will find at last that tree. But you also find the tree at the beginning of things. And where would that be?

Miss Hannah: In the Garden of Eden.

Prof. Jung: Yes, with the marvelous apples.

Mrs. Crowley: Also in the Osiris legend there is a wonderful tree, with all the birds flying over it.

Prof. Jung: You mean where he transforms into a tree? That is also at the end of things. And in the Germanic sagas when the end of the world comes, what happens to the last couple there?

Mrs. Brunner: They go back into the tree.

Prof. Jung: Into Yggdrasil, the world-tree. And the first couple came from trees. There was the same idea in Persia.

Now I have just been asked about the dream and the unconscious, in reference to the peculiarly fragmentary condition of the unconscious of which I was speaking. That fragmentary condition is the unconscious without disturbance, the presumable state of images in a truly unconscious condition. It is impossible to have a complete experience of such a state, because inasmuch as you experience the unconscious you touch it, you disturb it; when the rays of consciousness reach the unconscious it is at once synthesized. Therefore, I repeat, you cannot have an immediate experience of the original or elementary state of the unconscious. Certain dreams refer to it, or I would not dare to speak of that state, but such dreams only happen under very extraordinary conditions, either under toxic conditions or in the neighborhood of death or in very early childhood, when there is still a sort of faint memory of the unconscious condition from which the first consciousness emerges.

It was in connection with these remarks that I was asked how it is that in the beginning of the analytical treatment, dreams are usually much more complete, more synthesized, more plastic, than in the later stages. That fact has really nothing to do with the original or essential condition of the unconscious; it has very much more to do with the peculiar condition of consciousness in the beginning of the analytical treatment, and towards the end of it or in a later stage of it. In the beginning there is a very fragmentary consciousness in which many things which should belong to consciousness are not represented. These contents are semi-conscious; they are dark representations, or dark contents, which are not completely black. They are not in a completely unconscious condition, but in a relatively unconscious condition, and they form a substantial part of the personal subconscious.[2] It is a sort of fringe of semidarkness, and because there is so little light people assume that they can see nothing. They don't like to look; they turn away from it, and so they leave many things there which they could see just as well if they would take the trouble to be conscious. Therefore Freud quite rightly speaks of repressions. People disregard the contents of this fringe of consciousness because they are more of less incompatible with their ideals, their aspiring tendencies. But they have a vague consciousness of something there, and the more of that consciousness there is, the more there is that phenomenon of repression. There is a wilful inattention, a preference not to see or to know these things, but if they would only turn their head, they could see them.

It is a fact, then, that there are such highly synthetical contents in the unconscious, the shadow for instance, of which many people are unconscious—though not totally unconscious. They have a pretty shrewd notion that something is wrong with them on the other side. That highly synthesized figure appears in dreams and informs us of that other unconscious sphere. And these dreams are synthetical because they are built up of that synthetical material, which could be conscious just as well. Often it is a sort of negligence that it is not conscious. Now, if you analyze that material, if you integrate it into consciousness, you gradually remove the synthetical contents from the unconscious and clear up that sphere of twilight, the so-called subconscious, so that the collective unconscious can appear. The collective unconscious is normally in a state of absolute chaos—an atomic chaos—and that cannot become conscious; only synthesized figures can become conscious. Just as you cannot see the atomic world without applying all sorts of means to make it visible, so you cannot enter the unconscious unless there are

---

[2] In his published writing, Jung rarely used the concept of "the subconscious," but here it serves to distinguish the personal from the collective in the vast realm that lies outside consciousness.

certain synthesized figures. Now these later dreams are far less clear, far less synthetical than those in the beginning, because you have removed all the synthetical parts since they were capable of becoming conscious. But the collective unconscious is not inclined to become conscious, but needs very special conditions for it to become conscious at all. It needs a peculiar subjective condition, a sort of fatal condition—that you are vitally threatened by an external or internal situation, for instance, or that you are deeply connected with the general mind in a very serious crisis. Under such conditions the collective unconscious attracts so much consciousness that it begins to synthesize; then it forms the compensatory figures to the conscious.

So when the case is very serious, even in the second or third or 101st part of your analysis, you may suddenly develop a highly synthetical dream, which of course has then the character of a big dream, a big vision; such dreams often have a visionary character. But all the ordinary dreams in between are singularly chaotic and apparently not very meaningful. The rule is, that when you have gone through the inevitable analytical procedure, you will be left in the end with very few dreams, often none for months. Of course you always dream really, but they are impossible to remember, just a string of fragments. When you do happen to remember such dream material, it is very distorted, an unclear chaotic sequence, sometimes very difficult to interpret. Of course those dreams which you can remember can be tackled, because they are more or less synthetic. In the first part of an analysis, then, dreams are synthetic and well composed on account of the fact that they live on synthetic material. In the end the synthetic material is all gone, and you usually cannot remember the dreams; only very rarely do you have an important one. But that is as it should be. You see, dreams are, according to my idea, not aids to sleep as Freud says, but disturbers of sleep. When you remember your dreams the whole night through, you have a very light sleep. So it is perfectly normal when dreams are weak or seem to fail altogether, and if you only rarely have an important dream, that is all you can wish for. You see, that has nothing to do with the theoretical question of the actual state of the unconscious without the interference of consciousness. Well now, Mrs. Baumann has a contribution to the tree symbolism.

Mrs. Baumann: I thought it was very interesting that in the prehistoric mythology of the island of Crete, of which practically nothing is known, there is another example of a world-tree. In a picture on a gold seal ring called the "Ring of Nestor," the tree is depicted in connection with scenes in the underworld. The trunk of the tree and two large branches divide the picture into four scenes. In the first, there are two butterflies and two chrysalises over the head of the Mother Goddess, and they seem to represent the souls of a man and a woman who are shown greeting each other with surprise. In the lower part of the picture is a judgment scene, and the Mother Goddess is standing behind a table on which a griffin is seated, as the souls are brought before her by strange bird-headed beings. Another point is, that in some of the graves, miniature scales made of gold have been found. They are so small that they must be symbolic, and a butterfly is engraved on each of the golden discs which form the balance, so it looks as if the souls were weighed as butterflies, not as hearts as in Egypt. The highest development of the Minoan civilization in Crete was contemporary with that of Egypt, its earliest beginnings dating as far back as 3000 B.C.

Prof. Jung: That is a remarkable contribution to the tree and the butterfly symbolism. You remember Nietzsche applies that symbol of the butterfly to himself—quite aptly, because nobody gets beyond the world, outside the field of gravity, where he might see the world as an apple, unless he has become a soul. One must be a sort of ghost to get to such distances. To step out of the body and become the spirit or the soul itself, denotes a kind of *ekstasis.* Now, we have a number of associations about that tree, and we should try to understand what it means practically when Nietzsche reaches the promontory, the end of his world, the end of his consciousness, and meets there the tree. You have heard that the tree is always the symbol of the end as well as of the beginning, of the state before man and the state after man.

Mr. Bash: Would the tree not be the symbol of the *collectivum* out of which man is differentiated and into which his elements dissolve?

Prof. Jung: That is certainly so, and why is that *collectivum* symbolized by the tree?

Mrs. Sachs: The tree means vegetative life.

Prof. Jung: Yes. It might be the snake or any other animal or the earth, but no, it is the tree, and the tree means something specific; that is a peculiar symbol. It is the tree that nourishes all the stars and planets; and it is the tree out of which come the first parents, the primordial parents of humanity, and in which the last couple, also representing the whole of humanity, are buried. That of course means that consciousness comes from the tree and dissolves into the tree again—the consciousness of human life. And that surely points to the collective unconscious and to a *collectivum.* So the tree stands for a particular kind of life of the collective unconscious, namely, vegetative

1433

life, as Mrs. Sachs rightly said. Now what is the difference between the life of the plant and the life of the animal?

Miss Wolff: Two things. The plant is rooted to the spot and able to move in growth only, and then the respiratory system of the plant is different from that of the warm-blooded animals.

Prof. Jung: Yes, a tree is unable to move in space except for the moment of growth, whereas the animal can move about. And all animals are parasites on plants, while the tree lives on the elements. Or one can say that the plant is the kind of life which is nearest to the elements, a transition as it were, or the bridge, between the animal and inorganic nature.

Dr. Escher: The plant lives by the sun.

Prof. Jung: The source of energy for plant life is the sun, but that is true of animals also, since they are parasites on plants. But the plant depends immediately upon the sunlight, which is also one of the elements of life, while the animal depends on it only indirectly. Of course we need sunlight, most animals would perish without sunlight, though there are a few that are adapted to living without it.

Dr. Wheelwright: In plant life, anabolism exceeds katabolism. That is to say, as long as the tree is living, it is growing, whereas human beings stop growing at a certain point and their bodies begin to retrogress.

Prof. Jung: Yes, another characteristic of vegetative life is that it continues to grow till the end, while at a certain time an animal ceases to grow.

Mrs. Sigg: The tree receives its nourishment from above and below, which is like man in a way.

Prof. Jung: Yes, in contradistinction to the animal that expresses its life in horizontal movement. One can make the statement that vegetative life is vertical; it functions in living from below to above or from above to below. Therefore vegetative life is another aspect of the psyche within ourselves as well. So the plant is forever the symbol of what?

Answer: Of the soul.

Mrs. Crowley: Of the psychical experience.

Miss Hannah: Of impersonal life.

Prof. Jung: I would call it more definitely spirituality. The plant represents spiritual development, and that follows laws which are different from the laws of biological, animal life; therefore spiritual development is always characterized by the plant. For instance, the lotus is very typical as the symbol of spiritual life in India: it grows out of absolute darkness, from the depth of the earth, and comes up through the medium of the dark water—the unconscious—and blossoms above the water, where it is the seat of the Buddha. Or several gods may appear in the lotus.

Mrs. Crowley: Is there not also that idea of a serpentine movement?

Prof. Jung: Oh yes, that is another detail which of course points to the serpent, and the serpent is an animal. The roots of the tree have that obvious serpentine character, and water-plants look like snakes. Also plants under water seem to have snakelike movements due to the flowing water; the water flowing upon a flexible body naturally gives that undulating effect. There the two things come together: namely, that part of the psyche which approaches plant life is the snake—that is, the cerebro-spinal system, which leads down and eventually transcends into the vegetative system, the sympathetic nervous system. And there we approach the lowest form of life, a sedentary life that is rooted to the spot, like the sea-anemone and those colonies of the siphonophora that are exactly like plants; and they all have the undulating movement which is characteristic of the sympathetic nervous system. So even in animals we can see the transition into plants, and that is indicated at least in the oldest nervous system in the world, the sympathetic nervous system; there we are bordering upon plant life. If we have any idea of plant life it is through that analogy.

Now, the plant or the tree is clearly beyond human experience, but the snake is within human experience. That is, you can experience the life of the cerebro-spinal system within your own body, but you cannot experience the life of the tree in your own body: you have no connection, your whole being is totally different from that of a plant. Therefore the tree represents, one could say, a transcendental experience, something that transcends man and is beyond him; it is before his birth and after his death, a life which man has not within himself. So he has no experience of it, yet peculiarly enough he finds the symbol of it in the tree. You see, a sacred tree means to a primitive his life. Or sometimes people plant a tree when a child is born, with the idea of their identity. If the tree keeps well and sane, the child's health will be good; if the child dies, the tree will die, or if the tree dies, the child will die. This old idea is a representation of that feeling in man that his life is linked up with another life. It is as if man had always known that he was, like any other animal, a parasite on plants, that he would perish if there were no plants. Of course that is a biological truth, and it is also a spiritual truth, inasmuch as our psyche can only live through a parasitical life on the spirit. Therefore no wonder, when you come to the end of your conscious life, stepping out onto that promontory as Nietzsche did, that you begin to realize the condition upon which your life ultimately rests. And then the tree appears, the tree that is the origin of your life as it is your future abode, the sarcophagus into which your corpse will disappear; it is the place of death or rebirth.

Mr. Bash: How would you explain as spiritual symbols all the totemic symbols, for instance, which are almost always animals?

Prof. Jung: There are of course many symbols for psychic facts. If the symbol is a totem animal, it is clearly a matter of what an animal means: namely, it is a matter of the reconciliation or the reunion of man with his cerebro-spinal system, or, more probably, with his sympathetic system. But not with the tree. The tree symbolizes something much higher and much deeper. It has a specifically transcendental character. For instance, it is far more wonderful when a tree speaks to you than when an animal speaks to you. The distance between man and animal is not very great; but between the tree and the animal is an infinite distance, so it is a more primitive and yet a more advanced symbol. Therefore we find the tree as a symbol of the Yoga, or for the divine grace in Christianity. It is very advanced symbolism and at the same time exceedingly primitive.

Mr. Allemann: One important difference is that the tree is in Tao, following nature absolutely and accepting everything—there is no separate impulse; whereas in every animal there is that impulse.

Prof. Jung: Yes, and therefore deviation from the divine law. The animal is in a way already a deviation from the divine law because it doesn't surrender absolutely and indifferently to all the conditions provided by the creator, but is able to dodge them. And man with his consciousness has a far more wonderful opportunity for deviation. While the tree symbolizes the kind of life that cannot deviate for one single inch from the divine law, from the absolute law of conditions; it is rooted to the spot, exposed to every enemy that attacks it. There is a very nice story in one of the Buddhistic treatises, the *Samyutta Nikaya,* about the *deváta* of a tree; that is a sort of tree-soul, a semidivine being living in a tree. The story describes the despair of the *deváta* upon seeing that the termites are approaching the tree, because it cannot get away. The *Samyutta Nikaya* is an original collection of stories told by the disciples of Buddha, and containing many authentic sayings of Buddha himself, so it would go back to the 6th century B.C.

LECTURE VII

7 December 1938

Prof. Jung:

Here is a very valuable contribution from Mrs. Baumann, a photograph of Nestor's ring, that famous *intaglio* with the representation of the world-tree.

And here is a contribution from Mrs. Crowley about the tree in Egypt: "In the early Pyramid texts, there is a passage in which the Pharaoh on his way to Rē, comes upon a tree of Life on the Mysterious island, situated in the midst of the Field of Offerings. 'This king Pepi went to the great isle in the midst of the Field of Offerings, over which the gods make the swallows fly. The swallows are the imperishable stars. They give to this king Pepi this tree of Life, whereof they live, and Ye-Pepi and the Morning Star may at the same time live thereof.'

1437

This image belongs, prior to the Osiris faith, to the Solar religion of the old kingdom, about 3000 B.C."[1]

This tree in the photograph is not exactly the world-tree, but has more the aspect of the tree of life, what they called in India the soma tree, the *nyagrodha* tree. You know, the tree has many different aspects. It appears first in ancient mythologies as the cosmic tree, the tree of development—of cosmic as well as human evolution, like the great tree of the Germanic sagas, Yggdrasil. Another more specific aspect is the tree of life, the tree which gives life to human beings and animals and to the universe. And this tree has also the aspect of the world axis: the branches up above are the kingdom of the heavens; the roots below form the kingdom of the earth, the nether world; and the trunk is the world axis round which the whole world revolves, and at the same time a life-giving center or the main artery of life throughout the world. So the tree is more or less equivalent to the spinal column in a human body. You know in the interior of the cerebellum, a certain part in the middle part branches in such a way that it has a treelike appearance and is called the *arbor vitae*, the tree of life. Also this famous symbol of Osiris, the Tet, is a sort of tree form. It is identified with the *os sacrum*, that part of the spinal column which is inserted in the middle of the pelvic basin, and it also refers to the whole length of the spinal column, which maintains the straightness of the body and carries the arteries along the backbone. These anatomical facts are the same in animals, so naturally they have been known forever, practically. Moreover, they knew  that the arteries carried the blood, which was supposed to be the seat of the soul, so blood is itself a symbol for the soul, as warmth and breath symbolize blood, the indispensable essence of life. Then another aspect of the tree is the tree of knowledge. It is the carrier of revelation: out of the tree come voices; in the whispering of the wind in the tree words can be discerned, or the birds that live in the tree talk to one.

We have endless material as evidence for those traditions. The tree of paradise, for instance, is really one and the same tree but with a three-fold aspect: the tree which carries the evolution of the world, the tree which gives life to the universe, and the tree which gives understanding or consciousness. Then there is the Indian idea of the sacred

[1] Mrs. Crowley is drawing upon James Breasted (who cites the Pyramid text of 1212-1216), *The Dawn of Conscience* (New York, 1933), p. 134.

inverted tree. And the *nyagrodha* is the sacred tree of Buddha at the monastery of the Holy Tooth at Bodh Gaya, that famous Buddhist place of pilgrimage and worship in Ceylon. It is really a pipal tree, and looks like a willow. The soma tree is also sacred in Hinduism. According to its oldest definition, soma is a life-giving or intoxicating drink, but is also called a tree because it has the life-giving quality. One sees no resemblance to a tree, yet because it is life-giving they are identical. That is the primitive way of thinking: when two things function in the same way, even though they are utterly incommensurable, they are supposed to be one and the same thing. For instance, things that give life in the way of nourishment are identical. They say a sort of life-power or mana circulates through these different things, uniting them, making them one.

Then the tree is a very central symbol in the Christian tradition, having even taken on the quality of death—just as Yggdrasil is not only the origin of life, but also the end of life. As life originates in the tree, so everything ends in the tree of evolution; the last couple enters the tree again and disappears therein. So the mummy of Osiris transforms into a tree. And Christ ends on the tree. As I told you, the Christian cross was supposed to have been made from the wood of the tree of life, which had been cut down after the fall of the first parents and used later on for the two obelisks or pillars, Aachim and Boas, in front of Solomon's temple. Those are analogous to the Egyptian pillars or obelisks that flanked the way on which the sun-barque passed to and fro. One is now in Rome and another is in Paris, but happily enough, there are still a number left at Karnak. When Solomon's temple was destroyed those two pillars were thrown into one of the ponds of the river valley and much later discovered again, and tradition says the cross was made from the wood of those ancient beams. So Christ was crucified on the tree of life. Therefore those medieval pictures where Christ is represented as hanging crucified on a tree with branches and leaves and fruits. And that idea of Christ on the tree is not only medieval—there is also a famous antique representation of Christ among the vines. Do you remember it?

Mrs. Baumann: The chalice of Antioch.

Prof. Jung: Yes. It is now in America in a private collection, but was discovered together with other antique silver vessels at the bottom of an ancient well and is supposed to be part of the treasure of an early Christian church which had been thrown into the well at the time when Julian the Apostate was persecuting the Christians and destroying their churches. It consists of silver filigree work around a much more ancient silver bowl; it has even been suggested that it might be the vessel which Christ used at the Last Supper. But the chalice is most remarkable for its symbolism: Christ is represented as sitting among the leaves and grapes in the branches of a huge vine which is like a tree. That is the traditional antique form in which the Caesars were often depicted. There is a very similar representation of the Emperor Augustus, linking him up thus with Dionysos or Bacchus. Now, Christ was closely associated with Bacchus at the beginning of our era, and also with Orpheus, as we know from that famous inscription on the Gnostic seal. Orpheus and Bacchus were both old mystery gods of the period. Eisler's book *Orpheus—The Fisher* gives us the peculiar symbolism of those Bacchic mystery cults.[2] According to archeological discoveries, in Pompeii for instance, fish and fishing symbolism belonged to a contemporary cult—or possibly a pre-cult—of Bacchus. The seal to which I referred is in Berlin, and it represents quite indubitably the crucifixion, with the inscription "Orpheus-Bacchus," so those two heathen gods were obviously competitors of Christ in those days. We know from other sources also that there was a mystery god like Orpheus, who was therefore also called "Orpheus" and was explained by the same symbolism as both Orpheus and Dionysos. That representation of Christ also links him up with the age-old traditions about the tree of life, and the crucifixion would mean, according to that symbolism, a retrogression or a recession of Christ into the tree from which he originally came. Therefore in the medieval dialogue, Mary is confronted with the cross as the mother that has given birth to Christ and taken his life as well.

Miss Wolff: There are early medieval representations of the genealogical tree of Christ. On the branches, as the fruits of the tree, are the prophets and all Christ's ancestors. The roots of the tree grow out of the skull of Adam, and Christ is its central and more precious fruit.

Prof. Jung: Well, the tree sometimes grows out of Adam's naval, and on the branches, as you say, sit the prophets and kings of the Old Testament, Christ's ancestors, and then on top of the tree is the triumphant Christ. That life begins with Adam and ends with Christ is the same idea, or one might put it, that the fate of the wood of the cross parallels that tradition or symbolism. So the tree is a symbol which is found almost everywhere with a number of somewhat different meanings. I have given you the main aspects but there are a quantity of

[2] Robert Eisler, author of *Orpheus—The Fisher* (London, 1921). He spoke at Eranos in 1935 on "The Riddle of the Gospel of St. John."

lesser ones. Now we come to this tree on the promontory and also to the big round apple. I will read those two paragraphs again:

> As if a big round apple presented itself to my hand, a ripe golden apple, with a coolly-soft, velvety skin:—thus did the world present itself unto me:—
> As if a tree nodded unto me, a broad-branched, strong-willed tree, curved as a recline, and a foot-stool for weary travellers: thus did the world stand on my promontory:—

This is a most extraordinary way of putting it, unimaginable if you understand it as a world. Our idea of the world as a sort of globe would make a funny picture on that promontory. But a tree makes sense, and a bit farther on we shall see that he refers to a tree on the promontory again. So one could say the promontory stood for what in his imagination? Where is the tree of life?

Remark: In the Garden of Eden.

Prof. Jung: Of course, in paradise. Those who heard my German lecture will remember that I spoke of the *bodhi-druma*, the bodhi tree. Now where is the bodhi tree?

Mrs. Brunner: In paradise, on the round terrace of enlightenment.

Prof. Jung: Yes, and the text called it "the bodhi mandala." It is the *circulus quadratus*, which is a sort of *circumambulatio*, and in the center is the bodhi tree. So the promontory is the Garden of Eden. And that is characterized by what?

Mrs. Fierz: By the four rivers.

Prof. Jung: Yes. The tree is in the center and the four rivers issuing from the Garden of Eden make it the typical mandala. And the bodhi mandala contains also the idea of the square building inside, the corners of which are identical with the cardinal points of the horizon. North, south, east, and west are called the four corners of the world, or the four winds, and that gives the basis, the natural pattern, for the squaring of the circle. And inside the circle is a sort of stupa, a container, in which are the sacred relics. The most precious thing, the *cinta mani*, the pearl beyond price, is contained in the vessel in the center of the temple with the four corners.

Then if you follow it up psychologically, you arrive at the fact that consciousness has four corners as it were, four different ways or aspects, which we call the four functions. For since psychological consciousness is the origin of all the apperception of the world, it naturally understands everything, even the system of that axis, from that basis, as a sort of necessary bridge to all observation of facts. For instance, in looking through a telescope, you observe a cross inside of two thin threads, by which you measure the position of everything in the field of vision. That is an exact image of our consciousness, and the indispensable basis of all understanding, of all discernment; it is an intrinsic quality of consciousness that there are four elements or four different aspects. You could also say 360, but it must be a regular division of the horizon and the most satisfactory division is by four. Naturally it can be divided by five or six or by three, but that is more complicated or in some way not so satisfactory. If you want to divide a circle, you had best do it crossways. If I should give you the task of dividing it by five, I am sure a number of you would not know how to do it—it would demand all sorts of instruments. To divide a circle by four is the easiest and simplest way, and that comes from the fact that it coincides with the constitution of consciousness.

For you must have a function which tells you that there *is* something, and that is sensation. Then you must have a function which tells you what the thing is, and you can call that thinking. And then a function which tells you what it is worth to you, and that is feeling. You would then have a complete orientation for the moment, but the time axis is not considered: there is a past and a future, which is not given in the present moment, so you need a sort of divination in order to know where that thing comes from or where it is going, and that is called intuition. Now if you know of anything more, tell me. You see, that gives you a complete picture. We have no other criterion that I know of and need no other—I have often thought about it but I could never find any other—from the data these four functions give me I have a complete picture. It is the same as logic: when you examine carefully the aspects of causality, for instance, you arrive at a fourfold root. Schopenhauer has even written a treatise *Über die vierfache Wurzel des Satzes vom Grunde*, and it really has four aspects to which you can add nothing.[3] As you cannot add some other dimension to the horizon when you have named the four points, the four corners; that is enough, it is complete.

Apparently the ancients already had an intuition about it. So the saying that the soul is a square, and that four is the number of all living things, was attributed to Pythagoras by his pupils; he probably has an important vision or intuition about this truth. You can go on speculat-

---

[3] Schopenhauer's Inaugural Dissertation, *On the Fourfold Root of the Ground of Reason*, was published in 1813.

ing about it forever—there is plenty of matter for speculation. For instance, the main building material of the body is carbon, and carbon or coal is characterized chemically by the number four: it is chiefly quadrivalent; and the diamond is native carbon crystallized in the isometric system, often in the form of octahedrons. Then you know that the *lapis philosophorum*, the stone, is often called "the white stone," or "the white light," that perfect transparency which comes out of utter darkness. Coal is black and the diamond of the purest water is composed of the same substance. We know that now, but in those days of course nobody knew about the chemical formula of a diamond; it was taken to be like a ruby or an emerald. Now, the promontory which juts out into the ocean seems to be half in the sea and half on *terra firma*, so it is something between the sea and the earth. What does that remind you of?

Answer: A mandala that is half in the earth and half in the sky.

Prof. Jung: Yes, it is like the famous stupas of Sanchi or of Anuradhapura in Ceylon, the mandala composed of two bowls, one bowl being embedded in the earth and the other half in the air above. The two bowls make a globe, and the one underneath is supposed to contain the remains of the Lord Buddha. So that promontory in Nietzsche's unconscious is really a place of individuation, the very central place. He is in the place of the Emperor. There the apple is given to him. And there is always an increase of personality there; it is the coronation place, the place of exaltation. In mystery initiations the initiant climbs up the seven planetary steps to that place where he is worshipped as Helios, the sun god; he is supreme, there becoming the first man under the tree of paradise, or the very last man, who at the end of his days is again confronted with the tree. So Nietzsche is really at the origin and also at the top of the world. That is the psychology of the mandala, that is what mandalas mean and why they are made or imagined; they indicate the sacred place, the sacred condition, in which man is at the beginning as well as at the top of the world, where he is the child just being born and at the same time the lord of the universe. Now he goes on with the "as if":

> As if delicate hands carried a casket towards me—a casket open for the delectation of modest adoring eyes: thus did the world present itself before me today:—

What about this casket "open for the delectation of modest adoring eyes"?

Miss Wolff: In the German text it is a shrine, therefore it must mean a casket for relics, a holy thing.

Prof. Jung: You are quite right. The shrine usually contains the sacred figure or the relic, the most precious objects of worship. And that bears out what we were saying about the promontory and the contents of the mandala.

Mrs. Baumann: I wondered if the fact that it is a reliquary with dead bones in it might have something to do with the fact that he does not mention water here. It might mean that this is the tree of death rather than the tree of life. There is no mention of the four rivers of paradise or of the water of life. The world-tree is nearly always associated with a spring of living water, but here there is none—and it seems queer because Zarathustra has often before mentioned a well-spring.

Prof. Jung: The idea of water is completely absent, and it is true, as you say, that water is usually associated with the tree. You remember, at the foot of Yggdrasil there is a double spring in the alchemical colors, which is most remarkable. Also the tree of Pherekydes in Greek mythology is always associated with the idea of fertility.[4]

Miss Wolff: But Nietzsche's text implies not a well, but the sea.

Prof. Jung: The sea is also the water of life under certain conditions, but it is not exactly the life-giving water, rather the life-*preserving* water. The life-giving water is usually fresh water, like a spring. That idea is absent here, and why it is so is a question. Well, we have to state the facts: it just is so. Now this shrine surely expresses the idea that a most precious thing is contained or shown here for the delectation of adoring eyes. One is also reminded here of certain Christian motifs.

Mrs. Brunner: Of the Host?

Prof. Jung: Yes, of course, but why not be simple? There is something much nearer. Have you never seen a typical adoration?

Miss Foote: The Christ Child.

Prof. Jung: Yes, think of Christmas: there is the tree. The adoration of the Child that is given under the tree or by the tree. And here we are in Advent and don't remember that! Now Nietzsche goes on:

> Not riddle enough to scare human love from it, not solution enough to put to sleep human wisdom:—a humanly good thing was the world to me to-day, of which such bad things are said!

If you meditate upon that sentence in the light of what we have seen in the symbolism, you can understand a good deal of Nietzsche's dream.

---

[4] Pherekydes of Syros was a middle sixth-century B.C. mythologist and cosmologist—on some lists, one of the Seven Wise Men.

Now, would you assume that it was a dream, or was it a so-called poetical invention, or was it a vision? We have these three possibilities.

Mrs. Fierz: Is there not underlying it the vision of a woman? All through this text the picture of a woman is suggested. First there is the apple with its soft skin; out of it comes the winking tree, then the delicate hands bringing a shrine. The text also says that the world *stands* on the promontory, just as if it were a person. It reminds me of the statue of "Frau Welt" on the Basel Cathedral, which Nietzsche must have known: the woman with smiling face and devils and apes behind her. After having looked only at the devils and apes for such a long time, it is as if Nietzsche finally could see "Frau West" smiling. Anyhow, the picture of a woman is always underneath.

Prof. Jung: My question is: is it a vision or a dream or an invention? So you would be in favor of a vision, whatever that may mean. We shall come to that.

Mr. Allemann: It is surely not a poetical invention; it may be a dream or a vision.

Prof. Jung: And why do you assume that it cannot be a poetical invention?

Mr. Allemann: Because it hits the nail on the head. It must come directly from the unconscious, it couldn't be an invention.

Prof. Jung: Yes, it goes too deep, absolutely to the core of things. It is so incredibly rich, one cannot assume that a mere invention could express the essence of all mythologies, of all creeds, in three lines. It is too amazing.

Mrs. Jung: There is to me something not quite satisfactory in this whole imagery because there is such an inflation in it. I doubt whether one would have a feeling of being on top of the world if one were in the center of the mandala.

Prof. Jung: That is true, it is all seen through that awful veil of inflation. But we have thrown away for the moment that sad veil of inflation in order to see what appears behind the veil, in order to do justice to the background. We must be critical of the foreground, that is sure. There is that unsatisfactory element of inflation, and he identifies with it. His attitude is of course not at all correct. That still further proves that it is not invention. He himself doesn't understand it, doesn't know what is happening. But he cannot help it; he can do nothing against it. *It* appears in all the confusion and turmoil of his very restricted consciousness; the old picture that is at the bottom of all religious experiences comes through. For instance, if I should tell James Joyce that that came through in his *Ulysses*, he would deny it, as Spitteler would deny that anything came through the walls of his prejudice.[5] But it did nevertheless, and so it has happened to Nietzsche; despite his attitude, his inflation and identification, the eternal picture breaks through all those veiling mists and becomes visible—to us at least.

Miss Hannah: I think that it must have been a dream because it is so far from his conscious point of view.

Prof. Jung: You think it is a dream. What do you say, Mrs. Schevill?

Mrs. Schevill: I think it must be a vision because at the beginning of the chapter he says, "In my dream, in my last morning-dream," and that is generally the time of the coming of the vision. It is the end of the dreams of the night, and the beginning of day and of the coming of consciousness. Therefore the two things come together in the vision.

Prof. Jung: Yes. Physiologically that is true: the curve of sleep drops far down and then it gradually rises again. We drop out of consciousness, and then approach consciousness again towards morning; the dreams are then increasingly associated with consciousness. So when he accents the last morning dream, it probably means that it was the last thing which was still in the unconscious and yet already mixed up with consciousness. Comparing this with dreams of patients in general, I would say it was a vision. For a dream it is too synthetic; a dream is more grotesque. There is nothing grotesque about this. It is tremendously synthetic, as a matter of fact; that picture of being on a promontory weighing the world is synthesized to the utmost. We could not expect that of a dream. A dream may be very powerful and very beautiful but it would use a language which was not so near to consciousness; there would be something more like primitive lore, or there would be obvious allusions to certain mythical formations.

You see, he could have said just as well, "I am now as if standing on a ledge of rock jutting out into the ocean and behind me is the land of the living. I am looking out to the endless sea, the symbol of death, of non-existence; and I am weighing life, the whole of existence, all of humanity, against this fact of no humanity at all, this fact which was before humanity and which will be after humanity, when man is no more." For Nietzsche was the man who, when he looked at the Alps, realized the feeling: *Crimen laesae majestatis humanae.*[6] Those glaciers and peaks and snow fields—all that icy primeval world neither knows nor needs man; it will be itself, live its own life, in spite of man. It isn't

---

[5] For Jung's ambivalent response to *Ulysses*, see CW 15. Jung was irritated by Spitteler's claim that his works were only tales and not at all symbolic.

[6] Vexing complaint about human majesty.

concerned with man in the least. That is the horror of the cold-blooded animal also: a snake simply doesn't take man into account. It may crawl into his pocket, behave as if he were a tree trunk. One world is human and the other is inhuman, before man and after man, and Nietzsche is now weighing the two worlds in his scales. So he weighs his own world which he comes from; that is almost a conscious thought, and it is of course a direct logical outcome of the chapters before, where he came to the conclusion that it was all Maya and the people could go to hell— to be burned up like chaff was the only thing they were good for. He is at the end of the world and has to weigh the question whether existence in general is worthwhile or not. Is it worthwhile to live, to go on? If you consider the chapters before and put yourself into his place, you will realize it; but if you do not realize what went before, if you have no feeling heart, you are naturally confronted with a great riddle. But it is "not riddle enough to scare human love from it." Now he says,

> How I thank my morning-dream that I thus at today's dawn, weighed the world! As a humanly good thing did it come unto me, this dream and heart comforter!

We must go a little into the detail of this. He speaks of the "humanly good thing." What does he mean by that?

Mrs. von Roques: Good and evil together.

Prof. Jung: It is certain that if a thing is human, it is both good and evil, but he doesn't mean evil here.

Mrs. Sigg: It might mean something that remains in human proportions, not so very wide and not so very high.

Prof. Jung: That is a good idea.

Miss Hannah: I thought it made him not hate people quite so much.

Prof. Jung: Yes, it is positive, after his having said so many negative things. He must be afraid of human beings because they will strike back when they hear them.

Miss Hannah: He is afraid of revenge—that they will do the same to him.

Prof. Jung: Yes, that is the reason he is so critical about people—he anticipates their revenge, their misunderstanding. He was tremendously interested in the question of how *Zarathustra* would be taken by the public, whether they would revile him as he had reviled them. There was plenty of reason for being afraid that the public would turn down his book; after saying such unkind things he must naturally expect a bad reply. Now this vision gives him a positive feeling after all that negative feeling; it has a human character one could say, and a humanizing effect. He is no longer an outcast from the world, an exile who has driven himself into solitude. He heaped so much prejudice upon the world that he drove himself into isolation on the promontory, and this vision has a soothing reconciling effect. Also, he seems to realize—and this is probably important—that the expression "humanly good thing" alludes to something really human. This is evident in the line Mrs. Fierz alluded to: "as if delicate hands carried a casket towards me." So it is a sort of personification of the humanly good thing that carries this shrine or reconciling gift to him. Here we are allowed to consider a personification, and a woman's figure is the most likely. Now the main symbolism in the immediately preceding verses is the tree. You see, the tree produces the apples, the food of immortality, the golden apples of the Hesperides, or the revivifying apples from the tree of wisdom. And the tree itself is often personified as a woman; in old alchemistic books, for example, sometimes the trunk of the tree is a woman, and out of her head grow the branches with the golden apples, the fruit which gives new life to those who are fettered in Hades. This reminds one of the famous vision of Arisleus, one of the first visions, or the only big one really, in Latin alchemy. In Greek alchemy there are others, the visions of Zosimos, for instance, or of Krates.[7]

Arisleus sees, in his vision, himself and his companions on the shore of the sea, in a land where nothing thrives; the fields are not fertile, the cattle are sterile, and the people are sterile too, because the men mated with men and the women with women. The King, the Rex Marinus, therefore has Arisleus brought to him and asks him what to do about it. And Arisleus tells him that he needs a philosopher in his country, and advises that the king's two children, Gabricus and Beya, who were born out of his brain , should now copulate. But in so doing the prince dies (in some versions of this story Beya is said to have swallowed him), so the king is very much upset. Arisleus, however, promises to revivify the prince with the aid of Beya. The king then locks him and his companions with the dead prince and Beya, into a glass house with three

[7] Zosimos of Panopolis, a third-century Gnostic and alchemist, recorded a number of visions on which Jung comments at length, CW 13, pars. 85-144. It is perhaps worth noting too that Zosimos sometimes cited Zoroastrian texts and counted Zoroaster a prophet on the level of Jesus. Arisleus was a legendary alchemist, the presumed author of the *Turba Philosophorum* which is included in the compendium, *Theatrum Chemicum*, 6 vols. (Strasbourg, 1602-1661). The *Book of Krates* is yet another alchemical text, probably by an ancient Greek, but transmitted by the medieval Arabic scholars and reprinted in *La Chimie au moyen age*, ed. Marcell in Berthelot (Paris, 1893), vol. III, p. 50.

walls, deep under the sea; the house is like three vessels or alembics of glass, contained one in the other. There Arisleus is heated, practically boiled, so he is in great misery. He also suffers from hunger, as the hero in the whale-dragon's belly always suffers from hunger; but in that case the hero sustains himself by cutting off and eating part of the monster's body, usually the liver, *die Leber*, which is the life and soul according to primitive ideas. He nourishes himself from the life of the monster. And now, in the glass house, Arisleus has another vision: he sees his master Pythagoras and asks him for help. So Pythagoras sends a man named Horfoltus (also called Harpocrates) who brings the fruits of a mystical tree to those who are caught under the sea—in the unconscious. By that food, which is the *pharmakon athanasias*, the medicine of immortality, the prince is brought back to life, and the lives of Arisleus and his companions are renewed. They are all released from their prison, and Gabricus and Beya rule over the country thereafter. They have many children, and their people and their cattle and their fields all become fertile and prosper.

This old myth is very clearly a psychological archetype of initiation, or the revivification of an attitude which has gone dead, become sterile and useless, and so has disappeared into the unconscious, where it had to be boiled over, made new again. And it is also an old spring myth, the renewal of vegetation.

Now the tree from which the wonderful fruit comes is, as I said, represented as a woman in a certain alchemical treatise. And there are other pictures where the life-giving tree is represented as a woman, or the life-giving woman is represented by a tree. One also sees this in mere ornamental figures. It is used as an ornamental motif in those famous medieval chandeliers, for instance, where the tree is represented by the horns of a stag growing out of the head of a woman, usually a sort of nymph with bare breasts curving beneath and the stag's horns on top, each branch of the horns carrying a light. That is the light-giving woman. So it is quite within the symbolism when we encounter here this idea that delicate hands carry the shrine or the casket towards him. According to the primitive idea, it would be the tree-soul personified that in its kindness gives him the jewel. Now, since the tree is the world and since there is that association with the woman, the tree would be the positive aspect of his world which he has been reviling. It is as if his vision were saying to him, "This is the world, and when you come to the end of things and begin to weigh the world—when you make the ultimate judgment as if you were lord of the universe—you arrive at the conclusion that this world is mother nature and that she is kind and human." So it is an entirely compensatory vision, and it is quite understandable that he has a very positive feeling about it. But he doesn't realize what it means, so he cannot make the right use of it. He doesn't say to himself, "Here I made a great mistake. I should realize that the world and humanity is not so bad after all." He should be in a much better frame of mind. Of course he is already in a somewhat better frame of mind, but he doesn't come out of his state of inflation. So he continues,

> And that I may do the like by day, and imitate and copy its best, now will I put the three worst things on the scales, and weigh them humanly well.

You see he is backing his superior frame of mind, continuing that role which was really forced upon him by his solitude. He should say, "unfortunately enough I am forced to be the last man and the man at the beginning of the world. I am unfortunately made into God's own son." But he rather enjoys it and that is his misfortune.

> He who taught to bless taught also to curse: what are the three best cursed things in the world? These will I put on the scales.
> Voluptuousness, passion for power, and selfishness: these three things have hitherto been best cursed, and have been in worst and falsest repute—these three things will I weigh humanly well.
> Well! Here is my promontory, and there is the sea—it rolleth hither unto me, shaggily and fawningly, the old, faithful, hundred-headed dog-monster that I love!
> Well! Here will I hold the scales over the weltering sea: and also a witness do I choose to look on—thee, the anchorite-tree, thee, the strong-odoured broad-arched tree that I love!

In the face of his tree, which means life, knowledge, wisdom, consciousness, he is now weighing the three vices that carry the curse: voluptuousness, passion for power, and selfishness. Here we see how modern Nietzsche really is and to what extent he is a psychologist. If he had lived in our days, he couldn't have helped being an analyst; he would have gone into it right away. He was really more a psychologist than any philosopher except the very early ones, a psychologist inasmuch as he realized that philosophy is *au fond* psychology. It is simply a statement made by an individual psyche and it doesn't mean more than that. To what extent he is a modern psychologist we can see from the statement he makes here, for what does he anticipate in these three vices?

Miss Hannah: The present day.

Mrs. Fierz: Freud, Adler, and you.

Prof. Jung: Yes. Voluptuousness, the lust principle, is Freud; passion for power is Adler; and selfishness—that is myself, perfectly simple. You see my idea really is the individuation process and that is just rank selfishness. And Freud is supposed to be nothing but sex, and Adler nothing but power. Those are the three aspects and in the right order, mind you. First came Freud, then Adler who was about my age but an earlier pupil of Freud. I found him in the Freudian society when I went to Vienna the first time; he was already on the premises and I was newly arrived—so surely passion for power comes next. And mine is the last, and peculiarly enough it includes the other two, for voluptuousness and passion for power are only two aspects of selfishness. I wrote a little book saying that Freud and Adler looked at the same thing from different sides, Freud from the standpoint of sex, and Adler from the standpoint of will to power; they observed the same cases but from different angles.[8] Any case of hysteria or any neurosis can be explained just as well from the side of Freud as from the side of Adler, as unfulfilled sex wishes or as frustrated will to power. So this is in every respect a clear forecast of the way things actually developed. Nietzsche was really an extraordinary fellow. And it is true that "these three things have hitherto been best cursed, and have been in worst and falsest repute." Well, divide by two—he is always a little exaggerated—for the repute is not absolutely false; it is bad I admit but not really false, because these three things are definite vices. There is no doubt about that.

But you see, our religious point of view is that all vice is wrong, and that needs some rectification. We are not sufficiently aware that even a bad thing has two sides. You cannot say that any one of those vices is entirely bad. If it were entirely bad and you wanted to be morally decent, you could not live at all. You cannot prevent voluptuousness, because it *is*; you cannot prevent power, because it *is*; and you cannot prevent selfishness, because it *is*. If you did prevent them, you would die almost instantly, for without selfishness you cannot exist. If you should give all your food to the poor, there would be nothing left, and if you eat nothing you die—and then there would be nobody left to give them the food. You cannot help functioning; those vices are functions in themselves.

Such a judgment comes from the assumption that someone could es-

---

[8] "The Psychology of the Unconscious," in CW 7, pars. 1-201.

tablish a definite truth, could decide that such-and-such a thing was definitely bad for instance; but you never can. At no time can you make such a statement, because it always depends upon *who* has done it and under what conditions. There is no one vice of which we can say it is under all conditions bad. For all those conditions may be changed and different, and they are always different in different cases. You can only say if a thing happens under such-and-such conditions, and assuming that other conditions happen along the same line, that the thing is then most probably bad. You can judge to that extent, or you can say such-and-such a thing is in itself bad under such-and-such conditions, but all exceptions suffer when exposed to reality. So the mistake we make is in passing a moral judgment as if it were possible, as if we could really pass a general moral judgment. That is exactly what we cannot do. The more you investigate the crime, the more you feel into it, the less you are capable of judging it, because you find when you go deep enough, that the crime was exceedingly meaningful, that it was inevitable in that moment—everything led up to it. It was just the right thing, either for the victim or for the one who committed the crime. How can you say that particular man was bad, or that the victim was bad and deserved it? The more you know about the psychology of crime the less you can judge it; when you have seen many such cases, you just give up.

On the other hand if you give up judgment, you give up a vital function in yourself: namely, your hatred, your contempt, your revolt against evil, your belief in the good. So you come to the conclusion that you cannot give up passing judgment; as a matter of fact, practically, you have to pass judgment. When a man breaks into a house or kills people, you must stop it; it is disturbing to live in a town where such things are permitted, and therefore you must stop that fellow. And how do you do it? Well, you must put him in jail or behead him or something like that. And sure enough if somebody asks why you put that man in jail, you say because he is a bad man. Yes, he is bad, you cannot get away from it. Even if you yourself do something which is against the general idea of morality, no matter how you may *think* about it, you feel awkward, you get attacks of conscience—as a matter of fact you develop a very bad conscience. Perhaps that is not apparent: a man may say, "Oh, I haven't a bad conscience about what I have done as long as I know that nobody else knows it." But I hear such a confession from a man who comes to me with a neurosis, not knowing that his neurosis is due to the fact that he has offended his own morality. And so he excludes himself, for inasmuch as he has a neurosis, he is excluded from normal humanity; his neurosis, his isolation, is on account of the fact that he himself is a-social and that is on account of the fact that he is amoral, so he is excluded from regular social intercourse.

When you offend against those moral laws you become a moral exile, and you suffer from that state, because your libido can no longer flow freely out of yourself into human relations; you are always blocked by the secret of your misdeeds. So you suffer from an undue accumulation of energy which cannot be liberated, and you are in a sort of contrast and opposition to your surroundings, which is surely an abnormal condition. And it doesn't help that you have particularly enlightened ideas about good and evil, like Nietzsche, who said he was beyond good and evil and applied no moral categories. *It* applies moral categories for you; you cannot escape the judge in yourself. You see, that whole moral system in which we live has been brought about by history, by thousands of years of training. It is based upon archetypes of human behavior. Therefore you find the same laws in the lowest society as in the highest. As a matter of fact, there is no fundamental difference between the laws of a primitive society and those of a very highly developed society; the aspects may be different but the principles are the same. Everybody suffers when they commit an offense against the instinctive law, out of which the universal morality grows. It doesn't matter at all what your convictions are; something is against you and you suffer from a corresponding disintegration of personality, which may amount to a neurosis.

Now in such a case, you may have to sin against your better judgment. For instance, you observe a human being clearly forced to a certain course of life, to a certain kind of misdeed, and, understanding it, you can pity such an individual, can feel compassion, can even admire the courage with which he can live at all. You think: is it not marvelous, magnificent, the way he or she takes on that awful burden, lives that dirt? Nevertheless, you have to say it is bad, and if you don't, you are not accepting yourself. You commit a sin against your own law and are not fulfilling your own morality which is instinctive. And you don't do justice to the other fellow either, for the fellow who has to live like that must know that he is committing misdeeds, and if you tell him you admire his courage he says, "Thank you, that is awfully nice, but you see I *need* to suffer from my misdeed." A man is dishonored by the fact that he is not properly punished. His misdeed must be punished, must have compensation, or why in hell should he risk punishment? The things which are not allowed are full of vitality, because in order to put them through, you risk something. So if you deny a depreciative judgment, you perhaps deprive your fellow being of his only reward. He is merely attracted by the danger, by the adventure, the risk of being immoral, which is wonderful in a way; and you must give him the reward and call him a doer of evil deeds. And if it happens to yourself, if you yourself misbehave, you will be forced to admit that you are a doer of evil deeds, and it gives you a peculiar satisfaction. You can repent, for instance, and there is no greater and more wonderful satisfaction than to repent a thing from the bottom of your heart. I am sure that many people commit sins merely in order to repent; it is too marvelous, a sort of voluptuousness. You must watch them when they do it. Go to religious meetings; there you will see it.

So when you consider that whole problem, from whatever side you look at it, you come to the conclusion that it is perfectly understandable that those things are bad. And it is also quite understandable that people cannot avoid living them, doing them, and at the same time nobody can avoid cursing the people who do them. Therefore, whatever happens must happen, it is inevitable: that is the comedy of life. We know it is a comedy, we know it is illogical, but that is life, and you have to live that if you want to live at all. If you don't want to live, you can step out of all that nonsense; you don't need to pass the judgment. But the moment you fail to curse an offence, or call it "nothing but" a vice, or say it is admirable that this man is able to commit such marvelous crimes—such courage of life!—then you are no longer real, but are on the way to a neurosis, just a crank. Life is in the middle of all that comedy. For it is essentially a comedy, and the one who understands that it is illusion, Maya, can step out of it—provided it is his time. Then he doesn't risk a neurosis because he is then on the right way. So in the second half of life you may begin to understand that life is a comedy all round, in every respect, and that nothing is quite true and even that is not quite true; and by such insight you slowly begin to step out of life without risking a neurosis.

WINTER TERM

January / February 1939

LECTURE I

18 January 1939

Prof. Jung:
We stopped before Christmas at the 54th chapter, "The Three Evil Things." We were nearly at the end of the first part, but there is still one point in the last two verses which I should like to speak of.

> On what bridge goeth the now to the hereafter? By what constraint doth the high stoop to the low? And what enjoineth even the highest still—to grow upwards?
> Now stand the scales poised and at rest: three heavy questions have I thrown in; three heavy answers carrieth the other scale.

Now in order to link up what is coming with the past, we must realize where we stand in *Zarathustra*. How does he arrive at these three evil things? You remember they are voluptuousness, passion for power, and selfishness. What is the connection here? It is most difficult, but absolutely necessary, to keep one's head clear in wading through *Zarathustra*; one easily gets lost in the jungle of his talk. Therefore it is very useful to know the general theme with which we are concerned, the general trend of the whole argument, not only of the last chapter but of all the chapters before it.

Mrs. Brunner: He is always approaching the inferior man.

Prof. Jung: Exactly. All the previous chapters deal with the problem of the inferior man, or the shadow. And when did he first meet the shadow?

Answer: When the fool approached him in the beginning of the book.

Prof. Jung: And what was his attitude to it then?

Answer: He reviled the shadow.

Prof. Jung: And not only did he revile the inferior man in himself, but collectivity in general, representing the inferior man. For collectivity is practically always shadowy, always inferior, because the more people there are together, the more they become inferior. Just recently

1457

there has been an article in the *Neue Zürcher Zeitung* about a book, *The Mass Soul*, in which a man expressed his disagreement with the idea that the individual is lowered in a crowd.[1] Of course everybody in a crowd thinks that *he* is a fellow, that he is even quite superior to that rabble. Notice the way the crowd in a theater look at each other! You see everyone thinks God-knows-what of himself, something very wonderful. Therefore they all put on their best clothes and their jewelry, so that everybody will see that they are the superior people. They even stand up in the front rows and turn their backs on the orchestra—in such a position everybody must see them—and then they make important faces and stick out their bellies and stare up at the boxes. But that of course just shows how inferior they are. The fact is, when a man is in a crowd he is inferior, no matter what idea he may have about his greatness. The morality of a crowd is lower than the morality of each individual in the crowd. A crowd is overpowering naturally, since thousands are more than one, then one is overpowered; and to be overpowered or to overpower the others is inferior. So what can you do? You are just caught in inferiority and you are inferior too.

Nietzsche reviles not only his own shadow but also the shadow in masses, the collective man. I have often pointed out the stupidity of that, because he lives on the inferior man—perhaps a monkey man, perhaps an ape psychology. But that is the stuff of life and the source from which we spring, so there is no use in reviling it. Now in his attack on the inferior man and in his arguments concerning him, he cannot help discovering certain truths; he is now just about to recognize the demerits of the shadow as great merits. So in denying or reviling the shadow he enters the house by the back door. For instance, he says that collective man is a low brute, and then he slowly realizes the merit of brutality; he begins to recognize that the motives which move the collective man are really virtues. So he takes the three outstanding demerits of the shadow man, his voluptuousness, his lust for power, and his lust in himself, his selfishness, and makes them into virtues. He is now going to concern himself with that theme. But here he says something which is of particular importance; he asks, "On what bridge goeth the now to the hereafter? By what constraint doth the high stoop to the low? And what enjoineth even the highest still—to grow upwards?" Can you give the answer?

[1] Almost certainly Jung is here referring to José Ortega y Gasset's *The Revolt of the Masses*, which appeared in Spanish in 1930 and was anonymously translated into English in 1932 (New York). It is this work by the Spanish philosopher that made current the expression "mass-man."

Miss Hannah: Individuation.

Mrs. Fierz: I would say just by living.

Prof. Jung: No, it is so simple that you don't see it. It is already said here: By voluptuousness, by passion for power, and by selfishness. There the scales stand poised. You see these things are powers of life, therefore they are really merits. They are vital virtues because they are vital necessities in that they build the bridge to the hereafter. Virtues and high accomplishments are always an end; the incomplete is a beginning. The incomplete, the undifferentiated is the bridge to tomorrow; the fruit that is not ripe or that is a mere germ today, is the ripe fruit of two months hence. And what are the forces that move the world—that constrain the high to stoop to the low, for instance. Surely not merits, because they help him to rise even higher. He rightly says it "enjoineth even the highest still—to grow upwards," namely, to move far away from the low, because the effort to compensate vice forces you to great heights of virtue. If you had not to combat a very deep shadow you would never create a light. Only when it is very dark do you make a light, only when you are suffering from a vice do you begin to develop the virtue that will help you to grow upwards. Also, if you are high, what helps you to stoop to the low ones? Just such vices. By voluptuousness, by the will to power, you can stoop low, you can deteriorate. The man who assumes power over others simply lowers himself with their loss of power. He gives them the power they want but he has. He is just as low as those he is ruling. The slave is not lower than the tyrant; the slave receives the power of the tyrant and the tyrant takes power from the slave. It is the same coin whether you take it from someone or give it to someone. And that is so with power, or with voluptuousness or with selfishness: it is all the same. But those are the powers which make things move on. Unfortunately, the good thing, the high thing, the virtue, is always an accomplishment, always a summit, and the summit leads no farther. Only when you are down below can you rise, as only after the summit can you descend. But if there is nothing below, you cannot descend. Now that is Nietzsche's idea and it is to be considered.

Mrs. Fierz: Why is it that just at this moment the scales are even?

Prof. Jung: There is a sort of *enantiodromia* here, as I pointed out.

Mrs. Fierz: Is it because he has not yet accepted these three things?

Prof. Jung: But he has.

Mrs. Fierz: Then why doesn't it go down?

Prof. Jung: Ah, that is just Nietzsche's style. He recognizes the thing but other people must practice it. He merely preaches it, but it doesn't concern him. He doesn't realize when he preaches house-cleaning that it might be his own house. Everybody else has to clean house because his own house is dirty. It is like those people who always talk about the weeds in other people's gardens but never weed their own. He never asks: "Now what does that mean for myself?" That he never looks back on himself is the tragedy of this book; otherwise he would benefit from his book. But he looks for something else, for fame, or that other people should approve of it. It is as if he didn't want to know whether it was also right for him. You see, he recognizes these evil things as important powers of life, but again comes to the conclusion that of course those ordinary people do *not* recognize these facts, that they discredit these powers of life; again we see that the shadow, which consists of just these qualities, is reviled under that assumption. Naturally the inferior man doesn't recognize the philosophical aspect, but he is moved by these forces, he lives the shadow; and being overcome by these forces, he realizes their evil side. So the inferior man likes to be taught how to be different, how to extricate himself from such powers.

You see, a man who is not at home in his house is not held fast to his own personal and corporeal life, and so doesn't realize in how far he is overcome by these dark powers. Such a man naturally comes to the conclusion, which Nietzsche reaches, that they are merits because he doesn't possess them, doesn't see them or touch them. While one who is fettered, imprisoned, by these powers—who knows that he cannot extricate himself from voluptuousness, from passion for power, from selfishness—such a one gladly hears that he can liberate himself from these evils. These are the powers of hell, and here is the god who will help you to overcome them. To him it makes sense to liberate himself because he is too much under their suggestion. But the one who is quite outside and unaffected by them will gladly return to these powers, because to him they mean something positive. From the distance it looks fine, like the blond beast, a wonderful voluptuous beast, a powerful selfish beast, a sort of Cesare Borgia. The poor, amiable, half-blind Professor Nietzsche is anything but that, so if he could get something of the red beard of Cesare Borgia, or something of the voracity and power of the lion, or of the sexual brutality of a bull, it would naturally seem to him all to the good. So he begins to revile again the sad creatures who cannot see how wonderful these three vices are. In the sixth verse before the end of Part II he says, speaking of this blessed selfishness:

1460

Bad: thus doth it call all that is spirit-broken, and sordidly-servile—constrained, blinking eyes, depressed hearts, and the false submissive style, which kisseth with broad cowardly lips.
And spurious wisdom:—

That is a bad translation of *After-Weisheit*. Instead of spurious wisdom, it really should be "mock wisdom."

And spurious wisdom: so doth it call all the wit that slaves, and hoary-headed and weary ones affect; and especially all the cunning, spurious-witted, curious-witted foolishness of priests!

The spurious wise, however, all the priests, the world-weary, and those whose souls are of feminine and servile nature—oh, how hath their game all along abused selfishness!

And precisely *that* was to be virtue and was to be called virtue—to abuse selfishness! And "selfless"—so did they wish themselves with good reason, all those world-weary cowards and cross-spiders!

He just goes on reviling the ordinary man for not seeing what wonderful advantages, what marvelous powers of life, those three vices are, not taking into account that there are people who are just the prisoners of these powers. He only sees himself and projects himself naively all over the world as if his case were the universal one. He has grown outside of himself with his intuition, he is not in his body, but is an abstract number, and how does an abstract number feel with no blood for feet and hands and body to give him some relationship to such things? Of course he would welcome being a bit more overcome by the powers of life. But the vast majority of people are the victims of life, and you do them a great service in showing them the way out of their captivity—not into it. You can imagine the effect if he preaches such ideas to those who are in captivity, who are selfish and suffer from their selfishness; now they must realize that selfishness is a great virtue, that they must be more selfish, have more will to power. Then the inferior men become the canaille; then they are really the rabble which before they were not. Perhaps they were modest, and now they become immodest, because the vices from which they suffer—and there was a time when they knew that they suffered from them—are now called virtues. Then they take over the power, and see what becomes of a fellow like Nietzsche! What he has produced is just the contrary to what he tried to produce. If he had only looked back once, he would have seen the

shadow behind him, and then he would have known what he produced. But he never would have had the realization that Hannibal, for
instance, had. You remember Hannibal had a remarkable dream when
he was on his way to Rome: He felt that something was following him
and that he should not turn his head to see what it was; but he did turn
his head and he saw that it was a terrible dragon monster that devas-
tated a whole world. As you know, the outcome of his campaign against
Rome was the complete destruction of Carthage, which was not exactly
his plan, not what he was looking for. But that is what often happens
to people who do not see the shadow; they think they only mean the
best for a nation or for the whole world, never reckoning with the fact
of what they actually produce. If they looked back they would see.
Hannibal saw what he produced: first Italy was destroyed, and finally
Carthage was definitely and completely destroyed.

You see, one should always ask *who* is teaching a thing. As if it mat-
tered what the man says; it only matters that *he* says, not *what* he says.
In order to criticize it, you must always ask *who* has said it. For instance,
suppose you are in a bad financial situation, and somebody comes
along and says to give him your books and he will handle everything,
he will take over the responsibility. But I ask: who is that fellow that is
going to take the responsibility? Then we find out that he has gone
through a dozen bankruptcies already, that he is really a swindler, and
the man who would put his affairs into his hands would be a fool.

And so in reading a philosophy, it is not only the thought itself but
the man who produced the thought that counts. Ask what it meant to
him, for in reading those words you cannot help comparing them with
what he himself was. Or who delivers a sermon? Go back to his reality
and see whether it fits. You see, from the context you could conclude
here that a *condottiere* from the Renaissance, a hell of a fellow, was
speaking. While in reality you find a kindly, very nervous, half-blind
man who suffers from headaches and doesn't touch the world anywhere; he is up in a corner of a little house in the Engadine and disturbs not a fly. Then you would say that he was apparently monolog-
izing and that you must turn that thing round and see what was
happening. And you would decide that it should be broadcast chiefly
in university circles, but forbidden to any ordinary and instinctive
creature; that it was only to be handed out to doctors and professors
who suffer from insomnia and headaches and nobody else should read
it. You see if Nietzsche's inferior man could hear what he, the man
above, was preaching, his prophecy would be right, namely:

> But to all those cometh now the day, the change, the sword of judgment, the great noontide; then shall many things be revealed.

Revealed to Herr Professor Nietzsche you see.

> And he who proclaimeth the ego wholesome and holy, and self-ishness blessed, verily, he, the prognosticator, speaketh also what he knoweth: "Behold, it cometh, it is nigh, the great noontide!"

To Professor Nietzsche, actually living in Sils Maria, it would be the great noontide, where the evening joins the morning, where all things become complete, where he could come together with his shadow. But to nobody else.

Now we come to the next chapter, "The Spirit of Gravity." Nietzsche would never have spoken of the spirit of gravity if he had ever come down to it really. He never touched the shadow, but projected it into other people. If he had contacted his own shadow, this chapter would have had no purpose. But he realizes here that something is pulling him down, feels the gravity, an enormous weight, and therefore this chapter, "The Spirit of Gravity," follows. You see, he is still hovering six thousand feet above good and evil, still avoids the three evils which are such great virtues, and so feels the weight, the gravity of things. He rightly begins with the words, "My mouthpiece—is of the people"—not his own. The funny thing is that here he is not talking as if he were Professor Nietzsche; the shadow, the inferior man is talking out of him because the inferior man wants to be heard. And Nietzsche doesn't realize it—in spite of the fact that he is the megaphone of the worst people. You see, this is a very important anticipation.

> My mouthpiece—is of the people: too coarsely and cordially do I talk for Angora rabbits.

That is stupidly translated. Nietzsche uses the word "*Seidenhasen.*" Now rabbits are very cowardly and stupid animals, very tender, with silky fur; this does not mean Angora rabbits, but means that his opponents are touchy, tender-skinned, foolish, narrow-minded rabbits, living in holes and gnawing cabbage stumps. Of course those are all professors at Basel University. There are some like that sure enough, but he himself belongs to them: *he* is touchy and tender-skinned, and shrinks away from every coarse touch. Every cold wind tells on him. He cannot live in Basel on account of the mists in winter.

And still stranger soundeth my word unto all ink-fish and pen-foxes. *Who* lives by ink and pen?
My hand—is a fool's hand: . . .

That means: my shadow's hand, this is the work of my shadow. But he doesn't realize it at all.

woe unto all tables and walls, and whatever hath room for fool's sketching, fool's scrawling!

He is filling the empty space round himself with the noise of his own words, demonstrating his own ideas; nobody else is concerned with them. As other people write the name of their sweetheart on the walls, or obscene jokes, or their own name, as if that were of interest to anybody but themselves. So he says that of his own sermons; his own chatter, his own wisdom is the fool's voice.

My foot—is a horse-foot; . . .

Who has a horse's foot? The devil. So he is not only a fool, but is also the devil.

therewith do I trample and trot over stick and stone, in the fields up and down, and am bedevilled with delight in all fast racing.

Now we have the picture. He has horse's feet, so he cannot help his feet running away with him. He is chasing up and down through the fields—as if that were particularly helpful to the fields. He is simply destructive, running about like a mad horse. If Jakob Burckhardt had been malicious, he could have said of Nietzsche that he was like a mad bull in a china shop, or like a rhinoceros in a flower bed. He did not because he was too polite, and because he was definitely afraid of Nietzsche. And here Nietzsche takes the words out of his mouth; he is criticizing himself:

My stomach—is surely an eagle's stomach? For it preferreth lamb's flesh. Certainly it is a bird's stomach.

Do you think that a bird has a good stomach?
Mrs. Fierz: They can swallow anything, and then they make it into a ball in their stomach and spit it out.
Prof. Jung: That is the so-called *Gewölle*.
Mrs. Fierz: And they have sort-of stones in their stomachs, so they can grind things.
Prof. Jung: Yes, like iron balls. But Nietzsche's stomach was so weak

that he often suffered from vomiting and so on—an extraordinary contrast! Then that his eagle stomach particularly liked to digest lamb's meat refers to what?

Mrs. Fierz: To the Lamb in Christianity.

Prof. Jung: Yes, that most certainly refers to the *Agnus Dei,* so the eagle is a god-eater. Naturally Christ, as the *Agnus Dei,* the Lamb of God, would be dead, a dead lamb, and that is what eagles do eat; and Nietzsche is the great devourer of Christianity and he has an excellent stomach. Now that is not the conscious Nietzsche, but the shadow speaking all along, and it would be up to Nietzsche to realize that something had been said, and that perchance it was himself who was speaking. Then, as any reasonable individual would do, he should ask what that meant. Just as you naturally ask, if someone tells you that he has written such-and-such a thing, "But how did you arrive at it? What does it meant to you?" So Nietzsche might say to himself, "Eagles have wonderful eyes, but you are half blind; birds have wonderful stomachs, but your stomach is weak. [If it had been an ostrich, that would have been the acme of a stomach because—proverbially—they can even digest iron nails!] You say you are a most destructive devil trampling down the wheat fields of the peasants, but you see you are a fool, filling every empty space with this silly writing. Now what on earth does that mean?" But it is only today apparently that we begin to ask ourselves such a question, or to reflect at all upon such things. Formerly it seemed only important that something had been said and no matter by whom. At least that was Nietzsche's psychology—something has been said—it happens that I have said something; not *I* have said, but I have said *something.* That prejudice is very important psychologically: namely, that only the thing outside matters, the thing that is produced and not the person by whom it is produced. Then he goes on,

> Nourished with innocent things, and with few, ready and impatient to fly, to fly away—that is now my nature: why should there not be something of bird-nature therein!

How do you interpret this?

Mrs. Fierz: It is an illusion about bird nature really, for why should they be nourished with innocent things?

Prof. Jung: Ah, but the Lamb, the *Agnus Dei,* is innocent food and that is very becoming! It is very nice of the eagles to eat innocent lambs or the innocent chickens; therefore they are so much liked by the peasants! This simply means also that the bird of prey is not a particularly constructive animal and is much hated by mankind. And what does "ready and impatient to fly away" mean?

Miss Hannah: He is still wanting to escape the inferior man, to live above it.

Prof. Jung: Well, it is the shadow speaking. This is a French expression: *prendre son vol.* He is now on the wing, he can fly to the top. This is the liberation of the shadow. And what will happen when the shadow is liberated—when it becomes a bird?

Mrs. Fierz: It will descend upon something.

Prof. Jung: Yes, pounce on a prey. Now, what kind of picture do you see? There is a famous picture from antiquity.

Mrs. Fierz: Ganymede.

Prof. Jung: Of course, fetched by the eagle of Zeus. And we have another connection.

Mrs. Jung: Prometheus.

Prof. Jung: Yes, that is the classical case. There the eagle has found its prey and killed it practically. So when the shadow puts on wings and becomes a bird, when the shadow is liberated, it is an independent, autonomous thing, and it swoops down on Nietzsche and takes him up into another world. Eventually, the eagle will eat out his life exactly as the eagle of Zeus ate the liver of Prometheus when he was chained to a rock, chained to earth. There we have the whole story. Then he says,

> And especially that I am hostile to the spirit of gravity, that is bird-nature:—verily, deadly hostile, supremely hostile, originally hostile! Oh, whither hath my hostility not flown and misflown!

This is a statement as to the attitude of the bird of prey that is now ready to take its flight. The shadow speaks here as an eagle; he has become a volatile being, a bird, and as such he is hostile to the spirit of gravity. We have had passages enough before where Zarathustra expressed his particular disgust with the spirit of gravity, with anything that pulled him down, and here it comes to the acme. His idea is that the very nature of the bird is hostile to the spirit of gravity, and he cannot do enough to enhance this hostility. He repeats it three times: "verily, deadly hostile, supremely hostile, originally hostile!" He wants to express a complete, hopeless contrast, things which never come together, and he even acknowledges that his hostility is so great that it may mislead him—""misflown," he says. You see, he identifies here completely with the bird-being and our inference is that it is an eagle, because he speaks of an eagle's stomach and it is a bird of prey that kills lambs. And that means a spirit hostile to Christianity and to all innocent things, and particularly is it hostile to the inferior man, to the spirit of gravity that is held in the prison of the earth. So it is a being that is intensely hostile to ordinary humanity or to everything human. One cannot help thinking here of the totem animal of the place from which Nietzsche comes, as more or less the model for such symbolism. And what is that totem animal?

Mrs. Crowley: The eagle.

Prof. Jung: That is the totem animal of the whole country, but Nietzsche's immediate background was my good town of Basel, and there it is the basilisk, a sort of winged dragon with a scorpion's tail, also a flying thing, but with a very poisonous sting at the end of its tail. Now, one of the characteristics of people who come from Basel is their *médisance*, their poisonous sting. There is a story that in the Middle Ages, when it happened that a rooster produced an egg—at all events it was the assumption that he did, for nobody else could have produced that egg—the police arrested the rooster. They had a trial and the judge issued a sentence: the rooster was condemned to death, given to the executioner, and burned like a heretic. For if a rooster produces an egg in the country where the basilisk is the totem animal, it is quite possible that a toad will discover that egg and hatch it; and when a toad hatches a rooster's egg, a basilisk will creep out. Then the totem animal would have become real, which would have been the most awful catastrophe for the town of Basel. Therefore the rooster had to be declared a witch and removed. That this case happened in Basel is of course the expression of their fear of the totem animal. So the totem animal is a reality in Switzerland. There is another town here where they keep the totem animal alive, Berne.

They say the word *Berne* comes from *Bär*, but this is of course the vulgar etymology. The fact is that in the old Celto-Roman settlement—which was not exactly at Berne but on the next peninsula—the river making a loop there—they excavated the *Dea Artio*, a bear goddess. So a sanctuary of that pre-Christian goddess was there already, which explains why the local totem is the bear. And that idea is still so much alive at Berne that they have to have living bears in the *Bärengraben* in order to feel all right. Like the primitives, when they have lost their totem they are gone. Therefore we have to take such allusions very seriously. In this case the bird coincides with the bird that is characteristic for the whole country, the eagle. You can now draw your conclusions if you like. We don't need to do it publicly; we can do it in private meditation. So Nietzsche says:

Thereof could I sing a song—[I could sing a song too!] and *will* sing it: though I be alone in an empty house, and must sing it to mine own ears.

There was nobody to listen, nobody would understand; he was quite alone with that intuition, of course, in his days. Now, in the next part we will skip the first four verses, and then continue:

One must learn to love oneself—thus do I teach—with a wholesome and healthy love: that one may endure to be with oneself, and not go roving about.

This is a very reasonable idea, a very good intention obviously. In the verse before we find a measure of precaution and a realization:

Not, to be sure, with the love of the sick and infected, for with them stinketh even self-love!

So we are quite sure he doesn't mean the egotistical autoeroticism of a morbid being. But when one says, "Of course I don't mean that awful kind of self-love, that egocentric attitude of neurotics," one must be quite sure that one is not a neurotic oneself. Otherwise an indiscreet individual of our day will enquire, "Are *you* the one with that right kind of love?" And then one must be sure that one has a clean sheet, that one doesn't also suffer from egocentricity or neuroticism. Therefore, when Nietzsche says he doesn't mean that stinking kind of self-love, that is not enough. For *who* has been talking? The shadow, the inferior man, who, we know, has even become a bird that in time may swoop down upon Nietzsche, sweep him off his feet and carry him away. This bird is the fool who jumped over him in that first fatal vision. When Nietzsche-Zarathustra was a rope-dancer, the fool that leapt over him as if he were flying, was already this evil bird that would take possession of him; and that fool caused the downfall, the death even, of the poor rope-dancer, whose mind would be dead before his body. That was the prophecy even then. So when this bird-man is speaking, as he was definitely in the chapter before and still is here, we have to be critical. For even a truth works in the wrong way when spoken by the wrong man; the right means in the hands of the wrong man works evil. We will go back to the first verses in this second part of the chapter where it says.

He who one day teacheth men to fly will have shifted all landmarks; . . .

The one who can teach men to fly is the flier, the bird-man, and he will thereby shift all landmarks. So there will no longer be any definite borderlines. What does that mean?

Mrs. Fierz: It means just chaos.

Prof. Jung: Yes, indistinctness. Nobody knows what belongs to himself and what belongs to his neighbors; it will be a complete mixup. The bird-man will produce chaos.

to him will all landmarks themselves fly into the air; . . .

Now what are landmarks really? What would you call a landmark, Miss Hannah?

Miss Hannah: Something that is always there, that one is absolutely used to.

Prof. Jung: Well, you are used to a midday meal. Is that a landmark too? Please give me a definite description of a landmark.

Mr. Allemann: All laws or conventions, everything that has been exactly defined, like the two hedges between which a road goes. If they disappear in the air you don't know where you are.

Prof. Jung: Yes, a landmark is a definite characteristic of a country. It can be a boundary stone, a hedge, a river, a hill, a tree—any outstanding feature of a countryside is a landmark. And if all such features should fly up to heaven—which of course is a perfectly nonsensical picture—what happens then?

Mr. Allemann: No orientation is possible.

Prof. Jung: Yes, but we must be concrete. When a landmark flies into the air, what happens?

Mrs. Fierz: Then gravity has stopped.

Prof. Jung: Yes. Now if that should really happen on the earth, if there were no gravity, nothing would be changed in the moment, but I would only need to press on this table and I would float into the air and remain there. You lift your chair and up it goes to the ceiling and you remain with it. The slightest shock causes your house to rise into the air, and so everything, the whole surface of the earth, would be floating through space. So Nietzsche describes here a condition where gravity is gone completely, where every landmark rises into the air. And the text goes on,

the earth will he christen anew—as "the light body."

The earth has no weight, it is the light body. He has obliterated gravity, so the earth itself becomes a bird. Of course that is madness.

The ostrich runneth faster than the fastest horse, . . .

He could not suppress the ostrich on account of its stomach, and the horse's hoofs, the devil, must be brought in again . . .

> but it also thrusteth its head heavily into the heavy earth: thus is it with the man who cannot yet fly.

Nor could he suppress this picture, because it is again an opportunity to revile the inferior man who is already a bird, but he still has his head buried in the earth. He is again reviling the shadow, but the shadow is still speaking. That the shadow reviles itself is the devilish cunning of the unconscious. The old Fathers of the church have already pointed out that the devil is not dangerous as long as he appears with claws and a tail, or as long as he utters blasphemies, or causes one to sin. He is not even dangerous when he reads the Bible and sings hymns. But when the devil tells the truth, look out! For you then have to ask *who* has told it, and since that is never asked, there the greatest danger lies. Then it is like assuming that the tenor with a wonderful voice has a noble character.

> Heavy unto him are earth and life, and so willeth the spirit of gravity! But he who would become light, and be a bird, must love himself: thus do I teach.

Here is the devil, the bird-man who says you cannot get rid of the spirit of gravity without loving yourself. You see, this love of himself serves the aims of the bird-man, so that is not the right teaching. It leads into complete annihilation of order and law, and of nature as well, the nature that is heavy and has definite landmarks. It upsets the natural order of things, creating beings that have no soil under their feet. It changes everything heavy that has its own place in nature, its own uniqueness, into something indistinct and means the destruction and dissolution of all definite individual values. The end is a soup: everything is in the soup. This great truth is to be met with severe criticism, because the spirit or the bird-man is going to teach this truth to everybody indiscriminately. He says one must learn to love oneself with a wholesome and healthy love, but is everybody ready to understand and to accept such a teaching? That it is right for everybody is of course very questionable. Therefore one asks, "Did you apply that teaching to yourself? Did you love yourself with that love? Show me the result." And then Prof. Nietzsche is produced, with an upset stomach, taking a sleeping draught every night. Is that the bird-man or the spirit-man, or in any way a superior man? No, it is a poor sick man.

But the truth of this sentence is valid under certain conditions; if you understand properly what it means to love oneself with a wholesome and healthy love, that one may endure to be with oneself and not go roving about, then it is a very excellent truth. If that is told to the right man by the right man in the right moment, it is an excellent truth, and one of the most modern, most moral tasks you can imagine. For you have to love yourself just as you are, and then there is no reviling of the inferior man any more: there is no reviling at all. Then you are forced to even love the inferior man in yourself, the ape man perhaps; then you have to be nice to your own menagerie—if you can realize what that means. It is difficult to realize it, because you have to love them with such a love that you are able to endure being with yourself. Now, how can you endure to be with your menagerie unless you have your animals in cages? The only thing to do is to have cages, perhaps very nice cages with different species of water plants and such things, a sort of aquarium such as Hagenbeck makes for his animals: deep moats round your cages, no iron bars.[2] It looks as if they were free but they are not. So you see, you can only say, "Ah, I am civilized man but my menagerie has to be looked after." You can make a very cultural zoo of yourself if you love your animals.

For instance, innocent animals—antelopes, gazelles, and such animals—can be kept walking about as long as they cannot escape. But if they escape you have lost something. Even your birds must be kept in a *volière*; but it can be spacious and well equipped, so that they have a sort of Garden of Eden. That was the original idea: the Garden of Eden was a sort of cage for man and animals from which nobody could escape without getting into the desert, or a zoo where the animals had a pleasant existence and could not eat each other. That would be very awkward for the birds of prey, so we must assume they got horseflesh from outside perhaps, since they would not eat apples. This is of course an entirely different picture from what Nietzsche dreamed of. But if you don't love your menagerie, I don't see how you can endure to be with yourself. You couldn't very well be in the monkey cage or with the snakes—it would be too uncomfortable, and you would not

[2] Carl Hagenbeck (1844-1913), *Von Tieren und Menschen* (Berlin, 1909); abridged version, tr. H.S.R. Eliot and A. G. Thacker (London, 1909) under the title *Beasts and Men*. Hagenbeck was a German pioneer of the modern zoo.

love yourself when exposed to the hardships day and night, to the stench and also to the danger. So you must produce a relatively decent existence for yourself. You have probably a nice little house near the zoo, perhaps inside near the bird cage where you don't smell the wolves or the foxes. They are a bit further away, also the snake house. It must be nothing more and nothing less than a little Garden of Eden in which you are the lord god walking about and enjoying the different species of animals and plants.

Mrs. Jung: You said before that the shadow was speaking. Now, from the standpoint of the shadow it would be understandable that he wishes to lose his gravity so that he would become more differentiated.

Prof. Jung: Yes, the shadow was speaking, but we now detach that whole sentence from the shadow and take it for an impersonal truth. We put it under conditions where the right man uses the right means in the right moment with the right people. We assume the best possible conditions for this truth. Here it is not the best possible condition because it is told by the bird-man to everybody indiscriminately; and that is a great danger because the inferior man will not understand it properly. If you teach the inferior man to follow his voluptuousness, follow his passion for power, to have it all his own way, you will soon have a communistic chaos: that would be the inevitable result of such teaching. But here we are imagining that this truth is now told, not by the bird-man but by the right man; not to everybody, but to the right people; not just at any time in the world, but now, profiting by the right moment. For a truth in the wrong moment can have an entirely wrong effect. It must be said in the right moment. You see, when we assume that things are at their best, we can then make an extract of that truth, which is universal. And it is a tremendous problem of course: How shall we deal with all the different aspects of human nature? If you love the inferior man, if you love all those inferior qualities as you should, what does that mean?

For instance, if you love flies and lice, which you also have to do to a certain extent, they will simply eat you up in the end. But you have other animals that you have to love, so you must give each part of yourself a decent existence. Then naturally the different kinds of animals will check each other. The birds of prey will hinder a superabundance of mice or other little vermin. The big animals of prey will eat many of the sheep and cows, so there will not be an overproduction of milk and butter and so on. It is exactly the same in the human constitution: there are innumerable units with definite purposes, and each can overgrow

1472

all the others if you insist upon one particular unit. But if you love yourself, you have to love the whole, and the part has to submit to the necessities of the whole in the interest of democracy. You can say it is perfectly ridiculous, but we *are* ridiculous. The management of the whole psychological situation, like the management of a country, consists of a lot of ridiculous things. Like all nature, it is grotesque—all the funny animals you know—but they do exist and the whole is a symphony, after all. If it is one-sided, you disturb the whole thing: you disturb that symphony and it becomes chaos. Then it is also an excellent truth that one should not go roving about, as Nietzsche defines it:

> Such roving about christeneth itself "brotherly love"; with these words hath there hitherto been the best lying and dissembling, and especially by those who have been burdensome to everyone.

Those are the people who go about and tell everybody how much they love them or what they ought to do for their own good, always assuming that they know what is best for them. Or the people who want to get rid of themselves, so they unburden themselves on others. There are certain lazy dogs who want to get rid of their own destiny so they put it on somebody else by loving them. They fall on the neck of someone saying, "I love you," and so they put the bag on his back; they call that love. Or they go to someone and burden him with what he really ought to do and *they* never do. They never ask themselves what is good for themselves, but they know exactly what is good for him. Do it yourself first and then you will know if it is really good. So here Nietzsche tells other people they ought to fly—as if *he* could. He cheats them as he has cheated himself. It is the same mechanism that he blames Christian love for. But there is Christian love and Christian love. When someone applies Christian love in the right way, it is a virtue and of the highest merit; but if he misuses Christian love in order to put his own burdens on other people, he is immoral, a usurer, a cheat. You see, if he loves other people with the purpose of making use of them, it is not love; he simply uses love as a pretext, a cover under which he hides his own selfish interests. To really love other people, he must first give evidence that he can love himself, for to love oneself is the most difficult task. To love someone else is easy, but to love what you are, the thing that is yourself, is just as if you were embracing a glowing red-hot iron: it burns into you and that is very painful. Therefore, to love somebody else in the first place is always an escape which we all hope for, and we all enjoy it when we are capable of it. But in the long run, it comes back on us. You cannot stay away from yourself forever, you have to return, have to come to that experiment, to know whether you really can love. That is the question—whether you can love yourself, and that will be the test. So when Nietzsche blames Christian love, he is simply blaming his own type.

LECTURE II

25 January 1939

Prof. Jung:

We left off the second part of the 55th chapter at the verse:

> One must learn to love oneself—thus do I teach—with a whole-some and healthy love: that one may endure to be with oneself, and not go roving about.

This, as you remember, is said in connection with all the preceding chapters about the shadow man. Nietzsche has talked so much about him and has reviled him so often, that we might almost expect a reaction to take place: he should develop beyond it. You know, when you have occupied your mind with an object for a while, particularly when it is such an emotional object—or subject—as the shadow, you are almost forced into a reaction. For whether it is the shadow or any other unconscious figure, the preoccupation is of a rare, emotional kind, and you are drawn into the problem of it: you become almost identified with it. The fact that Nietzsche reviles the shadow shows to what extent he is already identical with it, and his vituperation is really a means of separating himself from it. You often find people swearing and kicking against things with which they are too closely connected: then they develop inner resistances and make attempts to liberate themselves. So it seems as if we might now expect something to happen, and here we find a trace of something new—one could almost say a way to deal with the shadow properly—though you cannot expect Nietzsche in his vague unconsciousness to deal quite clearly or properly with the shadow. Nevertheless, ways may suggest themselves. Even in dreams, where one is also in an unconscious condition, more or less clear statements may come through, which you can use if, with consciousness, you can understand them. While if you leave them in the dream state, they have only a faint effect and you can never really use them.

Therefore, I have often been asked what was the use of having a healing or helpful dream when you cannot understand it. That is ex-

1475

actly why we try to understand dreams, for the fact of having a helpful dream doesn't mean that you are really much helped. You may be benefitted even if you don't understand it—it may have a certain positive effect—but as a rule it is a transitory effect. It is too unimportant, too faint, and vanishes too soon, so that practically nothing happens. It is in order to gain ground, to enlarge our understanding of them, that we make the attempt to interpret dreams. It is just as if you had discovered that there was gold in the ground under your feet; you must dig it up or it always remains there. Or you may know that there is three or four percent of gold in a certain rock, yet it is so distributed in the substance of the rock that it is of no use to you. Therefore you must invent a special chemical procedure to extract that gold; then you get it, but it needs your conscious or even your scientific effort.

Of course in Nietzsche's case, there is nothing of the kind; he is in a sort of dream process. He swims along with the current of his problems, and only with our knowledge of psychology are we able to see what they really are. The problem of how to compensate the shadow appears on the surface and disappears, and then comes up again, like a log carried along by a muddy river; and there is nobody there to fish out that log and make a good beam of it. He is simply carried along by the stream of his associations, and he does bring up something of great value, but it is we who know it is of great value. He also has a feeling that it is worth something, but it is as if he didn't know that he could make that log into a pole which would be the foundation of a bridge perhaps, or which could be shaped into a boat to carry him across the river. So he lets it go, it passes by and forms a part of that great river, the eternal movement of life, and the river flows down into the sea. It is coming to an end. This book begins with the statement that this is the down-going of Zarathustra, the sunset—the river is nearing the end; and the mere moving current reveals many things, but nothing comes of it because there is nobody to take a hook and fish something out. What he says here is a great truth and an extraordinarily helpful one, the formula by which he could deal with or overcome his shadow. But if he did realize it, he would have to strike out with a blue pencil all the chapters before, for he would not be reviling the shadow because he would also *be* his shadow. And how could he love himself if he reviles himself? He could not blame the inferior man, because to love oneself means to love one's totality, and that includes the inferior man.

You see, the idea in Christianity is to love the least of our brethren, and as long as he is outside of us, it is a wonderful chance; we all hope that the least of our brethren is, for God's sake, outside ourselves. For you cut a very wonderful figure when you put a tramp at your table and feed him, and you think, "Am I not grand? Such a dirty chap and I feed him at my table!" And the devil of course is not lazy in that respect: he stands right behind you and whispers in your ear what a wonderful heart you have, like gold you know, and you pat yourself on the back for having done it. And everybody else says, "Is he not a wonderful fellow, marvelous!" But when it happens that the least of the brethren whom you meet on the road of life is yourself, what then? I have asked certain theologians this question, but they can only whisper that they don't know. Otherwise it would appear as if they were kind to the least of their brethren in themselves, that they didn't despise him on account of his inferiority; while the ordinary practice is that they revile themselves, so that again everybody will say, "What a grand fellow! What self-criticism! He sees his mistakes, his vices, and he rebukes himself." And then the whole of collectivity will agree.

Now, Nietzsche discovered the truth, that if you have to be kind to the least of your brethren, you have to be kind also when the least of your brethren comes to you in the shape of yourself, and so he arrives at the conclusion: love thyself. The collective Christian point of view is: "Love thy neighbor," and they hush up the second part "as thyself." Nietzsche reverses this; he says, "Love thyself," and forgets "as thou lovest thy neighbor." That is the anti-Christian point of view and so the truth is falsified both ways. It really should be: "Love thy neighbor as thou lovest thyself; or love thyself as thou lovest thy neighbor." That is a complete truth—if you love at all, or if you can afford to love at all. One could say also, "Hate your neighbor as you hate yourself, or hate yourself as you hate your neighbor." Nietzsche's understanding is quite complete, one could say—only he doesn't realize it. One *should* love oneself, one *should* accept the least of one's brethren in oneself, that one may endure to be with oneself and not go roving about. And how can we endure anything if we cannot endure ourselves? If the whole of mankind should run away from itself, life would consist on principle of running away all the time. Now that is not meant; God's creation is not meant to run away from itself. If the tiger runs away from itself and eats apples, or an elephant runs away from itself in order to study at the university library, or a man becomes a fish, it is a complete perversion. Therefore, the very foundation of existence, the biological truth, is that each being is so interested in itself that it does love itself, thereby fulfilling the laws of its existence. The individual gets cut off from his roots if he tries to use the roots of other people. Inasmuch as we run away from ourselves we are trying to use the roots of other people, to be parasites on other people, and that is a perversity, a monstrosity. That deviation or separation from oneself is what Nietzsche calls "roving about," and he explains in the next paragraph:

> Such roving about christeneth itself "brotherly love"; with these words hath there hitherto been the best lying and dissembling, and especially by those who have been burdensome to every one.

Here he makes a statement which is absolutely true. The Christian brotherly love is exactly that, loving thy neighbor and suppressing the second part of the sentence. In that case you are running away from yourself, so you come to your neighbor as the man who doesn't love himself, and then naturally you burden your neighbor with the task of loving you. You love him in the hope that he will love you again because you don't love yourself. Because you don't feed yourself, you tell your neighbor you love him, with the secret hope that he will feed you. Or because you don't earn money yourself, you tell your neighbor you love him in the hope that he will give you money. That is damnable. It is: "I give that thou givest," and that is not exactly what we call love. It is a plot, or an insinuation, or an intention, a definite plan to get something for yourself, and that contradicts the very idea of love. So when you hate yourself and pretend to love your neighbor, it is more than suspect, it is poison. You see, when you cannot love yourself, then in a way you cannot love, so it is really a pretense to say that you love your neighbor. The love of the man who cannot love himself is defective when he loves somebody else. It is like saying one cannot think one's own thoughts, but can only think the thoughts of other people. But that is not thinking; it is mere parrot talk, a sham, a fraud—one is simply pulling the wool over other people's eyes. So if you are full of desires and needs and pretend to love somebody else, it is merely in order that they shall fulfil what you really desire and need. That is what Nietzsche is emphasizing. Then he goes on,

> And verily, it is no commandment for to-day and tomorrow to learn to love oneself. Rather is it of all arts the finest, subtlest, last and patientest.

This is perfectly true: one could call it a great art, and I should say a great philosophy because it is the most difficult thing you can imagine, to accept your own inferiority. It needs more than art: it needs a great deal of philosophy, even of religion, in order to make that bond between yourself and your shadow a lasting one. When Nietzsche assumes that it is an art and even the highest art, he doesn't put it strongly enough, because he doesn't realize what it is. Now he continues,

> For to its possessor is all possession well concealed, and of all treasure-pits one's own is last excavated—so causeth the spirit of gravity.

He understands sloth, or whatever it is which hinders us from excavating our own treasure, to be the spirit of gravity. That is because it is understood to be, not a treasure, but a black hole full of evil spirits.

> Almost in the cradle are we apportioned with heavy words and worths: "good" and "evil"—so calleth itself this dowry. For the sake of it we are forgiven for living.

This means that the moral categories are a heavy, even a dangerous, inheritance, because they are the instruments by which we make it impossible to integrate the shadow. We condemn it and therefore we suppress it.

> And therefore suffereth one little children to come unto one, to forbid them betimes to love themselves—so causeth the spirit of gravity."

Here is a clear reference to what?

Miss Hannah: To Christ's remark.

Prof. Jung: Yes, so we see he means Christianity all along the line.

> And we—we bear loyally what is apportioned unto us, on hard shoulders, over rugged mountains! And when we sweat, then do people say to us: "Yea, life is hard to bear!"
> But man himself only is hard to bear!

This is a very important statement from a psychological point of view. We forget again and again that our fate, our lives, are just ourselves; it is in a way our choice all along. Of course one can say that we are born into overwhelming conditions, but the conditions don't depend upon the weather, don't depend upon the geological structure of the surface of the earth, don't depend upon electricity or upon the sunshine. They depend upon man, upon our contemporaries, and we are included. We are born into the after-war world, but we are the people who live there. We have the psychology that produces an after-war world, so we are in it, participating in those conditions, and if we have social responsibilities, it is because we are the makers of that kind of psychology. If everybody in his own place and in his own self would correct the atti-

1479

tude which has brought about those conditions, they would not exist. So we can only conclude that whatever we meet with, inasmuch as it is man-made, is the thing we have chosen, the result of our peculiar psychology. We are always inclined to say: "Oh, if *they* had not done this or that." But who are they? We are they too, for if you take one man out of the crowd that you accuse, and ask him who "they" are, he will say, "*You!*" You are in the same crowd, life is yourself, and if life is hard to bear, it is because it is very hard to bear yourself. That is the greatest burden, the greatest difficulty.

> The reason thereof is that he carrieth too many extraneous things on his shoulders. Like the camel kneeleth he down, and letteth himself be well laden.

Is that logical? He has just said, "But man himself only is hard to bear," and now he calls it the burden of life. It is the burden of himself, man is the burden.

Mrs. Jung: I thought it referred to what he said before, that one teaches the people good and evil, and because he thinks those are extraneous things, that might be what he means by the burden.

Prof. Jung: Quite so. No doubt Nietzsche assumes that those things would not have grown in that individual if he had not been taught them. But inasmuch as those so-called extraneous things are also in himself, he participates in it: he is also one of those who shares such concepts.

Remark: I thought it might mean that he has to carry the burden because of other people.

Prof. Jung: Oh yes, one can enumerate a number of things that are forced upon one by so-called external conditions. For instance, a person with an objectionable persona can say circumstances forced him to have such a persona. Perhaps he is stiff, proud, gives other people no access to himself; perhaps he refuses everything and is obstinate, and he can explain exactly why he is all that, can give me a complete list of the causes that made him into such a thing. He can say if his parents had behaved in a different way he would be quite different, or Mrs. So-and-So, or his professor in the university, or his wife, his children, his uncles and aunts—they all account for his attitude. And it would be perfectly true. But then one asks, "Why is his brother, who lived with him in the same family, an entirely different persona with an entirely different attitude to life? He was under the same influence, was at the same school, had the same education; but he has chosen a different attitude, has made a different selection. So it is not true that these external conditions have caused him to be what he is; he has chosen those external conditions in order to be what he is. If somebody else had chosen them, the very same conditions would have been made into something quite different. And the life of the one is miserable on account of his attitude, and the life of the other fellow is much nicer on account of *his* attitude. The life of the individual is his own making. So when the one is overburdened by a moral teaching, it is because he chooses it. Another one, taught the same thing, doesn't care a bit for that moral teaching. He takes it lightly, doesn't believe it perhaps, or he models those concepts to his own liking. He is not at all overburdened because he did not choose to be overburdened, did not accept it. You cannot blame external circumstances, but can only blame yourself for taking on that persona, for allowing yourself to be poisoned by circumstances.

So Nietzsche makes here a complete contradiction. For man himself is his own difficulty and if anyone is to blame, it is himself, because he has chosen it, has swallowed it. He was not critical enough, or he has preferred to make a special selection of circumstances in order to prove his point, which is himself. And if that proves to be wrong, perhaps, in the long run, it is not the world that is wrong: it is himself. Therefore, when he says: "Like the camel kneeleth he down, and letteth himself be well laden," we can only say, "Well yes, he *is* a camel, he is an ass." Now why does Nietzsche say a camel? He writes in German, and when a German says *Kamel* he can't help realizing the double meaning of that word. To a German-speaking man, a camel is not necessarily the wonderful ship of the desert that faithfully carries its loads, a true servant of man, the highly prized domestic animal of the nomad. Of course he knows that, but when I say to a man. "You are just a camel," he never will think that he is the true servant of God. He knows exactly what I mean and he will sue me for libel. So when Nietzsche designates himself as a camel, he needs all that exaggeration in order not to see what his unconscious really means. For he is that fellow who allows himself to be burdened, the camel that kneels down and laps up all the stuff he has been taught.

Especially the strong load-bearing man in whom reverence resideth.

He has to pat himself on the back for all the things he has carried. Yes, it is nice if it is not stupid.

Too many *extraneous* heavy words and worths loadeth he upon himself—. . .

Well, it is the camel that is doing it: it allows itself to be overburdened; that is just the difference between man and the camel. A man knows when the limit is reached and how much it is reasonable to carry, but a camel is supposed not to know that exactly. It is supposed to be a pretty stupid animal, and well deserves that "then seemeth life to him a desert!"

> And verily! Many a thing also that is our own is hard to bear!

Here he cannot help coming to himself. Naturally he would have come to himself long ago if he had realized what he was saying, but only now does it begin to dawn upon him that it is hard to bear oneself. This just shows again how little he realizes in the moment the meaning of his words. One thinks, because he says it, that he knows it, but he doesn't know it: it just flows out. As little as the river knows what it is carrying along, does he know what he is saying. It is as if he were slowly waking up and coming to the conclusion that even many a thing that is really our own, that is part of our own psychology, is hard to bear. So he is now going on in the same style, slowly realizing that this thing reaches pretty far, that it even reaches into the depths of psychology.

> And many internal things in man are like the oyster—repulsive and slippery and hard to grasp.

This is the resistance one naturally feels against the fact that the shadow is a reality; one can talk a mouthful about it, but to realize it is something else.

> So that an elegant shell, with elegant adornment, must plead for them. But this art also must one learn: to have a shell, and a fine appearance, and sagacious blindness.

One could not add much to this. It is perfectly true. But I should say that for the time being it would be very important if he could pierce the shell.

> Again it deceiveth about many things in man, that many a shell is poor and pitiable, and too much of a shell. Much concealed goodness and power is never dreamt of; the choicest dainties find no tasters!

Yes, one must admit that sometimes even great values are concealed, but also things which are not particularly valuable. Now we will skip the next paragraphs and go to:

Verily, I learned waiting also, and thoroughly so,—but only waiting for *myself*.

I emphasize this passage only because it will soon be completely contradicted. The idea of learning to wait, learning patience, would indeed be a good realization, and particularly to be patient with oneself. That would be the greatest asset. It would mean that he knew how to deal with himself, that he knew what it means to endure oneself, to be kind to oneself, to carry oneself. One is, of course, deeply impressed with this immense truth, but here again one has to understand that Nietzsche does not realize what he is saying. If he were really waiting for himself, why should he wait for man? Why does he wait and hope for the moment when he can leave his isolation in order to come down to overburdened man? One sees what such great insight is really worth from the second paragraph after this:

> With rope-ladders learned I to reach many a window, with nimble legs did I climb high masts: to sit on high masts of perception seemed to me no small bliss;—
> —To flicker like small flames on high masts: a small light, certainly, but a great comfort to cast-away sailors and shipwrecked ones!

So when he is isolated, when he is waiting for himself, he is really waiting for a shipwreck somewhere, waiting to be a beacon light of orientation to shipwrecked sailors, but for heaven's sake, not to himself. He must hope that many people will suffer shipwreck, otherwise he would not function at all. Now what is that flickering on high masts?

Miss Wolff: The fire of St. Elmo.

Prof. Jung: Yes, an electrical discharge which takes place when there is great electric tension. One sees it also on mountains before a thunderstorm: the electricity streams out of the top of the mountain, one feels it directly. So he compares himself to a sort of electric phenomenon that happens only on the summits of very high mountains. That is the truth: he is climbing into a world of very high thoughts. He is on the top of very high masts, just like such a flickering flame, a will o' the wisp which never settles down, has no roots—an intuitive function only. Of course that is only a side glance at his psychology. Now the next chapter, "Old and New Tables" should be "Old and New Tablets" really, like cuneiform writing tablets. That was the original idea, the parallel of those cuneiform tiles upon which the law of Moses was inscribed. In those days everything was written on clay which was then burned. So it means old and new laws, and here we can expect some further code of prescriptions of how to deal with the inferior man. He begins:

> Here do I sit and wait, old broken tables around me and also new half-written tables. When cometh mine hour?
>
> The hour of my descent, of my down-going: for once more will I go unto men.

This means: why in hell should I stay with myself? Why can I not escape at once the unendurable self?—which of course would come to him with tremendous realization. You see, when he is a flickering light on mast-tops he is escaping himself. He is only on the highest masts and what is there below? Apparently he doesn't know. He doesn't realize that all his intuitions mean nothing whatever if they don't become reality in himself. He is the *materia* through which these intuitions ought to come into life, to become really true, and then he would know what they mean. He can hardly wait for his coming down from the mast-tops, but that doesn't mean coming to himself, into his ordinary human reality, but out into a crowd; it means an audience to talk to and tell them what they ought to be. Now he says,

> For that hour do I now wait: . . .

He had better say, "I wait for myself," but no, he waits for the hour when he can give up the task of himself.

> for first must the signs come unto me that it is mine hour— namely, the laughing lion with the flock of doves.

Think of the picture—a laughing lion and a circle of pigeons sitting round him.

Now, I find that there is a little uncertainty about that question of being alone with oneself and going down to humanity. You see, in Nietzsche's case it was really a question of physical solitude, and man meant to him just society. Of course, enduring oneself would not mean sitting in the observatory on the top of Mont Blanc where there is nobody for the better part of a year. That is no opportunity for finding yourself; you don't find yourself in such utter solitude, but only fall into your own unconscious. What is meant is, that you should be *with yourself*, not alone but with yourself, and you can be with yourself even in a crowd. Inasmuch as you are in connection with other people, it makes sense to be with yourself, but it makes no sense at all when you are just alone, because solitude, if it is a bit exaggerated, is most conducive to becoming unconscious. Therefore a human being who wants to lose himself seeks solitude as a sure means of making him unconscious of himself. But the point is *not* to be unconscious: the point is to picture the unconscious of oneself but to be with oneself.

That forced, or chosen, solitude in which Nietzsche lived was a temptation, and one of the reasons why he lost himself in the unconscious. Because of his peculiar lack of realization, he got into the swift current of that stream which carried him away. If he had been forced to explain himself to a number of people whose connection he could not afford to lose, he would have been forced to self-realization; but if nobody has a claim, there is no contradiction, no opposition, no discussion. Then he is not forced to hold on to anything, even to himself. He can let go of himself, let himself disappear into that great underground river of the unconscious where one necessarily loses one's self-realization. That he desires company, that he wants to go down to humanity out of his solitude, is quite right; but inasmuch as he fails to realize that he doesn't possess himself in his solitude, but is possessed, then most certainly when he comes down among other people, humanity in general, he will be as if possessed. Then he will be as if surrounded by a glass wall, isolated against humanity, because he is possessed by an undigested unconscious. If he had digested his unconscious, if he had been in connection with people whom he could not afford to lose, he would have constantly broken through that wall of isolation. If you observe a man who is lost in the unconscious, possessed by the unconscious, simply identical with it, you always feel that peculiar isolation, that glass wall; you see him and he sees you but there is no connection. You cannot touch him; he is as if removed from human contact. Wherever you find a person of whom you have that feeling—provided that it is not yourself and that you project it—you can be sure that such a one is possessed.

I told you the alchemistic myth of Arisleus and his companions. You remember he got into the threefold glass house under the sea, which means that he went into the unconscious and was caught in the threefold glass house. You see, that is correct psychologically: he was not only under the sea, which would be enough in itself but he was even shut into a threefold glass house, which means that he was completely isolated against his surroundings. Of course, that may have also a positive aspect: there is no situation so bad that it has not some redeeming feature about it. In such isolation you may develop such a heat that it burns through the glass, in the end. In this case of Arisleus it was the preparation for resurrection, a rebirth. That it was so terribly hot inside the glass house is of course difficult to understand, but it was heated from within. Another simile is the old man in a glass house who is so hot that the vapor of his perspiration covers the glass walls and becomes a precious substance because it is sublimated: it is the dew of Gideon in the Old Testament. And that is the marvelous, divine or eternal water by which transformation is produced. So by that isolation, or within that isolation, something rises from you, something that is forced out of you in your tortured condition. The same situation is depicted in the biblical story of the three men in the fiery furnace where a fourth appeared. The fourth one is the Redeemer, the angel of God. Of course it isn't said there that he was the result or the outcome of the three, but in alchemy the idea is that by heating up the three, the fourth appears. You see, the glass house in which Arisleus and his companions, or the old man, suffer from heat, is a sort of sweat lodge, such as we find with the North American Indians. In India they call it *tapas*, which means creating a fertile warmth, a sort of brooding, hatching oneself out by evaporation. By remaining in that isolation one is heated up, and then something emanates which is the looked-for precious substance.

Now, to show psychologically what that substance is, is not so easy. If it were, those old philosophers would not have used such varied symbolism to explain it. That *aqua divina*, the divine water, has already been symbolized in innumerable ways—if I say a thousand it is too few—so you can be sure nobody has ever expressed what it really is, and you can be sure that if I should try to formulate it I would meet with the same obstacles. But we know what happened to Nietzsche in his isolation: this semidivine figure of Zarathustra, the word of Zarathustra, flowed out of him, a river of psychical material personified. Zarathustra represents the self, and that wonderful thing which is produced by the attempt, or enterprise, or by the opus of Hermetic philosophy, is the *lapis philosophorum*. So the divine being, a sort of subtle body, divine or semidivine, has been also called the *lux moderna*, which is greater than any light in the world. It is something like Christ himself, a Christ that comes after Christ, a new Savior. Or it is the Paraclete, the Comforter, that was promised by Christ. Or the baptismal water that brings a new fertility into the world, a transformation of something low into something that is valuable—so there is the idea of redemption.

Now, Zarathustra is all that too: the water of redemption. He tries to renew the world, to make man over into the superman that should rise up from the river of Zarathustra or from the glass house. So in this case the divine water is that flow of meaningful, helpful ideas or revelations which emerge from the state of torture in the fire. And it is again a case of that age-old symbolism of the hero who for the sake of mankind—or for his people, or for his friend—goes down into the belly of the monster, where it is so hot that he loses all his hair. He is quite bald when he comes out, like a new born child—which is of course the idea. Then he brings out the spirits of the dead, his parents, his friends, all the things that have been devoured by the great beast of time, and so he makes the world anew. This is very much the same thing, always the same old myth. And in our days we could give a psychological interpretation of that divine water as a sort of spiritual product—spiritual with the meaning of sublimated—something simply evaporated or perspired from him, the expression of immense torture. So this state of real isolation, real solitude, may be productive.

But what we are really looking for is the result. Is it really helpful? Did it really help him? Did Nietzsche have a full realization of what he produced? Or is he the one who inadvertently fell into the valley of the diamonds and thought they were pebbles or only semiprecious stones. I am afraid he is like an alchemist who has found a red or yellow or white powder, never knowing that that was *the* thing, or only half realizing it. Of course Nietzsche himself thought very highly of *Zarathustra*. It was a revelation to him; he even knew that he had encountered a god, and therefore he called it a Dionysian experience. In the first German edition of this book there are some comments upon Nietzsche's own understanding of *Zarathustra*, and we have other evidence also, from which we may conclude that to him it was really a sort of divine revelation. He really thought that he had produced something like a new religion. But there again is a mistaken idea, for no one can found a new religion. It is one man's experience and everything else is a matter of history. No one could say, or prophesy, that a thing one has produced is a revelation.

For instance, Meister Eckhart had an extraordinary revelation of truth, so he was the fellow who could have been followed by a great religious movement. But nothing happened. On the contrary, a certain sect who were influenced by Meister Eckhart and called themselves Brothers of the Free Spirit became sort-of highwaymen. They were so eaten up by the spirit and the feeling of the futility of life that they robbed people on the road, took their money and wasted it. They said it was not good for people to have money—it was sinful—so they must take it away; it was a merit to destroy it. They were sending it into eternity. They were sort of spiritual anarchists. That is what followed, and for six hundred years Meister Eckhart went under. His writings were condemned and one hardly knew of his existence. He died on his way to Rome, where he should have given an account of his ideas, and his works were only piece by piece discovered, here and there in the libraries of Switzerland. In Basel we have one of his manuscripts in his own handwriting, but it was only in about the middle of the 19th century that an edition was made of his works. Now of course we have practically the whole opus. You see, that is a case where nobody could have foretold what the development would be: he was thoroughly anachronistic. And Nietzsche too was anachronistic, for people were not ready to understand these truths, particularly because they are so enveloped, one could say. They are not on the surface; we have a lot of work in bringing out his specific ideas. They are all swimming along in one stream with so much talk, so much boasting, so many contradictions, that we never know whether it is really valuable or not. For instance, one might conclude when Nietzsche says "Love thyself," that it was just egocentricity; people have drawn the most ridiculous conclusions from *Zarathustra*.

One sees pretty much the same thing in the way the Christian revelation has been dealt with in the subsequent centuries. It has not developed to the realization that Christ himself meant, as we know from the Evangels. For instance, he said, "I will leave you a Comforter,"[1] which means that the holy spirit was to be there instead of himself, that every one should be filled with the holy spirit. That is, the Holy Ghost, that Comforter, was to be a source of original revelation in everybody. And what did the church make of it? They monopolized Christ as God, which put the whole thing into the past. Christ could be made real again by the rites of the church, by his incarnation in physical elements, the bread and the wine, but that was the prerogative of the church, came about only through the magic word of the church—which means the priests. Otherwise Christ's existence was in the past, and the Holy Ghost was merely the prerogative of the assembly of the highest priests. If anybody had been convinced that he possessed a revelation from the Holy Ghost, he would have gotten into hot water, or really into hot fire, for having such ambitions. So even Christ's very clear intention to leave a Comforter was obstructed. It did not work, and the whole thing became something quite different from what he intended. Nobody could have foretold that. The time was not ripe, and

[1] "And I will pray the Father and he shall give you another comforter, that he may abide with you forever" (John 14:16).

one really cannot see how it would be possible for everybody to be a source of revelation. In those days, and even today, it would be perfectly impossible; no one could found any such organization on such nonsense. One person would say, "My god has three—or four or five—heads," and no one would care. Therefore the church had to repress every attempt along that line. You see, we have to be careful with everything Nietzsche says. I try to give both the positive and the negative aspects so that you can see Nietzsche from all sides, a man who received a sort of revelation, yet in a mind which was clouded, an understanding which was not quite competent, so he was unable to realize the meaning of his own words.

Now, here he is anticipating going down to man: "For once more will I go unto men." And a picture appears before his inner eye of how that will look, for when *his* hour comes, that laughing lion with the flock of doves will appear. This is most extraordinary, and you remember that whenever Nietzsche uses such a picture, there is always something behind it. When he wrote that, he surely did not represent it to himself concretely, or he would have understood that one could express it also in other words. What parallel could you give—a sort of proverbial metaphor which would be an equivalent for this laughing lion and the flock of doves?

Miss Welsh: The lion lying down with the lamb?

Prof. Jung: Well, that is another aspect, the chiliastic idea of the state where the pairs of opposites are united, where the animal of prey is united with the innocent animal.

Mrs. Brunner: The *Salonlöwe*.

Prof. Jung: Yes, the lion of the salon, the *bel homme* in the drawing room with a flock of young girls round him. And then there is the rooster and the hens. That is a very covert metaphor for somebody whose audience contains a greater number of ladies.

Miss Wolff: It perhaps doesn't belong just here but I should like to recall the first appearance of the lion in the chapter called "The Three Metamorphoses": first the camel and then the lion and then the child. It may have some connection.

Prof. Jung: Yes, and now he is trying how the lion would do. That he really means something like that is rather evident from the next paragraph:

Meanwhile do I talk to myself as one who hath time. No one telleth me anything new, so I tell myself mine own story.

1489

So the laughing lion is obviously himself with an audience, and the doves are specifically feminine birds.

Mr. Allemann: It is the bird of Astarte, and of Aphrodite.

Prof. Jung: Yes, or Venus, the Asiatic form of Aphrodite. So the laughing lion is surrounded by lovebirds. The dove is also the symbol of the Holy Ghost, since the nature of the Holy Ghost is exceedingly feminine. How is that shown—and according to what interpretation?

Miss Hannah: As Sophia.

Prof. Jung: Yes, the Gnostic interpretation, which has also played a great role almost within the church: the "Acts of Thomas" contain that famous invocation to the Holy Spirit as the mother. And one finds ample evidence of the Gnostic interpretation in the *Pistis Sophia* as well. The Holy Ghost was supposed to be the wife of God and the mother of Christ, and Mary was herself the Holy Ghost. There is the same idea in the second part of *Faust*.[2]

Dr. Frey: Is it not interpreted also as the church?

Prof. Jung: Oh yes, but that is the official interpretation. That the church was the embodiment of the Holy Ghost was the way they taught it, the church as the great mother being very clearly the result or the production of the Holy Ghost, the crystallization as it were. So this flock of doves means really an assemblage of lovebirds. And what about the laughing lion?

Mrs. Sigg: Perhaps this connection of the lion and the doves is a remembrance of the Piazza di St. Marco in Venice.[3]

Prof. Jung: You are quite right. And, mind you, the Baroque lion is often laughing. That combination of doves and the laughing lion in the Piazza di St. Marco is surely the external origin; it is most impressive and Nietzsche was of course under that impression. But what is the interpretation of the lion? That is only the external origin of the picture.

Mrs. Fierz: The lion is the animal of hottest summer, of great heat, and that would relate to what you said about the heat of the lonely

---

[2] The Acts of Thomas contains the invocation to the Holy Spirit as mother: "Come Holy Dove, mother of two young twins. Come Hidden Mother, revealed in deeds alone" (Mead*, p. 423). On the *Pistis Sophia*, see Mead*, pp. 471-72. Jung often refers to that part of *Faust* II which deals with the Realm of the Mothers. In a Victorian translation: "Ye Mothers, in your name, who set your throne / In boundless Space, eternally alone, / And yet companioned! All the forms of Being, / In movement, lifeless, ye are round you seeing." (*Faust*, tr. Bayard Taylor [Boston, 1888]).

[3] Nietzsche often went to Venice, especially to visit his young musician friend, Peter Gast.

man. And if the lion is laughing, it would mean that Nietzsche had begun to like it.

Prof. Jung: He sees some light!

Mrs. Fierz: Yes, it is a kind of acceptance of the humor of it, instead of the terrible anger he has always expressed before. I mean, it is a contrary mood.

Mr. Allemann: Is it not the wise man who is above it all and laughs at the foolishness of the world?

Prof. Jung: That is the picture, you are quite right. But there is also a secret joke behind it which Mrs. Fierz was just trying to formulate. You see, in interpreting the lion we have to take into consideration that it is the age-old symbol of the sun, and the sun in July and August particularly, the *domicilium solis.* So for thousands of years the lion symbolized the hottest time of the year; it is the flashing sun itself. And the sun was a very powerful god, often the only god, of course with his consort the moon. The sun and the moon were representations of divine power, the divine parents in heaven. Now, we must assume that there was a time when the lion did not laugh. If he were always laughing there would be no point in even mentioning it; one would think it was just a silly animal—as people who always laugh are silly, while people who only laugh sometimes might be very witty. So when the lion doesn't laugh he is obviously in a condition where things don't move or develop as he wants them to; but when fulfillment comes, when he sees a light ahead or when a door opens, then he laughs: "Ah, there it comes!" Nietzsche doesn't see it exactly, but he senses something of the kind—that he might be the lion of the drawing room with the lovely flock of lovebirds. One supposes that the lovebirds would make a circle round him, as the pigeons on the Piazza di St. Marco are all over the place, swarming around the statue of the lion, so this is the female hovering round him. Zarathustra compares himself again and again with the setting sun and the rising sun, or the sun that comes out of the dark clouds, or out of the cave, and so on. It is very clear, therefore, that this lion is Zarathustra, and he is laughing because he sees the fulfilment, senses a completion. Completion is a circle and here it is a circle of lovebirds. That is the Shakti circling round Shiva. That is of course a pretty grand idea and not necessarily something to laugh about. But when that becomes concrete, the animal god in Nietzsche laughs. Then Eros comes up, and of course everybody will say, "I always told you so, that is the end of it." As Erasmus wrote to a friend when Luther married, "*Ducit monachus monacham,*" meaning, "That is the end of the story: the monk has married the nun." We would say nowadays that he simply got a bit funny on account of his celibacy, and we must now wait and see what comes of marriage. Then the animal laughs and says, "That is what I was looking for." Don't forget that in the end of *Zarathustra* comes "The Ass-Festival," and when he became insane Nietzsche produced the most shocking erotic literature. It was destroyed by his careful sister, but Professor Overbeck had a glimpse of it, and there is plenty of evidence of his pathological condition. He could not withhold that information—it slipped out—for the farther the river flows, the lower it goes, and finally it arrives at the bottom. Zarathustra turns into his own opposite, practically, by the law of *enantiodromia*. The book begins with that great spiritual solitude, and at the end come the Dionysian dithyrambs. Now arrives the ass, beautiful and strong, but the ass is the symbol of voluptuousness, which Nietzsche, as a philologist, knew very well. And when you look through his poems you see the same element.

Miss Wolff: Another meaning of the image of the lion and the doves might be this: In the lines just above, Zarathustra says that he is waiting for his hour of descent and decline. Once more, for the last time, he intends to go down to humanity. The image of the lion and the doves gives the idea of how this going-down is brought about. The image corresponds in a way to the astrological symbol of the solar course. The highest position of the sun, its greatest heat and strength, are expressed by the sign of Leo. Then follows Virgo, which is the first sign of the decline of the sun. Virgo would correspond here to the circle of doves, the feminine birds, and the birds of Aphrodite. So the lion, or sun, or hero, is confronted with the feminine principle, and that leads to the decline of Zarathustra.

Prof. Jung: The hour of descent is the hour of the coming-up of Yin, the feminine substance.

Miss Wolff: And by the coming-up of the feminine principle, the hero image is always overcome.

LECTURE III

1 February 1939

Prof. Jung:

Here is a question by Miss Hannah: "In speaking of the camel Nietzsche says: 'Too many extraneous heavy words and worths loadeth he upon himself.' As Nietzsche should preach to himself and does preach to other people, would not those 'heavy words' add themselves to his load? And are not the 'worths' of the best enemy the most annoying of all 'worths,' so would Nietzsche not have to carry this annoyance as a compensation for reviling his projected shadow? In this sense could not the word *extraneous* be correct? [This is a bit involved!] In other words does not projection, in spite of the apparent relief, actually *add* to the weight of carrying oneself?"

Well, one can only say, yes, it does. That is the drawback of any projection: it is only an apparent relief; it is like a narcotic: only apparently are you casting off a load. As a matter of fact, it cannot be cast off because it belongs to your own contents as part of the total of your personality. Even if it has become unconscious, it forms part of yourself, and if you throw it away you are still linked up with it. It is as if an elastic connection existed between that cast-off thing and yourself. So it is a sort of self-deception when one projects. Of course you really don't *make* projections: they *are*; it is a mistake when one speaks of *making* a projection, because in that moment it is no longer a projection, but your own property. It cannot be detached just at that moment perhaps; it may linger on as a relative projection, but at all events you know of your connection with that particular thing. So any kind of neurotic measure—a projection, a repression, or a transference, for instance—are mere self-deceptions which happen to you, and they have really a very transitory effect. In the long run, they are no asset whatever. Otherwise it would be wonderful: we could simply unload ourselves. There are certain religious movements which train people in just that respect—teach them to unload.

In the very modern Oxford Movement you unload all your sins

1493

upon Christ; anything that is bothering or annoying you, you hand over to Christ and he takes care of it.[1] And I have a very pious woman patient—she is not in the Oxford Movement, but in the Middle Ages—and whenever anything goes wrong or she wants something, perhaps something immoral like cheating (which she cannot accept in herself), she simply unloads it on Christ. She gets him to take it over for her. Then, marvelously enough, Christ decides upon a very modern trick, how to cheat the state of taxes, for instance. She has a wonderful economic system: so much set aside for the poor in one envelope, so much for the hospitals in another, and so on, and she is not allowed to take anything out for a different purpose. But Christ may decide that she can easily take five francs out of the envelope for the poor in order to pay the chauffeur of a taxi. If she has some pricks of conscience still, she asks me without telling me that Christ has already decided, and as a rule I happen to agree with Christ, so she has complete confidence in me because I also help her to cheat the poor or the state. You see, that principle must be broken through. It is impossible to live according to principles; you have to allow the necessary exceptions to every rule. Otherwise there would be no rules. So Christ decides in the higher sense of living realities. She would not be able to decide by herself on account of too narrow a consciousness. Of course it is a most medieval mental condition, but plenty of people nowadays are still living in the Middle Ages. They are absolutely unable to decide for themselves, so they need such a figure as Christ or God who can decide for them.

My point of view concerning projections, then, is that they are unavoidable. You are simply confronted with them; they are there and nobody is without them. For at any time a new projection may creep into your system—you don't know from where, but you suddenly discover that it looks almost as if you had a projection. You are not even sure at first; you think you are all right and it is really the other fellow, until somebody calls your attention to it, tells you that you are talking a bit too much of that fellow—and what is your relation to him anyhow? Then it appears that there is a sort of fascination. He may be a particularly bad character, and that is in a way fascinating and makes you talk of him day and night; you are fascinated just by that which you revile in him. Now, from that you can conclude as to your own condition: your attention is particularly attracted; that evil fascinates you.

---

[1] The Oxford Movement was an attempt dating from 1833 within the clergy at Oxford to reinstate in the Church of England certain doctrines and rituals of the Roman Catholic Church.

Because you have it, it is your own evil. You may not know how much is your own but you can grant that there is quite a lot; and inasmuch as you have it, you add to it, because as Christ says, "Unto everyone which hath shall be given," so that he has it in abundance.[2] Where there is the possibility of making a projection, even a slight one, you are tempted to add to it. If an ass walks past carrying a sack on its back, you say, "Oh, he can carry my umbrella as well, because he is already carrying something." If a camel passes you, anything which you don't want to carry just jumps out of your pocket onto the back of that camel.

There are people who even attract projections, as if they were meant to carry burdens. And others who are always losing their own contents by projecting them, so they either have a particularly good conscience or they are particularly empty people, because their surroundings have to carry all their loads. Empty people, or people who have an excellent opinion of themselves and cherish amazing virtues, have always somebody in their surroundings who carries all their evil. That is literally true. For instance, it may happen that parents are unaware of their contents and then their children have to live them. I remember a case, a man, who had no dreams at all. I told him that that was abnormal, his condition was such that he must have dreams, otherwise somebody in his surroundings must have them. At first I thought it was his wife, but she had no undue amount and they cast no light on his problems. But his oldest son, who was eight years old, had most amazing dreams which did not belong to his age at all. So I told him to ask his son for his dreams and bring them to me, and I analysed them as if they were his own. And they were his own dreams, and finally by that procedure they got into him and the son was exonerated.[3]

Such things can happen: a projection is a very tangible thing, a sort of semisubstantial thing which forms a load as if it had real weight. It is exactly as the primitives understand it, a subtle body. Primitives—also the Tibetans and many other peoples—inasmuch as they are aware of such things at all, understand projections as sort of projectiles, and of course they play a role chiefly in their magic. Primitive sorcerers throw out such projectiles. There are three monasteries in Tibet mentioned by name by Lama Kagi Dawa-Sandup, the famous Tibetan scholar who worked with John Woodroffe and Evans-Wentz, where

[2] Matthew 15:19-20.

[3] In mentioning this case (CW 17, par. 106), Jung identifies the father's problems as erotic and religious.

they train people in the art of making projections.[4] And that term was used by the alchemists for the final performance in the making of the gold. It was supposed that they projected the red matter—or the tinctura or the eternal water—upon lead or silver or quicksilver, and by that act transformed it into gold or into the philosopher's stone. It is interesting that they themselves explained the making of the stone as a projection. That is to say, it is something that is detached from one; you detach something and establish it as an independent existence, put it outside yourself. Now, that may be quite legitimate inasmuch as it is a matter of objectifying contents; or it may be most illegitimate if it is used for magical purposes, or if it is a simple projection where you get rid of something. But people are not to be blamed directly for making other people suffer under such projections because they are not conscious of them.

You see, our whole mental life, our consciousness, began with projections. Our mind under primitive conditions was entirely projected, and it is interesting that those internal contents, which made the foundation of real consciousness, were projected the farthest into space—into the stars. So the first science was astrology. That was an attempt of man to establish a line of communication between the remotest objects and himself. Then he slowly fetched back all those projections out of space into himself. Primitive man—well, even up to modern times—lives in a world of animated objects. Therefore that term of Tylor's, *animism*, which is simply the state of projection where man experiences his psychical contents as parts of the objects of the world. Stones, trees, human beings, families are all alive along with my own psyche and therefore I have a *participation mystique* with them.[5] I influence them and I am influenced by them in a magical way, which is only possible because there is that bond of sameness. What appears in the animal say, is identical with myself because it *is* myself—it is a projection. So our psychology has really been a sort of coming together, a confluence of projections. The old gods, for instance, were very clearly psychical functions, or events, or certain emotions; some are thoughts and some

[4] Lama Kazi Dawa-Sandup was the translator of *The Bardo Thodol* or *Liberation by Hearing on the After Death Plane*, which W. Evans-Wentz compiled and edited as *The Tibetan Book of The Dead* (see *Tibetan*); John Woodroffe (Avalon), *The Serpent Power* (Madras, 3rd rev., 11th edn., 1931), is an interpretation of Kundalini Yoga.

[5] Edward Burnett Tylor (1832-1917) English evolutionary anthropologist, invented the concept "animism" to explain how "the notion of a ghost-soul as the animating principle of man" can be readily extended to "souls of lower animals, and even lifeless objects. . . ." *Primitive Culture*, 2 vols. (Gloucester, Mass., 1958; orig. 1917), vol. I, p. 145.

are definite emotions. A wrathful god is your own wrathfulness. A goddess like Venus or Aphrodite is very much your own sexuality, but projected. Now, inasmuch as these figures have been deflated, inasmuch as they do not exist any longer, you gradually become conscious of having those qualities or concepts; you speak of *your* sexuality. That was no concept in the early centuries, but was the god, Aphrodite or Cupid or Kama or whatever name it was called by. Then slowly we sucked in those projections and that accumulation made up psychological consciousness.

Now, inasmuch as our world is still animated to a certain extent, or inasmuch as we are still in *participation mystique*, our contents are still projected; we have not yet gathered them in. The future of mankind will probably be that we shall have gathered in all our projections, though I don't know whether that is possible. It is more probable that a fair amount of projections will still go on and that they will still be perfectly unconscious to ourselves. But we have not made them; they are a part of our condition, part of the original world in which we were born, and it is only our moral and intellectual progress that makes us aware of them. So the projection in a neurosis is merely one case among many; one would hardly call it abnormal even, but it is more visible—too obvious. Nowadays, one might assume that a person would be conscious of his sexuality and not think that all other people were abnormal perverts; because one is unconscious of it, one thinks that other people are therefore wrong. Of course that is an abnormal condition, and to any normal, balanced individual, it seems absurd. It is an exaggeration, but we are always inclined to function like that to a certain extent; again and again it happens that something is impressive and obvious in another individual which has not been impressive at all in ourselves. The thought that we might be like that never comes anywhere near us, but we emphatically insist upon that other fellow having such-and-such a peculiarity. Whenever this happens we should always ask ourselves: Now have I that peculiarity perhaps because I make such a fuss about it?

You see, whenever you make an emotional statement, there is a fair suspicion that you are talking of your own case; in other words, that there is a projection because of your emotion. And you always have emotions where you are not adapted. If you are adapted you need no emotion; an emotion is only an instinctive explosion which denotes that you have not been up to your task. When you don't know how to deal with a situation or with people, you get emotional. Since you were not adapted, you had a wrong idea of the situation, or at all events you did not use the right means, and there was as a consequence a certain projection. For instance, you perhaps project the notion that a certain person is particularly sensitive and if you should say something disagreeable to him he would reply in such-and-such a way. Therefore you say nothing, though he would not have shown such a reaction because that was a projection. You wait instead until you get an emotion, and then you blurt it out nevertheless, and of course it is then far more offensive. You waited too long. If you had spoken at the time, there would have been no emotion. And usually the worst consequences of all are not in that individual but in yourself, because you don't like to hurt your own feelings, don't want to hear your own voice sounding disagreeable and harsh and rasping. You want to maintain the idea that you are very nice and kind, which naturally is not true. So sure enough, any projection adds to the weight which you have to carry.

Mr. Bush: Would you then endorse the concept of Dewey that whenever there is a conflict between the individual and his environment, the projection is an expression of that conflict and a provisional attempt to get rid of it?[6]

Prof. Jung: Well, I would avoid the idea of the conflict because one cannot always confirm the existence of a conflict; it is simply lack of adaptation, that you are not up to the situation. That very often causes a conflict, it is true, but it is not necessarily *caused* by a conflict. I think you get nearer to the root of the matter when you call it a lack of adaptation, because to be emotional is already on the way to a pathological condition. Any emotion is an exceptional, not a normal, state. The ego is momentarily suppressed by the emotion: one loses one's head, and that is an exceptional state. Therefore, primitives are always afraid of emotions in themselves as well as in their fellow beings. An emotion always has a magic effect, so they avoid emotional people, think they are dangerous and might use witchcraft or have a bad influence. So to have an emotion is to be on the way to a morbid condition, and a morbid condition always being due to inferior adaptation, one could call an emotion already an inferior adaptation. An old definition of disease is that it is a state of insufficient adaptation—one is incapacitated and so in an inferior state of adaptation—and that is also true of an emotion.

Dr. Frey: But you cannot forget the positive side of emotion. In the fire of emotion the self is created.

---

[6] Mr. Bush is alluding to Dewey's teaching that difficulties which impede customary action promote thinking to resolve the problem. See, for instance, *Democracy and Education* (New York, 1916), *passim.*

Prof. Jung: Quite so. Emotion is on the other hand a means by which you can overcome a situation in which you are inferior; the emotion can then carry you over the obstacle. That is the positive value of the emotion. So it is like that patient of mine who dares not decide by herself, but leaves it to Christ to decide for her. That carries her a long way naturally: he can carry her way beyond her moral scruples, so that she can do something which is not very nice or reasonable. And that is of course her emotion—Christ is her emotion.

Mrs. Sigg: Is it not that she has perhaps in her youth already projected some animus contents into the figure of Christ? So instead of saying the animus is her leader, she says Christ is her leader.

Prof. Jung: She has naturally had the Christian education and she smelt a wonderful opportunity, as all good Christians do, to say that Christ is *there* to facilitate life, to eliminate our sorrows. We are told that there is a good god, a shepherd of men, who will carry our burden. And anyone who says he didn't know how to decide and gave it to Christ to decide, will be considered an example of goodness: What a pious man! What belief in God! So no wonder that she adopted that mechanism. You see, she is far from any animus theory; the animus theory would not work in the Middle Ages. There are far more tangible figures than the animus; with her it is a real thing, not only a *façon de parler*. It is bordering on magic.

Mrs. Jung: It seems to me that there are cases where it is more adapted to have an emotion than to have none; it is not normal to have no emotions.

Prof. Jung: One could say that in certain circumstances it would be more normal to have an emotion, but you also could imagine mastering the situation without an emotion, and if you *can* handle it, I would not call it an emotion. For instance, suppose a patient behaves in a way which I cannot support—perhaps he won't listen at all. I say "You are not listening." But that makes no impression at all. Then I say, "If you don't listen you will gain nothing from your work." It doesn't register. I persist, "Well, if you don't listen, if you get nowhere, I can only kick you out." It doesn't register. So I decide that this is obviously a mental deafness. *"Damn you! You get out of here!"* That is primitive and that registers. I can kick somebody out of the door—if it is necessary you have to—and then I light my pipe. There are people who must be manhandled. In dealing with African primitives, it doesn't help to *tell* them things. It is a civilized idea that you can tell people what they should or should not do. I am often asked to tell such-and-such a nation how they should behave, that it is not reasonable to behave as they do. As if that would make any impression! Of course, you can apply emotion, but then it is not emotion, it is a force. You have an emotion when you are moved yourself; when you move others, it is not necessarily your emotion—it becomes your force, your strength. You can use emotion as strength where force is needed. But that is quite different from falling into an affect; that is on the way to morbidity, an inferior adaptation. While to speak forcefully means that one is adapted, for here is a block of lead and you can't brush it away with a feather, but have to apply a crowbar. So I understand emotion in the sense of an affect, that one is affected by an outburst of one's own unconscious.

Now of course that may be very useful. In an exceptional situation, for instance, or in a moment of danger, you get a terrible shock and fall into a panic—you are absolutely inferior—but it makes you jump so high that you may overcome the obstacle by a sort of miracle.[7] [. . .]

Another instance is that story which I have occasionally quoted of the man on a tiger hunt in India, who climbed up a tree near the waterhole where he expected the tiger to turn up. He was sitting in the branches of the tree when the night wind arose, and he got into a most unreasonable panic and thought he must get down. Then he said to himself that was altogether too damned foolish. He was in the tree in order to be out of reach of the tiger and to climb down would be walking into the tiger's jaws. So his fear subsided and he felt normal again. But a new gust of wind came and again he got into a panic. A third gust came and he could no longer stand it—he climbed down. Then a fourth gust came, stronger than before, and the tree crashed to the ground. It had been hollowed out by termites. I read that story in a missionary report and the title was, "The Finger of God." God helped that man down from the tree, he interfered.

But whoever has travelled in the jungle knows that when you pitch your tent in the evening, you must always examine the trees. Naturally you pitch your tent under a tree on account of the shelter, but it must never be under trees which you have not examined. Even trees that still have their foliage may already be hollowed out by termites to a dangerous degree. But you can see it, and if a tree is in such a bad condition that a gust of wind will blow it down, you couldn't help noticing it, particularly when you climbed it. Moreover, the tree is covered by canals. The termites never expose themselves to sunlight, but always work in the dark, making tunnels out of that red earth till there is a

---

[7] Jung repeats here the story of a man who, confronting a huge snake, leapt over a wall.

hole in the tree; and when a tree is really so foul and rotten, you feel that it is hollow in touching it. So that man could easily have seen that it was not safe, but in his excitement over the tiger hunt, he did not notice it. Of course, a man who goes to hunt tigers in the jungle is not a baby; he knew it, but in his excitement he paid no attention to it consciously, or he thought it was not so bad after all. He could have been aware of it himself, but he simply was not. Then the wind rose, and then he knew it, and when you are several meters high, there is danger of a bad fall. So sure enough it was the hand of God—it was his emotion which carried him out of the reach of danger. In that sense emotion can produce a miracle; it can have a very positive effect in such a unique situation. But many people have emotions in very banal situations which are not unique at all. They have emotions over every nonsense out of sheer foolishness and laziness; they have emotions instead of using their minds.

Now we must continue our text. You remember we were concerned with that most edifying symbolism of the laughing lion and the flock of doves. We will skip some of the following pages and look at the fourth part. This chapter consists of a series of parts which contain the old and new tablets, a system of values, a sort of decalogue like the laws of Moses, but a very modern edition. The fourth part reads as follows:

> Behold, here is a new table; but where are my brethren who will carry it with me to the valley and into hearts of flesh?—
>
> Thus demandeth my great love to the remotest ones: be not considerate of thy neighbour! Man is something that must be surpassed.

Here we have a statement which we have encountered already. Instead of loving your neighbor, Nietzsche emphasizes the contrary: "be not considerate of thy neighbour." What mistake does he make here?

Mr. Allemann: He goes too far to the other side.

Prof. Jung: Yes, the original suggestion was: "Love thy neighbor," with the famous omission of the second part "as thyself." But he only thinks of the first part, and then makes the anti-Christian statement: "be not considerate of thy neighbour," and the necessary compensation "as thyself" is again omitted. For if you cannot love yourself, you cannot love your neighbor.[8] [. . .] Whether you say you love or hate

---

[8] Nietzsche often proclaimed the importance—the necessity—of self-love. For instance, "The noble soul has reverence for itself" (*BG&E*, no. 276). Or again, "We have cause to fear him who hates himself, for we shall be the victims of his wrath and his revenge" (*Daybreak*, no. 517). Two repetitive sentences are omitted here.

your neighbor, it is just the same, because it is an uncompensated statement, the self is lacking. Then what does it mean, that "man is something that must be surpassed"? You see, Nietzsche doesn't hold that he is the only living being. He also speaks of brethren, and when some brother says, "Be not considerate of Mr. Nietzsche or Mr. Zarathustra," what then? If everybody surpasses everybody, everybody denies everybody, and what is the result?

Mrs. Jung: He only wants to consider the *Übermensch.*

Prof. Jung: Naturally, for inasmuch as he considers that he is the *Übermensch* himself, nobody can surpass him or leap over him: everybody has to consider him. He must be considered and he has to consider nobody because they only deserve to be overleapt. So naturally there can be only one Superman; if there were more they would be overleaping each other all the time and then the whole story would be in vain. It would be exactly like those boys who found a toad. One said, "I bet you five francs that you wouldn't eat that toad." And the other replied, "If you give me five francs I will eat it." He didn't think the first one had five francs, but he had, so he ate the toad. Then after a while they found another toad, and the one who had lost the five francs was quite angry, so he said, "Will you give me back the five francs if I eat this toad?" And the other one said he would, so he ate it. Then after a while they both had indigestion and they said to each other, "Now why have we eaten those toads?" And that would be the case if there were two or three supermen. They would eat each other and then ask, "Now why have we become supermen after all?" If Nietzsche were not in such an infernal haste, he would stop and think and would see what nonsense he was talking really. The text continues:

> There are many divers ways and modes of surpassing: see *thou* thereto! But only a buffoon thinketh: "man can also be *overleapt.*"

What distinction is Nietzsche making here when he says that man can also be overleapt—by a buffoon mind you, *ein Narr?*

Miss Hannah: He is talking of that time when the buffoon jumped over the rope-dancer.

Prof. Jung: And what makes him think of that? Something must have reminded him of that scene.

Mrs. Baumann: He has just said practically the same thing in different words.

Mrs. Jung: In German it is: "das *überwunden* werden muss," not *übersprungen.*

Prof. Jung: That is it, he makes a difference between leaping over a thing, and surmounting or surpassing it, a rather subtle distinction which should not be omitted. Perhaps in the following verses we shall get some light on this. He continues,

> Surpass thyself even in thy neighbor: . . .

That has nothing to do with it, but there is obviously a distinction in his mind between overleaping and surpassing, which makes him think of the fool who jumped over the rope-dancer and killed him. He also surpassed man in a way, but by leaping over him. This is only an allusion, but he lets us feel that he has the difference in mind and evidently intends to make a discrimination.

Dr. Wheelwright: It is the difference between intuitive attainment and real attainment.

Prof. Jung: Yes, an intuitive attempt would be overleaping, disregarding reality; and surpassing would be a rather laborious attempt at surmounting or overcoming man. So what he understands by surpassing is an effort, real work perhaps, at all events a somewhat lengthy and laborious procedure—it should not be just an intuitive leap. It is a critical distinction and a very important one, so one is again astonished that he doesn't insist upon it. It would be well worthwhile to remain here for a while and dwell upon that distinction. We should then hear how he understands the procedure by which the ordinary man of today would transform into the Superman; he would be forced to say how he images that procedure. But here he just touches upon it and instantly goes on, saying,

> and a right which thou canst seize upon, shalt thou not allow to be given thee.

This means first of all that to be a Superman is a right, and you can seize upon it, steal it: you don't need to wait until it is given to you. Even if somebody were quite ready to give it to you you must not wait. Hurry, take it by force. You see, he is just storming away over this most critical point. If anyone who is really serious, who really wants to know, asks, "But how on earth can man transform into the Superman, how is that done? Tell me," he only says that one would be a fool to jump over it. But what one ought to do he doesn't say. So he behaves intuitively with the problem, only touches upon that point, and of course it is *the* point. Once more we have to regret that Nietzsche is merely intuitive; he is always in that infernal haste, never settles down with the problem and chews on it to see what will come of it. He very clearly feels that here is something shallow, a danger zone, so he mentions it—then off he goes. So one doesn't see how that transition of the ordinary man into the Superman can be accomplished: the most interesting question in the whole of *Zarathustra* if it comes to practical issues—if one were to try to apply it.

Mrs. Sigg: Could it not be that we have a sort of self-regulating system in the psyche which helps us to keep it balanced?

Prof. Jung: We have it inasmuch as we are really balanced, but if one is unbalanced one is just unbalanced—that mechanism is out of gear. Of course Nietzsche is a very one-sided type, a fellow in whom one function is differentiated far too much and at the expense of the others. He is a speculative thinker, or not even speculative,—he doesn't reflect very much—he is chiefly intuitive and that to a very high degree. Such a person leaps over the facts of sensation, realities, and naturally that is compensated. This is the problem throughout the whole book. For about two years we have been working through the shadow chapters of *Zarathustra*, and the shadow is creeping nearer and nearer to him, his inferior function, sensation. The actual reality is ever creeping nearer with a terrible threat and a terrible fear. And the nearer it comes, the more he leaps into the air, like that man who saw the rattlesnake behind him. He performs the most extraordinary acrobatic feats in order not to touch or to see his shadow. So we have on the one side his extreme intuition, and on the other side the shadow always coming nearer.

Dr. Frey: But was he not nearer to the problem in the beginning—when he carried the corpse and buried it in the tree?

Prof. Jung: Yes, and not only in the beginning. In the course of *Zarathustra* he apparently deals with the shadow a number of times; his mind or psyche seems to function as everyone's psyche functions. There are always attempts at dealing with the problem. But then he again jumps away and doesn't deal with it adequately: things get difficult and he reviles and suppresses it. For instance, you remember that chapter not very long ago, where the fool came up and talked exactly like Zarathustra, reviling the low-down inferior people. And Nietzsche could not accept it; he reviled the fool despite the fact that he was repeating his own words, practically. You see, that was an attempt of the shadow, by disguising himself in the language of Zarathustra, to say, "I am yourself, I talk like yourself, now do accept me." When you hear a person cursing someone and quoting him—"He even said this and that"—you know those are the views of that fellow himself, of the one who is complaining. And if you said, "But that is what you say too," it might dawn upon him that what he was reviling in the other was so very much like himself that he didn't see it. So Nietzsche might have said to himself, "Since the fool talks my own language, is he not identical with me? Are we not one and the same?" And mind you, there are passages where he speaks of Zarathustra as the fool.

Some of you surely remember that famous *soreites syllogismos* which I made in the first *Zarathustra* seminar. That is a figure of logical conclusion, a statement with no preconditions; since the premises are true, the conclusion is true. There I proved that every figure we encounter in *Zarathustra* is Nietzsche himself. So he is the shadow, and if Nietzsche had only stopped to think for a moment, he would have seen it. Even here is an opportunity: Nietzsche says man is something that must be surpassed, which is what the fool showed him. He showed what one ought or ought not to do, for there the rope-dancer died, there Nietzsche should have learned that man is killed by that overleaping, that he himself would be killed. And he made there the famous prophecy that his mind would die before his body. You see, here again he remembers the fool, so here again he has a chance to understand that he is identical with him in that he is overleaping man. For what does he mean by surpassing man? He has never shown us how that is done. He definitely feels here that something is wrong; he feels that he should make a distinction so that the fool may be removed, so that he has not to acknowledge the buffoon. That is of course an exceedingly important point; we would expect here definite evidence that Zarathustra is not a buffoon. Nietzsche should by all means stop here and explain the difference between overleaping and surpassing. But having touched it a bit, he goes off as if he had touched a red hot iron. Yet he even goes so far as to say concerning the surpassing, "Don't wait until you get it legitimately. Take it by force, hurry, anticipate it. It must be caught at once." You have heard that tune before; you heard it in September: *Es muss jetzt sein und jetzt sofort.* Don't wait until it comes about quite naturally, take it by any means whatever, no time to wait. That is the wind nature: the wind doesn't wait, the wind moves, and quickly, at once. Farther on, Nietzsche comes to that statement that the wind is at work. Now we will skip what follows and go to the sixth part:

O my brethren, he who is a firstling is ever sacrificed. Now, however, are we firstlings!

We all bleed on secret sacrificial altars, we all burn and broil in honour of ancient idols.

To know how he gets to this idea, we must look at the end of the preceding part.

> One should not wish to enjoy where one doth not contribute to the enjoyment. And one should not wish to enjoy! Nei-
>
> For enjoyment and innocence are the most bashful things. Neither like to be sought for. One should *have* them,—but one should rather *seek* for guilt and pain!

What kind of language is this?

Mrs. Crowley: It is Christian language.

Prof. Jung: Yes, it sounds exactly like Tertullian, who admonished his young Christians to seek the arena rather than to avoid it. This is exceedingly Christian teaching. Therefore the next part begins with that idea that he and his brethren are firstlings to be sacrificed.

Mrs. Sigg: It is like the language of the New Testament, Christ being the firstling.

Prof. Jung: And what does that mean?

Mr. Allemann: The first fruits have always been sacrificed.

Prof. Jung: Yes, the Romans called the firstlings of spring, sacrificed to the gods, *ver sacrum*. The Christian analogy to this pagan custom or rite is that Christ, being the first born of God, is sacrificed. Nietzsche is now apparently in a very Christian mood, and one should ask what on earth has produced it in him.

Mrs. Crowley: In the chapter before, was he not saying that he had brought a new religion to man? We were discussing it.

Prof. Jung: That is a general reason. "Zarathustra" is the name of a founder of a religion, and of course it is something like a new religion. Also the new commandments he gives instead of the old suggest a new religion. But what is the immediate thought which produces this Christian analogy?

Dr. Wheelwright: It is the reaction against the desire to create a thing quickly. It is a compensation for that.

Prof. Jung: I would explain that, rather, as an immediate reaction against touching the hot iron, the shadow. Therefore he says to grasp that right to be a Superman quickly. Jump at it, take it by force, don't wait until it is given to you by a regular procedure! He as much as says that he doesn't want to know what the surpassing consists of. He feels that it would mean a long dissertation, one he should dwell upon a long time in order to tell us how to pass over from the ordinary man into the state of the Superman. And that is annoying to him because it is only reality. This is the impatience of the intuitive reaction against the half-conscious realization that that surpassing means something on which he could not dwell without getting into hot water.

Mrs. Jung: Because he has broken the old tables and put up a new law, he is the firstling of that new law and the victim at the same time.

Prof. Jung: That is certain, but I want to know the logical transition in the text.

Miss Hannah: One cannot possibly go in for a new religion like that without dealing with one's old religion, which he has not done. He has leapt over it; he has not come to any terms with his old religion.

Prof. Jung: That is true, but can't you see in the text how that transition is done in reality?

Miss Hannah: We are all burning and broiling in honor of ancient idols, and the new things burn and broil too, but he has not taken the trouble to find out what is burning and broiling him.

Prof. Jung: Yes, but I want you to establish the connection between the fifth and sixth parts. In the end of the fifth part we find that he has assumed an exceedingly Christian attitude, which explains in the beginning of the sixth part that he is a firstling that is to be sacrificed. Now I ask how he gets into that Christian attitude.

Mrs. Baumann: Are we allowed to read something which you did not read? There are the last two verses of the fourth part:

What thou doest can no one do to thee again. Lo, there is no requital.

He who cannot command himself shall obey. And many a one *can* command himself, but still sorely lacketh self-obedience.

Prof. Jung: There you can establish the connection. Now Mrs. Baumann, what is the connection between the end of the fifth and the beginning of the sixth parts? What follows from that—or why does he say that?

Mrs. Baumann: Because he has said that, he then becomes a sacrifice.

Prof. Jung: But how do you explain it?

Mrs. Baumann: He is jumping along intuitively but he feels it underneath just the same, because he is preaching that one can grasp something immediately without overcoming it. Then follows this about commanding and obeying.

Mr. Allemann: He says that there is no retribution, *Es gibt keine Vergeltung,* and then he has to realize the retribution, to become a sacrifice.

Mrs. Fierz: But does it not follow directly, when you want to find a way to surpass yourself, that a way then presents itself? But that is the Christian way so he thinks of it unwillingly.

Prof. Jung: Well, you and Miss Hannah are both about right, but I wanted you to establish the connection in the text.

Miss Hannah: He says one should command oneself but he cannot command his shadow, he thinks he can but he cannot, and therefore he has to be sacrificed. He is one who has to be commanded, and he makes the awful mistake of thinking he commands.

Prof. Jung: That is again near the truth—he says that himself.

Mr. Bash: Is the shadow, then, not the element which still remains in himself and in contrast with the Superman, which commands him but not consciously, not in accordance with his boasted ideal of the Superman, so that he obeys—but in a sense does not obey—himself?

Prof. Jung: Well, the subsequent paragraphs elucidate the point. But I should have liked you to establish the connection through the fifth part, beginning in the fourth. You see, Nietzsche overleaps his own statement that one ought to surpass man, for he doesn't know how that is done and it is disagreeable. So he jumps away from it and says to seize that right to be the Superman; don't wait for the disagreeable procedure which is making you into the Superman. Now of course that still rankles in his mind: how on earth is it done? It is like making a pretty broad statement with a doubt in your mind whether it is right. Then it begins to worry you, it nags at you. While you are talking big stuff, it bores its way further and further. It keeps on nagging at you. So that problem he has overleapt is not completely extinguished; it appears again in, "He who cannot command himself shall obey." This immediately points to the commandments—say Moses' commandments—and that is in fact the way by which something can be done: you simply command it, you make a statement and say, "Thou shalt." That is generally his intention here; instead of showing the way, he orders, makes laws, laws of behavior or laws of thinking, thereby establishing a new system of commandments by means of which one can surpass or surmount. But can everyone command himself? Obviously there are a number of people who cannot. There is the beginning of Nietzsche's doubts about the possibility of that development into the Superman. For instance, my shadow won't obey me. Well then, my shadow simply *has* to obey. "And many a one *can* command himself, but still sorely lacketh self-obedience." What does that mean?

Mr. Allemann: Many can see what would be good for them but cannot find the way to do it.

Prof. Jung: Man can invent all kinds of ways. He can say, "This is the right thing to do," and command himself to do it. But would you call that self-obedience? Whom would you be obeying then? You see, the ordinary case of moral behavior is that you obey a command which you hear or invent yourself. You give a command; you say, "I think this is the thing to do in this case? I am going to do it." Now have you then obeyed the self?

Mrs. Fierz: No, Mr. One.

Prof. Jung: Yes, if *I* think this is good for everybody, therefore *I* shall do it, I am obeying public opinion. That is not the self. Or you are obeying your unconscious, or the devil: *it* thinks and you do it; so you have obeyed a ghost. The command was simply given by the unconscious, by a fool perhaps. Therefore you should examine the ghosts that are whispering in your ear, because you are never quite sure whose voice it is. The spirit can say very funny things sometimes, so as St. Paul says, *prüfet die Geister.*[9] That old patient of mine tells me that Christ sometimes makes obscene jokes, particularly in church, which is shocking and makes it hard for her to maintain the theory that it is Christ. I don't say this is wrong: it happens as a necessary compensation for a pious attitude which is not too real. Then necessarily you would have obscene fantasies in order to see who you are. So the fact that you are able to command yourself doesn't mean that it is a particularly good thing to do, or that the self is really the source of that command. Even a man who can command himself and is able to obey his own command, may not obey the self. This passage betrays profound doubt in Nietzsche as to the usefulness of his commandments.

Yet that is the only way which is known—we don't know other ways. For instance, suppose you are in a psychological situation where you feel very inferior and would like to get out of it. So you go to an ordinary parson and ask his advice, and he says you ought to do this or that. But you know that as well as he and that is exactly what you cannot do. The reason you don't go to a parson is because you know exactly what he is going to say; you know it will be done in the way of a commandment or an order because this is the way that is known. And Nietzsche naively attempts the same way in making new commandments, because that is the only way *he* knows—it has been practically the only way for two thousand years. But that God could work it out in yourself by a slow and painful procedure is for curious reasons not accepted. Why is that idea, really a religious idea which would give us confidence in God, not generally accepted? Why should we suffer the law all the time?

Miss Wolff: Because we *want* a law. We want to be irresponsible, and

9 "Try the spirits" (John 4:1).

so we expect to be guided. We are no exceptions ourselves. We say, "I don't know what to do, but I shall have a dream about it." So somebody else is deciding for us, and we are getting out of all moral trouble.

Prof. Jung: Yes, you can always say, "Oh, I don't need to think; I simply behave according to the law." It gives us a sort of security. The law is a sure direction and a reliable staff, so we don't need to worry. But why should we not assume that God could work it in ourselves?

Mrs. Fierz: Because he is not so entirely good.

Prof. Jung: That is it—nor so entirely reliable; there is a certain risk about it. God might do something quite unconventional.

Mrs. Flower: May I ask how one knows that it is God who is replying?

Prof. Jung: That is exactly the point. If we knew for certain, *we* could make a law. The Catholic attitude is very reasonable in these matters. They say, "Anybody can suggest anything and call it God's own word, and how do we know? Well, we have the tradition of the church, the collegium of the cardinals, the concilium of priests, and that enormous apparatus is a measure by which to decide. If it agrees with the holy tradition it is good, if it does not agree it is bad. Now if we decide like that, what happens to God?

Mrs. Baumann: He is eliminated.

Prof. Jung: Yes, and who is eliminating him?

Mrs. Sigg: Man in collectivity.

Prof. Jung: Well, the popes and the cardinals or the Fathers of the concilium decide about such matters. There is a funny story about the concilium: They didn't know what to do about certain books, so they put them under the altar in the hope that God would decide about them. Then certain books were miraculously picked up and placed *upon* the altar, so they decided those were the right books, and the others that remained below were no good. So it is really man's own work, man's own mind, which decides that one thing is good and another bad. The attitude of the Catholic church is perfectly legitimate because it is built upon the system of commandments; the church must give sure guidance. The church is the stable for the herd or for the sheep, so that they won't get lost or be attacked by wolves. They are well protected within the walls of the church. That makes sense and therefore the church rightly holds: *extra ecclesiam nulla salus,* "outside of the church there is no salvation," only perdition. But the question is: *is* it only perdition? Or is it possible that God is free? For according to the teaching of the church, God cannot be free, having limited himself to the commands of the church. Of course theoretically they say: Naturally God is free, God's will is supreme and he can decide. But practically, since God has instituted the sacraments he cannot forsake them. So if the rite of baptism is administered, the grace will be there. In other words, when the priest is consecrated by the apostolic blessing and performs the rite of baptism or any other sacramental rite in the correct way, the rite has a magic effect upon God. God has to be there and he won't go back on his promise, he won't forsake his own institutions, he will support the rite with the presence of his grace. By that argument the church avoids the reproach that they believe in magic, that a priest is working magic in carrying out the correct rite. As a matter of fact, practically, God is limited: he is fettered by the magic rites of the church—he can't stop giving his grace. And since he never promised to give his grace to anything else, nothing else receives the grace of God. So one is held entirely in the church. If God wants to work at all, it must be in and through the church; he cannot work outside the church nor can he publish any other news, perhaps a still newer Testament. The last edition appeared two thousand years ago—nothing new since then. It would be too upsetting if there were, because it would be outside the dogma and that cannot be countered. So our whole idea of spiritual development is entirely linked up with the idea of commandments.

LECTURE IV

8 February 1939

Prof. Jung:

Mrs. Crowley calls our attention to the fact that the saying, "Love thy neighbor as thyself," is already contained in Leviticus, chapter 19, the 18th verse: "Thou shalt not avenge, nor bear any grudge against the children of thy people, but thou shalt love thy neighbour as thyself: I am the Lord."

Now we are still concerned with the question of the transition from the fourth part of the 56th chapter, which we had dealt with, to the sixth part. Have you thought about it?

Miss Hannah: I thought about it, but I am muddled about it. I wish you would repeat the question.

Prof. Jung: You remember we skipped the fifth part and went on to the sixth, which begins, "O my brethren, he who is a firstling is ever sacrificed." My question was, "How does Nietzsche arrive at the idea of the firstling? To what—or to whom—does that clearly point?"

Miss Hannah: To the Christian lamb really.

Prof. Jung: Yes, to Christ himself, who is the firstling among the dead, *der erste der Toten*, the paschal Lamb that is sacrificed in Spring. Now how does Nietzsche arrive at this idea from part 4? What is the transition? Please stick to what Nietzsche himself says in his text.

Mrs. Brunner: He preaches overcoming himself to himself, but he realizes that he cannot overcome himself, so he is thrown back to the Christian state of mind.

Prof. Jung: That is pretty close to the truth.

Mrs. Sigg: I think we should not overlook the fact that this chapter has for a title "Old and New Tablets," and the question of the firstling, the reason why the firstling must be sacrificed, is treated in just this chapter where breaking the tablets is discussed. There is a clear connection. So I think the identification with Moses plays an enormous role in *Zarathustra*, since Moses was the one who broke the old and made new tablets.

1512

Prof. Jung: The idea of the firstling is based upon the Mosaic law, but Moses himself has nothing to do with this question of the transition from Part IV to Part VI.

Remark: He says, "Be not considerate," and then that is put against him. He meets his own lack of consideration at once, for one is one's own neighbor.

Prof. Jung: Yes, you are also quite near to the truth.

Mr. Bash: It seems to me there are two trends of thought here: in the first place a feeling of his own inadequacy, which is given expression in the sentence, "And many a one can command himself, but still sorely lacketh self-obedience." Then he says later, one should not wish to enjoy, and somewhat later, that one should rather seek for guilt and pain. I wonder if those have not a personal application to himself as the first revealer of a new religion, which he rather self-consciously is, and if he does not still feel his own inadequacy to carry out his prophecies. He is the first prophet of the Superman, but he is not the Superman and never can be; furthermore, he feels that he himself must be overcome, that he himself must not command, but must be sacrificed to the real Superman, who is yet to come.

Prof. Jung: You are quite right, and you hit upon the decisive point in that question of seeking guilt and pain. That is an exceedingly Christian attitude which late Christianity has been blamed for: namely, that morality chiefly consists of doing unpleasant things, that to be moral one should do something unpleasant on principle. At certain times in the Middle Ages the highest ideal of piety, the highest ethical attitude, was that one should really seek torture, that one should seek only guilt and pain. That amounts to a complete suppression of the natural man, through a very one-sided ethical attitude. Well, we can now reconstruct the inner bridge of thought. You see, Nietzsche always induces us to skip things, to glide over them as he glides over abysses, creating the illusion that there is a bridge. We think we have passed an obstacle quite easily, when as a matter of fact we have only skipped it. We have not gone through it, we have not worked to overcome it, we have simply taken an intuitive flight—leaping like a grasshopper—and skipped it. So one has to pull oneself together and force oneself to go deeper into the underlying meaning of his words in order to become aware of the enormous difficulties he just leaves behind him.

In the fourth part, you remember, he is again reminded of the buffoon, the fool who thinks exactly like himself. In chapter after chapter Nietzsche has reviled the collective man, shown that he is no good at

all, not worthwhile. He has said so many negative things about the natural man that in the end he himself admits that only a fool could talk
like that. The realization comes to him that he is talking almost like the
buffoon who overleapt the rope-dancer. So he says only a fool would
think that the ordinary man can be overleapt—one has to *surpass* him.
Now, in this case we really could expect—as in such places before—an
explanation of the method, or the way, to integrate that inferior man,
so that he will not be merely overleapt. But here he says, "Surpass thyself even in thy neighbour," as if that were different from overleaping
thyself even in thy neighbor, yet he doesn't say of what the surpassing
consists. Instead of going into the depths of the problem, he simply
takes another word, as if something had thereby been done. But nothing is done. He immediately gets impatient again and says, ". . . and a
right which thou canst seize upon, shalt thou not allow to be given
thee!"—for heaven's sake don't wait, you must anticipate the Superman, seize upon the result even if you have no right to it, don't be patient, don't wait until the Superman naturally grows in you. Now,
could anything be more overleaping than such an attitude? He leaps
over the ordinary man all along the line.

You see, the natural man waits until a thing comes to him. To usurp
a place means too much spasm and cramp, he must make an enormous
effort to grasp anything which doesn't come to him naturally. If you
force people to jump at a conclusion, or to usurp a right which would
come anyhow, you are forcing them into an entirely unnatural attitude. All this demonstrates clearly that he is not at all minded to take
the inferior man into consideration: again the inferior man is overleapt. Then in that statement that "many a one *can* command himself,
but still sorely lacketh self-obedience" there is the doubt whether even
someone who is apparently in command of himself can obey the intimations of the self. The very justifiable doubt is naturally aroused in
him, whether he himself would be able to obey the command of a self
that is thought of as being supreme, or at least superior to the "I" that
is able to command himself. As Mr. Bash has pointed out, Nietzsche
has the feeling that he himself cannot live up to this superior heroic
attitude. Yet in the fifth part, he assumes an attitude which is again
overheroic: namely, one should not seek pleasure, but should seek
pain and guilt. That is a most unnatural attitude, because any natural
being seeks pleasure: it is morbid if he doesn't. And what has Nietzsche
said before about those people who are so degenerate that they only
want to suffer? Now he adopts that attitude simply because it fits in
with what he has said about the treatment of the inferior man—that

the inferior man is and shall be overleapt, *surpassing* being merely another kind of *overleaping*. So he quite consistently comes to that conclusion that the inferior man is not to be taken into account at all, because the ideal is to look only for pain—and no butter please, no pleasure.

We have heard that before. Such an overheroic attitude leads directly to the figure of Christ who overcomes the weakness of man, who sacrifices himself and identifies with the paschal Lamb. This is no criticism of the problem of Christ—that attitude, or symbol, was needed then, but nobody is allowed to identify to that extent with Christ unless he can have the same attitude. Mind you, Nietzsche *has* that attitude now. He is more than medieval in that seeking of guilt and pain: We are all followers of Zarathustra, we are the firstlings, we only live to be sacrificed. This is the attitude which you now find substantiated in Germany: it is the mood and the attitude of the *ver sacrum*, and it certainly overleaps the inferior man. You see, there is one continuous stream of thought through these chapters, a sort of Christian undercurrent, which clearly comes to the surface now and gives one the impression that Nietzsche, as a Christian individual or an individual who had once had a Christian education, had yet never understood what Christianity really meant. It was apparently something that merely happened in churches, or in the head.

And now, in the moment when the dogmatic ideas are discarded, they suddenly reappear in a psychological attitude. That is the tragedy of our time. Whatever was a creed in the Middle Ages, whatever ideal people kept before their eyes, was lost, and it is now in the flesh. So we see a whole nation really becoming Christian in a way, but without the idea of Christianity—with even an anti-Christian idea. But the idea that everybody must now be a sacrifice is essentially Christian. Never mind all the things you miss and that life is very hard anyway: everybody must sacrifice himself. That is *plus papal que le pape*, more Christian than ever before. We know of no time in history when a pope or a bishop would have educated his nation as Germany is now being educated under a so-called anti-Christian rule; it is much worse than it has ever been, without mercy, without redemption, without explanation. It is done in the name of the state, but it is a thoroughly Christian attitude. Now that is Nietzsche's logic, and that has come off as a political or sociological condition. In these paragraphs we have the same kind of thought, the same development. The Christian imagery is abolished, yet the psychological fact of Christianity remains. It is as if that child had been beheaded; as long as he had a head he was human, but now he has no head. There is simply the body of the child with all its strength, doing just what it was doing before but with no head, with no understanding of what it is doing. And so naturally everybody has to be sacrificed, not on the altar of any temple or deity or church, but on the altar of the state—a fiction. So Nietzsche continues:

> Now, however, are we firstlings!
> We all bleed on secret sacrifical altars, we all burn and broil in honour of ancient idols.

In the Middle Ages, they burned and broiled the heretics, and now people are doing it to themselves in honor of or in the name of the state. What is apparently a most advanced conception, as a matter of fact, is an old idol, and behind that are pagan gods that are not named. But they are secretly embodied in the state.

> Our best is still young: this exciteth old palates. Our flesh is tender, our skin is only lambs' skin:—how could we not excite old idol-priests!

How do you explain this passage?

Mrs. Brunner: He is the paschal Lamb.

Prof. Jung: Yes, that is clear, but understood not as a sacrifice exactly, more as the victim of an old idol-priest. Now, who are the old idol-priests?

Miss Hannah: Is it not Wotan? They actually did sacrifice sheep, did they not, at the beginning of the New Paganism movement?

Prof. Jung: Yes, they did. And old Wotan had human sacrifices offered to him: prisoners of war were suspended on a tree and speared in his honor, because that was the sort of sacrificial rite Wotan himself had undergone when he was suspended on the world-tree and wounded by the spear. His own original fate was repeated in the sacrifice of the prisoners of war. Of course the god of our time is Christ, and his symbol is the lamb: he was the sacrificed lamb. So if people were to be sacrificed in his honor, it should be a repetition of his own myth; they should be sacrificed as sheep. Now, that sheep are exceedingly gregarious is even proverbial, so that great crowds should be slaughtered: herds of sheep would be the appropriate sacrifice. In what easy way could such sheep sacrifices be performed in reality?

Miss Hannah: By war.

Prof. Jung: Yes, we have excellent machinery for that purpose: in a few seconds several thousand people could be killed. So the collective slaughter, the slaughter of the sheep, can be done technically quite easily by war. War is the sacrificial knife by which that can be accomplished. Now, the sacrificial knife does nothing by itself—a hand guides the knife—so if war is the sacrificial knife, who then is the priest?

Miss Wolff: The state that orders war.

Prof. Jung: Yes, but the state is supposed to be a modern concept, and behind the state are ancient deities, so who would the sacrificial priest be in reality?

Miss Hannah: Wotan.

Prof. Jung: You can say Wotan, or it would be a god of war; that is the ancient idol. The state is merely the modern pretense, a shield, a make-belief, a concept. In reality, the ancient war-god holds the sacrificial knife, for it is in war that the sheep are sacrificed. The Christian herd of sheep is now without a shepherd; it is brought to the sacrifice of the firstlings and killed gregariously, the most efficient way being war. That is the psychology which threatens Europe generally. The old shepherd is done for in practically every country—the herd is no longer led by a benevolent shepherd. Even the Pope, or any bishop in the past, was a more benevolent shepherd than the state. The state is impersonal, a dark power, the power which rules the masses—and that is forever a barbarous deity. So instead of human representatives or a personal divine being, we have now the dark gods of the state—in other words, the dark gods of the collective unconscious. It is the old assembly of the gods that begins to operate again because no other principle is on top. Where there is no recognized leading principle, the collective unconscious comes up and takes the lead. If our *Weltanschauung* is no longer in existence or is insufficient, the collective unconscious interferes. Wherever we fail in our adaptation, where we have no leading idea, the collective unconscious comes in, and in the form of the old gods. There the old gods break into our existence: the old instincts begin to rage again.

That is not only the problem of Germany; Germany is only a symptom. It is so in every country. For instance, France has finished with the old shepherds. It was not the shepherd idea that came back in France, but was rather the wolf idea: namely, the dissolution and disintegration of the people by socialistic ideas. Then the wolves come in. With the Germans the idea of the shepherd remained, but it took on the form of the old wind-god that blows all the dry leaves together, a funny kind of shepherd, an old sorcerer. But that is only the other aspect. The effect is just the same whether it is wolves, which also kill gregariously, or the wrong kind of shepherd. It is the same condition all over the earth that causes the disease. The old gods are coming to life again in a time when they should have been superceded long ago, and nobody can see it. That is now the problem of those old idol priests.

Miss Wolff: In the first part of chapter 9, "The New Idol," Nietzsche says the same thing, almost literally: the state is the new idol.

Prof. Jung: Yes. Just before that was the chapter on "War and Warriors," and then followed "The New Idol." There we have the same idea already.

Miss Wolff: I wondered if in this chapter we are dealing with now, the old idols and old priests are for Nietzsche not the Christian priests—as if the whole sacrificial idea were reversed, and the old priests or idols were slaughtering the new idea.

Prof. Jung: Naturally, to him it looks as if it were the old Christian priests. But as a matter of fact, they were never able to control a nation as is being done now by the state.

Miss Wolff: But he doesn't say it is a nation here. The firstlings seem to be himself and a few other firstlings.

Prof. Jung: Of course not—because he didn't know it. If he could have seen it clearly, he never would have spoken so clearly. Only inasmuch as they are modern people are they firstlings. Modern people follow Zarathustra. But he did not see that he was really anticipating the whole future development, that there would be a time when what he says here would come true. It is as if the whole world had heard of Nietzsche or read his books, and had consciously brought it about. Of course they had not. He simply listened in to that underground process of the collective unconscious, and he was able to realize it—he talked of it, but nobody else noticed it. Nevertheless, they all developed in that direction, and they would have developed in that direction even if there had been no Nietzsche. For they never understood it. Perhaps I am the only one who takes the trouble to go so much into the detail of Zarathustra—far too much, some people may think. So nobody actually realizes to what extent he was connected with the unconscious and therefore with the fate of Europe in general, for it is the same trouble all over the world.

Mrs. Crowley: I wondered if something you said last week was possibly another way of seeing it; you referred to projection and affect, and you spoke of the antique gods having been reassimilated by modern man because we have taken in their virtues or their powers, and that was done by overcoming them. Now, could you not say, in a way, that this complex of the modern world—which I see as a savior complex rather than a sheep complex, because everybody wants to save—is this same idea? We really assimilated the Christian God, but by overleaping instead of overcoming or surpassing. We have produced the shadow of the Christian God, because it was done by affect instead of by realization. That is what you mean, is it not?

Prof. Jung: Yes, it was by overleaping. If you simply destroy it, you create a ghost of the old value and you are possessed by that thing. So when we destroyed Christianity—of course it just happened that it was destroyed, to a great extent it destroyed itself—the ghost of Christianity was left, and we are now possessed. The Christian sacrifice is now produced in actuality, in the flesh. And so it was when the people threw away the old gods. They then had the conflict of their emotions in themselves, and had to assume an attitude which would rescue them from those battles and intrigues the gods were always having. Therefore, these savior religions arose, which saved the people from the gods in themselves. They were then planetary gods; it was the astrological influence, the continuous fear of the *heimarmene*,[1] all that compulsion of the bad stars. The soul was burdened with the influence of the bad stars; that was the so-called handwriting which was imprinted on the soul when it descended to earth through the spheres of the planets. And that had to be washed off by a savior; people had to be saved from the inexorable law of the old gods. The old gods were not exactly destroyed by Christianity: they died before Christ came. Therefore Augustus was obliged to regress to old Latin rites and ceremonies in order to do something toward restoring the old religion which was already giving out. It simply became obsolete, and then already people were filled with what the gods had been before. The gods became integrated in them.

For as soon as you cannot call an affect by a certain name—for instance, Cupid—it is in yourself. If you cannot say it is somewhere in space, in the planet Mars perhaps, it must be in yourself, and cannot be anywhere else. That causes a psychological disorder. We are apparently pretty far from these old facts because we don't realize the power of the archetypes; and we don't realize the mentality of a time when there were many gods, don't know what it would be like to be surrounded by divine, superior, demoniacal powers. We have the poetic conception, but that is nothing like the reality. So we don't know what it means to have lived in a time when these old gods descended upon man, when they became subjective factors, immediate magic. A wave of superstition went through the world at that time, the first centuries in Rome were swarming with sorcerers and amulets and magic of all

[1] *Heimarmene*: destiny in the Poimandres vision.

descriptions. People were as if beset by superstitious parasites, because they didn't know how to defend themselves. So they did the most amazing things in order to get rid of the swarm of gods that had settled down upon them like fleas or lice. That accounts for their extraordinary desire to be redeemed, liberated—to be lifted out of that awful swarm of vermin which infested the world.

Now, just as that happened in antiquity, a parallel phenomenon—of course not exactly the same thing—is taking place in our times, when the medieval Christian world is beginning to disappear. The essential truth comes back to us. Whatever has been in a metaphysical heaven is now falling upon us, and so it comes about that the mystery of Christ's sacrificial death, which has been celebrated untold millions of times by the masses, is now coming as a psychological experience to everybody. Then the lamb sacrifice is assimilated in *us*: we are becoming the lambs, and the lambs that are meant for sacrifice. We become gregarious as if we were sheep, and there will surely be a sacrifice. Now, we will go on with our text. Nietzsche says here.

In ourselves dwelleth he still, the old idol-priest, . . .

Of course Nietzsche doesn't mean this as we would interpret it; he means the old priests who preached a sort of metaphysical religion, and that we with our belief still support that old prejudice. What he says is true, but in an entirely different way, in a psychological way. The old idol-priest is *really* an old idol-priest, an archetypal figure of the priest-god or the sacrificed god; and "in ourselves dwelleth he still" means that we should never forget that the old gods, Wotan or any other, are still ready to spring up again when hitherto valid forms become obsolete.

who broileth our best for his banquet. Ah, my brethren, how could firstlings fail to be sacrifices!

This means the wholesale sacrifice, and they are all meant to die the ritual sacrifical death in order to produce redemption, as Christ chose death in order to become transformed. And into what did he become transformed through his death?

Miss Hannah: Into the subtle body.

Prof. Jung: You never read that in the New Testament!

Miss Hannah: The everlasting body, the resurrection body.

Prof. Jung: That is Paul's interpretation, but according to the dogma, what did Christ become after his death?

Answer: God.

Prof. Jung: Yes, the second person of the Trinity. He became the Logos, and then returned to God, to the metaphysical state in which he ever was; having been man he returned to God. So when we are sacrificed, we are all supposed to return to God. Now we will pass over the seventh part, and go to the last verse of the eighth part.

"Woe to us! Hail to us! The thawing wind bloweth!"—Thus preach, my brethren, through all the streets!

Here we have Wotan, the thawing wind. When things are generally at a standstill, when nothing happens and things are undecided, then someone is sure to see Wotan making ready. There are legends of his having been seen as a wanderer, and soon after a war would break out. When Wotan appears, it is like the thawing wind in Spring which melts the ice and snow, as Nietzsche says here very clearly. Now we will go to the ninth part:

There is an old illusion—it is called good and evil. Around soothsayers and astrologers hath hitherto revolved the orbit of this illusion.

Once did one *believe* in soothsayers and astrologers; and therefore did one believe, "Everything is fate: thou shalt, for thou must."

This is antiquity, you see.

Then again did one distrust all soothsayers and astrologers; and therefore did one believe, "Everything is freedom: thou canst, for thou willest!"

This is modern times, exactly what I have been pointing out. We will pass on now to the eleventh part, the third paragraph:

A great potentate might arise, an artful prodigy, who with approval and disapproval could strain and constrain all the past, until it became for him a bridge, a harbinger, a herald, and a cock-crowing.

What does he anticipate here?

Miss Hannah: The dictator.

Prof. Jung: Yes, a big fellow who welds the whole thing together with a hammer, doing away with the past, making it a bridge for the future. This is a very wonderful vision of the future.

This however is the other danger, and mine other sympathy:—
he who is of the populace, his thoughts go back to his grandfather,—with his grandfather, however, doth time cease.

Now what is that?

Miss Hannah: All the dictators come from the populace.

Prof. Jung: As we know them now, they come from the populace, and
their ideas do go back just to the grandfather—that is the funny thing.
That would be the 19th century or thereabouts. Before the grandfather, time ceases; there is no time. That is the case with the primitives. The so-called *alcheringa* or *altjiranga* time is before the grandfather.[2] You see, no primitive knows of anything further back than the
grandfather, so the heroic times when the great miracles happened,
the time of creation, was the time before the grandfather lived. Only a
few generations away we would say, but for the primitive it is utterly
remote: their knowledge of the past goes no further. Before the
grandfather was the *Urzeit*, the *alcheringa*, when the wonderful things
happened. That is exactly what Nietzsche says here. One sees examples of such primitivity in the examinations of recruits for the army.
They have heard of Napoleon—he was a contemporary of William
Tell and Caesar. That all happened practically at the same time; the
old Romans came just before Napoleon, and Martin Luther and Professor So-and-So are close together. They have no feeling for the
length of time and an extraordinary lack of historical vision, with only
a few dim scenes in their heads about heroes in the past and they are
all jumbled together. The discovery of America would have to do with
Genesis.

Mr. Bash: Is there not a parallel to this impression in Greek mythology, where there were just three generations of gods—Saturn,
Chronos, and Zeus—and before that nothing?

Prof. Jung: Yes, that is the very primitive fact. The grandfather is the
utmost limit; before the grandfather, time comes to an end. The Homeric time in Greece is an absolute parallel to the *altjiranga* time. The
altjirangamitjinas, to their primitive descendants, are the heroes of that
time when there was no time; as noble Greek families were supposed
to be descendants of Agamemnon or Odysseus or any of those Homeric heroes. Moreover, the heroes of the Homeric times were half
man, half beast, which explains the fact that the first founder of Ath-

---

[2] Ancestral souls, half man and half animal, are reinvoked by Australian aborigines in
a religious rite. CW 9 i, par. 114. Jung learned about this from Lucien Lévy-Bruhl's *Primitive Mythology*. See above, 23 May 1934, n. 3.

ens, Cecrops, was half man and half snake; and Erechtheus was worshipped in the form of a snake down under the Erechtheon on the Acropolis. There was the idea that heroes transform into snakes after death. The idea of the heroes being half beast is also related to the fact that all gods had animal attributes. Even the Evangelists had animal attributes. And the animal ancestors have been symbolized by the heraldic totemic animals, like the British lion and the unicorn, or the eagle, or the cock of France. The Eastern peoples have eagles because they have more to do with the wind: birds are their totemic animals. So those old ideas have left their traces.

Now, Nietzsche has an intuition of the danger that that great dictator might be of the populace, and that his thoughts would go back to his grandfather, which means that he would have somewhat antiquated ideas. And that is true of the present really prominent dictators, of Hitler himself, for example. In his book *Mein Kampf*, one sees that one set of his ideas comes from socialism—he imitates it, gets certain basic ideas from socialism (he himself says he is just one point better)—and the other set is from the Catholic church. Socialism is one aspect of realized Christianity, brotherly love with the ensuing disorder; and the other aspect is the Catholic church—discipline, organization, with the ensuing prison. These two are the main features of his ideas, the grandfather ideas. Now we will see what Nietzsche says about this.

> Thus is all the past abandoned: for it might some day happen for the populace to become master, and drown all time in shallow waters.

It is obviously possible when the leader is one of the populace, that the populace may get to the top; it has often happened that a dictator has been carried away by the masses he has roused.

> Therefore, O my brethren [now he comes to the remedy], a *new nobility* is needed, which shall be the adversary of all populace and potentate rule, and shall inscribe anew the word "noble" on new tables.

The remedy for all dictator habits and dangers would be a sort of oligarchy, a few rulers of noble quality, of noble birth. But that is of course the idea of any dictator. The Communist party is the nobility in Russia; they are paid several dozen times better than anyone else, have automobiles, etc., and they rule the workman who has nothing to say. He is a mere slave, worse than in the old feudal times. In Germany they are imitating that idea of nobility too. In those schools of the Ordensburgen, the young s.s. boys receive an education which makes them into a new order of knights—the knights of the new state. All that is foreseen, exactly as Nietzsche says here. But of course he doesn't mean that; he means a real nobility—not one that is made but one that creates itself. So he says,

> For many noble ones are needed, and many kinds of noble ones, *for a new nobility!*

People who are noble in themselves, not *made* into a sort of nobility, given a title or social prerogatives as is the case in Germany. Particularly in Russia they are given social prerogatives as members of the communist party.

> Or, as I once said in parable: "That is just divinity, that there are Gods, but no God!"

So what he means by the sacrifice of the many is that they are thereby transformed into gods. This bears out what we were assuming, that if one continues the Chrisitian attitude of self-sacrifice—wholesale sacrifice or wholesale slaughter—the inevitable outcome, according to the Christian dogma, is transformation. In that way gods should be made. Any sacrificial death has that meaning. That was true in the mysteries, and primitives always put the initiates through a symbolic death. Among the Kavirondos, a tribe in East Africa, the young men in the puberty initiations, for instance, are told that they are now going to die, or that they are already dead and have transformed into new beings, sort-of spirits; they get a new name, don't know their own family—their mother is no longer their mother, and so on. They are made anew into sort-of spirit beings. In modern times, of course, it happens more frequently that the young people do not undergo the initiations. They are not encouraged to do so, stupidly enough, by the officials, who, if they are military, don't believe in it and don't care anyway; and if they are missionaries they are absolutely against it because it is not Christian. They don't understand it at all; they even have a prejudice against it. But those who have undergone initiation say that the refractory ones are not human; they are nothing but animals, because they have not the spiritual quality which can only be acquired through the sacrificial death.

Mrs. Baumann: The American Indians have another expression for that: they speak of raw persons and cooked persons.[3]

---

[3] See Claude Lévi-Strauss, *The Raw and the Cooked,* tr. J. and D. Weightman (New York, 1969).

Prof. Jung: That is very good. It is exactly the same idea. Those who are cooked have gone through the pain and torture of the fire, have been transformed through pain. The essence of it is, of course, a sacrificial death. You see, in this way the Christian idea infiltrates into man and becomes real—it realizes itself; but then it happens blindly, which is, or can be, exceedingly dangerous. That accounts for the actual situation in Europe. The communistic state is equal to the dictator state inasmuch as it functions. If it is merely socialistic it doesn't function but simply disintegrates, as you have seen in France. Therefore automatically someone must pull the thing together and say, "Now we shall make order." So they are practically the same: the one is pulling asunder, the other is just disintegration. People say it should not be like that; of course it is never ideal. Both forms of social life lead into the most unsatisfactory condition, because they are automatically fulfilling the idea which has been the leading idea before. But now it is blind; it simply happens in reality, and the meaning is lost. So Nietzsche's idea that there should be a new nobility, an oligarchy of the good and valuable people, is the socialistic idea—all the socialistic leaders are very wonderful people naturally! In reality of course, they are corrupt. The dictators should be very wonderful people but look at them! Sure enough, there should be a nobility but it cannot be made; that can only grow. If it is fated that there shall be such a nobility, it must grow somehow. But it is surely not a social phenomenon, at least not at first. We have a parallel phenomenon in early Christianity in the idea of the elect: "Many are called, few are chosen" to form the kingdom of heaven, or the kingdom of God.[4] That is the nobility, but they stand against the world. That was the natural nobility of those days.

Mrs. Crowley: Is that not the *enantiodromia* in the progress of Christianity? Christ was the elect—the one—and with him a handful of people who had nothing to do with the state; and now we have again the one and the many who have only to do with the state.

Prof. Jung: Christ was the shepherd, the leader, a spiritual sort of dictator. That is all contained in his understanding that his kingdom was not of this world, but a spiritual kingdom of God—that form of nobility. It was not a sociological but a spiritual phenomenon, because it is only the contradiction of the spiritual with worldly affairs which creates that nobility.

Mrs. Jung: He says just before in Part VI ("But so wisheth our type," etc.) that the lambs or gregarious people really ask for the dictator, and

4 Matthew 22:14.

therefore in a socialistic or communistic state there must be a dictator.
The nobility on the other hand, is not gregarious: it consists of individuals.

Prof. Jung: Quite. Nobility cannot be a gregarious affair. Therefore
I say it cannot be a social phenomenon. I call it spiritual, but you can
call it a psychological affair. Those people must possess nobility of soul.
Otherwise it is an utterly impossible idea.

Miss Hannah: Is it not the same as Buddha's idea: the people who are
off the wheel?

Prof. Jung: Absolutely. Buddha formed such a nobility; the Buddhistic Sangha is the community of the elect who have forsaken the illusions of the world. Those who don't participate in the blindness of
Maya, who are freed from the wheel of the Samskaras—the cycle of repeated incarnations—those who have passed out of the state of concupiscentia are the elect ones, the leaders. It was the same in Manichaeism, where the term *electus* meant a definite degree of initiation. It
is even possible that Mani, who naturally knew the Christian tradition
since he lived in 220 or 230 A.D., got that idea of the elect from St. Paul
who based himself upon the Christian tradition: "Many are called but
few are chosen"—*electus*.

Miss Wolff: There is a parallel idea in the mystery cults of antiquity,
only there one was not *electus* because, being initiated by one's own effort, one became the special or outstanding one: one became "deified."

Prof. Jung: Yes, in the pagan mystery cults, or among the primitives,
the initiates were passed through those mysteries, and the achievement happened to them; while in Buddhism or Manichaeism or Christianity, it was really an individual achievement to be an *electus*. Naturally the more such a thing is an institution, the more it becomes a sort
of machine, so that anybody, practically, can become a chosen one. In
the Middle Ages any worldly prince could become a priest. He was simply passed through the consecration in a mechanical way, and it was
not at all a spiritual achievement, but entirely a worldly affair. Of
course that sort of thing upsets the apple cart after a while. Then that
system, which had become a factory for consecrating priests, was destroyed. The spiritual ideas disappeared through routine. Therefore,
the Reformation.

Now we must say a word more concerning this last sentence, "That
is just divinity, that there are Gods, but no God!" We know that
Nietzsche has declared God to be dead, and here it appears as if God
were not so dead; that is, as if there were no personal or monotheistic
God, but there was divinity. In the language of Meister Eckhart, it

would be the Godhead, not God.[5] The divine element, the divine factor, is still there, but not in the form of the monotheistic God, and Nietzsche thinks here of a peculiar transformation: namely, that through the abolition of Christianity the divine element will leave the dogmatic idea of God and will become incarnated in man, so there will be *gods*. That is a sort of intuition of an individuation process in man, which eventually leads to the deification of man or to the birth of God in man. Then we are confronted with that dilemma: is it the deification of man or the birth of God in man?

[5] Meister Eckhart uses *Godhead* when his emphasis is upon more than one member of the trinity as in ". . . persons in the godhead—on the one side, the begetter or Father, on the other, the offspring. . . ." "Commentary on John" in *Meister Eckhart*, tr. Bernard McGuise (New York, 1981), p. 143.

Prof. Jung:

I find here two contributions. One is a prayer, but because I am not God I cannot fulfil it. The other is from Mrs. von Roques: "There is a Russian fairy tale of a Czar who bade his three sons 'seek his traces and pick his flowers.' The two elder sons do not succeed, although they are given the best horses. But the youngest son takes the poorest horse, transforms it (by killing and magic) into the best of stallions, sits on it backwards and thus rides to his grandfather's cellar, strengthens himself by drinking his grandfather's wine, takes saddle and head-harness from there, and then is able to fulfill his task. In this case the 'grandfather' (dead) is regression 'pour mieux sauter,' and is probably 'pars pro toto' for *all the other side*. (Perhaps it is also the first step on the way.) Feeling at home there gives him (the hero) the necessary strength and possibilities."

I am not quite clear about this.

Mrs. von Roques: Nietzsche says in the fourth verse in part 11: . . . he who is of the populace, his thoughts go back to his grandfather,—with his grandfather, however, doth time cease." In this story, it is a going back also, but it has a more positive meaning; with Nietzsche it is negative.

Prof. Jung: Naturally it would be negative, but it also has a positive meaning—that the grandfather, as the term denotes, is the aggrandized father. In your fairy tale the grandfather is the primordial being that asks the great question, or sets the great task.

Mrs. von Roques: The father sets the task, and then the hero goes back to the grandfather.

Prof. Jung: Well, the grandfather really sets the task. He is the origin, because he is the representative of the *altjiranga*, which means psychologically, the representative of the collective unconscious. Since the collective unconscious, through the archetypes, sets the task, it is often called "the grandfather" directly. The primitives use that very term.

They call those powers that make people do the particular things, "grandfathers." They are the originators of the arts and crafts, for instance, and they have the knowledge of the country, the planting and hunting, the knowledge of medicinal herbs, and so on; all that is the grandfather's work: he taught it. But by "the grandfather" they mean the half man, half beast, that was in the beginning, in the *alcheringa* time, when they performed all those labors and tasks on the earth which became the models for mankind—what they must do in order to attain their ends. For instance, the half man, half beast—whatever he was—once came to a spot where he planted rice, which means that he transformed into rice, became the rice man, as you can still see. A stalk of rice has roots, a stem, a head, and even hair on the head; the roots are the feet, the stem is the body and neck, the grain is the head, and the little spikes are the hair. So it is clear that the grandfather was transformed into rice. And from that he transformed into something else, perhaps a bird. He is even believed to have transformed into a hoe which clearly consists of a head and a neck and a body.

Mrs. von Roques: So the hero goes back to the grandfather, and Nietzsche also.

Prof. Jung: Yes, the grandfather is simply the primordial image of the hero: the hero is embodied in the grandfather; or the grandfather is the first model of what a hero should be. The head man of a certain water-totem, for example, is a sort of grandchild of the grandfather, because he knows best what the *alcheringa* grandfather has done in order to produce the water—he transformed perhaps into rain—so he will repeat by a magic ceremony what the *alcheringa* ancestor did: he will be the rain-maker. Nietzsche is all depreciation. To him the grandfather's time conveys absolutely no meaning except that it is old-fashioned and antiquated—old nonsense even. We only spoke of the other significance of the grandfather because of Nietzsche's peculiar remark, "With his grandfather, however, doth time cease." He says those people who have the views of the grandfather never see further back, but merely repeat the ways and the words of the grandfather, because that is the only knowledge of history they possess. But curiously enough that fits in—that is exactly what happens with the primitives. Beyond the third or fourth generation there is nothing. Then comes the *alcheringa* time and there time comes to a standstill: as the Central Australians say, the time when there was no time. Only when man appeared was there time, and even then, having a time, they are still surrounded by no time because *altjiranga* is eternal. So the grandfathers, half man and half beast, have only gone underground; they sank down into the earth and left certain stones or trees or hillocks of plants as their relics. Therefore, there are certain sacred spots in which their respective ceremonies are celebrated, and they cannot be celebrated anywhere else.

In modern times farmers have taken land which originally belonged to the natives, and if they happened to occupy such a sacred place, the primitive was in this way killed. The vital ceremonies can only be celebrated in that one place, and if that is used for agriculture or any other purpose, it is desecrated. They cannot perform the *alcheringa* rites because the necessary food cannot be supplied. The relationship to nature is lost because the relationship to the ancestors is lost—only there are the *altjirangamitjinas* present and accessible. It is as if their connection with nature had been severed, and then those people are doomed; they decay when they lose the inner connection. All those primitive tribes are fertile and quite well off as long as they live in their natural haunts and have their natural religious relationship with nature, but the moment that is disrupted, they are gone. Then they form a sort of physical and mental proletariat—no good for anything. Like the so-called "mission boy" in Africa, who is no good at all. He is an animal speaking a sort of Christian slang which he doesn't understand. One sees at once that it is all bunk. They say, "I am a good Christian like you, I know all those fellows, Johnny and Marky and Lukey"; and when one asks about Jesus, they say he is a grasshopper and sing a hymn "Jesus, our grasshopper." To preach a highly developed religion, which even we do not understand, to such people is utterly ridiculous. Our missionaries work pure magic out there: they teach them prayers which they repeat with their lips, but their hearts cannot follow. Of course the missionary is much too uneducated to understand what he is doing. Even in the Catholic church where the priests are supposed to have a good education, one must seek far to find one who can tell you about the symbolism of the Mass or any other rite; they are just magically caught and don't know what they are doing.

Now I should like to speak again about the sentence in the end of the eleventh part: "That is just divinity, that there are Gods, but no God!" Nietzsche expresses something here which he has never said before, but we talked about it in the beginning when Nietzsche made the statement that God is dead. We said then that by that statement he dissolved the hitherto prevailing conception of a God existing in his own right. He destroyed that projection—the assumption that there is a God quite apart from man. For since God is not a mere assumption of pure reason but a very emotional fact, a very psychological fact, even a psychic fact, you deprive that fact of an abode when you say that God is dead. By that, you are saying that God no longer exists, but Nietzsche even means that there is no god, that God is not. Then that psychological fact which was originally called "God" has no place. It is no longer visible where you would expect to find it, in whatever form you have projected it into space—say, a venerable old man with a white beard, a father sitting on a throne in heaven and surrounded by a choir of angels singing eternally. Some such idea has been destroyed. In such a case the psychological fact, which is God, returns into the unconscious and one may say God is dead.

Nietzsche himself instantly reacts with an inflation and a dissociation, as we have seen. So he has to produce out of himself this one peculiar figure, Zarathustra, in order to have something in place of the fact, God. Zarathustra is the wise one, the great prophet, the founder of a religion, something like the messenger of God himself, as any great founder of a religion is considered to be. Christ is considered to be the son of God; and Mohammed is considered to be at least the messenger or prophet of God, as Moses, for instance, is a messenger of God, bringing the divine law. And so Zarathustra is the face of God, the Angel of the Face (*angelus* means messenger); he is that which is called in mystical Islam, in Sufism, the green one, the visible god Chidr. The prophet, or the messenger, or the angel of the god is always the visible god. Since all these religions have an idea of god which is unimaginable, you cannot make a picture of the deity, but you can at least make a picture of the messenger of God, the Angel of the Face. (That is the cabalistic expression. He is called the *metatron*.)[1]

Nietzsche was inflated by the regression of the image of the God into the unconscious, and that forces him to balance himself by a new projection in the form of Zarathustra. But Zarathustra is Nietzsche himself. Therefore throughout the whole text Nietzsche is somewhere in between Nietzsche the man and Zarathustra the messenger of God: they can hardly be separated. Only in certain places does it become apparent that Zarathustra is very probably speaking, and in other places that it is more like Nietzsche. Now here, in his decalogue, where he produces the new tablets which are meant for humanity, he realizes what happens when one declares that God is dead. He thinks here more or less in terms of his audience. He assumes that they have listened to his words and that they all agree with him that God is dead.

[1] *Metatron*, a word found in the *Zohar*, is yet another name for primordial man, the first human self that continues to exist in all his descendants. See CW 13, par. 168.

But then they are all gods. Here he has realized that if he declares God is dead, he is then the god; and if all his listeners or pupils have the same conviction, they also become gods: God regresses into them. The original projection of the image of God is destroyed, so God enters into them and they are gods. Now do you know the Christian model for that process? There is a wonderful example in the New Testament. Of course it is somewhat awkward for theologians.

Miss Wolff: After Christ is dead and risen to Heaven, the Holy Ghost descends upon the disciples at Pentecost.

Prof. Jung: That is it, the Pentecostal miracle. Christ said he would leave a Comforter, the Paraclete, and the spirit of God descended upon everyone present at that gathering. As the Holy Ghost was seen descending upon Christ in the form of a dove at the moment of his baptism in the Jordan—there he was made into the son of God. Then if the Holy Ghost descends upon every one of the disciples, they are also made into sons of God: every one of them becomes a Christ, an immediate son of God. Now, that was Christ's idea. But the Church has disregarded this fact in spite of its being authentic. It cannot be wiped out of the New Testament as a very much later interpolation. It is related in the Acts of the Apostles, as a peculiar *post mortem* phenomenon, one of the authentic *post mortem* effects; and inasmuch as we still celebrate Pentecost in the church it should be taken into account. It has been taken into account to a certain extent. Do you know in what institution the Holy Ghost really gives the character of divinity?

Mrs. Schlegel: In the consecration of the priests.

Prof. Jung: Yes, in the so-called Apostolic Succession in the Catholic church. The idea is that St. Peter received the immediate blessing of the Lord, so he stood in the place of the Lord. He was the Lord's deputy, and St. Peter passed on his blessing to his successors, the bishops of Rome. The Apostolic Succession goes on through the centuries in the Catholic church. It is something like a gift of the Holy Ghost, as the emanation of Christ would be the Holy Ghost. The Apostolic blessing is a small Holy Ghost, a small parcel of mana handed out to St. Peter and his successors, and therefore it gives an absolutely indestructible character to the priest, the *character indelebilis*. Even if the one who has received the Apostolic blessing is excommunicated, or even if he is a criminal, the *character indelebilis* cannot be taken away from him. He is marked by that touch. That is a special prerogative: only the priest has a *character indelebilis*, so he is separated from the rest of humanity as a sort of outstanding Superman. He holds a divine prerogative; in having received the Apostolic blessing, which means a part of Christ, the *character indelebilis* of the priest is a minor degree of deification. There- fore he is able to perform the rites, and above all the transubstantiation in the Mass, which is a miracle. The head of a nunnery, the abbess, can- not celebrate the Mass, so each nunnery has an affiliated priest who through his *character indelebilis* is able to do it for them. They entirely depend upon him because only a man can receive that divine charac- ter.

Now if the Holy Ghost *in toto* descends upon people, they receive the full imprint of divinity. The divine form enters them and they are even more than the priests; they *are*-instead-of-the-deity—as Christ, having received the imprint of God through the Holy Ghost, *is*-instead-of- God. He is the second person of the Trinity, between the Holy Ghost and the Father. Inasmuch as Christ promised that he would leave a Comforter and inasmuch as this Comforter has descended upon the disciples, they have received the divine imprint and they *are*-instead- of-Christ—not only St. Peter. He was selected by Christ himself and given the Apostolic blessing, but the others have the divine character nevertheless. The church doesn't dwell upon that however; the church dislikes this idea: no conclusion has ever been drawn from it.

Mrs. Brunner: Already St. Paul wrote against it.

Prof. Jung: Yes, right in the beginning that fact was hushed up. It was impossible for those days. It could not be maintained because it in- cluded the fact that God was not outside, but meant that he was within those people.

Miss Wolff: But then logically the same thing ought to happen after the Holy Communion because Christ is in the Host; in eating the Host one is eating Christ.

Prof. Jung: Yes, one should draw the same conclusion there. And the primitives do draw such a conclusion. They think that by eating the to- temic animal, they integrate all its virtues into themselves; inasmuch as the totem animal is the ancestor of the tribe, they integrate all the qual- ities that originally made the tribe. The original ancestors created the tribe by transforming into the first men and women of the tribe—the original idea of creation being not creation out of nothing, but trans- formation. As if in Genesis, instead of creating heaven and earth, God in the beginning transformed himself into heaven and earth. We still have a trace of that primitive idea in a classical text of the time of Al- exandria, the so-called *tabula smaragdina*, the emerald table. The story is that in the grave of Hermes the Thrice Greatest, a tablet of emerald was found, upon which a text was engraved saying that the world was created in the beginning through adaptation. This is a very peculiar idea. Adaptation means to fit one thing to another, or to shape a thing into an image; one adapts a thing to oneself or to a certain use. For instance, the idea that God has created man in his image is adaptation.

Now if God creates an image of himself, what is the difference? Since this image represents the deity, then if it is a living image, it is the deity. It is the face of the deity, the Angel of the Face. That is man, and since the Angel of the Face is God's power and virtue itself, man is that also; he is made in the image of God, created through adaptation. In the text of the *tabula smaragdina*, the whole world is made in the image of God, so the world represents God, is God, is the imaginable, perceptible, understandable, accessible God. Therefore the world is essentially round because God is round, perfect. It is said in Genesis that God himself was satisfied with the state of affairs, which means that it was perfect, like his image—except on the second day. Then he created the two things—there he made a split in the world, and he did not say it was good. The same idea is in the Old Zarathustrian religion, where the fatal split between Ormazd and Ahriman comes from a doubt, or a doubtful thought, in the divine mind, so it was perhaps due to that Persian influence. However that was, we have the incontestable fact that the *binarius* which God created on the second day never quite pleased him. I didn't find that out—an old alchemist wrote a long article about it.[2] That is only in parenthesis however. I wanted to give you a history of this peculiar statement that there is a sort of unconscious continuation of the problem of the descent of the Holy Ghost in the Acts of the Apostles. That idea continued. It remained as an open question which has never been properly answered, and it is quite understandable why it could not have been answered.

Mrs. Jung: The faith in the efficiency of the Holy Ghost seems not to have been very great, because the *character indelebilis* is not extended to the priest as a human person, but only in as far as he is a priest. If the Holy Ghost was really efficient, the whole person should be influenced by it.

Prof. Jung: It should be, but it is not.

Mrs. Jung: If it is believed to be real then its effect also ought to be real.

Prof. Jung: Absolutely, but you see it was altogether too obvious that the *character indelebilis* did not show in the person. Therefore that

---

[2] The second created thing introduced distinction (thus consciousness, in Jung's system) into what had been serenely single. This point was made by Gerhard Dorn, a 16th-century German alchemical physician whose writings are collected in *Theatrum Chemicum* (Strasbourg, 1659).

thought could not be pursued—it was impossible. Even with the Apostolic blessing it was not believable that those old bishops were divine. Well, of course man was never divine, as people understood divinity.

Miss Wolff: When the Pope took on his character of infallibility, did he connect it with that idea of the Holy Ghost?

Prof. Jung: Oh, quite. The infallibility of the Pope is exactly the same as the *character indelebilis,* only very much more so. A priest would not be able through his *character indelebilis* to establish a dogma, while the Pope, being the immediate successor of St. Peter, being in the place of the Lord—not as a human being mind you, but *in officio*—is filled with the Holy Spirit. He is a sort of incarnation of the Holy Spirit, so he *can* establish a dogma.

Miss Wolff: Is he only infallible in establishing the dogma?

Prof. Jung: Yes, only in this function is he infallible; as the head of the Collegium of the cardinals he can establish a dogma by his ultimate decision. But not even as the Pope has he an infallible character.

Miss Wolff: I would like to ask, in connection with Mrs. Jung's question: is not a priest supposed to be dead as a human being? Therefore his human side would not come into consideration. I mean, his human character is not important for the priest: he is sort of dead as a human being; so of course those prerogatives would not extend to his humanity, which is unimportant.

Prof. Jung: That is perfectly true. His humanity is in a way completely unimportant if he is looked at as a priest. But if he is a rascal, then where does his *character indelebilis* show?

Miss Wolff: He can be excommunicated.

Prof. Jung: Naturally, on account of his fallible humanity which is not touched by the *character indelebilis* of his priesthood. But one would expect that it would be touched if the *character indelebilis* really exists, and that was the original assumption. It was so much the assumption that Tertullian was convinced that a man who had received baptism could not sin any more, and if he did sin again, one should find out whether he had been baptized in the correct way. And even if one could not detect a fault, one should repeat the rite. Then if he sinned again he was lost, meant for eternal hell: then God simply had not allowed the rite of baptism to work in that case.

Mrs. Jung: I think the fact that a priest has to confess shows that they are considered as human beings; if they were considered non-existent as human beings, they would not have to confess.

Prof. Jung: Yes, even the Pope has a confessor. You have just read in the papers about the Pope's last confession. On the one side the Pope is a human being, and on the other side a priest, and he has that divine character in the highest degree because, besides the consecration as a priest, he is the representative of the Lord.

Mrs. Flower: Is the Holy Ghost transferred by the laying on of hands in the ceremony?

Prof. Jung: Yes, in the consecration of the priest, the bishop conveys the Apostolic blessing by laying on his hands. The mana goes through the hand, as Christ conveyed the divine mana by his hands. That also is a prerogative of the bishop; the priest cannot convey it. The bishop is supposed to contain more mana. Those are very primitive ideas and therefore peculiarly right.

Mrs. Crowley: When they made this separation between the office of the priest and his human side, is it not like the doubt in the deity's mind when he separated heaven and earth?

Prof. Jung: It is of course that psychologically, but the church has no intention of creating a dissociation between the priest's human character and his divinity. Experience shows, however, that there is a most regrettable little gap between the two, which of course has to do with the fact that God created the *binarius*, the two, that split which he did not call good. Perhaps he thought, "Now I am not quite certain whether that is right." The original Persian idea was that he himself was not quite certain whether the dogma would be a favorable one.

Well now, here Nietzsche fulfils, one could say, an unconscious expectation, for time and again in the Middle Ages that idea of the Holy Ghost played a very great role. Do you know where?

Mrs. Flower: With the Albigenses?

Prof. Jung: Yes, the Albigenses assumed that the descent of the Holy Ghost was the active religious principle, but that standpoint was not elaborated by the church.[3] Yet in the Middle Ages they already began to speak of the Kingdom of the Father representing the Old Testament, the Kingdom of the Son representing the New Testament, and the third Reich was the Kingdom of the Holy Ghost. This is the mystical hook in that term which catches on—that the third Reich is the Kingdom of the Holy Ghost. Unfortunately the Holy Ghost has the wind quality; it is a thawing wind, it is pneuma. Therefore a mighty wind filled the house at the time of the descent of the Holy Ghost. But it can have two aspects: the wind quality which is external, physical, and then it is a kingdom where the wind-god rules, a god of breath and

[3] The Albigenses were members of a Catharistic sect of southern France (Albi) in the eleventh to thirteenth centuries.

wind; or it may be the spirit within. And it is possible that the two things happen at the same time, that the one is a reaction against the other. The outside very often instigates the creation of the inside; the unfavorable external aspect can produce a reaction which contains the real meaning, or the meaningful thing, while the externals are utterly mistakable. That again explains something which quite decidedly belongs to this part. We are now coming to part 12, where the argument we have begun is continued: we are in the channel of Nietzsche's own thought.

> O my brethren, I consecrate you and point you to a new nobility: . . .

He is bestowing consecration upon all his imaginary disciples, his brethren. That he consecrates them means that he bestows the Apostolic blessing upon them, that he is in possession of the Holy Ghost or the Apostolic blessing originally received from Christ himself, and he thereby points them to a new nobility.

> ye shall become procreators and cultivators and sowers of the future;—

He is sending them out into the world, as Christ also said to go out into the world and preach the Evangels.

> —Verily, not to a nobility which ye could purchase like traders with traders' gold; for little worth is all that hath its price.
> Let it not be your honour thenceforth whence ye come, but whither ye go! Your Will and your feet which seek to surpass you—let these be your new honour!

It is clear from the text that he understands their new character as a will for the future, that the gold which is to be attained gives them their nobility. The task which he sets them, and the goal, is the mana. So it is not because they have received a certain character from the past: it is rather the task assigned to them which gives them their meaning and their goal. In other words, it doesn't matter who you are, provided that your goal is so-and-so; that you want to attain such-and-such a goal gives you character, not what you are but what you are looking for. Of course that is a very important point of view. It is really true that an individual is not only characterized by what he was originally, by birth and by inherited disposition; he is also that which he is seeking. His goal characterizes him—but not exclusively. For you sometimes set a task for yourself which is merely compensatory for what you are in

reality. It is not an entirely valid goal inasmuch as your original disposition is not valid under all conditions. Your own condition may be at
fault—you may have a very faulty disposition. Any human disposition
is somewhat imperfect, and the more it is imperfect, the more you will
seek a goal of perfection which compensates your defect. But then the
goal is equally faulty. Then the goal doesn't coincide with the goals of
other people, and under those conditions you really don't collaborate
with them.

For instance, a generous character with a certain tendency to waste-
fulness naturally will seek economy. And a thrifty person, or somebody who suffers from self-inflicted poverty, naturally will seek riches.
Now how do those two goals coincide? Therefore it is by no means indifferent where you come from or what you were originally. It depends very much upon whether you start from a basis which in itself is
solid or healthy, or whether you start from a faulty basis. Also when
you say, *my* goal is so-and-so, you are perhaps using a sort of slogan,
and I don't know what kind of goal it may be. And it doesn't mean that
you are the one who is going to attain that goal, or that you are even
the one who will work for it in a satisfactory way. With all doing there
is always the question, "*Who* is doing it? *Who* is the man who is so willing
to accept responsibility?"[4] [. . .]

Here again Nietzsche simply swings over to the other side. He thinks
a man is sanctified, almost deified, by the great goal he has in mind.
But he might be a miserable fool who never could attain to such a goal,
who has such a goal only because he is a fool. Of course you may say,
"We have no goal, we go nowhere, but we have quality, we have character," and that is no good either. You must have the two things: you
must have quality, virtue, efficiency, *and* a goal, for what is the good of
the qualities if they don't serve a certain end? But Nietzsche simply
swings over to the other extreme by the complete denial of all past values, of all the truth of the past, as if he were going to establish brand
new ideas, as if there had never been any past worth mentioning. In
that way he would create people who forgot all about themselves. They
would now be quite different, as they never had been before—entirely
new beings, capable of very great accomplishment. As if that were possible! A goal can only be realized *if* there is the stuff by which and
through which you can realize the goal. If the stuff upon which you
work is worth nothing, you cannot bring about your end. Now in the
third paragraph further on, he says.

---

[4] Here there is an excision of a repeated anecdote.

> Nor even that a Spirit called Holy, led your forefathers into promised lands, which I do not praise: for where the worst of all trees grew—the cross,—in that land there is nothing to praise!

He is obviously referring to the crusades to the Holy Land.

> And verily, wherever this "Holy Spirit" led its knights, always in such campaigns did—goats and geese, and wry-heads and guy-heads run *foremost!*—

Here he mentions the Holy Ghost, so we were following his underlying idea. Nietzsche usually realizes slowly, in subsequent paragraphs, what has been underlying before. It slowly rises to the surface, and if you are shrewd enough you can guess what is welling up from what lies underneath. So now he cannot help remembering the Holy Spirit and how close he is to the symbolism of Christianity. But in contradistinction to the Holy Ghost that in the past led the forefathers to the cross, Nietzsche's teaching would of course have a different end in view; his great goal is the creation of the superman—whatever the superman may be. Now what is the goal of Christianity? Is it really the cross—if you take it historically, not morally? Of course our theology tells us that the Holy Ghost led us to the cross, but that is only a partial truth. Christ did not mean that. He did not leave his Comforter in order to bring us to the cross.

Mrs. Sachs: He meant to find the Kingdom of God.

Prof. Jung: Yes, the early Christian idea was that we were all going forward into the Kingdom of God, not to the cross at all. That is a later, moralistic misunderstanding. The original Christian message was that the kingdom of God was coming near and that we were all making ready for it, so it was also a goal, and decidedly a social goal in the near future. Of course it was meant spiritually, yet it had its social aspects: it was a community of the saints, a wonderful condition in which all conflicts would be settled. The Superman is very much the same idea, a sort of redeemed man living in an entirely new spiritual condition. So Nietzsche's idea is not so different, but is simply another word for the kingdom of heaven or the kingdom of God; it is now the kingdom of man, but the Superman, a god-man, no longer the ordinary man. Then just before, he says something quite interesting which we passed over: "Your Will and your feet which seek to surpass you—let these be your new honour!" (third verse of part 12). What does that mean?

Mrs. Brunner: He alludes again to the concept of jumping over the primitive man.

Prof. Jung: Well, one should always make a vivid image of his metaphors, and what strikes one here is the will. Now where is the will?

Mrs. Crowley: In the head.

Prof. Jung: Yes, the will starts in the head because there is no will that is not a thought: one has always a goal, an end in mind. The will is a thoroughly conscious phenomenon. Then the feet are the other end, and something is in between.

Miss Hannah: The body.

Remark: The heart.

Prof. Jung: The whole body: the heart is only one of the series of chakras which are in between. So you are to go further with the head and the feet, and they are supposed to surpass you. But that would mean that your head might fly off your shoulders, rise up higher than your body, and your feet also. Your feet walk away with you and your head too, and whatever is between, the whole man practically, is perhaps carried—he doesn't know what happens to him, probably he is just left in the rear to rot away. It is an ugly metaphor. I should call it a schizophrenic metaphor, a dissociation. It is as if the will had liberated itself from the body, and the feet had dissociated themselves from the body and were now going away by themselves: they detach themselves and rise above you, and everything else is left in the rear. So the thing that arrives in the land of the superman is nothing but a head and two feet, just a head walking along. That is terribly grotesque. It looks as if there would be plenty of opportunity in such a kingdom of heaven for marching, feet walking about with nothing but heads above them. But how did things begin in Germany? With marching about. And they are all possessed by a will—will and feet: every other consideration had disappeared. This is really an extraordinary metaphor. It is a sort of abbreviated sign of man, a hieroglyph.

Mr. Bash: There is an interesting parallel to that in James Branch Cabell's *Figures of Earth*, in the peculiar way in which Dom Manuel serves Misery for thirty days in the forest.[5] Misery is simply a head which moves about, so it may be considered as having feet. And each of the thirty days is as a year to him, but he stays there in order to win from Misery the soul of the person he loved, to recover it again from Hades.

Prof. Jung: That is quite apt symbolism for misery, because the heart

---

[5] James Branch Cabell (1879-1958) a satirical, ironical American novelist, published *Figures of Earth* (1921) two years after his best known work, *Jurgen*, which created a furor over its open sexuality.

of the body is absolutely left out of the game. And if you go by your will you only get into a miserable condition, because the man doesn't follow. He is left behind, really surpassed.

Mrs. Crowley: It is also prophetic in another way if you think of the machinery, flying, etc.—nobody walks any more.

Prof. Jung: Oh, but these do. They can't drive in automobiles because they have none. Now we go on (ninth verse of part 12):

> O my brethren, not backward shall your nobility gaze, but *outward!* Exiles shall ye be from all fatherlands and forefather-lands.

That will happen, they will be uprooted. For it is the body, the feeling, the instincts, which connect us with the soil. If you give up the past you naturally detach from the past; you lose your roots in the soil, your connection with the totem ancestors that dwell in your soil. You turn outward and drift away, and try to conquer other lands because you are exiled from your own soil. That is inevitable. The feet will walk away and the head cannot retain them because it also is looking out for something. That is the Will, always wandering over the surface of the earth, always seeking something. It is exactly what Mountain Lake, the Pueblo chief, said to me, "The Americans are quite crazy. They are always seeking; we don't know what they are looking for." Well, there is too much head and so there is too much will, too much walking about, and nothing rooted.

Miss Hannah: I quite agree with the negative side, but could not the passage also have a positive meaning? We said last time that the new nobility were people who had stepped off the wheel and brought their Samskaras to an end. Are not such people able to dispense with looking back at the ancestral ways, for are they not in the mandala and able to look out on all the four sides through the gates of the four functions?

Prof. Jung: Of course that is the way Nietzsche understood it, but we are further away from him and we cannot help looking at it from the standpoint of subsequent events. Looked at from the standpoint of Germany as it was in those days, one understands that they really suffered from the weight of the past. Naturally they would begin to think: "If only there were a new wind somewhere that would blow away all that old dust so that we can move and breathe again." They would get the *Wandertrieb,*[6] would feel that they ought to get out of that leaden weight of the past and of tradition. But one cannot preach it one-sid-

---

[6] *Wandertrieb*: the impulse to wander, wanderlust.

edly. If one goes too far, if one loses too much connection with the past, one loses connection with one's ancestors.

Mrs. Jung: Dr. Heyer made a very good point in this connection when he spoke in his Ascona lecture of all this marching and trampling of the earth in order to get rid of the mother.[7] I think that also means the past.

Prof. Jung: Quite. There is decidedly an attempt to get rid of the weight of the earth—the spirit of gravity, as Nietzsche calls it—and that is absolutely justifiable as long as the weight rules, as long as one is really suppressed. But if you move so far away that you forget about the past, you lose the connection.

Mrs. Flower: This new analysis gives a frightful picture of what is going on in Germany, in being only one-sided when trying to get rid of the past.

Prof. Jung: Russia is a still better example. Russia was entirely suppressed by the past, suffering under an enormous weight of old traditions, so there was the desire to make their way through it, to move on, but then it all became one-sided. That is the terrible danger of unconsciousness. As soon as you get rid of one evil, you fall into another, from the fire into the water and from the water into the fire. If you could only hold on and see the two sides! If you want to get rid of a certain Christian tradition, try to understand what Christianity really is in order to get the true value—perhaps you may return to the true value of Christianity. Or if you move on farther, don't say that Christianity has been all wrong. It is only that we have had the wrong idea of it. To destroy all tradition, as has happened already in Spain and Russia and is about to happen in several other places, is a most regrettable mistake. And that is expressed by the head which walks with two feet and nothing between. Nietzsche says, "Exiles shall ye be from all fatherlands and forefather-lands!" For how can you be connected with the chthonic gods, how can you be connected with your blood, your soil, if you are uprooted from it all? The past is really the earth; all the past has sunk into the earth, as those primitives say. The ancestors, the *alcheringa* people, went underground and their people must remain there, because there they can contact them and only there, nowhere else. That is such a truth to them that they can't even dream of taking another country, because they would lose touch with the spirits and be injured. The women would get the wrong ancestor spirits and then the

---

[7] G. R. Heyer, a German neurologist, lectured on "The Great Mother in the Psyche of Modern Man" at the Eranos Conference in 1938.

children would have the wrong souls. They cannot live in the country of another tribe—it is absolutely impossible. They can only live where their totem ancestors have gone underground. That is an eternal truth, and whoever goes against it, gets the wrong ancestral souls, wrong influences; they get detached, they lose their instincts, and their civilization becomes strained and unnatural. They suffer from a pronounced dissociation between the conscious and the unconscious. The unconscious is with the ancestors down in the bowels of the earth, and their consciousness is a head on two feet, constantly marching about in an awful restlessness. That is the restlessness of our time, always seeking—seeking the lost ancestral body, seeking the ancestral instincts. But they are only to be found on the spot where they have gone underground.

Mrs. Crowley: In the myth of the hero, is it not one of his functions to assimilate his ancestors?

Prof. Jung: The real hero is swallowed by the earth—the mother, the dragon, the whale—and apparently he goes under, down to the totemic ancestors, but he returns with them and brings them back. That is the proper hero according to mythology, not the one who runs away with a will and two feet. Now he says.

> Your *children's land* shall ye love: let this love be your new nobility,—the undiscovered in the remotest seas! For it do I bid your sails search and search![8]

He directs his disciples into the greater distances, as far away as possible from their origins. And not for themselves should they seek that land, but for their children, which is worse still. You see, in a country like England, where people have had a very sound egotism and where each generation has sought to increase their wealth and comfort, they left very decent conditions to their offspring. But if they had run after all the countries in the world and deposited themselves there, what would have been left to the children? Nothing. When you neglect your own welfare in seeking the welfare of the children, you leave the children a bad inheritance, a very bad impression of the past. If you torture yourself in order to produce something for the children, you give them the picture of a tortured life. Therefore away with all that. It is all wrong, says the child, and it commits the other mistake. If you are always preparing for the happiness of the children, you don't know

---

[8] Jung's final citation from *Thus Spake Zarathustra* is from section 56 of Part III. Four other sections from this part and all of Part IV remain without his commentary.

how to look after your own happiness, nor do your children learn how to look after theirs. They in turn may go on to prepare for the happiness of your grandchildren, and the grandchildren for your great-grandchildren, and so happiness is always somewhere in the future. You think happiness is something to be attained in the future, that you cannot attain it, but your children will have it. So you fill your life with ambitions for that kingdom to come and it never comes. Every generation is doing something towards it. They all torture themselves in order that the children shall attain it, but the children grow up and are the same fools that we are. They receive the same evil teaching.

Try to make it here and now, for yourself. That is good teaching. Then the children will try to make it here and now for themselves—then it can come into the real world. Don't be unnatural and seek happiness in the next generations. If you are too concerned about your children and grandchildren, you simply burden them with the debts you have contracted. While if you contract no debts, if you live simply and make yourselves as happy as possible, you leave the best of conditions to your children. At all events, you leave a good example of how to take care of themselves. If the parents can take care of themselves, the children will also. They will not be looking for the happiness of the grandchildren, but will do what is necessary to have a reasonable amount of happiness themselves. And so when a whole nation is torturing itself for the sake of the children, an inheritance of misery is all that they leave for the future, a sort of unfulfilled promise. So instead of saying, "I do it for the children—it may come off in the future," try to do it for yourself here and now. Then you will see whether it is possible or not. If you postpone it for the children, you leave something which you have not dared to fulfil, or perhaps you were too stupid to fulfil it; or if you had tried to fulfil it you might have seen that it was impossible, or all nonsense anyhow. While if you leave it to the future you leave less than nothing to the children—only a bad example.

REFERENCES TO THE PSYCHOLOGICAL
ANALYSIS OF *THUS SPAKE ZARATHUSTRA*
BY CHAPTER

* Chapters 35–39 and 50 are passed over by Jung.
** The seminars ended at the discussion of chapter 56, part 13.

INDEX

Aargau, Canton of, 181
Abegg, Emile, 4n, 1306
Abraham, 1246, 1327
Abu Simbel, temple of, 936
Abudabad, 157
Accidents as punishments, 713-15
Acropolis, 756, 1523
Action, symbolic, 91, 109
Actor of roles, 1348-49
Adam, 105, 1418, 1423, 1440; and Eve, 1418; Cadmon, 1180; Primus, 1180
Adaptation, 1497-98, 1517, 1533
Adler, Alfred, xi, 1211, 1451
Aeneas, 1397
Aetna, Mt., 1217
Aetoi, 35
Affect, 1193, 1379. *See also* Emotion
Africa: Christianity in, 1530; dance, 46; and the dead, 176, 1191; myth of death, 1246; initiation rites, 1524; soul as serpent, 756-57
Agathodaimon, 1295, 1300, 1310
Agrippa von Nettesheim, 907
Ahriman, 7, 190n, 1086, 1095, 1368-69, 1534
Ahura Mazda, 6-9, 492-93. *See also* Ormuzd
Aion, 1282
Aischrologia, 953, 1283
Ajna chakra, 253, 257, 1375
Alberich, 868
Albertus Magnus (Albert the Great), 243, 1050
Albigenses, 1536
Albrecht, King, 241
Alchemy, 64, 167, 204, 243, 480, 653, 949, 1104, 1260, 1407, 1413; aim, 105-6, 444-45, 522, 549, 653; vision of Arisleus, 1448-49, 1485-88; Avicenna, 1413; *Cabala Chymica*, 311; problem of chaos, 105, 1400, 1404-10, 1418; relation to Christianity, 1048; *Chymical Marriage of Christian Rosenkreutz*, 312; colors

in, 547; eagle and toad, 967, 1413, 1419; fire, heat (*see also* Arisleus), 1067-68, 1079, 1486; Goethe and, 893-95; gold in, 444-45, 796, 1073, 1223; Herforetus (Harpocrates), 853; hermaphrodite in, 533; and lead, 1260; *materia*, 1046, 1073; Middle Ages, 311-12; old man in, 308; *ouroborus*, 1286; *prima materia*, 886, 954, 1046; projection in, 1496; three roses, 888; spirit, 1067; stone, 949; use of symbol, 1248-49; triangle, trinity, 1079, 1085; *vas Hermeticus*, 1085, 1086; water, 1079. *See also* Hermetic philosophy, Philosopher's stone
Alcheringa, 1266, 1522, 1528-30, 1531, 1542
Alcohol, 1039
Alexandria, 1533
Allah, 7, 369
Alphonse of Spain, 643
Altjiranga. See Alcheringa
Altruists, 1146
Alypius, 685
Ambrose, St., 879, 1049
Amenhotep IV, 252, 794, 1405
Amesha spentas, 9
Amfortas, 854, 866
Amor fati, 87, 275
Anahata, 394, 395
Analysis, 66-67, 84-85, 100, 106, 468, 486, 742, 758, 763, 1184, 1357, 1360; danger of, 278-79, 476; dreams in, 1302, 1411, 1430-31; problems in, 497-98; process of, 955-56, 1358; technique, 1320, 1321
Analyst, 1087; neurosis of, 154, 618; task of, 708, 1358
Analytical psychology, 329
Ancestors, 1530, 1541, 1542; represented by snakes, 1282
Ancestral life, 941-42; spirits, 160; units, 643, 1267-68, 1399-1403, 1404

LIBRARY OF CONGRESS

Library of Congress Cataloging-in-Publication Data

Jung, C. G. (Carl Gustav), 1875-1961.
Nietzsche's Zarathustra : notes of the seminar given in 1934-1939 / by C. G. Jung ;
edited by James L. Jarrett.
p. cm.—(Bollingen series ; 99)   Includes bibliographies and indexes.
ISBN 0-691-09953-7 (set : alk. paper)
1. Nietzsche, Friedrich Wilhelm, 1844-1900. Also sprach Zarathustra. 2. Philosophy. I.
Jarrett, James L. (James Louis), 1917-   . II. Title. III. Series.
B3313.A44J85   1988
193—dc19   87-32897
                                                                      CIP